Ninth Edition

Psychology Applied *to* Work

An Introduction
to Industrial and
Organizational
Psychology

Paul M. Muchinsky
University of North Carolina at Greensboro

Hypergraphic Press

Hypergraphic Press

Psychology Applied to Work: An Introduction to Industrial and Organizational Psychology, **Ninth Edition**
Paul M. Muchinsky

Production Service: Newgen–Austin
Compositor: Newgen–Austin
Interior Design: Newgen–Austin
Interior Design Image: A Red Mixture, Fotosearch Stock
   Photography, © 2004, Design Pics Inc.

Cover Design: Michael Lane
Cover Image: Getty Images
Printer: Signature Book Printing
Indexer: Wendy Allex

Hypergraphic Press, Inc.
P.O. Box 743
Summerfield, NC 27358

For permission to use material from this text, submit a
request to *info@hypergraphicpress.com.*

1 2 3 4 5 6 13 12 11 10 09 08

Library of Congress Control Number: 2008924259

ISBN: 978-0-9801478-0-3

To Sam
Eternally grateful

To Andrea and Brian
Partners!

To Frank and Michele
Thanks a million

About the Author

Paul M. Muchinsky was born and raised in Connecticut. He received his B.A. degree in psychology from Gettysburg College, his M.S. degree in psychology from Kansas State University, and his Ph.D. degree in industrial/organizational psychology from Purdue University. He was a faculty member of Iowa State University for twenty years. In 1993 he was appointed the Joseph M. Bryan Distinguished Professor of Business at The University of North Carolina at Greensboro. In 2004 Dr. Muchinsky was the inaugural recipient of the Distinguished Teaching Contribution Award from the Society for Industrial and Organizational Psychology for his outstanding educational contributions to the field. In 2008 Dr. Muchinsky was awarded the honorary Doctor of Science (D.Sc.) degree from Gettysburg College. He is a Fellow of four divisions of the American Psychological Association: the Society for Industrial and Organizational Psychology; the Society for the Teaching of Psychology; the Society of Consulting Psychology; and the Society of Counseling Psychology. He is a Diplomate of the American Board of Professional Psychology (in industrial/organizational psychology) and a licensed psychologist. Throughout his career, Dr. Muchinsky has been very active in a wide range of professional activities within the field of industrial/organizational psychology. Many of the cases and examples of concepts presented in this book come directly from his professional experiences. When not engaged as an I/O psychologist, Dr. Muchinsky fantasizes about playing baseball for the New York Yankees. He can be reached at pmmuchin@uncg.edu.

Brief Contents

Contents

Preface

Psychology Applied to Work and I have aged together. I wrote the first edition when I was in my early 30s. Now I am in my early 60s. I consider *Psychology Applied to Work* to be my legacy to industrial/organizational (I/O) psychology. For almost 30 years it has allowed me to tell the story of I/O psychology through the voices of the many people who have contributed to the field. Just as the world of business is now global, so is I/O psychology. Researchers from around the world are active contributors to the field. Today I/O psychology is as vibrant as the world of work is in the 21st century.

This 9th Edition of *Psychology Applied to Work* retains the standard design features long evidenced throughout the book's history. They include three Field Notes per chapter, case studies, cartoons, photographs, glossaries, and two special sections in each chapter: "Cross-Cultural I/O Psychology" and "The Changing Nature of Work." This 9th Edition contains over 150 new references published between 2006 and 2008. It is the most current, comprehensive, and engaging textbook in I/O psychology.

The chapter-by-chapter revisions for the 9th Edition include:

- **Chapter 1.** Update on the history of I/O psychology across all major areas of interest within the field. A discussion of why I/O psychology has limited visibility within psychology and the origin of the field's name.

- **Chapter 2.** Discussion of the meaning and importance of theory in I/O psychology. How a quantitative approach to I/O psychology evolved and why it is important to understand. The problems of "translating" scientific research findings into practical applications and a discussion of why I/O practitioners are often slow to adopt scientific findings.

- **Chapter 3.** The presentation of two new major criteria in I/O psychology: emotional labor and person-organization fit. Discussion of how job analysis came to be a prominent activity in I/O psychology. Expanded discussion of dynamic performance criteria and their importance for both the science and practice of I/O psychology.

- **Chapter 4.** Increased discussion of faking in personality assessment. Discussion of alternative methods for assessing personality beyond paper-and-pencil inventories: the job interview, telephone reference checks, and cognitive reasoning tests. Advances in internet testing and situational judgment tests.

- **Chapter 5.** Major new section explaining personnel selection from a non-quantitative, human perspective, and describing the reasons why employers make the personnel selection decisions they do. Increased discussion of Affirmative Action and the relevance of U.S. employment laws in an era of global business. Increased emphasis on "high stakes" testing, retesting, and the effects of candidates knowing their test scores on the application process.

- **Chapter 6.** New section on error management training. Increased discussion of how the global economy affects the need for organizational learning. Recent research advances in mentoring and sexual harassment.

- **Chapter 7.** Explanation of top-grading as a means of performance management. Added discussion of how performance appraisal is embedded in a larger organizational context. Discussion of a proposed construct of a "general factor" of job performance and its implications for personnel selection.

- **Chapter 8.** Discussion of major advances in Mintzberg's theory of organization, including two new dimensions: ideology and politics. A detailed description of how intended small organizational change can mushroom into unintended radical change. An explanation of the need for organizational change at all levels of society in a rapidly changing world. New material on organizational culture, Six Sigma, global organizations and distinctions among downsizing, outsourcing, and offshoring.

- **Chapter 9.** Discussion of the origins of teamwork and how society is dependent upon teamwork to function. Increased discussion of trust in teams and how contextual performance applies to teams.

- **Chapter 10.** Discussion of a new integrated theory of job satisfaction. Increased analysis of how moods affect emotions at work, gender differences in perceptions of altruistic behavior, breaches of the psychological contract, workplace cynicism, and the consequences to both employees and the organization of job loss.

- **Chapter 11.** Discussion of major reports by the U.S. Department of Labor on the worst forms of child labor throughout the world, and by the World Health Organization on night shift work causing cancer. Increased coverage of illicit drug usage in the workforce, cross-cultural differences in work/family conflict, the growing recognition of positive psychology, and the emergence of "happiness" as a meaningful scientific construct.

- **Chapter 12.** Recent research findings on self-regulation and work design theories of motivation. Discussion of a new theory of motivation proposed to explain how we must adapt to radical changes at work. Explanation of how the more recent theoretical advances describing motivated employees are similar to the research findings describing mentally healthy employees.

- **Chapter 13.** Major new section on entrepreneurship. Entrepreneurship is explained from the perspective of leadership: the interaction of a person and a situation. Recent research on psychopaths in the workplace and the value of researchers asking the right questions as they seek to understand leadership.

- **Chapter 14.** A new theoretical explanation of why workers join unions. Advances in online dispute settlement, hybrid dispute resolution methods, and women in organized labor.

I am honored that, after eight editions, *Psychology Applied to Work* has become the most widely read textbook in the history of I/O psychology. I sincerely believe that this is the finest edition yet. I look forward to continuing to chronicle our rapidly changing discipline in the years to come.

Ancillaries For Students and Instructors

For Students

Study Guide.   The *Study Guide* is electronically downloadable and is available at no cost to students. Its purpose is to provide additional assistance in understanding industrial/organizational psychology. It includes key terms and concepts, the main ideas of each chapter and how they relate to one another, practical exercises, quizzes, and lists of relevant websites. The free *Study Guide* can be accessed at *www.hypergraphicpress.com*.

For Instructors

Instructor's Manual with Test Bank.   The *Instructor's Manual with Test Bank* is electronically downloadable and is available to every registered instructor. It includes chapter outlines, learning objectives, test items (multiple choice, fill-in, and essay), instructional tips, and web links. Powerpoint slides are provided for each chapter that summarize the main points of the text; and the contents of the slides can be modified for individual instructor customization. The instructor should register online to access the *Instructor's Manual with Test Bank* at *www.hypergraphicpress.com*.

1

The Historical Background of I/O Psychology

Chapter Outline

Industrial/Organizational Psychology
Fields of I/O Psychology

Licensing of Psychologists

The History of I/O Psychology
The Early Years (1900–1916)
World War I (1917–1918)
Between the Wars (1919–1940)
World War II (1941–1945)
Toward Specialization (1946–1963)
Government Intervention
(1964–1993)
The Information Age (1994–Present)
Overview

The Changing Nature of Work:
I/O Psychology and 9/11/01

Cross-Cultural I/O Psychology

The Mandate of I/O Psychology

Chapter Summary

Learning Objectives

- Explain how I/O psychology relates to the profession of psychology as a whole.
- Be able to identify the major fields of I/O psychology.
- Understand how and why psychologists are licensed.
- Learn the history of I/O psychology, including major people, events, and eras.
- Give the reasons for cross-cultural interest in I/O psychology

Psychology is defined as the scientific study of thinking and behavior. It is a science because psychologists use the same rigorous methods of research found in other areas of scientific investigation. Some of their research is more biological in nature (such as the effects of brain lesions on a rat's food consumption); other research is more social in nature (such as identifying the factors that lead to bystander apathy). Because psychology covers such a broad spectrum of content areas, it is difficult to have a clear and accurate image of what a psychologist does. Many people think that every psychologist "is a shrink," "has a black couch," "likes to discover what makes people tick," and so on. In fact, these descriptions usually refer to the specialty of clinical psychology—the diagnosis and treatment of mental illness or abnormal behavior. Most psychologists do not treat mental disorders, nor do they practice psychotherapy. In reality, psychologists are a very diversified lot with many specialized interests.

Many psychologists are united professionally through membership in the American Psychological Association (APA), founded in 1892. As of 2007 the APA had more than 148,000 members. The broad diversity of interests among psychologists is reflected by the fact that the APA has 54 divisions representing special-interest subgroups. There are not really so many different specialty areas of psychology, just many fields in which the same basic psychological principles are applied. Although some APA members have no divisional affiliation, others belong to more than one. The APA publishes several journals—vehicles through which psychologists can communicate their research findings to other scholars. The APA also holds regional and national conventions, sets standards for graduate training in certain areas of psychology (that is, clinical, counseling, and school), develops and enforces a code of professional ethics, and helps psychologists find employment. In 1988 the American Psychological Society (APS) was founded, in part because the membership and emphasis of the APA had shifted significantly toward the health care practice areas of psychology. The purpose of the APS is to advance the discipline of psychology primarily from a scientific perspective. Most of its members are academic psychologists.

Industrial/Organizational Psychology

Society for Industrial and Organizational Psychology (SIOP)
The professional organization that represents I/O psychologists in the United States.

One of the specialty areas of psychology is industrial/organizational (I/O) psychology (represented by Division 14 of the APA, the **Society for Industrial and Organizational Psychology**, or **SIOP**). In 2007 SIOP had about 6,000 professional members (62% male and 38% female). The percentage of women entering the field has greatly accelerated in recent years. For example, in 2001 more than half of those who received doctorates in I/O psychology were women, and the trend is continuing. SIOP is the primary professional organization for I/O psychologists in this nation. SIOP has a website on the internet, *www.siop.org*, which provides information about careers in I/O psychology. In other countries what we call *I/O psychology* has other names. In the United Kingdom it is referred to as *occupational psychology*, in many European countries as *work and organizational psychology*, and in South Africa *industrial psychology*. The Japanese Association of I/O Psychology has almost 900 members (Author, 2002). Although the terminology varies around the world, the members of our profession share common interests. Warr (2007a) described the origins (typically the 1920s) of I/O psychology in several European nations, Japan, Australia, Israel, and Canada. He noted both the practice and science of the discipline were often influenced by the prevailing political, cultural, and economic forces operating at the time.

Approximately 4% of all psychologists work in the I/O area. Our relatively small representation in the total population of psychologists probably helps to explain why some people are unaware of the I/O area. As noted by Campbell (2007), the various applications of psychology are often directed toward enhancing the welfare of an individual or an institution (as a school or business organization). Clinical psychology, for example, is directed toward enhancing the lives of individuals. I/O psychology strives to enhance both the institution and the individual, but the image of the field is often portrayed as more aligned with institutional welfare.

I/O psychology has long grappled with its image. The general public is not as aware of I/O psychology as, for example, clinical psychology. Various efforts have been made to understand why I/O psychology has a low level of recognition. Payne and Pariyothorn (2007) reported that every year approximately 1.5 million students in the United States enroll in an introductory psychology course. To the extent students learn about the various areas of psychology in an introductory course, many I/O psychologists believe their area does not get much notice or coverage. Zickar and Gibby (2007) also commented on how I/O psychology is misperceived. "One I/O psychologist complained that the mere mention of 'psychology' often evokes images of Freud, couches, and psychoanalysis, not to mention sex therapy. . . . This problem of marginalization has existed throughout I/O psychology history; knowledge of I/O psychology remains fairly low among the general public" (p. 76). Another possibility is the linguistically unwieldy 14-syllable name the field has selected for itself: "industrial/organizational psychology." Highhouse (2007b) noted that a name conveys an image, and the field's image is unclear. Highhouse described the experience in 1969 of a British physicist who thought he made a monumental discovery. "He called his finding a 'gravitationally totally collapsed object' and the world responded with a collective yawn. Months later, he began to refer to his discovery as a 'black hole,' and it suddenly became headline news" (p. 56). I/O psychologists have discussed changing their name to help clarify its image to the public, but no apparent agreement has yet been reached on any other name. Ryan (2003) commented that I/O psychology does not have a clear identity and that relatively few people have ever heard of "industrial and organizational psychology," nor do they understand how our discipline differs from others.

I/O psychology
An area of scientific study and professional practice that addresses psychological concepts and principles in the work world.

As a specialty area, **I/O psychology** has a more restricted definition than psychology as a whole. Many years ago Blum and Naylor (1968) defined it as "simply the application or extension of psychological facts and principles to the problems concerning human beings operating within the context of business and industry" (p. 4). In broad terms, the I/O psychologist is concerned with behavior in work situations. There are two-sides of I/O psychology: science and practice. I/O psychology is a legitimate field of scientific inquiry, concerned with advancing knowledge about people at work. As in any area of science, I/O psychologists pose questions to guide their investigation and then use scientific methods to obtain answers. Psychologists try to form the results of studies into meaningful patterns that will be useful in explaining behavior and to replicate findings to make generalizations about behavior. In this respect, I/O psychology is an academic discipline.

The other side of I/O psychology—the professional side—is concerned with the application of knowledge to solve real problems in the world of work. I/O psychologists

Scientist–practitioner model
A model or framework for education in an academic discipline based on understanding the scientific principles and findings evidenced in the discipline and how they provide the basis for the professional practice.

can use research findings to hire better employees, reduce absenteeism, improve communication, increase job satisfaction, and solve countless other problems. Most I/O psychologists feel a sense of kinship with both sides: science and practice. Accordingly, the education of I/O psychologists is founded on the **scientist–practitioner model**, which trains them in both scientific inquiry and practical application.

As an I/O psychologist, I am pleased that the results of my research can be put to some practical use. But by the same token, I am more than a technician—someone who goes through the motions of finding solutions to problems without knowing why they "work" and what their consequences will be. I/O psychology is more than just a tool for business leaders to use to make their companies more efficient. So the I/O psychologist has a dual existence. Well-trained I/O psychologists realize that an effective application of knowledge can come only from sound knowledge, and they can therefore both contribute to knowledge and apply it. Dunnette (1998) believes that an emerging trend in I/O psychology is greater fusion of the science and practice aspects of our profession than we have witnessed in the past.

I/O psychologists work in four main employment settings: universities, consulting firms, industry, and government, with universities and consulting firms being the primary employers. Across these four areas, I/O psychologists are unevenly split in their scientist–practitioner orientation. Universities employ more scientists; consulting firms employ more practitioners; business and government have a good mix of both. As of 2006 the median annual income for M.S. graduates in I/O psychology was approximately $80,000, whereas Ph.D. graduates in I/O psychology earned approximately $103,000 (Khanna & Medsker, 2007). However, these annual salaries are heavily influenced by whether the I/O psychologist is employed primarily as an academic or a practitioner. Some members of our profession who work in consulting firms earn more than $1 million annually. Brooks et al. (2003) examined the values of I/O psychologists who elect to work as academics and as practitioners. Academics were found to place a higher value on autonomy (the desire to work independently) and scientific research, whereas practitioners placed a higher value on affiliation (the desire to work with others) and a structured work environment.

Fields of I/O Psychology

Like psychology in general, I/O psychology is a diversified science with several subspecialties. The professional activities of I/O psychologists can be grouped into six general fields.

Selection and Placement.   I/O psychologists who work in this field are concerned with developing assessment methods for the selection, placement, and promotion of employees. They are involved in studying jobs and determining to what degree tests can predict performance in those jobs. They are also concerned with the placement of employees and identifying those jobs that are most compatible with an individual's skills and interests.

Training and Development.   This field is concerned with identifying employee skills that need to be enhanced to improve job performance. The areas of training include technical skills enhancement (e.g., computer operations), managerial development programs, and training of all employees to work together effectively. I/O psychologists

DILBERT by Scott Adams

Dilbert: © Scott Adams/Dist. by United Feature Syndicate, Inc. Reprinted with permission.

who work in this field must design ways to determine whether training and development programs have been successful.

Performance Appraisal. Performance appraisal is the process of identifying criteria or standards for determining how well employees are performing their jobs. I/O psychologists who work in this field are also concerned with determining the utility or value of job performance to the organization. They may be involved with measuring the performance of work teams, units within the organization, or the organization itself.

Organization Development. Organization development is the process of analyzing the structure of an organization to maximize the satisfaction and effectiveness of individuals, work groups, and customers. Organizations grow and mature just as people do; thus the field of organization development is directed toward facilitating the organizational growth process. I/O psychologists who work in this field are sensitized to the wide array of factors that influence behavior in organizations.

Quality of Worklife. I/O psychologists who work in this field are concerned with factors that contribute to a healthy and productive workforce. They may be involved in redesigning jobs to make them more meaningful and satisfying to the people who perform them. A high-quality worklife contributes to greater productivity of the organization and to the emotional health of the individual.

Ergonomics. Ergonomics is a multidisciplinary field that includes I/O psychologists. It is concerned with designing tools, equipment, and machines that are compatible with human skills. I/O psychologists who work in this field draw upon knowledge derived from physiology, industrial medicine, and perception to design work systems that humans can operate effectively.

In summary, psychology as a discipline is composed of many specialty areas, one of which is I/O psychology. And I/O psychology consists of several subspecialties. Although some of these subspecialties overlap, many are distinct from one another. Thus I/O psychology is not really a single discipline; it is a mix of subspecialties bonded together by a concern for people at work. Each of the subspecialties of I/O psychology will be explored to various degrees in this book.

Licensing of Psychologists

What makes a psychologist a psychologist? What prevents people with no psychological training from passing themselves off as psychologists? One way professions offer high-quality service to the public is by regulating their own membership. Selective admission into the profession helps protect the public against quacks and charlatans who can cause great damage not only to their clients but also to the profession they allegedly represent.

Licensure
The process by which a professional practice is regulated by law to ensure quality standards are met to protect the public.

The practice of professional psychology is regulated by law in every state. A law that regulates both the title and practice of psychology is called a *licensing law*. **Licensure** limits those qualified to practice psychology as defined by state law. Each state has its own standards for licensure, and these are governed by regulatory boards. The major functions of any professional board are to determine the standards for admission into the profession and to discipline its members when professional standards are violated.

Typically, licensure involves education, experience, examination, and administrative requirements. A doctoral degree in psychology from an approved program is usually required as well as one or two years of supervised experience. Applicants must also pass an objective, written examination covering many areas of psychology, although the majority of questions pertain to the health care (i.e., clinical and counseling) areas of psychology. Specialty examinations (for example, in I/O psychology) usually are not given. Currently, psychologists must pass a uniform national examination to obtain a license. Finally, the applicant must meet citizenship and residency requirements and be of good moral character.

Licensing is intended to ensure that clients receive services from qualified practitioners. Even scrupulous I/O psychologists can never guarantee results, however, and they should never try. Companies have been duped by consulting firms and individuals into believing a wide range of claims that simply cannot be substantiated. The problems that the I/O psychologist faces are too complex for guarantees. Reasonable expectations on the part of both the I/O psychologist and the company are the best way to avoid such difficulties.

The licensure of I/O psychologists is controversial. The original purpose of licensure in psychology was to protect the public in the health care areas of psychology. Because I/O psychologists are not health care providers, the need for licensure to protect the public is not so pressing (Howard & Lowman, 1985). Also, some I/O psychologists object to the heavy emphasis placed on clinical and counseling psychology in the licensure process. Most states regard I/O psychologists as they do other types of applied psychologists who offer services to the public, however, and thus require them to be licensed. A few states regard I/O psychologists as having a sufficiently different mandate to exempt them from requiring licensure. The issue of licensing remains an ongoing professional concern for I/O psychologists (Macey, 2002).

The History of I/O Psychology

It is always difficult to write *the* history of anything; there are different perspectives with different emphases. It is also a challenge to divide the historical evolution of a discipline into units of time. In some cases, time itself is a convenient watershed (decades or centuries); in others, major events serve as landmarks. In the case of I/O psychology, the two world wars were major catalysts for changing the discipline. This historical overview will show how the field of I/O psychology came to be what it is and how some key individuals and events helped shape it.[1]

The Early Years (1900–1916)

In its beginnings, what we know today as I/O psychology didn't even have a name; it was a merging of two forces that gathered momentum before 1900. One force was the pragmatic nature of some basic psychological research. Most psychologists at this time were strictly scientific and deliberately avoided studying problems that strayed outside the boundaries of pure research. However, the psychologist W. L. Bryan published a paper (Bryan & Harter, 1897) about how professional telegraphers develop skill in sending and receiving Morse code. A few years later in 1903, Bryan's (1904) presidential address to the American Psychological Association touched on having psychologists study "concrete activities and functions as they appear in everyday life" (p. 80). Bryan did not advocate studying problems found in industry per se, but he emphasized examining real skills as a base upon which to develop scientific psychology. Bryan is not considered the father of I/O psychology but rather a precursor.[2]

The second major force in the evolution of the discipline came from the desire of industrial engineers to improve efficiency. They were concerned mainly with the economics of manufacturing and thus the productivity of industrial employees. Industrial engineers developed "time and motion" studies to prescribe the most efficient body motions per unit of time to perform a particular work task. For example, by arranging parts to be assembled in a certain pattern, a worker could affix a nut to a bolt every 6 seconds, or 10 per minute.

The merging of psychology with applied interests and concern for increasing industrial efficiency was the impetus for the emergence of I/O psychology. Koppes (2002) observed that in the late 19th century American society was undergoing rapid changes and developments because of industrialization, immigration, a high birthrate, education, and urban growth. A drive for social reform prevailed, Americans were ready for the useful, and society looked toward science for practical solutions. These societal demands forced psychologists to popularize their science and demonstrate the value of psychology in solving problems and helping society. As eloquently stated by Koppes and Pickren (2007), "The prevailing generation wanted to make the American society a better and safer place to live and work. Society turned to science for practical solutions to everyday problems. Improving the quality of work was part of a broad-based social effort to improve the quality of life" (p. 10). I/O psychology took its place upon the social stage to help achieve this result. By 1910 "industrial psychology" (the "organizational" appendage did not become official until 1973) was a legitimate specialty area of psychology.

---

[1] A more detailed treatment of the history of I/O psychology can be found in the book by Koppes (2007).

[2] The term *industrial psychology* was apparently used for the first time in Bryan's 1904 article. Ironically, it appeared in print only as a typographical error. Bryan was quoting a sentence he had written five years earlier (Bryan & Harter, 1899), in which he spoke of the need for more research in individual psychology. Instead, Bryan wrote "industrial" psychology and did not catch his mistake.

Walter Dill Scott

Four individuals stand out as the founding figures of I/O psychology. They worked independently of one another, and their major contributions deserve a brief review.

Walter Dill Scott.   Scott, a psychologist, was persuaded to give a talk to some Chicago business leaders on the need for applying psychology to advertising. His talk was well received and led to the publication of two books: *The Theory of Advertising* (1903) and *The Psychology of Advertising* (1908). The first book dealt with suggestion and argument as means of influencing people. The second book was aimed at improving human efficiency with such tactics as imitation, competition, loyalty, and concentration. By 1911 Scott had expanded his areas of interest and published two more books: *Influencing Men in Business* and *Increasing Human Efficiency in Business*. During World War I, Scott was instrumental in the application of personnel procedures in the army. Landy (1997) described Scott as the consummate scientist–practitioner who was highly respected in both spheres of professional activity. Scott had a substantial influence on increasing public awareness and the credibility of industrial psychology.

Frederick W. Taylor

Frederick W. Taylor.   Taylor was an engineer by profession. His formal schooling was limited, but through experience and self-training in engineering he went on to obtain many patents. As he worked himself up through one company as a worker, supervisor, and finally plant manager, Taylor realized the value of redesigning the work situation to achieve both higher output for the company and a higher wage for the worker. His best-known work is his book *The Principles of Scientific Management* (1911). Van De Water (1997) reported these principles as: (1) science over rule of thumb, (2) scientific selection and training, (3) cooperation over individualism, and (4) equal division of work best suited to management and employees. In perhaps the most famous example of his methods, Taylor showed that workers who handled heavy iron ingots (pig iron) could be more productive if they had work rests. Training employees when to work and when to rest increased average worker productivity from 12.5 to 47.0 tons moved per day (with less reported fatigue), which resulted in increased wages for them. The company also drastically increased efficiency by reducing costs from 9.2 cents to 3.9 cents per ton.

As a consequence of this method, it was charged that Taylor inhumanely exploited workers for a higher wage and that great numbers of workers would be unemployed because fewer were needed. Because unemployment was rampant at this time, the attacks on Taylor were virulent. His methods were eventually investigated by the Interstate Commerce Commission (ICC) and the U.S. House of Representatives. Taylor replied that increased efficiency led to greater, not less, prosperity and that workers not hired for one job would be placed in another that would better use their potential. The arguments were never really resolved; World War I broke out and the controversy faded.

Lillian Moller Gilbreth.   Koppes (1997) reported that Lillian Gilbreth was one of several female psychologists who made substantial contributions in the early era of

Underwood and Underwood/CORBIS

Lillian Moller Gilbreth

I/O psychology. Along with her husband, Frank, she pioneered industrial management techniques that are still used. Her husband was more concerned with the technical aspects of worker efficiency, while she was more concerned with the human aspects of time management. Lillian Gilbreth was among the first to recognize the effects of stress and fatigue on workers. Koppes noted that Gilbreth made a historic speech at a meeting of industrial engineers in 1908. She was asked for her opinion because she was the only woman at the meeting. According to Yost (1943), Gilbreth "rose to her feet and remarked that the human being, of course, was the most important element in industry, and that it seemed to her this element had not been receiving the attention it warranted. The engineer's scientific training, she said, was all for the handling of inanimate objects. She called attention to the fact that psychology was fast becoming a science and that it had much to offer that was being ignored by management engineers. The plea in her impromptu remarks was for the new profession of scientific management to open its eyes to the necessary place psychology had in any program industrial engineers worked out" (Koppes, 1997, p. 511). The mother of 12 children, Gilbreth combined a career and family and was called by a leading publication "a genius in the art of living." Two of her children wrote a book about her life, *Cheaper by the Dozen*, which was made into a motion picture in 1950 and remade in 2003.

Archives of the History of American Psychology at the University of Akron

Hugo Münsterberg

Hugo Münsterberg.   Münsterberg was a German psychologist with traditional academic training. The noted American psychologist William James invited Münsterberg to Harvard University, where he applied his experimental methods to a variety of problems, including perception and attention. He was a popular figure in American education, a gifted public speaker, and a personal friend of President Theodore Roosevelt. Benjamin (2006) stated, "Münsterberg's personality made him a natural for the role of scientific expert. . . . He was authoritarian in manner; he promoted the application of psychology. Indeed, he would argue that the contributions of psychological science were necessary for success in business and in everyday life" (p. 420). Münsterberg was interested in applying traditional psychological methods to practical industrial problems. His book *Psychology and Industrial Efficiency* (1913) was divided into three parts: selecting workers, designing work situations, and using psychology in sales. One of Münsterberg's most renowned studies involved determining what makes a safe trolley car operator. He systematically studied all aspects of the job, developed an ingenious laboratory simulation of a trolley car, and concluded that a good operator could comprehend simultaneously all of the influences that bear on the car's progress. Some writers consider Münsterberg *the* founder of industrial psychology. Landy (1992) reported that many prominent I/O psychologists throughout the 20th century can trace their professional roots back to Münsterberg. Münsterberg's influence in the history of the field is well evidenced by the coterie of I/O psychologists who were guided by his teachings.

When World War I broke out in Europe, Münsterberg supported the German cause. He was ostracized for his allegiance, and the emotional strain probably contributed to his death in 1916. Only the U.S. involvement in the war gave some unity to the profession. The primary emphasis of the early work in I/O psychology was on the economic gains that could be accrued by applying the ideas and methods of psychology to problems in business and industry. Business leaders began to employ psychologists, and some psychologists entered applied research. However, World War I caused a shift in the direction of industrial psychological research.

World War I (1917–1918)

World War I was a potent impetus to psychology's rise to respectability. Psychologists believed they could provide a valuable service to the nation, and some saw the war as a means of accelerating the profession's progress. Robert Yerkes was the psychologist most instrumental in involving psychology in the war. As president of the APA, he maneuvered the profession into assignments in the war effort. The APA made many proposals, including ways of screening recruits for mental deficiency and of assigning selected recruits to jobs in the army. Committees of psychologists investigated soldier motivation and morale, psychological problems of physical incapacity, and discipline. Yerkes continued to press his point that psychology could be of great help to our nation in wartime.

The army, in turn, was somewhat skeptical of the psychologists' claims. It eventually approved only a modest number of proposals, mostly those involving the assessment of recruits. Yerkes and other psychologists reviewed a series of general intelligence tests and eventually developed one that they called the **Army Alpha**. When they discovered that 30% of the recruits were illiterate, they developed the **Army Beta**, a special test for those who couldn't read English. Many military recruits in WWI were foreign-born and had limited capacity to read and write English. The Army Beta Test was used to assess such recruits, and contained information presented in the form of pictures and graphics (Salas, DeRooin, & Gade, 2007). Meanwhile, Walter Dill Scott was doing research on the best placement of soldiers in the army. He classified and placed enlisted soldiers, conducted performance ratings of officers, and developed and prepared job duties and qualifications for more than 500 jobs.

Plans for testing recruits proceeded at a slow pace. The army built special testing sites at its camps and ordered all officers, officer candidates, and newly drafted recruits to be tested. Both the Army Alpha and Army Beta group intelligence tests were used, as were a few individual tests. The final order authorizing the testing program came from the Adjutant General's office in August 1918. However, the war ended just three months later, and testing was terminated just as it was finally organized and authorized. As a result, the intelligence testing program didn't contribute as much to the war as Yerkes had hoped. Even though 1,726,000 individuals were ultimately tested in the program, actual use of the results was minimal.

Although psychology's impact on the war effort was not substantial, the very process of giving psychologists so much recognition and authority was a great impetus to the profession. Psychologists were regarded as capable of making valuable contributions to society and of adding to a company's (and in war, a nation's) prosperity. Also in 1917 the oldest and most representative journal in the field of I/O psychology—the *Journal of Applied Psychology*—began publication. Some of the articles in the first volume were "Practical Relations Between Psychology and the War" by G. S. Hall,

Army Alpha Test
An intelligence test developed during World War I by I/O psychologists for the selection and placement of military personnel.

Army Beta Test
A nonverbal intelligence test developed during World War I by I/O psychologists to assess illiterate recruits.

"Mentality Testing of College Students" by W. V. Bingham, and "The Moron As a War Problem" by F. Mateer. The first article published in the *Journal of Applied Psychology* not only summarized the prevailing state of industrial psychology at the time but also addressed the science-versus-practice issue that still faces I/O psychologists today.

> The past few years have witnessed an unprecedented interest in the extension of the application of psychology to various fields of human activity . . . . But perhaps the most strikingly original endeavor to utilize the methods and the results of psychological investigation has been in the realm of business. This movement began with the psychology of advertising . . . . Thence the attention of the applied psychologist turned to the more comprehensive and fundamental problem of vocational selection—the question, namely, of making a detailed inventory of the equipment of mental qualities possessed by a given individual, of discovering what qualities are essential to successful achievement in a given vocation, and thus of directing the individual to the vocational niche which he is best fitted to fill . . . . Every psychologist who besides being a "pure scientist" also cherishes the hope that in addition to throwing light upon the problems of his science, his findings may also contribute their quota to the sum-total of human happiness; and it must appeal to every human being who is interested in increasing human efficiency and human happiness by the more direct method of decreasing the number of cases where a square peg is condemned to a life of fruitless endeavor to fit itself comfortably into a round hole. (Hall, Baird, & Geissler, 1917, pp. 5–6)

After the war, there was a boom in the number of psychological consulting firms and research bureaus. The birth of these agencies ushered in the next era in I/O psychology.

Between the Wars (1919–1940)

Applied psychology emerged from World War I as a recognized discipline. Society was beginning to realize that industrial psychology could solve practical problems. Following the war, several psychological research bureaus came into full bloom. The Bureau of Salesmanship Research was developed by Walter Bingham at the Carnegie Institute of Technology. There was little precedent for this kind of cooperation between college and industry. The bureau intended to use psychological research techniques to solve problems that had never been examined scientifically. Twenty-seven companies cooperated with Bingham, each contributing $500 annually to finance applied psychological research. One of the early products of the bureau was the book *Aids in Selecting Salesmen*. For several years the bureau concentrated on the selection, classification, and development of clerical and executive personnel as well as salespeople.

Another influential group during the period was the Psychological Corporation, founded by James Cattell in 1921. Cattell formed it as a business corporation and asked psychologists to buy stock in it. The purpose of the Psychological Corporation was to advance psychology and promote its usefulness to industry. The corporation also served as a clearinghouse for information. To protect against quacks and charlatans, who were becoming increasingly prevalent, it provided companies with reference checks on prospective psychologists. Unlike many agencies that began at the time, the Psychological Corporation has remained in business. Over the years it has changed its early mission, and today it is one of the country's largest publishers of psychological tests.

In 1924 a series of experiments began at the Hawthorne Works of the Western Electric Company. Although initially they seemed to be of minor scientific significance, they became classics in industrial psychology. In the opinion of many writers, the **Hawthorne studies** "represent the most significant research program undertaken to show the enormous complexity of the problem of production in relation to efficiency" (Blum & Naylor, 1968, p. 306). The Hawthorne Works of the Western Electric Company is still in operation today (see Figure 1-1).

Hawthorne studies
A series of research studies that began in the late 1920s at the Western Electric Company and ultimately refocused the interests of I/O psychologists on how work behavior manifests itself in an organizational context.

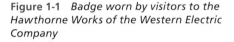

Figure 1-1 *Badge worn by visitors to the Hawthorne Works of the Western Electric Company*

The Hawthorne studies were a joint venture between Western Electric and several researchers from Harvard University (none of whom were industrial psychologists by training). The original study attempted to find the relationship between lighting and efficiency. The researchers installed various sets of lights in workrooms where electrical equipment was being produced. In some cases the light was intense; in other cases it was reduced to the equivalent of moonlight. Much to the researchers' surprise, productivity seemed to have no relationship to the level of illumination. The workers' productivity increased whether the illumination was decreased, increased, or held constant. The results of the study were so bizarre the researchers hypothesized that some other factors must be responsible for the increased productivity.

The results of the first study initiated four other major studies that were conducted over a 12-year period: (1) relay assembly test room, (2) mass interviewing program, (3) bank wiring observation room, and (4) personnel counseling. (For more information on these studies, see the original text by Roethlisberger and Dickson, 1939.) In essence, the Hawthorne studies revealed many previously unrecognized aspects of human behavior in a workplace. Researchers hypothesized that the study's results were caused by the employees' desire to please them. Flattered at having distinguished investigators from Harvard University take the time to study them, the workers had gone out of their way to do what they thought would impress them—namely, to be highly productive. They therefore had produced at a high level whether the room was too light or too dark. The researchers learned that factors other than purely technical ones (for example, illumination) influence productivity.

Hawthorne effect
A positive change in behavior that occurs at the onset of an intervention followed by a gradual decline, often to the original level of the behavior prior to the intervention. First identified in the Hawthorne studies, which is why it is so named.

One of the major findings from the studies was a phenomenon named the **Hawthorne effect**. The workers' job performance began to improve following the start of the researchers' intervention and continued to improve because of the novelty of the situation; that is, the employees responded positively to the novel treatment they were getting from the researchers. Eventually, however, the novelty began to wear off, and productivity returned to its earlier level. This phenomenon of a change in behavior following the onset of novel treatment, with a gradual return to the previous level of behavior as the effect of the novelty wears off, is the Hawthorne effect.

As Adair (1984) observed, however, the precise reason for the change in behavior (for example, the novelty of the situation, special attention, or prestige from being selected for study) is not always clear. Sometimes behavior change is due to just a change in the environment (for example, the presence of the researchers) and not to the effect of some experimentally manipulated variable (for example, the amount of illumination). The psychological literature indicates that Hawthorne effects may last from a few days to two years, depending on the situation.

The Hawthorne studies also revealed the existence of informal employee work groups and their controls on production as well as the importance of employee attitudes, the value of having a sympathetic and understanding supervisor, and the need to treat workers as people instead of merely human capital. Their revelation of the complexity of human behavior opened up new vistas for industrial psychology, which for nearly 40 years had been dominated by the goal of improving company efficiency. Today the Hawthorne studies, though regarded by some contemporary psychologists as having been based on flawed research methods (e.g., Bramel & Friend, 1981), are considered to be the greatest single episode in the formation of industrial psychology. They also showed that researchers sometimes obtain totally unexpected results. Because the investigators were not tied to any one explanation, their studies took them into areas never before studied by industrial psychology and raised questions that otherwise might never have been asked. Industrial psychology was never the same again.

This era in industrial psychology ended with the coincidental conclusion of the Hawthorne studies and the outbreak of World War II. Industrial psychologists were now faced with an immense task: helping to mobilize a nation for a global war.

World War II (1941–1945)

When the United States entered World War II, industrial psychologists were more prepared for their role in the war effort than they had been in 1917. By this time, psychologists had studied the problems of employee selection and placement and had refined their techniques considerably.

Walter Bingham chaired the advisory committee on classification of military personnel that had been formed in response to the army's need for classification and training. Unlike in World War I, this time the army approached the psychologists first. One of the committee's earliest assignments was to develop a test that could sort new recruits into five categories based on their ability to learn the duties and responsibilities of a soldier. The test that was finally developed was the **Army General Classification Test (AGCT)**, a benchmark in the history of group testing. Harrell (1992), in reflecting on his own involvement in developing the AGCT 50 years earlier, reported that 12 million soldiers were classified into military jobs on the basis of the test. The committee also worked on other projects, such as methods of selecting people for officer training, trade proficiency tests, and supplemental aptitude tests.

Psychologists also worked on the development and use of situational stress tests, a project undertaken by the U.S. Office of Strategic Services (OSS) (Murray &

Army General Classification Test (AGCT)
A test developed during World War II by I/O psychologists for the selection and placement of military personnel.

MacKinnon, 1946). The purpose of this testing program was to assess candidates for assignment to military intelligence units. During a three-day session of extremely intensive testing and observation, the candidates lived together in small groups under almost continuous observation by the assessment staff. Specially constructed situational tests, many modeled after techniques developed in the German and British armies, were used to assess candidates in nontraditional ways. One test, for example, involved constructing a 5-foot cube from a collection of wooden poles, pegs, and blocks. It was impossible for one person to assemble the cube in the allotted time, so two "helpers" were provided. These were actually psychologists who played prearranged roles. One helper acted very passive and contributed little; the other obstructed work by making impractical suggestions and ridiculing and criticizing the candidate. Of course, no candidate could complete the project with this kind of "help." The real purpose of the test was not to see whether the candidates could construct the cube but to assess their emotional and interpersonal reactions to stress and frustration. In general, the OSS assessment program was judged to be quite successful.

Another area of work was the selection and training of pilots to fly warplanes. The committee formed for this purpose consisted of psychologists, military personnel, and civilian pilots. The committee's policy was to move the traditional experimental test setting from the laboratory to the cockpit. Airplanes were outfitted with recording and monitoring devices to assess the problems and reactions of student pilots. This research resulted in two products. First, good candidates were selected and trained as pilots (the traditional domain of personnel psychology). Second, equipment was designed to make the pilot's job easier and safer (a contribution of the new field of engineering psychology).

Throughout the war, industrial psychology was also being used in civilian life. The use of employment tests in industry increased greatly. Because the nation needed a productive workforce, psychologists were called on to help reduce employee absenteeism. Industry discovered that many of the techniques of industrial psychologists were useful, especially in the areas of selection, training, and machine design, and industrial leaders were particularly interested in the applications of social psychology. New methods of measuring soldier attitude and morale could also be used in industry. In short, the techniques developed during the war could be applied to business and industry in peacetime. World War II was a springboard for refining industrial psychological techniques and honing the skills of applied psychologists.

Each of the two world wars had a major effect on industrial psychology but in a somewhat different way. World War I helped form the profession and give it social acceptance. World War II helped develop and refine it. The next era in the history of I/O psychology saw the discipline evolve into subspecialties and attain higher levels of academic and scientific rigor.

Toward Specialization (1946–1963)

In this era industrial psychology evolved into a legitimate field of scientific inquiry, having already been accepted as a professional practice. More colleges and universities began to offer courses in "industrial psychology," and graduate degrees (both M.S. and Ph.D.) were soon given. The Division of Industrial Psychology of the APA was created in 1946. Benjamin (1997) reported that earlier I/O psychologists had less professional identity, being represented in the family of "applied psychologists."

As in any evolving discipline, subspecialties of interest began to crystallize and industrial psychology became splintered. New journals emerged along with new professional associations. Engineering psychology (or ergonomics), born during World War II, was recognized as a separate area, in part because of such seminal books as *Applied Experimental Psychology* (Chapanis, Garner, & Morgan, 1949) and the *Handbook of Human Engineering Data* (1949). Engineering psychology entered an explosive period of growth from 1950 to 1960 due mainly to research done in affiliation with the defense industries. Engineering psychology's heritage was a mixture of both experimental and industrial psychology, as seen in its early label, "applied experimental psychology." That part of industrial psychology specializing in personnel selection, classification, and training also got its own identity, "personnel psychology." Sometime in the 1950s, interest grew in the study of organizations. Long the province of sociologists, this area caught the interest of psychologists. Elton Mayo was a founder of what became known as the human relations movement. Drawing upon the findings from the Hawthorne studies, it emphasized individual needs, informal groups, and social relationships as the primary bases for behavior within organizations. In the 1960s industrial psychology research took on a stronger organizational flavor. Investigators gave more attention to social influences that impinge on behavior in organizations. Terms such as *organizational change* and *organization development* appeared in the literature regularly. Industrial psychology addressed a broader range of topics. Classic textbooks of the 1950s, such as *Personnel and Industrial Psychology* by Ghiselli and Brown (1955), gave way in title (as well as in substance) to books with more of an organizational thrust. Traditional academic boundaries between disciplines began to blur in this postwar period. Engineering psychology was a fusion of experimental and industrial psychology; organizational behavior was a mix of industrial psychology, social psychology, and sociology. This melding of disciplines was healthy because it decreased the use of narrow, parochial attempts to address complex areas of research.

Government Intervention (1964–1993)

In the late 1950s and early 1960s, the nation was swept up in what became known as the "civil rights movement." As a nation we became more sensitized to the plight of minorities who had systematically been denied equal opportunities to various sectors of life, including housing, education, and employment. In 1964 Congress passed the Civil Rights Act, a far-reaching piece of legislation designed to reduce unfair discrimination against minorities. One component of the Civil Rights Act, Title VII, addressed the issue of discrimination in employment. The significance of the law to I/O psychologists is explained as follows: for years I/O psychologists were given a relatively free rein to use a wide variety of psychological assessment devices (that is, tests, interviews, and so on) to make employment decisions. The result of these employment decisions was the disproportionately small representation of minorities (most notably Blacks and women) in the workplace, particularly in positions above lower-level jobs. Because historically these decisions seemed to result in discrimination against minorities, Title VII authorized the government to monitor and remedy discriminatory employment practices.

By 1978 the government had drafted a uniform set of employment guidelines to which employers were bound. Companies were legally mandated to demonstrate that their employment tests did not uniformly discriminate against any minority group. In addition, the new government standards were not limited to just paper and-pencil tests or the personnel function of selection; they addressed all devices (interviews, tests, application blanks) used to make all types of personnel decisions (selection, placement, promotion, discharge, and so on).

The discipline of I/O psychology now had to serve two ultimate authorities. The first authority is what all disciplines must serve—namely, to perform high-quality work, be it conducting scientific research or providing services to clients. The second authority added was government scrutiny and evaluation. I/O psychologists now had to accept the consequences of being legally accountable for their actions. As professionals, I/O psychologists would continue to evaluate themselves, but government policies and agencies would also judge their actions. In 1990 President George H. W. Bush signed into law the Americans with Disabilities Act and in 1991 an updated version of the Civil Rights Act. Both acts were designed to remedy further inequities in the workplace. In 1993 President William Jefferson Clinton signed into law the Family and Medical Leave Act which grants workers up to 12 weeks of unpaid leave from work to attend to family and medical issues.

Much has been discussed about the overall effect of government intervention on the profession of I/O psychology. Some people believe it has been an impetus to the profession, compelling us to address issues and develop solutions that we might otherwise have ignored. Others believe that the profession has been compromised by the intrusion of political and legal influences that deflect activities into areas beyond our traditional domain. Some of the greatest advances in I/O psychology have been made in the past 30 years, and I attribute these advances, in part, to our being accountable to forces beyond our own profession. Legal oversight has, in my opinion, prompted I/O psychologists to broaden their horizons in both the problems they address and the solutions they propose. In any case, the reality of being an I/O psychologist in the 21st century involves attentiveness to legal standards, parameters that our professional predecessors never had to deal with.

I/O psychology also made a major contribution to the military during this era. Campbell (1990a) described the efforts of I/O psychologists to develop a test for the selection and classification of military personnel. This project involved many psychologists and took almost ten years to complete. Called "Project A," it involved developing the **Armed Services Vocational Aptitude Battery (ASVAB)**. Every year the ASVAB is administered to between 300,000 and 400,000 people; of that number, 120,000 to 140,000 individuals are selected.

Armed Services Vocational Aptitude Battery (ASVAB) A test developed in the 1980s by I/O psychologists for the selection and placement of military personnel.

The Information Age (1994–Present)

In the early 1980s the personal computer provided individuals with access to a technology previously limited to large businesses. By the late 1980s a new concept was established, the internet. The internet enabled individuals and businesses throughout the world to be connected electronically. Although several years might be identified as the start of the Information Age, I have selected 1994 in part because that was the year the total number of World Wide Web sites first surpassed 1,000. In one decade that number grew to exceed 45 million (Zakon, 2004). There has become a major shift in the way society functions, primarily revolving around the explosion in available information and how that information changes our lives. The critical theme of the current era is that change, dramatic change, is upon us, and both organizations and employees must find ways to adapt to this rapidly changing world.

Murphy (1999) described how the turbulent changes faced by organizations (such as the need to change products or services frequently in response to changing market conditions) have led to the need for frequent changes in workers' responsibilities, tasks, and work relationships. Organizations that once held rigid specifications for what employees are supposed to do in their job find it difficult to compete in an environment that must be responsive to change. Organizations are more likely to hire generalists (i.e., people who are intelligent, ambitious, and willing to adjust to the demands of change) rather than specialists (i.e., people hired to perform a single job with pre-established responsibilities). Electronic communication (like the internet) has revolutionized business and customer oriented service. The concept of "e business" entails networks of suppliers, distributors, and customers who make products and render services by exchanging information online (Pearlman & Barney, 2000). Additionally, there is greater urgency to deliver products and services quickly. In decades past the typical standards for judging organizations were the quality and quantity of their products and services. In the Information Age, we add a new critical standard, speed of delivery.

The very language of work is being challenged. A "job" is the traditional unit around which work is organized and the means by which individuals are linked to organizations. Duties and responsibilities are bundled together on the basis of the tasks performed and capabilities of people assigned to the job (Ilgen & Pulakos, 1999). As individuals we desire a sense of social identity about the job we hold. In the Information Age, tasks and duties are constantly changing, as are the skills needed to perform them. As such, a "job" as a useful and meaningful way to describe work performed is starting to erode. With the innovations of telecommuting (doing work at home and communicating it electronically to the office), virtual work teams and offices, and wireless communications, work is no longer a physical place. Furthermore, integrated work is now performed in different continents at the speed of electronic transmission. For example, assume a patient goes to see a doctor. The doctor speaks into a handheld voice recorder, describing the patient's condition and treatment. By the close of business that day, the verbal account of the visit to the doctor is sent electronically halfway around the world (which at that time is the start of the workday). The verbal account is rendered into a transcription format by typists and then electronically returned to the doctor by the next business day. The transcribing work is sent overseas because of much cheaper labor costs there, perhaps as much as 80% lower than wages paid to U.S. workers. The transcription is downloaded via a printer in the doctor's office and placed in the patient's file. As has been said regarding the irrelevance of national boundaries to the conduct of work, "geography is history." Information plays such a big role in the conduct of work today that many organizations have entire units or departments devoted to "IT"—information technology. The head of that unit often holds the title of "CIO"—chief information officer. Hesketh (2001) suggested that the objective of vocational psychology, which historically was devoted to helping people identify vocations suitable for them, should shift its emphasis to help workers cope with the stress caused by radical and rapid changes in the workplace.

By any reasonable standard, the past decade has witnessed a dramatic shift in how work is performed and where it is performed, if not a change in the meaning of the concept of work. Among the leading skills workers must possess today to remain competitive in the workplace is the willingness and capacity to effectively deal with change. These changes affect the very substance of I/O psychology.

Overview

The history of I/O psychology is rich and diverse. The field was born at the confluence of several forces, developed and grew through global conflict, and was woven into the societal fabric of which it is a part. Our history is relatively brief and our members are not great in number, but I believe I/O psychologists have contributed greatly to both economic and personal welfare. The year 1992 marked the 100th anniversary of the American Psychological Association. In celebration of our centennial, Katzell and Austin (1992) wrote a major review of the history of I/O psychology. They noted that our history is marked by a continuous interweaving of scientific and professional contributions. At certain points in our history the practice of I/O psychology has been at the vanguard of our professional efforts (particularly during wars) (see The Changing Nature of Work: I/O Psychology and 9/11/01).

At other times, our scientific advances have been more noteworthy. As stated earlier in this chapter, however, the science and practice of I/O psychology can never be too far apart. Katzell and Austin quoted a memorable statement by Morris Viteles, one of the early pioneers of our field, who aptly summarized the two domains of I/O psychology: "If it isn't scientific, it's not good practice, and if it isn't practical, it's not good science" (p. 826). Indeed, Vinchur and Koppes (2007) described Viteles as a "lifelong advocate" of combining science and practice in I/O psychology. Likewise, Farr and Tesluk (1997) cited the comment by the first president of Division 14, Bruce Moore, on the duality of the science and practice of I/O psychology: "The extreme applied practitioner is in danger of narrow, myopic thinking, but the extreme pure scientist is in danger of being isolated from facts" (p. 484).

Our profession, like many others, is subject to cycles of interest and activity. For example, Highhouse (1999) reported that the Great Depression in the 1930s led to the development of personnel counseling within organizations for helping employees solve personal problems. Questionable managerial support for such activity eventually led to its disappearance within the field of I/O psychology by the 1960s. Now, however, our profession has renewed interest in work/family conflict and the mental health of employees.

Today I/O psychology is multidisciplinary in both its content and its methods of inquiry. On reflection, it was the same at the turn of the 20th century—a confluence of interest in advertising research, industrial efficiency, and mental testing. In a sense, the evolution of I/O psychology is the chronicle of mushrooming interests along certain common dimensions as molded by a few seismic events. As we enter what some call the "global era" of civilization, where national and cultural boundaries are less confining, I/O psychology has also expanded its domains of interest and involvement. Entrance into the global era has compelled I/O psychology to become more knowledgeable of cultures other than those typified by Western civilization. We have learned that there are broad cultural differences in the importance placed on work in life.

The Changing Nature of Work: I/O Psychology and 9/11/01

I/O psychologists have long contributed to our nation's welfare. We have made some of our most enduring contributions during times of national crisis, as witnessed by our roles in World Wars I and II. So too did we contribute following the terrorist attacks on September 11, 2001. On November 19, 2001, President George W. Bush signed into law the Aviation and Transportation Security Act, which, among other things, established a new Transportation Security Administration (TSA). The law was designed to create a secure air travel system while ensuring freedom of movement for people and commerce. The TSA was faced with a Herculean task. It had to establish effective selection standards to hire airport security screening personnel, design new procedures to screen passengers and luggage, and do so in a matter of months. Several I/O psychologists played key roles in implementing this new program that was of extreme national urgency. The new TSA security screeners were to be a highly skilled workforce, meeting specific standards at date of hire and throughout their career (e.g., annual certifications), and they were to be provided ongoing training and development. Kolmstetter (2003) described the development of a day-long assessment of applicants for the job of security screener. The tests included assessments of English proficiency (e.g., reading, writing, listening), personality (e.g., integrity, positive work ethic, customer service orientation), and technical aptitudes (e.g., visual observation of X-ray images). The assessment also included a structured job interview, a physical abilities test (e.g., lifting and searching luggage), and a medical evaluation. The candidates who were hired were taught the job duties of each of five primary screening jobs, and they rotated their job assignments throughout each work shift.

Approximately 1,300 screeners were hired by March 2002. By November 2002 the TSA had processed more than 1.8 million applications, tested about 340,000 candidates, and hired about 50,000 screeners. These screeners were deployed at the nation's 429 commercial airports. Women made up 38% of the screeners, and ethnic minorities made up 44%. The size of the total TSA workforce (58,000) exceeds that of the FBI, Customs Service, and Secret Service combined. Through the skill, diligence, and commitment of a handful of people (many of whom were I/O psychologists), in record time a large, vitally important federal agency was created and staffed to meet a national mandate. As an I/O psychologist, I am proud of what my colleagues were able to contribute to ensuring our nation's safety. The belief that I/O psychologists must continue to make such contributions was well stated by Harris (2003): "I think we as I/O psychologists have much to offer in this arena, and I encourage all of you to extend your help in combating terrorism and making this world a safer place to live" (p. 79).

Cross-Cultural I/O Psychology

Cross-cultural psychology
An area of research that examines the degree to which psychological concepts and findings generalize to people in other cultures and societies.

Cross-cultural psychology studies "similarities and differences in individual psychological and social functioning in various cultures and ethnic groups" (Kagitcibasi & Berry, 1989, p. 494). When extended to I/O psychology, the investigation pertains to the work context. The globalization of business has compelled I/O psychology to examine how its theories and practices apply in cultures other than North America and Western Europe. The increased interest in cross-cultural I/O psychology stems from greater cultural diversity in the workforce, U.S. companies doing business overseas, partnerships or joint ventures between companies from different countries, and the development of new electronic means of communication that render geographic boundaries between nations meaningless. Smith, Fischer, and Sale (2001) posed the basic question: "Does I/O psychology contain an established body of well-researched knowledge, which organizations would be best advised to draw upon wherever their operation is located" (p. 148)? As a scientific discipline, I/O psychology is examining to what degrees and in what ways cultural differences influence the work world.

At a fundamental level, we can consider the degree to which words have the same meanings across cultures as work-related documents (questionnaires, company policies, selection tests, etc.) are translated from one language to another. Glazer (2002) cited research indicating that even relatively simple words such as *working* and *career*, though translatable, have different meanings in different cultures. In a multi-national study involving workers in Belgium, Germany, Israel, Japan, the Netherlands, and the United States, researchers found that the word *working* varied in meaning to include the reasons for engaging in work, the outcomes associated with work, and the controls placed on employees while performing work. Similarly, the word *career* can be translated into Hebrew, but for Israelis the word has a negative tone, implying egotism and self-promotion. Glazer concluded, "The results of these studies imply even 'simple' terms have complex and different meanings across cultures" (p. 147).

The amount of time people spend engaged in work varies greatly across cultures. Brett and Stroh (2003) reported that American workers work 137 hours per year more than Japanese workers and 499 hours per year more than French workers. The official workweek in France is 35 hours (compared to 40 in the United States), and Europeans at all job levels typically take four to six weeks of vacation per year. Further research reveals that U.S. managers work 50–70 hours per week. It has been proposed that American work hours are related to the American culture and that other cultures do not share this value. Is it correct to describe workers in cultures that work less than Americans as "lazy"? No, just as it is not correct to describe American workers as "compulsive." Work hours are a reflection of the values each culture has for the role that work plays in life. It is these types of cross-cultural differences that must be addressed in the melding of workers and work-related practices across different nations.

As this book will reveal, the full range of topics that I/O psychologists address is influenced by cross-cultural differences. Topics include preferences for how to select employees, the degree to which workers compete versus cooperate with each other, and preferred styles of leadership, among many others. The issue of cross-cultural I/O psychology is so salient that each chapter in this book contains a highlighted section on cross-cultural issues pertaining to a topic within the chapter. As Aycan and Kanungo (2001) aptly summarized, "In our business dealings we will encounter people of different nations across real and virtual borders. In this world order understanding the impact of culture on various aspects of organizations and their practices will become more critical than ever to increase synergy, productivity and welfare of the workforce within and across countries" (p. 385).

The Mandate of I/O Psychology

I/O psychology is confronted with a daunting task—to increase the fit between the workforce and the workplace at a time when the composition of both is rapidly changing. Today's workforce is unlike any other in our history. More people are seeking employment than ever before, and they have higher levels of education. There are more women entering the workforce seeking full-time careers, more dual-income couples, and more individuals whose native language is not English. Likewise, the nature of work is changing. There are increasing numbers of jobs in service industries, jobs that require computer literacy, and part-time jobs. Rapid economic changes are forcing large-scale layoffs, often requiring individuals to learn new job skills at midlife. Societal changes also influence employment, as evidenced by the growing problem of drug use in the workplace. Campbell and Campbell (2005) believe that I/O psychology has a role to play in understanding global warming. Climate change will produce social change on a massive scale, and I/O psychologists can contribute to helping people cope with these changes in their work lives.

I/O psychology is concerned with the worklives of people, and because those worklives are changing, so too is I/O psychology. As a profession, we find ourselves on the threshold of some areas where we have little prior experience. We would be remiss if we did not venture into these new territories, for they are legitimate and important concerns within the world of work. Furthermore, all of our work must be conducted according to our professional code of ethics (American Psychological Association, 2002). I find the mandate of I/O psychology to be very challenging, with the unending variety of issues we address being a great source of stimulation. Although some disciplines rarely change their content, I/O psychology most certainly is not the "same old stuff."

I can think of few other fields of work that are as critical to human welfare as I/O psychology. We spend more of our lifetimes engaged in working than in any other activity. Thus I/O psychology is devoted to understanding our major mission in life. As our nation faces increasing problems of economic productivity, the field of I/O psychology continues to contribute to making our world a better place in which to live. Indeed, Colarelli (1998) asserted that across the full spectrum of work organizations in society, psychological interventions designed to solve social and organizational problems are underutilized. Additionally, the scientific contributions that I/O psychologists have made are regarded as sufficiently noteworthy to occasion the revision of federal laws governing fair employment practices.

In general, we as professionals are striving to gain a complete understanding of the problems and issues associated with the world of work, embracing both its quantitative and humanistic dimensions. When you have finished reading this book, you should have a much better understanding of human behavior in the workplace. Perhaps some of you will be stimulated enough to continue your work in I/O psychology. It is a most challenging, rewarding, and useful profession.

Chapter Summary

- Industrial/organizational (I/O) psychology is one area of specialization within the broad profession of psychology.
- I/O psychologists generally function in one of two roles: scientists or practitioners.
- I/O psychology is practiced and studied throughout the world.
- The discipline of I/O psychology comprises several subfields.
- The history of I/O psychology is best represented by seven eras, the most recent being the Information Age (1994–present).

- Business is now conducted on a global scale, which presents many professional opportunities for I/O psychologists.
- The mandate of I/O psychology is to increase the fit between the workforce and the workplace when the composition of both is rapidly changing.
- As work assumes a more central role in our lives, the need for I/O psychology to balance work and family issues continues to grow.

2 Research Methods in I/O Psychology

Learning Objectives

- Understand the empirical research cycle.

- Know the relative advantages and disadvantages of the laboratory experiment, quasi-experiment, questionnaire, and observation research methods.

- Understand meta-analysis and qualitative research methods.

- Explain the statistical concepts of central tendency and variability.

- Understand the concept of correlation and its interpretation.

- Have an awareness and appreciation of the ethical issues associated with I/O psychological research.

Research
A formal process by which knowledge is produced and understood.

Generalizability
The extent to which conclusions drawn from one research study spread or apply to a larger population.

We all have hunches or beliefs about the nature of human behavior. Some of us believe that red-haired people are temperamental, dynamic leaders are big and tall, blue-collar workers prefer beer to wine, the only reason people work is to make money, and the like. The list is endless. Which of these beliefs are true? The only way to find out is to conduct **research**, or the systematic study of phenomena according to scientific principles. Much of this chapter is devoted to a discussion of research methods used in I/O psychology. Understanding the research process helps people solve practical problems, apply the results of studies reported by others, and assess the accuracy of claims made about new practices, equipment, and so on.

I/O psychologists are continually faced with a host of practical problems. Knowledge of research methods makes us better able to find useful solutions to problems rather than merely stumble across them by chance. An understanding of research methods also helps us apply the results of studies reported by others. Some factors promote the generalizability of research findings; others retard it. **Generalizability** is defined as the degree to which the conclusions based on one research sample are applicable to another, often larger, population. People often assert the superiority of some new technique or method; a knowledge of research methods helps us determine which ones are truly valuable. It has been suggested that science has three goals: description, prediction, and explanation. The descriptive function is like taking a photograph—a picture of a state of events. Researchers may describe levels of productivity, numbers of employees who quit during the year, average levels of job satisfaction, and so on. The second function is prediction. Researchers try to predict which employees will be productive, which ones are likely to quit, and which ones will be dissatisfied. This information is then used to select applicants who will be better employees. The explanatory function is perhaps the most difficult to unravel; it is a statement of *why* events occur as they do. It tries to find causes: why production is at a certain level, why employees quit, why they are dissatisfied, and so forth.

This chapter will give you some insight into the research process in I/O psychology. The process begins with a statement of the problem and ends with the conclusions drawn from the research. This chapter should help you become a knowledgeable consumer of I/O psychological research.

The Empirical Research Process

Figure 2-1 shows the steps that scientists take in conducting empirical research. The research process is basically a five-step procedure with an important feedback factor; that is, the results of the fifth step influence the first step in future research studies. First, the research process begins with a statement of the problem: what question or problem needs to be answered? Second, how do you design a study to answer the question? Third, how do you measure the variables and collect the necessary data? Fourth, how do you apply statistical procedures to analyze the data? (In other words, how do you make some sense out of all the information collected?) Finally, how do you draw conclusions from analyzing the data? Let's look at each of these steps in more detail.

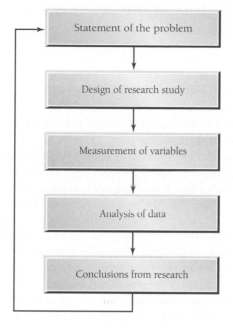

Figure 2-1 *The empirical research cycle*

Statement of the Problem

Questions that initiate research don't arise out of thin air. They are based on existing knowledge—your own and others' experiences with the problem, personal intuition or insight, or a theory. A **theory** is a statement that proposes to explain relationships among phenomena—for example, a theory of why individuals are attracted to each other. As researchers conduct their studies, they become more familiar with the problem and may expand the scope of their questions. One person's research may stimulate similar research by someone else; thus researchers often benefit from their colleagues' studies. After conducting much research on a topic, researchers may propose a theory about why the behavior occurs. The sequence that starts with data and culminates in theory is the **inductive method** of science. The opposite sequence is the **deductive method**, in which a researcher first forms a theory (perhaps by intuition or by studying previous research) and then tests the theory by collecting data. If the theory is accurate, the data will support it; if it is inaccurate, they will not.

The value of theory in science is that it integrates and summarizes large amounts of information and provides a framework for the research. Campbell (1990b) noted, however, that as a scientific discipline, psychology is much more difficult to investigate than physics or chemistry. People are far too variable, both across individuals and from day to day within one person, to be defined by a single formula or equation. "The situation is not the same in physics or chemistry. A molecule of water has the same formula no matter where in the universe it might be" (p. 46). Psychology has no equivalent of universal natural laws, such as Newton's three laws of motion. The following quotes illustrate three different yet valid views on theory:

- "There is nothing quite so practical as a good theory."—Kurt Lewin, noted social psychologist

Theory
A statement that proposes to explain relationships among phenomena of interest.

Inductive method
A research process in which conclusions are drawn about a general class of objects or people based on knowledge of a specific member of the class under investigation.

Deductive method
A research process in which conclusions are drawn about a specific member of a class of objects or people based on knowledge of the general class under investigation.

- "Research designed with respect to theory is likely to be wasteful."—B. F. Skinner, noted experimental psychologist
- "Theory, like mist on eyeglasses, obscures facts."—Charlie Chan, noted fictional detective

Lewin's statement is often cited in psychology. Its essence is that a theory is useful for conducting research. A theory synthesizes information, organizes it into logical components, and directs the researcher's efforts in future studies. But Skinner believes that too much effort is spent on "proving" theories; that is, the theory is master of the research. Skinner thinks that most theories eventually fall out of favor and that productive research does not require a theory. His position is an extreme case of empiricism. Charlie Chan thinks that researchers become too committed to proving their theories and become blinded to information that doesn't conform to the theory they want to believe. A good researcher doesn't let the theory obscure the facts. Rather than thinking of theories as "right" or "wrong," we try to think of them in terms of their usefulness. A useful theory gives meaning to the problem; it helps the subject matter make more sense. Theorizing or theory development is an on-going process. A theory is proposed, then tested with empirical data, which in turn may result in the theory being fine-tuned or sharpened in focus. Theories are not "born" fully intact with unquestioned adherence, but are the objects of scientific scrutiny and evaluation. Some theories may receive extensive empirical support and confirmation, while others may repeatedly be disconfirmed and ultimately dismissed by scientists. Vancouver (2005) expressed the process of theory development as follows: "Clearly, any theory should go through rigorous testing under a cloud of skepticism. This is what we do as scientists . . . Any theory that is still the focus of research is a work in progress. We do not know what it might explain or fail to explain. We do not know what past, present, or future revisions will make it better or worse" (pp. 49–50).

Campbell (1990b) believes that theories are only a means to an end and thus have no inherent value. He stated that theories should "help us develop better research questions, provide more useful interpretation of data, or guide the future investment of research resources" (pp. 66–67). A theory is an important way to specify research questions, but it is only one way to formulate a research problem. Other methods can also result in high-quality research. This is especially true in a pragmatic area like I/O psychology, where some research problems come from everyday experiences in industry. If 50% of a company's workforce quit every year, one doesn't need a theory to realize that this is a serious problem. However, a theory of turnover can help explain why the turnover is occurring. I believe the value of theory in I/O psychology is to provide a useful explanation for work-related behaviors as opposed to being the sole source of a research idea.

Design of the Research Study

Research design
A plan for conducting scientific research for the purpose of learning about a phenomenon of interest.

A **research design** is a plan for conducting a study. A researcher can use many strategies; the choice of method depends on the nature of the problem being studied as well as on cost and feasibility. Research strategies may be compared along several dimensions, but two are most important: (1) the naturalness of the research setting and (2) the investigator's degree of control over the study. No one strategy is the best

Internal validity
The degree to which the relationships evidenced among variables in a particular research study are accurate or true.

External validity
The degree to which the relationships evidenced among variables in a particular research study are generalizable or accurate in other contexts.

under all conditions; there are always tradeoffs. These two dimensions affect both the internal and external validity of the research. **Internal validity** is the extent to which the results of the research can be attributed to the variables investigated rather than to other possible explanations for the results. **External validity** is the extent to which findings from a research study are relevant to individuals and settings beyond those specifically examined in the study. External validity is synonymous with generalizability. If a study lacks internal validity, it can have no external validity.

Naturalness of the Research Setting.   In some research strategies, the problem can be studied in the environment in which it naturally occurs. This is desirable because we don't want the research strategy to destroy or distort the phenomenon under study. Some research strategies appear phony because they study the problem in unnatural ways. In contrast, for example, the Hawthorne studies were conducted right in the plant with actual employees performing their normal jobs. Some studies do not need to be conducted in a natural environment, however, because the behavior under investigation is assumed to be independent of the setting. For example, an engineering psychology study to test whether people react faster to red or green lights could be conducted as appropriately in a laboratory as in a natural field setting.

Degree of Control.   In some research strategies, the researcher has a high degree of control over the conduct of the study. In others, very little control is possible. In the Hawthorne studies, the researchers could control the exact amount of lighting in the work area by installing (or removing) lights, although it turned out that factors other than lighting affected the workers' performance. Suppose you want to study the relationship between people's ages and their attitudes toward I/O psychology. You are particularly interested in comparing the attitudes of people over age 40 with those under 40. You develop a questionnaire that asks their opinions about I/O psychology (is it interesting, difficult to understand, and so on) and distribute it to your classmates. It turns out that every person in the class is under 40. Now you have no information on the over-40 group, so you can't answer your research question. This is an example of a low degree of control (you cannot control the age of the people in your class). Low control is particularly endemic to the questionnaire research method.

Primary Research Methods

This section is a discussion of four primary research methods used in I/O psychology. A **primary research method** provides an original or principal source of data that bears on a particular research question. No one method is perfect; that is, none offers a high degree of both naturalism and control. Each method will be described and illustrated with an example.

Primary research methods
A class of research methods that generates new information on a particular research question.

Laboratory experiment
A type of research method in which the investigator manipulates independent variables and assigns subjects to experimental and control conditions.

Laboratory Experiment.   **Laboratory experiments** are conducted in contrived settings as opposed to naturally occurring organizational settings. In a laboratory, the researcher has a high degree of control over the conduct of the study, especially over those conditions associated with the observations of behavior. The experimenter designs the study to test how certain aspects of an actual environment affect behavior. The laboratory setting must mirror certain dimensions of the natural environment where the behavior normally occurs. A well-designed laboratory experiment will have some of the conditions found in the natural environment but will omit those that would never be present. Furthermore, in a laboratory experiment, the researcher randomly assigns the study participants to the various treatment conditions, which enhances control and facilitates drawing causal inferences.

Streufert et al. (1992) conducted a laboratory experiment on the effects of alcohol intoxication on visual-motor performance. A sample of adult men participated for two days; one day they consumed alcohol and the other day they consumed mineral water (disguised with a mild ethanol spray to provide the odor of alcohol). The mineral water served as a control condition against which to compare alcohol intoxication. The alcohol dosage was designed to produce breath alcohol levels of either .05 or .10. Visual-motor performance was measured on a task similar to a video game. The researchers studied several aspects of performance, including risk taking and errors. They compared performance under alcohol intoxication with performance under the control condition for each person. The results showed that error rates were dramatically higher under conditions of alcohol consumption. Serious performance deterioration was found even at the lower (.05) intoxication level. Under the effects of alcohol, some individuals exhibited greater cautiousness (i.e., slower reaction time) to the visual-motor task, trading off speed of response for fewer errors. The researchers regarded errors in the task to be equivalent to an air traffic controller's failure to ward off aircraft that have come too close to each other. Additionally, although reduced speed of response may decrease errors, it also may prevent engaging in needed defense maneuvers.

This study illustrates the defining characteristics of a laboratory experiment. By controlling for other factors, the researchers were able to determine the causal link between alcohol consumption and performance on a visual-motor task. They could also control the dosage of alcohol to produce precise breath alcohol levels of .05 or .10, typical levels of intoxication associated with drinking alcohol in naturalistic settings. Nevertheless, one can question the generalizability of the skills needed to perform the selected visual-motor task to real jobs. Some jobs, such as a surgeon, require even greater concentration and coordination. In such a case, the magnitude of the "errors" caused by alcohol intoxication would be greater. Other jobs, such as a manual laborer, have fewer visual-motor skill requirements, in which case the errors would be less. In short, the findings from the study pertain to the effects of alcohol on visual-motor performance, not the total spectrum of skills needed for performance across many jobs. Nevertheless, the laboratory experiment is a classic research method for addressing highly specific research questions, and the results from such experiments can often be interpreted with a high degree of clarity.

Quasi-Experiment.   *Quasi* is defined as "seemingly but not actually"; therefore, a **quasi-experiment** resembles an experiment but actually provides less control over the variables under investigation. A quasi-experiment is a research strategy in which independent variables are manipulated in a field setting (that is, the people in the study do not perceive the setting as having been created to conduct the research). As in a laboratory experiment, the researcher tests the effects of a few variables on the subjects' behavior. But there is also less control. In a laboratory experiment, all the variables are manipulated at the researcher's discretion and can be included or excluded according

Quasi-experiment
A type of research method for conducting studies in field situations where the researcher may be able to manipulate some independent variables.

to the design of the study. In a quasi-experiment, however, variables that occur in the field setting are also part of the investigation. Although they add to the richness and realism of the study, they also lessen the researcher's control. Furthermore, random assignment of study participants is often not possible in a field setting, which leads to less generalizable conclusions by the researcher (Shadish, 2002).

Latham and Kinne (1974) conducted a notable study that clearly demonstrates the quasi-experiment as a research method. It examined how a one-day training program on goal setting affected the job performance of pulpwood workers. The subjects in the study were 20 pulpwood logging crews. Their behavior was observed as they performed their normal job duties harvesting lumber in a forest. The experimenters split the subjects into two groups of ten crews each. They matched the two groups on a number of factors so that they were equal in terms of ability and experience. One group was given a one-day course on how to set production goals—that is, how many cords of wood to harvest per hour. The other group was not given any special instructions and worked in the usual way. The experimenters then monitored the job performance of the wood crews over the next three months. Results showed that the crews who were trained to set production goals for themselves harvested significantly more wood than the other crews. The study supported the use of goal setting in an industrial context.

The major strength of this study in terms of demonstrating the quasi-experiment method is that the context was real. Actual workers were used in the context of their everyday jobs. The setting was a forest, not a laboratory where the crews would have been pretending. Although the study's design was not complex enough to rule out competing explanations for the observed behavior, it did allow the researchers to conclude that the goal-setting technique probably caused the increase in job performance. This study also illustrates some weaknesses of the quasi-experiment method. Some workers who were supposed to participate in the goal-setting group decided not to. This forced the researchers to redesign part of the study. Also, few I/O psychologists are able to influence a company to change its work operations for research purposes. (In fact, one of the authors of this study was employed by the lumber company, which undoubtedly had some effect on the company's willingness to participate.)

Questionnaire
A type of research method in which subjects respond to written questions posed by the investigator.

Questionnaire.   **Questionnaires** rely on individuals' self-reports as the basis for obtaining information. They can be constructed to match the reading ability level of the individuals being surveyed. Questionnaires are a means of maintaining the anonymity of respondents if the subject matter being covered is sensitive. Furthermore, they are a highly effective means of collecting data.

Murphy, Thornton, and Prue (1991) used the questionnaire method to ascertain the acceptability of employee drug testing. The authors asked two samples of individuals (college-aged students and older, nontraditional students) to indicate the degree to which they view testing for illicit drug use as justified in each of 35 jobs (such as salesperson, surgeon, mechanic, and airline pilot). The students rated each job on a 7-point scale from low to high acceptance of drug testing. The jobs were carefully selected to represent different types of skills and temperaments needed for their successful conduct as well as physical conditions under which the jobs are performed. The results indicated that the degree to which different jobs involved danger to the worker, co-workers, or the public was most strongly related to the acceptability of employee drug testing. The authors concluded that it would be relatively easy to justify drug testing for some jobs, whereas substantial efforts may be necessary to overcome resistance to drug testing for other jobs. Furthermore, the responses by both sets of students were virtually the same; that is, the attitudes of college-aged students were the same as those of older individuals (average age of 35). However, the results also revealed a high degree of variability in attitudes toward drug testing among members of both groups. Some individuals were in favor of drug testing across all jobs, whereas other individuals were opposed to drug testing for any job.

Questionnaires are a very popular method of research in I/O psychology; however, they suffer from several practical limitations. Some people are not willing to complete a questionnaire and return it to the researcher. Roth and BeVier (1998) reported that a 50% return rate is considered adequate in survey research, yet the return rate of mailed questionnaires is often less than 50%. For example, in the Murphy et al. (1991) study, the return rate of questionnaires mailed to the homes of the nontraditional students was 31%. Such a low response rate raises the question of how representative or unbiased the responses are for the group as a whole. Indeed, Rogelberg et al. (2000) found that nonrespondents to an organizational survey exhibited more negative attitudes about various aspects of their work than did respondents to the survey. The researchers were able to ascertain the attitudes of both groups by means of interviews. Their findings cast doubt on the generalizability of the answers from respondents of some surveys to the larger population in question. More positively, Stanton (1998) found that responses to a survey using the internet contained fewer incomplete or missing answers than responses to the same survey administered via the mail. The author supported using the internet as an efficient means of collecting survey data. Church (2001) reported very small differences in the quality of data collected by various survey methods and suggested that researchers choose the method based on ease of administration.

Another issue is the truthfulness of the responses given by respondents to questions asked. Research indicates questions that are perceived to be sensitive or threatening are more likely to produce distorted responses than benign questions. For example, Tourangeau and Yan (2007) reported that as many as 70% of the people who tested positive for drug use in a urine analysis denied on a questionnaire having recently taken any illicit drugs.

Despite their limitations, questionnaires are used extensively in I/O psychology to address a broad range of research questions (see Cross-Cultural I/O Psychology: Cross-Cultural Research).

Observation
A type of research method in which the investigator monitors subjects for the purpose of understanding their behavior and culture.

Observation.   **Observation** is a method that can be used when the research is examining overt behaviors. In natural field settings, behavior may be observed over extended periods of time and then recorded and categorized. As a research method, observation is not used very frequently in I/O psychology, primarily because it requires substantial amounts of time and energy.

Komaki (1986) sought to identify the behaviors that differentiate effective and ineffective work supervisors. She had observers record the behaviors of 24 managers: 12 previously had been judged as effective in motivating others and 12 judged as relatively ineffective. Approximately twenty 30-minute observations were made of each manager's behavior over a seven-month period (232 hours of observation in total). The managers were observed as they conducted their normal day-to-day job duties.

Cross-Cultural I/O Psychology: *Cross-Cultural Research*

As noted in Chapter 1, the era of global interdependence is upon us. Nations and cultures can no longer operate in isolation. I/O psychologists need to understand to what degree our knowledge is universal versus culture-specific. Gelfand, Raver, and Ehrhart (2002) discussed how cross-cultural research can aid I/O psychologists in understanding work-related behavior around the world. Concepts developed in Western cultures by I/O psychologists might not be the same in other cultures. For example, there appear to be cultural differences in the motivation of workers. In the United States there is substantial support for the importance of individuals setting goals for themselves, directing their own behavior toward pursuit of the goals, and making evaluations regarding goal attainment. This motivational process is highly individualistic. In other cultures (most notably Eastern), motivation is an exchange process between a supervisor and subordinate. Subordinates strive to be accepted by their supervisor. If accepted, the subordinates are obligated to repay their supervisors with high performance. This motivational process is highly dyadic, involving a reciprocal exchange relationship between the two parties.

Even the process of participating in research varies across cultures. In the United States, the questionnaire method is a very popular approach to conducting research. This method is consistent with U.S. cultural values such as individualism, freedom of speech as a basic human right, and the comfort and willingness to express one's opinion. However, these values are not universal. In one study, despite the researcher's instructions to work independently, Russian participants worked collectively to complete the questionnaire. As a group, they read the questions aloud, decided upon a group answer, and all circled the same response. These participants found the individual questionnaire research method to be inconsistent with their own cultural experiences and values, and therefore they modified the instructions to achieve group consensus.

Gelfand et al. discussed additional cross-cultural issues in research, including the equivalence of concepts translated from one language to another, the acceptability of the researcher to the participants before truthful responses are given, and the willingness of participants to use the extreme ends of a rating scale (e.g., very satisfied or very dissatisfied) in responding. A prudent researcher must understand the prevailing social values in a particular culture before attempting to "export" a single research methodology derived in one culture to all others of interest.

The observer stood out of sight but within hearing distance of the manager and used a specially designed form for recording and coding the observations. Komaki found the primary behavior that differentiated the effective and ineffective managers was the frequency with which they monitored their employees' performance. Compared with ineffective managers, effective managers spent more time sampling their employees' work. The findings were interpreted as underscoring the importance of monitoring critical behaviors in producing effective supervisors. However, this conclusion requires corroborating empirical evidence because the two groups of managers were merely observed with no attempt to control for other variables that might account for the results.

Observation is often a useful method for generating ideas that can be tested further with other research methods. The observation method is rich in providing data from environments where the behavior in question occurs. But how successful can observers be in acting like "flies on the wall," observing behavior but not influencing it? In the Komaki study, the managers were aware that they were being observed. Given this, to what degree did the managers modify their conduct to project socially desirable behaviors (e.g., monitoring of their subordinates)? Perhaps effective managers are more sensitive to social cues than ineffective managers and thus are better able to be perceived in a positive fashion. Note that we are dealing with interpretations of the behavior (the "why"), not merely the behavior itself (the "what"). It has been suggested that acceptance and trust of the observers by the study participants are critical to the success of this research method. Stanton and Rogelberg (2002) suggested that the internet may become a fruitful mechanism for conducting observational research through the use of webcams and smartcards.

Table 2-1 compares the four primary research methods on two major dimensions: researcher control and realism. No method rates high on both factors. There is always a tradeoff; a researcher may sacrifice realism for control or vice versa, depending on the study's objectives. The choice of a strategy should be guided by the purpose of the research and the resources available. A well-trained I/O psychologist knows the advantages and disadvantages of each method.

Table 2-1   *Comparison of primary research strategies*

	Laboratory Experiment	Quasi-Experiment	Questionnaire	Observation
Control (potential for testing causal relationships)	High	Moderate	Low	Low
Realism (naturalness of setting)	Low	High	Moderate	High

Secondary Research Methods

Secondary research methods
A class of research methods that examines existing information from research studies that used primary methods.

Meta-analysis
A quantitative secondary research method for summarizing and integrating the findings from original empirical research studies.

While a primary research method gathers or generates new information on a particular research question, a **secondary research method** looks at existing information from studies that used primary methods. One particular secondary research method, meta-analysis (Hunter & Schmidt, 1990; Rosenthal, 1991), is being used with increasing frequency in I/O psychology. **Meta-analysis** is a statistical procedure designed to combine the results of many individual, independently conducted empirical studies into a single result or outcome. The logic behind meta-analysis is that we can arrive at a more accurate conclusion regarding a particular research topic if we combine or aggregate the results of many studies that address the topic, instead of relying on the findings of a single study. The result of a meta-analysis study is often referred to as an "estimate of the true relationship" among the variables examined because we believe such a result is a better approximation of the "truth" than would be found in any one study. A typical meta-analysis study might combine the results from perhaps 25 or more individual empirical studies. As such, a meta-analysis investigation is sometimes referred to as "a study of studies." Although the nature of the statistical equations performed in meta-analysis is beyond the scope of this book, they often entail adjusting for characteristics of a research study (for example, the quality of the measurements used in the study and the sample size) that are known to influence the study's results. Cohn and Becker (2003) explained how a meta-analysis increases the likelihood of achieving more accurate conclusions than could be reached in an individual study by reducing errors of measurement.

Despite the apparent objectivity of this method, the researcher must make a number of subjective decisions in conducting a meta-analysis. For example, one decision involves determining which empirical studies to include. Every known study ever conducted on the topic could be included or only those studies that meet some criteria of empirical quality or rigor. The latter approach can be justified on the grounds that the results of a meta-analysis are only as good as the quality of the original studies used. The indiscriminate inclusion of low-quality empirical studies lowers the quality of the conclusion reached. The findings derived from poorly conducted primary research studies cannot be elevated in quality by conducting a meta-analysis of them. Another issue is referred to as the "file drawer effect." Research studies that yield negative or nonsupportive results are not published (and thus not made widely available to other researchers) as often as studies that have supportive findings. The nonpublished studies are "filed away" by researchers, resulting in published studies being biased in the direction of positive outcomes. Thus a meta-analysis of published studies could lead to a conclusion distorted because of the relative absence of (unpublished) studies reporting negative results. McDaniel, Rothstein, and Whetzel (2006) found evidence of the file drawer effect among meta-analyses published by professional test vendors. By selectively excluding those studies that reported negative results for their tests, the findings from a meta-analysis are inevitably biased in an upward direction. Additionally, Ostroff and Harrison (1999) noted that original research studies on a similar topic sometimes differ in the **level of analysis** used by the researchers. For example, one original study may have examined the individual attitudes of employees in a work team, whereas another original study may have examined the attitudes of different teams working with each other. It would not be appropriate to meta-analyze the findings from these two studies because the level (or unit) of analysis in the first study was the individual, but in the second study it was the work team. Ostroff and Harrison argued that researchers must be careful meta-analyzing findings from original studies that focused on different topics. These are examples of the issues that psychologists must address in conducting a meta-analysis (Wanous, Sullivan, & Malinak, 1989).

Despite the difficulty in making some of these decisions, meta-analysis is a popular research procedure in I/O psychology. Refinements and theoretical extensions in meta-analytic techniques (Raju et al., 1991) attest to the sustained interest in this method across the areas of psychology. For example, many companies have sponsored smoking cessation programs for their employees to promote health and reduce medical costs. Visweswaran and Schmidt (1992) meta-analyzed the results from 633 studies of smoking cessation involving more than 70,000 individual smokers. They found that 18.6% of smokers quit after participation in a cessation program, but the results differed by type of program. Instructional programs were found to be twice as effective as drug-based programs. The results of this meta-analysis can be of considerable practical value in assisting organizations to develop effective smoking cessation programs for their employees.

Level of analysis
The unit or level (individuals, teams, organizations, nations, etc.) that is the object of the researchers' interest and about which conclusions are drawn from the research.

Hunter and Schmidt (1996) are very optimistic about the scientific value of meta-analysis. They believe it has the power to change how we conduct our research and to provide guidance on major social policy issues. Shadish (1996) contended that meta-analysis can also be used to infer causality through selected statistical and research design procedures. Schmidt and Hunter (2001) concluded, "It is hard to overemphasize the importance of [meta-analysis] in advancing cumulative knowledge in psychology" (p. 66).

Qualitative Research

Qualitative research
A class of research methods in which the investigator takes an active role in interacting with the subjects he or she wishes to study.

In recent years there has been an increase in interest among some disciplines in what is called **qualitative research**. Qualitative research is not new. As Locke and Golden-Biddle (2002) noted, its origins are from the ancient Greeks who desired to document the course of human history. The name is somewhat of a misnomer because it implies the absence of any quantitative procedures (i.e., statistical analyses), which is not true. Qualitative research involves new ways of understanding research questions and how these ways influence the conclusions we reach about the topic under investigation. Qualitative research (compared with traditional research methods) requires the investigator to become more personally immersed in the entire research process, as opposed to being just a detached, objective investigator. As Bartunek and Seo (2002) described, quantitative research uses predefined variables (organizational commitment, for example) that are assumed to have meaning across multiple settings (e.g., different organizations). Alternatively, the focus of qualitative research may be to increase understanding of what it means to the employees of a particular organization to feel committed to it.

Maxwell (1998) stated that qualitative research often begins by examining why the investigator is interested in conducting the research in the first place. He proposed three kinds of purposes for conducting a scientific study: personal, practical, and research. Personal purposes are those that motivate *you* to conduct a study; they can include a desire to change some existing situation or simply to advance your career as a researcher. Such personal purposes often overlap with the practical and research purposes. It is critical that you be aware of your personal purposes and how they may shape your research. To the extent that data analysis procedures are based on personal desires and you have not made a careful assessment of their implications for your methods and results, you are in danger of arriving at invalid conclusions. Practical purposes focus on accomplishing something—meeting some need, changing some situation, or achieving some goal. Research purposes, in contrast, focus on understanding something, gaining some insight into what is going on and why it is happening. Maxwell advised researchers to be fully cognizant of the multiple purposes for doing a study, and of how these purposes can interact to influence the conclusions we reach in our research.

Ethnography
A research method that utilizes field observation to study a society's culture.

The essence of qualitative research is to recognize the number of different ways we can reach an understanding of a phenomenon. We can learn through watching, listening, and in some cases participating in the phenomenon we seek to understand. Kidd (2002) offered this assessment of qualitative research: "It is a better way of getting at meaning, at how people construe their experiences and what those experiences mean to them. That's often difficult to capture statistically or with quantitative methods" (p. 132). One qualitative research approach is ethnography. Fetterman (1998) described **ethnography** as the art and science of describing a group or culture. The description

Emic
An approach to
researching phenomena
that emphasizes
knowledge derived
from the participants'
awareness and
understanding of their
own culture. Often
contrasted with etic.

Etic
An approach to
researching phenomena
that emphasizes
knowledge derived
from the perspective
of a detached objective
investigator in
understanding a culture.
Often contrasted with
emic.

Variable
An object of study
whose measurement can
take on two or more
values.

**Quantitative
variables**
Objects of study
that inherently have
numerical values
associated with them,
such as weight.

Categorical variables
Objects of study that
do not inherently
have numerical values
associated with them,
as gender. Often
contrasted with
quantitative variables.

Independent variable
A variable that can be
manipulated to influence
the values of the
dependent variable.

may be of any group, such as a work group or an organization. An ethnographer details the routine daily lives of people in the group, focusing on the more predictable patterns of behavior. Ethnographers try to keep an open mind about the group they are studying. Preconceived notions about how members of the group behave and what they think can severely bias the research findings. It is difficult, if not impossible, however, for a researcher to enter into a line of inquiry without having some existing problem or theory in mind. Ethnographers believe that both the group member's perspective and the external researcher's perspective of what is happening can be melded to yield an insightful portrayal of the group. The insider's view is called the **emic** perspective, whereas the external view is the **etic** perspective. Because a group has multiple members, there are multiple emic views of how group insiders think and behave in the different ways they do. Most ethnographers begin their research process from the emic perspective and then try to understand their data from the external or etic perspective. High-quality ethnographic research requires both perspectives: an insightful and sensitive interpretation of group processes combined with data collection techniques.

The field of I/O psychology has been relatively slow to adopt qualitative research methods. Historically our discipline has taken a quantitative approach to understanding phenomenon; meta-analysis is an example. However, I/O psychology is relying increasingly on more qualitative methods to facilitate our understanding of organizational issues. One example is researchers attempting to understand the processes of recruitment and selection from the perspective of the job applicant, not just the organization. With the growing use of work teams in organizations, ethnographic research methods may well aid us in understanding the complex interactions within a group (Brett et al., 1997). In the final analysis, there is no need to choose between qualitative and traditional research methods: rather, both approaches can help us understand topics of interest. Lee, Mitchell, and Sablynski (1999) suggested that the use of qualitative methods may be growing in I/O psychology because researchers want additional methods to better understand the topics of interest to them. This book will use case studies and field notes along with empirical research findings to facilitate an understanding of issues in I/O psychology.

Measurement of Variables

After developing a study design, the researcher must carry it out and measure the variables of interest. A **variable** is represented by a symbol that can assume a range of numerical values. **Quantitative variables** (age, time) are those that are inherently numerical (21 years or 16 minutes). **Categorical variables** (gender, race) are not inherently numerical, but they can be "coded" to have numerical meaning: female = 0, male = 1; or White = 0, Black = 1, Hispanic = 2, Asian = 3; and so forth. For research purposes, it doesn't matter what numerical values are assigned to the categorical variables because they merely identify these variables for measurement purposes.

Variables Used in I/O Psychological Research.   The term *variable* is often used in conjunction with other terms in I/O psychological research. Four such terms that will be used throughout this book are *independent, dependent, predictor*, and *criterion*. Independent and dependent variables are associated in particular with experimental research strategies. **Independent variables** are those that are manipulated or controlled by the researcher. They are chosen by the experimenter, set or manipulated to occur at a certain level, and then examined to assess their effect on some other variable. In the laboratory experiment by Streufert et al. (1992), the independent variable was the level of alcohol intoxication. In the quasi-experiment by Latham and Kinne (1974), the independent variable was the one-day training program on goal setting.

Experiments assess the effects of independent variables on the dependent variable. The **dependent variable** is most often the object of the researcher's interest. It is usually some aspect of behavior (or, in some cases, attitudes). In the Streufert et al. study, the dependent variable was the subjects' performance on a visual-motor task. In the Latham and Kinne study, the dependent variable was the number of cords of wood harvested by the lumber crews.

The same variable can be selected as the dependent or the independent variable depending on the goals of the study. Figure 2-2 shows how a variable (employee performance) can be either dependent or independent. In the former case, the researcher wants to study the effect of various leadership styles (independent variable) on employee performance (dependent variable). The researcher might select two leadership styles (a stern taskmaster approach versus a relaxed, easygoing one) and then assess their effects on job performance. In the latter case, the researcher wants to know what effect employee performance (independent variable) has on the ability to be trained (dependent variable). The employees are divided into "high-performer" and "low-performer" groups. Both groups then attend a training program to assess whether the high performers learn faster than the low performers. Note that variables are never inherently independent or dependent. Whether they are one or the other is up to the researcher.

Dependent variable
A variable whose values are influenced by the independent variable.

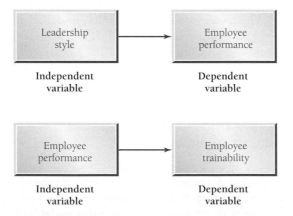

Independent variable → Dependent variable

Leadership style → Employee performance

Independent variable / Dependent variable

Employee performance → Employee trainability

Independent variable / Dependent variable

Figure 2-2 *Employee performance used as either a dependent or an independent variable*

Predictor variable
A variable used to predict or forecast a criterion variable.

Criterion variable
A variable that is a primary object of a research study; it is forecasted by a predictor variable.

Predictor and criterion variables are often used in I/O psychology. When scores on one variable are used to predict scores on a second, the variables are called **predictor** and **criterion** variables, respectively. For example, a student's high school grade point average might be used to predict his or her college grade point average. Thus, high school grades are the predictor variable; college grades are the criterion variable. As a rule, criterion variables are the focal point of a study. Predictor variables may or may not be successful in predicting what we want to know (the criterion). Predictor variables are similar to independent variables; criterion variables are similar to dependent variables. The distinction between the two is a function of the research strategy. Independent and dependent variables are used in the context of experimentation. Predictor and criterion variables are used in any research strategy where the goal is to determine the status of subjects on one variable (the criterion) as a function of their status on another variable (the predictor). Independent variables are associated with making causal inferences; predictor variables may not be.

Analysis of Data

After the data have been collected, the researcher has to make some sense out of them. This is where statistics come in. Many students get anxious over the topic of statistics. Although some statistical analytic methods are quite complex, most are reasonably straightforward. I like to think of statistical methods as golf clubs—tools for helping to do a job better. Just as some golf shots call for different clubs, different research problems require different statistical analyses. Knowing a full range of statistical methods will help you better understand the research problem. It is impossible to understand the research process without some knowledge of statistics. A brief exposure to statistics follows.

Descriptive statistics
A class of statistical analyses that describe the variables under investigation.

Descriptive statistics simply describe data. They are the starting point in the data analysis process; they give the researcher a general idea of what the data are like. Descriptive statistics can show the shape of a distribution of numbers, measure the central tendency of the distribution, and measure the spread or variability in the numbers.

Distributions and Their Shape.   Suppose a researcher measures the intelligence of 100 people with a traditional intelligence test. Table 2-2 is a list of those 100 scores. To make some sense out of all these numbers, the researcher arranges the numbers according to size. Figure 2-3 (p. 38) shows what those 100 test scores look like in a frequency distribution. Because so many scores are involved, they are grouped into categories of equal size, with each interval containing ten possible scores.

Table 2-2   *One hundred intelligence test scores*

133	141	108	124	117
110	92	88	110	79
143	101	120	104	94
117	128	102	126	84
105	143	114	70	103
151	114	87	134	81
87	120	145	98	95
97	157	99	79	107
108	107	147	156	144
118	127	96	138	102
141	113	112	94	114
133	122	89	128	112
119	99	110	118	142
123	67	120	89	118
90	114	121	146	94
128	125	114	91	124
121	125	83	99	76
120	102	129	108	98
110	144	89	122	119
117	127	134	127	112

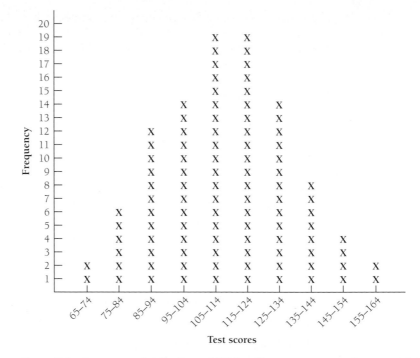

Figure 2-3   *Frequency distribution of 100 intelligence test scores (grouped data)*

The figure tells us something about the intelligence test scores. We can see that the most frequently occurring scores are in the middle of the distribution; extreme scores (both high and low) taper off as we move away from the center. The general shape of the distribution in Figure 2-3 is called *normal* or *bell shaped*. Many variables in psychological research are distributed normally—that is, with the most frequently occurring scores in the middle of the distribution and progressively fewer scores at the extreme ends. Figure 2-4a shows a classic normal distribution. The curve in Figure 2-4a is smooth compared to the distribution in Figure 2-3 because the inclusion of so many test scores takes the "kinks" out of the distribution.

Not all distributions of scores are normal in shape; some are lopsided or pointed. If a professor gives an easy test, a larger proportion of high scores results in a pointed or *skewed* distribution. Figure 2-4b shows a negatively skewed distribution (the tail of the distribution is in the negative direction). The opposite occurs if the professor gives a difficult test; the result is a positively skewed distribution (the tail points in the positive direction), as in Figure 2-4c. Thus, plotting the distribution of data is one way to understand it. We can make inferences based on the shape of the distribution. (In the case of the negatively skewed distribution of test scores, we infer that the test was easy.)

Measures of Central Tendency.   After we learn the shape of the distribution, the next step is to find the typical score. One of three measures of central tendency is usually used for this, depending on the shape of the distribution.

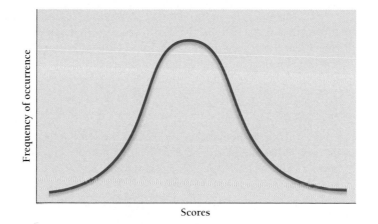

Figure 2-4a   *A normal or bell-shaped distribution of scores*

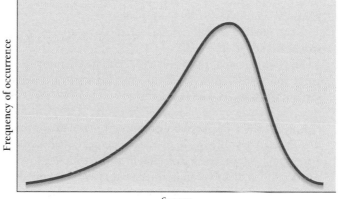

Figure 2-4b   *A negatively skewed distribution of scores*

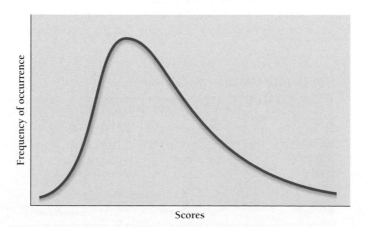

Figure 2-4c   *A positively skewed distribution of scores*

Mean
The arithmetic average of a distribution of numbers.

The **mean** is the most common measure of central tendency. The mean is the arithmetic average score in the distribution. It is computed by adding all of the individual scores and then dividing the sum by the total number of scores in the distribution. The formula for computing the mean is

$$\bar{X} = \frac{\Sigma X}{N}$$ [Formula 2-1]

where $\bar{X}$ is the symbol for the mean, Σ is the symbol for summation, X is the symbol for each individual score, and N is the total number of scores in the distribution. The mean for the data in Table 2-2 (p. 37) is found as follows:

$$\bar{X} = \frac{11,322}{100} = 113.22$$ [Formula 2-2]

The average intelligence test score in the sample of people tested is 113.22 (or 113 rounded off). The entire distribution of 100 scores can be described by one number: the mean. The mean is a useful measure of central tendency and is most appropriately used with normally distributed variables.

Median
The midpoint of all the numbers in a distribution.

The **median** is the midpoint of all the scores in the distribution, so 50% of all scores are above the median and 50% are below. If we have a distribution of four scores, 1, 2, 3, and 4, the median is 2.5; that is, half the scores (3 and 4) are above this point and half (1 and 2) are below it. (The statistical procedure used to compute the median for graphed data is lengthy and will not be presented here. For your information, the median of the scores in Table 2-2 is 112.9.) The median is the best measure of central tendency for skewed distributions that contain some extreme scores. The median is relatively insensitive to extreme scores, whereas the mean is affected by them. For example, if we have a distribution of three scores, 1, 2, and 3, the mean is 2. Alternatively, if the distribution of three scores were 1, 2, and 30, the mean would be 11.

Mode
The most frequently occurring number in a distribution.

The **mode** is the least common measure of central tendency. It is defined as the most frequently occurring number in a distribution. The mode is not used for many statistical analyses, but it has a practical purpose. Some concepts are best understood in whole numbers (that is, integers), not in fractions or decimals. For example, it makes more sense to say "The modal number of children in a family is 3" rather than "The mean number of children in a family is 2.75." It is difficult to imagine three-fourths

FRANK AND ERNEST by Bob Thaves

Frank & Ernest: © Thaves/Dist. by Newspaper Enterprise Association, Inc. Reprinted with permission.

of a child. In cases such as this, the mode is the preferred measure of central tendency. Although the mean is more appropriate than the mode for describing the data in Table 2-2, the mode is 114.

In the normal distribution, the mean ($\overline{X}$), median (Md), and mode (Mo) are equal, as shown in Figure 2-5a. In a skewed distribution, the mean and median are pulled toward the tail of the distribution, as shown in Figure 2-5b.

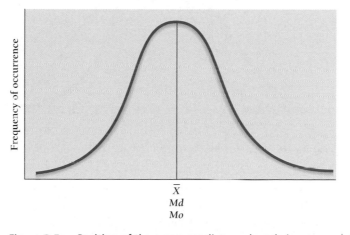

Figure 2-5a *Position of the mean, median, and mode in a normal distribution*

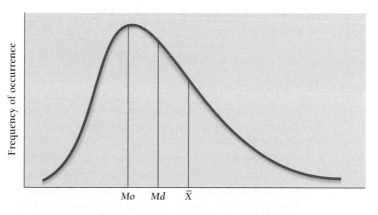

Figure 2-5b *Positions of the mean, median, and mode in a skewed distribution*

One of the three measures of central tendency can be used to describe a typical score in a distribution.

Measures of Variability.   In addition to describing a set of scores by the shape of their distribution and central tendency, we can talk about the spread of the scores or their variability. The scores' **variability** is an indication of how representative the mean is as a measure of central tendency. Several numerical indices are used to describe variability in scores. The simplest index, the **range**, is found by subtracting the lowest score from the highest score. The range of the data in Table 2-2 is $157 - 67 = 90$.

Variability
The dispersion of numerical values evidenced in the measurement of an object or concept.

Range
A descriptive statistical index that reflects the dispersion in a set of scores; arithmetically, the difference between the highest score and the lowest score.

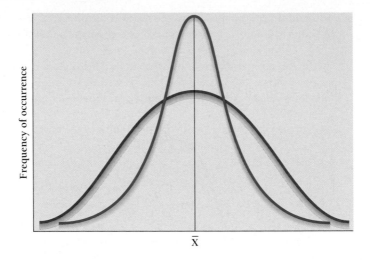

Frequency of occurrence

$\overline{X}$

Figure 2-6   *Two distributions with the same mean but different variability*

Standard deviation
A statistic that shows
the spread or dispersion
of scores around the
mean in a distribution of
scores.

Consider Figure 2-6. The two normal distributions have equal means but unequal variability. One distribution is peaked with a small range; the other is flatter with a large range. In addition to having different ranges, these distributions differ with regard to another measure of variability, the standard deviation. The **standard deviation** is a measure of the spread of scores around the mean. The formula for the standard deviation is

$$s = \sqrt{\frac{\Sigma(X - \overline{X})^2}{N}}$$ [Formula 2-3]

where s is the standard deviation, X is each individual score, Σ is the symbol for summation, $\overline{X}$ is the mean of the distribution, and N is the total number of scores in the distribution. To compute the standard deviation, we subtract the mean ($\overline{X}$) from each individual score (X) in the distribution, square that number, add all the numbers, divide that total by the number of scores in the distribution, and then take the square root of the figure. By applying this formula to the data in Table 2-2, we find the standard deviation for that distribution is 19.96 (or 20 rounded off).

The standard deviation is particularly important when used with the normal distribution. Given the mathematical properties of the normal curve, we know that theoretically 68% of all scores fall within ±1 standard deviation of the mean. So from the data in Table 2-2 (which has a mean of 113 and a standard deviation of 20), we know that theoretically 68% of all the scores should fall between 93 (113 − 20) and 133 (113 + 20). Furthermore, the mathematical derivation of the normal curve indicates that theoretically 95% of all the scores should fall within ±2 standard deviations from the mean—that is, between 73 (113 − 40) and 153 (113 + 40). Finally, theoretically 99% of all the scores should fall within ±3 standard deviations from the mean, between 53 (113 − 60) and 173 (113 + 60). The actual percentages of scores from the data in Table 2-2 are very close to the theoretical values; 69% of the scores fall within 1 standard deviation, 96% fall within 2 standard deviations, and 100% fall within

3 standard deviations. Although other measures of variability besides the range and standard deviation are also used, these two measures suffice for the purposes of this book. Variability is important because it reveals the spread of scores in a distribution. And this can be just as important as knowing the most typical score in a distribution.

Correlation.   So far we have been concerned with the statistical analysis of only one variable: its shape, typical score, and dispersion. But most I/O psychological research deals with the relationship between two (or more) variables. In particular, we are usually interested in the extent that we can understand one variable (the criterion or dependent variable) on the basis of our knowledge about another (the predictor or independent variable). A statistical procedure useful in determining this relationship is called the correlation coefficient. A **correlation coefficient** reflects the degree of linear relationship between two variables, which we shall refer to as X and Y. The symbol for a correlation coefficient is r, and its range is from -1.00 to $+1.00$. A correlation coefficient tells two things about the relationship between two variables: the direction of the relationship and its magnitude.

The direction of a relationship is either positive or negative. A positive relationship means that as one variable increases in magnitude, so does the other. An example of a positive correlation is between height and weight. As a rule, the taller a person is, the more he or she weighs; increasing height is associated with increasing weight. A negative relationship means that as one variable increases in magnitude, the other gets smaller. An example of a negative correlation is between production workers' efficiency and scrap rate. The more efficient workers are, the less scrap is left. The less efficient they are, the more scrap is left.

The magnitude of the correlation is an index of the strength of the relationship. Large correlations indicate greater strength than small correlations. A correlation of .80 indicates a very strong relationship between the variables, whereas a correlation of .10 indicates a very weak relationship. Magnitude and direction are independent; a correlation of $-.80$ is just as strong as one of $+.80$.

It is instructive to consider why the correlation coefficient became important to the field of I/O psychology. Zickar and Gibby (2007) identified an emphasis on quantification and correlational analysis as one of the enduring themes throughout the history of I/O psychology. I/O psychologists have long believed that better decisions (for example, as in personnel selection) can be made on the basis of a statistical analysis of the relationship between how well people perform on an employment test and how well they perform on the job. Such quantification leads to more confidence and soundness of the resulting selection decision than impressionistic or "gut feel" approaches. The quantitative approach provides an empirically-based justification for why we do what we do (e.g., use employment tests to assess job applicants). The correlation coefficient is the most frequently used method in I/O psychology for revealing the statistical relationship between two variables.

The four parts of Figure 2-7 (pp. 44–45) are graphic portrayals of correlation coefficients. The first step in illustrating a correlation is to plot all pairs of variables in the study. For a sample of 100 people, record the height and weight of each person. Then plot the pair of data points (height and weight) for each person. The stronger the relationship between the two variables, the tighter is the spread of data points around the line of best fit that runs through the scatterplot.

Correlation coefficient
A statistical index that reflects the degree of relationship between two variables.

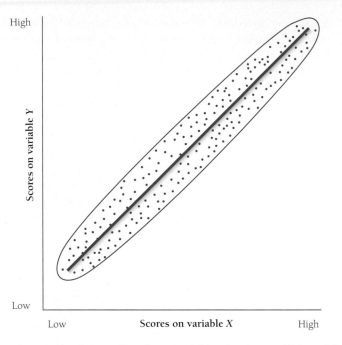

Figure 2-7a   *Scatterplot of two variables that have a high positive correlation*

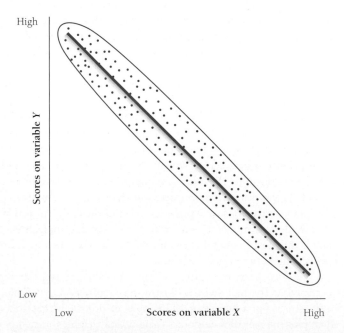

Figure 2-7b   *Scatterplot of two variables that have a high negative correlation*

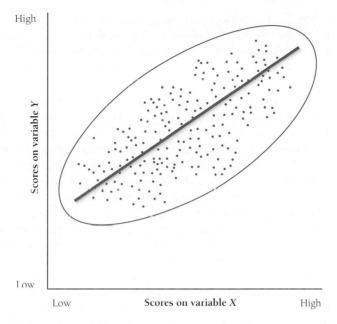

Figure 2-7c *Scatterplot of two variables that have a low positive correlation*

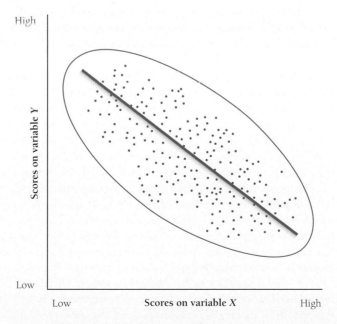

Figure 2-7d *Scatterplot of two variables that have a low negative correlation*

Figure 2-7a shows a scatterplot for two variables that have a high positive correlation. Notice that the line of best fit through the data points slants in the positive direction, and most of the data points are packed tightly around the line. Figure 2-7b shows a scatterplot for two variables that have a high negative correlation. Again, notice that the data points are packed tightly around the line, but in this case, the line slants in the negative direction. Figure 2-7c shows a scatterplot for two variables that have a low positive correlation. Although the line slants in the positive direction, the data points in the scatterplot are spread out quite widely around the line of best fit. Finally, Figure 2-7d shows a scatterplot for two variables that have a low negative correlation. The line of best fit slants in the negative direction, and the data points are not packed tightly around the line.

The stronger the correlation between two variables (either positive or negative), the more accurately we can predict one variable from the other. The statistical formula used to compute a correlation will not be presented in this book because it is available in statistics books and it will not be necessary for you, as you read this book, to compute any correlations. However, it is important that you know what a correlation is and how to interpret one. The only way to derive the exact numerical value of a correlation is to apply the statistical formula. Although the eyeball-inspection method of looking at a scatterplot gives you some idea of what the correlation is, research has shown that people are generally not very good at inferring the magnitude of correlations by using this method.

The correlation coefficient does not permit any inferences to be made about causality—that is, whether one variable *caused* the other to occur. Even though a causal relationship may exist between two variables, just computing a correlation will not reveal this fact.

Suppose you wish to compute the correlation between the amount of alcohol consumed in a town and the number of people who attend church there. You collect data on each of these variables in many towns in your area. The correlation coefficient turns out to be .85. On the basis of this high correlation, you conclude that because people drink all week, they go to church to repent (alcohol consumption causes church attendance). Your friends take the opposite point of view. They say that because people have to sit cramped together on hard wooden pews, after church they "unwind" by drinking (church attendance causes alcohol consumption). Who is correct? On the basis of the existing data, no one is correct because causality cannot be inferred from a single correlation coefficient. Proof of causality must await experimental research. In fact, the causal basis of this correlation is undoubtedly neither of the opinions offered. The various towns in the study have different populations, which produces a systematic relationship between these two variables along with many others, such as the number of people who eat out in restaurants or attend movies. Just the computation of a correlation in this example does not even determine whether the churchgoers are the drinkers. The effect of a third variable on the two variables being correlated can cloud our ability to understand the relationship between the variables in purely correlational research.

To what degree can we determine causality in I/O research? Making a clear determination of causality in research is never easy, but two basic approaches have been developed. Both involve the critical factor of control—to control for other explanations for the obtained results. The classic approach is the laboratory experiment. In this case, a small number of factors are selected for study, the experiment is carefully designed to control other variables, and the causal-based conclusions are limited to only the variables examined in the study. The Streufert et al. (1992) study on the effects of alcohol intoxication on visual-motor performance is one example. The second approach to assessing causality is more recent. It is based on advances in mathematical techniques for abstracting causal information from nonexperimental data. These mathematical approaches require restrictive assumptions, such as the availability of well-developed theoretical formulations, the measurement of all critical variables, and high precision of measurement. Under these conditions, assessments of causality are permissible. Answering the question "why" is not only the ultimate objective of scientific research but also the means by which we make sense out of the events in our environment (Silvester & Chapman, 1997).

Because correlation is a common analytical technique in I/O psychological research, many of the empirical findings in this book will be expressed in those terms. However, the concept of correlation will not magically yield accurate inferences in I/O psychological research. As Mitchell (1985) noted, a poorly designed research study cannot be "saved" by the use of correlation to draw valid conclusions. Researchers must plan studies carefully, use sound methodological procedures, and use appropriate statistical analyses to arrive at meaningful conclusions. Over the past few decades our profession has made major advances in the sophistication and precision of our statistical methods. This increased precision can lead to increased understanding of the phenomena we seek to understand. Murphy and De Shon (2000) argued that such advances are of sufficient magnitude to cause us to question some long-held assumptions about major topics of interest to us. Kirk (1996) added that statistical results must also be judged in terms of their practical significance—that is, whether the result is useful in the real world. Practical significance is a most reasonable standard for judging research findings in I/O psychology.

Conclusions from Research

After analyzing the data, the researcher draws conclusions. A conclusion may be that alcohol intoxication impairs certain skills more than others, or jobs that require skills more adversely impaired by alcohol consumption warrant more restrictive standards than other jobs. Latham and Kinne's study (1974) concluded that goal setting increased the rate of wood harvesting. So a company might decide to implement the goal-setting procedure throughout the firm. Generally, it is unwise to implement any major changes based on the results of only one study. As a rule, we prefer to know the results from several studies. We want to be as certain as possible that any organizational changes are grounded in repeatable, generalizable results.

Sometimes the conclusions drawn from a study modify beliefs about a problem. Note in Figure 2-1 (p. 25) that a feedback loop extends from "Conclusions from research" to "Statement of the problem." The findings from one study influence the research problems in future studies. Theories may be altered if empirical research fails to confirm some of the hypotheses put forth. One of the most critical issues in conducting research is the quality of the generalizations that can be drawn from the conclusions. A number of factors determine the boundary conditions for generalizing the conclusions from a research study to a broader population or setting. One factor is the representativeness of individuals who serve as the research subjects. The generalizability of conclusions drawn from research on college students has been questioned on the grounds that college-aged students are not representative of the population. This is why it is advisable to explicitly assess the generalizability of findings across groups, as was done in the Murphy et al. (1991) study on attitudes toward drug testing. A second factor is the degree of fit between the subjects and the research task. Studying what factors high school students believe is important in selecting a college is a reasonable fit between subjects and the task. Studying what factors high school students believe is important in selecting a nursing home for the elderly is not. A third factor that determines the generalizability of conclusions is the research method. Dipboye (1990) argued that research topics get studied in either laboratory *or* field (i.e., naturally occurring) settings. He suggested that laboratory *and* field research strategies should be used in coordination with each other rather than in competition. Dipboye believes that each basic strategy has something to offer and that researchers can gain understanding by studying a problem with both methods. Laboratory research has traditionally been regarded as more scientifically rigorous, whereas field research is seen as more representative of real-world conditions. Locke (1985) reached the conclusion that most findings from laboratory experiments can be generalized beyond the lab, but other individuals (for example, Mook, 1983) are more skeptical.

The generalizability of research conclusions based on college students (typically 18–22 years old) is particularly open to questions in I/O psychology. Much research is conducted in university settings, and university students often serve as subjects in research studies because they are an available sample. It has been a matter of great debate within the entire field of psychology whether the conclusions reached from studying college students generalize to a larger and more diverse population. There is no simple answer to this question: it depends greatly on the research topic under consideration. Asking typical college students to describe their vocational aspirations is highly appropriate. Asking typical college students to describe how they will spend their retirement years, 50 years from now, would have limited scientific value. Because I/O psychology is concerned with the world of work, and thus the population of concern to us is the adult working population, we are generally cautious in attempting to generalize findings based on studies of college students.

Research is a cumulative process. Researchers build on one another's work in formulating new research questions. They communicate their results by publishing articles in journals. A competent researcher must keep up to date in his or her area of expertise to avoid repeating someone else's study. The conclusions drawn from research can affect many aspects of our lives. Research is a vital part of industry; it is the basis for changes in products and services. Research can be a truly exciting activity, although it may seem tedious if you approach it from the perspective of only testing stuffy theories, using sterile statistics, and inevitably reaching dry conclusions. Daft (1983) suggested that research is a craft, and a researcher, like an artist or craftsperson, has to pull together a wide variety of human experiences to produce a superior product. Being a researcher is more like unraveling a mystery than following a cookbook (see Field Note 1). However, research is not flash-in-the-pan thrill seeking; it involves perseverance, mental discipline, and patience. There is no substitute for hard work. I can recall many times when I anxiously anticipated seeing computer analyses that would foretell the results of a lengthy research study. This sense of anticipation is the fun of doing research—and research, in the spirit of Daft's view of researchers being

Field Note 1: Researcher as Detective

Being a good researcher is a lot like being a good detective. You have to use all of your senses to buttress information collected by traditional research methods. I often administer and interpret attitude surveys for my industrial clients. The results of these surveys reveal a wealth of information about the companies. If it is judged only in statistical terms, however, this information often seems dry and bland. Therefore, I decided to experience the organizations in person to better understand and appreciate the statistical results. I have smelled acid fumes in a metal fabricating company that burned my nose and eyes after only a few minutes of exposure. I have tasted a rancid bologna sandwich from a vending machine situated by a big window in the company cafeteria (the sun shining through the window heated the machine and spoiled the food). I have walked (and slipped) across a company parking lot that was a solid 2- to 3-inch sheet of ice during January and February. I have been in a "sound-sensitive" room that was so quiet I could hear my heartbeat. And in the president's office of one status-conscious organization, I have seen a white llama-wool carpet thick enough to swallow most of your shoes as you walked across it. In and of themselves, these events have little meaning, but when considered as part of the total organizational fabric, they provide a rich texture to I/O psychological research findings.

craftspersons, is a craft I try to pass on to my students. Klahr and Simon (1999) believe researchers from all scientific disciplines, though differing in the methods used in their respective disciplines, are all basically problem solvers. They invoke research methods to solve problems and answer questions of interest to them. Researchers are driven by a sense of curiosity, like that of a child. Klahr and Simon added: "Perhaps this is why childlike characteristics, such as the propensity to wonder, are so often attributed to creative scientists and artists" (p. 540).

McCall and Bobko (1990) noted the importance of serendipity in scientific research. *Serendipity* refers to a chance occurrence or happening. "The history of science is filled with chance discoveries. [For example] a contaminated culture eventually led [Alexander] Fleming to learn about and recognize the properties of penicillin" (p. 384). Rather than discarding the culture because it was contaminated, Fleming sought to understand how it had become so. The lesson is that we should allow room for lucky accidents and unexpected observations to occur and be prepared to pursue them.

Ethical Issues in Research

The American Psychological Association (2002) has a code of ethics that must be honored by all APA members who conduct research. The code of ethics was created to protect the rights of subjects and to avoid the possibility of unqualified people conducting research. It is the responsibility of the researcher to balance ethical accountability and the technical demands of scientific research practices. It is not at all unusual for psychologists to face ethical conflicts in the conduct of their work, including research (Bersoff, 1999).

As stated by Aguinis and Henle (2002), participants in psychological research are granted five rights that are specified in the code of ethics:

1. **Right to informed consent.** Participants have the right to know the purpose of the research, the right to decline or withdraw participation at any time without negative consequences, and the right to be informed of any risks associated with their participation in the research. This right is perhaps the most fundamental because most research aims to meet the needs of the researcher, not the participants.

2. **Right to privacy.** Researchers must respect the participants' right to limit the amount of information they reveal about themselves. How much information the participants might be required to reveal and the sensitivity of this information may offset their willingness to participate.

3. **Right to confidentiality.** Confidentiality involves decisions about who will have access to research data, how records will be maintained, and whether participants will be anonymous. Participants should have the right to decide to whom they will reveal personal information. By guaranteeing participants' confidentiality, researchers may be able to obtain more honest responses.

4. **Right to protection from deception.** Deception refers to a researcher intentionally misleading a participant about the real purpose of the research. Examples are withholding information and producing fake beliefs and assumptions. Deception is sometimes used by researchers in the belief that it is critical to understanding the phenomenon of interest. Researchers who wish to use deception must demonstrate to an institutional review board that the value of the research outweighs the harm imposed on participants and that the phenomenon cannot be studied in any other way. It has been argued that deception does not respect participants' rights, dignity, and freedom to decline participation and may result in participants being suspicious of psychological research. In short, deception can be used in research, but participants are assured that it is used only as a last resort.

5. **Right to debriefing.** After the study is completed, debriefing must take place to answer participants' questions about the research, to remove any harmful effects brought on by the study, and to leave participants with a sense of dignity. Debriefing should include information about how the current study adds to knowledge of the topic, how the results of the study might be applied, and the importance of this type of research.

Researchers who violate these rights, particularly in studies that involve physical or psychological risks, are subject to professional censure and possible litigation. Wright and Wright (1999) argued that organizational researchers should be concerned with the welfare of research participants not only during the research but also after it.

They asserted that participants as well as researchers should benefit from the research. Aguinis and Henle also noted that many countries have developed codes of ethics regarding research. Although nations differ in the breadth of research issues covered, every country emphasizes the well-being and dignity of research participants in their ethics code by addressing informed consent, deception, protection from harm, and confidentiality.

The researcher is faced with additional problems when the participants are employees of companies. Even when managers authorize research, it can cause problems in an organizational context. Employees who are naive about the purpose of research are often suspicious when asked to participate. They wonder how they were "picked" for inclusion in the study and whether they will be asked difficult questions. Some people even think a psychologist can read their minds and thus discover all sorts of private thoughts. Research projects that arouse emotional responses may place managers in an uncomfortable interpersonal situation.

Mirvis and Seashore (1979) described some of the problems facing those who conduct research with employees. Most problems involve role conflict, the dilemma of being trained to be a good researcher yet having to comply with both company and professional standards. For example, consider a role-conflict problem I faced in doing research with industrial employees. I used a questionnaire to assess the employees' opinions and morale. Management had commissioned the study. As part of the research design, all employees were told that their responses would be anonymous. One survey response revealed the existence of employee theft. Although I did not know the identity of the employee, with the information given and a little help from management, that person could have been identified. Was I to violate my promise and turn over the information to management? Should I tell management that some theft had occurred but I had no way to find out who had done it (which would not have been true)? Or was I to ignore what I knew and fail to tell management about a serious problem in the company? In this case, I informed the company of the theft, but I refused to supply any information about the personal identity of the thief. This was an uneasy compromise between serving the needs of my client and maintaining the confidentiality of the information source.

Lowman (1999) presented a series of cases on ethical problems for I/O psychologists. Taken from real-life experiences, the multitude of ethical dilemmas cover such issues as conflict of interest, plagiarizing, and "overselling" research results. The pressures to conduct high-quality research, the need to be ethical, and the reality of organizational life sometimes place the researcher in a difficult situation (see Field Note 2, p. 52). These demands place constraints on the I/O psychologist that researchers in other areas do not necessarily face. Lefkowitz (2003) noted that I/O psychology is sometimes portrayed (incorrectly) as being value-free in science and research. This view is advanced by those who believe the field is entirely objective, despite our service to the highly competitive world of business. If our personal values are consistent with those of the larger social system within which we act, it can create the illusion that our systems are value-free. In theory, research may be value-free; in practice, researchers are not. The code of ethics was written and is enforced to assure respect for the principles that guide the society of which we are a part (see The Changing Nature of Work: Genetic Research, p. 53).

Field Note 2: An Ethical Dilemma

Many ethical problems do not have clear-cut solutions. Here is one I ran into. I was trying to identify some psychological tests that would be useful in selecting future salespeople for a company. As part of my research, I administered the tests to all the employees in the sales department. With the company's consent, I assured the employees that the test results would be confidential. I explained that my purpose in giving the tests was to test the tests—that is, to assess the value of the tests—and that no one in the company would ever use the test results to evaluate the employees. In fact, no one in the company would even know the test scores. The results of my research were highly successful. I was able to identify which tests were useful in selecting potentially successful salespeople.

A few weeks later the same company's management approached me and said they now wanted to look into the value of using psychological tests to promote salespeople to the next higher job in the department, sales manager. In fact, they were so impressed with the test results for selecting new salespeople that they wanted to assess the value of these very same tests for identifying good sales managers. And since I had already given the tests to their salespeople and had the scores, all I would have to do is turn over the scores to the company, and they would determine whether there was any relationship between the scores and promotability to sales manager. I said I couldn't turn over the test results because that would violate my statement that the results were confidential and that no one in the company would ever know how well the employees did on the tests. I offered two alternatives. One

was to readminister the same tests to the employees under a different set of test conditions—namely, that the company *would* see the test results and in fact the results could be used to make promotion decisions. The second alternative was for me (not the company) to determine the value of these tests to make promotion decisions. In that way I would maintain the confidentiality of the test scores.

Management totally rejected the first alternative, saying it made no sense to readminister the same tests to the same people. I already had the test results, so why go back and get them a second time? The second alternative was also not approved. They said I was deliberately creating a need for the company to pay me for a second consulting project when they were perfectly capable of doing the work, with no outside help and at no extra cost. They said, in effect, I was holding the test results "hostage" when I would not release them. In my opinion, the company's management was asking me to compromise my professional integrity by using the test results in a way that violated the agreement under which the tests were originally administered.

The issue was never really resolved. The company soon faced some major sales problems caused by competitors and lost interest in the idea of using psychological tests for identifying sales managers. The management is still angry about my decision, asserting that I am assuming ownership of "their" test results. I have not been asked to do any more consulting work for them, but it is also quite possible that they would no longer have needed my services even if I had turned the test results over.

The Changing Nature of Work: Genetic Research

As a scientific discipline, psychology posits two fundamental bases of human behavior: environment and heredity. Since its inception, I/O psychology has focused on environmental explanations for behavior in the workplace. The list of topics that I/O psychologists have researched over the past century is lengthy. For example, we have researched why employees are satisfied with their jobs, what behaviors are associated with being an effective leader, and how to enhance work motivation. The implicit assumption behind all of this research is that organizations can make changes in the workplace (e.g., the environment) to increase satisfaction, leadership, and motivation.

Psychology has, for the most part, not examined heredity or genetics as a basis for behavior. What we have learned about the role heredity plays in behavior has come in large part from the study of identical twins reared apart. This research paradigm permits psychologists to investigate both genetic (i.e., identical twins) and environmental (i.e., different patterns of upbringing) causes of behavior. Although I/O psychology has certainly been aware of the heredity basis of behavior, the study of genetics is beyond our scientific purview.

In 1990 a major scientific investigation was begun, entitled the *Human Genome Project* (Patenaude, Guttmacher, & Collins, 2002). Its stated goal was to identify the 30,000 genes that make up human DNA, the biochemical "building blocks" of our genetic structure. Furthermore, the project had a mandate to determine the 3 billion possible *sequences* of genes that make up DNA. One intent of the research was to facilitate the identification of mutant genes that cause individuals to develop certain diseases, such as cancer. Over the past decade researchers have identified genes associated with obesity and the proclivity to alcoholism, among other findings. Individuals diagnosed with these mutant genes might submit themselves to gene replacement therapy, thereby changing their genetic structure and thus gaining a greater chance of leading longer, healthier lives. Five percent of the Human Genome Project budget is devoted to studying the ethical implications of identifying and possibly altering mutant genes. Without question, the primary focus of the genomic research has been on clinical and medical issues.

Does this genetic research have any implications for I/O psychology? It would appear so. Research has revealed that individuals with certain genetic structures are more likely to develop diseases associated with exposure to chemicals found in the workplace. These research findings might be used to screen applicants out of jobs for which they are genetically ill-suited. However, what if continued research on the genome reveals that a gene is responsible for how satisfied we are in life (including our work), whether we are likely to be an effective leader, or to be highly motivated? It is at least plausible there is a genetic explanation for three areas that I/O psychologists have long examined from an environmental perspective. Thus the identification of a gene that contributes to our motivation level, for example, might not be "science fiction." What are the ethical implications of using gene replacement therapy to make individuals more motivated in the workplace? This approach certainly differs from the current path of using genetic research findings to treat disease. As the ethics of genomic research have already posed, just because we *could* alter genes to achieve some outcome, *should* we? Although it may be many years before researchers identify genes that directly influence human behavior in the workplace, the prospects of them doing so seems plausible. Our profession will then have to debate the ethics of genetically "engineering" people to achieve work-related outcomes. I doubt that the founding figures of I/O psychology ever imagined such discourse within our profession!

Research in Industry

Although the empirical research steps in Figure 2-1 (p. 25) are followed in most I/O psychological research, research conducted in industry (as opposed to universities or research centers) often has some additional distinguishing features. First, Boehm (1980) observed that research questions in industry inevitably arise from organizational problems. For example, problems of excessive employee absenteeism, turnover, job dissatisfaction, and so on may prompt a research study designed to reduce their severity. Rarely are research questions posed just to "test a theory." In fact, a study by Flanagan and Dipboye (1981) revealed that psychologists who view organizations simply as laboratories to test theories are not looked on favorably. Hulin (2001) claimed the goals of science and the goals of practice are different. Specifically, the goal of research is to contribute to knowledge, not simply to find solutions for practice. Rynes, McNatt, and Bretz (1999) investigated the process of academic research conducted within work organizations. They found that such collaborative research narrows the gap between the science and practice of I/O psychology, in part by increasing the likelihood of the research findings being implemented by the organizations. Latham (2001) asserted that the goals of the science and practice of I/O psychology are overlapping, and research benefits both sides of the profession. Kehoe (2000) offered this description of the difference between science and practice:

> In a research role, psychologists use previous research to form conclusions, raise questions, and generalize across conditions of interest. In a practice role, selection psychologists depend on previous research to determine solutions, inform decisions, and generalize to the particular set of conditions in the organization. The needs of practice are to decide on and implement solutions; the needs of researchers are to create information, raise possibilities, and expand the horizon for questions. Practice is about reaching closure; research is about opening for discovery. (pp. 409–410)

A second distinguishing feature of research in industry is how the results will be used. In industry, if the results of the study turn out to be positive and useful, the research unit of the organization will try to "sell" (that is, gain acceptance of) the findings throughout the organization. For example, if providing job applicants with a candid and realistic preview of the organization reduces turnover, then the researchers will try to persuade the rest of the organization to use such procedures in recruiting new employees. If the results of a study turn out negative, then the organization will look for side products or secondary ideas that will be of value. In research outside industry, less attention is given to implementing the findings and convincing other people of their utility.

Third, industry has practical motives for conducting research. Industrial research is done to enhance the organization's efficiency. Among private-sector employers, this usually translates into greater profitability. For example, research can be of vital importance in finding out how consumers respond to new products and services, identifying ways to reduce waste, and making better use of employees. In university settings, research may not have such an instrumental purpose. The research questions have relevance to industry, but the link between the findings and their implementation may not be so direct (see Field Note 3).

I am reminded of a student who approached an organization with a research idea. The student needed a sample of managers to test a particular hypothesis. After patiently

Field Note 3: Win the Battle but Lose the War

Industry based research is always embedded in a larger context; that is, it is conducted for a specific reason. Sometimes the research is successful, sometimes it isn't, and sometimes you can win the battle but lose the war. A client of mine gave promotional tests—tests that current employees take to be advanced to higher positions in the company at higher rates of pay. These tests were important to the employees because only through the tests could they be promoted. The company gave an attitude survey and discovered that many employees did not like the tests. They said many test questions were outdated, some questions had no correct answers, and most questions were poorly worded. As a result of these "bad" questions, employees were failing the tests and not getting promoted. I was hired to update and improve the promotional tests (there were 75 of them). Using the full complement of psychological research procedures, I analyzed every question on every test, eliminated the poor questions, developed new questions, and

in general "cleaned up" each of the tests. By every known standard, the tests were now of very high quality. Both the company's management and I felt confident the employees would be delighted with these revised tests. We were wrong. In the next attitude survey given by the company, the employees still thought poorly of the (new) tests, but their reasons were different from before. Now they complained that the tests were too hard and too technical and required too much expertise to pass. The employees failed the new tests with the same frequency they had failed the old tests and were just as unhappy. In fact, they may have been even more unhappy; their expectations about the tests had been elevated because the company had hired me to revise them. I felt I had done as good a job in revising the tests as I possibly could have, but in the final analysis I didn't really solve the company's problem. I was hired to revise the tests, but what the management really wanted was to have the employees be satisfied with the tests, which didn't occur.

listening to the student's request, the organization's representative asked, "Why should we participate in this study? How can this study help us?" Industries that sponsor and participate in research do so for a reason: to enhance their welfare. Universities also conduct research for a reason, but it may be nothing more than intellectual curiosity. Some studies have examined the extent to which research influences policy makers—that is, how much the results of research studies influence important decisions. Rogelberg and Brooks-Laber (2002) stated that researchers in I/O psychology must become more skilled in demonstrating the value of research to people not trained in how to evaluate it. There can be an unhealthy gap between the academics who research topics (the "knowledge producers") and the practitioners who want to implement research findings (the "knowledge users"). Austin, Scherbaum, and Mahlman (2002) believe the gap could be narrowed if researchers were more aware of the possible audiences for their research, and as a profession we were better at "translating" our scientific research findings into practical action. Shapiro, Kirkman, and Courtney (2007) identified two types of "translation" issues with scientific research findings that inhibit their use in making real world decisions. One is that day-to-day challenges faced by managers are not related to what scientists study. They both live in their own separate worlds. The second issue is that even if the topics of interest are common to both managers and researchers, researchers tend to report findings that are not actionable. Recall from earlier in the chapter that the statistical index most commonly used by I/O researchers is the correlation coefficient. Bazerman (2005) considers correlational research findings to be *descriptive* ("what is the statistical relationship between *X* and *Y* "), while managers prefer findings that are *prescriptive* in nature ("if *X* occurs, do *Y* "). Argyris (1996) referred to these findings as **actionable knowledge**. Ruback and Innes (1988) concluded that to have the greatest impact, I/O psychologists need to study dependent variables that are important to decision makers, such as human lives and dollars saved. They also believe we should focus our attention on independent variables that policy makers have the power to change.

> **Actionable knowledge**
> Knowledge produced from research that helps formulate policies or action to address a particular issue.

Although academic and industrial research may be guided by somewhat different factors, both have contributed heavily to the I/O psychological literature. The infusion of research from both sectors has in fact been healthy and stimulating for the profession. What should I/O psychologists study? Strasser and Bateman (1984) surveyed both managers and nonmanagers as to what they would like to see researched. The predominant answer from both groups related to how people can learn to get along with one another in a work context. As one respondent in their survey said, "People all have different personalities and some people we just can't get along with. How can we avoid personality conflicts and still have a good working relationship?" (p. 87). The second most pressing research need was communication among people.

Although it may be tempting to say that researchers should tackle big, socially important problems, such problems are usually very complex and difficult to research. Nevertheless, some psychologists (Moghaddam, 2005) believe that a global problem such as terrorism must first be understood from a psychological perspective before any long-term solutions can be enacted. I/O psychological research has been instrumental in enhancing our nation's productivity and the quality of our worklife. An understanding of research methods is vital for psychologists to resolve problems that confront humankind in an increasingly complex world.

Case Study   How Should I Study This?

Robin Mosier had just returned from her psychology class and was eager to tell her roommate about an idea she had. Julie Hansen had taken the same class the previous semester, so Robin was hopeful that Julie could help her out. The psychology professor gave the class an assignment to come up with a research design to test some hypothesis. Robin's idea came from the job she had held the past summer.

Robin began to describe her idea. "Last summer I worked in data entry of the records department of a bank. Sometimes it wasn't always clear how we should fill out certain reports and forms. I was always pretty reluctant to go to my supervisor, Mr. Kast, and ask for help. So were the other female workers. But I noticed the guys didn't seem to be reluctant at all to ask him for help. So I got this idea; see, I think women are more reluctant than men to ask a male superior for help."

"Okay," replied Julie. "So now you have to come up with a way to test that idea?"

"Right," said Robin. "I was thinking maybe I could make up a questionnaire and ask students in my class about it. I think people would know if they felt that way or not."

"Maybe so," Julie said, "but maybe they wouldn't want to admit it. You know, it could be one of those things that either you don't realize about yourself, or if you do, you just don't want to say so."

"Well, if I can't just ask people about it, maybe I could do some sort of experiment," Robin commented. "What if I gave students some tasks to do, but the instructions weren't too clear? If I'm right, more men than women will ask a male experimenter for help."

"Do you think you'd get the opposite effect with a female experimenter?" asked Julie.

"You mean, would more women than men ask a female experimenter for help? I don't know. Maybe," answered Robin.

"If that's the case," said Julie, "you might want to test both male and female experimenters with both male and female subjects."

Robin scratched some notes on a pad. Then she said, "Do you think an experimenter in a study is the same thing as a boss on a job? You see your boss every day, but you may be in an experiment for only about an hour. Maybe that would make a difference in whether you sought help."

"I'm sure it could," replied Julie. "I know I would act differently toward someone I might not see again than toward someone I'd have to work with a long time."

"I know what I'll do," Robin responded. "I won't do the experiment in a lab setting, but I'll go back to the company where I worked last summer. I'll ask the male and female office workers how they feel about asking Mr. Kast for help. I saw the way they acted last summer, and I'd bet they tell me the truth."

"Wait a minute," cautioned Julie. "Just because some women may be intimidated by Mr. Kast doesn't mean that effect holds for all male supervisors. Mr. Kast is just one man. How do you know it holds for all men? That's what you want to test, right?"

Robin looked disconsolate. "There's got to be a good way to test this, although I guess it's more complicated than I thought."

Questions

1. What research method should Robin use to test her idea? How would you design the study?
2. If this idea were tested using a laboratory or quasi-experiment method, what variables should be eliminated or controlled in the research design?
3. If this idea were tested with a questionnaire, what questions should be asked?
4. If this idea were tested with the observation method, what behaviors would you look for?
5. What other variables might explain the employees' attitude toward Mr. Kast?

Chapter Summary

- Research is a means by which I/O psychologists understand issues associated with people at work.
- The four primary research methods used by I/O psychologists are experiments, quasi-experiments, questionnaires, and observation.

- The four primary research methods differ in their extent of control (potential for testing causal relationships) and realism (naturalness of the research setting).
- Meta-analysis is a secondary research method that is useful in integrating findings from previously conducted studies.
- I/O psychologists measure variables of interest and apply statistical analyses to understand the relationships among the variables.
- All psychological research is guided by a code of ethics that protects the rights of research participants.
- Research is conducted in both academic (university) and applied (industry) settings, but usually for different purposes.
- As a profession, I/O psychology has a broad base of knowledge derived from both academic and applied research.
- There are cross-cultural differences in both people's willingness to serve as research participants and their responses.

Criteria: Standards for Decision Making

Learning Objectives

- Understand the distinction between conceptual and actual criteria.
- Understand the meaning of criterion deficiency, relevance, and contamination.
- Explain the purpose of a job analysis and the various methods of conducting one.
- Identify the major types of criteria examined by I/O psychologists.

Criteria
Standards used to help make evaluative judgments.

Each time you evaluate someone or something, you use criteria. **Criteria** (the plural of *criterion*) are best defined as evaluative standards; they are used as reference points in making judgments. We may not be consciously aware of the criteria that affect our judgments, but they do exist. We use different criteria to evaluate different kinds of objects or people; that is, we use different standards to determine what makes a good (or bad) movie, dinner, ball game, friend, spouse, or teacher. In the context of I/O psychology, criteria are most important for defining the "goodness" of employees, programs, and units in the organization as well as the organization itself.

When you and some of your associates disagree in your evaluations of something, what is the cause? Chances are good the disagreement is caused by one of two types of criterion-related problems. For example, take the case of rating Professor Jones as a teacher. One student thinks he is a good teacher; another disagrees. The first student defines "goodness in teaching" as (1) preparedness, (2) course relevance, and (3) clarity of instruction. In the eyes of the first student, Jones scores very high on these criteria and receives a positive evaluation. The second student defines "goodness" as (1) enthusiasm, (2) capacity to inspire students, and (3) ability to relate to students on a personal basis. This student scores Jones low on these criteria and thus gives him a negative evaluation. Why the disagreement? Because the two students have different criteria for defining goodness in teaching.

Disagreements over the proper criteria to use in decision making are common. Values and tastes also dictate people's choice of criteria. For someone with limited funds, a good car may be one that gets high gas mileage. But for a wealthy person, the main criterion may be physical comfort. Not all disagreements are caused by using different criteria, however. Suppose that both students in our teaching example define goodness in teaching as preparedness, course relevance, and clarity of instruction. The first student thinks Professor Jones is ill-prepared, teaches an irrelevant course, and gives unclear instruction. But the second student thinks he is well-prepared, teaches a relevant course, and gives clear instruction. Both students are using the same evaluative standards, but they do not reach the same judgment. The difference of opinion in this case is due to discrepancies in the meanings attached to Professor Jones's behavior. These discrepancies may result from perceptual biases, different expectations, or varying operational definitions associated with the criteria. Thus, even people who use the same standards in making judgments do not always reach the same conclusion.

Austin and Villanova (1992) traced the history of criterion measurement in I/O psychology over the past 75 years. Today's conceptual problems associated with accurate criterion representation and measurement are not all that different from those faced at the birth of I/O psychology. Furthermore, the profession of I/O psychology does not have a monopoly on criterion-related issues and problems. They occur in all walks of life, ranging from the criteria used to judge interpersonal relationships (communication, trust, and respect, for example) to the welfare of nations (literacy rates, per capita income, and infant mortality rates, for example). Since many important decisions are made on the basis of criteria, it is difficult to overstate their significance in the decision-making process. Because criteria are used to render a wide range of judgments, I define them as the evaluative standards by which objects, individuals, procedures, or collectivities are assessed for the purpose of ascertaining their quality. Criterion issues have major significance in the field of I/O psychology.

Conceptual Versus Actual Criteria

Psychologists have not always thought that criteria are of prime importance. Before World War II, they were inclined to believe that "criteria were either given of God or just to be found lying about" (Jenkins, 1946, p. 93). Unfortunately, this is not so. We must carefully consider what is meant by a "successful" worker, student, parent, and so forth. We cannot plunge headlong into measuring success, goodness, or quality until we have a fairly good idea of what (in theory, at least) we are looking for.

Conceptual criterion
The theoretical standard that researchers seek to understand.

A good beginning point is the notion of a conceptual criterion. The **conceptual criterion** is a theoretical construct, an abstract idea that can never actually be measured. It is an ideal set of factors that constitute a successful person (or object or collectivity) as conceived in the psychologist's mind. Let's say we want to define a successful college student. We might start off with intellectual growth; that is, capable students should experience more intellectual growth than less capable students. Another dimension might be emotional growth. A college education should help students clarify their own values and beliefs, and this should add to their emotional development and stability. Finally, we might say that a good college student should want to have some voice in civic activities, be a "good citizen," and contribute to the well-being of his or her community. As an educated person, the good college student will assume an active role in helping to make society a better place in which to live. We might call this dimension a citizenship factor.

Thus these three factors become the conceptual criteria for defining a "good college student." We could apply this same process to defining a "good worker," "good parent," or "good organization." However, because conceptual criteria are theoretical abstractions, we have to find some way to turn them into measurable, real factors. That is, we have to obtain **actual criteria** to serve as measures of the conceptual criteria that we would prefer to (but cannot) assess. The decision is then which variables to select as the actual criteria.

Actual criterion
The operational or actual standard that researchers measure or assess.

A psychologist might choose grade point average as a measure of intellectual growth. Of course, a high grade point average is not equivalent to intellectual growth, but it probably reflects some degree of growth. To measure emotional growth, a psychologist might ask a student's adviser to judge how much the student has matured over his or her college career. Again, maturation is not exactly the same as emotional growth, but it is probably an easier concept to grasp and evaluate than the more abstract notion of emotional growth. Finally, as a measure of citizenship, a psychologist might count the number of volunteer organizations (student government, charitable clubs, and so on) the student has joined over his or her college career. It could be argued that the sheer number (quantity) of joined organizations does not reflect the quality of participation in these activities, and that "good citizenship" is more appropriately defined by quality rather than quantity of participation. Nevertheless, because of the difficulties inherent in measuring quality of participation, plus the fact that one cannot speak of quality unless there is some quantity, the psychologist decides to use this measure. Table 3-1 shows the conceptual criteria and the actual criteria of success for a college student.

Table 3-1   *Conceptual and actual criteria for a successful college student*

Conceptual Criteria	Actual Criteria
Intellectual growth	Grade point average
Emotional growth	Adviser rating of emotional maturity
Citizenship	Number of volunteer organizations joined in college

How do we define a "good" college student in theory? With the conceptual criteria as the evaluative standards, a good college student should display a high degree of intellectual and emotional growth and should be a responsible citizen in the community. How do we operationalize a good college student in practice? Using the actual criteria as the evaluative standards, we say a good college student has earned high grades, is judged by an academic adviser to be emotionally mature, and has joined many volunteer organizations throughout his or her college career. In a review of the relationship between the two sets of criteria (conceptual and actual), remember that the goal is to obtain a reasonable estimate of the conceptual criterion by selecting one or more actual criteria that we think are appropriate.

Criterion Deficiency, Relevance, and Contamination

Criterion deficiency
The part of the conceptual criterion that is not measured by the actual criterion.

Criterion relevance
The degree of overlap or similarity between the actual criterion and the conceptual criterion.

Criterion contamination
The part of the actual criterion that is unrelated to the conceptual criterion.

We can express the relationship between conceptual and actual criteria in terms of three concepts: deficiency, relevance, and contamination. Figure 3-1 shows the overlap between conceptual and actual criteria. The circles represent the contents of each type of criterion. Because the conceptual criterion is a theoretical abstraction, we can never know exactly how much overlap occurs. The actual criteria selected are never totally equivalent to the conceptual criteria we have in mind, so there is always a certain amount (though unspecified) of deficiency, relevance, and contamination.

Criterion deficiency is the degree to which the actual criteria fail to overlap the conceptual criteria—that is, how deficient the actual criteria are in representing the conceptual ones. There is always some degree of deficiency in the actual criteria. By careful selection of the actual criteria, we can reduce (but never eliminate) criterion deficiency. Conversely, criteria that are selected because they are simply expedient, without much thought given to their match to conceptual criteria, are grossly deficient.

Criterion relevance is the degree to which the actual criteria and the conceptual criteria coincide. The greater the match between the conceptual and the actual criteria, the greater the criterion relevance. Again, because the conceptual criteria are theoretical abstractions, we cannot know the exact amount of relevance.

Criterion contamination is that part of the actual criteria that is unrelated to the conceptual criteria. It is the extent to which the actual criteria measure something other than the conceptual criteria. Contamination consists of two parts. One part,

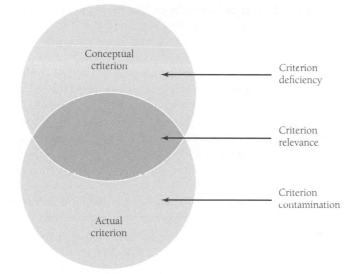

Figure 3-1   *Criterion deficiency, relevance, and contamination*

called *bias*, is the extent to which the actual criteria systematically or consistently measure something other than the conceptual criteria. The second part, called *error*, is the extent to which the actual criteria are not related to anything at all.

Both contamination and deficiency are undesirable in the actual criterion, and together they distort the conceptual criterion. Criterion contamination distorts the actual criterion because certain factors are included that don't belong (that is, they are not present in the conceptual criterion). Criterion deficiency distorts the actual criterion because certain important dimensions of the conceptual criterion are not included in the actual criterion.

Let us consider criterion deficiency and contamination in the example of setting criteria for a good college student. How might the actual criteria we chose be deficient in representing the conceptual criteria? Students typically begin a class with differing amounts of prior knowledge of the subject matter. One student may know nothing of the material, while another student may be very familiar with it. At the end of the term, the former student might have grown more intellectually than the latter student, but the latter student might get a higher grade in the course. By using the grade point average as our criterion, we would (falsely) conclude that the latter student grew more intellectually. So the relationship between good grades and intellectual growth is not perfect (that is, it is deficient). A rating of emotional maturity by an academic adviser might be deficient because the adviser is not an ideal judge. He or she might have only a limited perspective of the student. Finally, it is not enough to just count how many volunteer groups a student belongs to. Quality of participation is as important as (if not more important than) quantity.

How might these actual criteria be contaminated? If some academic majors are more difficult than others, then grades are a contaminated measure of intellectual growth; students in "easy" majors will be judged to have experienced more intellectual growth than students in difficult majors. This is a bias between earned grade point averages and the difficulty of the student's academic major. The source of the bias affects the actual criterion (grades) but not the conceptual criterion (intellectual growth). A rating of emotional maturity by the student's adviser could be contaminated by the student's grades. The adviser might believe that students with high grades have greater emotional maturity than students with low grades. Thus the grade point average might bias an adviser's rating even though it probably has no relationship to the conceptual criterion of emotional growth. Finally, counting the number of organizations a student joins might be contaminated by the student's popularity. Students who join many organizations may simply be more popular rather than better citizens (which is what we want to measure).

If we know that these criterion measures are contaminated, why would we use them? In fact, when a researcher identifies a certain form of contamination, its influence can be controlled through experimental or statistical procedures. The real problem is anticipating the presence of contaminating factors. Komaki (1998) noted that a problem with some criteria is that they are not under the direct control of the person being evaluated. For example, two salespeople may differ in their overall sales volumes because they have different-sized sales territories, not because one is a better salesperson than the other.

As Wallace (1965) observed, psychologists have spent a great deal of time trying to discover new and better ways to measure actual criteria. They have used various analytical and computational procedures to get more precise assessments. Wallace recommended that rather than dwelling on finding new ways to measure actual criteria, psychologists should spend more time choosing actual criteria that will be adequate measures of the conceptual criteria they really seek to understand. The adequacy of the actual criterion as a measure of the conceptual criterion is always a matter of professional judgment—no equation or formula will determine it. As Wherry (1957) said in a classic statement, "If we are measuring the wrong thing, it will not help us to measure it better" (p. 5).

Job Analysis

Job analysis
A formal procedure by which the content of a job is defined in terms of tasks performed and human qualifications needed to perform the job.

I/O psychologists must often identify the criteria of effective job performance. These criteria then become the basis for hiring people (choosing them according to their ability to meet the criteria of job performance), training them (to perform those aspects of the job that are important), paying them (high levels of performance warrant higher pay), and classifying jobs (jobs with similar performance criteria are grouped together). A procedure useful in identifying the criteria or performance dimensions of a job is called job analysis; it is conducted by a job analyst. Harvey (1991) defined **job analysis** as "the collection of data describing (a) observable (or otherwise verifiable) job behaviors performed by workers, including both *what is accomplished* as well as *what technologies are employed* to accomplish the end results, and (b) verifiable characteristics of the job environment with which workers interact, including physical, mechanical, social, and informational elements" (p. 74). A thorough job analysis documents the tasks that are performed on the job, the situation in which the work is performed (for example, tools and equipment, working conditions), and the human attributes needed to perform the work. These data are the basic information needed to make many personnel decisions. Their use is mandated by legal requirements, and estimated annual costs for job analyses have ranged from $150,000 to $4,000,000 in a large organization (Levine et al., 1988).

Wilson (2007) offered an insightful statement about the role that job analysis serves within I/O psychology. "The field of job analysis is especially important because it is the precursor to many other areas of I/O psychology. Job analysis often serves as a first step that cannot be ignored even though the investigator's primary interests may be in other areas" (p. 219). Wilson's statement that job analysis is a "first step that cannot be ignored" is most accurate. Using the peg-and-hole analogy written over 70 years ago as presented in Chapter 1, job analysis serves to define or describe the "shape of the hole." Failing to conduct a job analysis leaves us in the perilous position of trying to fit a given peg into a hole of unknown size or shape. Thus job analysis is often regarded as a required first step in many areas of I/O psychology for practical, theoretical, and legal reasons.

Sources of Job Information

The most critical issue in job analysis is the accuracy and completeness of the information about the job. There are three major sources of job information, and each source is a **subject matter expert (SME)**. The qualifications for being a SME are not precise, but a minimum condition is that the person has direct, up-to-date experience with the job for a long enough time to be familiar with all of its tasks.

Subject matter expert (SME)
A person knowledgeable about a topic who can serve as a qualified information source.

The most common source of information is the *job incumbent*—that is, the holder of the job. The use of job incumbents as SMEs is predicated upon their implicit understanding of their own jobs. Landy and Vasey (1991) believe that the sampling method used to select SMEs is very important. They found that experienced job incumbents provide the most valuable job information. Given the rapid changes in work caused by changing technology, Sanchez (2000) questioned whether job incumbents are necessarily qualified to serve as SMEs. New jobs, jobs that don't currently exist in an organization and for which there are no incumbents, also have to be analyzed. Sanchez proposed the use of statistical methods to forecast employee characteristics needed in the future as technology shifts the way work is conducted. A second source of information is the *supervisor* of the job incumbent. Supervisors play a major role in determining what job incumbents do on their jobs, and thus they are a credible source of information. Although supervisors may describe jobs somewhat more objectively than incumbents, incumbents and supervisors can have legitimate differences of opinion. It has been my experience that most differences occur not in what is accomplished in a job, but in the critical abilities actually needed to perform the job. The third source of job information is a trained *job analyst*. Job analysts are used as SMEs when comparisons are needed across many jobs. Because of their familiarity with job analysis methods, analysts often provide the most consistent across-job ratings. Job analyst expertise lies not in the subject matter of various jobs per se, but in their ability to understand similarities and differences across jobs in terms of the tasks performed and abilities needed.

Task
The lowest level of analysis in the study of work; a basic component of work (such as typing for a secretary).

Position
A set of tasks performed by a single employee. For example, the position of a secretary is often represented by the tasks of typing, filing, and scheduling.

Job
A set of similar positions in an organization.

Job family
A grouping of similar jobs in an organization.

In general, incumbents and supervisors are the best sources of descriptive job information, whereas job analysts are best qualified to comprehend the relationships among a set of jobs. The most desirable strategy in understanding a job is to collect information from as many qualified sources as possible, as opposed to relying exclusively on one source.

Job Analysis Procedures

The purpose of job analysis is to explain the tasks that are performed on the job and the human attributes needed to perform the job. A clear understanding of job analysis requires knowledge of four job-related concepts, as shown in Figure 3-2. At the lowest level of aggregation are tasks. **Tasks** are the basic units of work that are directed toward meeting specific job objectives. A **position** is a set of tasks performed by a single employee. There are usually as many positions in an organization as there are employees. However, many positions may be similar to one another. In such a case, similar positions are grouped or aggregated to form a **job**. An example is the job of secretary; another job is that of receptionist. Similar jobs may be further aggregated based on general similarity of content to form a **job family**—in this case, the clerical job family.

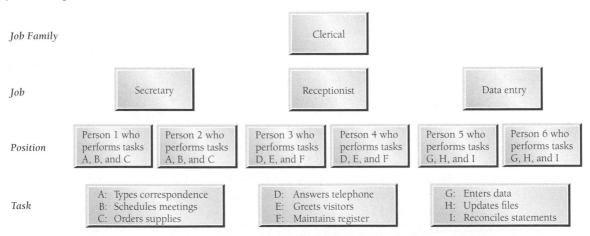

Figure 3-2 *Relationships among tasks, positions, jobs, and job families*

Task-oriented procedure
A procedure or set of operations in job analysis designed to identify important or frequently performed tasks as a means of understanding the work performed.

It is possible to understand jobs from either a task-oriented or a worker-oriented perspective. Both procedures are used in conducting job analyses.

Task-Oriented Procedures.   A **task-oriented procedure** seeks to understand a job by examining the tasks performed, usually in terms of *what* is accomplished. The procedure begins with a consideration of job duties, responsibilities, or function. Williams and Crafts (1997) defined a job duty as "a major part of the work that an incumbent performs, comprised of a series of tasks, which together accomplish a job objective" (p. 57). Tasks thus become the basic unit of analysis for understanding a job using task-oriented procedures. The job analyst develops a series of *task statements*, which are concise expressions of tasks performed. Examples are "splice high-voltage cables," "order materials and supplies," and "grade tests." Task statements should not be written in too general terminology, nor should they be written in very detailed language. They should reflect a discrete unit of work with appropriate specificity. Clifford (1994) estimated that the number of tasks required to describe most jobs typically is between 300 and 500.

Following the development of task statements, SMEs (most often incumbents) are asked to rate the task statements on a series of scales. The scales reflect important dimensions that facilitate understanding the job. Among the common scales used to rate task statements are frequency, importance, difficulty, and consequences of error. For example, the frequency scale would indicate whether a particular task was performed *rarely* (as once or twice per year) to *very often* (several times per day). Based on an analysis of the ratings (especially with regard to the mean and standard deviation), we acquire an understanding of a job in terms of the rated frequency, importance, difficulty, and other dimensions of the tasks that make up the job.

Functional job analysis (FJA)
A method of job analysis that describes the content of jobs in terms of People, Data, and Things.

A classic example of a task-oriented method of job analysis is **Functional Job Analysis (FJA)**, developed by Fine and Cronshaw (1999). FJA obtains two types of task information: (1) *what a worker does*—the procedures and processes engaged in by a worker as a task is performed, and (2) how *a task is performed*—the physical, mental, and interpersonal involvement of the worker with the task. These types of information are used to identify what a worker does and the results of those job behaviors. The critical component in analyzing a job is the proper development of task statements. These task statements are then rated by SMEs using specific rating scales. The ratings serve as a basis for inferring worker specifications needed to perform the tasks.

Perhaps the most notable characteristic of FJA is that tasks are rated along three dimensions: People, Data, and Things. When a task requires involvement with People, the worker needs interpersonal resources (sensitivity, compassion, etc.). When a task requires involvement with Data, the worker needs mental resources (knowledge, reasoning, etc.). When a task is defined primarily in relation to Things, the worker needs physical resources (strength, coordination, etc.). Each of these three dimensions (People, Data, Things) is presented in a hierarchy ranging from high to low. Thus, a given job may be defined as requiring a medium level of People, a high level of Data, and a low level of Things, for example. FJA has been used to analyze jobs in many sectors of society but most frequently in the federal government. The method is regarded as one of the major systematic approaches to the study of jobs.

Worker-oriented procedure
A procedure or set of operations in job analysis designed to identify important or frequently utilized human attributes as a means of understanding the work performed.

Worker-Oriented Procedures.   A **worker-oriented procedure** seeks to understand a job by examining the human attributes needed to perform it successfully. The human attributes are classified into four categories: knowledge (K), skills (S), abilities (A), and other (O) characteristics. *Knowledge* is specific types of information people need in order to perform a job. Some knowledge is required of workers before they can be hired to perform a job, whereas other knowledge may be acquired on the job. *Skills* are defined as the proficiencies needed to perform a task. Skills are usually enhanced through practice—for example, skill at typing and skill at driving an automobile. *Abilities* are defined as relatively enduring attributes that generally are stable over time. Examples are cognitive ability, physical ability, and spatial ability. Skills and abilities are confused often and easily, and the distinction is not always clear. It is useful to think of skills as cultivations of innate abilities. Generally speaking, high levels of (innate) ability can be cultivated into high skill levels. For example, a person with high musical ability could become highly proficient in playing a musical instrument. Low levels of (innate) ability preclude the development of high skill levels. *Other* characteristics are all other personal attributes, most often personality factors (e.g., remaining calm in emergency situations) or capacities (e.g., withstanding extreme temperatures). Collectively these four types of attributes, referred to as **KSAOs**, reflect an approach to understanding jobs by analyzing the human attributes needed to perform them.

KSAOs
An abbreviation for "knowledge, skills, abilities, and other" characteristics.

Like task statements, KSAO statements are written to serve as a means of understanding the human attributes needed to perform a job. They are written in standard format, using the wording "Knowledge of," "Skill in," or "Ability to." Examples are "Knowledge of city building codes," "Skill in operating a pneumatic drill," and "Ability to lift a 50-pound object over your head." The KSAO statements are also rated by SMEs, reflecting whether they are of *little importance* on the job, up to being *critically important*. Similar to analyzing the ratings of task statements, the ratings of KSAO statements are analyzed (i.e., mean and standard deviation) to provide an understanding of a job based on the human attributes needed to successfully perform the job.

Linkage analysis
A technique in job analysis that establishes the connection between the tasks performed and the human attributes needed to perform them.

Other analytic procedures can be followed to gain greater understanding of a job. A **linkage analysis** unites the two basic types of job analysis information: task-oriented and worker-oriented. A linkage analysis examines the relationship between KSAOs and tasks performed. The results of this analysis reveal which particular KSAOs are linked to the performance of many important and frequently performed tasks. Those KSAOs that are linked to the performance of tasks critical to the job become the basis of the employee selection test. That is, the linkage analysis identifies what attributes should be assessed among job candidates. While incumbents are typically regarded as the most credible source for information about the jobs they perform, the linkage analysis that ties KSAOs to tasks performed have been found more reliable when provided by job analysts than incumbents (Baranowski & Anderson, 2006).

How to Collect Job Analysis Information

Some written material, such as task summaries and training manuals, may exist for a particular job. A job analyst should read this written material as a logical first step in conducting a formal job analysis. Then the job analyst is prepared to collect more extensive information about the job to be analyzed. Three procedures are typically followed: the interview, direct observation, and a questionnaire.

Procedures for Collecting Information.   In the first procedure, the *interview*, the job analyst asks SMEs questions about the nature of their work. SMEs may be interviewed individually, in small groups, or through a series of panel discussions. The job analyst tries to gain an understanding of the tasks performed on the job and the KSAOs needed to perform them. The individuals selected to be interviewed are regarded as SMEs, people qualified to render informed judgments about their work. Desirable characteristics in SMEs include strong verbal ability, a good memory, and cooperativeness. Also, if SMEs are suspicious of the motives behind a job analysis, they are inclined to magnify the importance or difficulty of their abilities as a self-protective tactic (see Field Note 1).

The second method is called *direct observation*: Employees are observed as they perform their jobs. Observers try to be unobtrusive, observing the jobs but not getting in the workers' way (see Field Note 2, p. 70). Observers generally do not talk to the employees because it interferes with the conduct of work. They sometimes use cameras or videotape equipment to facilitate the observation. Direct observation is an excellent

Field Note 1: A Memorable Lesson

When interviewing employees about their jobs, job analysts should explain what they are doing and why they are doing it. If they do not fully explain their role, employees may feel threatened, fearing the analysts may somehow jeopardize their position by giving a negative evaluation of their performance, lowering their wages, firing them, and so on. Although job analysts do not have the power to do these things, some employees assume the worst. When employees feel threatened, they usually magnify the importance or difficulty of their contributions to the organization in an attempt to protect themselves. Therefore, to ensure accurate and honest responses, all job analysts should go out of their way to allay any possible suspicions or fears.

I learned the importance of this point early in my career. One of my first job analyses focused on the job of a sewer cleaner. I had arranged to interview three sewer cleaners about their work. However, I had neglected to provide much advance notice about myself, why I would be talking to them, or what I was trying to do. I simply arrived at the work site,

introduced myself, and told the sewer cleaners that I wanted to talk to them about their jobs. Smelling trouble, the sewer cleaners proceeded to give me a memorable lesson on the importance of first establishing a nonthreatening atmosphere. One sewer cleaner turned to me and said: "Let me tell you what happens if we don't do our job. If we don't clean out the sewers of stuff like tree limbs, rusted hubcaps, and old tires, the sewers get clogged up. If they get clogged up, the sewage won't flow. If the sewage won't flow, it backs up. People will have sewage backed up into the basements of their homes. Manhole covers will pop open, flooding the streets with sewage. Sewage will eventually cover the highways, airport runways, and train tracks. People will be trapped in their homes surrounded by sewage. The entire city will be covered with sewage, with nobody being able to get in or out of the city. And that's what happens if we don't do our job of cleaning the sewers." Sadder but wiser, I learned the importance of not giving employees any reason to overstate their case.

Field Note 2: Unintentional Obstruction of Work

Although logically it may not seem so, it takes talent to watch people at work. Observation is one of the methods job analysts use to study jobs. The object is to unobtrusively observe the employee at work. The analyst doesn't need to hide; he or she simply needs to blend in. In attempts to avoid interfering with employees, I have inadvertently positioned myself too far away to see what was really happening. I have also learned to bring earplugs and goggles to work sites because, when watching people at work, the observer is exposed to the same environmental conditions they are. Although you can be "too far" from a worker to make accurate observations, you can also get "too close." Cascio (1982) described this true story:

> While riding along in a police patrol car as part of a job analysis of police officers, an analyst and an officer were chatting away when a call came over the radio regarding a robbery in progress. Upon arriving at the scene the analyst and the officer both jumped out of the patrol car, but in the process the overzealous analyst managed to position himself between the robbers and the police. Although the robbers were later apprehended, they used the analyst as a decoy to make their getaway from the scene of the crime. (p. 56)

Taxonomy
A classification of objects designed to enhance understanding of the objects being classified.

method for appreciating and understanding the adverse conditions (such as noise or heat) under which some jobs are performed; however, it is a poor method for understanding *why* certain behaviors occur on the job.

The third procedure for collecting job information is a structured *questionnaire* or inventory. The analyst uses a commercially available questionnaire that organizes existing knowledge about job information into a taxonomy. A **taxonomy** is a classification scheme useful in organizing information—in this case, information about jobs. The information collected about a particular job is compared with an existing database of job information derived from other jobs previously analyzed with the questionnaire. Peterson and Jeanneret (1997) referred to this procedure as being *deductive* because the job analyst can deduce an understanding of a job from a preexisting framework for analyzing jobs. Alternatively, the interview and direct observation procedures are *inductive* because the job analyst has to rely on newly created information about the job being analyzed. Because job analysts are often interested in understanding more than one job, the structured inventory is a very useful way to examine the relationships among a set of jobs. Most of the recent professional advances in job analysis within the field of I/O psychology have occurred with deductive procedures.

Position Analysis Questionnaire (PAQ)
A method of job analysis that assesses the content of jobs on the basis of approximately 200 items in the questionnaire.

Taxonomic Information.   There are several sources of taxonomic information for job analysis. One is the **Position Analysis Questionnaire (PAQ)** (McCormick & Jeanneret, 1988), which consists of 195 statements used to describe the human attributes needed to perform a job. The statements are organized into six major categories: information input, mental processes, work output, relationships with other persons, job context, and other requirements. Some sample statements from the Relationships with Other Persons category are shown in Figure 3-3. From a database of thousands of similar positions that have been previously analyzed with the PAQ, the job analyst can come to understand the focal job.

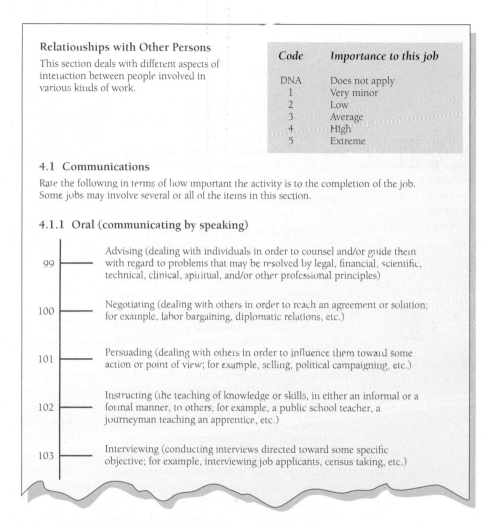

Relationships with Other Persons
This section deals with different aspects of interaction between people involved in various kinds of work.

Code	Importance to this job
DNA	Does not apply
1	Very minor
2	Low
3	Average
4	High
5	Extreme

4.1 Communications
Rate the following in terms of how important the activity is to the completion of the job. Some jobs may involve several or all of the items in this section.

4.1.1 Oral (communicating by speaking)

99 — Advising (dealing with individuals in order to counsel and/or guide them with regard to problems that may be resolved by legal, financial, scientific, technical, clinical, spiritual, and/or other professional principles)

100 — Negotiating (dealing with others in order to reach an agreement or solution; for example, labor bargaining, diplomatic relations, etc.)

101 — Persuading (dealing with others in order to influence them toward some action or point of view; for example, selling, political campaigning, etc.)

102 — Instructing (the teaching of knowledge or skills, in either an informal or a formal manner, to others; for example, a public school teacher, a journeyman teaching an apprentice, etc.)

103 — Interviewing (conducting interviews directed toward some specific objective; for example, interviewing job applicants, census taking, etc.)

Figure 3-3   Sample items from the PAQ

From *Position Analysis Questionnaire* by E. J. McCormick, P. R. Jeanneret, and R. C. Mecham. Copyright © 1989. All rights reserved. Reprinted by permission of PAQ Services.

A second source of taxonomic information is the research of Fleishman and his associates in developing a taxonomy of human abilities needed to perform tasks (Fleishman & Quaintance, 1984). Fleishman identified 52 abilities required in the conduct of a broad spectrum of tasks. Examples of these abilities are oral expression, arm–hand steadiness, multilimb coordination, reaction time, selective attention, and night vision.

Fleishman calibrated the amount of each ability needed to perform tasks. For example, with a scale of 1 (low) to 7 (high), the following amounts of *arm–hand steadiness* are needed to perform these tasks:

Cut facets in diamonds   6.32
Thread a needle   4.14
Light a cigarette   1.71

Fleishman's method permits jobs to be described in terms of the tasks performed and the corresponding abilities and levels of those abilities needed to perform them. Such a taxonomic approach classifies jobs on the basis of requisite human abilities.

The third source of taxonomic information available for job analyses is the U.S. Department of Labor. Based on analyses of thousands of jobs, massive compilations of information provide users with broad job and occupational assessments. The **Occupational Information Network (O*NET)** is a national database of worker attributes and job characteristics. It contains information about KSAOs, interests, general work activities, and work contexts. The database provides the essential foundation for facilitating career counseling, education, employment, and training activities. Additional information about the O*NET can be found at *www.onetcenter.org*.

Figure 3-4 shows the conceptual model upon which the O*NET is based. There are six domains of descriptions (e.g., worker requirements), with each domain containing more refined information (e.g., basic skills within worker requirements). The worker requirements and worker characteristics of the O*NET contain the kind of descriptions called "worker-oriented," while the occupational requirements, occupational-specific requirements, and organizational characteristics contain the kind of descriptions called "task-oriented." The experience requirements domain presents descriptions positioned between the worker- and task-oriented domains.

The O*NET offers a series of assessment instruments designed to assist individuals in exploring careers and making career decisions. The instruments are intended to help individuals assess their skills and interests and identify occupations that match their profiles. Information is also available on the O*NET pertaining to characteristics of an organization that affect all jobs within the organization (Peterson, Mumford, et al., 2001). Additionally, the O*NET presents economic information on labor markets, levels of compensation, and an occupational outlook for the future. As such, the O*NET provides a highly integrated approach to the world of work, greatly expanding upon previous taxonomic approaches to presenting job information (see Cross-Cultural I/O Psychology: Wage Rates Around the World, p. 74).

Jeanneret, D'Egido, and Hanson (2004) described an application of the O*NET in Texas to assist individuals who lost their jobs to become re-employed. The process involves several phases. Individuals search for new occupations based on their self-reported interests, abilities, and skills. The first phase allows individuals to take online self-assessments to identify occupations that fit with their work values and/or interests. The next phase identifies potential occupations based on selected criteria such as abilities, interests, general work activities, and work values. The third phase determines other occupations that are the best relative match to the individual's values and skills.

It is intended that a large number of applications will be developed that utilize the O*NET data, including job descriptions, job classification schemes, selection,

Occupational Information Network (O*NET)
An online computer-based source of information about jobs.

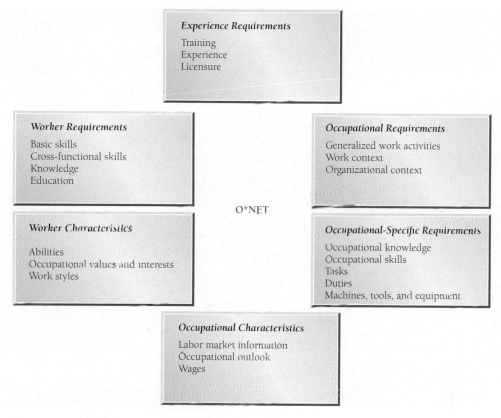

Figure 3-4 *Content model of the O*NET*

From "The O*NET Content Model: Structural Considerations in Describing Jobs," by M. D. Mumford and N. G. Peterson, 1999. In N. G. Peterson, M. D. Mumford, W. C. Borman, P. R. Jeanneret, and E. A. Fleishman (eds.), *An Occupational Information System for the 21st Century: The Development of O*NET*. Copyright © 1999 American Psychological Association. Reprinted by permission.

training, and vocational counseling. The O*NET is anticipated to be a major contribution of I/O psychology to enhancing our knowledge and use of job-related information (Peterson et al., 1999).

Managerial Job Analysis

With an emphasis on work activities that are performed on the job, traditional job analysis methods are typically well suited to traditional blue-collar and clerical jobs. In such jobs the work performed is evidenced by overt behaviors, such as hammering, welding, splicing wires, typing, and filing. These behaviors are observable, and the product of the work (e.g., a typed letter) flows directly from the skill (e.g., typing). In managerial-level jobs the link between the KSAOs and the work output is not nearly so direct. Managerial work involves such factors as planning, decision making, forecasting, and maintaining harmonious interpersonal relations. Managerial work involves

Cross-Cultural I/O Psychology: *Wage Rates Around the World*

There are various levels of compensation for jobs that differ in their overall value to the organization. However, the lowest possible level of compensation for jobs in the United States is determined by federal law. The Fair Labor Standards Act (FLSA) has a provision for a minimum wage, which is currently $6.55 (scheduled to be raised to $7.25 in July 2009) per hour. Since the passage of the FSLA in 1938, the minimum wage has increased, on average, about 3% per year. The guaranteed minimum wage was designed to ensure that all workers earned enough money to maintain at least a minimum standard of living. From an organization's perspective, however, the existence of a minimum wage in the United States has motivated companies to send work to countries that don't have a minimum wage. Labor costs (i.e., the costs associated with paying workers to do their jobs) can be a significant portion of an organization's total budget. Thus, exporting jobs that workers in other countries can perform can result in great cost savings. For example, suppose a company cuts and sews fabric into articles of clothing. The cost of the fabric is the same whether it is cut and sewn in the United States or elsewhere, but the labor costs can be far less. In Honduras, for example, textile jobs may pay 85¢ per hour. In Cambodia, wage rates may pay 45¢ per hour. The reduced cost of making the garments is translated into lower costs for the consumer. Would you rather pay $20 for a child's shirt made in the United States or $8 for a comparable child's shirt made overseas? Many consumers are cost conscious and will choose the less expensive shirt. Paying $8 for that shirt would not be possible if it weren't for overseas labor markets. Many manufacturing jobs that used to be performed in the United States have been exported overseas (a concept called *offshoring*, discussed in greater detail in Chapter 8). This fact adds a new consideration to the career choices people are making. What is the likelihood this job will still exist in the United States in another five or ten years?

mainly cognitive and social skills, which are not so readily observable or identifiable. As such, it is often more difficult to conduct an accurate job analysis for managerial-level jobs because of the greater inferential leap between the work performed and the KSAOs.

Several job analysis methods have been developed in order to assist in the understanding of managerial jobs. Mitchell and McCormick (1990) developed the *Professional and Managerial Position Questionnaire*, which examines work along the dimensions of complexity, organizational impact, and level of responsibility. Raymark, Schmit, and Guion (1997) developed the *Personality-Related Position Requirements Form*, which analyzes jobs on the basis of the personality factors needed to perform them. Some of the personality dimensions measured are general leadership, interest in negotiation, sensitivity to interest of others, thoroughness and attention to details, and desire to generate ideas. These personality dimensions are based on previous research that links them to managerial-level job activities. As a rule, however, the level of precision and accuracy of managerial job analyses are not as high as those for clerical jobs because the variables measured are more abstract.

Uses of Job Analysis Information

Job analysis information produces the criteria needed for a wide range of applications in I/O psychology, as the ensuing chapters will show. A brief introduction to its uses is instructive.

First, an analysis of KSAOs reveals those attributes that are needed for successful job performance, including those needed upon entry into the job. The identification of these attributes provides an empirical basis to determine what personnel selection tests should assess. Thus, rather than selection tests being based on hunches or assumptions, job analytic information offers a rational approach to test selection. This topic will be described in Chapter 4. Second, job analytic information provides a basis to organize different positions into a job and different jobs into a job family. Such groupings provide a basis for determining levels of compensation because one basis of compensation is the attributes needed to perform the work. Third, job analytic information helps determine the content of training needed to perform the job. The tasks identified as most frequently performed or most important become the primary content of training. This topic will be discussed in Chapter 6. Finally, job analytic information provides one basis to determine the content of performance evaluation or appraisal. A job analysis reveals the tasks most critical to job success, so the performance appraisal is directed at assessing how well the employee performs those tasks. This topic will be discussed in Chapter 7. In addition to these uses of job analytic information, the information can be used in vocational counseling, offering insight into the KSAOs needed to perform successfully in various occupations. Although not discussed in this book, the application of job analytic information in vocational counseling provides guidance in career selection. It is anticipated that one of the major uses of O*NET will be for vocational counseling.

Job analysis has special relevance at both a practical and a conceptual level in the recent history of I/O psychology. At a practical level, the Americans with Disabilities Act requires employers to make adjustments for accommodating people with disabilities. As Brannick and Levine (2002) described, job analysis can help ascertain what is a "reasonable accommodation" versus an "undue hardship" for the employer. Although what is "reasonable" is a matter of opinion, employers can provide disabled workers with wheelchair ramps and flexible work schedules (for example) to facilitate the conduct of one's job. At a conceptual level, the changing nature of jobs (as described in Chapter 1) calls into question the role and value of job analysis in the 21st century. Sanchez and Levine (2001) believe the focus of job analysis might shift from establishing the rigid boundaries of a job to understanding how the job facilitates the overall effectiveness of the organization. Specifically, Sanchez and Levine stated: "Although static 'jobs' may be a thing of the past, studying work processes and assignments continues to be the foundation of any human resource system today and in the foreseeable future" (p. 86). Work teams have increased in frequency of use as the means by which many organizations accomplish their objectives. Work teams involve the coordinated activity of several individuals, often with different skill sets, to achieve an outcome of higher quality or greater speed than could be achieved by a single employee. Brannick, Levine, and Morgeson (2007) discussed how the analysis of work performed by teams is more complex than the analysis of work performed by individuals. The selection of a new team member may involve consideration of more factors than the selection of an individual to perform a single job.

Evaluating Job Analysis Methods

A study by Levine et al. (1983) compared seven major questionnaire methods of job analysis, and the results reflect what the I/O profession as a whole has come to understand about job analysis methods. The authors found that different methods are regarded as differentially effective and practical depending on the purposes for which they may be used. No one method was consistently best across the board. I believe that a well-trained job analyst can draw accurate inferences and conclusions using any one of several questionnaire methods. The converse is also true. No method can ensure accurate results when used by someone who is inexperienced with job analysis. A related opinion was reached by Harvey and Lozada-Larsen (1988), who concluded that the most accurate job analysis ratings are provided by raters who are highly knowledgeable about the job. Morgeson and Campion (1997) outlined a series of potential inaccuracies in job analytic information caused by such factors as biases in how job analysts process information about the jobs they are analyzing, and loss of motivation among SMEs who are less than enthusiastic about participating in job analyses. Morgeson and Campion believe the chances for inaccuracies are considerably lower in task-oriented job analysis than in worker-oriented job analysis. That is, the ratings of observable and discrete tasks are less subject to error than the ratings of some abstract KSAOs. However, there is always an element of subjectivity in job analysis. Sackett and Laczo (2003) summarized the prevailing professional status of job analysis: "Job analysis is an information-gathering tool to aid researchers in deciding what to do next. It always reflects subjective judgment. With careful choices in decisions about information to collect and how to collect it, one will obtain reliable and useful information. . . . [T]he use of sound professional judgment in job analysis decisions is the best that can be expected" (pp. 34–35).

Competency Modeling

Competency modeling
A process for determining the human characteristics (i.e., competencies) needed to perform successfully within an organization.

A recent trend in establishing the desired attributes of employees is called **competency modeling**. A *competency* is a characteristic or quality of people that a company wants its employees to manifest. In traditional job analytic terms, a competency is a critical KSAO. *Modeling* refers to identifying the array or profile of competencies that an organization desires in its employees. Experts (e.g., Schippmann, 1999; Schippmann et al., 2000) agree that job analysis and competency modeling share some similarities in their approaches. Job analysis examines both the work that gets performed and the human attributes needed to perform the work, whereas competency modeling does not consider the work performed. The two approaches differ in the level of generalizability of the information across jobs within an organization, the method by which the attributes are derived, and the degree of acceptance within the organization for the identified attributes.

First, job analysis tends to identify specific and different KSAOs that distinguish jobs within an organization. For example, one set of KSAOs would be identified for a secretary, while another set of KSAOs would be identified for a manager. In contrast, competencies are generally identified to apply to employees in all jobs within an organization or perhaps a few special differentiations among groups of jobs, as for senior executives. These competencies tend to be far more universal and abstract than KSAOs, and as such are often called the "core competencies" of an organization. Here are some examples of competencies for employees:

- Exhibiting the highest level of professional integrity at all times
- Being sensitive and respectful of the dignity of all employees
- Staying current with the latest technological advances within your area
- Placing the success of the organization above your personal individual success

As can be inferred from this profile or "model," such competencies are applicable to a broad range of jobs and are specifically designed to be as inclusive as possible. KSAOs are designed to be more exclusive, differentiating one job from another. As Schippmann et al. (2000) stated, "Although job analysis can at times take a broad focus (e.g., when conducting job family research), the descriptor items serving as a basis for the grouping typically represent a level of granularity that is far more detailed than is achieved by most competency modeling efforts" (p. 727).

Second, KSAOs are identified by job analysts using technical methods designed to elicit specific job information. As such, the entire job analysis project is often perceived by employees to be arcane. In contrast, competency modeling is likely to include review sessions and group meetings of many employees to ensure that the competencies capture the language and spirit that are important to the organization. As a result, employees readily identify with and relate to the resulting competencies, an outcome rarely achieved in job analysis.

Third, competency modeling tries to link personal qualities of employees to the larger overall mission of the organization. The goal is to identify those characteristics that tap into an employee's willingness to perform certain activities or to "fit in" with the work culture of the organization (Schippmann et al.). We will discuss the important topic of an organization's culture in Chapter 8. Job analysis, on the other hand, does not try to capture or include organizational-level issues of vision and values. Traditional job analysis does not have the "populist appeal" of competency modeling by members of the organization.

Schippmann et al. asked whether competency modeling is just a trend or fad among organizations. Competency modeling does not have the same rigor or precision found in job analysis. However, competency modeling does enjoy approval and adoption by many organizations. The authors note somewhat ironically that "the field of I/O psychology has not led the competency modeling movement, despite the fact that defining the key attributes needed for organizational success is a 'core competency' of I/O psychology" (p. 731). They believe the future might see a blurring of borders as the competency modeling and job analysis approaches evolve over time.

Job Performance Criteria

Desirable job performance criteria are represented by three general characteristics. First, they must be appropriate: relevant and representative of the job. Second, they must be stable: enduring over time or across situations. Finally, they must be practical: they cannot be too expensive or hard to measure. Other authors think that different issues are important—for example, the time at which criterion measures are taken (after one month on the job, six months, and so on), the type of criterion measure taken (performance, errors, accidents), and the level of performance chosen to represent success or failure on the job (college students must perform at a C level in order to graduate). Criteria are often chosen by either history or precedent; unfortunately, sometimes criteria are chosen because they are merely expedient or available.

Bartram (2005) cogently stated the importance of first understanding criteria before we undertake the development of psychological assessments designed to predict the criteria. "Perhaps we have been preoccupied for too long with the wonderful personality questionnaires and ability tests we have constructed to measure all sorts of aspects of human potential. In so doing, we may have lost sight of why it is important to measure these characteristics. As a consequence, [I/O] practitioners have often had difficulty explaining to their clients the value of what we have to offer. We need to realize that this inability may be due in no small part to our failure to address the issues that actually concern clients: performance at work and the outcome of that performance" (p. 1200). What criteria are used to evaluate job performance? No single universal criterion is applicable across all jobs. The criteria for success in a certain job depend on how that job contributes to the overall success of the organization. Nevertheless, there is enough commonality across jobs that some typical criteria have been identified. You may think of these criteria as the conventional standards by which employees are judged on the job. However, successful performance may be defined by additional criteria as well. The criteria we study and seek to understand are an implied statement of what we think is important.

Job performance criteria may be objective or subjective. **Objective performance criteria** are taken from organizational records (payroll or personnel) and supposedly do not involve any subjective evaluation. **Subjective performance criteria** are judgmental evaluations of a person's performance (such as a supervisor might render). Although objective criteria may involve no subjective judgment, some degree of assessment must be applied to give them meaning. Just knowing that an employee produced 18 units a day is not informative; this output must be compared with what other workers produce. If the average is 10 units a day, 18 units clearly represents "good" performance. If the average is 25 units a day, 18 units is not good.

Objective performance criteria A set of factors used to assess job performance that are (relatively) factual in character.

Subjective performance criteria A set of factors used to assess job performance that are the product of someone's (e.g., supervisor, peer, customer) judgment of these factors.

Nine Major Job Performance Criteria

Production.   Using units of production as a criterion is most common in manufacturing jobs. If an organization has only one type of job, then setting production criteria is easy. But most companies have many types of production jobs, so productivity must be compared fairly. That is, if average productivity in one job is 6 units a day and in another job it is 300 units a day, then productivities must be equated to adjust for these differences. Statistical procedures are usually used for this. Other factors can diminish the value of production as a criterion of performance. In an assembly-line job, the speed of the line determines how many units are produced per day. Increasing the speed of the line increases production. Furthermore, everyone working on the line has the same level of production. In a case like this, units of production are determined by factors outside of the individual worker, so errors that are under the worker's control may be the criterion of job performance. Errors are not fair criteria if they are more likely in some jobs than others. Due to automation and work simplification, some jobs are almost "goof-proof." Then error-free work has nothing to do with the human factor.

Sales.   Sales are a common performance criterion for wholesale and retail sales work, but variations must be considered. Using the sheer number of sales as a criterion is appropriate only if everyone is selling the same product(s) in comparable territories. A person who sells toothbrushes should sell more units than a person who sells houses. Also, someone selling tractors in Iowa should sell more than a person whose sales territory is Rhode Island. Not only is Iowa bigger than Rhode Island but also more farming is done proportionately in Iowa than in Rhode Island. Total sales volume is equally fallible as a criterion. A real estate salesperson can sell a $100,000 house in one afternoon, but how long would it take to sell $100,000 worth of toothbrushes?

The solution to these types of problems is to use norm groups for judging success. A real estate salesperson should be compared with other real estate salespeople in the same sales territory. The same holds for other sales work. If comparisons have to be drawn across sales territories or across product lines, then statistical adjustments are needed. Ideally, any differences in sales performance are then due to the ability of the salesperson, which is the basis for using sales as a criterion of job performance.

Tenure or Turnover.   Length of service (or tenure) is a very popular criterion in I/O psychological research. Turnover not only has a theoretical appeal (for example, Hom & Griffeth, 1995) but also is a practical concern. Employers want to hire people who will stay with the company. For obvious practical reasons, employers don't want to hire chronic job-hoppers. The costs of recruiting, selecting, and training new hires can be extremely high. Turnover is perhaps the most frequently used nonperformance criterion in the psychological literature. It is a valuable and useful criterion because it measures employment stability.

Campion (1991) suggested that many factors should be considered in the measurement of turnover. One is *voluntariness* (whether the employee was fired, quit to take another job with better promotional opportunities, or quit because of dissatisfaction with a supervisor). Another factor is *functionality* (whether the employee was performing the job effectively or ineffectively). Williams and Livingstone (1994) meta-analyzed studies that examined the relationship between turnover and performance, and concluded that poor performers were more likely to voluntarily quit their jobs than good performers.

Absenteeism.   Absence from work, like turnover, is an index of employee stability. Although some employee turnover is good for organizations, unexcused employee absenteeism invariably has bad consequences. Excused absenteeism (e.g., personal vacation time) is generally not a problem because it is sanctioned and must be approved by the organization. Rhodes and Steers (1990) and Martocchio and Harrison (1993) reviewed many studies on why people are absent from work. Absence appears to be the product of many factors, including family conflicts, job dissatisfaction, alcohol and drug abuse, and personality. However, as Johns (1994) noted, employees are likely to give self-serving justifications for their absence. For example, being absent from work to care for a sick child is more socially acceptable than acknowledging deviant behavior such as drug use. Accordingly, self-reports of why employees are absent can be highly inaccurate.

Absenteeism is a pervasive problem in industry; it costs employers billions of dollars a year in decreased efficiency and increased benefit payments (for example, sick leave) and payroll costs. Absenteeism has social, individual, and organizational causes, and it affects individuals, companies, and even entire industrial societies.

Accidents.   Accidents are sometimes used as a criterion of job performance, although this measure has a number of limitations. First, accidents are used as a criterion mainly for blue-collar jobs. (Although white-collar workers can be injured at work, the frequency of such accidents is small.) Thus accidents are a measure of job performance for only a limited sample of employees. Second, accidents are difficult to predict, and there is little stability or consistency across individuals in their occurrence (Senders & Moray, 1991). Third, accidents can be measured in many ways: number of accidents per hours worked, miles driven, trips taken, and so on. Different conclusions can be drawn depending on how accident statistics are calculated. Employers do not want to hire people who, for whatever reason, will have job-related accidents. But in the total picture of job performance, accidents are not used as a criterion as often as production, turnover, or absence.

Theft.   Employee theft is a major problem for organizations, with annual losses estimated to be $200 billion annually (Greenberg & Scott, 1996). Hollinger and Clark (1983) administered an anonymous questionnaire about theft to employees at three types of organizations. The percentages of employees who admitted to stealing from their employer were 42% in retail stores, 32% in hospitals, and 26% in manufacturing firms. Thus, employee theft is a pervasive and serious problem. From an I/O psychologist's perspective, the goal is to hire people who are unlikely to steal from the company, just as it is desirable to hire people who have a low probability of having accidents. The problem with theft as a criterion is that we know very little about the individual identity of employees who do steal. Hollinger and Clark based their survey results on anonymous responses. Furthermore, those responses came from people who were willing to admit they stole from the company. Those employees who were stealing but chose not to respond to the survey or who did not admit they stole were not included in the theft results. Greenberg and Scott (1996) asserted that some employees resort to theft as a means of offsetting perceived unfairness in how their employer treats them. Figure 3-5 shows a program one retail company uses to curtail theft by its own employees. For a cash award, employees are provided an opportunity to report coworkers who are stealing from the company.

SILENT WITNESS INCENTIVE AWARD PROGRAM

The Silent Witness Incentive Award Program provides every associate the opportunity to share in substantial cash awards and at the same time help reduce our losses caused by dishonest associates.

CASH AWARDS
$100.00 to $1,000.00

HOW YOU CAN PARTICIPATE

When somebody causes an intentional loss to our company, each associate pays for it. If you observe or become aware of another associate causing loss to our company, you should report it immediately. Your Loss Prevention Department investigates all types of shortage including the theft of Cash, Merchandise, Underrings, and all types of Credit Card Fraud.

MAIL-IN INFORMATION

1. Associate's name involved? _____

2. Where does associate work? Store _____ Dept. _____

3. What is associate doing?   a) taking money   b) taking merchandise _____
   c) under-ringing merchandise   d) credit card fraud _____

4. How much has been stolen? $ _____

5. Is there anything else you wish to add? _____

_____

_____

_____

Figure 3-5 *Incentive award method for reporting employee theft*

A drawback in using theft as a job performance criterion is that only a small percentage of employees are ever caught stealing. The occurrence of theft often has to be deduced on the basis of shortages calculated from company inventories of supplies and products. In addition, many companies will not divulge any information about theft to outside individuals. Although companies often share information on such criteria as absenteeism and turnover, theft records are too sensitive to reveal. Despite these limitations, I/O psychologists regard theft as an index of employment suitability, and we will probably see much more research on theft in the years ahead (see Field Note 3, p. 82).

Field Note 3: Theft of Waste

Many organizations experience problems of theft by employees. Thefts include office supplies used in work, such as staplers and tape dispensers, as well as items that are intended for sale to customers. Sometimes cash is stolen. What all these items have in common is that they are assets or resources of the company.

I once had an experience with a company where the biggest concern was not the theft of resources, but the theft of waste! The company printed U.S. postage stamps. The worth of each stamp was the value printed on the stamp—usually the cost of 1 ounce of first-class postage, currently 42¢. Although there was some concern that employees would steal the postage stamps for their personal use, the bigger concern was the theft of misprints or errors. Printing errors occur when a stamp is printed off-center or, in extreme cases, when the printing on the stamp is correct but the image is inverted, or upside down. One 42¢ stamp printed with an inverted image may be worth thousands of dollars to philatelists, or stamp collectors. In the printing of postage stamps, errors occur as they do in all other types of printing. In this case, however, the errors have very high market value. To reduce the possibility of theft of misprints that were scheduled to be destroyed, the company had three elaborate and extensive sets of search and security procedures for anyone leaving the company. Somewhat paradoxically, there was no security for people entering the building. All the security procedures involved people leaving the building, as they were searched for the theft of highly valuable waste or scrap.

Counterproductive Workplace Behavior.   Counterproductive workplace behavior (or deviant behavior) includes a broad range of employee actions that are bad (i.e., counterproductive) for the organization. Theft and absenteeism are the two most prominent examples. As Cullen and Sackett (2003) described, other counterproductive behaviors are destruction of property, misuse of information, misuse of time, poor-quality work, alcohol and drug use, and inappropriate verbal (e.g., argumentation) and physical (e.g., assaults) actions. Berry, Ones, and Sackett (2007) proposed a further refinement in the classification of deviance: interpersonal and organizational. Interpersonal deviant behavior is targeted toward other individuals, and is represented by gossip, threats of violence, and theft from co-workers. Organizational deviant behavior is targeted against the organization as a whole, and includes intentionally working slowly, damaging company property, and disclosing confidential information. A common thread running through all of these counterproductive behaviors is intentionality; that is, the employee deliberately engages in them. From a personnel selection standpoint, the goal of the organization is to screen out applicants who are predicted to engage in these behaviors. As will be described in Chapter 4, I/O psychologists have developed methods to identify such individuals in the selection process. In contrast to criteria that are used to "select in" applicants because they reflect positive or desirable work behaviors, counterproductive workplace behaviors are reflected in criteria used to "screen out" applicants who are predicted to exhibit them on the job.

Emotional labor
The requirement
in some jobs that
employees express
emotions to customers
or clients that are
associated with
enhanced performance
in the job.

Emotional Labor.   The term "labor" (as opposed to "behavior", for example) was selected deliberately to connote toil, or a sense of onerous duty on the part of the employee whose job requires it. Most jobs calling for the employee to exhibit emotions "appropriate" for the context are positive in nature. Examples of such emotions include warmth, caring, and gratitude. Employees who must exhibit these emotions are trained to engage in *display rules*. Display rules are specific behavioral acts that reflect the underlying emotions customers expect. Examples include smiling, voice inflection, and eye contact. These display rules and corresponding emotions are typically found in the service industry, and are generally referenced as "service with a smile" (Grandey, Fisk, & Steiner, 2005).

However, not all required emotions need be positive. For jobs such as security personnel and bill collectors, the desired emotions would include aggressiveness, suspicion, and skepticism. The corresponding display rules would include a stern tone of voice, facial scowling, and arms crossed against the chest to indicate a defensive posture (Beal, Trougakos, Weiss, & Green, 2006). Rupp and Spencer (2006) noted that display rules can be considered a form of social acting, and differentiated shallow from deep acting. One major difference between the two is the length of time the "actor" (the employee) must engage in the behavior. A food server at a restaurant, for example, may only have to exhibit a warm, cheerful, and attentive demeanor for a few minutes at a time while taking orders and also when delivering the food to the table. Conversely, a funeral director would be required to exhibit the emotions of shared grief, compassion, and empathy for several hours in succession with the relatives of the deceased. Rupp and Spencer proposed that the shallow acting exhibited by the food server may be more stressful because of the intermittent chronicity associated with having to exhibit the display rules (e.g., alternating "on/off" interactions of short duration with many customers). Conversely, the deep acting exhibited by the funeral director may require the employee to regulate his or her own internal emotions. The duration of the interaction (several hours per funeral) may require deeper immersion in the emotion to sustain the requisite behaviors. As such, deep acting may induce less stress in employees because the emotions are internalized by the employee, which is not required in surface acting. In summary, employees who must project certain emotions through display rules as part of their jobs may not allow their own personal emotional states to interfere with the emotional front they must exhibit for their customers.

Person-organization fit
A criterion for
employment with an
organization that reflects
the belief the candidate
exhibits attributes
and values consistent
with those held by the
organization.

Person-Organization Fit.   The concept of **person-organization fit** is an extension of the classic conception of person-job fit (i.e., "a round peg in a round hole"). Instead of the hole being limited to a job, it is re-configured to be the entire organization. In a survey of organizations that described what constitutes desirable job candidates, Rynes, Brown, and Colbert (2002) discovered that the degree to which a candidate was a "good fit" with the organization (not just the job) was becoming an increasingly used criterion for making personnel selection decisions. As stated by Kristof-Brown and Jansen (2007), "If jobs are becoming increasingly fluid and companies are requiring employees to be able to move easily between roles, hiring for fit with the organization's culture may be just as important as hiring someone who is qualified" [to fill a specified job] (p. 125). Arthur, Bell, Villadu, and Doverspike (2006) proposed that people find it more desirable to interact with others who have similar psychological characteristics because the interaction verifies their own beliefs, values, and behaviors. Arthur et al. reported that person-organization fit was not associated with performance within a job, but proposed it may be related to the employee's length of service with the organization. A related explanation for the appeal of person-organization fit as a major criterion in personnel selection is that employees who fit within a company are less of a threat to disrupting its prevailing culture, and ultimately are more controllable by the organization.

Summary of Job Performance Criteria.   A consideration of the nine major job performance criteria reveals marked differences not only in what they measure but also in how they are measured. They differ along an objective/subjective continuum. Some criteria are highly objective, meaning they can be measured with a high degree of accuracy. Examples are units of production, days absent, and dollar sales volume. There are few disagreements about the final tally because the units, days, or dollars are merely counted. Nevertheless, there could be disagreements about the interpretation or meaning of these objectively counted numbers. Other criteria are less objective. Theft, for example, is not the same as being caught stealing. Based on company records of merchandise, an organization might know that employee theft has occurred but not know who did it. As was noted, although employee theft is a major problem, relatively few employees are ever caught stealing. The broader criterion of counterproductive work behavior includes dimensions that are particularly subjective. For example, we all probably waste some time on the job, but only at some point is it considered "counterproductive." Likewise, there is probably a fine line between being "outspoken" (it is good to express your feelings and opinions) and "argumentative" (it is bad to be negative and resist progress). Customer service behavior is a highly subjective criterion. An employee's customer service performance is strictly a product of other people's perceptions, and there may be as many judgments of that behavior as there are customers. Chapter 7 will examine sources of agreement and disagreement in assessing job performance.

"We've done a computer simulation of your projected
performance in five years. You're fired."

From this discussion, it is clear that no single measure of job performance is totally adequate. Each criterion may have merit, but each can also suffer from weakness along other dimensions. For instance, few people would say that an employee's absence has no bearing on overall job performance, but no one would say that absence is a complete measure of job performance. Absence, like production, is only one piece of the broader picture. Don't be discouraged that no one criterion meets all our standards. It is precisely because job performance is multidimensional (and each single dimension is a fallible index of overall performance) that we are compelled to include many relevant aspects of work in establishing criteria (see The Changing Nature of Work: The New Recipe for Success).

Relationships Among Job Performance Criteria

Several job performance criteria can be identified for many jobs, and each criterion frequently assesses a different aspect of performance. These criteria are usually independent of one another. If they were all highly positively intercorrelated—say, $r = .80$ or $r = .90$—there would be no point in measuring them all. Knowing an employee's status on one criterion would give his or her status on the others. Several studies have tried to identify interrelationships among criteria.

A classic study by Seashore, Indik, and Georgopoulos (1960) revealed multiple job performance criteria and also showed that the criteria were relatively independent

The Changing Nature of Work: The New Recipe for Success

For many decades the recipe for success in employment had two ingredients: skill and ambition. To be successful at work, you have to have some talent or skill that organizations value and you have to be a hardworking, reliable person who can be counted on to perform. The shift in the nature of the work world has introduced two additional criteria, so now the recipe has four ingredients. You still have to have some skill and you still have to be hardworking, but now you must also accept change and have good interpersonal skills. Accepting change is important because the work world is evolving at a rapid pace. New technologies, pressure from competition, and the need to develop new products and services require workers to adapt to continuously changing conditions. Workers who resist change will not be as successful as those who find ways to adjust to it. Also, because many jobs today involve employees interacting with coworkers in teams and with customers, a high priority is placed on the ability to communicate effectively and to get along with all types of people. Jobs in which employees function in relative isolation are becoming increasingly scarce. The changing nature of work has shifted the importance of communication and sociability from a few jobs to many jobs in our economy. In the 21st century the most successful employees will be those who have a valued skill, work hard, adapt to rapidly changing conditions, and have good interpersonal skills.

of one another. For example, Seashore and associates studied delivery people for whom five job performance criteria were available: productivity (objectively measured by time standards), effectiveness (subjectively rated based on quality of performance), accidents, unexcused absences, and errors (based on the number of packages not delivered). The data showed that the five criteria were relatively independent of one another. These results demonstrate that there really is no single measure of overall performance on the job; each criterion measures a different facet.

Bommer et al. (1995) conducted a meta-analytic study examining the relationship between subjective ratings of job performance and objective measures of job performance. They reported an average correlation of .39 between these two types of assessment. Quite clearly, you can arrive at different conclusions about a person's job performance depending on how you choose to assess it.

There is also a relationship between job level and the number of criteria needed to define job performance. Lower-level, relatively simple jobs do not have many dimensions of performance; more complex jobs have many. In fact, the number of job performance criteria can differentiate simple jobs from complex ones. Manual laborers who unload trucks might be measured by only three criteria: attendance (they have to show up for work), errors (they have to know how to stack the material), and speed. More complex jobs, as in the medical field, might be defined by as many as 15 independent criteria. The more complex the job, the more criteria are needed to define it and the more skill or talent a person has to have to be successful.

Dynamic Performance Criteria

Dynamic performance criteria
Aspects of job performance that change (increase or decrease) over time.

The concept of **dynamic performance criteria** applies to job performance criteria that change over time. It is significant because job performance is not stable or consistent over time, and this dynamic quality of criteria adds to the complexity of making personnel decisions. Steele-Johnson, Osburn, and Pieper (2000) identified three potential reasons for systematic changes in job performance over time. First, employees might change the way they perform tasks as a result of repeatedly conducting them. Second, the knowledge and ability requirements needed to perform the task might change because of changing work technologies. Third, the knowledge and abilities of the employees might change as a result of additional training.

Consider Figure 3-6, which shows the levels of three job performance criteria—productivity, absence, and accidents—over an eight-year period. The time period represents a person's eight-year performance record on a job. Notice that the patterns of behavior for the three criteria differ over time. The individual's level of accidents is stable over time, so accidents is not a dynamic performance criterion. A very different pattern emerges for the other two criteria. The individual's level of productivity increases over the years, more gradually in the early years and then more dramatically in the later years. Absence, on the other hand, follows the opposite pattern. The employee's absence was greatest in the first year of employment and progressively declined over time. Absence and productivity are dynamic performance criteria, whereas accidents is a static criterion.

When a job applicant is considered for employment, the organization attempts to predict how well that person will perform on the job. A hire/no hire decision is then made on the basis of this prediction. If job performance criteria are static (like accidents in Figure 3-6), the prediction is more accurate because of the stability of the behavior. If job performance criteria are dynamic, however, a critical new element is added to the decision, *time*. It may be that initially productivity would not be very impressive, but over time the employee's performance would rise to and then surpass a satisfactory level. Dynamic performance criteria are equivalent to "hitting a moving target," as the level of the behavior being predicted is continuously changing. Furthermore, the pattern of change may be different *across* individuals. That is, for some people productivity may start off low and then get progressively higher, whereas for others the pattern may be the reverse.

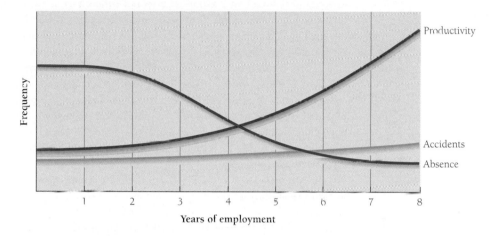

Figure 3-6 *Performance variations in three criteria over an eight-year period*

Sturmin (2007) proposed that dynamic performance criteria can be explained by a learning curve. Work productivity improves based on the accumulation of experience, and employees exhibit different rates of learning-by-doing. Some individuals may exhibit a steep learning curve, meaning they acquire new knowledge and skills quickly and thus make substantial contributions to the organization relatively faster. Conversely, individuals with a relatively flat learning curve will be much slower, in comparison, to exhibit performance improvements in their jobs. In short, both groups of employees may start off at the same level of performance, but one group accelerates at a much faster rate than the other. From an empirical perspective, our ability to understand and predict learning curves can only be achieved by studying employee behavior over an extended time period. In practice, however, most research on employee behavior has tended to be cross-sectional (i.e., at one point in time).

Expanding Our View of Criteria

Throughout the history of I/O psychology, our concept of criteria has been primarily *job-related*. That is, we have defined the successful employee primarily in terms of how well he or she meets the criteria for performance on the job. As Borman (1991) noted, however, it is possible to consider ways employees contribute to the success of the work group or organization that are not tied directly to *job* performance criteria. One example is being a "good soldier"—demonstrating conscientious behaviors that show concern for doing things properly for the good of the organization. Another example is prosocial behavior—doing little things that help other people perform their jobs more effectively.

Brief and Motowidlo (1986) found that in some organizations it is explicitly stated that part of an employee's own job performance is to support and provide guidance to other individuals. A military combat unit is one such example. However, in many other organizations, going beyond the call of duty to help out a fellow employee or the organization is outside the formally *required* job responsibilities. The proclivity of some individuals in a group to help out others can at times be detrimental to the organization. For example, two group members may frequently assist a highly likeable but unskilled coworker, and in doing so not complete their own work assignments. In most cases, however, prosocial behavior enhances the overall welfare of the organization. The topic of prosocial behavior will be discussed in more detail in Chapter 10.

Research on prosocial behavior shows that the criteria for a successful employee may transcend performance on job tasks. It is thus conceivable that some employees may be regarded as valuable members of the organization because they are quick to assist others and be "good soldiers"—and not because they perform their own job tasks very well. The concept of a "job" has historically been a useful framework for understanding one's duties and responsibilities and, accordingly, for employees to be held accountable for meeting job performance criteria. However, there are circumstances and conditions (such as demonstrating prosocial behavior) that lead I/O psychologists to question the value of criteria strictly from a job perspective. Some researchers believe it is more beneficial to think of employees as performing a series of roles for the organization, as opposed to one job. The relationship between roles and jobs will be discussed in Chapter 8.

Case Study   Theft of Company Property

Wilton Petroleum Company was a wholesale distributor of a major brand of gasoline. Gasoline was shipped on barges from the refinery to the company. The company then delivered the gasoline to retail gas stations for sale to motorists. Each gasoline tanker truck was a huge, 18-wheel vehicle that held 9,000 gallons of gasoline. The gasoline that was pumped out of the truck into underground holding tanks at the gas stations was monitored precisely. The company knew exactly how many gallons of gasoline were pumped into the holding tanks at each gas station, and it knew exactly how many gallons were pumped out of each tanker truck. A meter on the tanker truck recorded the amount of gasoline that left the truck. A 20-foot hose extending from the truck permitted the driver to fill the tanks at each gas station. Every day each driver recorded the total volume of gasoline delivered. The total volume pumped out of the truck had to equal the total volume of gasoline deposited in the holding tanks. Any discrepancy was regarded as evidence of theft of the gasoline by the drivers.

Based on years of experience the company knew there was a slight flaw in the system used to monitor the flow of gasoline out of the tanker. The meter recorded the flow of gasoline out of the tanker; however, about 3 gallons of gasoline in the 20-foot hose was always unrecorded. That was the gasoline that had flowed out of the truck but did not enter the holding tanks.

One truck driver, Lew Taylor, believed he knew a way to "beat the system" and steal gasoline for his personal use. After making all his scheduled deliveries for the day, he extended the full length of the hose on the ground and let gravity drain out the 3 gallons of gasoline in the hose. The pump and the meter were not turned on, so there was no record of any gasoline leaving the tank. Company officials knew that Taylor was siphoning the gasoline based on the very small but repeated shortage in his records compared with those of other drivers. The value of the stolen gasoline each day was only about $9, but the cumulative value of the losses was considerable.

Michael Morris, operations manager of the company, knew Taylor was stealing the gasoline but couldn't prove it. Taylor had found a loophole in the monitoring system and had found a way to steal gasoline. Morris decided to lay a trap for Taylor. Morris "planted" a company hand tool (a hammer) on a chair at the entrance to the room where the drivers changed their clothes after work. Morris had a small hole drilled in the wall to observe the chair. He thought that if Taylor stole the gasoline, he might be tempted to steal the hammer. The trap worked: Taylor was spied placing the company tool under his jacket as he walked out the door. On a signal from Morris, security officers approached Taylor and asked about the hammer. Taylor produced the hammer, was led by the security officers to Morris's office, and was immediately fired. Although Taylor had stolen hundreds of dollars worth of gasoline from his employer, he was terminated for the theft of a hammer worth about $10.

Questions

1. If Taylor had a perfect attendance record, made all his deliveries on time, had effective interpersonal skills, and in all other ways was a conscientious employee, would you still have fired Taylor for committing theft if you had been Morris? Why or why not?
2. Do you think Taylor "got what was coming to him" in this case, or was he "set up" by Morris and thus was a victim of entrapment?
3. What do you think of the ethics of companies that spy on their employees with peepholes and cameras to detect theft? Why do you feel as you do?
4. What effect might Taylor's dismissal by Wilton Petroleum have on other employees of the company?
5. Have you ever "taken" a paperclip, pencil, or sheet of paper home with you from your place of work? If so, do you consider it to be a case of theft on your part? Why or why not, and what's the difference between "theft" of a paperclip versus a hammer?

Chapter Summary

- Criteria are evaluative standards that serve as reference points in making judgments. They are of major importance in I/O psychology.

- The two levels of criteria are conceptual (what we would like to measure if we could) and actual (what we do measure). All actual criteria are flawed measures of conceptual criteria.
- Job analysis is a procedure used to understand the work performed in a job and the worker attributes it takes to perform a job. Job analysis establishes the criteria for job performance.
- Worker attributes are best understood in terms of job knowledge, skills, abilities, and other (KSAOs) characteristics as well as organizational competencies.
- The Occupational Information Network (O*NET) is a national database of worker attributes and job characteristics. I/O psychologists use it for a wide range of purposes.
- Vast differences in compensation levels paid around the world have led to the exporting of jobs out of the United States to other countries.
- Job performance criteria typically include production, sales, turnover, absenteeism, accidents, theft, counterproductive workplace behavior, emotional labor, and person-organization fit.
- The level of job performance criteria can change over time for workers, making long-term predictions of job performance more difficult.
- Valuable workers not only perform their own jobs well but also contribute to the welfare and efficiency of the entire organization.

4

Predictors: Psychological Assessments

Learning Objectives

- Identify the major types of reliability and what they measure.
- Understand the major manifestations of validity and what they measure.
- Know the major types of psychological tests categorized by administration and content.
- Explain the role of psychological testing in making assessments of people, including ethical issues and predictive accuracy.
- Explain nontest predictors such as interviews, assessment centers, work samples, biographical information, and letters of recommendation.
- Understand the controversial methods of assessment.

A **predictor** is any variable used to forecast a criterion. In weather prediction, barometric pressure is used to forecast rainfall. In medical prediction, body temperature is used to predict (or diagnose) illness. In I/O psychology, we seek predictors of job performance criteria as indexed by productivity, absenteeism, turnover, and so forth. Although we do not use tea leaves and astrological signs as fortune-tellers do, I/O psychologists have explored a multitude of devices as potential predictors of job performance criteria. This chapter will review the variables traditionally used, examine their success, and discuss some professional problems inherent in their application.

Assessing the Quality of Predictors

Psychometric
Literally, the measurement ("metric") of properties of the mind (from the Greek word "psyche"). The standard used to measure the quality of psychological assessments.

All predictor variables, like other measuring devices, can be assessed in terms of their quality or goodness. We can think of several features of a good measuring device. We would like it to be consistent and accurate; that is, it should repeatedly yield precise measurements. In psychology we judge the goodness of our measuring devices by two **psychometric** criteria: reliability and validity. If a predictor is not both reliable and valid, it is useless.

Reliability

Reliability
A standard for evaluating tests that refers to the consistency, stability, or equivalence of test scores. Often contrasted with validity.

Reliability refers to the consistency, stability, or equivalence of a measure. A measure should yield the same estimate on repeated use if the measured trait has not changed. Even though that estimate may be inaccurate, a reliable measure will always be consistent. Three major types of reliability are used in psychology to assess the consistency or stability of the measuring device, and a fourth assessment of reliability is often used in I/O psychology.

Test–retest reliability
A type of reliability that reveals the stability of test scores upon repeated applications of the test.

Test–Retest Reliability.   **Test–retest reliability** is perhaps the simplest assessment of a measuring device's reliability. We measure something at two different times and compare the scores. We can give an intelligence test to the same group of people at two different times and then correlate the two sets of scores. This correlation is called a *coefficient of stability* because it reflects the stability of the test over time. If the test is reliable, those who scored high the first time will also score high the second time, and vice versa. If the test is unreliable, the scores will "bounce around" in such a way that there is no similarity in individuals' scores between the two trials.

When we say a test (or any measure) is *reliable*, how high should the coefficient of stability be? The answer is the higher the better. A test cannot be too reliable. As a rule, reliability coefficients around .70 are professionally acceptable, although some frequently used tests have test–retest reliabilities of only around .50. Furthermore, the length of time between administrations of the test must be considered in the interpretation of a test's test–retest reliability. Generally the shorter the time interval between administrations (e.g., one week vs. six months), the higher will be the test–retest reliability coefficient.

Equivalent-form reliability
A type of reliability that reveals the equivalence of test scores between two versions or forms of the test.

Equivalent-Form Reliability.   A second type of reliability is parallel or **equivalent-form reliability**. Here a psychologist develops two forms of a test to measure the same attribute and gives both forms to the same group of people. The psychologist then correlates the two scores for each person. The resulting correlation, called a *coefficient of equivalence*, reflects the extent to which the two forms are equivalent measures of the same concept. Of the three major types of reliability, this type is the least popular because it is usually challenging to come up with one good test, let alone two. Many tests do not have a "parallel form." Furthermore, research (e.g., Clause et al., 1998) reveals it is by no means easy to construct two tests whose scores have similar meanings and statistical properties such that they are truly parallel or equivalent measures. However, in intelligence and achievement testing (to be discussed shortly), equivalent forms of the same test are sometimes available. If the resulting coefficient of equivalence is high, the tests are equivalent and reliable measures of the same concept. If it is low, they are not.

Internal-consistency reliability
A type of reliability that reveals the homogeneity of the items comprising a test.

Internal-Consistency Reliability.   The third major assessment is the **internal-consistency reliability** of the test—the extent to which it has homogeneous content. Two types of internal-consistency reliability are typically computed. One is called split-half reliability. Here a test is given to a group of people, but in scoring the test (though not administering it), the researcher divides the items in half, into odd- and even-numbered items. Each person thus gets two sets of scores (one for each half), which are correlated. If the test is internally consistent, there should be a high degree of similarity in the responses (that is, right or wrong) to the odd- and even-numbered items. All other things being equal, the longer a test, the greater its reliability.

A second technique for assessing internal-consistency reliability is to compute one of two coefficients: Cronbach's alpha or Kuder-Richardson 20 (KR20). Both procedures are similar though not statistically identical. Conceptually, each test item is treated as a minitest. Thus a 100-item test consists of 100 minitests. The response to each item is correlated with the response to every other item. A matrix of inter-item correlations is formed whose average is related to the homogeneity of the test. If the test is homogeneous (the item content is similar), it will have a high internal-consistency reliability coefficient. If the test is heterogeneous (the items cover a wide variety of concepts), it is not internally consistent and the resulting coefficient will be low. Internal-consistency reliability is frequently used to assess a test's homogeneity of content in I/O psychology.

Inter-rater reliability
A type of reliability that reveals the degree of agreement among the assessments of two or more raters.

Inter-Rater Reliability.   When assessments are made on the basis of raters' judgments, it is possible for the raters to disagree in their evaluations. Two different raters may observe the same behavior yet evaluate it differently. The degree of correspondence between judgments or scores assigned by different raters is most commonly referred to as **inter-rater reliability**, although it has also been called *conspect reliability*. In some situations raters must exercise judgment in arriving at a score. Two examples are multiple raters analyzing a job and multiple interviewers evaluating job candidates. The score or rating depends not only on the job or candidate but also on the persons doing the rating. The raters' characteristics may lead to distortions or errors in their judgments. Estimation of inter-rater reliability is usually expressed as a correlation and reflects the degree of agreement among the ratings. Evidence of high inter-rater reliability establishes a basis to conclude that the behavior was reliably observed, and in turn we conclude that such observations are accurate. Inter-rater reliability is frequently assessed in I/O psychology.

Validity

Validity
A standard for evaluating tests that refers to the accuracy or appropriateness of drawing inferences from test scores. Often contrasted with reliability.

Reliability refers to consistency and stability of measurement; validity refers to accuracy. A valid measure is one that yields "correct" estimates of what is being assessed. However, another factor also distinguishes validity from reliability. Reliability is inherent in a measuring device, but validity depends on the use of a test. **Validity** is the test's appropriateness for predicting or drawing inferences about criteria. A given test may be highly valid for predicting employee productivity but totally invalid for predicting employee absenteeism. In other words, it would be appropriate to draw inferences about employee productivity from the test but inappropriate to draw inferences about absenteeism. There are several manifestations of validity, and they all involve determining the appropriateness of a measure (test) for drawing inferences.

Validity has been a controversial topic within the field of psychology. For many years psychologists believed there were "types" of validity, just as there are types of reliability (test–retest, internal consistency, etc.). Now psychologists have come to believe there is but a single or unitary conception of validity. Psychologists are involved in the formulation, measurement, and interpretation of constructs. A *construct* is a theoretical concept we propose to explain aspects of behavior. Examples of constructs in I/O psychology are intelligence, motivation, mechanical comprehension, and leadership. Because constructs are abstractions (ideas), we must have some real, tangible ways to assess them; that is, we need an actual measure of the proposed construct. Thus a paper-and-pencil test of intelligence is one way to measure the psychological construct of intelligence. The degree to which an actual measure (i.e., a test of intelligence) is an accurate and faithful representation of its underlying construct (i.e., the construct of intelligence) is **construct validity**.

Construct validity
The degree to which a test is an accurate and faithful measure of the construct it purports to measure.

Construct validity.   In studying construct validity, psychologists seek to ascertain the linkage between what the test measures and the theoretical construct. Let us assume we wish to understand the construct of intelligence, and to do so we develop a paper-and-pencil test that we believe assesses that construct. To establish the construct validity of our test, we want to compare scores on our test with known measures of intelligence, such as verbal, numerical, and problem-solving ability. If our test is a faithful assessment of intelligence, then the scores on our test should converge with these other known measures of intelligence. More technically, there should be a high correlation between the scores from our new test of intelligence and the existing measures of intelligence. These correlation coefficients are referred to as *convergent validity coefficients* because they reflect the degree to which these scores converge (or come together) in assessing a common concept, intelligence.

Likewise, scores on our test should *not* be related to concepts that we know are *not* related to intelligence, such as physical strength, eye color, and gender. That is, scores on our test should diverge (or be separate) from these concepts that are unrelated to intelligence. More technically, there should be very low correlations between the scores from our new test of intelligence and these concepts. These correlation coefficients arc referred to as *divergent validity coefficients* because they reflect the degree to which these scores diverge from each other in assessing unrelated concepts. Other statistical procedures may also be used to establish the construct validity of a test.

After collecting and evaluating much information about the test, we accumulate a body of evidence supporting the notion that the test measures a psychological construct. Then we say that the test manifests a high degree of construct validity. Tests that manifest a high degree of construct validity are among the most widely respected and frequently used assessment instruments in I/O psychology.

Binning and Barrett (1989) described construct validation as the process of demonstrating evidence for five linkages or inferences, as illustrated in Figure 4-1. Figure 4-1 shows two empirical measures and two constructs. X is a measure of construct 1, as a test of intelligence purports to measure the psychological construct of intelligence. Y is a measure of construct 2, as a supervisor's assessment of an employee's performance purports to measure the construct of job performance. Linkage 1 is the only one that can be tested directly because it is the only inference involving two variables that are directly measured (X and Y). In assessing the construct validity of X and Y, one would be most interested in assessing linkages 2 and 4, respectively. That is, we would want to know that the empirical measures of X and Y are faithful and accurate assessments of the constructs (1 and 2) they purport to measure. Because our empirical measures are never perfect indicators of the constructs we seek to understand, Edwards and Bagozzi (2000) believe researchers should devote more attention to assessing linkages 2 and 4. For the purpose of constructing theories of job performance, one would be interested in linkage 3, the relationship between the two constructs. Finally, Binning and Barrett noted that in personnel selection, we are interested in linkage 5—that is, the inference between an employment test score and the domain of performance on the job. Thus the process of construct validation involves examining the linkages

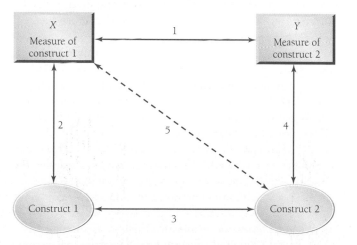

Figure 4-1   *Inferential linkages in construct validation*

Adapted by permission from "Validity of Personnel Decisions: A Conceptual Analysis of the Inferential and Evidential Bases," by J. F. Binning and G. V. Barrett, 1989, *Journal of Applied Psychology, 74*, p. 480. Copyright © 1989 American Psychological Association.

among multiple concepts of interest to us. We always operate at the empirical level (X and Y), yet we wish to draw inferences at the conceptual level (constructs 1 and 2). Construct validation is the continuous process of verifying the accuracy of an inference among concepts for the purpose of furthering our ability to understand those concepts (Pulakos, Borman, & Hough, 1988). Messick (1995) furthermore believes that issues of construct validation extend to how test scores are interpreted and the consequences of test use.

Criterion-Related Validity.

Criterion-related validity
The degree to which a test forecasts or is statistically related to a criterion.

One manifestation of construct validity is the **criterion-related validity** of a test. As its name suggests, criterion-related validity refers to how much a predictor relates to a criterion. It is a frequently used and important manifestation of validity in I/O psychology. The two major kinds of criterion-related validity are concurrent and predictive. Concurrent validity is used to diagnose the existing status of some criterion, whereas predictive validity is used to forecast future status. The primary distinction is the time interval between collecting the predictor and criterion data.

In measuring *concurrent* criterion-related validity, we are concerned with how well a predictor can predict a criterion at the same time, or concurrently. Examples abound. We may wish to predict a student's grade point average on the basis of a test score, so we collect data on the grade point averages of many students, and then we give them a predictor test. If the predictor test is a valid measure of grades, there will be a high correlation between test scores and grades. We can use the same method in an industrial setting. We can predict a worker's level of productivity (the criterion) on the basis of a test (the predictor). We collect productivity data on a current group of workers, give them a test, and then correlate their scores with their productivity records. If the test is of value, then we can draw an inference about a worker's productivity on the basis of the test score. In measurements of concurrent validity, there is no time interval between collecting the predictor and criterion data. The two variables are assessed concurrently, which is how the method gets it name. Thus the purpose of assessing concurrent criterion-related validity is so the test can be used with the knowledge that it is predictive of the criterion.

In measuring *predictive* criterion-related validity, we collect predictor information and use it to forecast future criterion performance. A college might use a student's high school class rank to predict the criterion of overall college grade point average four years later. A company could use a test to predict whether job applicants will complete a six-month training program. Figure 4-2 graphically illustrates concurrent and predictive criterion-related validity.

The conceptual significance of predictive and concurrent validity in the context of personnel selection will be discussed in the next chapter. The logic of criterion-related validity is straightforward. We determine whether there is a relationship between predictor scores and criterion scores based on a sample of employees for whom we have both sets of scores. If there is a relationship, we use scores on those predictor variables to select applicants on whom there are no criterion scores. Then we can predict the applicants' future (and thus unknown) criterion performance from their known test scores based on the relationship established through criterion-related validity.

Validity coefficient
A statistical index (often expressed as a correlation coefficient) that reveals the degree of association between two variables. Often used in the context of prediction.

When predictor scores are correlated with criterion data, the resulting correlation is called a **validity coefficient**. Whereas an acceptable reliability coefficient is in the

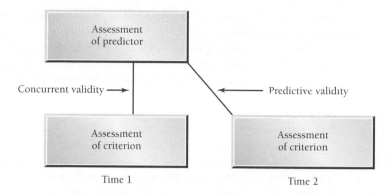

Figure 4-2 *Portrayal of concurrent and predictive criterion-related validity*

.70–.80 range, the desired range for a validity coefficient is .30–.40. Validity coefficients less than .30 are not uncommon, but those greater than .50 are rare. Just as a predictor cannot be too reliable, it also cannot be too valid. The greater the correlation between the predictor and the criterion, the more we know about the criterion on the basis of the predictor. By squaring the correlation coefficient (r), we can calculate how much variance in the criterion we can account for by using the predictor. For example, if a predictor correlates .40 with a criterion, we can explain 16% (r^2) of the variance in the criterion by knowing the predictor. This particular level of predictability (16%) would be considered satisfactory by most psychologists, given all the possible causes of performance variation. A correlation of 1.0 indicates perfect prediction (and complete knowledge). However, as Lubinski and Dawis (1992) noted, tests with moderate validity coefficients are not necessarily flawed or inadequate. The results attest to the complexity of human behavior. Our behavior is influenced by factors not measured by tests, such as motivation and luck. We should thus have realistic expectations regarding the validity of our tests.

Some criteria are difficult to predict no matter what predictors are used; other criteria are fairly predictable. Similarly, some predictors are consistently valid and are thus used often. Other predictors do not seem to be of much predictive value no matter what the criteria are, and thus they fall out of use. Usually, however, certain predictors are valid for predicting only certain criteria. Later in this chapter there will be a review of the predictors typically used in I/O psychology and an examination of how accurate they are in predicting criteria.

Content validity

The degree to which subject matter experts agree that the items in a test are a representative sample of the domain of knowledge the test purports to measure.

Content Validity.   Another manifestation of construct validity is **content validity**. Content validity is the degree to which a predictor covers a representative sample of the behavior being assessed. It is limited mainly to psychological tests but may also extend to interviews or other predictors. Historically, content validity was most relevant in achievement testing. Achievement tests are designed to indicate how well a person has mastered a specific skill or area of content. In order to be "content valid," an achievement test on Civil War history, for example, must contain a representative sample or mix of test items covering the domain of Civil War history, such as battles, military and political figures, and so on. A test with only questions about the dates of famous battles would not be a balanced representation of the content of Civil War history. If a person scores high on a content-valid test of Civil War history, we can infer that he or she is very knowledgeable about the Civil War.

How do we assess content validity? Unlike criterion-related validity, we do not compute a correlation coefficient. Content validity is assessed by subject matter experts in the field the test covers. Civil War historians would first define the domain of the Civil War and then write test questions about it. These experts would then decide how content valid the test is. Their judgments could range from "not at all" to "highly valid." Presumably, the test would be revised until it showed a high degree of content validity.

Face validity
The appearance that items in a test are appropriate for the intended use of the test by the individuals who take the test.

A similar type of validity based on people's judgments is called **face validity**. This is concerned with the appearance of the test items: do they look appropriate for such a test? Estimates of content validity are made by test developers; estimates of face validity are made by test takers. It is possible for a test item to be content valid but not face valid, and vice versa. In such a case, the test developers and test takers would disagree over the relevance or appropriateness of the item for the domain being assessed. Within the field of psychology, content validity is thought to be of greater significance or importance than face validity. However, the face validity of a test can greatly affect how individuals perceive the test to be an appropriate, legitimate means of assessing them for some important decision (such as a job offer). Individuals are more likely to bring legal challenges against companies for using tests that are not face valid. Thus issues of content validity are generally more relevant for the science of I/O psychology, whereas issues of face validity are generally more relevant for the practice of I/O psychology.

Content validity has importance for I/O psychology. Once used mainly for academic achievement testing, it is also relevant for employment testing. There is a strong and obvious link between the process of job analysis (discussed in Chapter 3) and the concept of content validity. Employers develop tests that assess the knowledge, skills, and abilities needed to perform a job. How much the content of these tests is related to the actual job is assessed by content-validation procedures. First, the domain of job behavior is specified by employees and supervisors. Then test items are developed to assess the factors needed for success on the job. The content validity of employment tests is thus the degree to which the content of the job is reflected in the content of the test. Goldstein, Zedeck, and Schneider (1993) asserted that content validity is established by the careful linkage between the information derived from job analysis and its use in test construction. Content validity purports to reveal that the knowledge and skills required to perform well on the job and on the employment test are interchangeable. In short, a test's validity can be described in terms of its content *relevance*, criterion *relatedness*, and construct *meaning*.

There is the tendency to think of test validity as being equivalent to an on/off light switch—either a test is valid or it isn't. The temptation to do so is probably based on other uses of the word *valid* in our language, such as whether or not a person has a valid driver's license. However, this either/or type of thinking about test validity is not correct. It is more accurate to think of test validity as a dimmer light switch. Tests manifest varying degrees of validity, ranging from none at all to a great deal. At some point along the continuum of validity, practical decisions have to be made about whether a test manifests "enough" validity to warrant its use. To carry the light switch analogy further, a highly valid test sheds light on the object (construct) we seek to understand. Thus the test validation process is the ongoing act of determining the amount of "illumination" the test projects on the construct. Another analogy is to think of validity as the overall weight of evidence that is brought before a jury in a legal trial. Different types of evidence may be presented to a jury, such as eyewitness reports, fingerprint analysis, and testimony. No one piece of evidence may be compelling to the jury; however, the weight of all the evidence, taken in its totality, leads the jury to reach a decision. In this case we can think of the validity of a test as the overall weight of the evidence showing that it measures the construct it purports to measure. The very meaning of the term *validity* in psychology is continually evolving and being refined (Jonson & Plake, 1998) due to the inherent complexity of the concept.

Predictor Development

The goal of psychological assessment is to know something about the individual being assessed for the purpose of making an inference about that person. In I/O psychology the inference to be made often pertains to whether the individual is likely to perform well in a job. What the "something" is that we seek to know is a construct we believe is important to success on the job. That "something" could be the individual's intelligence, ambition, interpersonal skills, ability to cope with frustration, willingness to learn new concepts or procedures, and so on. How do we assess these characteristics of individuals? I/O psychologists have developed a broad array of predictor measures designed to help us make decisions (i.e., hire or not hire) about individuals. A discussion of these predictor measures is presented in the rest of this chapter. For the most part, these predictor measures can be classified along two dimensions.

The first dimension is whether the predictor seeks to measure directly the underlying psychological construct in question (e.g., mechanical comprehension), or whether it seeks to measure a sample of the same behavior to be exhibited on the job. For example, let us assume we want to assess individuals to determine whether they are suitable for the job of a mechanic. On the basis of a job analysis we know the job of mechanic requires the individual to be proficient with tools and equipment and with diagnosing mechanical problems. We could elect to assess mechanical ability with a paper-and-pencil test of mechanical comprehension. Such a test would reveal to what degree the individual possesses mechanical knowledge, but it would not assess proficiency in the use of tools (i.e., because it is a paper-and-pencil test). Alternatively, we could present the individual with a mechanical object in a state of disrepair and say, "This appears to be broken. Figure out what is wrong with it and then fix it." The individual's behavior in diagnosing and repairing the object would be observed and rated by knowledgeable individuals (i.e., subject matter experts). This latter type of assessment is called "behavioral sampling" because it samples the types of behavior exhibited on the job (in this case, diagnosing and repairing mechanical objects). This particular assessment would measure the individual's proficiency with tools used in diagnosis and repair; however, it is limited to only one particular malfunctioning mechanical object. The assessment lacks the breadth of coverage of a paper-and-pencil test. Furthermore, the behavioral sampling method of assessment measures whether the individual can perform the diagnosis and repair at this time, but not whether he or she could learn to do so with proper training. These types of issues and others will be presented in the discussion of predictor methods.

A second distinction among predictors is whether they seek to measure something about the individual currently or something about the individual in the past. A job interview is a current measure of a person's characteristics because the interviewer assesses voice quality, interpersonal demeanor, and poise. An assessment of these factors would be used to predict whether the individual will succeed in a job. Alternatively, a predictor measure could assess whether the individual exhibited these behaviors in the past, not concurrently. An example would be a letter of recommendation solicited from a former employer who supervised the individual in a previous job. Here the intent is to make a prediction about future behavior (in the new job) on the basis of past behavior (in the old job). Thus predictor measures are used to make inferences about future behavior on the basis of current or past behavior. Some predictor measures can be developed that measure both past and current behaviors. The job interview is one example. The interviewer can assess the individual's behavior in the interview as it is happening and can also ask questions about the individual's previous work history.

Not all predictor measures fall neatly into either the construct/behavioral sampling categories or the assessment of past/present characteristics of individuals. However, this classification approach is a reasonable way to understand the varieties of predictor measures and their respective intents. In all cases predictor measures are designed to forecast future behavior. They differ in the approaches they take in making these predictions. The degree to which these approaches differ in reliability, validity, fairness, social acceptability, legal defensibility, time, and cost has been the subject of extensive research in I/O psychology.

Psychological Tests and Inventories

Psychological tests and inventories have been the most frequently used predictors in I/O psychology. The difference between the two is that in a test the answers are either right or wrong, but in an **inventory** there are no right or wrong answers. Usually, though, the terms *tests* and *psychological testing* refer to the family of tests and inventories.

Inventory
Method of assessment in which the responses to questions are recorded and interpreted but are not evaluated in terms of their correctness, as in a vocational interest inventory.

History of Psychological Testing

Testing has a long multinational history in the field of psychology. Sir Francis Galton, an English biologist, was interested in human heredity. During the course of his research, he realized the need for measuring the characteristics of biologically related and unrelated persons. He began to keep records of people on such factors as keenness of vision and hearing, muscular strength, and reaction time. By 1880 he had accumulated the first large-scale body of information on individual differences. He was probably the first scientist to devise systematic ways of measuring people. In 1890 the American psychologist James Cattell introduced the term *mental test*. He devised an early test of intelligence based on sensory discrimination and reaction time. Hermann Ebbinghaus, a German psychologist, developed math and sentence-completion tests and gave them to schoolchildren. In 1897 he reported that the sentence-completion test was related to the children's scholastic achievement.

The biggest advances in the early years of testing were made by the French psychologist Alfred Binet. In 1904 the French government appointed Binet to study procedures for educating impaired children. To assess mental impairment, Binet (in collaboration with Theodore Simon) developed a test of intelligence. It consisted of 30 problems covering such areas as judgment, comprehension, and reasoning, which Binet regarded as essential components of intelligence. Later revisions of this test had a larger sampling of items from different areas. Binet's research on intelligence testing was continued by the American psychologist Lewis Terman, who in 1916 developed the concept of IQ (intelligence quotient). These early pioneers paved the way for a wide variety of tests that would be developed in the years to come, many of which were used by industrial psychologists to predict job performance. Although most of the early work in testing was directed at assessing intellect, testing horizons expanded to include aptitude, ability, interest, and personality.

Types of Tests

Tests can be classified either by their administration or by their content.

Speed Versus Power Tests.   **Speed tests** have a large number of easy questions; the questions are so easy that the test taker will always get them right. The test is timed (for example, a 5-minute limit) and contains more items than can possibly be answered in the allotted time period. The total score on such a test is the number of items answered and reflects the test taker's speed of work.

Power tests have questions that are fairly difficult; that is, the test taker usually cannot get them all right. Often there is no time limit. The total score on a power test is the number of items answered correctly. Most tests given in college are power tests. If time limits are imposed, they are mostly for the convenience of the test administrator.

Individual Versus Group Tests.   **Individual tests** are given to only one person at a time. Such tests are not common because of the amount of time needed to administer them to all applicants. For example, if a test takes one hour and ten people are to take it, ten hours of administration time will be required. The benefits of giving such a test must be balanced against the costs. Certain types of intelligence tests are individually administered, as are certain tests for evaluating high-level executives. In these tests the administrator has to play an active part (for example, asking questions, demonstrating an object) as opposed to just monitoring.

Group tests are administered to several people simultaneously and are the most common type of test. They do not involve the active participation of an administrator. The Army Alpha and Army Beta tests were early group intelligence tests used during World War I. Most tests used in educational and industrial organizations are group tests because they are efficient in terms of time and cost.

Paper-and-Pencil Versus Performance Tests.   **Paper-and-pencil tests** are the most common type of test used in industrial and educational organizations. They do not involve the physical manipulation of objects or pieces of equipment. The questions asked may require answers in either multiple-choice or essay form. The individual's physical ability to handle a pencil should not influence his or her score on the test, however. The pencil is just the means by which the response is recorded on a sheet of paper.

Speed test
A type of test that has a precise time limit; a person's score on the test is the number of items attempted in the time period. Often contrasted with a power test.

Power test
A type of test that usually does not have a precise time limit; a person's score on the test is the number of items answered correctly. Often contrasted with a speed test.

Individual test
A type of test that is administered to one individual test taker at a time. Often contrasted with a group test.

Group test
A type of test that is administered to more than one test taker at a time. Often contrasted with an individual test.

Paper-and-pencil test
A method of assessment in which the responses to questions are recorded on a piece of paper.

Performance test
A type of test that requires the test taker to exhibit physical skill in the manipulation of objects, as in a typing test.

In a **performance test** the individual has to manipulate an object or a piece of equipment. The score is a measure of the person's ability to perform the manipulation. A typing test and a test of finger dexterity are examples of performance tests. Sometimes paper-and-pencil and performance tests are used jointly. To get a driver's license, for example, most people have to pass both a written and a behind-the-wheel performance test.

Ethical Standards in Testing

Maintaining ethical standards in testing is one of the more important ethical issues confronting the entire profession of psychology (APA, 2002). To prevent the misuse of psychological tests, the American Psychological Association has developed standards (AERA, APA, NCME, 1999). The APA has also issued guidelines and user qualifications to ensure that tests are administered and interpreted correctly (Turner et al., 2001). Sometimes the user must be a licensed professional psychologist, particularly in clinical psychology. In industry fewer qualifications are required to administer employment tests. To prevent their misuse and to maintain test security, restrictions are also placed on who has access to tests (Author, 1999). However, Moreland et al. (1995) concluded that educational efforts will ultimately be more effective in promoting good testing practices than efforts to limit the use of tests. Test publishers are discouraged from giving away free samples or printing detailed examples of test questions as sales promotions, which could invalidate future test results.

Invasion of privacy
A condition pertaining to the asking of questions that are unrelated to the assessment's intent or are inherently intrusive.

Other ethical issues are the invasion of privacy and confidentiality. **Invasion of privacy** occurs when a psychological test reveals more information about a person than is needed to make an informed decision. Tests should be used for precise purposes; they should not be used to learn information that is irrelevant to performing the job. For example, if a mechanical comprehension test is used to hire mechanics, then the company should not also give an interest inventory just to learn about potential employees' hobbies and recreational activities. Using an interest inventory that has no relationship to job performance could be an invasion of the applicant's privacy. Furthermore, some types of questions are inherently invasive (for example, about one's religious beliefs), regardless of the merit or intent of the questions.

Confidentiality
A condition associated with testing pertaining to which parties have access to test results.

Confidentiality refers to who should have access to test results. When a person takes an employment test, he or she should be told the purpose of the test, how the results will be used, and which people in the company will see the results. Problems arise if a third party (another prospective employer, for example) wants to know the test results. The scores should be confidential unless the test taker gives a written release.

Another ethical problem in this area is the retention of records. Advances in computer technology have made it possible to store large quantities of information about people. Who should have access to this information, and what guarantees are there that it will not be misused? The results of an intelligence test taken in sixth grade may become part of a student's permanent academic record. Should a potential employer get the results of this elementary school test? Furthermore, the test probably doesn't predict job performance, so why would anyone want the results? Indeed, recent research (e.g., Chan, Dragsow, & Sawin, 1999; Farrell & McDaniel, 2001) revealed that time diminishes the predictive accuracy of cognitive ability measures. These types of questions are central to problems of confidentiality.

Sources of Information About Testing

Because testing is a rapidly changing area, it is important to keep up with current developments in the field. Old tests are revised, new tests are introduced, and some tests are discontinued. Fortunately, several key references are available. Perhaps the most important source of information about testing is the series of **Mental Measurements Yearbooks (MMY)**. The MMY was first published in 1938 and is now revised every two years. Each yearbook includes tests published during a specified period, thus supplementing the tests reported in previous yearbooks. The *Seventeenth Mental Measurements Yearbook* (Geisinger, Spies, Carlson & Plake, 2007), for example, deals mainly with tests that appeared between 2004 and 2006. Each test is critically reviewed by an expert in the field and documented with a complete list of references. Information about price, publisher, and versions of the test is also given. The MMY is the most comprehensive review of psychological tests available in the field. It is also available online at www.unl.edu/buros.

Less-detailed books, such as *Tests in Print VII* (Murphy, Spies, & Plake, 2006), resemble bibliographies and help locate tests in the MMY. Online services provide information on more restricted applications of tests, such as *Health and Psychosocial Instruments*. Some psychological journals review specific tests, and various professional test developers publish test manuals. The test manual should give the information needed to administer, score, and evaluate a particular test as well as data on the test's reliability and validity. Although these manuals are useful, they are usually not as complete and critical as reviews in the MMY.

The test user has an obligation to use the test in a professional and competent manner. Tests should be chosen with extreme care and concern for the consequences of their use. Important decisions are based on test scores, and the choice of test is equally important. A test should be thoroughly analyzed before it is considered for use. Whittington (1998) reported that test developers and test reviewers should be more thorough in providing information to help potential users make more informed decisions about test usage. Figure 4-3 reveals the range of professional responsibilities in

Figure 4-3 *Professional responsibilities in psychological assessment*

Adapted from the National Council on Measurement in Education's *Code of Professional Responsibilities in Educational Measurement* (available at http://www.ncme.org/about/prof_respons.doc). Copyright 1995 by the National Council on Measurement in Education. Reproduced with permission of the publisher.

psychological assessment, including test development, marketing and selling the tests, scoring, interpretation and use, and educating others about psychological assessment, among others.

Test Content

Tests can be classified according to their content. This section will discuss the major types of constructs assessed by tests used in industry. Also presented will be information on how valid the various types of tests have been in personnel selection as documented from their use in the psychological literature.

Intelligence Tests

Intelligence or cognitive ability is perhaps the most heavily researched construct in all of psychology. Interest in the assessment of intelligence began more than 100 years ago. Despite the length of time the construct of intelligence has been assessed, however, there remains no singular or standard means to assess it. Furthermore, recent research suggests intelligence is even more complex than we have believed.

g
The symbol for "general mental ability," which has been found to be predictive of success in most jobs.

What is generally agreed upon regarding intelligence? Intelligence traditionally has been conceptualized as having a singular, primary basis. This concept is known as *general mental ability* and is symbolized by *g*. By assessing *g*, we gain an understanding of a person's general level of intellectual capability. Tests that measure *g* have been found to be predictive of performance across a wide range of occupations (e.g., Ree, Earles, & Teachout, 1994). The criterion-related validity of *g* is impressive, often in the range of .40–.60. Many researchers believe it is the single most diagnostic predictor of future job performance. Simply put, if we could know only one attribute of a job candidate upon which to base a prediction, we would want an assessment of intelligence. General intelligence is regarded to be a ubiquitous predictor of a wide variety of performance criteria, prompting Brand (1987) to observe: "*g* is to psychology what carbon is to chemistry" (p. 257). Reeve and Hakel (2002) summarized the prevailing scientific status of general mental ability: "A wealth of data has confirmed that there is virtually no circumstance, no life outcome, no criterion for which even minimal cognitive functioning is required in which *g* is not at least moderately predictive of individual differences . . ." (p. 49).

Although research clearly supports the validity of general intelligence as a predictor, some researchers believe that conceptualizing intelligence merely as *g* encourages oversimplification of the inherent complexity of intelligence. Murphy (1996) asserted that intelligence is not a unitary phenomenon, and other dimensions of intelligence are also worthy of our consideration. Ackerman (1992), for example, reported superior predictive power of multiple abilities over general intelligence in complex information-processing tasks, as in the job of air traffic controller. Ackerman and Kanfer (1993) developed a useful selection test for air traffic controllers based in large part on the assessment of spatial ability. From an I/O psychology perspective, therefore, the controversy regarding the assessment of intelligence rests primarily on the adequacy of measuring general intelligence (*g*) only or assessing multiple cognitive abilities in forecasting job behavior. The current body of research seems to indicate that in most cases measuring the *g* factor of intelligence offers superior predictive accuracy in forecasting success in training and job performance over measuring specific (math, spatial, and verbal) cognitive abilities (Carretta & Ree, 2000; Roznowski et al., 2000). Salgado et al. (2003) likewise demonstrated that in a major study of ten European countries general mental ability forecasts success in training and on the job.

Sternberg (1997) proposed a triarchic (or three-part) theory of intelligence. Sternberg contended that there are multiple kinds of intelligence. He posited academic intelligence as representing what intelligence tests typically measure, such as fluency with words and numbers. Table 4-1 shows two sample test questions from a typical intelligence test. Sternberg proposed two other important kinds of intelligence that conventional intelligence tests don't measure. One is *practical intelligence*, which he stated is the intelligence needed to be competent in the everyday world and is not highly related to academic intelligence. The second (nontraditional) kind of intelligence Sternberg called *creative intelligence*, which pertains to the ability to produce work that is both novel (i.e., original or unexpected) and appropriate (i.e., useful). Manifestations of this kind of intelligence are critical in writing, art, and advertising. Sternberg believes that all three kinds of intelligence may be necessary for lifelong learning and success, depending upon the nature of our vocation.

Table 4-1 *Sample test questions from a typical intelligence test*

1. What number is missing in this series?
   3–8–14–21–29–(?)
2. SHOVEL is to DITCHDIGGER as SCALPEL is to:
   (a) knife   (b) sharp   (c) butcher   (d) surgeon   (e) cut

As Daniel (1997) stated, our means of assessing intelligence (i.e., a test) are heavily guided by how we view what we are trying to assess (see Field Note 1, p 106). A view of intelligence dominated by academic intelligence will lead us to assess that particular kind to the relative exclusion of practical and creative intelligence. Wagner (1997) asserted that we need to expand our criteria to show the various manifestations of intelligence, such as over time and over different aspects of job performance (e.g., task proficiency vs. successfully interacting with other people). Hedlund and Sternberg (2000) asserted that the contemporary world of business seeks employees who are adaptable to highly changing conditions. Real-life problems tend to be ill-defined, ambiguous, and dynamic, and such problems do not match the types of problems on which intelligence traditionally has been assessed. Hedlund and Sternberg believe the concept of practical intelligence is intended to complement, rather than to contradict, the narrower views of *g*-based theories of intelligence.

As can be inferred from the foregoing discussion, the construct of intelligence is highly complex. From an I/O psychology perspective, we are concerned with the degree to which cognitive ability forecasts job performance. Murphy (1996) summarized the prevailing conclusion: "Research on the validity of measures of cognitive ability as predictors of job performance represents one of the 'success stories' in I/O psychology" (p. 6). While other abilities and attributes are also necessary for different jobs, "I/O psychologists generally agree that cognitive ability tests are valid and fair, that they provide useful information, although perhaps not complete information about the construct of general cognitive ability" (Murphy, Cronin, & Tam, 2003, p. 670).

Field Note 1: What is Intelligence?

The construct of intelligence is highly complex, perhaps more complex than researchers have realized. Theorists have long debated whether intelligence is a unitary concept or whether there are various forms of intelligence, such as verbal and quantitative. Tests of intelligence are designed and interpreted based on these theoretical formulations. The questions on traditional tests of intelligence have a correct answer and only one correct answer. Examples include the answers to questions about mathematics and vocabulary. However, recent research by Sternberg suggests that there are other manifestations of intelligence. Many problems in life do not have any correct answer; other problems may have more than one correct answer. Furthermore, in real life, solutions to problems are not so much "correct" and "incorrect" as they are "feasible" and "acceptable." Examples include dealing with interpersonal problems at the individual level and with global problems at the national level. It takes intelligence to solve such problems, but these types of questions do not appear on typical tests of intelligence. There is an adage that "young people are smart and old people are wise." Perhaps wisdom is a form of intelligence that is derived through many years of successfully dealing with problems that lack single correct solutions. Psychologists refer to knowledge that helps solve practical problems as procedural or tacit knowledge. Indeed, Sternberg and Horvath (1999) described how tacit knowledge contributes to success in a broad array of occupations, such as law, military command, medicine, and teaching. As Marchant and Robinson (1999) stated on the subject of legal expertise, all lawyers are knowledgeable of the law. That is what they are taught in law school. But the truly successful lawyers understand how to interpret the law and the dynamics of the entire legal system. The capacity to derive feasible and acceptable solutions to complex problems that do not have any correct answer is, as current research supports, a legitimate form of intelligence.

Mechanical Aptitude Tests

Mechanical aptitude tests require a person to recognize which mechanical principle is suggested by a test item. The underlying concepts measured by these items include sound and heat conductance, velocity, gravity, and force. One of the more popular tests of mechanical reasoning is the Bennett Test of Mechanical Comprehension (Bennett, 1980). The test is a series of pictures that illustrate various mechanical facts and principles. Other tests of mechanical comprehension have also been developed.

Muchinsky (2004a) reported that tests of mechanical ability are highly predictive of performance in manufacturing/production jobs. However, women traditionally perform worse than men on tests of mechanical ability. Recent attempts to include test questions pertaining to kitchen implements and other topics about which women are more familiar (e.g., high-heel shoes) have reduced, but not eliminated, the male/female score differential (Wiesen, 1999).

Personality Inventories

Unlike the previously cited tests, which have objective answers, personality inventories do not have right or wrong answers. Test takers answer how much they agree with certain statements (e.g., "People who work hard get ahead"). In personality inventories similar types of questions typically make up a scale, which reflects a person's introversion, dominance, confidence, and so on. Items are scored according to a predetermined key such that responding one way or another to an item results in a higher or lower score on a particular scale. These scale scores are then used to predict job success. The basic rationale is that successful employees possess a particular personality structure, and scales reflective of that structure become the basis for selecting new employees.

Personality has been assessed in a variety of ways. One of the more popular assessments is the Myers-Briggs Type Indicator® (MBTI®). The MBTI is predicated upon 16 personality types. Each type is created by a person's status on four bipolar dimensions: Extraversion–Introversion, Sensing–Intuition, Thinking–Feeling, and Judgment–Perception. Questions are asked that require individuals to state their personal preference for how they direct their energies, process information, make decisions, and organize their lives. When scored, the MBTI yields a profile of the individual in terms of these four bipolar dimensions—for example, Introversion–Sensing–Feeling–Perception. This particular profile is classified as the ISFP personality type. According to the Myers-Briggs theory of personality, each of 16 personality types can be characterized in terms of job or role preferences that best match their personality. Among the strengths of the MBTI are its ease of understanding, high face validity, and appeal among a wide population of users. Critics of the MBTI question whether it is useful to conceptualize personality into "types," the validity of the four dimensions (the strongest support is for Introversion–Extraversion), and the lack of differentiation in interpretation between a high score and low score on a given dimension. For example, a person who is a strong extravert and another person who is mildly extraverted both are classified as the same type (E). Despite criticisms of the test and its underlying theory, the MBTI is widely used to make personnel selection decisions and to help people understand their own personality.

Personality assessment is one of the fastest growing areas in personnel selection. The five-factor model of personality has received more scientific support than the MBTI. It is often referred to as the **"Big 5" theory of personality**. These are the five personality factors:

Big 5 personality theory
A theory that defines personality in terms of five major factors: neuroticism, extraversion, openness to experience, agreeableness, and conscientiousness. Also called the "Five Factor" theory of personality.

- *Neuroticism*—the person's characteristic level of stability versus instability
- *Extraversion*—the tendency to be sociable, assertive, active, talkative, energetic, and outgoing
- *Openness to experience*—the disposition to be curious, imaginative, and unconventional
- *Agreeableness*—the disposition to be cooperative, helpful, and easy to get along with
- *Conscientiousness*—the disposition to be purposeful, determined, organized, and controlled

Extensive empirical support for its validity was provided by McCrae and Costa (1987) and R. T. Hogan (1991). Personality inventories have also been developed based upon this theory—for example, the NEO-PI (P. T. Costa, 1996) and the Hogan Personality Inventory (Hogan & Hogan, 1992). Barrick and Mount (1991) concluded from a meta-analysis that extraversion is a valid predictor of performance in occupations that involve social interactions, such as managers and salespeople. Tokar, Fisher, and Subich (1998) revealed that personality is linked to many aspects of work behavior, including job performance, career progression, and vocational interests. Conscientiousness shows consistent correlations with job performance criteria for all occupations and across different cultures (Salgado, 1997). In a major meta-analytic review of the five-factor model, Hurtz and Donovan (2000) cautioned that the validity coefficients for predicting job performance criteria were only modest, about .20. Collins and Gleaves (1998) reported that the five personality factors were equally applicable for evaluating Black and White job applicants. These five factors are a durable framework for considering personality structure among people of many nations, and they have prompted McCrae and Costa (1997) to refer to their pattern of interrelationships as a "human universal." Furthermore, such personality measures provide *incremental* predictive validity beyond measures of intelligence (Judge et al., 1999).

A long-standing concern with using personality tests for personnel selection is that job applicants might not give truthful responses. Rather, applicants may fake their responses to give what they believe are socially desirable responses. Morgeson et al. (2007) concluded that faking on personality inventories is unavoidable because job candidates will necessarily try to project highly positive images of themselves to hiring organizations. The degree of faking on such inventories is typically detected by the responses to certain items. Schmitt and Oswald (2006) questioned what actions organizations should take with candidates who faked their responses. Two options seem possible: to statistically correct the test scores (i.e., essentially "re-score" the test), or to eliminate the fakers from further employment consideration. However, the authors noted that the goal of any personnel selection system is to get good employees on the job and neither method has been found to substantially increase the quality of the workforce. The prevailing opinion among I/O psychologists is that faking on personality inventories occurs, although some researchers deny that it is a significant problem in personnel selection decisions (Hogan, Barrett, & Hogan, 2007).

Hogan, Hogan, and Roberts (1996) concluded that personality tests should be used in conjunction with other information, particularly the applicant's technical skills, job experience, and ability to learn. More specifically, Ackerman and Heggestad (1997) believe "abilities, interests, and personality develop in tandem, such that ability level and personality dispositions determine the probability of success in a particular task domain, and interests determine the motivation to attempt the task" (p. 239). Simply put, the influence of personality on job performance should not be overestimated, but it should also not be underestimated.

On a conceptual level intelligence and personality have typically been viewed as separate constructs. Intelligence traditionally has reflected the "can do" dimension of an individual; namely, the person "can do" the work because he or she is judged to possess an adequate level of intelligence. Personality traditionally has reflected the "will do" dimension of an individual; namely, the person "will do" the work because he or she is judged to possess the demeanor to do so. Kehoe (2002) explained how intelligence and personality can both be predictive of job performance, each in its own way. Assume a personality test and a test of *g* both correlate equally with job performance.

The employees selected by each of these tests will not be the same. "The 'personality' employees might achieve their overall performance by being relatively more dependable, persistent, attentive, helpful, and so on. The 'cognitive' employees might achieve their overall performance by being relatively more accurate, faster, effective problem solvers, and the like" (pp. 103–104). Hofstee (2001) proposed the existence of a "*p* factor" (a general personality factor reflecting the ability to cope), which is parallel to the *g* factor in intelligence. Further research may lead to a melding of these two constructs, which have typically been viewed as distinct.

Recently there have been developments in alternative assessments of personality to the traditional self-report paper-and-pencil method. Self-report measures are prone to response distortion in the form of faking to create a favorable impression. Van Iddekinge, Raymark, and Roth (2005) assessed personality through two traditional methods of personnel selection: the structured interview and the self-report personality inventory. The Big 5 theory of personality was the theoretical basis of the research. Individuals were instructed to take the personality inventory under two instructional conditions: reporting honestly and as a job applicant seeking employment. Interviewer ratings of personality were more similar to the responses under the respond honestly instructions. The authors concluded that personality assessments in an employment context might be more accurate with a structured interview than a self-report personality inventory.

Taylor, Pajo, Cheung, and Stringfield (2004) developed a telephone reference check for evaluators to describe applicants on three dimensions of personality: Conscientiousness, Agreeableness, and Customer Focus. The telephone reference check took 10-15 minutes to administer. The correlation between the score on the reference check and subsequent supervisor rating of job performance was .25. This level of predictive accuracy is higher than those typically found for self-report personality inventories.

A third method of personality assessment was developed by James (1998), and is called "conditional reasoning." On the surface, the questions posed to the applicant appear to measure a cognitive dimension (reasoning), but the assessment purports to measure the personality dimension of aggression. LeBreton, Barksdale, Robin, and James (2007) stated: "In contrast to traditional self-report surveys, which are designed to directly measure explicit (i.e., conscious) self-perceptions, **conditional reasoning tests** (CRTs) are designed to indirectly measure the implicit (i.e., unconscious) biases and rationalizations linked to various latent motives" (p. 1). CRTs represent a psychologically complex form of assessment. The candidate is presented with a description of a logical problem and is asked to indicate which of several justifications for a situation is most likely. For example, the logical problem may be the occurrence of automobile accidents. The presented justifications for the accidents might include bad road conditions, excessive speed, high traffic volume, and drivers under the influence of illicit performance impairing drugs. The choices candidates make to justify the likely cause of the problem is an assessment of their unconscious biases that are used to justify their choices (especially in the absence of any additional information). In particular, CRTs are designed to assess the unconscious bias of social aggression. While all of the presented justifications for automobile accidents may be plausible to some degree, the choice of illicit performance impairing drugs reflects a bias of aggression toward others.

Although there is not a large body of research on CRTs, the authors believe that CRTs may hold promise for providing an assessment of personality that would be more

Conditional reasoning test
A type of personality test that appears to be measuring reasoning.

difficult to fake than traditional self-report measures of personality. CRTs might best be used in combination with the self-report inventory and the interview to triangulate personality assessment, which in turn would lead to greater predictive accuracy.

Integrity Tests

Integrity test
A type of test that purports to assess a candidate's honesty or character.

The prevalence of personality assessment in personnel selection is also demonstrated by the recent development and growing use of honesty or integrity tests. **Integrity tests** are designed to identify job applicants who will not steal from their employer or otherwise engage in counterproductive behavior on the job. These tests are paper-and-pencil tests and generally fall into one of two types (Sackett & Wanek, 1996). In the first type, an *overt integrity test*, the job applicant clearly understands that the intent of the test is to assess integrity. The test typically has two sections: one deals with attitudes toward theft and other forms of dishonesty (namely, beliefs about the frequency and extent of employee theft, punitiveness toward theft, perceived ease of theft, and endorsement of common rationalizations about theft), and a second section deals with admissions of theft and other illegal activities (such as dollar amounts stolen in the past year, drug use, and gambling). There is some evidence (Cunningham, Wong, & Barbee, 1994) that the responses to such tests are distorted by the applicants' desire to create a favorable impression. Alliger, Lilienfeld, and Mitchell (1995) found that the questions in integrity tests are value-laden and transparent (e.g., "Are you a productive person?"), which makes it easy for applicants to distort their responses to affect the desired result. Berry, Sackett, and Wiemann (2007) concluded that respondents appear able to fake an integrity test when instructed to do so. This conclusion was reached by comparing the scores of people who were instructed to "respond honestly" and also to "respond as a job applicant who wanted to fake good to beat the test." The second type of test, called *a personality-based measure*, makes no reference to theft. These tests contain conventional personality assessment items that have been found to be predictive of theft. Because this type of test does not contain obvious references to theft, it is less likely to offend job applicants. These tests are primarily assessments of conscientiousness and emotional stability personality factors (Hogan & Brinkmeyer, 1997).

Research findings have shown that integrity tests are valid. Collins and Schmidt (1993) conducted a study of incarcerated offenders convicted of white-collar crimes, such as embezzlement and fraud. Compared with a control sample of employees in upper-level positions of authority, offenders had greater tendencies toward irresponsibility, lack of dependability, and disregard of rules and social norms. In a meta-analytic review, Ones, Viswesvaran, and Schmidt (1993) concluded that integrity tests effectively predict the broad criterion of organizationally disruptive behaviors like theft, disciplinary problems, and absenteeism. Self-reported measures of counterproductive behavior were found to be more predictable than objective measures (such as detected workplace theft). Cullen and Sackett (2004) concluded that "integrity tests make an independent contribution above and beyond Big Five measures [of personality] in the prediction of job performance" (p. 162).

Problems are inherent in validating tests designed to predict employee theft. First, the issue is very sensitive, and many organizations choose not to make information public. Organizations may readily exchange information on employee absenteeism, but employee theft statistics are often confidential. Second, the criterion isn't really theft so much as being caught stealing because many thefts go undetected. Third, the percentage of employees caught stealing in an organization is usually very small—2% to 3% is the norm. Consequently, there are statistical difficulties in trying to predict what is essentially a rare event. Furthermore, Camara and Schneider (1994) noted that test publishers classify integrity tests as proprietary, meaning that access to these tests is not provided to researchers interested in assessing their validity. Some people argue that the value of integrity tests for personnel selection is greater than the typical validity coefficient suggests. They argue that applicants who pass an integrity test are sensitized to the organization's concern for honesty and that other theft-reducing measures (such as internal surveillance systems) may well be used to monitor employees. Such procedures reduce the occurrence of employee theft but are not evidenced in the predictive accuracy of the honesty test.

Wanek (1999) offered the following summation of the use of integrity tests for personnel selection: "Between otherwise equal final candidates, choosing the candidate with the highest integrity test score will lead, over the long run, to a work force comprised of employees who are less likely to engage in counter-productive activities at work, and more likely to engage in productive work behaviors" (p. 193).

Physical Abilities Testing

Psychological assessment has long focused on cognitive abilities and personality characteristics. However, research (e.g., Fleishman & Quaintance, 1984) has also examined the assessment of physical abilities, and in particular how these physical abilities relate to performance in some jobs. Fleishman and Quaintance (pp. 463–464) presented the set of abilities relevant to work performance. These are some critical physical abilities:

- *Static strength*—"the ability to use muscle force to lift, push, pull, or carry objects"
- *Explosive strength*—"the ability to use short bursts of muscle force to propel oneself or an object"
- *Gross body coordination*—"the ability to coordinate the movement of the arms, legs, and torso in activities where the whole body is in motion"
- *Stamina*—"the ability of the lungs and circulatory (blood) systems of the body to perform efficiently over time"

An analysis (J. Hogan, 1991b) revealed that the total set of physical abilities may be reduced to three major constructs: strength, endurance, and movement quality. These three constructs account for most of the variation in individual capacity to perform strenuous activities. Arvey et al. (1992) established the construct validity of a set of physical ability tests for use in the selection of entry-level police officers. The findings suggested that two factors—strength and endurance—underlie performance on the physical ability tests and performance on the job. The results further showed that women scored considerably lower than men on the physical ability tests. However, the findings did not suggest how much importance physical abilities compared to cognitive abilities should be accorded in the selection decision.

In general the research on physical abilities reveals they are related to successful job performance in physically demanding jobs, such as firefighters, police officers, and factory workers. Indeed, Hoffman (1999) successfully validated a series of physical ability tests for selecting employees for construction and mechanical jobs. Future research needs to consider the effects of aging on the decline of physical abilities and the legal implications of differences in physical abilities across groups.

Situational Judgment Tests

Advances are being made in the format of test questions. Traditional multiple-choice test questions have one correct answer. Given this characteristic, test questions have to be written such that there is indeed a correct answer to the question, and only one correct answer (Haladyna, 1999). In real life, however, many problems and questions don't have a single correct answer. Rather, an array of answers is possible, some more plausible or appropriate than others. There is a growing interest in designing tests that require the test taker to rate a series of answers (all correct to some degree) in terms of their overall suitability for resolving a problem. One name given to this type of assessment is **situational judgment test** (McDaniel et al., 2001). An example of a situational judgment test question is presented in Table 4-2. Research on this type of test reveals that it measures a construct similar to intelligence, but not the same as the traditional conception of *g*. Situational judgment tests reflect the theoretical rationale of practical intelligence discussed earlier in the chapter.

Situational judgment test
A type of test that describes a problem to the test taker and requires the test taker to rate various possible solutions in terms of their feasibility or applicability.

Table 4-2 *Sample question from a situational judgment test*

You are a leader of a manufacturing team that works with heavy machinery. One of your production operators tells you that one machine in the work area is suddenly malfunctioning and may endanger the welfare of your work team. Rank order the following possible courses of action to effectively address this problem, from most desirable to least desirable.

1. Call a meeting of your team members to discuss the problem.
2. Report the problem to the Director of Safety.
3. Shut off the machine immediately.
4. Individually ask other production operators about problems with their machines.
5. Evacuate your team from the production facility.

Interest in situational judgment tests as a means of personnel selection is growing among I/O psychologists. The concept of judgment refers to the ability to comprehend situations and anticipate the consequences associated with actions taken in those situations. Brooks and Highhouse (2006) stated that situational judgment test items are constructed to measure the candidate's fluency with this concept. The authors explained the importance of having a strong theoretical understanding of judgment and its relationship to general mental ability. The two constructs are related, but empirical evidence indicates they are not equivalent.

McDaniel, Hartman, Whetzel, and Grubb (2007) conducted a meta-analysis on the validity of situational judgment tests (SJTs) as related to the response instructions given to candidates. Two types of instructions are typically given with situation judgment tests: behavioral tendency (assessing how a person would likely behave in a given situation); and knowledge instruction (evaluating the effectiveness of possible responses to a given situation). The authors found that scores on SJTs administered under knowledge instructions correlated more highly with general mental ability, while the behavioral tendency instructions produced scores more strongly related to personality. The authors concluded that SJTs are a valuable means of assessing personnel because they provide incremental validity beyond cognitive and personality measures combined.

Lievens (2006) questioned whether SJTs developed in one culture could be transplanted to and used as a valid predictor in another culture. SJTs describe situations that are inherently embedded within a cultural context, and a highly appropriate action to take in one culture may not be highly appropriate in another (i.e., "We would never shake hands with a woman in our culture"). In constructing SJT questions that might be generalizable across different cultures, one would have to focus on "universally acceptable" responses to such situations. An alternative approach would be to use the SJT assessment approach, but tailor the question to each cultural context. In the former case, both the assessment method (SJT) and the specific items would be used across all cultures. In the latter case the SJT method would be used across all cultures, but not the same situations (or the desired responses would differ).

Computerized Adaptive Testing

Computerized adaptive testing (CAT)

A form of assessment using a computer in which the questions have been precalibrated in terms of difficulty, and the examinee's response (i.e., right or wrong) to one question determines the selection of the next question.

One of the major advances in psychological testing is called **computerized adaptive testing (CAT)**, or "tailored testing" (Wainer, 2000). Here is how it works: CAT is an automated test administration system that uses a computer. The test items appear on the video display screen, and the examinee answers using the keyboard. Each test question presented is prompted by the response to the preceding question. The first question given to the examinee is of medium difficulty. If the answer given is correct, the next question selected from the item bank of questions has been precalibrated to be slightly more difficult. If the answer given to that question is wrong, the next question selected by the computer is somewhat easier. And so on.

The purpose of CAT is to get as close a match as possible between the question-difficulty level and the examinee's demonstrated ability level. In fact, by the careful calibration of question difficulty, one can infer ability level on the basis of the difficulty level of the questions answered correctly. CAT systems are based on complex mathematical models. Proponents believe that tests can be shorter (because of higher precision of measurement) and less expensive and have greater security than traditional paper-and-pencil tests. The military is the largest user of CAT systems, testing thousands of examinees monthly. Tonidandel, Quinones, and Adams (2002) reported that two-thirds of all military recruits were assessed via a CAT version of the ASVAB. In an example of CAT used in the private sector, Overton et al. (1997) found their CAT system achieved greater test security than traditional paper-and-pencil tests. Additionally, traditional academic tests like the Graduate Record Exam (GRE) are now available for applicants using an online CAT system. An added benefit is that the results of the test are available to the applicant immediately upon completion of the test.

CAT systems will never completely replace traditional testing, but they do represent the cutting edge of psychological assessment (Meijer & Nering, 1999). Computers have made possible great advances in science, as evidenced in I/O psychology by this major breakthrough in testing. Furthermore, with the creation of national information networks, the traditional practice of using psychological tests late in the selection process may change as it becomes possible to have access to test results at the time a job application is made. There have also been recent technical advances in the use of pen-based notebook computer testing (Overton et al., 1996).

Testing on the Internet

In recent years the biggest change in psychological testing is in the way tests are administered and scored. Psychological assessment is moving inexorably from paper-and-pencil testing to online computer testing. As Thompson et al. (2003) described, the movement "from paper to pixels" is affecting all phases of assessment. As a society we are growing more comfortable with computer-based services in life and that includes psychological assessment. Naglieri et al. (2004) described how the internet offers a faster and cheaper means of testing. Test publishers can download new tests to secure testing sites in a matter of moments. Updating a test is also much easier because there is no need to print new tests, answer keys, or manuals. Nevertheless, computer-based testing produces potential problems as well. One is test security and whether test content can be compromised. A second issue pertains to proctoring. With unproctored web-based testing, the applicant completes the test from any location with internet access and without direct supervision of a test administrator. With proctored web-based testing, the applicant must complete the test in the presence of a test administrator, usually at a company-sponsored location. Ployhart et al. (2003) reported that many organizations will accept the results from only proctored web-based testing. As increasingly more testing is done online, our profession will have to respond to a new range of issues associated with this means of assessment. The growing use of internet testing has prompted researchers to compare internet tests to traditional paper-and-pencil tests. Tippins et al. (2006) stated that one of the goals of internet testing is to reduce the time between candidate assessment and the personnel selection decision. As such, a candidate can take a test on the internet at any time, and in so doing, the test taking would not be proctored by a test administrator. The authors raised serious questions about unproctored internet testing, including whether the candidate had others assist in answering the questions. In short, unproctored internet testing provides opportunities for forms of cheating that are less likely with paper-and-pencil tests.

Potosky and Bobko (2004) examined many practical differences between internet and paper-and-pencil testing. For example, in a paper-and-pencil test the candidates can flip through the pages and answer questions in whatever order they wish. "Flipping the pages" in a paper-and-pencil test is replaced with "scrolling up and down" in an internet test, which can take more time. Furthermore, some computer-based tests do not allow the next set of questions to be presented until all of the first set have been answered. Thus, paper-and-pencil tests are generally more conducive to "skipping around" the questions than are internet tests. The authors believe this difference can influence the scores on the two types of tests, with possible implications for selection decisions based on these test scores.

The Value of Testing

As Haney (1981) observed, society has tended to imbue psychological tests with some arcane mystical powers, which, as the evidence reviewed in this chapter indicates, is totally unwarranted. There is nothing mysterious about psychological tests; they are merely tools to help us make better decisions than we could make without them. The

"Let's put it this way—if you can find a village without an idiot, you've got yourself a job."

Reprinted with permission from *The Industrial-Organizational Psychologist*

psychological testing profession has a large number of critics. The criticism relates more to the inappropriate use of good tests than to poor quality. For example, because tests of vocational interest were not originally intended to predict managerial success, we really shouldn't be too surprised or unhappy when we find they do not. Testing has been oversold as a solution to problems. Many people have decried the "tyranny of testing"—the fact that critical decisions (say, entrance into a college or professional school) that affect an entire lifetime are based on a single test. Testing has its place in our repertoire of diagnostic instruments; tests should help us meet our needs and not be the master of our decisions. This is sound advice that psychologists have long advocated. However, it is advice that both the developers and users of psychological tests have occasionally ignored or forgotten. It is also the case that many people don't like to be tested, find the process intimidating or anxiety-producing, and are highly concerned about what use will be made of their test results. Tenopyr (1998) described organized efforts by some groups of people opposed to testing to get laws passed pertaining to the legal rights of test takers, bearing such titles as "The Test Takers' Bill of Rights." We cannot seriously hope to abolish testing in society because the alternative to testing is not testing at all. What we can strive to accomplish is to make testing highly accurate and fair to all parties concerned.

In a major review of psychological testing, Meyer et al. (2001) concluded that psychological test validity is compelling and comparable to medical test validity. In practice we often get validity coefficients in the .10–.40 range. If we compare these correlations with the perfect upper limit of 1.00, we may feel disappointed with our results. Meyer et al. stated:

> However, perfect associations are never encountered in applied psychological research, making this benchmark unrealistic. Second, it is easy to implicitly compare validity correlations with reliability coefficients, because the latter are frequently reported in the literature. However, reliability coefficients (which are often in the range of $r = .70$ or higher) evaluate only the correspondence between a variable and itself. As a result, they cannot provide a reasonable standard for evaluating the association between two distinct real-world variables. (pp. 132–133)

What we have learned about psychological tests from an I/O perspective is that some tests are useful in forecasting job success and others are not. As an entire class of predictors, psychological tests have been moderately predictive of job performance. Yet some authors believe that, all things considered, psychological tests have outperformed all other types of predictors across the full spectrum of jobs. Single-validity coefficients greater than .50 are as unusual today as they were in the early years of testing. Although test validity coefficients are not as high as we would like, it is unfair to condemn tests as useless. Also, keep in mind that validity coefficients are a function of both the predictor and the criterion. A poorly defined and constructed criterion will produce low validity coefficients no matter what the predictor is like. Because of the limited predictive power of tests, psychologists have had to look elsewhere for forecasters of job performance. The balance of this chapter will examine other predictors that psychologists have investigated.

Interviews

Posthuma, Morgeson, and Campion (2002) described an employment interview as a social interaction between the interviewer and applicant. As such, various social factors can influence the outcome of the interview, quite apart from the objective qualifications of the applicant. Examples include the degree of similarity between the interviewer and applicant (in terms of gender, race, and attitudes), nonverbal behavior (smiling, head nodding, hand gestures), and verbal cues (pitch, speech rate, pauses, and amplitude variability). Because of these additional sources of variance in the outcome of the interview (hire or reject), interviews are a more dynamic means of assessment than traditional testing (e.g., a test of general mental ability). Thus information derived from a job analysis should be the primary basis for the questions posed in an interview. Because interviews are used so often in employment decisions, they have attracted considerable research interest among I/O psychologists.

Degree of Structure

Interviews can be classified along a continuum of structure, where *structure* refers to the amount of procedural variability. In a highly **unstructured interview**, the interviewer may ask each applicant different questions. For example, one applicant may be asked to describe previous jobs held and duties performed, whereas another applicant may be asked to describe career goals and interests. In a highly **structured interview**,

Unstructured interview
A format for the job interview in which the questions are different across all candidates. Often contrasted with the structured interview.

Structured interview
A format for the job interview in which the questions are consistent across all candidates. Often contrasted with the unstructured interview.

the interviewer asks standard questions of all job applicants. Whatever the focus of the questions (e.g., past work experiences or future career goals), they are posed to all applicants in a similar fashion. It is not unusual for the interviewer to use a standardized rating scale to assess the answers given by each candidate. In reality, most employment interviews fall somewhere along the continuum between the highly unstructured and the highly structured interview. However, research results indicate a higher validity for the structured interview than for the unstructured type. Huffcutt et al. (2001) determined that the predictor constructs most often assessed by interviewers of candidates were personality traits (conscientiousness, agreeableness, etc.) and applied social skills (interpersonal relations, team focus, etc.). However, highly unstructured and highly structured interviews do not tend to measure the same constructs. In particular, highly unstructured interviews often focus more on constructs such as general intelligence, education, work experience, and interests, whereas highly structured interviews often focus more on constructs such as job knowledge, interpersonal and social skills, and problem solving.

Campion, Palmer, and Campion (1997) examined procedures to increase the degree of structure in the interview. Among their suggestions are to base the questions on an analysis of the job, to limit prompting by the interviewer, to rate the answers given to each question asked, and to use multiple interviewers per candidate. Campion et al. reported that while some techniques increase structure, such as limiting prompting and not accepting any questions from the applicant, neither the interviewer nor the applicant likes being so constrained. Therefore, although these procedures reduce the likelihood that different applicants are treated unequally in the interview, they also produce negative reactions among the participants. The preference for more unstructured interviews by participants was confirmed by Kohn and Dipboye (1998). In a study that examined interview structure and litigation outcomes, Williamson et al. (1997) reported that organizations were more likely to win when their interviews were job related (e.g., the interviewer was familiar with the job requirements) and based on standardized administration (e.g., minimal interviewer discretion) and the interviewer's decision was reviewed by a superior. Furthermore, research on the validity of structured interviews (e.g., Cortina et al., 2000) indicated that they predict job performance as well as mental ability. Increasing the degree of structure in the interview is also associated with greater fairness among minority group members (Huffcutt & Roth, 1998; Moscoso, 2000).

Despite these reasons for using a structured interview, Dipboye (1997) reported there are also reasons that unstructured interviews have value to the organization. A primary reason is that interviews serve purposes besides assessing the candidate's suitability for a job. They also provide an opportunity for the interviewer to convey information about the organization, its values, and its culture. The unstructured interview can be akin to a ritual conveying to others the important attributes of the organization and sending the message that great care is being taken to select a qualified applicant. Dipboye concluded that a semistructured interview procedure may be the best compromise for meeting the multiple purposes of employment interviews.

Maurer and Salomon (2006) reported that candidates can be successfully coached to perform well in an employment interview. Given the popularity of the employment interview in personnel selection, candidates may be well served by investing time and effort in how to be more favorably assessed in the interview.

Situational Interviews

Situational interview
A type of job interview in which candidates are presented with a problem and asked how they would respond to it.

Situational interviews present the applicant with a situation and ask for a description of the actions he or she would take in that situation. Some situational interviews focus on hypothetical, future-oriented contexts in which the applicants are asked how they would respond if they were confronted with these problems. Other situational interviews focus on how the applicants have handled situations in the past that required the skills and abilities necessary for effective performance on the job. Pulakos and Schmitt (1995) referred to the latter type of interviews as "experience-based," and they offered the following examples to illustrate differences in focus (p. 292):

- *Experience-based question*: Think about a time when you had to motivate an employee to perform a job task that he or she disliked but that you needed the individual to do. How did you handle that situation?

- *Situational question*: Suppose you were working with an employee who you knew greatly disliked performing a particular job task. You were in a situation where you needed this task completed, and this employee was the only one available to assist you. What would you do to motivate the employee to perform the task?

A candidate's responses to such questions are typically scored on the type of scale shown in Figure 4-4. The interviewer has to use his or her best judgment to evaluate the candidate's response because the question clearly has no one correct answer. Thus the situational judgment interview is the oral counterpart of the written situational judgment test. Each candidate responds to several such situational questions, and the answers to each question might be evaluated on different dimensions, such as "Taking Initiative" and "Problem Diagnosis."

Low	*Medium*	*High*
Responses showed limited awareness of possible problem issues likely to be confronted. Responses were relatively simplistic, without much apparent thought given to the situation.	Responses suggested considerable awareness of possible issues likely to be confronted. Responses were based on a reasonable consideration of the issues present in the situation.	Responses indicated a high level of awareness of possible issues likely to be confronted. Responses were based on extensive and thoughtful consideration of the issues present in the situation.
1	2 3 4	5

Figure 4-4   *Example of rating scale for scoring a situational interview*

The situational interview has grown in frequency of use and has been found particularly helpful in evaluating candidates for supervisory jobs. Latham and Finnegan (1993) reported that the use of the situational interview as a selection method was a source of pride among those who passed and were hired. The current employees who had gone through it themselves believed the people being hired were well qualified for the job. There is also recent evidence (Weekley & Jones, 1997) that situational judgments can be assessed through video-based tests. Thus the use of situational contexts, which was originally developed through the interview format, is now being expanded with different technologies. Although visual and vocal cues in an interview have been found to be predictive of job success (DeGroot & Motowidlo, 1999), research shows that interviews have validity even when the interviewer and candidate don't meet in person. Schmidt and Rader (1999) reported a validity coefficient of .40 for tape-recorded interviews that are scored based on a transcript of a telephone interview.

McDaniel et al. (1994) estimated the criterion-related validity of the interview to predict job performance to be .39. This level of predictive accuracy is less than for tests of general mental ability but superior to some other nontest predictors of job performance. The interview is still the most commonly used personnel selection methods. Arvey and Campion (1982) postulated three reasons for its persistent use. First, the interview really is more valid than research studies indicate. Due to methodological problems and limitations in our research, however, we can't demonstrate how valid it actually is (Dreher, Ash, & Hancock, 1988). Second, people generally place confidence in highly fallible interview judgments; that is, we are not good judges of people, but we think we are—a phenomenon called the *illusion of validity*. Finally, the interview serves other personnel functions unrelated to employee selection, such as selling candidates on the value of the job and of the organization as an attractive employer. Judge, Higgins, and Cable (2000) proposed that the interview is perceived to be an effective means for both the candidate and the organization to gauge the degree of fit or congruence between them, which in large part accounts for the popularity of the method. Whatever the reasons for the interview's popularity, few companies are willing to do something as important as extending a job offer without first seeing a person "in the flesh" (see The Changing Nature of Work: Video-Interpretive Assessment).

The Changing Nature of Work: Video-Interpretive Assessment

Research reveals that the most commonly used method of personnel selection is the interview. Companies are usually reluctant to offer a job to candidates without first meeting with them. We place a high degree of confidence in our ability to judge people after we have met them. As discussed by Posthuma, Morgeson, and Campion (2002), the face-to-face interview is a social exchange between the interviewer and the candidate, with both parties drawing upon facial, verbal, and nonverbal cues in their assessment of each other. A telephone interview is based on only verbal cues. With the advent of video-interactive technology, however, we can approximate the face-to-face interview without the two parties ever actually meeting in person. We do not have much scientific evidence on the validity or social acceptability of this type of interview format, yet it is being used with increasing frequency in the work world. How much confidence would you have in *accepting* a job offer from an employer based on this technology? Alternatively, as an employer, how much confidence would you have in *offering* a job to a candidate without ever having met the individual in person? Would it depend on the job level? That is, would such a technique be more acceptable for lower-level than for upper-level jobs? In any event, we have long felt that "seeing is believing" in establishing employment relationships. The changing nature of work technologies now permits "pseudo-seeing."

Assessment Centers

Assessment center
A technique for assessing job candidates in a specific location using a series of structured, group-oriented exercises that are evaluated by raters.

Assessment centers involve evaluating job candidates, typically for managerial-level jobs, using several methods and raters. They were originally developed by researchers at AT&T who were interested in studying the lives of managers over the full span of their careers. **Assessment centers** are a group-oriented, standardized series of activities that provide a basis for judgments or predictions of human behaviors believed or known to be relevant to work performed in an organizational setting. They may be a physical part of some organizations, such as special rooms designed for the purpose. They may also be located in a conference center away from the normal workplace. Because these centers are expensive, they have been used mainly by large organizations; however, consulting firms also offer assessment center appraisals for smaller companies.

Here are four characteristics of the assessment center approach:

1. Those individuals selected to attend the center (the assessees) are usually management-level personnel that the company wants to evaluate for possible selection, promotion, or training. Thus assessment centers can be used to assess both job applicants for hire and current employees for possible advancement.

2. Assessees are evaluated in groups of 10 to 20. They may be divided into smaller groups for various exercises, but the basic strategy is to appraise individuals against the performance of others in the group.

3. Several raters (the assessors) do the evaluation. They work in teams and collectively or individually recommend personnel action (for example, selection, promotion). Assessors may be psychologists, but usually they are company employees unfamiliar with the assessees. They are often trained in how to appraise performance. The training may last from several hours to a few days.

4. A wide variety of performance appraisal methods are used. Many involve group exercises—for example, leaderless group discussions in which leaders "emerge" through their degree of participation in the exercise. Other methods include personality inventories, personal history information forms, and interviews. The program typically takes from one to several days.

Given the variety of tests, the assessee provides substantial information about his or her performance. Raters evaluate the assessees on a number of performance dimensions judged relevant for the job in question. These dimensions involve leadership, decision making, practical judgment, and interpersonal relations skills—the typical performance dimensions for managerial jobs. Based on these evaluations, the assessors prepare a summary report for each assessee and then feed back portions of the report to the assessee. Raters forward their recommendations for personnel action to the organization for review and consideration. When giving feedback to assessees about their performance in the assessment center, there is a debate about whether the feedback should be situation-based (e.g., "You didn't do well in the work delegation case") or trait-based (e.g., "You excessively seek to avoid conflict"). Lievens, Chasteen, Day, and Christianson (2006) recommended combining the two by identifying the specific situations that activate a given trait (e.g., "You score poorly in situations where you try to please everyone").

Klimoski and Strickland (1977) proposed a source of bias in assessment center evaluation. They contended that assessment center evaluations are predictive because both assessors and company supervisors hold common stereotypes of the effective employee. Assessors give higher evaluations to those who "look" like good management talent, and supervisors give higher evaluations to those who "look" like good "company" people. If the two sets of stereotypes are held in common, then (biased) assessment center evaluations correlate with (biased) job performance evaluations. The danger is that organizations may hire and promote those who fit the image of the successful employee. As Lievens and Klimoski (2001) stated, "Assessors do not judge assessees exclusively on the basis of the prescribed dimensions but also take into account the fit of the applicants into the culture of the organization" (p. 259). The long-term result is an organization staffed with people who are mirror images of one another. Opportunity is greatly limited for creative people who "don't fit the mold" but who might be effective if given the chance.

Work Samples and Situational Exercises

Work Samples

Work samples
A type of personnel selection test in which the candidate demonstrates proficiency on a task representative of the work performed in the job.

Motowidlo, Hanson, and Crafts (1997) classified **work samples** as "high-fidelity simulations," where *fidelity* refers to the level of realism in the assessment. A literal description of a work sample is that the candidate is asked to perform a representative sample of the work done on the job, such as using a word processor, driving a forklift, or drafting a blueprint.

A classic example of a work sample was reported by Campion (1972), who wanted to develop a predictor of job success for mechanics. Using job analysis techniques, he learned that the mechanic's job was defined by success in the use of tools, accuracy of work, and overall mechanical ability. He then designed tasks that would show an applicant's performance in these three areas. Through the cooperation of job incumbents, he designed a work sample that involved such typical tasks as installing pulleys and repairing gearboxes. The steps necessary to perform these tasks correctly were identified and given numerical values according to their appropriateness (for example, 10 points for aligning a motor with a dial indicator, 1 point for aligning it by feeling the motor, 0 points for just looking at the motor). Campion used a concurrent criterion-related validity design, and each mechanic in the shop took the work sample. Their scores were correlated with the criterion of supervisor ratings of their job performance. The validity of the work sample was excellent: it had a coefficient of .66 with use of tools, .42 with accuracy of work, and .46 with overall mechanical ability. Campion showed that there was a substantial relationship between how well mechanics performed on the work sample and how well they performed on the job. In general, work samples are among the most valid means of personnel selection.

But work samples do have limitations (Callinan & Robertson, 2000). First, they are effective primarily in blue-collar jobs that involve either the mechanical trades (for example, mechanics, carpenters, and electricians) or the manipulation of objects. They are not very effective when the job involves working with people rather than things. Second, work samples assess what a person can do; they don't assess potential. They seem best suited to evaluating experienced workers rather than trainees. Finally, work samples are time-consuming and costly to administer. Because they are individual tests, they require extensive supervision and monitoring. Few work samples are designed to be completed in less than one hour. If there are 100 applicants to fill 5 jobs, it may not be worthwhile to give a work sample to all applicants. Perhaps the applicant pool can be reduced with some other selection instrument (for example, a review of previous work history). Yet, despite their limitations, work samples are useful in personnel selection.

Truxillo, Donahue, and Kuang (2004) reported that job applicants favor work samples as a means of assessment because they exhibit a strong relationship to job content, appear to be both necessary and fair, and are administered in a non–paper-and-pencil format. Roth, Bobko, and McFarland (2005) reported that work samples continue to have appeal as a personnel selection method because of such factors as favorable applicant reactions and reduced bias compared to paper-and-pencil tests. However, the authors cautioned that the validity of work samples, while still high, may not be as generalizable as previous research has suggested.

Situational Exercises

Situational exercise
A method of assessment in which examinees are presented with a problem and asked how they would respond to it.

Situational exercises are roughly the white-collar counterpart of work samples; that is, they are used mainly to select people for managerial and professional jobs. Unlike work samples, which are designed to be replicas of the job, situational exercises mirror only part of the job. Accordingly, Motowidlo, Hanson, and Crafts (1997) referred to them as "low-fidelity simulations" because they present applicants with only a description of the work problem and require them to describe how they would deal with it.

Situational exercises involve a family of tests that assess problem-solving ability. Two examples are the In-Basket Test and the Leaderless Group Discussion. The In-Basket Test has applicants sort through an in-basket of things to do. The contents are carefully designed letters, memos, brief reports, and the like that require the applicant's immediate attention and response. The applicant goes through the contents of the basket and takes the appropriate action to solve the problems presented, such as making a phone call, writing a letter, or calling a meeting. Observers score the applicant on such factors as productivity (how much work got done) and problem-solving effectiveness (versatility in resolving problems). The In-Basket Test is predictive of the job performance of managers and executives, a traditionally difficult group of employees to select. But a major problem with the test is that it takes up to three hours and, like a work sample, is an individual test. If there are many applicants, too much time is needed to administer the test. Schippmann, Prien, and Katz (1990) reported the typical validity coefficient for the In-Basket Test is approximately .25.

In a Leaderless Group Discussion (LGD), a group of applicants (normally, two to eight) engage in a job-related discussion in which no spokesperson or group leader has been named. Raters observe and assess each applicant on such factors as individual prominence, group goal facilitation, and sociability. Scores on these factors are then used as the basis for hiring. The reliability of the LGD increases with the number of people in the group. The typical validity coefficient is in the .15–.35 range.

Although neither the In-Basket Test nor the LGD has as high a validity as a typical work sample, remember that the criterion of success for a manager is usually more difficult to define. The lower validities in the selection of managerial personnel are as attributable to problems with the criterion and its proper articulation as anything else.

As Motowidlo et al. noted, although high-fidelity simulations (like work samples) are often highly valid, they are also time-consuming to administer and costly to develop. However, the converse is also undesirable—a selection method that is inexpensive but also has little predictive accuracy. The authors recommend low-fidelity simulations as a reasonable compromise between the twin goals of high validity and low cost.

Biographical Information

The theory of using biographical information as a method of personnel selection is based on our development as individuals. Our lives represent a series of experiences, events, and choices that define our development. Past and current events shape our behavior patterns, attitudes, and values. Because there is consistency in our behaviors, attitudes, and values, an assessment of these factors from our past experiences should be predictive of such experiences in the future. **Biographical information** assesses constructs that shape our behavior, such as sociability and ambition. To the extent that these constructs are predictive of future job performance, through biographical information we assess previous life experiences that were manifestations of these constructs.

Biographical information
A method of assessing individuals in which information pertaining to past activities, interests, and behaviors in their lives is considered.

Biographical information is frequently recorded on an application blank. The application blank, in turn, can be used as a selection device on the basis of the information presented. The questions asked on the application blank are predictive of job performance criteria. Mael (1991) recommended that all biographical questions pertain to historical events in the person's life, as opposed to questions about behavioral intentions or presumed behavior in a hypothetical situation. Table 4-3 lists 16 dimensions

Table 4-3   *Sixteen biographical information dimensions*

Dimension	Example Item
Dealing with people	
1. Sociability	Volunteer with service groups
2. Agreeableness/cooperation	Argue a lot compared with others
3. Tolerant	Response to people breaking rules
4. Good impression	What a person wears is important
Outlook	
5. Calmness	Often in a hurry
6. Resistance to stress	Time to recover from disappointments
7. Optimism	Think there is some good in everyone
Responsibility/dependability	
8. Responsibility	Supervision in previous jobs
9. Concentration	Importance of quiet surroundings at work
10. Work ethic	Percent of spending money earned in high school
Other	
11. Satisfaction with life	How happy in general
12. Need for achievement	Ranking in previous job
13. Parental influence	Mother worked outside home when young
14. Educational history	Grades in math
15. Job history	Likes/dislikes in previous job
16. Demographic	Number in family

Adapted with permission from "From Dustbowl Empiricism to Rational Constructs in Biographical Data," by L. F. Schoenfeldt, 1999, *Human Resource Management Review, 9*, pp. 147–167. Copyright © 1999.

of biographical information and an example item for each dimension, as reported by Schoenfeldt (1999).

Although using biographical information for personnel selection has generated considerable interest on the part of researchers, there are concerns about fairness, legal issues, and honesty of responses. One aspect of the fairness problem is equal access by all respondents to the behavior or experience being questioned. For example, assume the response to a question about participation in high school football is found to be predictive of subsequent performance on a job. The strategy would then be to include this question on an application blank to evaluate job candidates. The problem is that only males are allowed to play high school football, thereby prohibiting females from having access to this type of experience. Female job applicants would be disadvantaged in being evaluated by this question. The problem is not that females *didn't* have this experience but that they *couldn't* have it (i.e., females didn't have equal access). The "solution" to this problem is not to ask different questions of male and female applicants because laws governing fair employment practice emphasize consistency of treatment to all job applicants.

Another concern is that questions should not be invasive. Invasiveness addresses whether the respondent will consider the item content to be an invasion of his or her privacy. As Nickels (1994) noted, asking questions about certain types of life experiences that are generally regarded as private matters (e.g., religious beliefs) is off limits for assessment. Mael, Connerly, and Morath (1996) reported two types of biodata questions that are regarded as intrusive: a question that refers to an event that could have been explained away if the applicant had the chance to do so, and a question with a response that does not reflect the type of person the respondent has since become. Questions that are perceived to invade privacy invite litigation against the hiring organization by job applicants (see Field Note 2).

A final issue is the question of fakability: To what extent do individuals distort their responses to create a more socially desirable impression? Research (Becker & Colquitt, 1992; Kluger, Reilly, & Russell, 1991) revealed that faking does occur in responses to certain types of questions. The questions most likely to be faked in a socially desirable direction are those that are difficult to verify for accuracy and have the appearance of being highly relevant to the job. Stokes and Cooper (2004) proposed a way to control faking by asking questions that have no obvious desired answer. One such item is: "I frequently help coworkers with their tasks so they can meet their deadlines even when I have not finished my assigned task" (p. 262).

Despite these limitations, using biographical information is a logically defensible strategy in personnel selection. Mumford and Stokes (1992) portrayed biographical information as revealing consistent patterns of behavior that are interwoven throughout our lives. By assessing what applicants have done, we can gain considerable insight into what they will do.

Letters of Recommendation

One of the most commonly used and least valid of all predictors is the letter of recommendation. Letters of recommendation and reference checks are as widespread in personnel selection as the interview and the application blank. Unfortunately, they often

Field Note 2: Inappropriate Question?

Biographical items sometimes lack content validity and face validity for the job in question even though they manifest empirical criterion-related validity. The seeming irrelevance of biographical questions is always a concern in personnel selection. Here is a case in point.

A city had developed a biographical inventory that was to be used along with some psychological tests to evaluate police officers for promotion to police detectives. All the questions in the biographical inventory were predictive of job performance as a detective, as determined by a criterion-related validity study. One of the questions on the inventory was: "Did you have sexual intercourse for the first time before the age of 16?" Some police officers who took this promotional exam and failed it sued the city for asking such a question in an employment test, a question so obviously lacking face validity. The officers said the question had absolutely no relevance to the conduct of a detective's job, and furthermore it was an in-

vasion of their privacy. They had been denied a detective's job because of a totally inappropriate question, and therefore they wanted the entire test results thrown out.

The case was heard at the district court. The judge ruled in favor of the officers, saying that the question totally lacked content validity and was an invasion of their privacy. Therefore the officers should be reconsidered for promotion to detective. The city appealed the verdict to the state supreme court. The supreme court reversed the lower court ruling and allowed the test results to stand, meaning the officers would not get promoted. The state supreme court based its decision on the grounds that the answer to that question did correlate with job performance as a detective. From a practical and legal standpoint, it is advisable to avoid asking such invasive questions in the first place, even though in this case a lengthy legal battle ultimately resulted in a decision favorable to the city.

lack comparable validity. Letters of recommendation are usually written on behalf of an applicant by a current employer, professional associate, or personal friend. The respondent rates the applicant on such dimensions as leadership ability and written and oral communication skills. The responses are then used as a basis for hiring.

Letters of recommendation are one of the least accurate forecasters of job performance. Some people even make recommendations that have an inverse relationship with the criterion; that is, if the applicant is recommended for hire, the company would do best to reject him or her! One of the biggest problems with letters of recommendation is their restricted range. As you might expect, almost all letters of recommendation are positive. Most often, the applicants themselves choose who will write the letters, so it isn't surprising that they pick people who will make them look good. Because of this restriction (that is, almost all applicants are described positively), the lack of predictive ability of the letter of recommendation is not unexpected.

Although a few studies using specially constructed evaluation forms have reported moderate validity (e.g., McCarthy & Goffin, 2001), the typical validity coefficient is estimated to be .13. Therefore letters of recommendation should not be taken too

Field Note 3: Intentional Deception in Letters of Recommendation

I was the director of a graduate program to which about 100 students seek admission annually. One of the requirements for admission is a letter of recommendation. Over the years I received several memorable letters of recommendation, but on one occasion I received a letter (actually, two) that clearly illustrates why such letters have little predictive value. This letter came from the president of a foreign university where the student was enrolled. It made the student sound incredibly strong academically: the class valedictorian, the only recipient of the native king's fellowship program, the only student who received a special citation from the university, and so forth. Needless to say, I was most impressed by this letter.

About two weeks later I got another application for admission from a second student from that same university. Accompanying this application was another letter supposedly written by the university president. This letter was identical to the first. The only difference was the name of the student typed at the top of the letter. Thus both students had been the class valedictorian, both were the only recipient of the fellowship, and so on.

I then called a different academic department and discovered that it had received the identical letter on yet a third student from that university who was applying for graduate work in that department. What we had was literally a form letter in which every student in the university was being described, word for word, as the best. The university apparently provided this "service" to its students seeking admission to graduate schools in the United States. Such attempts at deception do nothing to portray fairly a candidate's strengths and weaknesses—and most certainly do not enhance the validity of the letter of recommendation as a personnel selection method.

seriously in making personnel selection decisions. The only major exception to this statement is the following condition: on those rare occasions when the applicant is described in negative terms (even if only mildly), the letter is usually indicative of future problems on the job. Those types of letters should be taken seriously. On average, though, very few letters of recommendation contain nonsupportive information about an applicant (see Field Note 3).

Drug Testing

Drug testing
A method of assessment typically based on an analysis of urine that is used to detect illicit drug use by the candidate.

Drug testing is the popular term for efforts to detect *substance abuse*, the use of illegal drugs and the improper and illegal use of prescription and over-the-counter medications, alcohol, and other chemical compounds. Substance abuse is a major global problem that has far-reaching societal, moral, and economic consequences. The role that I/O psychology plays in this vast and complex picture is to detect substance abuse in the workplace. Employees who engage in substance abuse jeopardize not only their own welfare but also potentially the welfare of fellow employees and other individuals.

I/O psychologists are involved in screening out substance abusers among both job applicants and current employees.

Unlike other forms of assessment used by I/O psychologists that involve estimates of cognitive or motor abilities, drug testing embraces chemical assessments. The method of assessment is typically based on a urine sample (hair samples can also be used). The rationale is that the test will reveal the presence of drugs in a person's urine. Therefore a sample of urine is treated with chemicals that will indicate the presence of drugs if they have been ingested by the person. There are two basic types of assessments. A screening test assesses the potential presence of a wide variety of chemicals. A confirmation test on the same sample identifies the presence of chemicals suggested by the initial screening test. I/O psychologists are not directly involved with these tests because they are performed in chemical laboratories by individuals with special technical training. The profession of I/O psychology does become involved in drug testing because it assesses suitability for employment, with concomitant concerns about the reliability, validity, legality, and cost of these tests.

Drug abuse issues are very complex. The reliability of the chemical tests is much higher than the reliability of traditional paper-and-pencil psychological assessments. However, the reliability is not perfect, which means that different conclusions can be drawn about substance abuse depending on the laboratory that conducts the testing. Questions of validity are more problematic. The accurate detection of drug use varies as a function of the type of drug involved because some drugs remain in our systems for days and others remain for weeks. Thus the timing of taking the urine sample is critical. It is also possible that diet can falsely influence the results of a drug test. For example, eating poppy-seed cake may trigger a confirmatory response to heroin tests because heroin is derived from poppy seeds. The legality of drug testing is also highly controversial. Critics of drug testing contend it violates the U.S. Constitution with regard to unreasonable search and seizure, self-incrimination, and the right to privacy. It is also a matter of debate which jobs should be subject to drug testing. Some people argue for routine drug testing; others say drug testing should be limited to jobs that potentially affect the lives of others (for example, transportation workers). Yet another issue is the criteria for intoxication and performance impairment. What dose of a drug constitutes a level that would impair job performance? Thus the validity of drug tests for predicting job performance may well vary by type of job and the criteria of job performance. Drug use may be a valid predictor of accidents among truck drivers or construction workers, but may not predict gradations of successful job performance among secretaries. Finally, there is the matter of cost. Screening tests cost about $25 per specimen, but confirmatory tests can cost up to $100 per specimen. These costs will eventually have to be passed on to consumers as part of the price they pay for having their goods and services rendered by a drug-free workforce. A major investigation by the National Research Council (Normand, Lempert, & O'Brien, 1994) underscored the particular danger of unfairness to job applicants who are falsely classified as drug users. Drug testing thus must balance the economic goals of workforce productivity with individual rights to fair treatment in the workplace.

Normand, Salyards, and Mahoney (1990) conducted a study on the effects of drug testing and reported sobering results. A total of 5,465 job applicants were tested for the use of illicit drugs. After 1.3 years of employment, employees who tested positive for illicit drugs had an absenteeism rate 59.3% higher than employees who tested negative. The involuntary turnover rate (namely, employees who were fired) was 47% higher among drug users than nonusers. The estimated cost savings of screening out drug users in reducing absenteeism and turnover for one cohort of new employees was $52,750,000. This figure does not reflect the compounded savings derived by cohorts of new employees added each year the drug-testing program is in existence.

As can be seen, drug testing is an exceedingly complex and controversial issue. Although the analysis of urine is beyond the purview of I/O psychology, making decisions about an applicant's suitability for employment is not. I/O psychology has been drawn into a complicated web of issues that affects all of society. Our profession must now address problems unimaginable a century ago.

Controversial Methods of Assessment

This final section is reserved for three controversial methods of assessing job applicants.

Polygraphy or Lie Detection

Polygraph
An instrument that assesses responses of an individual's central nervous system (heart rate, breathing, perspiration, etc.) that supposedly indicate giving false responses to questions.

A **polygraph** is an instrument that measures responses of the autonomic nervous system—physiological reactions of the body such as heart rate and perspiration. In theory these autonomic responses will "give you away" when you are telling a lie. The polygraph is attached to the body with electronic sensors for detecting the physiological reactions. Polygraphs are used more to evaluate people charged with criminal activity in a *post hoc* fashion (for example, after a robbery within a company has occurred) than to select people for a job, although it is used in the latter capacity as well.

Is a polygraph foolproof? No. People can appear to be innocent of any wrongdoing according to the polygraph but in fact be guilty of misconduct. Research conducted by the Federal Bureau of Investigation (Podlesny & Truslow, 1993) based on a crime simulation reported that the polygraph correctly identified 84.7% of the guilty group and 94.7% of the innocent group. Bashore and Rapp (1993) suggested that alternative methods that measure brain electrical activity can be used to complement the polygraph and would be particularly effective in detecting people who possess information but are attempting to conceal it (i.e., the guilty group). Countermeasures are anything that a person might do in an effort to defeat or distort a polygraph examination. It is unknown how effective countermeasures are because funding for research on countermeasures is limited to the Department of Defense Polygraph Institute and all findings from such research are classified (Honts & Amato, 2002). In 1988 President Ronald Reagan signed into law a bill banning the widespread use of polygraphs for preemployment screening by private-sector employers. However, as Honts (1991) reported, polygraph use by the federal government continues to grow. It is used extensively in the hiring process of government agencies involved in national security as well as in law enforcement. The U.S. Joint Security Commission offered the following summation of the polygraph as a method of personnel selection. "Despite the controversy, after carefully weighing the pros and cons, the Commission concludes that with appropriate standardization, increased oversight, and training to prevent abuses, the polygraph program should be retained. In the Central Intelligence Agency and the National Security Agency, the polygraph has evolved to become the single most important aspect of their employment and personnel security programs" (Krapohl, 2002, p. 232).

Graphology

Graphology
A method of assessment in which characteristics of a person's handwriting are evaluated and interpreted.

Graphology, or handwriting analysis, is popular in France as a selection method. Here is how it works: a person trained in handwriting analysis (called a *graphologist*) examines a sample of a candidate's handwriting. Based on such factors as the specific formation of letters, the slant and size of the writing, and how hard the person presses the pen or pencil on the paper, the graphologist makes an assessment of the candidate's personality. This personality assessment is then correlated with criteria of job success.

Rafaeli and Klimoski (1983) had 20 graphologists analyze handwriting and then correlated their assessments with three types of criteria: supervisory ratings, self-ratings, and sales production. Although the authors found some evidence of inter-rater agreement (meaning the graphologists tended to base their assessments on the same facets of handwriting), the handwriting assessments did not correlate with any criteria. Ben-Shakhar et al. (1986) reported that graphologists did not perform significantly better than chance in predicting the job performance of bank employees. Graphology has been found to be predictive of affective states such as stress (Keinan & Eilat-Greenberg, 1993), but its ability to predict job performance has not been empirically established.

Tests of Emotional Intelligence

Recently I/O psychology has begun to address what has historically been regarded as the "soft" side of individual differences, including moods, feelings, and emotions. For many years the relevance of these constructs to the world of work were denied. They were regarded as transient disturbances to the linkages between abilities (e.g., intelligence) and performance. However, we are beginning to realize that moods, feelings, and emotions play a significant role in the workplace, just as they do in life in general. The concept of **emotional intelligence** was initially proposed by Salovey and Mayer (1990).

Emotional intelligence
A construct that reflects a person's capacity to manage emotional responses in social situations.

It is proposed that individuals differ in how they deal with their emotions, and those who effectively manage their emotions are said to be "emotionally intelligent." Some theorists believe that emotions are within the domain of intelligence, rather than viewing "emotion" and "intelligence" as independent or contradictory.

Goleman (1995) differentiated people who are high in traditional intelligence (i.e., cognitive ability) from those high in emotional intelligence as follows: people with high cognitive ability (alone) are ambitious and productive, unexpressive, detached, and emotionally bland and cold. In contrast, people who are high in emotional intelligence are socially poised, outgoing, and cheerful. They are sympathetic and caring in their relationships. They are comfortable with themselves, others, and the social environment they live in. These portraits are of extreme types, when in reality most of us are a mix of traditional and emotional intelligence. However, each construct adds separately to a person's attributes. Goleman (1995) believes "of the two, emotional intelligence adds far more of the qualities that make us more fully human" (p. 45).

Ciarrochi and Mayer (2007) described practical applications of emotional intelligence training programs; including developing interpersonal skills for professionals and leaders and improving the well-being, social skills, and grades of school children.

Perrewe and Spector (2002) stated, "Few constructs in psychology have generated as much controversy as emotional intelligence. Exaggerated claims of its importance and relevance for both life and career success have made many researchers skeptical about its value as a topic of scientific research" (p. 42). Because the concept of emotional intelligence is relatively new, we don't know a great deal about it. A few tests (e.g., Mayer, Salovey, & Caruso, 2002) of emotional intelligence have been developed, but they are not used widely in personnel selection. Furthermore, it is a matter of professional debate whether emotional intelligence is a distinct construct (Murphy, 2006) or just a new name for selected dimensions of personality. There is conceptual overlap between personality and emotions, but they are not identical. Psychology has not yet reached a verdict on the scientific status of emotional intelligence, and what it addresses is certainly not well understood within the field of I/O psychology. In an empirical study on emotional intelligence, Law, Wong, and Song (2004) reported that emotional intelligence was distinct from the Big 5 personality measures and was predictive of job performance ratings provided by supervisors. I anticipate that the relationship between emotional intelligence and job performance will be more fully explored in the near future.

Overview and Evaluation of Predictors

Personnel selection methods can be evaluated by many standards. I have identified four major standards that I think are useful in organizing all the information we have gathered about predictors.

1. *Validity* refers to the ability of the predictor to forecast criterion performance accurately. Many authorities argue that validity is the predominant evaluative standard in judging selection methods; however, the relevance of the other three standards is also substantial.

2. *Fairness* refers to the ability of the predictor to render unbiased predictions of job success across applicants in various subgroups of gender, race, age, and so on. The issue of fairness will be discussed in greater detail in Chapter 5.

3. *Applicability* refers to whether the selection method can be applied across the full range of jobs. Some predictors have wide applicability in that they appear well suited for a diverse range of jobs; other methods have particular limitations that affect their applicability.

4. The final standard is the *cost* of implementing the method. The various personnel selection methods differ markedly in their cost, which has a direct bearing on their overall value.

Table 4-4 presents 12 personnel selection methods appraised on each of the four evaluative standards. Each standard is partitioned into three levels: low, moderate, and high. This classification scheme is admittedly oversimplified, and in some cases the evaluation of a selection method did not readily lend itself to a uniform rating.

Nevertheless, this method is useful in providing a broad-brush view of many personnel selection methods.

Table 4-4   *Assessment of 12 personnel selection methods along four evaluative standards*

Selection Method	Evaluative Standards			
	Validity	Fairness	Applicability	Cost
Intelligence tests	High	Moderate	High	Low
Mechanical aptitude tests	Moderate	Moderate	Low	Low
Personality inventories	Low	High	Moderate	Moderate
Physical ability tests	High	Moderate	Low	Low
Situational judgment tests	Moderate	Moderate	High	Low
Interviews	Moderate	Moderate	High	Moderate
Assessment centers	High	High	Low	High
Work samples	High	High	Low	High
Situational exercises	Moderate	(Unknown)	Low	Moderate
Biographical information	Moderate	Moderate	High	Low
Letters of recommendation	Low	(Unknown)	High	Low
Drug tests	Moderate	High	Moderate	Moderate

Average validity coefficients in the .00–.20, .21–.40, and over .40 ranges were labeled low, moderate, and high, respectively. Selection methods that have many, some, and few problems of fairness were labeled low, moderate, and high, respectively. The applicability standard, the most difficult one to appraise on a single dimension, was classified according to the ease of using the method in terms of feasibility and generalizability across jobs. Finally, direct cost estimates were made for each selection method. Methods estimated as costing less than $25 per applicant were labeled low; $26–$50, moderate; and more than $50, high. The ideal personnel selection method would be high in validity, fairness, and applicability and low in cost. Inspection of Table 4-4 reveals that no method has an ideal profile. The 12 methods produce a series of tradeoffs among validity, fairness, applicability, and cost. This shouldn't be surprising; if there were one uniformly ideal personnel selection method, there probably would be little need to consider 11 others.

In terms of validity, the best methods are intelligence tests, work samples, assessment centers, and physical abilities tests. However, each of these methods is limited by problems with fairness, applicability, or cost. Ironically, the worst selection method in terms of validity, letters of recommendation, is one of the most frequently used. This method is characterized by high applicability and low cost, which no doubt accounts for its popularity.

Fairness refers to the likelihood that the method will have differential predictive accuracy according to membership in any group, such as gender or race. Although the issue of fairness has generated a great deal of controversy, no method is classified in Table 4-4 as having low fairness. Insufficient information is available on two of the methods (situational exercises and letters of recommendation) to render an evaluation of their fairness, but it seems unlikely they would be judged as grossly unfair. Although several methods have exhibited some fairness problems (thus warranting caution in their use), the problems are not so severe as to reject any method as a means of selecting personnel.

The applicability dimension was the most difficult to assess, and evaluation of this dimension is most subject to qualification. For example, work samples are characterized by low applicability because they are limited to only certain types of jobs (that is, jobs that involve the mechanical manipulation of objects). However, this limitation appears to be more than offset by the method's high validity and fairness. Simply put, the problem with this method is its feasibility for only a selected range of jobs. In contrast, other methods have high applicability (such as the interview) and qualify as an almost universal means of selection.

The cost dimension is perhaps the most arbitrary. Selection methods may have indirect or hidden costs—costs that were not included in their evaluation but perhaps could have been. The break points in the classification scheme are also subjective. For example, I considered a $40-per-applicant cost to be moderate; others might say it is low or high. These issues notwithstanding, one can see a full range of cost estimates in Table 4-4. Some methods do not cost much (for example, letters of recommendation), but they do not appear to be worth much either.

This chapter has examined the major types of predictors used in personnel selection. These predictors have been validated against a number of different criteria for a variety of occupational groups. Some predictors have been used more extensively than others. Furthermore, certain predictors have historically shown more validity than others. The ideal predictor would be an accurate forecaster of the criterion, equally applicable across different groups of people, and not too lengthy or costly to administer. But predictors rarely meet all these standards in practice. Furthermore their frequency of use varies across nations (see Cross-Cultural I/O Psychology: Cross-Cultural Preferences in Assessing Job Applicants).

This chapter has described the diversity of methods that organizations use to predict whether an individual will succeed on the job. All of the methods involve candidates being administered assessments (test, interview, work sample, etc.), receiving scores on those assessments, and then employers deciding whether a candidate's score profile meets the organization's standards for selection. However, there is another way that suitability for employment can be judged—an examination of work experience (Quinones, Ford, & Teachout, 1995). The logic of this selection method is captured by a quotation from the philosopher Orison Swett Marden:

> Every experience in life, everything with which we have come in contact in life, is a chisel which has been cutting away at our life statue, molding, modifying, shaping it. We are part of all we have met. Everything we have seen, heard, felt, or thought has had its hand in molding us, shaping us.

Levine, Ash, and Levine (2004) proposed three dimensions to judgments of job-related experience. *Personal attributes* are affected by exposure to work-related settings and activities. The *perceived outcome of experience* is the meaning we attach to our experiences, the perceived changes in our attributes we derive from them. Finally, *aspects of experience judged relevant and important* are determined from the perspective of the evaluation of the experience. Hiring organizations attempt to understand how past experiences of candidates will be translated into future job performance. As with all personnel selection methods, assessments of education and experience must meet federal standards for test fairness. Buster, Roth, and Bobko (2005) developed a content

Cross-Cultural I/O Psychology: *Cross-Cultural Preferences* in Assessing Job Applicants

Responding to growing interest in cross-cultural I/O psychology, several studies have examined differences across nations in the predictors used to forecast job performance. There are differences *within* countries (i.e., not all companies in a given nation use the same predictors) as well as substantial differences across nations. Newell and Tansley (2001) reported the following differences:

- Although a significant number of French companies use graphology to assess candidates, this method is rarely used elsewhere in Europe.
- Situational tests and assessment centers are used more often in the United Kingdom, Germany, and the Netherlands than in France and Belgium, and assessment centers are not used at all in Spain.
- There is a greater use of tests in France and Belgium than in the United Kingdom and Germany.
- There is somewhat greater use of letters of recommendation by British companies compared with France, Germany, and Belgium.

- In Greece selection methods are primitive and simple compared with methods used in other European countries.
- Drug testing and integrity testing are becoming popular in the United States, but they are rarely used elsewhere.
- In China selection decisions rely heavily on personal and economic information and little emphasis is placed on assessing whether the candidate has the competencies to perform the job.
- Italian companies make little use of any method except the interview.

Newell and Tansley believe that the increasing globalization of business will help diffuse knowledge about our best (valid) predictors, which will reduce the variability in how selection decisions are made across nations. However, if the different selection methods used in these countries are part of their national cultures, then their differential use will continue.

valid process for assessing education and experience-based minimum qualifications approved by federal courts.

As Tesluk and Jacobs (1998) stated, I/O psychology is just beginning to understand the linkage between work experience and future job behavior. Our discipline has much to learn about candidates who, for example, have rich and lengthy work experience yet score poorly on some form of psychological assessment. Currently we have no professionally established and accepted system for equating or even comparing assessment results with work experience.

As noted in Chapter 1, I/O psychology has entered the global era. We have become aware of business customs and practices that are considerably different from those practiced in Western cultures. These include the methods by which employees are selected and promoted. Currently in Japan personnel decisions are made, in part, on the basis of blood type. The four types of blood are O, A, B, and AB. D'Adamo (1996) offered this explanation:

> Termed *ketsu-eki-gata*, Japanese blood type analysis is serious business. Corporate managers use it to hire workers, market researchers use it to predict buying

habits, and most people use it to choose friends, romantic partners, and lifetime mates. Vending machines that offer on-the-spot blood type analysis are widespread in train stations, department stores, restaurants, and other public places. There is even a highly respected organization, the ABO Society, dedicated to helping individuals and organizations make the right decisions, consistent with blood type. . . . This happens every day in Japan—for example, when a company advertises that it is looking for Type Bs to fill middle management positions. (pp. 46–47)

Although the methods used to select employees vary across cultures, what is constant is the need for all organizations to make good personnel decisions. This process is the subject of the next chapter.

Case Study   How Do We Hire Police Officers?

Bay Ridge, a city with a population of about 125,000, experienced remarkable growth over a short time for two major reasons. First, several large industries were attracted to the area; with more jobs came more people. Second, due to a rezoning plan, several small townships were incorporated into Bay Ridge, which caused a sudden burgeoning in the city's official population. As a consequence of this growth, the city needed to expand its police force. For many years, Bay Ridge had a relatively small force and used only a brief interview to select the officers. Recently, however, there had been several complaints about the city's selection interview. Due to the complaints and the need to hire many more officers, the city council decided to abandon the old method of hiring. The city commissioned a job analysis for police officers and determined that three major factors contributed to success on the job. The next step was to develop selection measures to assess each of the three factors. The city council called a meeting with the city personnel director to get a progress report on the selection measures being proposed. Four city council members and Ron Davenport, the city personnel director, attended.

> Davenport: I'm pleased to report to you that we have made substantial progress in our study. The job analysis revealed that the following factors determine success on the police force: physical agility, sensitivity to community relations, and practical judgment. We are fairly pleased with the tests developed to assess two of the factors, although one of them is causing us some problems.
>
> Councilmember DeRosa: Would you kindly elaborate on what these factors mean?
>
> Davenport: Certainly. Physical agility is important in being able to apprehend and possibly disarm a suspect. It is also important in being able to carry a wounded officer out of the line of hostile fire. Sensitivity to community relations involves knowledge of racial and ethnic problems in the city, plus an ability to work with the community in preventing crime. Practical judgment reflects knowing when it is advisable to pursue a criminal suspect and what methods of action to use in uncertain situations.

Councilmember Flory: How do you propose to measure physical agility?

Davenport: It looks as if we'll go with some physical standard—being able to carry a 150-pound dummy 25 yards, or something similar. We might also use some height and weight requirements. We could have some problems with gender differences in that women are not as strong as men, but I think we can work it out.

Councilmember Reddinger: Are all of these tests going to be performance tests?

Davenport: No, that's the only one so far. For the community relations factor, we're going to use a situational interview. We'll ask the candidates how they would go about dealing with some hypothetical but realistic problem, such as handling a domestic argument. The interviewers will grade their answers and give a total score.

Councilmember Hamilton: What will be a passing score in this interview?

Davenport: We haven't determined that yet. We're still trying to determine if this is the best way to measure the factor.

Councilmember Flory: How do you plan to measure practical judgment?

Davenport: That's the problem case. We really haven't figured out a good test of that yet.

Councilmember DeRosa: How about a test of general intelligence?

Davenport: It appears that practical judgment is related to intelligence, but it's not the same thing. A person can be very intelligent in terms of verbal and numerical ability but not possess a great deal of practical judgment.

Councilmember Reddinger: Hasn't some psychologist developed a test of practical judgment?

Davenport: Not that we know of. You also have to remember that the type of judgment a police officer has to demonstrate is not the same as the type of judgment, say, a banker has to show. I guess I'm saying there appear to be different kinds of practical judgment.

Councilmember Hamilton: Could you use some personality inventory to measure it?

Davenport: I don't think so. I doubt that practical judgment is a personality trait. At least I'm not aware of any direct measures of it.

Councilmember Flory: How about using the interview again? A police officer has to demonstrate practical judgment in handling community relations. Can't you just expand the interview a bit?

Davenport: That's a possibility we're considering. Another possibility is to put candidates in a test situation where they have to demonstrate their practical judgment. It could be a pretty expensive method, all things considered, but it may be the best way to go.

Councilmember DeRosa: I have a feeling, Mr. Davenport, that your success in measuring practical judgment will determine just how many good officers we get on the force.

Questions

1. The city will have to validate whatever predictors it develops to select police officers. What method or methods of validation do you think it should use?
2. Do you think biographical information might be useful in predicting one's success as a police officer? If so, what types of items might be useful?
3. Describe a work sample or situational exercise that might measure practical judgment.
4. What might be a problem in using a physical ability test to select police officers?
5. The personnel department has asked you to assist in developing or selecting predictors of police officer performance. What advice would you give?

Chapter Summary

- Predictors are variables (such as a test, interview, or letter of recommendation) used to forecast (or predict) a criterion.
- High-quality predictors must manifest two psychometric standards: reliability and validity.
- Psychological tests and inventories have been used to predict relevant workplace criteria for more than 100 years.
- Psychological assessment is a big business. There are many publishers of psychological tests used to assess candidates' suitability for employment.
- The most commonly used predictors are tests of general mental ability, personality inventories, aptitude tests, work samples, interviews, and letters of recommendation.
- Predictors can be evaluated in terms of their validity (accuracy), fairness, cost, and applicability.
- Online testing is a major trend in psychological assessment.
- Controversial methods of prediction include the polygraph, graphology, and tests of emotional intelligence.
- There are broad cross-cultural differences in the predictors used to evaluate job candidates. The interview is the most universally accepted method.

Personnel Decisions

The Social Context for Personnel Decisions

I/O psychologists have historically contributed to the process of making personnel decisions by developing assessment instruments, conducting validational research on the boundaries of an instrument's usability, and explaining the consequences of how the instrument is used (e.g., the implications of determining the passing score). Members of an organization are also involved in making personnel decisions, including professionals in human resources, managers of the prospective employees, and in some cases coworkers of the prospective employees. Furthermore, personnel decisions are influenced by organizational values, such as an organization's preference for hiring only applicants who possess superior credentials. Additionally, organizations operate within a social or cultural context in which they are embedded. These larger-scale forces have a direct bearing on who gets hired and who doesn't. For example, hiring only the very best applicants will create a chronically unemployed segment of society. Every applicant can't be the "best," yet all people benefit from employment. Unemployment results in a host of serious ills for individuals and society as a whole, a topic we will discuss in Chapter 11. There are also cultural differences in what makes for a desirable employee. Many Western cultures consider the hiring of family members of employees to be undesirable. The term *nepotism* refers to showing favoritism in the hiring of family members. In the United States nepotism is usually viewed negatively because it results in unequal opportunity among job applicants, which is anathema to our cultural values. In some non-Western cultures, however, nepotism in hiring is viewed positively. The logic is that a family member is a known commodity who can be trusted to be loyal, unlike an anonymous applicant. Why *not* give preferential treatment to applicants who are associated by birth or marriage with members of the hiring organization? Personnel decisions are always embedded in a larger organizational and social context. They do not "stand apart" in a vacuum unrelated to the larger social system.

Guion (1998a) developed a schematic representation of the forces that affect personnel decisions, as shown in Figure 5-1. At the top of the diagram is the organization, which reflects that all personnel decisions are designed to serve the needs of the organization. I/O psychology draws heavily upon scientific theory (e.g., the concept of validity) to conduct research and develop assessment instruments. The instruments are used to assess candidates and help reach a decision about those candidates. The boxes in Figure 5-1 represent the traditional areas of activity among I/O psychologists in making personnel decisions. However, there is another important concept shown in the diagram that typically does not draw as much attention among I/O psychologists. It is the social and cultural context in which the total organization exists. The end product of the personnel selection process is to offer employment to some candidates and deny it to others. Some issues that affect this outcome transcend the scientific and technical.

The science of personnel selection is sometimes dismissed because it does not reflect the way hiring occurs "in the real world." There is truth to the assertion that some organizations make hiring decisions without regard to the forces presented in Figure 5-1. Guion (1998b) noted that the way some organizations hire people in real life tends to be more intuitive, nonquantitative, often not based on validated, empirically derived factors. This chapter will discuss the science and practice of making personnel decisions with the full realization that some organizations' practices are only loosely linked to science.

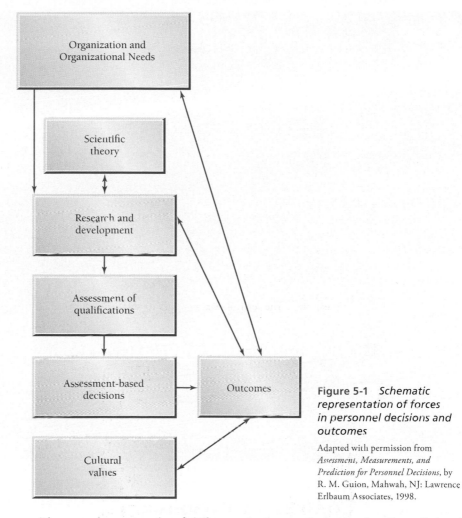

Figure 5-1 *Schematic representation of forces in personnel decisions and outcomes*

Adapted with permission from *Assessment, Measurements, and Prediction for Personnel Decisions*, by R. M. Guion, Mahwah, NJ: Lawrence Erlbaum Associates, 1998.

There are also cross-cultural differences in personnel selection (see Cross-Cultural I/O Psychology: Cross-Cultural Preferences in Ideal Job Candidates). The challenge of finding a good match between the qualifications of people and the demands of work seems to be more daunting today than ever before. However, the process of trying to figure out the best way to select people for organizations is ancient. The means of matching people and work are the subject of cultural lore since antiquity. Salgado (2000) recounted the following tale from long ago:

> A farmer did not know what profession he should choose for his son. One day, in order to orient himself, he gave a Bible, an apple, and a coin to the boy. The farmer thought:
>
>> If the boy eats the apple, he will be a gardener; if he reads the Bible, he will serve to be ecclesiastic; and if he puts the money in his pocket, he will be a merchant. Some time later, the farmer found the boy seated on the Bible, with the money in his pocket, and eating the apple. "Aha," said the farmer, "a clever boy. He has the makings of a politician." (p. 191)

Cross-Cultural I/O Psychology: *Preferences in Ideal Job Candidates*

In Chapter 4 we noted that graphology is an accepted means of personnel selection in France but highly unacceptable in most other countries. There are also national and cultural differences in how the results from the same method are interpreted. Nyfield and Baron (2000) described trends in selection practices around the world. Universalist cultures follow what they see as universal codes of practice and rules. They favor rational arguments. Particularist cultures put more emphasis on relationships and are willing to bend the rules in making selection decisions. They consider the particular relationship between the parties to be more important than a set of rules or procedures. The United States, Canada, and Australia are universalist cultures, whereas France, Greece, and Italy are much more particularist. Particularist countries rely more extensively on the interview, which is regarded as an open-ended conversation between two individuals. Attempts to structure and formalize the interview are likely to be resisted.

Countries also differ in their general preference for a calm, neutral style of interacting versus a strongly emotional one. In a neutral approach more emphasis is placed on the candidate's intellectual skills, whereas in an emotional culture the interviewer's emotional response to the candidate has more influence than what the candidate can actually do. The Japanese and Chinese are renowned for their neutral, reserved approach, whereas southern European and South American countries are more emotional. To an emotional interviewer, a calm, rational presentation by the candidate might be interpreted as dullness or lack of interest. Concentrating on the facts of an experience might be seen as a failure to understand the emotional impact of the experience. The reverse can also be true. To a neutral interviewer, an emotional candidate might seem overly excitable and undependable. The interviewer might be frustrated by the difficulty of understanding the facts of a particular experience. As Nyfield and Baron concluded, there may be similarities in cross-cultural methods of selection, but there can be strong cultural differences in the desired performance of the candidate.

The Legal Context for Personnel Decisions

Civil Rights Act of 1964

For the first 60 years or so of I/O psychology, there was virtually no connection between psychologists and the legal community. Psychological tests were developed, administered, and interpreted by psychologists, and as a profession psychologists governed themselves. However, during the late 1950s and early 1960s, the nation was swept up in the civil rights movement. At that time civil rights concerned primarily the conditions under which Blacks lived and worked in this country. Blacks were denied access to colleges, restaurants, and jobs—in short, their civil rights were denied. Under the administrations of Presidents Kennedy and Johnson steps were taken to change this aspect of American society. In 1964 the Civil Rights Act, a major piece of federal legislation aimed at reducing discrimination in all walks of life, was passed. The section of the law most relevant to I/O psychology is Title VII, which pertains to employment discrimination. In essence, this was the message: Blacks were grossly underemployed throughout the country in both private- and public-sector jobs, particularly in jobs above the lower levels of organizations. To reduce discrimination in employment (one of the mandates of the Civil Rights Act), the federal government began to intervene in employment decisions; in essence, it would monitor the entire procedure to ensure fairness in selection. Thus personnel decisions became deeply embedded within a legal context in the 1960s. As Guion (1998a) asserted, previously the federal government had regulated *things* (e.g., food and drugs), but with this Act it regulated *behavior*. The Civil Rights Act was expanded to cover other people as well. In fact, five groups were identified for protection: race, gender, religion, color, and national origin. They were referred to as the **protected groups**. The Civil Rights Act included all personnel functions—training, promotion, retention, and performance appraisal—in addition to selection. Furthermore, any methods used for making personnel decisions (tests, interviews, assessment centers, etc.) were subject to the same legal standards.

Title VII specifies several unlawful employment practices, including the following:

- Employers may not fail or refuse to hire, or discharge, anyone on the basis of their status in one of the five protected groups.

- Employers may not separate or classify employees or applicants so as to deprive anyone of employment opportunities on the basis of any of the five protected groups.

- Advertising employment or training opportunities may not indicate preferences for any group, as witnessed, for example, in separate classified advertisements for "Help Wanted—Men" and "Help Wanted—Women."

In 1967 the Age Discrimination in Employment Act (ADEA) was passed, which extends to people aged 40 and over the same legal protection granted to the five protected groups under the Civil Rights Act. Although most charges of discrimination in employment pertain to race and gender, Gutman (2002) believes that allegations of discrimination based on religion and national origin will become more frequent following the terrorist attacks of September 11, 2001.

Americans with Disabilities Act

In 1990 the Americans with Disabilities Act (ADA) was signed into law by President George H. W. Bush. The ADA is the most important piece of legislation ever enacted for persons with disabilities (O'Keeffe, 1994). A *disability* is defined by the ADA as "a physical or mental impairment that substantially limits one or more (of the) major life activities; a record of such impairment; or being regarded as having such an impairment." A major life activity is seeing, hearing, walking, learning, breathing, and working. An employment test that screens out an individual with a disability must be job-related and consistent with business necessity. The law states that employers must provide disabled persons *reasonable accommodation* in being evaluated for employment and in the conduct of their jobs. Employers are required to modify or accommodate their business practices in a reasonable fashion to meet the needs of disabled persons. This can include providing elevators or ramps for access to buildings for those who cannot walk, or providing readers for those who have dyslexia or are blind. The ADA extends protection to individuals who are alcoholics and former illegal drug users (Jones, 1994) as well as to individuals with psychiatric disabilities (Carling, 1994). The fundamental premise of the law is that disabled individuals can effectively contribute

Protected group
A designation for members of society who are granted legal status by virtue of a demographic characteristic, such as race, gender, national origin, color, religion, age, and disability.

to the workforce, and they cannot be discriminated against in employment decisions because of their disabilities. If a reasonable accommodation on the employer's part is needed to meld these individuals into the workforce, it is so prescribed by the ADA. As Klimoski and Palmer (1994) noted, organizations are expected to act in good faith in responding to the ADA and be committed to make it work effectively. Campbell and Reilly (2000) noted the ADA also extends to the selection procedures organizations use to evaluate disabled applicants for employment. Accommodations for assessing disabled applicants include the use of Braille, enlarged print, readers, and extended time limits for assessment. The challenge to employers under the ADA is that they must choose solutions that accommodate an applicant's disability yet still permit a valid assessment of that applicant's qualifications for the job.

In 2001 the U.S. Supreme Court ruled on the case of *Martin v. PGA Tour*. Martin was a professional golfer who suffered from a physical disability in his right leg that restricted his ability to walk a golf course. He asked The PGA of America for permission to ride a golf cart during tour competition. The PGA refused on the grounds that riding in a cart would give Martin an unfair advantage over other golfers who are compelled by PGA rules to walk the course. Martin sued the PGA for the right to use a golf cart under the ADA, claiming that his riding in a cart was a reasonable accommodation the PGA could make in his pursuit of earning a living as a golfer. Furthermore, Martin contended it would not be an "undue burden" (or hardship) on the PGA to allow Martin to ride. The U.S. Supreme Court ruled in favor of Martin, saying that making shots was an essential job function but walking between shots was not.

Adverse impact
A type of unfair discrimination in which the result of using a particular personnel selection method has a negative effect on protected group members compared with majority group members. Often contrasted with disparate treatment.

Disparate treatment
A type of unfair discrimination in which protected group members are afforded differential procedures in consideration for employment compared with majority group members. Often contrasted with adverse impact.

FRANK AND ERNEST   by Bob Thaves

Frank & Ernest: © Thaves/Dist. by Newspaper Enterprise Association, Inc. Reprinted with permission.

Adverse Impact

Under the Civil Rights Act discrimination may be charged under two legal theories. One is **adverse impact** (also called *disparate impact*), in which discrimination affects various groups (vis-à-vis the protected groups) differently. Evidence that one group (e.g., women) as a whole is less likely to be hired is evidence of discrimination against those group members. The second theory is **disparate treatment**, which refers to evidence that a member of a protected group is treated differently from other individuals in the employment process. All job applicants should receive the same treatment with regard to selection methods and hiring standards. Singling out some applicants for different employment procedures is evidence of disparate treatment.

Of the two legal bases of discrimination, adverse impact has garnered greater attention among I/O psychologists. Adverse impact exists when employment procedures result in a differential effect between protected and majority group members. A simple rule of thumb was created to operationalize the concept of adverse impact: the "80%" (or "4/5ths") rule. The rule states that adverse impact occurs if the selection ratio (that is, the number of people hired divided by the number of people who apply) for any group of applicants (such as Blacks) is less than 80% of the selection ratio for another group. Suppose 100 Whites apply for a job and 20 are selected. The selection ratio is thus 20/100, or .20. By multiplying .20 by 80%, we get .16. If fewer than 16% of the Black applicants are hired, the selection test produces adverse impact. So if 50 Blacks apply for the job and if at least 8 (50 × .16) Blacks are not selected, then the test produces adverse impact.

If adverse impact is found to exist, the organization faces two alternatives. One is to demonstrate that the test is a valid predictor of job performance. The second alternative is to use a different test that has no adverse impact (but may also be less valid than a test that does manifest adverse impact). If adverse impact does not result from the selection method, then the organization is not required to validate it. Obviously, however, it is a sound business decision to validate any selection method at any time. A company would always want to know whether its method is identifying the best candidates for hire. As Gutman (2004) noted, multiple legal interpretations of adverse impact can be inferred from court rulings. Other interpretations in addition to the 80% rule are possible. What they all have in common, however, is their intent of determining whether a disproportionately large percentage of one group of applicants is rejected for employment compared with another group.

As part of the Civil Rights Act, the Equal Employment Opportunity Commission (EEOC) was established to investigate charges of prohibited employment practices and to use conciliation and persuasion to eliminate prohibited practices. The EEOC subsequently produced the *Uniform Guidelines on Employee Selection Procedures* for organizations to follow in making employment decisions. When there is a conclusion of "just cause" to believe charges of employment discrimination are true, the EEOC can file suit in court. If the organization cannot be persuaded to change its employment practices, then the issue is brought before the court for adjudication. Organizations that lose such cases are obligated to pay financial damages to the victims of their employment practices. The financial awards in these cases can be class-action settlements (the individual who is suing represents a class of similar people), back-pay settlements (the organization has to pay a portion of what victims would have earned had they been hired), or both. The courts have granted multi-million-dollar awards in single cases. However, not everyone who fails an employment test automatically gets his or her day in court. A lawsuit must be predicated on just cause, and sometimes the two parties reach an agreement without resorting to litigation.

Table 5-1 (p. 144) shows 2006 statistics from the EEOC on the number of cases received regarding various types of employment discrimination, the number of cases in which financial damages were awarded, and the total monetary settlement. As can be seen, the largest financial settlements pertained to gender discrimination. The large difference between the number of cases received and the number of cases in which monetary damages were awarded is because most cases were found to have no reasonable cause for judicial review. Additional information about the EEOC can be found at *www.eeoc.gov*.

Table 5-1   *EEOC statistics on six types of employment discrimination in 2006**

Type of Discrimination	Cases Received	Cases Resolved	Total Monetary Settlement (millions)
Gender	23,000	5,700	$99
Race	27,000	5,000	$61
Age	16,500	2,800	$51
Disability	15,500	3,000	$49
National origin	8,500	1,800	$21
Religion	2,500	500	$6

*Figures have been rounded.
EEOC, 2006

Major Court Cases

A trial court applies the facts of a given case to the relevant law. If a case is appealed, a higher court (or appellate court) can issue a written opinion that becomes *case law* (or "precedent"). Several landmark decisions rendered by the U.S. Supreme Court have shaped the interpretation of the Civil Rights Act. In *Griggs v. Duke Power Company*, the Court ruled in 1971 that individuals who bring suit against a company do not have to prove that the company's employment test is unfair; rather, the company has to prove that its test is fair. Thus the burden of proving the fairness of the test rests with the employer. This finding is referred to as "Griggs' Burden." One effect of the Griggs case was to curtail the use of employment tests in the 1970s by organizations in making selection decisions for fear they would invite charges of illegal discrimination. In *Albemarle v. Moody*, the Court ruled that the EEOC's Guidelines have the "deference of law," even though they were issued by an administrative agency and not written by Congress and signed by the President. In *Bakke v. University of California*, the Court ruled that Whites can be the victims of discrimination as well as Blacks. Bakke (a White man) sued the University of California on the grounds that his race had been a factor in his being denied admission to its medical school. The Court ruled in Bakke's favor and required the University of California to admit Bakke to the medical college. This case was heralded as a classic case of "reverse discrimination," which technically is incorrect. First, the name connotes that only Blacks can be discriminated against, which obviously is not true. Second, reversal of the process of discrimination results in nondiscrimination. In *Watson v. Fort Worth Bank & Trust*, the Court ruled that the *cost* of alternative selection procedures must be considered in making decisions about selection methods. Previously, cost had not been a concern of the courts or the EEOC. In *Wards Cove Packing Company v. Atonio*, the U.S. Supreme Court modified both the applicant's and employer's responsibilities in employment litigation pertaining to such issues as burden of proof. Literally thousands of cases have been adjudicated in the district, appellate, state supreme courts, and U.S. Supreme Court on employment law issues. These five cases (all from the U.S. Supreme Court) represent a very small sampling.

A consideration of these court cases might lead one to the conclusion that employment testing is a risky business strategy and that the prudent employer should abandon testing in making personnel decisions. However, that is not the case at all. Sharf and Jones (2000) stated:

> The use of demonstrably job-related employment tests is a winning strategy for minimizing the risk of employment litigation. Forty-plus percent of employment decisions in the private sector are based on the results of employment tests. Litigation challenging employment test use, however, occurs in less than one-half of 1 percent of all discrimination claims. So the tides have turned from the post-Griggs days, when employers abandoned the casual use of employment tests. Legally defensible employment testing is now one of the safest harbors offering shelter from the howling gales of class-action EEO litigation. (p. 314)

Zickar and Gibby (2007) aptly summarized how federal employment laws came to influence I/O psychology:

> The Civil Rights Act of 1964 and successive U.S. Supreme Court decisions expressively forbid using hiring devices that resulted in adverse impact against several protected classes . . . unless the test was shown to be valid for the particular personnel decision for which it was being used. Although these rulings frightened employers from using employment tests (for fear of being sued), these rulings highlighted the importance of using well-developed selection testing practices. I/O psychologists quickly assumed the role of experts in deciding whether particular tests were biased in particular test usages. (p. 71)

Societal Values and Employment Law

Employment laws reflect our societal values about what we regard as "fairness" in the work world. As our conceptions of fairness have changed over time, so have employment laws. Guion (1998a) stated, "Changes follow or accompany (or are accompanied by) changes in the ideas and attitudes of society in general, whether emerging spontaneously or in response to leadership. Even imperfect law is an expression of, and an understanding of, social policy" (p. 205). Perhaps the next federal employment law pertaining to discrimination in the workplace will address sexual orientation. Tenopyr (1996) asserted that there is a strong linkage between measurement issues in psychology (e.g., validity) and social policy pertaining to employment. Tenopyr argued that psychologists should have addressed many of the issues long before national policy debates practically mandated the research. She believed psychologists "should undertake an organized effort to anticipate social issues of the future and to begin the research necessary to address them" (p. 360). Zedeck and Goldstein (2000) echoed similar thoughts: "Indeed, we believe that I/O psychologists have much to offer in the public policy arena on many important issues that relate to work behavior . . . " (p. 394).

The Civil Rights Act of 1964 provides for equal access to employment by all protected groups. Access to employment is often gained by passing tests used to make employment decisions. Psychological research has revealed that different groups of people do not score equally on all standard employment tests. An example is a test of physical fitness for the job of firefighter. Because men have, on average, greater upper body strength than women, more men than women pass a test requiring the lifting of a heavy object. This difference between genders in upper body strength increases the likelihood that men and women are not hired in equal proportions, thereby increasing the likelihood of adverse impact against women. Psychologists are thus sometimes compelled to consider two undesirable tradeoffs: either use tests that have validity but produce adverse impact, or use tests that do not produce adverse impact but are less valid. Selection methods that uniformly have high validity and no adverse impact are elusive, although various strategies have been proposed (e.g., Hattrup, Rock, & Scalia, 1997; Hoffman & Thornton, 1997). One strategy that had been used was to set different passing scores for various groups to avoid adverse impact. However, in 1991 President George H. W. Bush signed into law an amendment to the Civil Rights Act that prohibited test score adjustments as a means of attaining employment fairness. Specifically, the amended Civil Rights Act stated that it shall be an unlawful practice for an employer "in connection with the selection or referral of applicants or candidates for employment or promotion to adjust the scores of, use different cutoffs for, or otherwise alter the results of employment related tests on the basis of race, color, religion, sex, or national origin."

Wigdor and Sackett (1993) described the development of employment laws as reflecting attempts to reach ultimate societal goals of workforce productivity and provide opportunities for all social groups to achieve their employment potential. Some authors are of the opinion that there is no likely way to resolve the conflict between these goals in a fashion that is mutually satisfying to both sides. Our society is divided on the relative importance that should be attached to attaining these two goals (e.g., Gottfredson, 1994; Sackett & Wilk, 1994). The ensuing years will witness how the courts adjudicate the complicated interplay among the societal goals that surround employment testing. The profusion of laws and court cases testifies to the continuing debate within our country over issues of *social justice* in employment. This topic will be discussed in several contexts throughout this book.

Affirmative Action

Affirmative action
A social policy that advocates members of protected groups will be actively recruited and considered for selection in employment.

Affirmative action is a social policy aimed at reducing the effects of prior discrimination. It is not a requirement under the Civil Rights Act, although it is included in the EEOC guidelines. The original intent of affirmative action was aimed primarily at the recruitment of new employees—namely, that organizations would take positive (or affirmative) action to bring members of minority groups into the workforce that had previously been excluded.

Campbell (1996) described four goals of affirmative action:

1. *Correct present inequities.* If one group has "more than its fair share" of jobs or educational opportunities because of current discriminatory practices, then the goal is to remedy the inequity and eliminate the discriminating practices.

2. *Compensate past inequities.* Even if current practices are not discriminatory, a long history of past discrimination may put members of a minority group at a disadvantage.

3. *Provide role models.* Increasing the frequency of minority group members acting as role models could potentially change the career expectations, educational planning, and job-seeking behavior of younger minority group members.

4. *Promote diversity.* Increasing the minority representation in a student body or workforce may increase the range of ideas, skills, or values that can be brought to bear on organizational problems and goals.

As straightforward as these goals may appear, there is great variability in the operational procedures used to pursue the goals. The most passive interpretation is to follow procedures that strictly pertain to recruitment, such as extensive advertising in sources most likely to reach minority group members. A stronger interpretation of the goals is *preferential selection*: organizations will select minority group members from the applicant pool if they are judged to have substantially equal qualifications with nonminority applicants. The most extreme interpretation is to set aside a specific number of job openings or promotions for members of specific protected groups. This is referred to as the *quota interpretation* of affirmative action: organizations will staff themselves with explicit percentages of employees representing the various protected groups, based on local or national norms, within a specific time frame. Quotas are legally imposed on organizations as a severe corrective measure for prolonged inequities in the composition of the workforce. Quotas are not the typical interpretation of affirmative action. Harrison et al. (2006) asserted there is a common belief that Affirmative Action involves the abandonment of merit as an employment principle. Rather than presuming that Affirmative Action compels organizations to hire employees with less merit, Affirmative Action programs should be regarded as an attempt to get qualified employees who are representative of their proportion in the relevant labor market.

Affirmative action has been hotly debated by proponents and critics. In particular, over the past 15 years the subject of affirmative action has been a major political issue (Crosby & VanDeVeer, 2000). Criticism of the quota interpretation in particular has been strident, claiming the strategy ignores merit or ability. Under a quota strategy it is alleged that the goal is merely "to get the numbers right." Proponents of affirmative action believe it is needed to offset the effects of years of past discrimination against specific protected groups. The State of California reversed its commitment to affirmative action in the admission of students into its universities. Preliminary evidence indicates the new admission policy has resulted in less representation of some minority groups in the student population.

Has affirmative action been effective in meeting national goals of prosperity in employment for all people? Some experts (e.g., Guion, 1998a; Heilman, 1996) questioned its overall effectiveness, asserting that unemployment rates are much higher and average incomes much lower now for some groups (particularly Blacks) than they were at the inception of affirmative action more than 40 years ago. Although there appears to be consensus that affirmative action has not produced its intended goals (Murrell & Jones, 1996), there is considerable reluctance to discard it altogether. President William Jefferson Clinton stated the nation should "amend it, not end it." It is feared that its absence may produce outcomes more socially undesirable than have occurred with its presence, however flawed it might be. Dovidio and Gaertner (1996) asserted that affirmative action policies are beneficial in that they emphasize outcomes rather than intentions and they establish monitoring systems that ensure accountability.

Ward Connerly, founder and chairman of the American Civil Rights Institute, is an outspoken critic of racial and gender preferences in selection decisions. Connerly offered the following opinion on the perception of affirmative action by the general public (as reported in Evans, 2003): "Every day that I walk into class I have this feeling that people are wondering whether I'm there because I got in through affirmative action. The reality is the stigma exists. It exists, and they know it exists" (p. 121). Critics of affirmative action contend that it creates the stigma of incompetence among beneficiaries of its practices. Heilman, Block, and Lucas (1992) reported that individuals viewed as having been hired because of affirmative action were not believed to have had their qualifications given much weight in the hiring process. The stigma of incompetence was found to be fairly robust, and the authors questioned whether the stigma would dissipate in the face of disconfirming information about the individuals' presumed incompetence. Similar results have been reported by Heilman and Alcott (2001). Highhouse et al. (1999) found that subtle differences in the way jobs were advertised reflected a company's commitment to affirmative action and influenced the attitudes of Black engineers to pursue employment with the company. The authors concluded that minority applicants are sensitive to the manner in which a company projects its stance on minority recruitment and selection. Related findings were reported by Slaughter, Sinar, and Bachiochi (2002) and Avery (2003). Kravitz and Klineberg (2000) identified differences within minority group populations with regard to their support for affirmative action. Blacks were found to support affirmative action more strongly than Hispanics.

In June 2003 the U.S. Supreme Court ruled on two major cases involving affirmative action. Both involved the admission of students into the University of Michigan. The first case, *Gratz v. Bollinger*, challenged the process used by the University of Michigan in admitting students into the undergraduate program. As an attempt to comply with the intent of affirmative action (increase minority representation), the University of Michigan assigned points to all the variables examined in the student's application, such as points for SAT scores, high school grade point average, extracurricular activities, and so on. For admission 100 points were needed (out of 150 possible points). The university automatically assigned 20 points (or one-fifth of the total needed for admission) if a candidate was an "under-represented minority race." The Supreme Court ruled against the university, deciding that giving points for membership in certain races was unconstitutional. The second case, *Grutter v. Bollinger*, challenged the process used by the University of Michigan in admitting students into the law school. The law school did consider race in making selection decisions but did not use any point system to evaluate candidates for admission. Race could be considered a "plus" in each candidate's file, yet the entire selection system was flexible enough to consider the particular qualifications of each candidate. The Supreme Court ruled in favor of the University of Michigan's law school admissions system. If we consider both cases in their totality, it appears the Supreme Court recognized the legitimate need to have a broad representation of all groups in those candidates selected for admission, but it opposed the general practice that creates two groups of candidates based exclusively on group membership (in the *Gratz* case, those candidates who did and did not get points on the basis of their race).

The two opposing rulings by the Supreme Court illustrate the complexity of the issues raised by affirmative action. On the one hand, we recognize that society will be better served by having all segments of our population enjoying the benefits of admission into school or employment. On the other hand, it is not fair or lawful to explicitly reward some applicants (and in effect, punish others) for their particular group membership. Perhaps more than any other country, the United States is populated by an amalgam of citizens who (with the exception of native American Indians) originally came to this country from someplace else. Given the extreme diversity of people from various racial, cultural, and religious backgrounds, conflicts over who gets to participate in social benefits (education and employment) are perhaps inevitable. Affirmative action is an attempt to recognize the paramount need for all segments of society to be fairly represented in receiving these benefits. Nevertheless, there is ambiguity and disagreement over how best to achieve these goals. As Gutman (2003) noted, it is plausible for a law school with 4,000 applicants to scrutinize all or most of the applicants. It is implausible for an undergraduate program with 50,000 applicants to do likewise.

Recruitment

Recruitment
The process by which individuals are solicited to apply for jobs.

The personnel function of **recruitment** is the process of attracting people to apply for a job. Organizations can select only from those candidates who apply. Attracting and keeping competent employees are critical to the success of most organizations. Rynes and Cable (2003) said:

> In a recent survey of worldwide executives, 80% said that attracting and retaining people will be the number one force in business strategy by the end of the decade. Even if labor shortages ease in the future, increasing recognition of the economic value of hiring the best possible people will continue to keep recruitment at the forefront of corporate strategy—particularly for key positions. (pp. 72–73)

Rynes (1993) noted that most of the emphasis on personnel decisions from an I/O perspective centers on how employers can make better decisions in assessing applicants. As Rynes observed, however, the process can be viewed from the opposite perspective—that is, the extent to which applicants consider the company to be a desirable employer. Specifically, what impressions of the company do the company's recruitment and assessment practices generate? Schuler (1993) referred to the quality of a selection process that makes it acceptable to job applicants as "social validity," an extension of face validity discussed in Chapter 4. Steiner and Gilliland (1996), for example, reported that the social validity of selection procedures was the strongest correlate with applicants' favorable reactions to the organization. Furthermore, there were cultural differences in the social validity of various selection procedures. French college students were more favorably disposed to graphology as a selection method, whereas U.S. college students were more accepting of biographical information. Ployhart and Ryan (1998) found that job applicants held negative views of an organization for using what they considered unfair selection procedures, even when the applicants were hired. Schleicher et al. (2006) studied the reactions of candidates to a full-day multistage personnel selection procedure (e.g., ability tests, situational interview, analysis of past work history, etc.). At the end of the day, candidates were informed by trained assessors whether they had been accepted or rejected for hire. The authors found that the rejected candidates viewed the assessment process as fair and reasonable to the extent they felt the various assessments allowed them the "opportunity to perform" (i.e., to show the organization their skills). It was recommended that perceptions of fairness in personnel selection are enhanced when candidates have sufficient time and resources to be assessed under conditions free of distraction. Applicant reactions to assessment procedures are often vividly personal and highly emotional. Harris (2000) observed that it might be a wiser investment for organizations to explain to rejected candidates why they were denied employment in a way that reduces negative feelings and damage to self-esteem than to gird for potential litigation. Rynes (1993) offered the following examples of applicant reactions to the recruiting and assessment tactics of companies:

- A married graduate student with a 3.9 grade point average reported that the first three questions in a company's psychological assessment procedure involved inquiries about her personal relationship with her husband and children. Although the company asked her what she thought of the procedure before she left, she lied because she was afraid that telling the truth would eliminate her from future consideration. Because of dual-career constraints, she continued to pursue an offer, but noted that if she got one, her first on-the-job priority would be to try to get the assessor fired.

- A student told how he had originally planned to refuse to submit to psychological testing, but was persuaded by his girlfriend that it would be a more effective form of protest to pursue the offer and then pointedly turn it down.

- The first interview question asked of a female student was, "We're a pretty macho organization. . . . Does that bother you?" Unfortunately it did, and she simply wrote the company out of her future interviewing plans. (p. 242)

These examples illustrate that job applicants are not merely passive "receptors" of selection procedures. Rather, applicants react to what they are asked to do or say to get a job. Sometimes a negative experience results in withdrawal from the application process. Smither et al. (1993) found that applicant reactions to selection methods were positively related to their willingness to recommend the employer to others. Bauer, Truxillo, and Paronto (2004) summarized the importance of these findings: "[T]he literature on applicant reactions to selection systems seems clear: It is possible to help or hinder your chances of job offer acceptances and job pursuit intention" (p. 504). Chapman et al. (2005) stated how job applicants perceive the behavior of organizational recruiters and the applicants' perceived fit with the organization are positively related to various aspects of the recruiting process, ranging from the intention to submit a resume to actual job acceptance. Companies and applicants should realize that the recruitment and selection process is mutual—both parties are engaged in assessing the degree of fit with each other (see Field Note 1).

A Model of Personnel Decisions

Figure 5-2 (p. 152) is a model that shows the sequence of factors associated with making personnel decisions. Several of these factors have been discussed in earlier chapters. The process of job and organizational analysis initiates the sequence and was described in Chapter 3. An analysis of the job and organization establishes the context in which the personnel decisions will be made. The results of these analyses provide information useful in determining the criteria of job performance (also discussed in Chapter 3) as well as provide insights into predictor constructs useful in forecasting job performance (as discussed in Chapter 4). The linkage between the predictors and criteria is the essence of validity—the determination of how well our predictors forecast job performance (discussed in Chapter 4). The Society for Industrial and Organizational Psychology has issued a set of principles for the validation and use of personnel selection procedures (SIOP, 2003). The *Principles* specify established scientific findings

Field Note 1: The Left-Handed Dentist

One of the more unusual personnel selection consulting projects I've worked on involved hiring a dentist. A dentist in my town had just experienced an unpleasant breakup with his partner. They disagreed on many major issues surrounding dentistry, including the relative importance of preventive dental maintenance versus treatment, pain management for patients, and so on. Their parting was not amicable. The dentist who remained solicited my help in getting a new partner. He described at great length the characteristics he was looking for in a new partner. Some related to certain dentistry skills, while others dealt with attitudinal or philosophical orientations toward dentistry.

I didn't envision any major problems in picking a new partner because the desired characteristics seemed reasonable and I knew dental schools turned out many graduates each year (thus I would have a large applicant pool). Then came a curve ball I neither anticipated nor understood initially. The dentist said to me, "And, of course, my new partner must be left-handed." The dumb look on my face must have told the dentist I didn't quite catch the significance of left-handedness. The dentist then explained to me something I had never realized despite all the years I have gone to dentists. Dental partners often share instruments in their practice, and there are both left-handed and right-handed dental instruments. The dentist was left-handed himself, so therefore his new partner would also have to be left-handed. I then asked the dentist what proportion of dentists were left-handed. He said he didn't know for sure, but knew it was a small percentage. Suddenly, my task had become much more difficult.

It was one thing to find a new dentist who met the specifications for the job and who would like to set up a practice in a small Iowa town. It was another thing to have the size of the potential applicant pool greatly reduced by such a limiting factor as left-handedness. There is a technical term for left-handedness in this case: "bona fide occupational qualification" (BFOQ). For a qualification to be a BFOQ, it must be "reasonably necessary to the operation of that particular business or enterprise." Thus an employer could use left-handedness as a BFOQ in dentistry, but left-handedness would not be a BFOQ in accounting, for example. I am happy to tell you I found a dentist who met all the qualifications. The two dentists have been partners for more than 25 years now.

and generally accepted professional practices in the field of personnel selection. The *Principles* describe the choice, development, evaluation, and use of personnel selection procedures designed to measure constructs relating to work behavior with a focus on the accuracy of the inferences that underlie employment decisions. These *Principles* outline our responsibilities as I/O psychologists to assist in making accurate and fair personnel selection decisions. As Boutelle (2004) stated, "Based upon a set of test results, we are making judgments about people and their abilities and their suitability to perform specific jobs. These judgments have enormous impact upon people and their careers and we, as I/O psychologists, need to be very diligent in providing strong evidence supporting outcomes derived from test scores" (p. 21). We are now in a position to continue the sequence used by I/O psychologists—examining issues pertaining

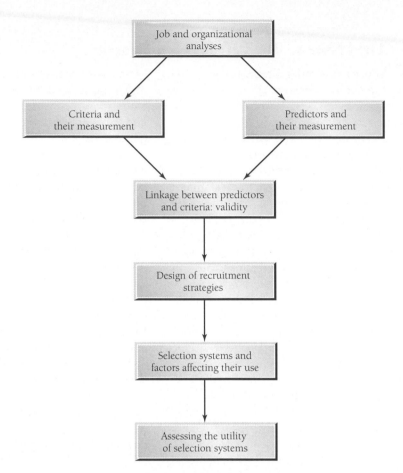

Figure 5-2   *Model of personnel decisions in organizations*

to recruiting, designing selection systems, and assessing the utility of those systems. However, before a discussion of these issues, the next topic is a method of statistical analysis often used by I/O psychologists in assessing the linkage between predictors and criteria. It is called regression analysis.

Regression Analysis

Regression analysis
A statistical procedure used to predict one variable on the basis of another variable.

The statistical technique used to predict criterion performance on the basis of a predictor score is called **regression analysis**. Although a correlation coefficient is useful for showing the degree of relationship between two variables, it is not useful for predicting one variable from the other. Regression analysis, however, does permit us to predict a person's status on one variable (the criterion) based on his or her status on another variable (the predictor). If we assume that the relationship between the two variables is linear (as it usually is), it can be described mathematically with a regression equation:

$$\hat{Y} = a + bX \qquad \text{[Formula 5-1]}$$

where

$\hat{Y} =$ the predicted criterion score

$a =$ a numerical value reflecting where the regression line intercepts the ordinate (or Y axis)

$b =$ a numerical value reflecting the slope of the regression line

$X =$ the predictor score for a given individual

The values of a and b are derived through mathematical procedures that minimize the distance between the regression line (that is, a line useful for making predictions) and the pairs of predictor–criterion data points.

To develop a regression equation, we need predictor and criterion data on a sample of people. Let us say we have a sample of 100 employees. Supervisor ratings of job performance are the criterion, and the predictor test we wish to investigate is an intelligence test. We administer the intelligence test to the workers, collect the criterion data, and then see whether we can predict the criterion scores on the basis of the intelligence test scores. From the predictor–criterion data, we derive the following regression equation:

$$\hat{Y} = 1 + .5X \qquad \text{[Formula 5-2]}$$

The relationship between the two variables is shown in Figure 5-3. Note that the regression line crosses the Y axis at a value of 1 (that is, $a = 1$). Also, for every 2-unit increase in X, there is a corresponding 1-unit increase in Y. Thus the slope of the regression line, defined as the change in Y divided by the change in X, equals 1/2 or .5 (that is, $b = .5$).

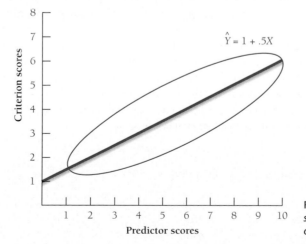

Figure 5-3 *Predictor–criterion scatterplot and regression line of best fit*

For any value of X, we can now predict a corresponding Y score. For example, if someone scores 10 on the intelligence test, the predicted criterion rating is

$$\hat{Y} = 1 + .5(10) = 6 \qquad\qquad \text{[Formula 5-3]}$$

If a supervisor rating of 5 represents adequate job performance (and we do not want anyone with a lower rating), the regression equation can be worked backward to get the minimum passing score:

$$5 = 1 + .5X$$
$$X = 8$$

So, if we use the intelligence test to make hiring decisions, we will not accept any applicant who scores less than 8 because those scores would result in a predicted level of job performance lower than we want. There is also another way to find the passing score. In Figure 5-3, locate the value of 5 on the Y axis (the criterion). Move horizontally to the regression line, and then drop down to the corresponding point of the X axis (the predictor). The score is 8.

Multiple Predictors

Better personnel decisions are made on the basis of more than one piece of information. Combining two or more predictors may improve the predictability of the criterion depending on their individual relationships to the criterion and their relationship to each other. Suppose two predictors both correlate with the criterion but do not correlate with each other. This relationship is illustrated by the Venn diagram in Figure 5-4. The darker shaded area on the left shows how much the first predictor overlaps the criterion. The overlap area is the validity of the first predictor, symbolized by the notation r_{1c}, where the subscript 1 stands for the first predictor and the subscript c stands for the criterion. The darker shaded area on the right shows the extent to which the second predictor overlaps the criterion; its validity is expressed as r_{2c}. As can be seen, more of the criterion can be explained by using two predictors. Also note that the two predictors are unrelated to each other, meaning that they predict different aspects of the criterion. The combined relationship between two or more predictors and the criterion is

Multiple correlation
The degree of predictability (ranging from 0 to 1.00) in forecasting one variable on the basis of two or more other variables. Often expressed in conjunction with multiple regression analysis.

referred to as a **multiple correlation**, R. The only conceptual difference between r and R is that the range of R is from 0 to 1.0, whereas r ranges from -1.0 to 1.0. When R is squared, the resulting R^2 value represents the total amount of variance in the criterion that can be explained by two or more predictors. When predictors 1 and 2 are not correlated with each other, the squared multiple correlation (R^2) is equal to the sum of the squared individual validity coefficients, or

$$R^2_{c.12} = r_{1c}^2 + r_{2c}^2 \qquad\qquad \text{[Formula 5-4]}$$

For example, if $r_{1c} = .60$ and $r_{2c} = .50$, then

$$R^2_{c.12} = (.60)^2 + (.50)^2 \qquad\qquad \text{[Formula 5-5]}$$
$$= .36 + .25$$
$$= .61$$

The notation $R^2_{c.12}$ is read "the squared multiple correlation between the criterion and two predictors." In this condition (when the two predictors are unrelated to each other), 61% of the variance in the criterion can be explained by two predictors.

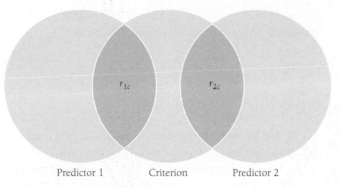

Predictor 1   Criterion   Predictor 2

Figure 5-4   *Venn diagram of two uncorrelated predictors*

In most cases, however, it is rare that two predictors related to the same criterion are unrelated to each other. Usually all three variables share some variance with one another; that is, the intercorrelation between the two predictors (r_{12}) is not zero. Such a relationship is presented graphically in Figure 5-5, where each predictor correlates substantially with the criterion (r_{1c} and r_{2c}) and the two predictors also overlap each other (r_{12}). The addition of the second predictor adds more criterion variance than can be accounted for by one predictor alone. Yet all of the criterion variance accounted for by the second predictor is not new variance; part of it was explained by the first predictor. When there is a correlation between the two predictors (r_{12}), the equation for calculating the squared multiple correlation must be expanded to

$$R_{c.12}^2 = \frac{r_{1c}^2 + r_{2c}^2 - 2r_{12}r_{1c}r_{2c}}{1 - r_{12}^2}$$ [Formula 5-6]

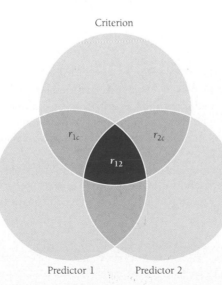

Criterion

Predictor 1   Predictor 2

Figure 5-5   *Venn diagram of two correlated predictors*

For example, if the two predictors intercorrelated .30, given the validity coefficients from the previous example and $r_{12} = .30$, we have

$$R_{c.12}^2 = \frac{(.60)^2 + (.50)^2 - 2(.30)(.60)(.50)}{1 - (.30)^2}$$

$$= .47 \qquad \text{[Formula 5-7]}$$

As can be seen, the explanatory power of two intercorrelated predictor variables is diminished compared with the explanatory power when they are uncorrelated (.47 versus .61). This example provides a rule about multiple predictors: it is generally advisable to seek predictors that are related to the criterion but are uncorrelated with each other. In practice, however, it is difficult to find multiple variables that are statistically related to another variable (the criterion) but at the same time statistically unrelated to each other. Usually variables that are both predictive of a criterion are also predictive of each other. Also note that the abbreviated version of the equation used to compute the squared multiple correlation with uncorrelated predictors is just a special case of the expanded equation when r_{12} is equal to zero.

Multiple Regression Analysis

Multiple regression analysis
A statistical procedure used to predict one variable on the basis of two or more other variables.

The relationship between correlation and regression is the foundation for the relationship between multiple correlation and multiple regression. Just as regression analysis permits prediction on the basis of one predictor, **multiple regression analysis** permits prediction on the basis of multiple predictors. The logic for using multiple regression is the same as the logic for using multiple correlation: it usually enhances prediction of the criterion.

As noted before, the formula for a regression equation with one predictor is

$$\hat{Y} = a + bX \qquad \text{[Formula 5-8]}$$

When we expand this equation to the case of two predictors, we have

$$\hat{Y} = a + b_1 X_1 + b_2 X_2 \qquad \text{[Formula 5-9]}$$

where X_1 and X_2 are the two predictors and b_1 and b_2 are the regression weights associated with the two predictors. As before, the b values are based in part on the correlation between the predictors and the criterion. In multiple regression the b values are also influenced by the correlation among the predictors. However, the procedure for making predictions in multiple regression is similar to that used in one-predictor (or simple) regression.

Suppose we have criterion data on a sample of industrial workers who take two tests we think may be useful for hiring future workers. We analyze the data to derive the values of a, b_1, and b_2 and arrive at this regression equation:

$$\hat{Y} = 2 + .4 X_1 + .7 X_2 \qquad \text{[Formula 5-10]}$$

If a person scores 30 on test 1 and 40 on test 2, his or her predicted criterion performance is

$$\hat{Y} = 2 + .4(30) + .7(40) = 42$$

The degree of predictability afforded by the two predictors is measured by the multiple correlation between the predictors and the criterion. If the multiple correlation is large enough to be of some value for prediction purposes, we might use the two tests to hire future workers. The company would undoubtedly set a minimum predicted criterion score at a certain value—say, 40. In this example, the person's predicted job performance score (42) was higher than the minimum score set by the company (40), so the person would be hired.

Multiple regression is not limited to just two predictors; predictors can be added to the regression equation until they no longer enhance prediction of the criterion. The k-predictor regression equation is simply an extension of the two-predictor regression equation, and all terms are interpreted as before. The equation looks like this:

$$\hat{Y} = a + b_1 X_1 + b_2 X_2 + b_3 X_3 + \cdots + b_k X_k \qquad \text{[Formula 5-11]}$$

There comes a point at which adding more predictors does not improve the prediction of the criterion. Regression equations with four or five predictors usually do as good a job as those with more. The reason is that the shared variance among the predictors becomes very large after four to five predictors, so adding more does not explain unique variance in the criterion. If we could find another predictor that was (1) uncorrelated with the other predictors and (2) correlated with the criterion, it would be a useful addition to the equation. Multiple regression is a very popular prediction strategy in I/O psychology and is used extensively.

Validity Generalization

Validity generalization
A concept that reflects the degree to which a predictive relationship empirically established in one context spreads to other populations or contexts.

The concept of **validity generalization** refers to a predictor's validity spreading or generalizing to other jobs or contexts beyond the one in which it was validated. For example, let us say that a test is found to be valid for hiring secretaries in a company. If that same test is found useful for hiring secretaries in another company, we say its validity has *generalized*. That same test could also be useful in selecting people for a different job, such as clerks. This is another case of the test's validity generalizing. Murphy (2003) stated, "Validity generalization represents a specialized application of meta-analysis . . . to draw inferences about the meaning of the cumulative body of research in a particular area" (p. 3). Schmitt and Landy (1993) graphically depicted the domains across which validity can generalize, as shown in Figure 5-6 (p. 158). Validity generalization has long been a goal of I/O psychologists because its implication would certainly make our jobs easier. However, the problem is that when we examined whether a test's validity would generalize across either companies or jobs, we often found that it did not; that is, the test's validity was specific to the situation in which it was originally validated. The implication, of course, was that we had to validate every test in every situation in which it was used. We could not assume that its validity would generalize.

Schmidt and Hunter (1978, 1980) supported validity generalization as a means of selecting personnel. They argued that the problem of situational specificity of test validity was based on psychologists' erroneous belief in the "law of small numbers," the belief that whatever results hold for large samples will also hold for small samples. They thought this belief was incorrect—that small-sample results were highly unstable and gave highly variable test validities. Schmidt and Hunter believed that in most cases

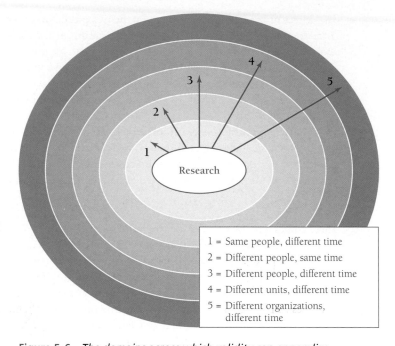

Figure 5-6 *The domains across which validity can generalize*

Source: From *Personnel Selection in Organizations*, by N. Schmitt and F. J. Landy. Copyright © 1993 John Wiley & Sons, Inc. Reprinted with permission of John Wiley & Sons, Inc.

psychologists use small samples (40 to 50) to validate tests. Indeed, Salgado (1998) reported the average sample size in typical criterion-related validity studies is too small to produce stable, generalizable conclusions, resulting in the (erroneous) conclusion that test validity is situation-specific. Schmidt and Hunter argued that if tests were validated in large samples, the results would generalize (not be situation-specific).

Validity generalization means that there is a single "true" relationship between a test and job performance, as for a secretary. Let us say that relationship has a correlation of .40 based on validity studies involving thousands of subjects each. In theory, we could generalize the validity of these findings from huge sample sizes to more typical employment situations with small samples. Organizations with immense sample sizes (such as the military or federal government) would validate certain tests; the rest of the business world would simply "borrow" these validities as a basis for using the tests for hiring. Alternatively, appropriately large samples can be found by pooling results from many smaller studies through meta-analysis.

In support of their position, Schmidt and Hunter (1978) presented data based on a sample of more than 10,000 individuals. The sample was drawn from the army. Data were reported on ten predictors that were used to forecast success in 35 jobs. The results indicated highly similar validity coefficients across different jobs, meaning that differences among jobs did not moderate predictor–criterion relationships. The researchers concluded that the effects of situational moderators disappear with appropriately large sample sizes. One psychological construct that is supposedly common for success in all jobs (and which accounts for validity generalizing or spreading) is intelligence and, in particular, the dimension of intelligence relating to information processing.

Meta-analyses of the relationship between tests of cognitive ability and job performance have consistently yielded evidence that the validity of intelligence does indeed generalize across a wide variety of occupations. Schmidt and Hunter (1981) stated, "Professionally developed cognitive ability tests are valid predictors of performance on the job and in training for all jobs" (p. 1128). This conclusion increases our reliance on measures of g to forecast job performance. However, as Guion (1998a) observed, the validity generalization conclusion about cognitive ability does not indicate that all cognitive tests are *equally* valid predictors across all jobs, all criteria, or all circumstances. Thus, although cognitive ability does predict job performance across many occupations, it is not comparably predictive in all cases. Even in lower-level jobs, however, cognitive ability still exhibits respectable levels of predictive validity.

Murphy (1997) concluded that the most important message of validity generalization research is that "validation studies based on small samples and unreliable measures are simply a bad idea" (p. 337). Such studies are more likely to mislead us into believing that validity varies greatly across situations. The impact of validity generalization research has been to improve the way researchers design validation studies. When research is designed improperly, the conclusions will most likely be erroneous. Guion (1998a) believes that validity generalization is one of the major methodological advances in personnel selection research in the past 30 years. It has allowed personnel selection specialists to infer criterion-related evidence and therefore use cognitive ability tests in situations where a local validity study would have been infeasible and might therefore preclude the use of cognitive ability testing. Murphy (2000) stated:

> The greatest single contribution of validity generalization analyses to personnel selection is the demonstration that the results of empirical research can indeed be applied, with considerable success, to help solve important and practical problems. . . . One implication is that hiring organizations do not have to "reinvent the wheel" every time a new selection system is developed. Rather, they can often use the accumulated literature on the validity of selection tests to make reasonably accurate forecasts of how well particular tests or methods of assessment will work for them. (p. 204)

A Model of Performance

When we speak of wanting to hire competent employees, individuals who will perform well, what exactly do we mean? More specifically, what are the components of performance? Johnson (2003) developed a model of individual job performance that is instructive. The model was an extension of research originally done by Campbell (1999). Individual job performance can be conceptualized at various levels of specificity. At its broadest or most general level, performance has three major components. Each component can be refined into more specific dimensions.

1. *Task performance.* Task performance refers to being effective in the tasks that make up one's job. Every job (plumber, teacher, police officer, salesperson, etc.) can be defined by the tasks performed in that job. This component might be further refined into such factors as written communication, oral communication, decision making, providing guidance to others, planning and organizing, and so on. This dimension of performance is clearly job oriented and refers to performing one's job effectively.

2. *Citizenship performance.* Citizenship performance refers to being a good organizational citizen, helping to make the organization run more smoothly by contributing in ways that go beyond one's particular job. More specific factors include being conscientious and responsible, maintaining personal discipline, handling work stress, helping others, and being committed to the organization. This dimension of performance clearly goes beyond one's job and refers to being effective in contributing to the overall welfare of the *organization*.

3. *Adaptive performance.* Adaptive performance is the most recently identified dimension of performance. Its importance has emerged as a result of the rapid pace of change in the work world and the need for employees to adapt to this changing environment. Borman et al. (2003) described this dimension:

> Adaptive job performance is characterized by the ability and willingness to cope with uncertain, new, and rapidly changing conditions on the job. . . . Today's technology is changing at an unprecedented rate. To adapt, personnel must adjust to new equipment and procedures, function in changing environments, and continuously learn new skills. Technological change often requires the organization of work around projects rather than well-defined and stable jobs, which in turn requires workers who are sufficiently flexible to be effective in poorly defined roles. (p. 293)

Perhaps a generation ago job performance was viewed primarily from the perspective of task performance. Statements such as "I'm just doing my job" and "That's not in my job description" conveyed the boundary between one's job and everything else within the organization. Today the effective performer must make additional contributions. Task performance is still relevant because employees must perform the job for which they were hired. But also expected are the capacity and willingness to go beyond one's job, to help the organization in whatever ways present themselves, and to be adaptive to rapidly changing work conditions. The effective performer of today has to exhibit a wider range of skills than found in generations past. Beal et al. (2005) examined whether performance within a job is stable over short periods of time. The authors concluded that emotional experiences encountered by individual employees lead not only to "good days and bad days", but also "good hours and bad hours". They further concluded that emotional changes in employees can occur episodically and with more variability across a shorter time period than had been previously recognized.

Personnel Selection

Personnel selection
The process of determining those applicants who are selected for hire versus those who are rejected.

Personnel selection is the process of identifying from the pool of recruited applicants those to whom a job will be offered. As long as there are fewer job openings than applicants, some applicants will be hired and some won't. Selection is the process of separating the selected from the rejected applicants. Ideally, the selected employees will be successful on the job and contribute to the welfare of the organization. Two major factors determine the quality of newly selected employees and the degree to which they can affect the organization: the validity of the predictor and the selection ratio.

Predictor Validity.   Figure 5-7 shows a predictor–criterion correlation of .80, which is reflected in the oval shape of the plot of the predictor and criterion scores. Along the predictor axis is a vertical line—the **predictor cutoff**—that separates passing from failing applicants. People above the cutoff (or cutscore) are accepted for hire; those below it are rejected. Also, observe the three horizontal lines. The solid line, representing the criterion performance of the entire group, cuts the entire distribution of scores in half. The dotted line, representing the criterion performance of the rejected group, is below the performance of the total group. Finally, the dashed line, which is the average criterion performance of the accepted group, is above the performance of the total group. The people who would be expected to perform the best on the job fall above the predictor cutoff. In a simple and straightforward sense, that is what a valid predictor does in personnel selection: it identifies the more capable people from the total pool.

Predictor cutoff

A score on a test that differentiates those who passed the test from those who failed; often equated with the passing score on a test.

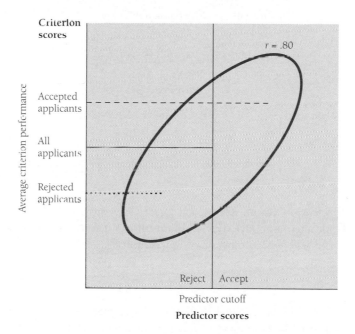

Figure 5-7   *Effect of a predictor with a high validity (r = .80) on test utility*

A different picture emerges for a predictor that has no correlation with the criterion, as shown in Figure 5-8 (p. 162). Again, the predictor cutoff separates those accepted from those rejected. This time, however, the three horizontal lines are all superimposed; that is, the criterion performance of the accepted group is no better than that of the rejected group, and both are the same as the performance of the total group. The value of the predictor is measured by the difference between the average performance of the accepted group and the average performance of the total group. As can be seen, these two values are the same, so their difference equals zero. In other words, predictors that have no validity also have no value.

On the basis of this example, we see a direct relationship between a predictor's value and its validity: the greater the validity of the predictor, the greater its value as

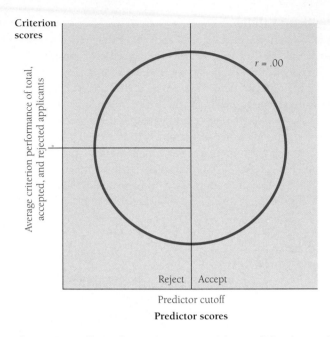

Criterion scores

Average criterion performance of total, accepted, and rejected applicants

r = .00

Reject | Accept

Predictor cutoff

Predictor scores

Figure 5-8   *Effect of a predictor test with no validity (r = .00) on test utility*

measured by the increase in average criterion performance for the accepted group over that for the total group.

Selection ratio
A numeric index ranging between 0 and 1 that reflects the selectivity of the hiring organization in filling jobs; the number of job openings divided by the number of job applicants.

Selection Ratio.   A second factor that determines the value of a predictor is the selection ratio (SR). The **selection ratio** is defined as the number of job openings (*n*) divided by the number of job applicants (*N*):

$$SR = \frac{n}{N}$$ [Formula 5-12]

When the SR is equal to 1 (there are as many openings as there are applicants) or greater (there are more openings than applicants), the use of any selection device has little meaning. The company can use any applicant who walks through the door. But most often, there are more applicants than openings (the SR is somewhere between 0 and 1) and the SR is meaningful for personnel selection.

The effect of the SR on a predictor's value can be seen in Figures 5-9 and 5-10. Let us assume we have a validity coefficient of .80 and the selection ratio is .75, meaning we will hire three out of every four applicants. Figure 5-9 shows the predictor–criterion relationship, the predictor cutoff that results in accepting the top 75% of all applicants, and the respective average criterion performances of the total group and the accepted group. If a company hires the top 75%, the average criterion performance of that group is greater than that of the total group (which is weighted down by the bottom 25% of the applicants). Again, value is measured by this difference between average criterion scores. Furthermore, when the bottom 25% is lopped off (the one applicant out of four who is not hired), the average criterion performance of the accepted group is greater than that of the total group.

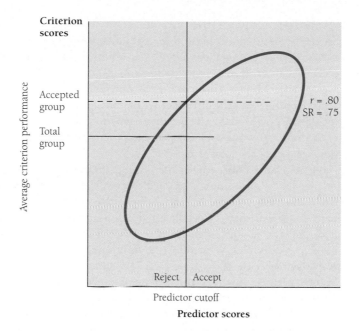

Figure 5-9   *Effect of a large selection ratio (SR = .75) on test utility*

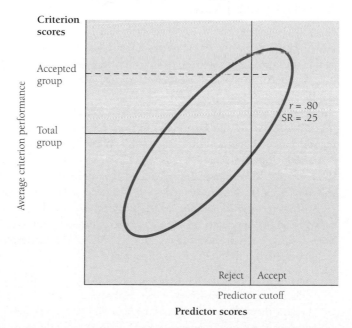

Figure 5-10   *Effect of a small selection ratio (SR = .25) on test utility*

In Figure 5-10 we have the same validity coefficient ($r = .80$), but this time the SR is .25; that is, out of every four applicants, we will hire only one. The figure shows the location of the predictor cutoff that results in hiring only the top 25% of all applicants and the average criterion performances of the total and accepted groups. The average criterion performance of the accepted group is not only above that of the total group as before, but the difference is also much greater. In other words, when only the top 25% are hired, their average criterion performance is greater than the performance of the top 75% of the applicants, and both of these values are greater than the average performance of the total group.

The relationship between the SR and the predictor's value should be clear: the smaller the SR, the greater the predictor's value. This should also make sense intuitively. The fussier we are in hiring people (that is, the smaller the selection ratio), the more likely it is that the people hired will have the quality we desire. A third factor (albeit of lesser significance) also affects the value of a predictor in improving the quality of the workforce. It is called the **base rate**, defined as the percentage of current employees who are performing their jobs successfully. If a company has a base rate of 99% (that is, 99 out of every 100 employees perform their jobs successfully), it is unlikely that any new selection method can improve upon this already near-ideal condition. If a company has a base rate of 100%, obviously no new selection system can improve upon a totally satisfactory workforce. The only "improvement" that might be attained with a new test is one that takes less time to administer or one that costs less (but still achieves the same degree of predictive accuracy).

Base rate
The percentage of current employees in a job who are judged to be performing their jobs satisfactorily.

Selection Decisions

As long as the predictor used for selection has less than perfect validity ($r < 1.00$), we will always make some errors in personnel selection. The object is, of course, to make as few mistakes as possible. With the aid of the scatterplot, we can examine where the mistakes occur in making selection decisions.

Part (a) of Figure 5-11 shows a predictor–criterion relationship of about .80, where the criterion scores have been separated by a criterion cutoff. The criterion cutoff is the point that separates successful (above) from unsuccessful (below) employees. Management decides what constitutes successful and unsuccessful performance (see Field Note 2, p. 166). Part (b) shows the same predictor–criterion relationship, except this time the predictor scores have been separated by a predictor cutoff. The predictor cutoff is the point that separates accepted (right) from rejected (left) applicants. The score that constitutes passing the predictor test is determined by the selection ratio, cost factors, or occasionally law.[1] Part (c) shows the predictor–criterion relationship intersected by both cutoffs. Each of the resulting four sections of the scatterplot is identified by a letter representing a different group of people:

True positives
A term to describe individuals who were correctly selected for hire because they became successful employees.

Section A: Applicants who are above the predictor cutoff and above the criterion cutoff are called **true positives.** These are the people we think will succeed on the job because they passed the predictor test, and who in fact turn out to be successful employees. This group represents a correct decision: we correctly decided to hire them.

---

[1] In some public-sector organizations (for example, state governments), the passing score for a test is determined by law. Usually a passing score is set at 70% correct.

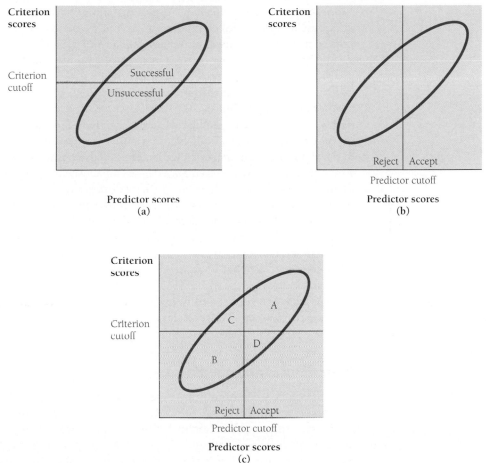

Figure 5-11 *Effect of establishing (a) criterion cutoff, (b) predictor cutoff, and (c) both cutoffs on a predictor–criterion scatterplot*

True negatives
A term to describe individuals who were correctly rejected for employment because they would have been unsuccessful employees.

False negatives
A term to describe individuals who were incorrectly rejected for employment because they would have been successful employees.

False positives
A term to describe individuals who were incorrectly accepted for employment because they were unsuccessful employees.

Section B: The people in this group are those we thought would not succeed on the job because they failed the predictor test and who, if hired anyway, would have performed unsatisfactorily. This group represents a correct decision: we correctly predicted they would not succeed on the job. These people are **true negatives**.

Section C: People who failed the predictor test (and are thus predicted not to succeed on the job) but who would have succeeded had they been given the chance are called **false negatives**. We have made a mistake in our decision-making process with these people. They would really turn out to be good employees, but we mistakenly decided they would not succeed. These are "the good ones we let get away."

Section D: The people who passed the predictor test (and are thus predicted to succeed on the job) but perform unsatisfactorily after being hired are called **false positives**. We have also erred with these people. They are really ineffective employees who should not have been hired, but we mistakenly thought they would succeed. They are "the bad ones we let in."

Positive/negative refers to the result of passing/failing the predictor test; *true/false* refers to the quality (good/bad) of our decision to hire the person. In personnel selection we want to minimize the false positives and false negatives.

If there is no difference between making false positive and false negative decisions (that is, letting a bad worker in is no worse than letting a good one get away), it does no good to "juggle" the predictor cutoff scores. By lowering the predictor cutoff in Figure 5-11c (moving the line to the left), we *decrease* the size of section C, the false negatives. But by reducing the number of false negatives, we *increase* the space in section D, the false positives. The converse holds for raising the predictor cutoff (moving the line to the right). Furthermore, classification errors (false positives and false negatives) are also influenced by extreme base rates. For example, when the behavior being predicted occurs very rarely (such as employees who will commit violent acts in the workplace), the differential likelihood of one type of error over the other is great (Martin & Terris, 1991). However, cutoff scores cannot be established solely for the purpose of minimizing false positives or false negatives. Cascio, Alexander, and Barrett (1988) indicated that there must be some rational relationship between the cutoff score and the purpose of the test (see Field Note 2). Issues pertaining to the cutoff score will be discussed in the next section.

For many years, employers were *not* indifferent between making false positive and false negative mistakes. Most employers preferred to let a good employee get away (in

Field Note 2: Raising the Bar

A popular expression heard in organizations is the desire to "raise the bar"—meaning to elevate the organization's standards above current levels. If the organization believes it is necessary to have higher standards associated with its operations, then it will "raise the bar" regarding what it considers to be acceptable or satisfactory. A good way to visualize this metaphor (both literally and figuratively) is with regard to personnel selection. Assume an organization uses a test that manifests criterion-related validity to select employees for its sales jobs. Further assume that the standard of satisfactory performance (or the criterion cutoff) is selling $1,000,000 in products per year. Assume the minimum score that corresponds to that sales figure is 87 on the test. Now the company decides that $1,000,000 per year no longer represents acceptable job performance; it decides to elevate the

sales standard to $1,250,000 per year. Think of the horizontal line reflecting the criterion cutoff in Figure 5-12a as the "bar." By "raising the bar," or elevating the minimum standard from $1,000,000 to $1,250,000, the organization seeks a higher level of job performance. To select employees who can attain this new higher level of job performance also entails raising the passing score on the test—for example, from 87 to 92. Because the test manifests criterion-related validity, the better people perform on the test, the better they perform on the job. To perform on the job at a level of $1,250,000 in sales per year now requires scoring 92 on the test. The expression "raising the bar" in this case refers to elevating the standard, first the criterion and then the concomitant effect of that decision on raising the standard passing score on the test.

the belief that someone else who is good could be hired) rather than hire a bad worker. The cost of training, reduced efficiency, turnover, and so on made the false positive highly undesirable. Although most employers still want to avoid false positives, false negatives are also important. The applicant who fails the predictor test and sues the employer on the grounds of using unfair tests can be very expensive. If people do fail an employment test, employers want to be as sure as possible that they were not rejected because of unfair and discriminatory practices. Denying employment to a qualified applicant is tragic; denying employment to a qualified minority applicant can be both tragic and expensive. An organization can reduce both types of selection errors by increasing the validity of the predictor test. The greater the validity of the predictor, the smaller the chance that people will be mistakenly classified.

Personnel Selection from a Human Perspective

Amid all the statistical equations, Venn diagrams, and graphs, it may be tempting to forget that personnel selection is, first and foremost, about people; real people with real lives, who apply for admission into real organizations. The word "personnel" means "people". In an attempt to humanize the statistical approach to personnel selection, consider Figure 5-12.

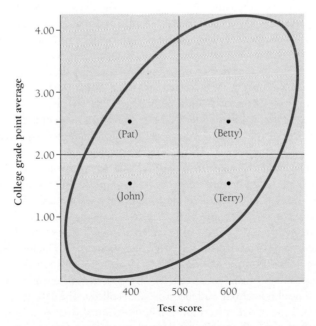

Figure 5-12 *Graphic depiction of four high school students' performance on admission test and subsequent performance in college.*

Figure 5-12 is similar to Figure 5-11c (p. 165), except it will be explained by reference to four individual people. The organization in question is a college. The criterion of successful performance in college is the student's grade point average. The criterion cutoff is 2.00 (a C average) with a maximum of 4.00. The predictor is a standardized test of verbal ability. The college has set the predictor cutoff at a score of 500 on the verbal ability test. Applicants who score 500 and above are admitted, and applicants who score below 500 are rejected. Figure 5-12 shows four data points. These "data points" are people, four high school students among the many who applied for college admission. Two of the applicants have the same test score, a score of 400. We will call these two students "Pat" and "John", respectively. Because both Pat and John scored below the predictor cutoff of 500, both were denied admission into the college. However, if the college had admitted them anyway, without regard to their test score, two very different outcomes regarding their performance in college would have occurred. John's college grade point average would have been below the criterion cutoff, approximately 1.50. As such, the college would have made the correct decision to reject John for admission, because he would not have earned a sufficiently high grade point average to receive his degree. Using the terminology of personnel selection, John is a *true negative*. Conversely, Pat, who also scored 400 on the test would, in fact, have succeeded in college. Pat's college grade point average would have been approximately 2.50, well above the criterion cutoff of 2.00 needed to receive a degree. The college made a mistake in rejecting Pat, and Pat would be termed a *false negative*. Why didn't the college "know" that Pat would have been successful in college, while John would have been unsuccessful? It wouldn't, and it couldn't. Based on an inspection of Figure 5-12, it is evident that far more applicants who scored 400 on the test would have been true negatives (the larger area) than false negatives (the smaller area). The college made the best use of the information available to it in attempting to make correct personnel selection decisions on Pat and John. In hindsight, the decision to reject John was correct, but the decision to reject Pat was incorrect.

We now examine two other applicants who scored *above* the predictor cutoff, and accordingly, both were admitted into the college. Both of these applicants scored 600 on the test. These two "data points" are also people, who we will call "Terry" and "Betty". Despite having identical test scores, two very different outcomes occurred for them in college. Betty's college grade point average of approximately 2.50 was well above the criterion cutoff, and thus she received her degree from the college. As such, Betty would be termed a *true positive*, and the college made a correct decision to admit her. Terry, however, never earned a college grade point average needed to receive a degree. Terry's college grade point average (approximately 1.50) was below the criterion cutoff. The college made a mistake in admitting Terry, and Terry would be termed a *false positive*. Why didn't the college "know" Betty would be successful and Terry would be unsuccessful? It wouldn't, and it couldn't. The logic for their selection is the same as the logic for Pat and John. More applicants who scored 600 on the test are true positives (the larger area) than false positives (the smaller area).

Four high school students applied to college. The college admitted two and rejected two. Of the two that were admitted, one (Betty) went on to get her degree. Of the two that were rejected, one (Pat) would have graduated if given the chance. The lives of John, Pat, Terry, and Betty were all affected by the high stakes personnel selection decisions made by the college. Across all applicants, as evidenced in Figure 5-13, the college made more correct decisions (true positives and true negatives) than incorrect decisions (false positives and false negatives). Two of the incorrect decisions (Pat and Terry) were caused by the imperfect validity of the predictor test upon which selection decisions are made. Selection mistakes will *always* occur when predictor tests have imperfect validity, and

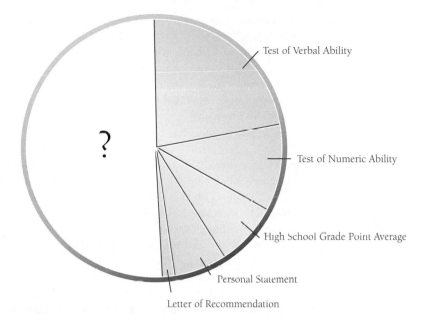

Figure 5-13 *Graphic depiction of the predictability of college grade point average using five assessment methods.*

no test has perfect validity. Thus personnel selection "errors", "mistakes", or "incorrect decisions" always occur. However, the number of incorrect decisions the college made is exceeded by the number of correct decisions that were made. As the validity of the selection process increases, the number of incorrect decisions is further reduced.

Because every predictor test has imperfect validity, the use of any single selection test will yield imperfect results. However, the validity of a personnel selection process can be increased by using multiple selection tests, with each one contributing to increased predictive accuracy. As noted previously in this chapter, the incremental value of adding more tests or assessments typically ceases at four or five predictors. Just how good are we in predicting the criteria of interest to us? There is no one answer to this question, as it all depends upon the particular criterion in question. Consider Figure 5-13. The circle represents the variance in the criterion we are trying to predict. Assume the criterion is again success in earning a college degree. Five assessments have been found valid in predicting this criterion and are indicated by the shaded area of the circle. Each of the five predictors accounts for a "slice" or portion of the criterion variance. The five predictors are: 1) a standardized test of verbal ability; 2) a standardized test of numeric ability; 3) the student's high school grade point average; 4) a personal statement written by the student; and 5) letters of recommendation submitted on behalf of the student. The degree to which each assessment predicts academic success in college is shown by each of the respective slices of the circle. Using multiple regression analysis the combined predictive capability of all five predictors results in a multiple correlation (R) of .70. The squared multiple correlation (R^2) would thus be .49. The unshaded portion of the circle is the amount of criterion variance that *cannot* be predicted. A question mark has been placed in this unshaded area to indicate it is that portion of the criterion variance that is unknown. The statistical term for the squared multiple correlation is the *coefficient of determination*, so named because it reflects the amount of criterion variance that can be determined from using the predictors. In this case, the coefficient of determination is .49, which can be interpreted as 49% of the criterion variance that can be predicted or explained. The statistical term for that portion of the criterion variance that *cannot* be predicted or explained is the *coefficient of non-determination*. It is computed by simply subtracting the coefficient of determination from 1.00. In this case,

$$1.00 - .49 = .51$$

which again is interpreted as a percentage, or 51%. We thus can predict 49% of what we want to know, and cannot predict 51% of what we want to know.

People unfamiliar with the science of personnel selection may make statements like, "I could flip a coin and have a 50% chance of making a correct personnel decision". However, a coin, used as a method of personnel selection, has no validity. That is, 0% of the criterion variance is predicted by whether the coin turns up heads or tails. The probability (p) of getting a head or tail on a coin flip must not be confused with the coefficient of determination (R^2). A probability of .50 associated with a coin flip is *not* indicative of a slightly more accurate personnel selection method than evidenced by a selection method that produces a coefficient of determination of .49. Personnel selection by coin flipping would produce random hiring decisions, the "worst case scenario" in staffing. The reason I/O psychologists have spent 100 years developing valid personnel selection tests is to improve upon random hiring decisions. The more strongly performance on a selection test is associated with performance on the job, the more correct selection decisions will be made. Flipping coins produces as many incorrect selection decisions as correct ones. The history of personnel selection in I/O psychology has been directed at making more correct selection decisions than incorrect ones. Even with our best tests, incorrect personnel decisions are still made. But their frequency is far less than what would result from random selection.

A literal interpretation of Figure 5-13 is that there is slightly more (51%) that we can't predict than what we can predict (49%) about success in college. What is the reason for the unexplained variance? This has been the subject of debate since psychological assessments were invented over 100 years ago. There is no one reason for the unexplained variance. Human behavior is very complex, and thus difficult to predict. However, we know that success in any life activity is a function of the mix of the "can do" and "will do" factors. In this example the best predictors are ability (verbal and numeric) tests, classic "can do" factors. The absence of a single predictive "will do" test has been the bane of predicting human behavior. "Will do" tests would assess personality traits like motivation or ambition, and test questions that seek to measure ambition are prone to faking by applicants. The "will do" factor is a major determinant of successful performance; the problem is our limited capacity to measure it and understand it. Thus, some students might have the ability to succeed in college, but they lack the ambition necessary to achieve it. Some students do not earn the needed grade point average to graduate (they "flunk out"), while others lose their ambition for college before graduating (they "drop out"). Success in college can also be a function of the area of study, and having the resources (typically time and money) needed to complete the degree requirements. In short, there are multiple reasons for the unexplained variance in the criterion of academic success in college. In an employment context, the overall level of predictability is often considerably less ($R^2 = .25$ would be more typical) than in an academic context.

We conclude with a final consideration of John, Pat, Terry, and Betty. Betty was admitted to the college and went on to earn her degree. John was denied admission, and would not have graduated even if he had been admitted. Pat would have graduated if given the opportunity. What Pat lacked in the "can do" factors would have been offset by Pat's level of ambition (the "will do" factor). Terry had sufficient ability to earn a college degree, but lacked the needed ambition to succeed. From an organizational perspective, applicants with lower ability are less likely to be selected, despite the organization's awareness that high ambition can overcome lesser ability. As such, organizations give more weight to ability measures than may be warranted, but they have no better way to make personnel selection decisions in a practical and efficient manner.

Determination of the Cutoff Score

Have you ever wondered how certain cutoff scores came to be? Why is 70% correct associated with passing a test (such as a driving test)? In educational institutions, why are the cutoffs of 90%, 80%, and 70% usually associated with the grades of A, B, and C, respectively? It has been reported that several thousand years ago a Chinese emperor decreed that 70% correct was needed to successfully pass a test. That 70% correct figure, or a relatively close approximation, has been used throughout history in a wide range of assessment contexts as a standard to guide pass/fail decisions. Although I/O psychologists are primarily limited to assessment decisions in employment contexts, we too have had to wrestle with issues pertaining to where to set the cutoff score and how to interpret differences in test scores (e.g., Strickler, 2000).

Cascio, Alexander, and Barrett (1988) addressed the legal, psychometric, and professional issues associated with setting cutoff scores. As they reported, there is a wide variation regarding the appropriate standards to use in evaluating the suitability of established cutoff scores. In general, a cutoff score should be set to be reasonable and consistent with the expectations of acceptable job proficiency in the workplace. As Zieky (2001) commented, "There are two types of errors of classification that are made when cutscores are used operationally. If the cutscore is set relatively high, people who deserve to pass will fail. If the cutscore is set relatively low, then people who deserve to fail will pass. It is important to realize that adjusting the cutscore up or down to reduce one type of error will automatically increase the other type of error. Setting a sensible cutscore requires a determination of which error is more harmful" (p. 46). Thus it would be sensible to set a high cutscore for airline pilots and a low cutscore for manual laborers.

There is no such thing as a single, uniform, correct cutoff score. Nor is there a single best method of setting cutoff scores for all situations. Cascio et al. (1988) made several suggestions regarding the setting of cutoff scores. Here are three:

- The process of setting a cutoff score should begin with a job analysis that identifies relative levels of proficiency on critical knowledge, skills, and abilities (KSAs).
- When possible, data on the actual relationship of test scores to criterion measures of job performance should be considered carefully.
- Cutoff scores should be set high enough to ensure that minimum standards of job performance are met.

In summarizing the process of determining a passing score, Ebel (1972) noted: "Anyone who expects to discover the 'real' passing score . . . is doomed to disappointment, for a 'real' passing score does not exist to be discovered. All any examining authority . . . can hope for, and all any of their examinees can ask, is that the basis for defining the passing score be defined clearly, and that the definition be as rational as possible" (p. 496).

Banding
A method of interpreting test scores such that scores of different magnitude in a numeric range or band (e.g., 90–95) are regarded as being equivalent.

Banding is an alternative method to setting cutoff scores (Murphy, Osten, & Myors, 1995). The traditional approach to personnel selection is to rank applicants on the basis of their test scores and select the applicants with the highest scores. In test score banding, some differences in test scores are ignored, and individuals whose scores fall within the same band are selected on some basis other than the test score (such as gender or race), thereby eliminating or greatly reducing adverse impact. The width of the band is a function of the reliability of the test. Highly reliable tests produce relatively narrow bands, whereas less reliable tests produce wider test score bands. Thus a one-point difference in test scores (e.g., a score of 90 versus 89) is not judged to be of sufficient magnitude to reflect a meaningful difference in the applicants' respective abilities. One then extends this logic to a two-point difference in test scores, a three-point difference, and so on. Eventually, a certain magnitude of difference in test scores is determined to reflect a meaningful difference in ability. It is at this point where this band ends, and other bands may be formed from the distribution of test scores. De Corte, Lievens, and Sackett (2007) offered an alternative solution to banding to the perplexing problem of balancing validity and workplace diversity. The authors proposed mixing and matching predictors that are valid but do not produce adverse impact. Such an approach would achieve the social goal of workplace diversity, but would likely entail some reduction in predictive accuracy.

Banding is a controversial interpretation of test scores. The dual purposes of banding are to hire qualified workers and promote diversity within the workforce (Campion et al., 2001). Proponents of the method (e.g., Siskin, 1995; Zedeck et al., 1995) argued that banding achieves the objectives of hiring able candidates while avoiding adverse impact. Critics of the method (e.g., Schmidt, 1991; Schmidt & Hunter, 1995) contended that banding leads to the conclusion that random selection (i.e., ignoring test scores altogether) is logically defensible, which is anathema to the classic principles of measurement. Arnold (2001) reported that one recent court ruling accepted the use of banding of test scores in employment selection, stating it is the equivalent of assigning letter grades in college. The court said, "Banding is best legitimized from the perspective that it aids in the interpretation of test data and is appropriate from a scientific and/or common sense perspective" (p. 153). The court decision also underscores the point raised by Ebel (1972) that there is no one professionally agreed-upon method to determine passing scores on tests. Furthermore, sometimes selection decisions are made for reasons that have little to do with passing scores (see Field Note 3).

Overview of Personnel Selection

The foregoing discussion of personnel selection addressed several interrelated issues. These issues will be briefly reviewed and summarized to capture the empirical, social, and legal context in which personnel selection decisions are made.

Field Note 3: Dirty Politics

This chapter is devoted to explaining how personnel decisions are made. Many factors have been identified and explained, but one has been left out. I've rarely seen it discussed in any book or article on personnel selection, but (unfortunately) it is sometimes a critical, if not deciding, factor. It is called politics. Consider this experience I had.

I was hired for a very important consulting project: to pick the chief of police for a large city. The job has tremendous visibility, high influence, and great responsibility. I didn't want to "blow it" as the consultant. The city recruited applicants for the opening, and a total of 50 applicants met the minimum qualifications for consideration set by the city. I was handed the 50 applications and told to identify the best candidates in the applicant pool.

My first step was to evaluate each candidate in terms of education and experience using a weighted application-blank procedure. That got the applicant pool down to 25. These 25 quarter-finalists then had to submit written answers to three essay test questions about how they would handle some difficult police problems. These answers were evaluated, and the 15 best applicants proceeded to the semifinalist stage. Here the candidates took a series of personality inventories and intelligence tests. Based on those results, 10 finalists were selected and in turn were subjected to a lengthy oral interview. From all the assessment results, I rank ordered the 10 finalists and submitted the list to the city council, which had the judicial authority to approve the new chief of police. The candidate ranked first was from a different state; the candidate ranked second was the current assistant chief of police, the second in command.

The candidate ranked first was clearly the best person for the job, far and away better than anyone else. I thought the city council (composed of seven people) had an easy job: to approve the top candidate as the new chief of police. It is here that politics came in, and it got rather dirty.

The assistant chief of police was a close friend of three city council members. They played cards together, as did their wives. From the very beginning, the three city council members had known the assistant chief of police would rank high in the selection process. In fact, nearly everyone had thought he would be the next chief of police. When I presented the city council with my list of the 10 candidates, things got very awkward: "Their man" was not first on the list. The press followed the selection process carefully because it was a hot news item. The media announced the rank order of the 10 finalists. The public's general reaction was to have the city council approve the candidate who had been ranked first. But the head of the city council was not about to sell out his old friend.

The head of the city council (one of the three friends) then made this startling announcement. Because every rookie cop on the force dreams about one day rising to be the chief, to award the chief's job to an "outsider" (that is, a candidate not native to the city) would destroy the morale of the police force and take away every rookie's dream forever. Therefore he was going to advise the city council to select as the next chief of police not the person ranked first (the outsider) but the person ranked second (the assistant chief, and his friend). This was the first time anyone had made any reference at all to the insider/outsider

(continued)

Field Note 3 (Continued)

distinction. It was a new hurdle imposed at the eleventh hour as a means of bumping the top-ranked candidate from the list. Some members of the community howled in protest at this announcement, as did the media, declaring it was a "fix" to install the council's personal choice. All the three city council members had to do was convince a fourth member to vote for the second-ranked person and he would be in. In a highly electrified meeting of the city council in a council chamber jam-packed with reporters and camera crews, the city council members publicly cast their votes. By a 4–3 vote, the number-one-ranked candidate (the outsider) was approved and became the new chief of police.

I would like to believe the four "yes" votes came from people who recognized the quality of the top candidate, but I know better. Politics being what it is, strange things can happen. They voted the way they did not simply because they supported the stronger candidate but because they wanted to even a score with the three council members against whom they had held a grudge from a previous political episode. In short, the right decision was made, but for the wrong reason.

I wish to emphasize that there was absolutely nothing in my graduate training to prepare me for this experience. Similarly, there is no section of this book titled "How to Cope with Political Intrigue." But politics is a driving force in all organizations at all levels. Given this fact, sometimes I wonder how I/O psychologists accomplish as much as they do.

The two goals of any personnel selection system are to hire qualified applicants and to fairly assess the ability of all applicants. The issue of "hiring qualified applicants" is subsumed under validity and reflects the correspondence between how well people perform on a test and how well they perform on the job. The issue of "fairly assessing the ability of all applicants" is subsumed under test fairness and reflects that tests are not biased against certain groups of people in our society. Furthermore, these two goals are embedded not only in a social context but also in a legal one. Laws have been passed to help achieve social goals, and personnel selection decisions are held to these legal standards.

Tests of cognitive ability are frequently used in making "high stakes" personnel selection decisions in educational and organizational settings. Hausknecht et al. (2007) estimated that one-fourth to one-half of applicants to jobs in those settings take a selection test a second time because they are dissatisfied with their original test score. The authors examined what effect retesting has on cognitive ability test scores. They concluded that retesting does improve scores, especially when accompanied by coaching and when the same form of the test was administered in both occasions.

Kuncel and Klieger (2007) examined a topic rarely considered in personnel selection. To what degree do candidates simply not apply to institutions if they know their test scores are not high and the institution is very selective in admitting candidates? Based on a large sample of college students who took a standardized test for admission into law school, a high percentage of the students did not even bother to make formal application to the law school once they learned their (low) test score. Kuncel and Klieger concluded that people who know their test scores in advance behave differently than those who don't.

What we have learned about the value of our tests is that they are very good. Schmidt and Hunter (1998) reviewed 85 years of research on many personnel selection methods. Their findings led them to conclude that general mental ability (*g*) was the single most valid predictor (*r* = .51) of job performance. When *g* was combined with a second predictor, the three best combinations in maximizing validity (expressed as a multiple correlation) were *g* plus an integrity test (.65), *g* plus a structured interview (.63), and *g* plus a work sample test (.63). The vast majority of other predictor variables also increased the overall predictive accuracy of a selection system beyond *g*. Personnel selection tests are as accurate as diagnostic tests in medicine, but they are far from perfect. Accordingly, selection errors (i.e., false negatives and false positives) always occur. Do these errors occur evenly across all group of applicants, or do they fall disproportionately more on some groups than others? This is the subject of the fairness of our tests. The population of the United States is a melting pot or amalgam of a broad range of racial, ethnic, and religious groups. As a nation we want that diversity reflected in our workforce. The constant tension in our society regarding personnel selection revolves around meeting these two goals—selecting qualified applicants and achieving diversification in the workforce.

There is often a direct relationship between people's preference for one of these two goals and their stance on affirmative action (see The Changing Nature of Work: Affirmative Action and the Conduct of Work, p. 176). Over the past 40 years (since passage of the Civil Rights Act of 1964) the pendulum for the relative social preference for these two goals has swung back and forth. Sackett et al. (2001) described what they call "high-stakes testing," which reflects that important decisions in life (e.g., admission into a school or job) often depend on the results of a test. Caught in the bind of using valid tests to make hiring decisions that produce adverse impact, some institutions have sought to use less valid tests that produce less adverse impact. However, doing so weakens the institution's commitment to selecting the most qualified applicants. Some universities have abandoned the use of tests (e.g., the SAT) in making admissions decisions to greater increase their chances of having diversified student populations. Sackett et al. believe the massive amount of research findings on psychological assessment reveals that it is not possible to simultaneously maximize the twin goals of having a highly diversified workforce (or student population) and selecting the most qualified applicants. Nevertheless, attempts to find ways to both maximize the quality of the selected workforce and reduce the level of adverse impact continue (e.g., De Corte, 1999; Ryan, Ployhart, & Friedel, 1998).

Indeed, Posthuma, Roehling, and Campion (2006) identified complex legal issues regarding the applicability of U.S. employment laws (such as the Civil Rights Act, the Age Discrimination in Employment Act, and the Americans with Disabilities Act) to foreign companies operating in the U.S., as well as U.S. companies operating overseas. The era of global business has compelled consideration of legal issues regarding employment to contexts that were not envisioned when the laws were enacted.

The conflict between the pursuit of these two goals is addressed within the legal system. Ultimately the courts decide what is judged to be the fairest resolution of the conflict. In an employment context, the *Uniform Selection Guidelines* define the standards for validating tests. In reality, it is often difficult for employers to validate

The Changing Nature of Work: Affirmative Action and the Conduct of Work

The national debate on affirmative action often addresses the social importance of diversity. It is proposed that because our nation is a melting pot of different races and nationalities, these differences should be proportionately distributed across the full spectrum of social activities, including participation in all levels of employment. The theme is social justice or fairness. Thus diversity should be sought because it is the morally right thing to do. However, another argument in favor of using affirmative action to achieve diversity has little to do with social justice. It is argued that diversity helps achieve success or effectiveness. From the perspective of a company that makes products or offers services, the market for its products or services is often diverse; that is, people of different races, religions, and ethnic backgrounds are likely customers. Because people of different races, religion, and ethnic backgrounds have different preferences, styles, and values, the organization can increase its sales by hiring employees who are as diverse as the markets they serve. Diversity in the employees will help the organization better serve the needs of its diverse customers.

Crosby et al. (2003) described how responding to the need for diversity increased an organization's effectiveness by changing the conduct of its work. In the 1970s the New York City Fire Department was sued for sex discrimination. A test of physical strength was required for all candidates. The test measured such dimensions of physical strength as endurance, explosive strength, and manual flexibility. Because men (on average) have larger bones and more muscle mass than women (on average), the test of physical strength had adverse impact against women. The basis for using the test as a selection method was to ensure that each firefighter was strong enough to perform those tasks in firefighting that required great strength. After the lawsuit the administrators of the fire department decided to move from an individual firefighter approach to a team approach. A team would consist of the coordinated efforts of individual firefighters, who performed different tasks within the team. Not all firefighting activities require intense physical strength. Women can perform many of the tasks within a firefighting unit, such as treating burn victims and responding to spills of hazardous material. Here is a case where understanding why (gender) diversity was not being achieved and redesigning the manner in which work was performed resulted in increased effectiveness of the unit.

tests because of the large sample sizes needed to do so accurately. Simply put, most organizations don't employ enough people in specific jobs to satisfy the conditions needed to conduct empirical validation research. The problem of insufficient sample sizes in validation has been of great concern among employers (i.e., Hoffman, Holden, & Gale, 2000; Peterson, Wise, et al., 2001). Psychologists have proposed the concept of validity generalization as a means of demonstrating the validity of tests, and the concept enjoys support among I/O psychologists. Court cases are judged by legal standards, however, not psychological concepts, and it is a matter of debate whether the courts would fully accept validity generalization as a means of demonstrating the appropriateness of a personnel selection method. As Hoffman and McPhail (1998) stated, "Depending on the stringency with which the job analysis and investigation of fairness [of the *Guidelines*] are enforced, the use of validity generalization arguments in support of test use in a particular setting may or may not be acceptable. . . . (S)ole reliance on validity generalization to support test use is probably premature" (p. 990). New-man, Jacobs, and Bartram (2007) proposed a statistical method whereby the results from both local validation studies and validity generalization could be used to establish the validity of personnel selection systems that satisfy both legal requirements and business objectives. The authors believe that the local validation study and the validity generalization concept both have something to offer.

In conclusion, personnel selection is predicated upon a complex mix of technical and social factors embedded in a legal framework. I/O psychologists are called upon to render our best professional judgments to facilitate the flow of people into the workforce. They must be highly aware of the dual goals of any selection system, with the full realization that simultaneously achieving both goals is often very difficult. Our profession can contribute knowledge regarding the scientific and technical aspects of personnel selection, but social preferences for what constitutes justice or fairness are at the core of the issues to be addressed.

Vinchur (2007) concluded that personnel selection has been a core activity of I/O psychology for over 100 years. The basic criterion-related paradigm for determining validity has endured, as well as many of the techniques, predictors, and criteria used by early psychologists. "The 'criterion problem' and the need to differentiate scientifically sound from unsound practice is still a matter of concern today . . . There is consistency underlying selection practice and research that would make much present-day practice recognizable to the early pioneers in the field" (p. 213).

Test Utility and Organizational Efficiency

Many resources contribute to the success of an organization; employees are just one of them. Each resource must contribute to the organization's overall success. If the company is a profit-making firm (as many are) or just wants to improve its operating efficiency (as all organizations should), a basic question is how much improved personnel selection techniques contribute to its overall profitability or efficiency. If more productive workers are hired as a result of a new selection technique, how much value or utility will they have to the company? The **utility** of a test is literally its value—where "value" is measured in monetary or economic terms. Several studies have shown just how much utility a valid testing program can provide.

Utility
A concept reflecting the economic value (expressed in monetary terms) of making personnel decisions.

Based on such factors as the validity of the selection test, the selection ratio, and the estimated dollar worth of hiring "good" employees, researchers have calculated the utility of an organization using the test to enhance the overall economic benefit to the company. The results were calculated in the millions of dollars per year for the hiring organization, depending on the number of employees hired and the value of the jobs to the organization. Yoo and Muchinsky (1998) found that employees who perform very well in jobs that require complex interpersonal skills (e.g., mentoring, negotiating) add great value to their organizations. The key element in improved utility is test validity. The impact of test validity on subsequent job performance is dramatic; there is no substitute for using "good" selection techniques.

Despite the impressive dollar values of using valid selection procedures, the acceptability of the statistical procedures used to derive the utility values among organizational decision makers is often low (Carson, Becker, & Henderson, 1998). A method

Benchmarking
The process of comparing a company's products or procedures with those of the leading companies in an industry.

that is highly accepted among managers in getting organizations to adopt testing procedures is called *benchmarking*. **Benchmarking** is the process of comparing leading organizations in terms of their professional practices. Jayne and Rauschenberger (2000) stated, "Executives are fascinated with comparing practices of their own firms with those of others. [T]hey provide decision makers with specific real-world examples that a proposed intervention works" (p. 140). In short, business leaders are skeptical of the ability to assess the exact dollar value of using selection tests. However, if other leading companies in an industry are using tests, it becomes prudent to follow their practices.

Placement and Classification

The vast majority of research in personnel psychology is on selection, the process by which applicants are hired. Another personnel function (albeit less common) involves deciding which jobs people should be assigned to after they have been hired. This personnel function is called either *placement* or *classification*, depending on the basis for the assignment. In many cases selection and placement are not separate procedures. Usually people apply for particular jobs. If they are hired, they fill the jobs they were applying for. In some organizations (and at certain times in our nation's history), however, decisions about selection and placement have to be made separately.

Placement and classification decisions are usually limited to large organizations that have two or more jobs an applicant could fill. It must be decided which job best matches the person's talents and abilities. A classic example is the military. Thousands of applicants used to be selected each year, either voluntarily or through the draft. The next question was where to assign them. Placement and classification procedures are designed to get the best match between people and jobs.

Placement
The process of assigning individuals to jobs based on one test score.

Classification
The process of assigning individuals to jobs based on two or more test scores.

Placement differs from classification on the basis of the number of predictors used to make the job assignment. **Placement** is allocating people to two or more groups (or jobs) on the basis of a single predictor score. Many middle school students are placed into math classes on the basis of a math aptitude test. **Classification** is allocating people to jobs on the basis of two or more valid predictor factors. For this reason, classification is more complex; however, it results in a better assignment of people to jobs than placement. Classification uses smaller selection ratios than placement, which accounts for its greater utility. The reason classification is not always used instead of placement is that it is often difficult to find two or more valid predictors to use in assigning people to jobs. The military has been the object of most classification research. Military recruits take a battery of different tests covering such areas as intelligence, ability, and aptitude. On the basis of these scores, recruits are assigned to jobs in the infantry, medical corps, military intelligence, and so on. Other organizations that have to assign large numbers of people to large numbers of jobs also use this procedure. Given this constraint, relatively few companies need to use classification procedures.

At one time, placement and classification were as important as (if not more so than) selection. During World War II, industry needed large numbers of people to produce war material. The question was not whether people would get a job but what kind of job they would fill. A similar situation occurred in the military, as thousands of candidates were selected each month. The next phase was to assign them to the jobs for which they were best suited. Today the military continues to have the most interest in classification (Campbell, Harris, & Knapp, 2001). The problems and issues faced in the classification of military personnel are traditional—trying to balance the needs of the organization with the abilities of the individual (Rosse, Campbell, & Peterson, 2001). Attending to the preferences and aspirations of individuals who enter the military is not a trivial matter, however. As Walker and Rumsey (2001) noted, military recruiters and guidance counselors must fill openings with candidates from an all-volunteer applicant pool. This contrasts with a time in U.S. history where military service was compulsory.

Researchers interested in classification have addressed many of the same issues that are confronted in selection. For example, Bobko (1994) reported that the most vexing issues facing classification decisions revolve around values, such as attaining ethnic and gender balance versus maximizing performance. The relative importance of general mental ability (g) versus other factors is also a matter of debate in making classification decisions. Zeidner and Johnson (1994) believe other factors besides g must be considered in efficiently assigning individuals to jobs. In addition to cognitive ability, Alley (1994) recommended the assessment of personality, interests, and knowledge. The rationale behind placement and classification remains the same: certain people will perform better than others in certain jobs. To this end, placement and classification are aimed at assigning people to jobs in which their predicted job performance will be the best.

Case Study   Just Give Me a Chance

Hugh Casey slumped at his desk, totally dejected. He just read the letter from Fulbright University informing him that his application for admission into the school of medicine had been rejected. It had been his dream since high school to become a doctor, and in particular to be a heart surgeon. Hugh had been an excellent student in high school and was admitted to the highly selective Seymour College despite achieving only a modest score on the college admissions test. His interest in medicine was sparked when his father had triple-bypass heart surgery. The surgeon who performed the operation, Dr. Charles Dressen, was a friend of the family. Dr. Dressen had graduated from Fulbright University's medical school, which was nationally renowned for its high standards. Fulbright was the premier medical school in the region. Hugh wanted to emulate Dr. Dressen, to become a heart surgeon who saved lives, just as Dr. Dressen had saved his father's life. Fulbright was not only his first choice for medical school, it was his only choice. Hugh felt it almost was his destiny to graduate with a medical degree from Fulbright and follow in Dr. Dressen's footsteps.

At Seymour College, Hugh made the dean's list during the last four semesters. His overall grade point average was 3.60. After a rough freshman year, which many first-year students experience, he settled down and performed very well in the pre-med curriculum. At the start of his senior year he took the medical college admissions test and did not score extremely well. It was the same story with the admissions test used by Seymour. He just didn't test well in standardized three-hour examinations. However, Hugh felt he had more than proved himself by his performance at Seymour. He believed that doing well over a four-year period should count more in his application to medical school than his performance in a three-hour test.

Furthermore, three professors at Seymour wrote what they said were very positive letters of recommendation on Hugh's behalf. Even Dr. Dressen, a graduate of

Fulbright's medical school, wrote a letter to his alma mater in support of Hugh. Finally, Hugh traveled to Fulbright for an interview with the medical school's admissions committee. Although he was admittedly nervous, Hugh felt the interview had gone very well. He was particularly delighted to tell the committee about his coming to know Dr. Dressen, and how Dr. Dressen had become his inspirational role model. Hugh got goose bumps when he walked through the halls of the medical school during his visit to Fulbright. He just knew Fulbright was the place for him.

Hugh stared at the rejection letter feeling devastated and angry. How could Fulbright do this to him? How did the admissions committee reach its decision? Hugh had earned excellent grades in high school and college, and he just knew he would do equally well in medical school. Hugh reasoned their rejection implied they thought he wouldn't make it through medical school. What would he have to do to prove himself, to prove to the admissions committee he would be a successful medical school student and then a successful heart surgeon? Hugh decided he would ask Fulbright to admit him on a conditional basis, not even knowing whether the medical school had such a policy. He would agree to be evaluated after one year in medical school. If he were performing poorly, he would leave Fulbright and accept that the admissions committee's initial decision on his application was correct. But if he performed well in that year, then he would want to be fully admitted to the medical school and no longer be under their scrutiny. Hugh wanted to prove to himself, to Fulbright, and to the world that he would become as great a heart surgeon as Dr. Dressen. All he wanted was a chance.

Questions

1. Which type of selection mistake (false positive or false negative) do you think Fulbright wants to avoid? Why does Fulbright feel this way?
2. Do you believe Fulbright thinks Hugh won't be successful in medical school, and that is why they rejected his application? Or do you believe Fulbright probably concluded Hugh would be successful in medical school, but there were simply other candidates who had better credentials?
3. If organizations are faced with evaluating many qualified applicants and they have more qualified applicants than there are openings, should a personal experience of the type Hugh had with Dr. Dressen be a factor in determining admission? Why or why not?
4. If you were on the admissions committee at Fulbright, how would you make decisions about applicants in a way that is fair and reasonable to both the medical school and the applicants?
5. What do you think about Hugh's plea to be given a chance to prove himself? Is Hugh unreasonable? Given the imperfect validity of our selection methods, should organizations give applicants a chance to prove themselves in a trial period on the job (or in school)? Why or why not?

Chapter Summary

- Personnel decisions are decisions made in organizations that affect people's worklives, such as selection, placement, and discharge.

- All business organizations must make personnel decisions about their employees. Some organizations use less formal and scientifically based methods than others.
- In the United States (and in most countries) personnel decisions are made in a strong legal context. Many laws protect the rights of individuals as employees.
- Affirmative action is a social policy designed to achieve a diverse and productive workforce. There is much controversy and social debate about the merits of affirmative action.
- Recruitment is the process by which individuals are encouraged to apply for work. The individuals selected for employment can be drawn only from those who have applied.
- Two statistical procedures, regression and multiple regression analysis, are useful for making personnel selection decisions.
- Validity generalization is the principle that the predictive capacity of a test generalizes or is applicable to a wide range of job applicants and employment contexts.
- A useful model is that effective employees are those who are skilled in performing their own jobs, contribute to the well-being of the organization, and are adaptable to changing conditions.
- Because our tests do not have perfect validity, errors or mistakes in hiring occur. We can falsely hire a poor employee or falsely reject someone who would have been a good employee. True positives and negatives and false positives and negatives are useful concepts to consider in selection decisions.
- It has been demonstrated that using valid personnel selection methods leads to large economic gains for the hiring organization.
- Placement and classification decisions refer to assigning workers to those jobs for which they are best suited.

Learning Objectives

- Explain the relationship between learning and task performance.
- Describe the assessment of training needs through organizational, task, and person analysis.
- Know the major methods of training and their associated strengths and weaknesses.
- Describe the importance of cultural diversity training, expatriate training, sexual harassment training, mentoring, and executive coaching in management development.
- Explain the evaluation of training and development programs.

As we have discussed throughout this book, the work world is changing rapidly. The economic and social pressures brought to bear on organizations affect the conduct of work and make it necessary for employees to serve larger strategic business needs. A generation ago employees were hired primarily to fill jobs that had specified KSAOs and tasks to be performed. Emphasis was placed on selection, finding the "round peg (the person) for the round hole (the job)." Metaphorically speaking, today the shape of the hole is continuously changing, thereby weakening the meaning of a "job." One implication of this changing nature of work is that greater relative importance is placed on skill *enhancement*. Organizations need to hire intelligent workers who are willing to learn new skills, skills determined by external conditions. For example, the skills may require increased technological sophistication, a greater emphasis on teamwork, the ability to deal with a diverse customer base, or any other issue related to the success of the organization. Simply put, organizations (and their employees) must continually learn new skills to adapt to a rapidly changing business world. The title of this chapter is therefore "Organizational Learning," which encompasses issues associated with **training** and developing the workforce.

Training
The process through which the knowledge and skills of employees are enhanced.

The importance of organizational learning is escalating. Blanchard and Thacker (2004) reported that in 2002, $60 billion was spent on training and development activities in U.S. companies that had 100 or more employees. The job title of the person in the organization responsible for these activities is evolving from "Director of Training and Development" to "Chief Learning Officer" (Danielson & Wiggenhorn, 2003). Thus "learning" has ascended to the same level previously reserved for finance (Chief Financial Officer) and operations (Chief Operating Officer). Danielson and Wiggenhorn offered the following assessment of the importance of organizational learning:

> Today's progressive corporations have moved from treating learning as an obligatory cost factor to regarding it as a weapon in the battle for competitive advantage. . . , The escalating level of investment corporations have made in learning, and the accompanying expectations of the investment's enhancing firm performance, have combined to create greater urgency in the search for models or tools for evaluating and improving transfer of learning. (p. 17)

In Chapter 1 the current era in the history of I/O psychology was called the Information Age. Kraiger and Ford (2007) stated that around 1990, the modern global business era compelled organizations to enter the era of strategic learning. The strategic learning approach was necessitated by the intense pressures associated with organizations having to increase their opportunity to learn, adapt, and change in response to these pressures. Organizations promoted continuous learning cultures, and recognized "the potential for improving organizational effectiveness was vastly increased when knowledge at every level was focused on the goals of quality, innovation, and continuous improvement" (p. 296). We are awash in a sea of information in our lives, and how we convert this information to usable knowledge is the basis of our modern economy. Tannenbaum (2002) stated, "An increasing percentage of people in the workforce can be thought of as knowledge workers—they work with information and ideas or solve problems and carry out creative tasks" (p. 15). The U.S. Department of Labor estimated that today on average 50% of an employee's knowledge and skills become outdated every 30–60 *months*, compared with an estimated 12–15 *years* in the 1970s. Although not all work is changing as rapidly as work that is information-intensive, we have reached a point where the skills we bring to a job are dwarfed in comparison to the new skills we must acquire as part of "learning a living."

Learning and Task Performance

Learning
The process by which change in knowledge or skills is acquired through education or experience.

Learning can be defined as the process of encoding, retaining, and using information. This view of learning prompted Howell and Cooke (1989) to refer to individuals as "human information processors." The specific procedures by which we process information for both short-term and long-term use has been the subject of extensive research in cognitive psychology (Weiss, 1990). This section will examine some useful findings from this body of research that facilitate our understanding of how learning affects the training and development process.

Anderson (1985) suggested that skill acquisition be segmented into three phases: declarative knowledge, knowledge compilation, and procedural knowledge. **Declarative knowledge** is knowledge about facts and things. The declarative knowledge of skill acquisition involves memorizing and reasoning processes that allow the individual to attain a basic understanding of a task. During this phase the individual may observe demonstrations of the task and learn task-sequencing rules. Individuals must devote nearly all of their attention to understanding and performing the task. Performance in the declarative knowledge stage is slow and prone to error. Only after the person has acquired an adequate understanding of the task can he or she proceed to the second phase, the **knowledge compilation** phase.

Declarative knowledge
A body of knowledge about facts and things. Often compared with procedural knowledge.

During this second stage of skill acquisition, individuals integrate the sequences of cognitive and motor processes required to perform the task. Various methods for simplifying or streamlining the task are tried and evaluated. Performance then becomes faster and more accurate than in the declarative knowledge phase. The attentional demands on the individual are reduced as the task objectives and procedures are moved from short-term to long-term memory.

Knowledge compilation
The body of knowledge acquired as a result of learning.

Procedural knowledge is knowledge about how to perform various cognitive activities. This final phase of skill acquisition is reached when the individual has essentially automatized the skill and can perform the task efficiently with little attention (Kanfer & Ackerman, 1989). After considerable practice, the person can do the task with minimal impairment while devoting attention to other tasks. DuBois (2002) reported this procedural knowledge becomes second nature to expert performers, so that they report difficulty in describing what they know that others do not know.

Procedural knowledge
A body of knowledge about how to use information to address issues and solve problems. Often compared with declarative knowledge.

Ackerman (1987) proposed that three major classes of abilities are critically important for performance in the three phases of skill acquisition. *General intellectual ability (g)* is posited to be the most important factor in acquiring declarative knowledge. When the individual first confronts a novel task, the attentional demands are high. As he or she begins to understand the demands of the task and develops a performance strategy, the attentional demands decrease and the importance of intellectual ability for task performance is lessened.

As the individual moves along the skill acquisition curve from declarative to procedural knowledge, *perceptual speed abilities* become important. The individual develops a basic understanding of how to perform the task but seeks a more efficient method for accomplishing the task with minimal attentional effort. Perceptual speed abilities seem most critical for processing information faster or more efficiently at this phase.

Finally, as individuals move to the final phase of skill acquisition, their performance is limited by their level of *psychomotor ability*. "Thus individual differences in final, skilled performance are not necessarily determined by the same abilities that affect the initial level of task performance or the speed of skill acquisition" (Kanfer & Ackerman, 1989, p. 664). Farrell and McDaniel (2001) found empirical support for this model of skill acquisition when examined in an applied setting. Therefore psychomotor abilities (such as coordination) determine the final level of task performance in the procedural knowledge phase.

It should be evident based on these research findings from cognitive psychology that there are complex relationships between individual abilities and phases of task performance. These findings offer an explanation of why some individuals may be quick to acquire minimal competency in a task but do not subsequently develop a high degree of task proficiency. Alternatively, other individuals may initially learn a task slowly but gradually develop a high level of task proficiency. Research by Morrison and Brantner (1992) revealed that learning the requirements of jobs in the military occurred in stages, with plateaus in learning followed by subsequent periods of growth. It appears that the relationship between learning and task performance is more complex than many researchers have believed. These findings bear not only on why certain individuals learn at different rates of speed but also on how training and development processes have to be targeted to enhance selected individual abilities. This conclusion was also supported by the research of Kluger and DeNisi (1996). Their meta-analysis of the effects of feedback on performance revealed that learning to perform tasks depends on a complex set of factors that affect gains in performance as well as the duration of the performance. The process of how we learn to perform tasks appears more complex than we have long believed.

Several major studies have been conducted that reveal the process by which learning occurs and transfers to the job. Ford and Kraiger (1995) identified three distinguishing characteristics of people who are regarded as experts on a topic versus novices. The first is proceduralization and automaticity. *Proceduralization* refers to a set of conditional action rules: if Condition A exists, then Action B is needed. *Automaticity* refers to a state of rapid performance that requires little cognitive effort. Automaticity enables a person to accomplish a task without conscious monitoring and thus allows concurrent performance of additional tasks. Experts not only "know" things but also know when that knowledge is applicable and when it should not be used. Novices may be equally competent at recalling specific information, but experts are much better at relating that information in cause-and-effect sequences. The second characteristic is *mental models*, which is the way knowledge is organized. The mental models of experts are qualitatively better because they contain more diagnostic cues for detecting meaningful patterns in learning. Experts have more complex knowledge structures, resulting in faster solution times. The third characteristic is *meta-cognition*. Meta-cognition is an individual's knowledge of and control over his or her cognitions. Experts have a greater understanding of the demands of a task and their own capabilities. Experts are more likely to discontinue a problem-solving strategy that would ultimately prove to be unsuccessful.

Ford et al. (1998) and Chen et al. (2000) both described the importance of a task-specific individual attribute for learning. Chen et al. distinguished "trait-like" and "state-like" individual differences. Trait-like attributes include cognitive ability and personality, which are not specific to a certain task or situation and are stable over time.

Self-efficacy
A sense of personal control and being able to master one's environment.

State-like attributes are task-specific. The most critical state-like attribute for learning is **self-efficacy**. Self-efficacy is the belief in one's own capabilities to mobilize the motivation, cognitive resources, and courses of action needed to meet given situational demands. A sense of self-efficacy, tied to a specific task, is reflected in the belief that "I can do this" and a feeling of getting "up" for a task. In contrast, low self-efficacy is reflected in the belief that there are some types of tasks (e.g., math problems) you are not good at. Ford et al. asserted it is important to develop a sense of self-efficacy in trainees—namely, that they feel confident and positive about being able to learn the material. The authors advise trainers to teach not only knowledge and skills but also other learning traits that facilitate the development of self-efficacy.

The Pretraining Environment

Tannenbaum and Yukl (1992) reviewed evidence suggesting that events that take place prior to training (i.e., the pretraining environment) can influence the effectiveness of training. Management actions and decisions provide cues that signal employee motivation for training (see The Changing Nature of Work: The Pretraining Environment and Workplace Safety). Employees start to learn about the way training is viewed in the organization early in the socialization process and continue to gather information with each training activity they attend. Some actions signal to trainees whether training is important (e.g., supervisory and peer support). Other actions reveal to employees the amount of control, participation, or input they have in the training process (e.g., participation in needs assessment).

The Changing Nature of Work: The Pretraining Environment and Workplace Safety

The topic of workplace safety represents a dilemma for those individuals responsible for it. On the one hand, workplace safety is a major concern for a wide range of employers. Concerns about safety are stereotypically associated with industrial work, but they also extend to office work that involves eye, neck, and hand strain with data entry. On the other hand, safety training programs are often described as boring by participants. It is often difficult to get employees inspired about the topic. Whereas most training programs are designed to help achieve or attain positive outcomes, safety training programs are designed to help prevent negative outcomes (accidents and injuries).

   A consistent finding from contemporary safety research is that the most critical need is not a list of dos and don'ts or even a set of policies and procedures to follow in workplace behavior. Rather it is the general environment or climate the organization establishes about the importance of safety. Organizations with a positive safety climate have training programs that may be based on the latest computer-based methods, give executive authority to safety officials, have high-ranking managers on safety committees, and may offer financial incentives to employees for accident-free behavior. If the organization actively shows its commitment and support to safety and establishes consequences associated with employee behavior, then the likelihood of effective safety training is much higher. The importance of the pretraining environment is no more evident than in the area of safety training.

Cohen (1990) found that trainees who had more supportive supervisors entered training with stronger beliefs that training would be useful. Supportive supervisors discussed upcoming training courses with their employees, established training goals, provided them release time to prepare, and generally encouraged the employees. Baldwin and Magjuka (1991) found that trainees who entered training expecting some form of follow-up activity or assessment afterward reported stronger intentions to transfer what they learned back on the job. The fact that their supervisor required them to prepare a posttraining report meant they were held accountable for their own learning and apparently conveyed the message that the training was important. The converse is also true. Mathieu, Tannenbaum, and Salas (1990) found that trainees who reported many limitations in their job (e.g., lack of time, equipment, and resources) entered training with lower motivation to learn. These trainees had little incentive to learn new skills in an environment where they could not apply them.

As Tannenbaum and Yukl (1992) articulated, several factors representative of the organizational environment in which training occurs bear directly on its effectiveness. Training does not occur in a vacuum; it is but a means to an end. Factors that strengthen the linkage between training and relevant outcomes can be as critical as the training itself.

Assessing Training Needs

The entire personnel training process has a rational design as proposed by Goldstein and Ford (2002). The design of personnel training begins with an analysis of training needs and ends with the assessment of training results. Important intermediate steps involve developing objectives, choosing methods, and designing an evaluation. Training directors must keep up with the current literature on training methods because previous successes or failures can help shape the selection or design of a training program. It is equally important to determine a means of evaluating the program before it is implemented; that is, evaluative criteria must be selected to serve as the program's scorecard. The bulk of this chapter will discuss the major steps in the design of personnel training.

The assessment of training needs consists of a classic three-step process: organizational analysis, task analysis, and person analysis.

Organizational Analysis

Organizational analysis
A phase of training needs analysis directed at determining whether training is a viable solution to organizational problems, and if so, where in the organization training should be directed.

In the evolution of thinking on training and development, the early focus of organizational analysis was on factors that provided information about where and when training could be used in the organization. More contemporary thinking has transformed **organizational analysis** into an examination of systemwide components that determine whether the training program can produce behavior that will transfer to the organization. Organizational analysis should provide information on whether training is even necessary, whether training is the right approach, whether resources are available to develop and conduct training, and whether management and employees will support its implementation. Goldstein (1991) noted that trainees are presented with an inherent contrast. They learn or develop skills in one context (the training environment) and are expected to apply these skills in a different context (the work environment). An analysis of a successful training program includes not only the specific content of the training but also the factors that facilitate the application of skills on the job that were learned in training. The topic of transfer of training will be discussed in more detail later in the chapter.

In summary, organizational analysis examines systemwide factors that facilitate or retard the transfer of skills from training to the job. Whatever factors facilitate the development of new skills in training should also be present on the job to facilitate maintenance of those skills.

Task Analysis

Task analysis
A phase of training needs analysis directed at identifying which tasks in a job should be targeted for improved performance.

A **task analysis** is used to determine the training objectives that are related to the performance of particular activities or job operations. Information relevant to a task analysis could conceivably be taken from a job analysis, as discussed in Chapter 3. A task analysis specifies the activities performed on the job as well as other factors pertaining to the conduct of work.

Development of Task Statements.   The goal of task analysis is to understand the work performed by an employee as well as how the work is conducted and its purpose. The topic of task analysis was also referenced in Chapter 3. The following two examples of task statements were provided by Goldstein (1991, p. 529):

> *From the job of a secretary*: "Sorts correspondence, forms, and reports to facilitate filing them alphabetically."
> *From the job of a supervisor*: "Inform next shift supervisor of departmental status through written reports so that the number of employees needed at each workstation can be determined."

It would not be unusual to have as many as 100 task statements to describe the tasks performed in a job. The more varied the job, the greater the number of task statements.

Development of KSAs and Relevant Tasks.   A useful way for specifying the human capabilities needed to perform tasks is through knowledge, skills, and abilities (KSAs). *Knowledge* (K) refers to a body of information learned through education or experience that is relevant to job performance. Examples include knowledge of accounting, electricity, and geography. *Skill* (S) refers to specific behaviors that may be enhanced through training. Examples include skill in dribbling a basketball, driving an automobile, and repairing a damaged object. *Ability* (A) refers to cognitive or physical attributes that are primarily genetically determined (i.e., "natural ability") and as such cannot be enhanced through training. Examples include mental ability, musical ability, and artistic ability. The purpose of this analysis is to establish the KSAs needed to perform particular tasks. Most often, persons who directly supervise the job being analyzed serve as SMEs to provide this information because they often think about what a job incumbent needs to know or what skills and abilities the incumbent needs in order to perform the tasks. Goldstein (1991, p. 532) proposed that among the questions asked of SMEs to elicit KSA information are these:

- "What are the characteristics of good and poor employees on [tasks in cluster]?"
- "Think of someone you know who is better than anyone else at [tasks in cluster]. What is the reason he or she does it so well?"

- "What does a person need to know in order to [tasks in cluster]?"

The researcher then develops linkages between the tasks performed on a job and the knowledge, skills, and abilities needed to perform them.

Development of Training Programs from the KSA–Task Links.   The linkages between the KSAs and tasks provide the basis for developing training programs to enhance those KSAs that are critical to job performance. The relevance of the training for KSA enhancement is established through the linkage. Mager (1984) recommended that after the tasks have been specified and the KSAs have been identified, effective behaviors should be established that will indicate the task has been performed correctly. It can also be helpful to identify what ineffective behaviors are being exhibited when a task is performed incorrectly. It is to the advantage of both the trainer and trainee that there be agreement and understanding of those specific behaviors that must be acquired and the standards to which the trainee will be held. A task-based system of training needs cannot usually provide the entire foundation for a training system. If training is provided on the exact tasks that exist on the job, the training system has very high **physical fidelity**. However, most training systems cannot achieve perfect physical fidelity. Therefore training usually consists of some variation in the tasks or conditions found on the job. The goal is to design training in such a way that permits a trainee to call forth the skills and abilities that need to be learned. An effective training environment is one that has a high degree of **psychological fidelity** in that it sets the stage for the trainee to learn the KSAs that will be applied on the job.

Person Analysis

Person analysis is directed at differences among employees in their individual training needs. It identifies specific individuals in the organization who could benefit from training and the specific type of training that would benefit them. On many occasions the need for individual training is revealed through an appraisal of the employee's performance. Performance appraisal is the subject of Chapter 7, and the issues inherent in its use will be discussed soon. For the moment, however, realize that performance appraisal is typically conducted for two reasons. One is to diagnose the employees' strengths and weaknesses as an aid in their development. The other reason is to evaluate the employees for the purpose of making administrative decisions, such as pay raises and promotions. Person analysis is predicated upon the diagnostic purpose of performance appraisal—to provide learning experiences helpful to the employee. To the extent that person analysis is directed solely to developmental issues and not administrative ones, there is usually little employee resistance to it. There is also some evidence that self-evaluations of ability may be of value in identifying individual training needs. Finally, it is possible to direct a person analysis of training needs not only to the present but also to the future in terms of what KSAs need to be learned to reach the next level of the organization. In this case, SMEs, usually upper-level managers, articulate the KSAs needed to perform future job requirements. An example (Frisch, 1998) of the results of a person analysis that shows the developmental needs of employees is shown in Figure 6-1, p. 190.

In summary, Ostroff and Ford (1989) concluded that the classic tripartite approach of needs analysis (organization, task, and person) is entrenched in the profession as the basis for all subsequent training issues. Although we still regard these three

Physical fidelity
The degree of similarity between the physical characteristics of the training environment and the work environment. Often compared with psychological fidelity.

Psychological fidelity
A concept from training pertaining to the degree of similarity between the knowledge, skills, and abilities (KSAs) learned in training and the KSAs needed to perform the job.

Person analysis
A phase of training needs analysis directed at identifying which individuals within an organization should receive training.

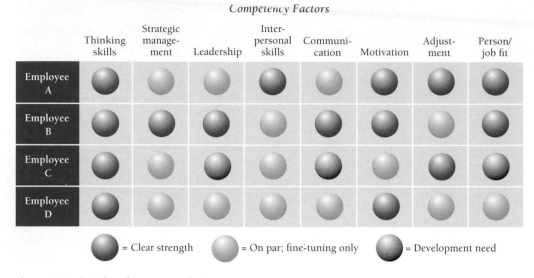

Figure 6–1   *Results of person analysis*

Source: Adapted from "Designing the Individual Assessment Process," by M. H. Frisch. In R. Jeanneret and R. Silzer (eds.), *Individual Psychological Assessment*, Jossey-Bass, 1999.

perspectives as a useful framework for determining training needs, the specific content of each continues to evolve over time. The most recent advances in training have demonstrated the critical importance of cues and consequences that promote the transfer of skills from training to the job. We are now more aware of the need to examine factors that enable us to successfully apply training to the job. These factors are just as critical as (if not more so than) the specific nature of the training.

Methods and Techniques of Training

Brown and Ford (2002) stated that in just the past few years there has been a dramatic shift away from instructor-led, classroom training toward learner-centered, technology-mediated training. A study of leading companies found a 20% reduction in classroom training between 1997 and 2000, with much of that time converted to training delivered via CD-ROMs, intranets, or the internet. That trend has undoubtedly continued, "thus computer-based training, in its many forms, is the future of training—and the future has arrived" (Brown & Ford, p. 192). Therefore the major focus of this section will be on computer-based training methods (see Field Note 1). Four of these methods will be presented, followed by three non–computer-based training methods that are used with considerable frequency.

Computer-Based Training

Blanchard and Thacker (2004) presented a comprehensive description of various computer-based training methods. The social acceptance and adoption of electronic technology and computer networks witnessed since the birth of the internet in the

Field Note 1: Distance Learning

Computers are having a profound impact in the field of education at all levels. Children in the early grades of elementary school are learning how to operate a computer. Today's high school graduates have a level of computer literacy that greatly exceeds that of college graduates less than a generation ago. Computer-aided instruction is changing the very nature of the educational process at the college level. An increasingly large number of students want a college education, yet they work during the day and may not have a university nearby that offers evening instruction. A solution to this problem is called *distance learning*, meaning that students can enroll in college courses yet not be physically present at the college. Course lectures offered at the college are videotaped and made available for viewing by students on their personal computers, at whatever time the students have available. Thus a course can be offered without regard to time or space because computer technology delivers the course to the student. Some universities are now offering entire degree programs to students through this technology. A student can earn a degree from a university without ever having physically attended the university. Such degree programs are in their infancy, and they do require the technical support needed to make such an offering possible. However, their very existence attests to the power of the computer in being the dominant technological innovation at the beginning of the 21st century.

Computer-based training
A method of training that utilizes computer technology (such as CD-ROM) to enhance the acquisition of knowledge and skills.

early 1990s created this general class of training methods. Van Buren (2001) estimated that "about 75% of organizations surveyed indicated they provided training to employees through the internet or an intranet (accessible only to those in the particular organization)" (Blanchard & Thacker, 2004, p. 243). **Computer-based training** is simply a form of training that occurs through the use of a computer and does not require a human trainer. Among the advantages of computer-based training Blanchard and Thacker discussed are:

- Learning time is reduced.
- Cost of training is reduced.
- Privacy of learning is increased.
- Access to training is increased.

The disadvantages to computer-based training include:

- There can be high developmental costs to create the training course.
- A sufficient number of employees must take the course to make it a cost-efficient means of training.
- The content of the course must remain sufficiently stable.

Blanchard and Thacker offered this assessment of computer-based training methods: "Developing any CBT [computer-based training] program from scratch is a labor intensive process requiring knowledge and skills in learning, programming, and computer systems, so initial costs tend to be substantial. The software development typically requires significant lag time between when the need is identified and completion of the CBT [computer-based training] program" (pp. 249–250). Nevertheless, there are commercial vendors of such programs that can make the transition to this method of training highly accessible to most companies.

Programmed instruction
The most basic computer-based training that provides for self-paced learning.

Programmed Instruction.   **Programmed instruction** is regarded as the basis from which all other computer-based training methods have been derived. It was developed as a manual training system long before the advent of the computer. It is a method of self-paced learning managed by both the trainee and the computer system. The basic framework of programmed instruction is as follows: information is presented to the trainee, a question is posed regarding the information, and depending on the trainee's response to the question, the program proceeds to the next question. If the trainee provides a correct answer, the trainee moves on to new information. If the answer is incorrect, the trainee is taken back to review the relevant information. This format allows trainees to move through the material at their own pace. Trainees who answer more questions correctly move rapidly through the material. Van Buren (2001) estimated that 80% of leading companies use programmed instruction in some form.

Intelligent tutoring systems
A sophisticated type of computer-based training that uses artificial intelligence to customize learning to the individual.

Intelligent Tutoring Systems.   **Intelligent tutoring systems** are more sophisticated than programmed instruction and use the concept of artificial intelligence to guide the instructional process. Based on the trainee's responses to questions posed, the system continuously modifies the level of instruction presented to the trainee. An intelligent tutoring system involves several components. The domain expertise is the set of knowledge to be learned. According to Blanchard and Thacker (2004), "The trainee model stores information about how the trainee is performing during training. As the trainee responds to items, the information is used to tutor the trainee. The training session manager is the component that interprets the trainee's responses and responds with either more information, helping the trainee further explore the topic, or guiding the trainee toward the correct answer" (pp. 246–247). Intelligent tutoring systems are also capable of varying the order and difficulty of the questions presented. The method differentiates itself from programmed instruction by its level of sophistication in tailoring the learning process to the pattern of trainee responses.

Interactive multimedia training
A type of computer-based training that combines visual and auditory information to create a realistic but nonthreatening environment.

Interactive Multimedia Training.   **Interactive multimedia training** is a more technologically sophisticated system than intelligent tutoring. As the term *multimedia* suggests, the training combines text, photos, graphics, videos, animation, and sound to achieve a rich simulation of a real-life situation. The method is "interactive" in that it allows the trainee to make decisions and then receive immediate feedback on the quality of the decisions. Interactive multimedia training provides an opportunity to learn skills in a nonthreatening environment, where the consequences of errors are not as serious as in a real-life setting. Blanchard and Thacker (2004) described an application of multimedia training in teaching medical students:

> This training, all computer-based, allows a medical student to take a medical history of a (hypothetical) patient, conduct an examination, and run lab tests. As part of the examination the medical student may choose to examine the patient's chest. The student checks the "examine chest" button and is then asked to choose a type of examination to conduct (visual inspection, palpitation, and auscultation). Imagine

you are the student and you click on auscultation (listen to the sounds made by the lungs). You would hear the chest sounds that would be made by the particular patient. Based on your interpretation of the sounds, you would make a diagnosis and click the button that represented your diagnosis. You would then be informed of the accuracy of your diagnosis. If your diagnosis were incorrect you would be given an explanation and moved to supplementary materials designed to provide you with the knowledge needed to make a correct diagnosis. (p. 248)

The development of CD-ROM and DVD technology has added to the rapid growth of interactive multimedia training methods. Van Buren reported that about 40% of companies surveyed indicated they often used the method for training.

Virtual reality training
A type of computer-based training that uses three-dimensional computer-generated imagery.

Virtual Reality Training.   **Virtual reality training** is designed to simulate a work environment in an artificial three-dimensional context. Virtual (meaning "almost") reality training permits trainees to learn skills that, if developed in an actual work environment, could result in harm to the trainee or damage to the environment. For example, Blanchard and Thacker (2004) reported that virtual reality training has been used to train police officers in how to safely stop a speeding car. The method is effective because the trainee experiences a sense of "telepresence" in the environment. Virtual reality training requires a trainee to wear devices designed to produce sensory effects, such as a headset (for visual and auditory information), gloves (for tactile information), and possibly a treadmill (to create the sense of movement). By looking up, down, left, or right, a trainee experiences different visual images. How the trainee is responding to this virtual reality is monitored by sensory devices. In general, virtual reality is the least commonly used of the computer-based training methods because of its narrow range of purpose.

Non–Computer-Based Training

Although the preponderance of recent advances in training methods have involved computers, other training methods are available as well.

Business games
A method of training that simulates a business environment with specific objectives to achieve and rules for trainees to follow.

Business Games.   **Business games** model the conduct of a company. They typically involve a hypothetical company, a stated business objective (e.g., to reach a certain level of profitability), and a set of rules and procedures for the trainees to follow. The participants are presented with information regarding a business context or situation and, within the rules of the game, must make decisions about what to do. The game progresses until a certain objective has been met, such as a predetermined level of profitability. Some business games present trainees with an opportunity to reach certain desired objectives but at the cost of engaging in unethical or questionable behavior. The trainees are thus faced with conflicting objectives and as part of the game must defend the choices they made. It is also possible to design business games that reward competition or cooperation among the participants, depending on the objective of the game. Well-crafted games contain surprises, interdependent outcomes, and twists and turns that engage the trainee.

Role playing
A training method directed primarily at enhancing interpersonal skills in which training participants adopt various roles in a group exercise.

Role Playing.   **Role playing** is a training method often aimed at enhancing either human relations skills or sales techniques. Role playing often involves many people. The method originally evolved out of clinical psychology, in which problems involving human interaction, real or imaginary, are presented and then spontaneously acted out. The enactment is normally followed by a discussion to determine what happened and why. Participants suggest how the problem could be handled more effectively in the future.

Role playing is less tightly structured than acting, where performers have to say set lines on cue. Participants are assigned roles in the scenario to be enacted. For example, the scenario may be a department store. One person takes the role of an irate customer who is dissatisfied with a recent purchase. A second person is assigned the role of the clerk who has to attend to the customer's complaint. Aside from observing some general guidelines about the process, the participants are free to act out their roles however they wish. Their performance is judged by people who do not have an active part in the role playing. In an educational setting the observers may be other students in the class; in a business setting they might be supervisors.

Many variations of role playing are possible. In some exercises participants repeat the enactment several times but switch roles. In other cases participants reverse the role they play in real life; for example, the supervisor plays a union representative. The role forces the participant to adopt the other side's position and then defend it.

FRANK AND ERNEST   by Bob Thaves

Source: Frank & Ernest: © Thaves/Dist. by Newspaper Enterprise Association, Inc. Reprinted with permission.

Behavior modeling
A method of training that makes use of imitative learning and reinforcement to modify human behavior.

Behavior Modeling.   **Behavior modeling** is based on the technique of imitating or modeling the actions of another person whose performance on some task is highly regarded. An expert is used as a model for the behavior. The method provides opportunities for the trainer and other trainees to give reinforcement for appropriate imitation of the expert's behavior. The method typically has a narrow focus with the intent of developing specific behavior skills. Behavior modeling is used for training in interpersonal skills, sales, industrial safety, employment interviews, and so on. One variation of the method involves videotaping the trainee's performance and comparing it with the expert's behavior. With the use of split-screen technology, the expert and the trainee can be shown side by side, and the trainee can see where his or her behavior needs to be improved. Behavior modeling is predicated upon a set of behaviors (e.g., a salesperson handling an irate customer) that can be successfully imitated irrespective of the personal attributes (as age or gender) of the trainee in question. Taylor et al. (2005) conducted a meta-analysis of behavioral modeling training. The authors concluded that skill development was greatest when learning points were presented with specific behavioral-based guidelines as opposed to general descriptions. For example, training is more effective when trainees are taught to "listen and respond with empathy to reduce defensiveness" rather than "listen carefully".

In summary, a wide array of training methods exist, including some others not described here. They differ in the breadth of skills they seek to enhance. Behavioral modeling, for example, has a narrow focus, whereas business games have a broader focus. The methods also differ in the types of skills they seek to enhance. Role playing is designed primarily to enhance social interpersonal skills, whereas intelligent tutoring systems tend to enhance cognitive skills. The biggest trend in training methods is the shift toward computer-based training, or *e-learning*. Kraiger (2003) believes that the new era of organizational learning extends to the way companies are organized to conduct their business operations. "[T]he very form of instructional delivery is changing as e-learning explodes, and training and development is even becoming an integral mechanism for restructuring organizations" (p. 186).

Error Management Training

One of life's great truths is that we learn from experience. In particular, making mistakes, and learning from those mistakes, is a very powerful form of learning. Yet there is a seeming paradox to making errors: while we learn from them, we are punished for committing them. In school, low grades are assigned to students who make errors. In the workplace, employees can be disciplined for making an error; even fired. As such, we learn to avoid making errors to avoid being punished. However, from a psychological perspective, errors enhance learning and could be a strategic component of training. This principle has led to **error management training**, a concept where participants are explicitly encouraged to make errors and learn from them. Ellis, Mendel, and Nir (2006) stated that people can learn from their mistakes and perform better in the future provided there is a careful review and explanation of what specific actions of the individual led to the mistake. Creating an organizational culture that does not take a punitive approach to errors was proposed by van Dyck et al. (2005). The authors believe that two factors are critical to this organizational culture: open communication about errors; and early detection and recovery from errors.

Error management training has the potential to be a very useful approach to learning. However, two issues must be squarely addressed in its consideration. First, it represents an inversion of conventional thinking about what contributes to our perception of a top performer within a company. Instead of employees who are highly regarded because "they rarely (if ever) make a mistake", the emphasis would switch to employees who "make many mistakes, and they have learned from their errors". The second issue is the practical reality that whatever mistakes are made must not inflict harm to the organization. As such, the "best" mistakes would be those that produce few or no negative consequences to the organization. Their learning value to the individual is high, they are generalizable across other situations, and are acceptable to all parties with vested interests in the outcome. Accordingly, perhaps such errors would be more acceptable in training environments as simulations and trial runs, where the potential negative consequences to the organization are artificially constrained. In short, the fundamental premise of error management training is sound: we learn from our mistakes. However, it is possible that despite the learning potential of mistakes to the

Error management training
A system of training in which employees are encouraged to make errors, and then learn from their mistakes.

individual, such employees may acquire the stigma of being "error-prone", while the error-avoidant employee may be regarded more favorably for assignments where the negative consequences of errors are potentially high.

Management Development Issues

Management development
The process by which individuals serving in management or leadership positions are trained to better perform the job.

Management development is the process by which individuals learn to perform effectively in managerial roles. Organizations are interested in management development in large part because they recognize its value as a strategy to improve organizational performance. Kotter (1988) argued the one factor that seems to distinguish excellent companies from others is the amount of time and energy spent in the planning, design, and execution of developmental activities. Baldwin and Padgett (1993) estimated that more than 90% of organizations worldwide engage in some form of development activities for managers. Tharenou (1997) reported that many managers seek continual advancement, not just until they reach a particular level in the organization. For them, successful development activities are particularly critical because they contribute greatly to what Tharenou called "career velocity." The literature on management development tends to focus on major issues or processes managers address as part of their professional maturation. In contrast, the literature on personnel training tends to be more concerned with specific methods or techniques of training. However, the larger systems issues of needs assessment, skill enhancement, and transfer are equally applicable to both training and development.

Whetten and Cameron (1991) identified critical management skills and linked them to successful performance on the job. Three *personal skills* were noted: developing self-awareness, managing stress, and solving problems creatively. Four *interpersonal skills* were also identified: communicating supportively, gaining power and influence, motivating others, and managing conflict. The authors pointed out that these skills overlap and managers must draw upon all of them to perform effectively in a managerial role. Yukl, Wall, and Lepsinger (1990) developed a survey that assesses managerial practices based on these skills. Subordinates and peers describe how much a manager uses these practices and make recommendations on whether the manager's behavioral style should be modified. Managers compare this feedback with their own self-assessment of behavior. Ratings of the importance of these behaviors for the manager's job provide additional information for identifying relevant developmental activities. Lombardo and McCauley (1988) proposed that underutilization of selected managerial skills and practices contributes to *derailment*. Derailment occurs when a manager who has been judged to have the ability to go higher fails to live up to his or her full potential and is fired, demoted, or plateaued below the expected level of achievement.

There is also considerable interest in gender differences in management development (Ragins & Sundstrom, 1989). Many organizations have created a male managerial hierarchy—one composed predominately of men—which is thought to be a critical structural influence on the processes that affect men's and women's managerial advancement. There is evidence of a "glass ceiling" for women in their professional advancement through an organization. This transparent barrier is created by organizations that regulate access to developmental experiences as part of a pattern that grooms men for powerful positions. Lyness and Thompson (1997) found that even women who "broke through" the glass ceiling into the highest-level executive jobs reported having less authority, fewer stock options, and less international mobility than men. Tharenou, Latimer, and Conroy (1994) reported that developmental activities had a more positive influence on the managerial advancement of men than of women. Men were more likely than women to attend company-sponsored training courses, especially between the ages of 35 and 54. Development may lead to more advancement for men than for women because men are thought to gain more skills and knowledge from professional development than women do. In turn, men gain skills and knowledge that are more relevant to managerial work, thus becoming better prepared for advancement than women. The authors believe organizations need to ensure that women's contributions of education, work experience, and development are perceived as similarly conducive to productivity as men's, and thus are rewarded with similar advancement.

Five issues of contemporary relevance to the management development process deserve discussion: cultural diversity, expatriates, sexual harassment, mentoring, and executive coaching.

Cultural Diversity Training

Triandis, Kurowski, and Gelfand (1994) offered an insightful analysis of the consequences of our nation's increasing cultural heterogeneity or diversity. Cultural diversity has been a defining characteristic of our nation since its inception. The vast majority of U.S. citizens (or their ancestors) emigrated to this country from other parts of the world. The modern conception of cultural heterogeneity is the realization (and its associated organizational implications) that the diversity evidenced in our society is also mirrored in the workforce and the customers it serves. Changes in the composition of the workforce are driven by labor and market trends, legislation, and demographics. For example, Brief and Barsky (2000) reported that 45% of all net additions to the labor force in the 1990s were non-White and almost two-thirds were women. Chrobot-Mason and Quinones (2002) summarized the practical importance of cultural diversity:

> As the workplace continues to diversify, organizations will have to make a choice: either ignore this trend and continue business as usual or take steps to prepare for diversity. Ignoring demographic changes may cause such problems as an inability to attract and retain minority employees or a hostile work environment that increases risk of litigation. In contrast, organizations that work to change or create organizational practices and policies that support a diverse workforce may not only minimize exposure to discrimination lawsuits but also realize the benefits of the creativity and problem-solving capabilities that a diverse workforce can provide. (p. 151)

Historically, there have been two ways to approach cultural differences. One is the color-blind perspective (Ferdman, 1992), which advocates ignoring cultural differences. Its basic rationale is thus "Do not pay attention to differences." The second approach accepts cultural differences and proposes to improve relationships by teaching people from each culture to appreciate the perspectives of people from other cultures. Triandis (1995) classified these two approaches as the **melting pot conception**, where cultural differences are homogenized, and the **multiculturalism conception**, which assumes each cultural group should maintain as much of its original culture as possible while contributing to the smooth functioning of society. Research indicates that both

Melting pot conception
A concept behind facilitating relationships among people of different cultures based on them relinquishing their individual cultural identities to form a new, unified culture as a means of coexisting. Often contrasted with multicultural conception.

Multicultural conception
A concept behind facilitating relationships among people of different cultures based on them retaining their individual cultural identities as a means of coexisting. Often contrasted with melting pot conception.

perspectives have merit, and an optimal approach may emphasize both what people universally have in common and what makes them different. Triandis, Kurowski, and Gelfand (1994) suggested that approximately half of all psychological theories are universally relevant and the other half are the products of Western cultures. The task of cross-cultural psychology is to sort out the two halves.

Schneider, Hitlan, and Radhakrishnan (2000) developed a survey to measure racial and ethnic harassment. The survey includes questions pertaining to whether a person has encountered the following types of experiences, which reflect the breadth and sensitivity of this issue:

- Someone at work makes derogatory comments, jokes, or slurs about your ethnicity.
- Someone at work excludes you from social interactions during or after work because of your ethnicity.
- Someone at work fails to give you information you need to do your job because of your ethnicity.
- Someone at work makes you feel as if you have to give up your ethnic identity to get along at work.

Cultural diversity training
A method of training directed at improving interpersonal sensitivity and awareness of cultural differences among employees.

The goal of **cultural diversity training** is to reduce barriers, such as values, stereotypes, and managerial practices, that constrain employee contributions to organizational goals and personal development (Noe & Ford, 1992). Diversity training programs differ on whether attitude or behavior change is emphasized to achieve these goals.

Attitude change programs focus on an awareness of diversity and the personal factors that most strongly influence our behavior toward others. Many programs involve self-assessment of perceived similarities and differences between different groups of employees, and attributions for success and failure of minority employees. These programs may use videotapes and experiential exercises to increase employees' awareness of the negative effects of stereotypes on minority group members. It is assumed that this heightened awareness will result eventually in behavior change.

The *behavior change* approach emphasizes changing organizational policies and individual behaviors that limit employee productivity. Programs with the behavioral emphasis identify incidents that discourage employees from working to their potential. Perceptions regarding the degree to which the work environment and management practices are congruent with a philosophy of valuing differences among employees are often collected. Specific training programs are then directed at developing employee skills that are needed to create a workplace that supports diversity.

Rynes and Rosen (1995) conducted a major survey of human resource professionals about diversity issues in their organizations. Organizations that had successfully adopted diversity programs had strong support from top management and placed a high priority on diversity relative to other competing organizational objectives. Diversity training success was also associated with mandatory attendance for all managers, long-term evaluation of training results, managerial rewards for increasing diversity, and a broad inclusionary definition of what is meant by "diversity" in the organization. However, some critics believe that diversity training has been largely unsuccessful. Hemphill and Haines (1997) cited that Texaco paid a record settlement of $176 million in a racial discrimination suit, and the U.S. Army has been confronted with potential sexual harassment claims from more than 5,000 women. Both of these organizations had previously implemented diversity training. The authors believe organizations can do little to compel changes in how people feel about each other, but organizations should adopt a zero-tolerance policy for discrimination and harassment practices.

The current emphasis on cultural diversity training seems attributable in part to two general factors. The first is the increasing awareness of our differences as people, and the second is the reality that we all have to get along with one another to have an amicable and productive society. In a sense it is somewhat of a paradox—seeking ways to find similarities among differences.

Expatriate Training

Expatriate
A person native to one country who serves a period of employment in another country.

The term **expatriate** refers to an employee who serves on an overseas assignment (typically for a defined time period, such as 2–5 years). The need for expatriate training has grown for two reasons. The first is the increase in the number of individuals so assigned, and the second is the relatively high failure rate of managers in such assignments. Spreitzer, McCall, and Mahoney (1997) developed an assessment for the early identification of international executive potential. It is based on rating aspiring international executives on selected competencies and the ability to learn from experience. Dotlich (1982) reported the findings from a survey of U.S. managers who lived or traveled abroad on the reasons for difficulties in overseas assignments. The following two quotes were representative of the findings:

> Time as a cultural value is something which we don't understand until we are in another culture. It took me six months to accept the fact that my staff meeting wouldn't begin on time and more often would start thirty minutes late and nobody would be bothered but me.
>
> Communication can be a problem. I had to learn to speak at half the speed I normally talk. (p. 28)

Another problem area is family members adjusting to a different physical or cultural environment. Arthur and Bennett (1995) determined from a study of internationally assigned managers from many countries that family support is the most critical factor in accounting for successful international assignments. The results suggest the advisability of including a manager's spouse and other family members in cross-cultural training and, if feasible, sending them overseas to preview their new environment. Shaffer and Harrison (2001) studied the spouses (typically women) who accompany their partners in international assignments. The authors concluded that for the most part international organizations do relatively little to help the managers understand the needs of their expatriate spouses and to help the spouses adjust to new cultures. The following discussion by an expatriate spouse depicts her as an organizational asset and highlights the costs associated with being an expatriate spouse:

> The very worst aspect of being an expat spouse is that one is completely disenfranchised. You become a nonperson. For 30 years, I have moved my kids, my pets, my household, trailing after my husband to places where there are few other expats, no work permit for me, therefore, no job opportunities. I could not get money (he gets it from the company), am at the beck and call as a "corporate wife" (unpaid!), could not leave a country without permits or air tickets. I've moved to lands where no one

spoke English (where we were living), many foods were unavailable, *very* poor health facilities, electricity and water would go off for hours or days. The few friends one might make leave for long vacations and leave permanently. One spends one's time volunteering, fund raising for the destitute, etc., and filled with guilt! After all, you *do* have water which occasionally comes out of a tap—you didn't have to walk one mile each way for it—you are not watching your child die of starvation or for lack of a measles shot. So you spend your time slogging away to help a few when thousands need it. The plusses? Drop me down in any culture, any language, unknown script—I am not afraid and neither are my now adult kids. I've learned to live without a support system of people who care about me. I've also learned that the world is peopled with lovely people. Sound bitter? You bet! I'm 52 soon—still have no college degree, no equity, no profession, no home (not even a house of my own). The people I care about are thousands of miles away. I once told a banker at one of the hundreds of corporate functions I attend and organize when asked what I do: "Oh, I move!" That's my job—unpaid. It's a shame my husband's company doesn't pay wives for all the "corporate" work we do—I'd be worth a fortune paid by the hour! (Shaffer & Harrison, p. 252)

Stahl and Caligiuri (2005) studied a sample of German expatriates on assignment in either Japan or the United States. They found maladjusted expatriates viewed the culture of the host nation as inferior to their own. They would tend to withdraw into an enclave of fellow German expatriates because they felt uncomfortable interacting with members of the host nation. Ronen (1989) identified four abilities considered critical for successful overseas assignments: tolerance for ambiguity, behavioral flexibility, nonjudgmentalism, and cultural empathy. The selection decision for overseas assignments is usually predicated upon the candidate's technical skills in applied functional areas (such as engineering or finance), but usually the reasons for a failed assignment have little to do with deficient technical skills. Major areas recommended for enhancement through training include information about the host country's geography, political system, history, religion, and general customs and habits. It is also recommended that managers learn to understand their own listening ability, reaction to feedback, and predisposition toward judgmental attitudes. Cultures differ in the strength of their social norms in sanctioning acceptable behavior. Gelfand, Nishii, and Raver (2006) place the norms on a continuum of sanctioning strength. Cultures with tight social norms are heavily guided by rules of behavior. Cultures with a loose system of norms are more flexible and permit a wider range of acceptable behavior. If an expatriate goes from a country with tight norms to a country with loose norms, the person may experience ambiguity about what behavior to exhibit, based upon the seeming normless nature of the culture. Conversely, a person going from a loose to a tight culture would likely experience high stress over the perceived narrowness in the range of acceptable behavior.

Sexual harassment
Unwelcome sexual advances, requests for sexual favors, and other verbal or physical conduct of a sexual nature that creates an intimidating, hostile, or offensive work environment.

Sexual Harassment Training

The Equal Employment Opportunity Commission (EEOC) (1980) defined **sexual harassment** as

> unwelcome sexual advances, requests for sexual favors, and other verbal or physical conduct of a sexual nature when submission to or rejection of this conduct explicitly

or implicitly affects an individual's employment, unreasonably interferes with an individual's work performance, or creates an intimidating, hostile, or offensive work environment.

In this definition are the two kinds of sexual harassment actionable under federal law: *quid pro quo* harassment and hostile-environment harassment. **Quid pro quo harassment** occurs when sexual compliance is made mandatory for promotion, favors, or retaining one's job. **Hostile-environment harassment** is less blatant than *quid pro quo* and refers to conditions in the workplace that are regarded as offensive, such as unwanted touching and off-color jokes. In the vast majority of cases, women rather than men have suffered from sexual abuse at work. Such abuse may constitute illegal sex discrimination in the form of unequal treatment on the job. In 1998 the U.S. Supreme Court upheld same-sex sexual harassment. More than 12,000 complaints were filed with the EEOC in 2006 (15% of the complaints were filed by men); $49 million dollars was paid in settlements. Sexual harassment is not so much about sex as about power and the power differential between managers and employees (Cleveland & Kerst, 1993). Organizations devote considerable training resources to deter the likelihood of sexual harassment in the workplace.

Much of the research on sexual harassment has focused on how men and women define it and whether men's definitions differ markedly from women's. Gutek (1985) reported that women consistently were more likely than men to label a behavior as sexual harassment. Men and women tend to disagree on whether uninvited sexual teasing, jokes, remarks, or questions represent sexual harassment. Rotundo, Nguyen, and Sackett (2001) reported in a meta-analysis of gender differences in perceptions of sexual harassment that women perceive a broader range of social sexual behaviors as harassing. Generally, as an act becomes more overt and coercive, women and men are more likely to agree that it is sexual harassment (Wiener & Hurt, 2000). Nevertheless, Schneider, Swan, and Fitzgerald (1997) found that low-level but frequent types of sexual harassment can have significant negative consequences for working women.

Sexual harassment training frequently consists of teaching sensitivity to other people's values and preferences. It should not be assumed, for example, that people prefer to be touched (as on the hand or arm) when engaged in conversation. There are also broad cultural differences in the degree to which physical contact between people is regarded as acceptable. People differ in the degree to which verbal statements, including profanity, are considered offensive or inappropriate. One organizational response to fear of allegations of sexual harassment is to engage in highly defensive behavior, including having a third party present when one talks with a member of the opposite sex and interacting with people only in an open, highly visible work area. Other examples are prohibiting any comments about physical appearance (e.g., "Those are attractive shoes you are wearing") and the reciprocal exchange of gifts among employees on special occasions (e.g., flowers or cards on birthdays). Some defensive behaviors are more personalized, such as a male manager refusing to mentor any female protégé. Lobel (1993) questioned the long-term benefit of these types of prohibitions on male/female relationships in the workplace. In an attempt to limit opportunities for potentially sexual harassing behaviors to occur, we may also be precluding opportunities for beneficial across-gender relationships to develop. Furthermore, the workplace can be a setting where people meet and mutually enter into a romantic relationship.

Quid pro quo sexual harrassment
A legal classification of harassment in which specified organizational rewards are offered in exchange for sexual favors. Often compared with hostile environment sexual harassment.

Hostile environment sexual harassment
A legal classification of sexual harassment in which individuals regard conditions in the workplace (such as unwanted touching or off-color jokes) as offensive. Often compared with *quid pro quo* sexual harassment.

Pierce, Byrne, and Aguinis (1996) asserted that although a successful relationship can be beneficial to both parties, the breakup of a relationship can lead to charges of sexual harassment. Thus allegations of sexual harassment can be spawned by what were once mutually positive experiences.

Recent research on sexual harassment has been extended to include the organizational context in which it occurs. Extensive previous research has established that sexual harassment is associated with a loss of commitment to work, reduced satisfaction from work, and the occurrence of ill physical and mental health. Willness, Steel, and Lee (2007) found that in addition to the harassment itself, the culture of the workplace that tolerates such behavior in the first place also contributes to the negative effects. Berdahl (2007) challenged the conception that sexual harassers target females based upon perceived desirable characteristics of women (e.g., deference, attractiveness, and warmth). Berdahl proposed that, in contrast, sexual harassment is often motivated by hostility toward women who violate typical gender ideals rather than by desire for those who meet them. Thus the more likely targets of sexual harassment would be women with assertive and dominant personalities. Finally, Gettman and Gelfand (2007) identified another organizational arena in which sexual harassment can occur. As we move to a more service-oriented economy, organizations place strong emphasis on employees being highly attentive to customer needs. However, employees in service jobs can also be targeted for sexual harassment by clients and customers; the people that the organization relies on for business. Thus the potential for sexual harassment for employees can transcend the traditional boundaries of an organization to include other individuals not directly under the organization's control.

Mentoring

Mentor

Typically an older and more experienced person who helps to professionally develop a less experienced person.

Protégé

Typically a younger and less experienced person who is helped and developed in job training by a more experienced person.

One method for facilitating management development is mentoring. **Mentors** are older, more experienced individuals who advise and shepherd new people (**protégés**) in the formative years of their careers. Mentors are professionally supportive and serve in a "godparent" role. Hunt and Michael (1983) discovered four states of the mentor relationship. The first is the *initiation phase*, when the more powerful and professionally recognized mentor looks on the apprentice as a protégé. The second is the *protégé phase*, when the apprentice's work is recognized not for its own merit but as the by-product of the mentor's instruction, support, and advice. The third is the *breakup stage*, when the protégé goes off on his or her own. If the mentor–protégé relationship has not been successful, this is the final stage. If it has been successful, however, both parties continue on to the *lasting-friendship stage*. Here the mentor and the protégé have more of a peer relationship. The protégé may become a mentor but does not sever ties with the former mentor.

Wanberg, Welsh, and Hezlett (2003) developed a three-factor model of mentoring relationships. *Frequency* refers to the frequency of meetings between mentor and protégé, which influences the amount of time mentors and protégés spend together. *Scope* addresses the breadth of mentoring functions received by the protégé in tandem with the breadth of subjects addressed during the mentoring relationship. *Strength of influence* is the degree to which the protégé is influenced by the mentor. Some mentors offer only superficial ideas and suggestions to protégés. Allen et al. (2004) differentiated task-related from psychosocial mentoring of protégés. Mentoring behaviors such as sponsorships, exposure, visibility, and coaching are more directly related to enhancing task-related aspects of work that facilitate objective career success. Behaviors associated with psychosocial mentoring, such as role modeling, acceptance and confirmation, counseling, and friendship, are more highly related to satisfaction with the mentor than with career success (see Cross-Cultural I/O Psychology: The Acceptability of Mentoring Across Cultures, p. 204).

Some recent research on mentoring has focused on the factors that contribute to successful or unsuccessful mentor/protégé relationships. Eby et al. (2004) examined protégés who had marked negative experiences with their mentors. The negative experiences were so profound that they often induced depression in the protégés and increased their desire to quit their jobs. Examined from the mentor perspective, it was learned that some mentors were not skilled in developing protégés. They didn't know how to be a good mentor, despite being aware their protégés wanted them to be effective mentors. Not knowing how to be a good mentor, they psychologically distanced themselves from their protégés, which in turn lead to the negative reactions by the protégés. Allen, Eby, and Lentz (2006b) reported a related finding. In general, the expectation of protégés for a successful mentoring relationship are typically clear and well-reasoned. However, the mentor side of the relationship is more ambiguous. Some mentors are not clear on the goals of the organizational mentoring program, their particular role in it, and what exactly they are supposed to do to help their protégés develop. Allen, Eby, and Lentz (2006a) identified the importance of both mentors and protégés having mutual input in the mentoring process, including the process by which a particular protégé is matched to a particular mentor. Although mentoring programs were in fact based on input from both participants, some participants were not aware their inputs were considered. The study highlighted the importance of not only mutual participation, but also mutual awareness of their contribution to the process.

Given the sensitivity of gender issues and the power differential between senior and junior managers, women may be more likely than men to pursue peer relationships to facilitate their career development. Kram and Isabella (1985) described the importance of peer relationships. They found three types of peers. One is the *information peer*, a person with whom you can exchange information about work in the organization. You share a low level of disclosure and trust, and there is little mutual emotional support. The second type is the *collegial peer*, with whom you have a moderate level of trust and engage in some self-disclosure. Collegial peers provide emotional support and feedback and engage in more intimate discussions. The third type is the *special peer*, with whom there are no pretenses and formal roles. You reveal ambivalence and personal dilemmas as you would to few other people in your life. You need not limit peer relationships to members of the same gender, but special peers are most likely of your gender. The value of peer relationships to career development is not limited to women. However, because of the constraints women have in mentoring relationships, the importance of the peer relationship in their career development is accentuated for women.

Executive Coaching

Executive coaching
An individualized developmental process for business leaders provided by a trained professional (the coach).

Executive coaching is one of the newer forms of professional development. As the name implies, it is directed toward top-level employees of an organization. Two parties are involved: the coach (a role that can be filled by an I/O psychologist) and the

Cross-Cultural I/O Psychology: *The Acceptability of Mentoring Across Cultures*

The acceptability of mentoring as a means of professional development varies across nations. One underlying factor that accounts for its acceptability is *power distance*. Power distance is based on human inequality, that people differ in such areas as prestige, wealth, and power. Power differentials are highly evident and formalized in boss–subordinate relationships. Part of the effectiveness of mentoring is that someone who *does* have more power, status, and expertise can use such resources to develop a protégé. Furthermore, the mentor is *willing* (if not desirous) to do so. In cultures that have a small power differential, mentoring is a more common means of professional development. Although the mentor has more formal power at work than does the protégé, the differential power is not used to distance the two parties from each other. In cultures that have a large power differential, the degree of inequality between the boss and subordinate is a defining characteristic of their relationship. For a boss to mentor a subordinate would, in effect, serve to lessen the distance between them.

Based on research by Hofstede (2001), countries with a small power distance are found in northern Europe (e.g., Austria, Denmark, England) and North America. Countries with a large power distance are more typically found in Asia (e.g., Malaysia, Philippines, Singapore) and South America (e.g., Guatemala, Panama, Mexico). A large power distance is not compatible with mentoring, particularly the psychosocial dimensions. Serving as a counselor, confidant, and friend lessens the inequality between the two parties. In cultures with a small power distance, mentoring is a manifestation of power (i.e., choosing to help someone when it is possible to do so). In cultures with a large power distance, not mentoring is a manifestation of power (i.e., asserting the inequality between the two parties).

manager being coached. Coaching is more than counseling, although the two have some similarities. Counseling involves intensive listening on the part of the therapist (who provides a supportive environment for the client), and often the client arrives at his or her own solutions to problems. In coaching, the coach also listens carefully and provides a supportive environment but then takes an active and direct role in preparing solutions and developing plans of action for the manager to follow.

A fundamental tenet of coaching is learning. The coach helps the executive learn new adaptive skills. Peterson (2002, p. 173) offered the following types of skills that can be enhanced through coaching:

- Interpersonal skills, including relationship building, tact, sensitivity, assertiveness, conflict management, and influencing without authority
- Communication, including listening skills, presentations, and speaking with impact
- Leadership skills, including delegating, mentoring, and motivating others
- Certain cognitive skills, such as prioritizing, decision making, and strategic thinking
- Self-management skills, including time management, emotion and anger management, and work–life balance.

A common theme among executives is time pressures. Part of the value of coaching is that it is specifically geared to the person's problems and needs (see Field Note 2). As a one-on-one activity, coaching has no general curriculum designed to appeal to a wide audience. According to Peterson, one leading consulting firm offers coaching as the primary development tool for its 110 highest-performing senior partners.

Field Note 2: Low Skill, High Tech

One of the principles of organizational learning is that *all* employees, including upper management, need to continuously develop new skills to compete in the ever-changing world of work. CEOs are also not immune from having to acquire new skills, but rank does have its privileges.

One company that I know purchased a highly sophisticated multimedia communication system. People around the world could now simultaneously both hear and see each other in a multi-site conference presentation. The system also had basic communication features, such as a speaker phone for telephone calls. Late one afternoon, the CEO and a company salesperson were meeting in the high-tech communication room. The company was located on the east coast, and a question came up about an important supplier on the west coast. The CEO wanted to show off his new communication system to the salesperson, who had not seen it before. The CEO turned on the system, hit a button that had the supplier's telephone number on speed-dial, and within seconds was talking to the supplier. The call lasted only a few minutes, whereupon the meeting ended. Both the CEO and salesperson left the room and went home for the day.

The next morning at 9:00 A.M., the CEO had scheduled a high-level staff meeting in the communication room. The purpose of the meeting was to discuss a highly confidential plan for the company to market more of its products on a global basis. If consensus was reached among the CEO's staff, other locations of the company around the world would join in the discussion. The CEO left strict word with his Administrative Assistant that the meeting was not to be interrupted.

Around 10:50 A.M. Eastern time, the CEO's office received an urgent telephone call. The caller said it was imperative to speak with the CEO. The Administrative Assistant dutifully said the CEO was not available. The caller again pressed the point the call was extremely urgent. The Administrative Assistant reiterated the CEO's unavailability, and added he was in an extremely important meeting and left instructions that he was not to be disturbed. The caller dryly stated he knew the CEO was in a meeting, and was discussing a confidential global marketing strategy. The Administrative Assistant said she was surprised the caller knew about the important meeting and its confidential agenda. The caller stated it would be difficult for him not to know, because when he arrived at his office a few minutes previously, he could hear every word spoken in the meeting over *his* high-tech communication system. The Administrative Assistant rushed to the communication room, whispered something to the CEO, who in turn asked aloud, "Does anyone here know how to turn this thing off?" The CEO had neglected to shut the system off from his late afternoon phone (continued)

Coaches are people who can relate well to the person and the world that person lives in and can effectively help this person develop. Coaches must have professional credibility, but they need not be licensed psychologists. Coaching can be conducted in person, online, or over the phone. Once the two parties have agreed to work together, the coaching typically has three phases. The first is the initial contract between the two parties, where the coach pays special attention to building trust and rapport by understanding what the person hopes to accomplish through training. The second phase is the essence of the coaching process. The coach uses instruction, modeling, feedback, and discussion to facilitate the intended learning. The final phase is the development of an action plan for the person to follow back on the job. The two parties decide how the new skills will be implemented and in what context, discuss likely impediments, and determine how the outcome of the newly learned skills will be judged.

No large-scale empirical research studies have assessed the effectiveness of coaching. By its very design coaching is a private and confidential interaction between two parties. Given the diverse range of issues addressed in coaching and the variety of styles used by coaches, it will be difficult to arrive at a singular judgment as to the effectiveness of the method (Kilburg, 2000). Coaching is geared to meeting the developmental needs of top leaders who are responsible for the company's welfare. As such, the effectiveness of coaching may well be determined more by *results* criteria than most other forms of professional development.

The Posttraining Environment

Tannenbaum and Yukl (1992) noted that the effectiveness of a training program can be influenced by events that occur after a trainee returns to the job. Some employees leave training with new skills and with strong intentions to apply those skills to their job, but limitations in the posttraining environment interfere with the actual transfer of training (see Field Note 3). As Machin (2002) stated, "When training does not transfer it is likely that employees will perceive training to be a waste of their time and employers will continue to question the benefit of their investment in it" (p. 263).

Transfer of training is defined as the extent to which trainees effectively apply the knowledge, skills, and attitudes gained in a training context back to the job. Holton and Baldwin (2003) proposed that training can transfer across different "distances"

Transfer of training
The degree of generalizability of the behaviors learned in training to those behaviors evidenced on the job that enhance performance.

Field Note 3: The Willingness to Be Trained

When I was in graduate school, I helped a professor with a study of the coal mining industry. Many on-the-job accidents occurred in coal mines, and our assignment was to develop a safety training program to reduce them. My personal assignment was to observe and interview the coal miners about their work. While down in the mines, I noticed that the miners engaged in dangerous behaviors, such as not wearing their hard hats, leaving off their masks (which filtered out coal dust), and smoking in the mine (where an open flame could trigger an explosion). In addition to being unsafe, some of these behaviors were blatant violations of safety rules.

After the miners finished their work shifts, I interviewed them about their jobs. I was particularly interested in why they did such hazardous things. Since our goal was to develop a training program to reduce accidents, I felt that eliminating these unsafe behaviors was an obvious place to start. So I asked them why they didn't wear safety equipment at times. I did not expect their answer. They said they believed there was no relationship between what they did in the mine and what happened to them. They felt their lives were in the hands of luck, fate, or God, and it did not really matter how they conducted themselves. They all seemed to have personal anecdotes about other miners who were extremely safety conscious (that is, always wore all the safety equipment and were exceedingly cautious people in general) yet suffered serious injuries or death in accidents through no fault of their own, such as a cave-in. In short, the miners were highly fatalistic. They believed that if "your number was up," you would get hurt or killed, and there was nothing you could do about it. Although a hard hat was a fine thing to wear, it would not do much good if five tons of rock fell on you. Therefore the miners were not interested in engaging in safe behavior because their behavior did not matter one way or another.

This experience taught me many lessons about training. The major one is that if people are not motivated to be trained, to learn some new behaviors, it is pointless to try. As every teacher can tell you, if students do not want to learn or just do not care, there is nothing you can do to force them to learn. The coal miners simply did not want to learn new behaviors because in their minds their lives and welfare were determined by factors beyond their control. Trainers are like chefs: they can prepare the finest meals, but they cannot make you eat if you are not hungry.

through two phases, with six key events representing points along the progression from cognitive learning to broad performance applications, as shown in Figure 6-2, p. 208. Baldwin and Ford (1988) noted the distinction between *generalization*, the extent to which trained skills and behaviors are exhibited in the transfer setting, and *maintenance*, the length of time that trained skills and behaviors continue to be used on the job. They believe that supervisory support is a major environmental factor that can affect the transfer process. In the posttraining environment, supervisor support includes reinforcement, modeling of trained behaviors, and goal-setting activities. Another factor that can influence transfer is the extent to which the posttraining environment

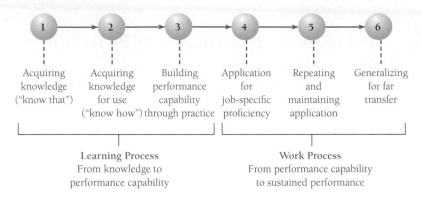

Figure 6-2   *Conceptual model of how training transfers from knowledge acquisition to sustained performance*

Source: From "Making Transfer Happen: An Active Perspective on Learning Transfer Systems," by E. F. Holton and T. T. Baldwin, in *Improving Learning Transfer in Organizations*, edited by E. F. Holton and T. T. Baldwin (San Francisco: Jossey-Bass, 2003). This material is used by permission of John Wiley & Sons, Inc.

provides opportunities for trainees to apply what they have learned. Ford et al. (1991) studied technical trainees after they completed training and found significant differences in opportunities to apply the training and wide variations in the lengths of time before trainees first performed the tasks for which they had been trained. Tracey, Tannenbaum, and Kavanagh (1995) concluded that posttraining knowledge and behavior are more likely to perseverate in organizations that have strong social support systems. Specifically, transfer of training is enhanced in organizations that have a culture that recognizes the importance of continuous learning.

Some studies have examined whether transfer is facilitated by relapse-prevention training, an approach derived from research on physical addictions (Marx, 1982). Relapse-prevention training is designed to prepare trainees for the posttraining environment and to anticipate and cope with "high-risk" situations. Marx and Karren (1988) found that trainees who received relapse-prevention training after a regular training seminar demonstrated more of the trained behaviors than trainees with no relapse-prevention training.

It appears that limitations in the posttraining environment may inhibit the application of skills acquired during training. Furthermore, supervisory actions taken after one training course may become pretraining cues for subsequent training courses. Tannenbaum and Yukl (1992) recommended that the transfer environment be examined carefully to identify situational facilitators and inhibitors, and they proposed means either to prepare trainees to deal with the inhibitors or to modify the posttraining environment to encourage transfer.

Evaluation Criteria of Training Programs

As is the case with any assessment or evaluation, some measure of performance must be obtained. Measures of performance refer to criteria, and the criteria used to evaluate training are just as important as those used in personnel selection. Relevance, reliability, and freedom from bias are all important considerations. One distinction between criteria used in personnel selection and criteria used to evaluate training is that training criteria are more varied and are used to evaluate multiple aspects of a training program.

Alliger et al. (1997) developed a taxonomy of training criteria based on the original research of Kirkpatrick (1976). Four types of training criteria are represented in the taxonomy. **Reaction criteria** refer primarily to the participants' reaction to the training program. These criteria measure impressions and opinions about the training; for example, did they believe it was useful or added to their knowledge? Reaction criteria are treated as a measure of the face validity of the training program. Most trainers believe that initial receptivity provides a good atmosphere for learning in the instructional program, but as Goldstein (1991) cautioned, it does not necessarily cause high levels of learning.

Learning criteria refer to what has been learned as a result of training. Three measures can be taken. The first is immediate knowledge learned, which is often assessed at the conclusion of the training. The second is knowledge retention, where evaluators assess what has been learned at a later time. The third measure, as proposed by Alliger et al., is a behavioral/skill demonstration. This measure is more than a score on a knowledge test, as perhaps a demonstration in a role-playing exercise or a simulation that is a behavioral manifestation of the knowledge learned in training. Collectively, reaction and learning criteria are called *internal criteria*; that is, they refer to assessments internal to the training program itself.

Behavioral criteria refer to actual changes in performance once the employee is back on the job. These criteria are most clearly reflected in the concept of transfer of training. These criteria address such questions as to what extent the desired changes in the job behaviors of the trainee are realized by the training program. If the goal of the training program is to increase production, then the behavioral criterion assesses output before and after training. Other behavioral criteria are absenteeism, scrap rate, accidents, and grievances. All of these are objective criteria; they can be measured easily and have relatively clear meaning, as discussed in Chapter 3. But if the goal of the training program is to increase managers' sensitivity toward people with handicaps, then "increased sensitivity" has to be translated into some objective behavioral criteria. Note that scores on learning criteria and on behavioral criteria do not always correspond to a high degree. Some people who perform well in training do not transfer their new knowledge or skills back to the job. This is particularly true for training programs aimed at changing attitudes or feelings.

Results criteria relate to the economic value of the training program to the company. Cascio (1989) developed a procedure to apply utility analysis to the assessment of training outcomes. One premise is if the training program has any effect, then the average job performance of the trained group should exceed that of the untrained group. Cascio proposed the use of a break-even analysis to determine that the economic value of the training program to the organization is greater than zero. Utility analyses are based on a careful assessment of the costs associated with developing training, training materials, training time, and production losses. Although such analyses are often difficult to perform, the failure to analyze training programs in dollars makes it more likely that training will be viewed as a cost rather than a benefit to the organization.

Collectively, behavioral and results criteria are called *external criteria*; they are evaluations external to the training program itself. Consideration of these four criteria

---

Reaction criteria
A standard for judging the effectiveness of training that refers to the reactions or feelings of individuals about the training they received.

Learning criteria
A standard for judging the effectiveness of training that refers to the amount of new knowledge and skills acquired through training.

Behavioral criteria
A standard for judging the effectiveness of training that refers to changes in performance that are exhibited on the job as a result of training.

Results criteria
A standard for judging the effectiveness of training that refers to the economic value that accrues to the organization as a function of the new behaviors exhibited on the job.

sometimes produces different conclusions about the effectiveness of training than a judgment reached by just one or two criteria. For example, Campion and Campion (1987) compared two methods for improving a person's interview skills. An experimental group received multiple instruction techniques on improving their interview skills, while a control group engaged in self-study of relevant material. The results revealed that the experimental group performed better on reaction and learning criteria, but the two groups were equivalent on behavioral and results criteria. Alliger and Janak (1989) concluded that there is not a causal flow among the four types of criteria but that each serves as a standard for evaluating training. Warr, Allan, and Birdi (1999) found that reaction criteria were more strongly related to learning criteria than to subsequent job behavior criteria.

In a major meta-analytic review of the effectiveness of training in organizations, Arthur et al. (2003) concluded that organizational training exerted a moderate effect on reaction, learning, behavior, and results criteria. Although there were differences in various types of training, on the whole organizational training is moderately effective in enhancing performance outcomes. Training programs that produce a large effect are relatively scarce. Sitzmann et al. (2006) compared web-based instruction to human instruction on two criteria: the effectiveness of the method (i.e., amount learned) and the trainee satisfaction's with the method. The two instructional methods were found to be equivalent on both criteria. The implications of this type of research have profound consequences for how organizations deliver training and educational programs. Web-based instruction is much less costly than a human instructor. If the quality of the instruction is the same and the participants are equally satisfied with the two methods, such findings invite the feasibility of reversing the traditional process of learning. Instead of the trainee receiving instruction in a certain classroom at a particular time, the instruction goes to the trainee through the boundless and timeless capacity of the internet.

In the final analysis, the success of any training and development system is intimately tied to the culture of the organization. The organization sets the tone for the relative importance and need placed on enhancing the skills of its employees. Training and development activities are a mirror of the organization's deeper values. Smith, Ford, and Kozlowski (1997) spoke to the need for *alignment* between the organization's culture and training initiatives. For example, a traditional authoritarian organization may not be supportive of individuals who attempt to take risks and try out new strategies. Mistakes and errors may be viewed as actions to be avoided rather than as opportunities from which to learn and develop. Kraiger and Jung (1997) described the importance of linking training objectives to training evaluation criteria. Given the subtleties of how we learn, what we learn, and the duration of our learning, methods of assessing learning must be appropriately refined. Learning is the foundation of training and development, and organizational learning is the foundation for organizational growth.

Case Study   Yet Again

Every employee of the Excelsior Furniture Company received the same message on the company's intranet. Excelsior had decided to implement a new, fully integrated information and data management system that would affect each business operation within the company. Every employee in the company (including marketing, operations, finance, human resources, sales, and information technology) was required to attend eight hours of training to learn the new system. The vendors of the new system had developed a specific training program for each separate business function and would explain to the employees how their work lives would be affected. This was the second time in three years Excelsior had adopted a new information system. For many years the company had department-specific systems. Thus the finance area managed its own functions (e.g., payroll and benefits) with its system, human resources managed its functions (e.g., selection and training) with its system, and so on. However, important information kept "falling through the cracks," not entered into any department's system. So Excelsior had decided to implement an integrated system that was common to all business functions. All employees had to learn how to enter relevant data and use the data in their work operations. That was three years ago. In the past 12 months Excelsior came under pressure to upgrade from two sources. First, they acquired two other furniture businesses, one specializing in office furniture and the other in lightweight wicker furniture, typically used on patios and porches. The second source of pressure was a big increase in overseas suppliers and customers. The two new acquisitions had to be melded into Excelsior's system, including information and data management. The new overseas businesses demanded greater speed of response to matters halfway around the world. In short, the three-year-old system could no longer handle the volume and complexity of Excelsior's new information needs.

Most employees readily accepted the need to implement the new information system. Learning the system was onerous, but it meant that business was good, sufficiently good to warrant a new way to keep track of everything. All the employees worked with computers in one form or another in their jobs, so using a computer-based information system was not alien to them. However, some employees didn't understand why the current system couldn't be modified to meet the new needs. After all, it took several months to become proficient in the current system, and now they had to start all over again with yet another system. It also seemed that some business areas would be more heavily affected by the changes than others, yet all business areas in the company had to adopt the system for it to work effectively.

Nick Chappel was not particularly pleased to have to learn an entire new information system. Learning the current one was not easy for him, and the rumor was the new system was even more complex. Nick went to his boss, Carol Hardy, and asked what exactly this new information system could do. Carol said she was told it was so sophisticated that "if someone in Florida bought a bag of French fries, it told a farmer in Idaho to plant a potato." Nick replied, "Farmers in Idaho have been planting potatoes for over 100 years. I don't think they need to be told when to do it."

Questions

1. What issues do you think Excelsior considered in making the decision to adopt a new information and data management system?
2. What factors in the company would facilitate employees learning the new system?
3. What factors in the company might cause some employees to resist learning the new system?

4. Why might employees like Nick Chappel question the value of a new information system?
5. What knowledge and skills should supervisors like Carol Hardy possess to get their employees to be more enthusiastic about learning the new system?

Chapter Summary

- Organizational learning is the process by which employees as well as the entire organization acquire new skills to better adapt to the rapidly changing work world.
- Skill acquisition is the process by which individuals acquire declarative and procedural knowledge.
- Training employees to acquire new skills is best done in organizations that encourage employees to learn and give them the opportunity to use their new skills on the job.
- Training needs are determined by a process that focuses on three levels of analysis: the organization, the task, and the person.
- Many contemporary training methods use computer technology. Among the more frequently used are programmed instruction, intelligent tutoring systems, interactive multimedia, and virtual reality.
- Management development is the process of cultivating skills in upper-level employees, who affect the lives of many workers.
- Cultural diversity training is designed to make employees understand how employees with different backgrounds and experiences can contribute to the welfare of the organization.
- Expatriate training is designed to facilitate the adjustment of an employee who is serving in an international assignment.
- Sexual harassment training is designed to make employees understand the unacceptability of behavior in the workplace that is regarded to be sexual or offensive in nature.
- Mentoring is a process by which older, more established employees (mentors) facilitate the career development of younger employees (protégés).
- Executive coaching is a one-on-one developmental relationship between a coach and a manager designed to facilitate the manager's career progression.
- The key to successful learning is the transfer between what has been learned in training to behavior on the job. The four major criteria used to assess the effectiveness of training are reaction, learning, behavioral, and results.
- There are cultural differences in the acceptability of various training methods.

Performance Management

Learning Objectives

- Understand why organizations manage employee performance.
- Know the sources of performance appraisal data and the limitations of each.
- Explain the purpose of rater training.
- Understand the bases of rater motivation.
- Understand peer assessment, self-assessment, and 360-degree feedback.
- Explain the use of performance appraisal interviews.

Employees continually have their job performance evaluated, whether on a formal or an informal basis. On one hand, informal evaluations may be made from haphazard observation, memory, hearsay, or intuition. On the other hand, with a formal and rational system, evaluations are more accurate, fair, and useful to all concerned. Rotchford (2002) differentiated three concepts associated with assessing employee performance. Performance *appraisal* is the process of assessing performance to make decisions (for example, about pay raises). The focus is on the administrative use of the information. Performance *development* refers to the assessment of performance with the goal of providing feedback to facilitate improved performance. The focus is on providing useful information that employees need to enhance their KSAOs to perform well in a current or future position. Performance *management* is the process that incorporates appraisal and feedback to make performance-based administrative decisions and help employees improve.

Before the discussion of performance management, it should be noted that there is no uniform understanding of what constitutes "performance," let alone how to assess it. Campbell et al. (1993) asserted that the concept of performance is poorly understood. They stated that performance is to be distinguished from effectiveness. *Performance* is synonymous with behavior; it is what people actually do, and it can be observed. Performance includes those actions that are relevant to the organization's goals and can be measured in terms of each individual's proficiency (that is, level of contribution). *Effectiveness* refers to the evaluation of the results of performance, and it is beyond the influence or control of the individual. Measures of effectiveness, though of major importance to the organization, are contaminated by factors over which the employee has little influence. An example of effectiveness is how many promotions an employee has had in a certain period of time—say, three years. The number of promotions is affected by the availability of job openings to which one can be promoted and the qualifications of other candidates. Furthermore, it is the organization and not the individual that makes promotion decisions. Rewarding or punishing individuals on the basis of their effectiveness may be unfair and counterproductive. Although there is a relationship between performance and effectiveness, the two concepts should not be confounded. The significance of the distinction is that appraisals of employee performance should be directed at job-related behaviors that are under the control of the employee.

Murphy and Cleveland (1995) believe that performance appraisals can help organizations in several ways. These factors are the primary reasons most organizations have formal performance appraisal systems. First, they can enhance the quality of organizational decisions ranging from pay raises to promotions to discharges. The purpose of the human resource function in an organization is to maximize the contributions of employees to the goals of the organization, and assessments of employee job performance can play a major role in accomplishing that function.

Second, performance appraisals can enhance the quality of individual decisions, ranging from career choices to the development of future strengths. Accurate performance feedback is an important component of success in training and provides critical input for forming realistic self-assessments in the workplace. Performance feedback is also a key to maintaining high levels of work motivation.

Third, performance appraisals can affect employees' views of and attachment to their organization. An organization's successful performance appraisal system may help to build employee commitment and satisfaction. Employees who believe that an organization's decisions are irrational or unfair are unlikely to develop a strong commitment to that organization.

Finally, formal performance appraisals provide a rational, legally defensible basis for personnel decisions. As discussed in Chapter 5, personnel decisions must be based on reason, not caprice. There must be a defensible explanation for why some employees are promoted or discharged or receive differential pay raises compared with others. As will be discussed shortly, personnel decisions based on performance appraisals are subject to the same legal standards as tests. Both tests and performance evaluations are used as techniques in the personnel function. Although performance appraisals may trigger discordant reactions from some employees, the alternative of making personnel decisions with no rational basis is simply unacceptable. Cardy (1998) summarized employer and employee reasons for conducting appraisals, as shown in Table 7-1.

Table 7-1   *Employer and employee reasons for conducting appraisals*

Employer Perspective
1. Despite imperfect measurement, individual differences in performance make a difference.
2. Documentation of performance appraisal and feedback may be needed for legal defense.
3. Appraisal provides a rational basis for constructing a bonus or merit system.
4. Appraisal dimensions and standards can operationalize strategic goals and clarify performance expectations.
5. Providing individual feedback is part of a performance management process.
6. Despite the traditional individual focus, appraisal criteria can include teamwork and teams can be the focus of appraisal.

Employee Perspective
1. Performance feedback is needed and desired.
2. Improvement in performance requires assessment.
3. Fairness requires that differences in performance levels across workers be measured and have an impact on outcomes.
4. Assessment and recognition of performance levels can motivate improved performance.

Source: From "Performance Appraisal in a Quality Context: A New Look at an Old Problem," by R. L. Cardy, in *Performance Appraisal*, edited by J. W. Smither, p. 142. Copyright 1998 Jossey-Bass. Reprinted with permission.

Using the Results of Performance Appraisals

The results of a performance appraisal program may be applied to many other management functions (see Figure 7-1, p. 216). As discussed in Chapter 3, criteria are derived from job analysis procedures; the criteria, in turn, are the basis for appraisals. The major uses of performance appraisal information are described in the following paragraphs.

Personnel Training.   Perhaps the main use of performance appraisal information is for employee feedback; this is the basis for the person analysis discussed in the preceding chapter. Feedback highlights employees' strengths and weaknesses. Of course, the appraisal should pertain to job-related characteristics only. Deficiencies or weaknesses

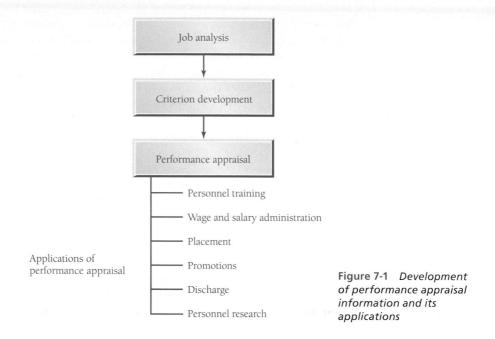

Figure 7-1 *Development of performance appraisal information and its applications*

then become the targets for training. Training should involve only those areas where poor performance can be attributed to the individual and not to aspects of the work environment. The supervisor plays a key role in helping to develop the employee's skills. Although, by definition, performance appraisals are evaluative, in this context they serve more as diagnostic aids. Because some employees will not acknowledge their weaknesses, a supportive supervisor is more effective than one who is threatening or critical. More will be said about this later in the chapter.

Wage and Salary Administration.   Perhaps the second most common use of performance appraisals is to determine raises. Pay increases are often made, in part, on the basis of job performance. Appraisal programs can be designed so that there is a direct relationship between the evaluation results and the size of the raise. For example, an employee who is judged to be performing in the top 10% of the workforce might get a 12% raise. An employee who performs in the bottom 10% might get only a 2% raise.

Unfortunately, the "personnel development" and "salary administration" aspects of appraisal are often uncomfortable partners. Many employees attach far more meaning to raises because they are more immediate and real than revelations about weaknesses on the job. If the two functions are combined in the same appraisal, employees can become defensive. When admitting weaknesses means getting a smaller raise, personnel development may take a backseat.

In a classic article, Meyer, Kay, and French (1965) talked about the need for "split roles" for supervisors in conducting appraisals. One role is a counselor or coach in discussing employee development or performance improvement. The other is a judge in making salary decisions. Evidence shows that most supervisors cannot play both roles simultaneously. The problem may be addressed by having two appraisals—for example, one in January for employee development and the other in June for salary. Or the supervisor may handle development while the human resources department handles salary. Although both functions are important, it is customary practice that they not be conducted at the same time by the same person.

Placement.   Performance appraisal information is vital for placement decisions. New employees (such as management trainees) are often exposed to many tasks or jobs at first. Over a 12-month period, a trainee might have jobs in marketing, finance, and accounting. After being appraised in each, the trainee might be permanently assigned to that area where he or she performed best. By identifying the employee's strengths, performance appraisal indicates where the person's talents might best be used.

Promotions.   Promotions may be based on how well an employee performs on his or her current job. Appraisals identify the better-performing employees, and an employee who cannot perform well on his or her current job will not be considered for promotion. Succession planning is a concept in which fairly long-term projections (typically three to five years) about future staffing needs in an entire company are based on the anticipated promotion of current employees. However, performance is not the sole determinant of promotion. Promotions are usually granted based on a combination of seniority and merit. If they are based strictly on seniority, there is nothing to ensure that competent people get promoted. Promotions based strictly on performance are more defensible, but most experts agree that experience in a job should also be considered. Promotions have often served as the criterion in validating assessment center ratings.

Discharge.   Termination of employment should be predicated on just cause. A typical just cause is inadequate job performance, as determined through performance appraisal. It is also highly advisable for organizations to document that efforts were made to enhance the employee's performance and that the decision to terminate employment was the organization's last resort. Many lawsuits stemming from performance appraisals allege the fired employee was the victim of a "wrongful discharge." In such cases the organization should demonstrate the fairness, job-relatedness, and accuracy of the performance appraisal process that led to the termination decision.

Personnel Research.   In many criterion-related validity studies, assessments of the criterion are derived from performance appraisals. Recall that the criterion is a measure of job performance, and that is what performance appraisals are supposed to measure. When I/O psychologists want to validate a new predictor test, they correlate scores with criterion measures, which are often exhumed from a company's performance appraisal files. Any selection device is only as good as the criterion it tries to predict, so the appraisal must be a relevant measure of job success. Research (e.g., Harris, Smith, & Champagne, 1995) has found that for the purpose of personnel research, specially constructed performance appraisal instruments yielded more useful and less biased information than evaluations originally collected for administrative purposes (for example, salary administration). Harris et al. recommended that more attention be given to the purposes behind performance appraisal and how these purposes influence the quality and usefulness of the evaluation.

Performance Appraisal and the Law

Federal law on fair employment practices also pertains to performance appraisal. Unfair discrimination can occur not only on the predictor (test) side of the equation but also in the job behavior the test is trying to predict.

Malos (1998) stated that the importance of legal issues in performance appraisal has "skyrocketed" in recent years. He reviewed many court cases involving alleged discrimination and found that charges of discrimination frequently related to the assessment of the employee's job performance. Charges of discrimination may be brought under the laws discussed in Chapter 5, including Title VII of the Civil Rights Act of 1964, the Civil Rights Act of 1991, the Age Discrimination in Employment Act (ADEA), and the Americans with Disabilities Act (ADA). Litigation can also result from charges of employer *negligence* (breach of duty to conduct appraisals with due care), *defamation* (disclosure of untrue unfavorable performance information that damages the reputation of the employee), and *misrepresentation* (disclosure of untrue favorable performance information that presents a risk of harm to prospective employees or third parties).

Malos synthesized the findings from many court cases and arrived at recommendations for employers regarding both the content and the process of performance appraisals. The *contents* of performance appraisal are the criteria of job performance that are evaluated. Table 7-2 gives Malos's recommendations for legally sound performance appraisals. Conducting the appraisals on job-related factors, usually derived from a job analysis, is particularly important. Werner and Bolino (1997) likewise found that whether or not the company based its performance appraisals on criteria derived from job analyses was often a deciding factor in court rulings. Malos also made *procedural* recommendations for legally sound performance appraisals. These recommendations are presented in Table 7-3. Malos concluded by stating that as our economy continues to move toward a service and information emphasis, there will be the tendency to use subjective performance criteria, particularly at the professional and managerial levels. Also, more organizations are increasingly relying on multiple sources of evaluation (customers, subordinates, and peers). Using both subjective criteria and untrained raters can lead to discrimination claims that are difficult to defend. It is recommended that when such criteria and raters are used, they should be used in conjunction with objective criteria and trained raters whose input is given greater weight.

Chapter 3 addressed the concept of organizationally-based competencies. Competencies are desired skills in all employees within the organization, irrespective of what

Table 7-2   *Content recommendations for legally sound performance appraisals*

Appraisal Criteria
■ Should be objective rather than subjective
■ Should be job-related or based on job analysis
■ Should be based on behaviors rather than traits
■ Should be within the control of the ratee
■ Should relate to specific functions, not global assessments

Source: From "Current Legal Issues in Performance Appraisal," by S. B. Malos, in *Performace Appraisal*, edited by J. W. Smither, p. 80. Copyright 1998 Jossey-Bass. Reprinted with permission.

Table 7-3 *Procedural recommendations for legally sound performance appraisal*

Appraisal Procedures
■ Should be standardized and uniform for all employees within a job group
■ Should be formally communicated to employees
■ Should provide notice of performance deficiencies and of opportunities to correct them
■ Should provide access for employees to review appraisal results
■ Should provide formal appeal mechanisms that allow for employee input
■ Should use multiple, diverse, and unbiased raters
■ Should provide written instructions for training raters
■ Should require thorough and consistent documentation across raters that includes specific examples of performance based on personal knowledge
■ Should establish a system to detect potentially discriminatory effect or abuses of the system overall

Source: From "Current Legal Issues in Performance Appraisal," by S. B. Malos, in *Performance Appraisal*, edited by J. W. Smither, p. 83. Copyright 1998 Jossey-Bass. Reprinted with permission.

particular job they held and their respective KSAOs. Examples of organizational-based competencies would include such factors as service orientation toward customers, interpersonal relations, and adaptability. Catano, Darr, and Campbell (2007) concluded that a performance assessment of broad-based competencies can be just as valid and legally acceptable as a job based system of performance appraisal. The desired attributes of performance assessment (e.g., behavioral based judgments, training supervisors how to appraise and coach employees, reviewing results with employees, etc.), are equally applicable to job-based and organization-based assessments.

Theory of Person Perception

Person perception
A theory that asserts how we evaluate other people in various contexts is related to how we acquire, process, and categorize information.

At a fundamental level performance appraisal involves the perception of people. That is, how you appraise a person is related to how you perceive that person. Psychologists have developed a theory of **person perception** that is a useful foundation for understanding performance appraisal. The theory is also called social cognition or attribution theory of person perception.

London (2001) outlined the theory as follows. We all have fairly fixed views of the way things should be when we enter into interpersonal interactions. These views act as filters to help us process large amounts of information about other people. We thereby tend to eliminate or ignore information that doesn't fit our initial views. We process information automatically whenever we can, avoid cognitive effort, and maintain consistency in our judgments. When something out of the ordinary happens, we may be compelled to think more carefully to interpret the unusual information and reformulate our opinions of a person or group. Automatic processing of information and the biases and distortions that result from it can be avoided with various interventions, such as training.

Klimoski and Donahue (2001) developed a framework to understand person perception. It is shown graphically in Figure 7-2, p. 220. The three parts of the framework

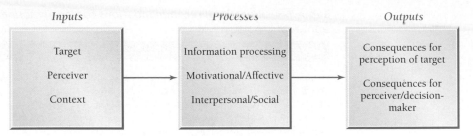

Inputs   *Processes*   *Outputs*

Figure 7-2   *Input–process–output framework of person perception*

Source: Adapted from "Person Perception in Organizations: An Overview of the Field," by R. J. Klimoski and L. M. Donahue, in *How People Evaluate Others in Organizations*, edited by M. London, p. 6. Mahwah, NJ: Lawrence Erlbaum Associates, 2001.

are inputs, processes, and outputs. *Inputs* are characteristics of the perceiver, characteristics of the person being perceived (the target), and contextual factors. Perceivers differ with regard to their level of affect toward others, their level of motivation, and their cognitive abilities. Characteristics of the target include age, race, and gender as well as nonverbal cues such as physical attractiveness, eye contact, body orientation, and interpersonal warmth. Contextual factors are represented by the presence of other group members, who influence the judgment of the target and provide the perceiver with information for making cognitive judgments.

The second component of the framework, *processes*, includes a broad range of variables pertaining to the way the perceiver uses information to make a judgment. Perceivers use approaches to social cognition that are good enough to accomplish their goals, which for the most part involve trying to "make sense" out of another person so they can make better choices regarding their own actions. For example, a perceiver would use a certain cognitive approach to assess the level of potential physical threat of a passerby on the sidewalk, a social exchange lasting only a few seconds. Alternatively, another cognitive approach would be used in a situation of greater length and purpose, such as a job interview in which the person wants to create a favorable impression. These cognitive structures are called **schemas**. Schemas are used to understand people in situations where the perceiver is confronted with incomplete or ambiguous information. They allow the perceiver to make rapid inferences about the characteristics and intentions of the target. Sometimes these inferences are correct and sometimes they are not. Heslin, Latham, and VandeWalle (2005) concluded the initial assessment of an employee by a manager may serve to establish an implicit expectation regarding future evaluations of performance. The manager may become overly vigilant to subsequent actions by the employee that corroborate the manager's initial impression, even actions that would not have otherwise garnered the manager's attention.

The third component of the person perception framework is *outputs*, which are the consequences of the processing to the perceiver and the target. The consequences for the perceiver might include less monitoring of a target who is perceived to be highly trustworthy. The consequences for the target are performance ratings and written evaluations that formally document a worker's performance. Jelley and Goffin (2001) advised designing performance appraisal methods to more closely parallel the cognitive processes by which memory is stored and retrieved by raters in making evaluations.

Schema

A cognitive approach to processing information that results in making sense of events and actions that in turn influence how decisions are made on the basis of that information.

Barnes-Farrell (2001) noted that changing demographics are creating a workforce in which supervisors and work-group members may have little common background to draw upon when making inferences, thus increasing the potential for using stereotypes to make appraisals. As will be discussed in Chapter 9, the emphasis on teamwork in organizations provides incentives that emphasize interpersonal functioning and the appraisal of performance in a team, not an individual, context. The current overall importance of performance appraisal in the design of work contexts in which these judgments are made is changing. The input–process–output framework proposed by Klimoski and Donahue offers a basis to understand the underlying psychological mechanisms associated with how people form judgments of others.

Sources of Performance Appraisal Information

As stated in Chapter 3, job performance may be characterized by many criteria. Three different types of data are used: objective production data, personnel data, and judgmental data.

Objective Production Data

Using objective production data as an index of how well an employee is performing on the job is limited in its frequency and value. For a person in the job of a machine operator, job performance may be measured by counting the number of objects produced per day, per week, and so forth. Similarly, salespeople are appraised by assessing (counting) their sales volume over a given period. It is even possible to evaluate the performance of firefighters by counting the number of fires they extinguish.

Although each of these objective production measures has some degree of intuitive appeal, none is a complete measure of job performance. Two problems in particular affect each of these measures. First, we would like to assume that differences in performance across people reflect true differences in how well these people perform their jobs. Unfortunately, variability in performance can be due to factors beyond the individual's control. One machine operator may produce more because he or she works with a better machine. A salesperson might have a larger sales volume because his or her territory is better. Firefighters who put out fewer fires might be responsible for an area with relatively fewer buildings. This problem of variation in performance stemming from external factors should sound familiar: it represents a form of criterion contamination (a topic discussed in Chapter 3).

The second problem with objective performance measures is that they rarely tell the whole story. A machine operator who produces more objects per day but who also produces more defective objects should not be described as the "best." Quality may be as important as quantity, but this cannot be recorded in a simple count of objects produced. A salesperson spends a lot of time recruiting new customers, an aspect that must be weighed against simply making calls on established customers. Creating new customers can be as important as maintaining business with old ones. The sales volume might be lower at first, but in the long run, the new customers will increase total sales volume. Extinguishing fires is but one aspect of a firefighter's job; preventing fires is another one. The "best" firefighters conceivably may not have put out many fires but might have contributed heavily toward preventing fires in the first place. There is growing use of electronic performance monitoring (EPM) to assess the performance of workers engaged in computer-based tasks. An EPM system records the objective aspects of performance on computer-based tasks, such as volume and speed of entries (Lund, 1992). Research (Westin, 1992) has revealed that such systems are regarded as unfair and inaccurate assessments of work performance because they ignore the discretionary or judgmental component of work, which is inherent in all jobs. In short, all of these actual criteria suffer from criterion deficiency. They are deficient measures of the conceptual criteria they seek to measure.

Relevance of Objective Production Data.   For the jobs mentioned, objective production data have some relevance. It would be absurd to say that sales volume has no bearing on a salesperson's performance. The salesperson's job is indeed to sell. The issue is the degree of relevance. It is a mistake to give too much importance to objective production data in performance appraisal (see Field Note 1). This is sometimes a great temptation because these data are usually very accessible, but the meaning of these clear-cut numbers is not always so evident. Finally, for many jobs, objective performance measures do not exist or, if they do, they have little relevance to actual performance. Criterion relevance is a question of judgment. For some jobs, objective performance data are partially relevant measures of success; in many others, such relevance is lacking.

Personnel Data

The second type of appraisal information is personnel data, the data retained by a company's human resources office. The two most common indices of performance are absenteeism and accidents. The critical issue with these variables is criterion relevance. To what extent do they reflect differences in job performance?

Field Note 1: What Is "High" Performance?

Usually we think of high performance as a positive score, a gain, or some improvement over the status quo. Conversely, when individuals perform "worse" than they did last year, it is tempting to conclude they didn't perform as well. However, such is not always the case. Performance must be judged in terms of what is under the control of the individuals being evaluated rather than those influences on performance that are beyond their control. There can be broad, pervasive factors, sometimes of an economic nature, that suppress the performance of everyone being judged. One example is in sales. If there is a general downturn in the economy, and products or services are not being purchased with the same frequency as in the previous year, sales could be down, for example, by an average of 15%. This 15% (actually −15%) figure would then represent "average" performance. Perhaps the best salesperson in the year had only a 3% drop in sales over the previous year. Then "good" performance in this situation is a smaller loss compared with some average or norm group. This example illustrates that there is always some judgmental or contextual component to appraising performance and that sole reliance on objective numbers can be misleading.

Absenteeism is probably the most concrete measure of performance. In almost all jobs, employees who have unexcused absences are judged as performing worse than others, all other factors being equal. Indeed, an employee can be fired for excessive absence. Most organizations have policies for dealing with absenteeism, which attests to its importance as a variable in judging overall performance. However, the measurement and interpretation of absenteeism are not clear-cut. Absences can be "excused" or "unexcused" depending on many factors pertaining to both the individual (for example, seniority) and the job (for example, job level). An employee who has ten days of excused absence may still be appraised as performing better than an employee with five days of unexcused absence. Whether the absence was allowed must be determined before performance judgments are made. Measuring absenteeism is a thorny problem, but it is seen as a highly relevant criterion variable in most organizations.

Accidents can be used as a measure of job performance but only for a limited number of jobs. Frequency and severity of accidents are both used as variables, as are accidents that result in injury or property damage. Accidents are a more relevant criterion variable for blue-collar than for white-collar jobs. People who drive delivery trucks may be evaluated in part on the number of accidents they have. This variable can be contaminated by many sources, though. Road conditions, miles driven, time of day, and condition of the truck can all contribute to accidents. Although their relevance is limited to certain jobs, accidents can contribute greatly to appraisal. Companies often give substantial pay raises to drivers who have no accidents and fire those who have a large number.

Relevance of Personnel Data.   There is no doubt that factors such as absences and accidents are meaningful measures of job performance. Employees may be discharged for excessive absences or accidents. Employers expect employees to come to work and not incur accidents on the job. Therefore these indicators are more likely to reflect levels of poor performance rather than good performance. However, as was the case with production data, personnel data rarely give a comprehensive picture of the employee's performance. Other highly relevant aspects of job performance often are not revealed by personnel data. It is for this reason that judgmental data are relied upon to offer a more complete assessment of job performance.

Judgmental Data

Rating Errors.   The most common means of appraising performance is through judgmental data or evaluations from raters. Because errors occur in making ratings, it is important to understand the major types of rating errors. In making appraisals with rating scales, the rater may unknowingly commit errors in judgment. These can be placed into three major categories: halo errors, leniency errors, and central-tendency errors. All three stem from rater bias and misperception.

Halo errors are evaluations based on the rater's general opinions about an employee. The rater generally has a favorable attitude toward the employee that permeates all evaluations of this person. Typically the rater has strong feelings about at least one important aspect of the employee's performance. The feelings are then generalized to other performance factors, and the employee is judged (across many factors) as uniformly good. The rater who is impressed by an employee's idea might allow those

Halo error
A type of rating error in which the rater assesses the ratee as performing well on a variety of performance dimensions, despite having credible knowledge of only a limited number of performance dimensions.

feelings to carry over to the evaluation of leadership, cooperation, motivation, and so on. This occurs even though the "good idea" is not related to the other factors. The theory of person perception offers a conceptual basis to understand halo error. In the schemas we use to assess other people, it may make sense to us that they would be rated highly across many different dimensions of performance, even dimensions we have little or no opportunity to observe.

Raters who commit halo errors do not distinguish among the many dimensions of employee performance. A compounding problem is that there are two manifestations of halo, but only one of them is truly a rating error. The first manifestation, called *invalid* halo, involves the failure to differentiate an employee's performance across different dimensions. The second manifestation, called *valid* halo, involves giving uniformly high ratings to an employee when these ratings are in fact justified. That is, the employee truly performs well across many dimensions. Solomonson and Lance (1997) concluded that a valid halo (actual job dimensions that are positively interrelated) does not affect rater halo error (raters who allow general impressions to influence their ratings). In general, halo errors are considered to be the most serious and pervasive of all rating errors (Cooper, 1981). Research on halo error has revealed it is a more complex phenomenon than initially believed. Murphy and Anhalt (1992) concluded that halo error is not a stable characteristic of the rater or ratee, but rather is the result of an interaction of the rater, ratee, and evaluative situation. Balzer and Sulsky (1992) contended that halo error may not be a rating "error" so much as an indicator of how we cognitively process information in arriving at judgments of other people. That is, the presence of a halo does not necessarily indicate the ratings are inaccurate. In a related view, Lance, LaPointe, and Fisicaro (1994) noted there is disagreement as to whether halo error can be attributed to the rater or to the cognitive process of making judgments of similar objects.

Leniency errors are the second category. Some teachers are "hard graders" and others "easy graders," so raters can be characterized by the leniency of their appraisals. Harsh raters give evaluations that are lower than the "true" level of ability (if it can be ascertained); this is called *severity* or *negative leniency*. Easy raters give evaluations that are higher than the "true" level; this is called *positive leniency*. These errors usually occur because raters apply personal standards derived from their own personality or previous experience. Kane et al. (1995) found that the tendency to make leniency errors was stable with individuals; that is, people tend to be consistently lenient or harsh in their ratings. Bernardin, Cooke, and Villanova (2000) found that the most lenient raters had the personality characteristics of being low in Conscientiousness and high in Agreeableness.

Central-tendency error refers to the rater's unwillingness to assign extreme—high or low—ratings. Everyone is "average," and only the middle (central) part of the scale is used. This may happen when raters are asked to evaluate unfamiliar aspects of performance. Rather than not respond, they play it safe and say the person is average in this "unknown" ability.

Even though we have long been aware of halo, leniency, and central-tendency errors, there is no clear consensus on how these errors are manifested in ratings. Saal, Downey, and Lahey (1980) observed that researchers define these errors in somewhat different ways. For example, leniency errors are sometimes equated with skew in the distribution of ratings; that is, positive skew is evidence of negative leniency and negative skew of positive leniency. Other researchers say that an average rating above the

Leniency error
A type of rating error in which the rater assesses a disproportionately large number of ratees as performing well (positive leniency) or poorly (negative leniency) in contrast to their true level of performance.

Central-tendency error
A type of rating error in which the rater assesses a disproportionately large number of ratees as performing in the middle or central part of a distribution of rated performance in contrast to their true level of performance.

midpoint on a particular scale indicates positive leniency. The exact meaning of central tendency is also unclear. Central-tendency errors occur if the average rating is around the midpoint of the scale but there is not much variance in the ratings. The amount of variance that separates central-tendency errors from "good" ratings has not been defined. Saal and associates think that more precise definitions of these errors must be developed before they can be overcome. Finally, the absence of these three types of rating errors does not necessarily indicate *accuracy* in the ratings. The presence of the rating errors leads to inaccurate ratings, but accuracy involves other issues besides the removal of these three error types. I/O psychologists are seeking to develop statistical indicators of rating accuracy, some based on classical issues in measurement.

Judgmental Data Used in Performance Appraisal.   Judgmental data are commonly used for performance appraisal because finding relevant objective measures is difficult. Subjective assessments can apply to almost all jobs. Those who do the assessments are usually supervisors, but some use has also been made of self-assessment and peer assessment. A wide variety of measures have been developed, all intended to provide accurate assessments of how people are performing (Pulakos, 1997). These are the major methods used in performance appraisal:

1. Graphic rating scales
2. Employee-comparison methods
    a. Rank order
    b. Paired comparison
    c. Forced distribution
3. Behavioral checklists and scales
    a. Critical incidents
    b. Behaviorally anchored rating scale (BARS).

Graphic Rating Scales.   Graphic rating scales are the most commonly used system in performance appraisal. Individuals are rated on a number of traits or factors. The rater judges "how much" of each factor the individual has. Usually performance is judged on a 5- or 7-point scale, and the number of factors ranges between 5 and 20. The more common dimensions rated are quantity of work, quality of work, practical judgment, job knowledge, cooperation, and motivation. Examples of typical graphic rating scales are shown in Figure 7-3, p. 226.

Employee-Comparison Methods.   With employee-comparison methods, individuals are compared with one another, not against some defined standard. Variance is thereby forced into the appraisals. Thus the concentration of ratings at one part of the scale caused by rating error is avoided. The major advantage of employee-comparison methods is the elimination of central-tendency and leniency errors because raters are compelled to differentiate among the people being rated. However, halo error is still possible because it manifests itself across multiple evaluations of the same person. All methods of employee comparison involve the question of whether variation represents true differences in performance or creates a false impression of large differences when

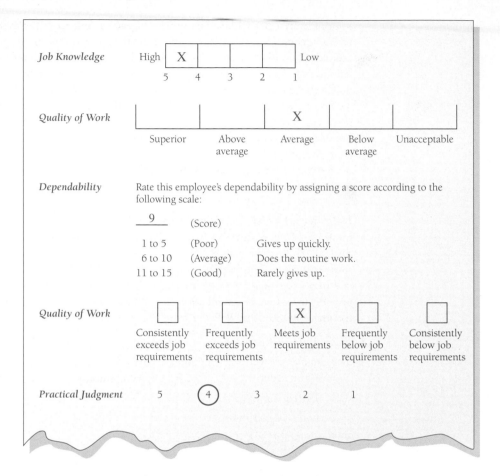

Figure 7-3   *Examples of graphic rating scales for various performance dimensions*

they are in fact small. The three major employee-comparison methods are rank order, paired comparison, and forced distribution.

With the *rank-order method*, the rater ranks employees from high to low on a given performance dimension. The person ranked first is regarded as the "best" and the person ranked last as the "worst." However, we do not know how good the "best" is or how bad the "worst" is. We do not know the level of performance. For example, the Nobel Prize winners in a given year could be ranked in terms of their overall contributions to science. But we would be hard pressed to conclude that the Nobel laureate ranked last made the worst contribution to science. Rank-order data are all relative to some standard—in this case excellence in scientific research. Another problem is that it becomes quite tedious and perhaps somewhat meaningless to rank order large numbers of people. What usually happens is that the rater can sort out the people at the top and bottom of the pile. For those with undifferentiated performance, however, the rankings may be somewhat arbitrary.

With the *paired-comparison method*, each employee is compared with every other employee in the group being evaluated. The rater's task is to select which of the two is better on the dimension being rated. The method is typically used to evaluate employees on a single dimension: overall ability to perform the job. The number of evaluation pairs is computed by the formula $n(n - 1)/2$, where n is the number of people to be evaluated. For example, if there are 10 people in a group, the number of paired comparisons is $10(9)/2 = 45$. At the conclusion of the evaluation, the number of times each person was selected as the better of the two is tallied. The people are then ranked by the number of tallies they receive.

A major limitation is that the number of comparisons made mushrooms dramatically with large numbers of employees. If 50 people are to be appraised, the number of comparisons is 1,225; this obviously takes too much time. The paired-comparison method is best for relatively small samples.

The *forced-distribution method* is most useful when the other employee-comparison methods are most limited—that is, when the sample is large. Forced distribution is typically used when the rater must evaluate employees on a single dimension, but it can also be used with multiple dimensions. The procedure is based on the normal distribution and assumes that employee performance is normally distributed. The distribution is divided into five to seven categories. Using predetermined percentages (based on the normal distribution), the rater evaluates an employee by placing him or her into one of the categories. All employees are evaluated in this manner. The method "forces" the rater to distribute the employees across all categories (which is how the method gets its name). Thus it is impossible for all employees to be rated excellent, average, or poor. An example of the procedure for a sample of 50 employees is illustrated in Figure 7-4.

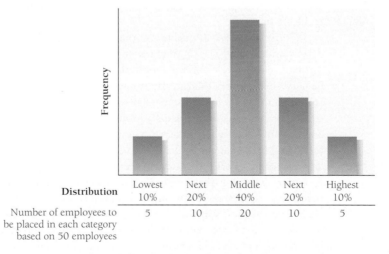

Distribution	Lowest 10%	Next 20%	Middle 40%	Next 20%	Highest 10%
Number of employees to be placed in each category based on 50 employees	5	10	20	10	5

Figure 7-4   *The forced-distribution method of performance appraisal*

Some raters react negatively to the forced-distribution method, saying that the procedure creates artificial distinctions among employees. This is partly because the raters think that performance is not normally distributed but rather negatively skewed; that is, most of their employees are performing very well. The dissatisfaction can be partially allayed by noting that the lowest 10% are not necessarily performing poorly, just not as well as the others. The problem (as with all comparison methods) is that performance is not compared with a defined standard. The meaning of the differences among employees must be supplied from some other source.

A frequently used method of performance appraisal predicated on the forced distribution method is **top-grading** (Smart, 2005). The method involves identifying the bottom 10% of a company's workforce (as shown in Figure 7-4), and firing those employees. The loss of the bottom 10% of the workforce not only removes the lowest performing employees, but also serves to induce even higher performance in the remaining 90% of the workforce. This forced distribution method of evaluation is repeated year after year, with the result that the workforce gets progressively better, as well as progressively smaller. The slang term for top-grading is "rank and yank." Scullen, Bergey, and Aiman-Smith (2005) examined the effectiveness of the top-grading method of performance appraisal. The results of their study supported such a strategy for improving workforce quality, but its effectiveness diminished substantially beyond its initial years of implementation. It is a statistical fact that no matter how well employees are performing, every year 10% of the workforce must be ranked in the bottom 10%. After repeated "yankings" the bottom 10% may well be performing their jobs successfully, and it is a matter of debate how much more work the surviving employees can absorb due to the annual departure of 10% of the workforce.

Behavioral Checklists and Scales.

Most recent advances in performance appraisal involve behavioral checklists and scales. The key term is *behavior*. Behaviors are less vague than other factors. The greater the agreement on the meaning of the performance appraised, the greater the chance that the appraisal will be accurate. All of the methods in this category have their origin directly or indirectly in the critical-incidents method.

Critical incidents are behaviors that result in good or poor job performance. Anderson and Wilson (1997) noted that the critical-incidents technique is flexible and can be used for performance appraisal as well as job analysis. Supervisors record behaviors of employees that greatly influence their job performance. They either keep a running tally of these critical incidents as they occur on the job or recall them at a later time. Critical incidents are usually grouped by aspects of performance: job knowledge, decision-making ability, leadership, and so on. The end product is a list of behaviors (good and bad) that constitute effective and ineffective job performance.

The original critical-incidents method did not lend itself to quantification (that is, a score reflecting performance). It was used to guide employees in the specifics of their job performance. Each employee's performance can be described in terms of the occurrence of these critical behaviors. The supervisor can then counsel the employee to avoid the bad and continue the good behaviors. For example, a negative critical incident for a machine operator might be "leaves machine running while unattended." A positive one might be "always wears safety goggles on the job." Discussing performance in such clear terms is more understandable than using such vague statements as "poor attitude" or "careless work habits."

Behaviorally anchored rating scales (BARS) are a combination of the critical-incidents and rating-scale methods. Performance is rated on a scale, but the scale points

---

Top-grading
A method of performance management whereby employees are graded on their overall contribution to the organization, and each year the bottom 10% of the employees are dismissed.

Behaviorally anchored rating scales (BARS)
A type of performance appraisal rating scale in which the points or values are descriptions of behavior.

are anchored with behavioral incidents. The development of BARS is time-consuming, especially in reaching agreement on expected job behaviors.

One of the major advantages of BARS is unrelated to performance appraisal. It is the high degree of involvement of the persons developing the scale. The participants must carefully examine specific behaviors that lead to effective performance. In so doing, they may reject false stereotypes about ineffective performances. The method has face validity for both the rater and ratee and also appears useful for training raters. However, one disadvantage is that BARS are job specific; that is, a different behaviorally anchored rating scale must be developed for every job. Furthermore, it is possible for employees to exhibit different behaviors (on a single performance dimension) depending on situational factors (such as the degree of urgency), and so there is no one single expectation for the employee on that dimension. For example, consider the dimension of interpersonal relations. When conditions at work are relatively free of tensions, a person may be expected to behave calmly. When operating under stress, however, a person may act irritably. Thus the expectation of behavior depends on the circumstances in effect.

Relevance of Judgmental Data.   The relevance of judgmental data in performance appraisal, like the relevance of any type of performance appraisal data, refers to the extent to which the observed data are accurate measures of the "true" variable being measured. The "true" variable can refer to a global construct, such as overall job performance, or a dimension of job performance, such as interpersonal relations ability. One method of assessing the relevance of judgmental data is to correlate them with performance appraisals from another method, such as objective production or personnel data. In studies that have conducted this type of analysis, the resulting correlations have been only moderate. Although these results may be interpreted to mean that judgmental data have only moderate relevance, the key question is whether the objective production data or the personnel data can be assumed to represent "true" ability. Those types of data might be just as incomplete or remotely relevant as judgmental data. Because we never obtain measures of the conceptual criterion (that is, "true" ability), we are forced to deal with imperfect measures that, not surprisingly, yield imperfect results. Research (e.g., Weekley & Gier, 1989) showed the existence of rater disagreement and halo error even among such expert raters as Olympic judges who were intensely trained to make accurate evaluations. DeNisi and Peters (1996) reported that instructing raters to keep a structured diary for continuous record keeping of performance (rather than using memory recall) produced more accurate assessments of the employees. Wagner and Goffin (1997) concluded that performance appraisal ratings produced by behavioral-observation methods are no more accurate than those produced by employee-comparison methods.

Borman (1978) had another approach to assessing the relevance of judgmental data. He made videotapes of two employment situations: a manager talking with a problem employee and a recruiter interviewing a job candidate. Sixteen videotapes were made, eight of each situation. Each tape showed a different degree of performance—for example, from a highly competent recruiter to a totally inept one. Similar levels of performance were shown of the manager–subordinate meeting. Professional actors were used in the tapes. The same actor played the recruiter in all eight tapes, but

"Barkley, I perceive my role in this institution not as a judge but merely as an observer and recorder. I have observed you to be a prize boob and have so recorded it."

a different actor played the new employee in each tape. Thus the performance level (the "true" ability of the manager or recruiter) was "programmed" into the scripts.

Raters were asked to rate the performance of the manager and recruiter with a series of rating scales. The evaluations were correlated with the performance levels depicted. Correlations between ratings and levels of performance across several job dimensions (organizing the interview, establishing rapport, and so on) ranged from .42 to .97. The median was .69. Although this study used a simulation rather than actual job performance, it did show that various types of rating procedures are susceptible to differences in validity. The study also revealed that certain dimensions of performance are more accurately evaluated ("answering recruitee's questions," $r = .97$) than others ("reacting to stress," $r = .42$). Borman concluded that raters are limited in their ability to appraise performance; they could not accurately evaluate the levels of "true" performance that were acted out in the scripts. He suggested a practical upper limit to validity that is less than the theoretical limit ($r < 1.0$) (see Field Note 2). After many years of research on various types of performance appraisal rating scales, I/O psychologists have concluded that the variance in rated performance due to the rating scale format is slight, typically less than 5%. Other sources of variance in rated performance are more substantial. These topics will be discussed next.

Field Note 2: Good Research Isn't Cheap

Many times unexpected costs are associated with performance appraisal. Here is the story of one of the more unusual expenses I have ever encountered in a research study.

One of the uses of performance appraisal information is as a criterion of job performance. In turn, criteria of job performance may be used to validate selection tests. I had a colleague who needed to collect both performance appraisal (criterion) data and test score (predictor) data to develop a selection test battery for a company. He traveled to the company and had all the supervisors convene in the company cafeteria. He explained the nature of the performance ratings he wanted them to make. Then he explained that all their subordinates would be taking a 30-minute test, and the scores would be correlated with the supervisors' performance appraisal ratings, as is done in a concurrent criterion-related validity study. My colleague then asked the supervisors whether they wanted to take the same test their subordinates would be taking just to get a feel for what it was like. They agreed. He passed out the test and informed them they would have 30 minutes to complete it. He wanted the testing procedure to be exact, giving everyone precisely 30 minutes. His watch did not have a second hand, so he was about to ask if he could borrow someone else's watch, when he spied the company's microwave oven on the wall in the cafeteria. He went over to the microwave, set the timer for 30 minutes, told the supervisors to begin the test, and started the microwave.

About 20 minutes into the test, a terrible odor began to fill the cafeteria. Somebody noticed it was coming from the microwave. My colleague had failed to place anything in the microwave when he started it, so for 20 minutes the microwave cooked itself, ultimately suffering terminal meltdown. The microwave cost $800 to replace and is one of the more unusual test-validation expense items I have ever heard of. Incidentally, the test turned out to be highly predictive of the performance appraisal ratings, so the exercise was not a complete waste.

Rater Training

Rater training
The process of educating raters to make more accurate assessments of performance, typically achieved by reducing the frequency of halo, leniency, and central-tendency errors.

Raters can be trained to make better performance appraisals. **Rater training** is a formal process in which appraisers are taught to make fewer halo, leniency, and central-tendency errors. For example, Latham, Wexley, and Pursell (1975) randomly assigned 60 managers who appraised performance to one of these three groups:

- *Workshop group.* This group was shown videotapes on evaluating individuals. Members then discussed appraisal procedures and problems in making appraisals, with the intent of reducing rating errors.

- *Discussion group.* This group received training similar in content, but the main method was discussion.

- *Control group.* This group received no training.

Six months later the three groups were "tested." They were shown videotapes of several hypothetical job candidates along with job requirements. The managers were asked to evaluate the candidates' suitability for the jobs in question. The groups showed major differences in the rating errors they made. The workshop group had no rating errors, the discussion group made some rating errors, and the control group performed the worst, making all three types of errors.

Zedeck and Cascio (1982) considered the purpose for which performance appraisal ratings are made—merit raise, retention, and development—and found that training works better for some purposes than others. Training typically enhances the accuracy of performance appraisals as well as their acceptability to those who are being appraised.

Not all research on rater training has shown positive results, however. Bernardin and Pence (1980) reported that raters who were trained to reduce halo errors actually made less accurate ratings after training. This may be because, as Bartlett (1983) noted, there are two types of halo; reduction of invalid halo increases accuracy, but reduction of valid halo decreases it. Hedge and Kavanagh (1988) concluded that certain types of rater training reduce classic rating errors such as halo and leniency but do not increase rating accuracy. It is possible to reduce the occurrence of rating errors and also reduce accuracy because other factors besides the three classic types of rating errors affect accuracy. The relationship between rating errors and accuracy is uncertain because of our inability to know what "truth" is (Sulsky & Balzer, 1988).

One type of rater training appears particularly promising. Frame-of-reference training (Sulsky & Day, 1992) involves providing raters with common reference standards (i.e., frames) by which to evaluate performance. Raters are shown vignettes of good, poor, and average performances and are given feedback on the accuracy of their ratings of the vignettes. The intent of the training is to "calibrate" raters so that they agree on what constitutes varying levels of performance effectiveness for each performance dimension. Research by Woehr (1994) and Day and Sulsky (1995) supported the conclusion that frame-of-reference training increases the accuracy of individual raters on separate performance dimensions. In a meta-analytic review of rater training for performance appraisal, Woehr and Huffcutt (1994) examined the effectiveness of rater training methods on the major dependent variables of reduced halo error, reduced leniency error, and increased rating accuracy. The authors concluded that rater training has a positive effect on each dependent variable. However, the training strategies are differentially effective in addressing the aspect of performance ratings they are designed to meet. Because raters are influenced by numerous attribution errors or biases, Kraiger and Aguinis (2001) encouraged reliance on multiple sources of information and questioned the veracity of judgments made by raters.

Rater Motivation

It is not unusual for the majority of employees in a company to receive very high performance evaluations. These inflated ratings are often interpreted as evidence of massive rater errors (i.e., leniency or halo) or a breakdown in the performance appraisal system. The typical organizational response to rating inflation is to make some technical adjustment in the rating scale format or to institute a new training program for raters. However, another explanation for rating inflation is unrelated to rater errors.

Murphy and Cleveland (1995) posited that the tendency to give uniformly high ratings is an instance of adaptive behavior that is, from the rater's point of view, an eminently logical course of action. These ratings are more likely to be a result of the rater's *unwillingness* to provide accurate ratings than of their *capacity* to rate accurately. If the situation is examined from the rater's perspective, there are many sound reasons to provide inflated ratings. **Rater motivation** is often adjusted to achieve some particular result.

Rater motivation
A concept that refers to organizationally induced pressures that compel raters to evaluate ratees positively.

First, there are typically no rewards from the organization for accurate appraisals and few if any sanctions for inaccurate appraisals. Official company policies often emphasize the value of accurate performance appraisals, but organizations typically take no specific steps to reward this supposedly valued activity. Second, the most common reason cited for rating inflation is that high ratings are needed to guarantee promotions, salary increases, and other valued rewards. Low ratings, on the other hand, result in these rewards being withheld from subordinates. Raters are thus motivated to obtain valued rewards for their subordinates. Third, raters are motivated to give inflated ratings because the ratings received by subordinates are a reflection of the rater's job performance (Latham, 1986). One of the duties of managers is to develop their subordinates. If managers consistently rate their subordinates as less than good performers, it can appear that the managers are not doing their jobs. Thus high ratings make the rater look good and low ratings make the rater look bad. Fourth, raters tend to inflate their ratings because they wish to avoid the negative reactions that accompany low ratings (Klimoski & Inks, 1990). Negative evaluations typically result in defensive reactions from subordinates, which can create a stressful situation for the rater. The simplest way to avoid unpleasant or defensive reactions in appraisal interviews is to give uniformly positive feedback (i.e., inflated ratings).

Kozlowski, Chao, and Morrison (1998) described "appraisal politics" in organizations. If there is a sense that most other raters are inflating their ratings of their subordinates, then a good rater has to play politics to protect and enhance the careers of his or her own subordinates. To the extent that a rating inflation strategy actually enhances the prospects of the better subordinates, it may be interpreted as being in the best interests of the organization to do so. Kozlowski et al. stated: "Indeed, if rating distortions are the norm, a failure to engage in appraisal politics may be maladaptive" (p. 176). Supporting this conclusion, Jawahar and Williams (1997) meta-analyzed performance appraisals given for administrative purposes (e.g., promotions) versus developmental or research purposes. Their results showed that performance appraisals conducted for administrative purposes were one-third of a standard deviation higher than those obtained for development or research purposes. As these authors stated, performance appraisals are much more lenient when those appraisals are "for keeps" (see Field Note 3, p. 234).

There is no simple way to counteract a rater's motivation to inflate ratings. The problem will not be solved by just increasing the capability of raters. In addition, the environment must be modified in such a way that raters are motivated to provide accurate ratings. Murphy and Cleveland (1995) believe accurate rating is most likely to occur in an environment where the following conditions exist:

- Good and poor performance are clearly defined.
- Distinguishing among workers in terms of their levels of performance is widely accepted.

Field Note 3: Are High Ratings a "Problem"?

Research on performance appraisal ratings has typically regarded high ratings as reflecting some kind of error. This error then becomes the focus of corrective action, as methods (i.e., different rating techniques, rater training) are applied to produce lower evaluations. However, an examination of just the statistical properties of ratings, apart from the organizational context in which they are rendered, fails to capture *why* they occur. As recent research has revealed, managers who give high evaluations of their employees are behaving in an eminently reasonable fashion, not making errors per se. Managers (or other supervisors) have a vested interest in the job performance of their subordinates. The subordinates are socialized and coached to exhibit desired behaviors on the job. Those who don't exhibit these behaviors are often dismissed.

Those who do are rewarded with social approval, if nothing more than being allowed to retain their jobs. The performance of subordinates is also regarded as a measure of the manager's own job performance. It is then logical for a manager to cultivate an efficient work group. Finally, managers often feel a sense of sponsorship for their employees. They want their employees to do well and have in fact often invested a sizable portion of their own time and energy to produce that outcome. Thus, when it comes time for a formal performance review of their subordinates, managers often respond by rating them highly. Rather than errors of judgment, the high evaluations could represent little more than the outcome of a successful socialization process designed to achieve that very outcome.

- There is a high degree of trust in the system.
- Low ratings do not automatically result in the loss of valued rewards.
- Valued rewards are clearly linked to accuracy in performance appraisal.

The authors know of organizations in which *none* of these conditions is met, but they don't know of any in which *all* of them are met. It is clear that we need more research on the organizational context in which performance appraisals are conducted. Mero and Motowidlo (1995) also reported findings that underscored the importance of the context in which ratings are made. They found that raters who are held accountable for their performance ratings make more accurate ratings than raters who are not held accountable. The problem of rating inflation will ultimately be solved by changing the context in which ratings are made, not by changing the rater or the rating scale.

Contextual Performance

Borman and Motowidlo (1993) contended that individuals contribute to organizational effectiveness in ways that go beyond the activities that make up their jobs. They can either help or hinder efforts to accomplish organizational goals by doing many things that are not directly related to their main functions. However, these contributions are important because they shape the organizational or psychological context that serves as a catalyst for work. The authors argued that these contributions are a valid component of overall job performance, yet they transcend the assessment of performance in specific tasks. This aspect of performance is referred to as **contextual performance**, organizational citizenship behavior, and extra-role performance. We will also discuss this topic in more detail in Chapter 10.

Contextual performance
Behavior exhibited by an employee that contributes to the welfare of the organization but is not a formal component of an employee's job duties. Also called prosocial behavior and extra-role behavior.

These are some examples of contextual performance:

- Persisting with enthusiasm and extra effort as necessary to complete one's own task activities successfully
- Volunteering to carry out task activities that are not formally part of one's own job
- Helping and cooperating with others
- Endorsing, supporting, and defending organizational objectives.

Borman and Motowidlo (1993) believe that an accurate assessment of job performance must include such contextual factors as well as task performance. Motowidlo and Van Scotter (1994) found that both task performance and contextual performance contributed independently to overall performance in a sample of U.S. Air Force mechanics. Experience was more highly related to task performance than to contextual performance, whereas personality variables were more highly related to contextual performance than to task performance. Borman, White, and Dorsey (1995) concluded that supervisors weigh contextual performance approximately as high as task performance when making overall performance ratings. Conway (1999) found that peers were particularly sensitive to the contextual job performance of managers. In general, it appears that knowledgeable raters are sensitized to the general contributions employees make in enhancing organizational welfare. Consideration of these contributions is as important in an overall evaluation as performance in the more narrow and specific behavior associated with task performance. Johnson (2001) examined the degree to which task performance and contextual performance contributed to the overall evaluation of the employee. The findings revealed that evaluations of contextual performance made both a unique and substantial contribution to overall performance.

However, to the extent that contextual performance is formally evaluated in making appraisals of job performance, it is no longer strictly contextual. Rather contextual performance becomes part of the formal job requirements, even though the behaviors are exhibited or directed toward activities that more accurately pertain to the functioning of the overall organization. The movement to include formal assessments of contextual performance into the overall assessment is part of the general view that an employee's value to the organization extends beyond his or her particular job (Fletcher, 2001).

A major study by Viswesvaran, Schmidt, and Ones (2005) proposed a bold departure from both the traditional theory and practice of performance appraisal. The authors contend the existence of a "general factor" of job performance that pervades the evaluation of the typical separate individual dimensions of job performance (as presented in Figure 7-3, p. 226). The basis for this general factor is contextual performance; that is, how the employee's overall job performance contributes to the overall welfare of the organization. Their research findings suggest that this general factor of job performance is not only evidenced in highly context based dimensions (as effort, leadership, and interpersonal relations), but also to such seemingly non-contextual performance domains as job knowledge and productive output. Their conclusions specifically refer to how job performance is rated within the organization, and not to "actual" job performance in a totally objective sense (that rarely can ever be measured). The practical implications of these findings would be substantial. As opposed to using multiple assessments (as discussed in Chapter 4) to predict multiple job performance criteria (as discussed in Chapter 3), the entire personnel selection process would become greatly simplified. An assessment of the "can do" factor (e.g., general mental ability) would be coupled with an assessment of the "will do" factor (e.g., an interview) to predict general job performance. Future research will be needed to determine the extent to which such a reductionistic approach to performance management will be scientifically and practically supported.

Peer and Self-Assessments

Most research on judgmental performance appraisal deals with evaluations made by a superior (supervisor, manager). However, valuable information about job performance can also be provided by colleagues or peers. Self-evaluations have also been discussed. Our knowledge is somewhat limited, but these methods do offer added understanding of performance.

Peer Assessments

Peer assessment
A technique of performance appraisal in which individuals assess the behavior of their peers or coworkers. Peer assessments include nominations, ratings, and rankings.

Peer nomination
A technique of appraising the performance of coworkers by nominating them for membership in a group.

Peer rating
A technique of appraising the performance of coworkers by rating them on a dimension of their job behavior.

Peer ranking
A technique of appraising the performance of coworkers by ranking them on a dimension of their job behavior.

In **peer assessment**, members of a group appraise the performance of their fellows. Three techniques are commonly used. One is **peer nomination**, in which each person nominates a specified number of group members as being highest on the particular dimension of performance. The second is **peer ratings**, in which each group member rates the others on a set of performance dimensions using one of several kinds of rating scales. The third technique is **peer ranking**, where each member ranks all others from best to worst on one or more performance dimensions.

The reliability of peer assessments is determined by the degree of inter-rater agreement. Most studies report high reliability coefficients (in the .80s and .90s), indicating that peers agree about the job performance of group members. The validity of peer assessments is determined by correlating them with criterion measures usually made later, such as who successfully completed a training program, who got promoted first, the size of raises, and so on. What is uncanny is that group members who have known one another a relatively short time (two to three weeks) can be quite accurate in their long-term predictions about one another. Validity coefficients are impressive, commonly in the .40–.50 range. The peer nomination technique appears best in identifying people who have extreme levels of attributes as compared with other members of the group. Peer ratings are used most often but have only marginal empirical support. It has been suggested that their use be limited to giving feedback to employees on how others perceive them. Relatively few data are available on the value of peer rankings, although they may be the best method for assessing overall job performance.

There is some evidence that peer assessments are biased by friendship (that is, employees evaluate their friends most favorably), but friendships may be formed on the basis of performance. Also, many work group members do not like to evaluate one another, so part of the method's success hinges on convincing participants of its value. Indeed, Cederblom and Lounsbury (1980) showed that lack of user acceptance may be a serious obstacle to this otherwise promising method. They found that a sample of college professors thought peer assessments were heavily biased by friendship. They thought peers would rate and be rated by their friends more favorably than would be justified. Problems with knowing the people to be rated and fostering a "mutual admiration society" caused the professors to question the value of peer assessment. They also felt that the method should be used for feedback, not for raises and promotions. Dierdorff and Surface (2007) noted that although peers may have the same or similar job titles, there can be contextual differences in their jobs that serve to diminish their equivalence as peers (or equals). For example, the manager of human resources, the manager of sales, and the manager of finance are all managers. However, despite being at the same organizational level (manager) they may have considerably different responsibilities and perspectives, thereby weakening their degree of comparability. Despite reluctance to use peer assessments for administrative decisions, research continues to support their predictive accuracy. Shore, Shore, and Thornton (1992) found peer assessments to be superior to self-assessments in predicting advancement.

Self-Assessments

Self-assessment
A technique of performance appraisal in which individuals assess their own behavior.

With **self-assessment**, as the term suggests, each employee appraises his or her own performance. The procedure most commonly used is a graphic rating scale. Meyer (1980) reported a study in which engineers rated their own performance against their views of the performance of other engineers in the company. On average, each engineer thought he or she was performing better than 75% of the rest of the engineers in the study. Statistically, it is quite a trick to have 100% of the workforce be in the top 25% of job performers. This underscores the biggest problem with self-assessment: positive leniency. Most people have higher opinions of their own performance than others do.

Anderson, Warner, and Spencer (1984) demonstrated in a clever study just how prevalent and pervasive inflation bias is in self-assessments of ability. They asked applicants to rate their own abilities in real clerical tasks as well as in bogus tasks that sounded real but were nonsense. Three of the bogus tasks were "operating a matriculation machine," "typing from audio-fortran reports," and "circumscribing general meeting registers." The clerical applicants rated themselves high on the real tasks (where their ability was not verified) and also on the tasks that did not even exist! Beehr et al. (2001) reported that self-ratings of job performance were *negatively* correlated with the personnel selection test scores used to hire the employees into their jobs. Mount (1984) found that managers evaluated themselves more leniently compared with both how they evaluated their supervisors and how their supervisors evaluated them. Bernardin et al. (1998) suggested that the reason for this pertains to perceptions of factors beyond the control of the individual. When we rate ourselves, we tend not to lower our own evaluations if we perceive that any shortcomings in our performance were beyond our control. When other people rate us, however, they tend to perceive us as being responsible for our performance.

Thornton (1980) reported that despite leniency problems, self-assessments have few halo errors. People apparently recognize their own strengths and weaknesses and appraise themselves accordingly. Thornton also reported little agreement in most studies that compare self-assessments and supervisor assessments. Superiors do not evaluate employees in the same way that employees evaluate themselves. This does not mean that one appraisal is "right" and the other "wrong." It just means that the two groups do not agree in evaluating the same performance. Thornton suggested this may be healthy because it provides a basis for discussing differences and may foster an exchange of ideas. Greguras et al. (2003) concluded that self-assessments are of higher quality when used for developmental purposes rather than for administrative purposes. Although self-assessments have documented value for developmental purposes, their frequency of use as a component of a performance appraisal process is approximately only 5% among U.S. companies (Atwater, 1998).

Peer and self-assessments are part of an overall performance appraisal system. The information generated cannot be isolated from information gained using other methods. Holzbach (1978) showed that superior, peer, and self-assessments all contribute information about performance, but information from each source was subject to halo errors. Borman (1974) showed that peers, superiors, and subordinates (if any) hold unique pieces of the puzzle that portrays a person's job performance. Thus, rather than having raters at just one level of the organization, it is better to have each level contribute the portion it is able to evaluate most effectively. Each performance dimension should be defined precisely enough to obtain the information unique to the relevant source. The appraisal system should include compatible and mutually supporting segments. Each segment should be assigned the role to which it is best suited. Performance appraisal should not be seen as simply selecting the best method. What is "best" varies with the use made of the information, the complexity of the performance appraised, and the people capable of making such judgments.

360-Degree Feedback

360-degree feedback
A process of evaluating employees from multiple rating sources, usually including supervisor, peer, subordinate, and self. Also called multisource feedback.

The technique of **360-degree feedback** is the practice of using multiple raters, often including self-ratings, in the assessment of individuals. It is also called multisource feedback (MSF). Advancements in the acceptability and use of multisource feedback represent some of the biggest changes in performance management in recent years. Typically feedback about a target manager is solicited from significant others, including the individual's coworkers, subordinates, and superiors. The original purpose for 360-degree feedback was to enhance managers' awareness of their strengths and weaknesses to guide developmental planning. However, it is increasingly being used as a method of performance appraisal (Bracken et al., 1997). According to Tornow (1993), 360-degree assessment activities are usually based on two key assumptions: (1) awareness of any discrepancies between how we see ourselves and how others see us enhances self-awareness, and (2) enhanced self-awareness is a key to maximum performance as a manager and thus becomes a foundation for management and leadership development programs.

The term *360-degree feedback* derives from the geometric rationale for multiple-rater assessment, as shown in Figure 7-5. The target manager is evaluated by other individuals who interact in a social network. The target manager also provides

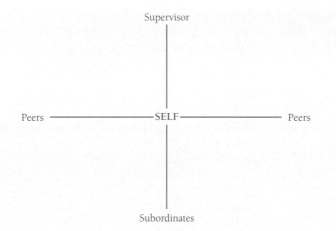

Figure 7-5   *360-degree feedback relationships*

self-assessments. The typical assessment includes evaluations along three dimensions (Van Velsor, Ruderman, & Young, 1991):

- *People*—dealing effectively with people, and building good relationships
- *Change*—setting, communicating, and implementing a goal or vision
- *Structure*—structuring and organizing information, time, and work.

The multiple raters make their assessments of an individual, and then the assessments are compared. Van Velsor et al. reported the following findings from their study, which are representative of most 360-degree feedback studies:

- Only 10% of the managers saw themselves as others saw them; the rest had substantial discrepancies (i.e., more than half of a standard deviation) on one, two, or three of the scales.
- Overrating oneself was the most common profile across scales. This difference was especially noteworthy in the *People* scale, where overrating was almost twice as common as underrating oneself or showing self–other agreement.
- About 80% of the managers modified their self-assessment in the expected direction on one or more scales after feedback. This change was most pronounced in the area of interpersonal skills.

It is particularly instructive to understand how disagreement among raters in 360-degree feedback is interpreted. The classic measurement perspective treats disagreement among raters as error variance—that is, something undesirable that reduces inter-rater reliability. With 360-degree feedback, however, differences in rater perspectives are regarded as potentially valuable and useful and are not treated as variations to be reduced. Such differences provide an opportunity for professional development and personal learning, to understand why individuals are perceived as they are by others (see Cross-Cultural I/O Psychology: Cultural Differences in the Acceptability of Multisource Feedback, p. 240).

Cross-Cultural I/O Psychology: *Cultural Differences in the Acceptability of Multisource Feedback*

As discussed in Chapter 6, the acceptability and usefulness of mentoring as a developmental method are influenced by cultural factors. Likewise, the acceptability and usefulness of some performance appraisal methods are also subject to cultural consideration. MSF has been described as an "American product" based on the cultural values of the United States, including a strong sense of individualism and participative democracy. Individual achievement is regarded as a virtue, and opinions from a wide range of people are solicited in addressing social problems. As discussed previously, nations differ in power distance, and they also differ in individualism. Power distance influences who provides performance feedback and appraisals in an organization (Fletcher & Perry, 2001). In countries with a large power distance, employee appraisal is most often conducted by a person who has more power than the person being evaluated. Because there is the perception that managers and subordinates are unequal, it may be particularly inappropriate to have employees of less power evaluate their managers (the basis of subordinate evaluations). Conversely, employees in cultures with a small power distance are less dependent on their supervisors, and thus MSF systems including upward appraisals are likely to be more acceptable.

It is the inherent nature of performance appraisal to compare and contrast employees. This is the perceived intent of forced-choice rating methods. Employees who get higher evaluations often receive greater rewards (e.g., pay raise) than employees with lower evaluations. In an individualistic culture, this type of appraisal is acceptable because it affirms interpersonal competition for rewards. Cultures low on individualism, in contrast, place greater emphasis on group unity and maintaining harmonious group relations. A performance appraisal system that seeks to differentiate employees within a group is far less likely to be regarded as useful to the overall goals of the organization. Uncritically transplanting performance management processes developed in the United States to nations that have different cultural values is doomed to fail. As Fletcher and Perry concluded, managerial techniques (such as performance appraisal) are most effective when they are congruent with a country's cultural values.

How important is it that managers see themselves as others see them? Nilsen and Campbell (1993) proposed that job performance is a function of an individual's aptitude, task understanding, decision about how intensely to work, decision about how long to persist in the face of obstacles, and facilitating or inhibiting conditions not under the individual's control. Self-assessments are important because individuals make judgments about themselves that are relevant to these determinants of performance. Individuals have beliefs about their aptitude and whether or not they understand the task they are asked to perform. If individuals overestimate their aptitude, they will devote less effort to the task than is needed to perform it adequately. If individuals believe that they fully understand a task, they will probably devote little or no effort to obtaining additional task-relevant information. If, however, individuals do not in fact understand what is expected, they may utilize their aptitude and devote their effort yet still fail to perform the task correctly. Additionally, London, Smither, and Adsit (1997) believe that 360-degree feedback will have little impact on changing behaviors when (1) the ratees are not accountable for using the feedback and (2) the raters are not accountable for the accuracy or usefulness of the feedback they provide. Smither, London, and Reilly (2005) found that multisource feedback is most likely to improve performance if the individual reacts favorably to the feedback, appropriate goals are set to direct the behavior in question, and it is possible to take specific actions that lead to performance improvement. Inherent in performance feedback is the likelihood that improving performance is under the control of the individual employee, as opposed to (for example) not having an adequate financial budget (that is determined by the organization, not the employee) to achieve the desired results.

In general, it appears that accurate self-assessors are better able to improve their performance than are inaccurate self-assessors. Self-awareness and self-perception are becoming recognized as critical factors in determining managerial job performance, a job that typically entails working with many other people. What exactly people agree or disagree on is not totally clear, however. Greguras and Robie (1998) found that there is not only disagreement *across* types of raters but also *within* the same type of rater (e.g., peers). Research has also been conducted on the measurement equivalence of ratings from different sources (Facteau & Craig, 2001; Maurer, Raju, & Collins, 1998). Using sophisticated analytic techniques, the authors concluded that ratings from different sources are comparable, although they may produce differential assessments of the target person.

A disturbing finding regarding the accuracy of multisource feedback was reported by Scullen, Mount, and Goff (2000). Based on a large number of 360-degree assessments, the authors partitioned the total amount of variance in the assessments into three components: the target's actual job performance, the raters' biases in the perception and recall of that performance, and random (uncontrollable) measurement error. The results revealed that only 25% of the variance in multisource feedback is attributable to the target's actual job performance, the intended object of the ratings. More than twice that amount of variance (54%) was due to rater bias in evaluating that performance. Thus the amount of performance-related variance is only moderate and differs by the perspective of the rater. The authors concluded that what multisource feedback measures is largely the idiosyncratic rating tendencies of the raters. Accordingly, Mount and Scullen (2001) stated that in the context of developmental feedback, rater biases can be interpreted as meaningful information that represents the rater's unique perceptions of the individual. However, when used to make personnel decisions, multisource feedback ratings should be averaged across types of raters, which will result in a more accurate understanding of the performance level of the individual.

I/O psychologists are divided in their opinions about the use of 360-degree feedback for both developmental and administrative purposes. The term *feedback* suggests that the method is best suited for its original intent, providing developmental feedback to employees. However, in recent years some organizations have shifted to use 360-degree feedback for both developmental *and* administrative purposes. Balzer, Greguras, and Raymark (2004) presented various issues associated with using 360-degree feedback for dual purposes, as shown in Table 7-4, p. 242. The major practical differences between the two purposes include source anonymity (i.e., the actual identity of the peers and subordinates), the implications of negative feedback, and adherence to legal guidelines. In short, both the employer's responsibilities and the employee's adaptive behavior differ as a function of how multisource feedback is used by the organization

Table 7-4 *The effects of purpose on MSF systems*

Decision Points	Feedback Purposes	Administrative Purposes
1. Content of instrument	Tied to employee short- and long-term developmental needs	Tied to job description or established performance goals
2. Frequency of use	As needed	Consistent with performance review timetable
3. Source anonymity	Of less importance	Of critical importance
4. Threat/implications of negative feedback	Low (limited consequences)	High (potentially serious consequences)
5. Data ownership	Individual receiving feedback	Organization
6. Adherence to legal guidelines	Of less importance	Of great importance

Source: From Balzer, W. K., Greguras, G. J., and Raymark, P. H., "Multisource Feedback," in J. C. Thomas (ed.), *Comprehensive Handbook of Psychological Assessment*, Vol. 4. Copyright © 2004 John Wiley & Sons. This material is used by permission of John Wiley & Sons, Inc.

(see The Changing Nature of Work: The Use of Multisource Feedback in Evaluating Students). Balzer et al. offered the following: "[D]ecisions about the design and implementation of an MSF system may be quite different for the most frequently discussed purposes of the system: feedback versus administrative. It is therefore critical to determine carefully the purpose(s) of an MSF system, communicate the purpose(s) to all who will participate in the system, and carefully monitor adherence to the purpose(s)" (p. 405). Simply put, an organization should not state that multisource feedback is used for only developmental purposes and then discharge an employee because he or she got low evaluations (as from peers). Some experts think that over time it may be possible to gradually shift from development-only multisource feedback to a system that also is used for administrative decision making. Others are far less confident.

Feedback of Appraisal Information to Employees

In the final step of appraisal, the employee and his or her superior review and discuss the evaluation, usually referred to by the misnomer "performance appraisal interview." Performance was appraised before the interview; the interview is just the means of giving the employee the results. Both superior and subordinate are usually very uneasy about the interview. Employees often get defensive about negative performance aspects. Superiors are often nervous about having to confront employees face to face with negative evaluations. For an appraisal system to be effective, however, interview objectives must be met with the same rigor as the other system objectives.

The interview typically has two main objectives. The first is reviewing major job responsibilities and how well the employee has met them. The second objective is future planning, or identifying goals the employee will try to meet before the next review. Both employee and superior should provide input in setting goals.

Much research has focused on factors that contribute to success in meeting the two objectives of the interview. Feedback on job performance has two properties: information and motivation; that is, feedback can tell the employee how to perform

The Changing Nature of Work: The Use of Multisource Feedback in Evaluating Students

Imagine you are enrolled in a class in which your grade will be determined by three assessments: two tests and an in-class oral presentation. The class is divided into five-person teams, and each person in the team makes a different presentation on a topic assigned to the team. You rehearse your presentation in front of your teammates, and they give you feedback on your performance. Furthermore, at the end of the semester the professor asks you to submit an assessment of how much you learned in the class and how the class might better be structured to enhance your learning. If all of this sounds plausible and reasonable, it is the essence of using MSF for developmental purposes. Although the professor is solely in charge of determining your grade, you have the opportunity to get helpful feedback from your teammates as well as yourself.

Now consider a different situation. There are still two tests, but they are the only portion of your course grade determined by the professor. These two tests are worth 40% of your final course grade. Instead of your teammates giving you helpful feedback on your planned presentation, your teammates formally evaluate your performance in the team as well as your oral presentation. These evaluations also represent 40% of your course grade. Finally, your end-of-the-semester evaluation of your own performance in the class is weighted 20% of your course grade. This system represents using MSF for administrative purposes (i.e., determining a final course grade). The three inputs are the assessments from your professor, your peers, and yourself. How would you adapt your own behavior in this class to using MSF to determine your grade? Would you study less for the tests because the professor's evaluation of you is worth only 40% of your final grade? Would you give yourself a high rating (no matter how much you learned in the class) to increase the likelihood of getting a high grade in the class? If you would, this would be an example of inflation bias in self-assessment. Would you interact with your teammates differently knowing they control 40% of your grade? Would you be tempted to "strike a deal" with your teammates—you all agree to give each other high ratings? If this use of MSF causes you some discomfort, these are the same concerns of employees who receive MSF for administrative purposes.

From a performance evaluation perspective, which system do you think would provide the more accurate assessment of your performance in the class? Which system would be more acceptable to you as a student? With the growing use of MSF for administrative purposes, these are some of the issues confronting both organizations and employees.

better as well as increase his or her desire to perform well. Ilgen, Fisher, and Taylor (1979) showed that how the employee perceives the superior greatly influences his or her response to feedback. They think that credibility and power are the most important traits. *Credibility* is the extent to which the superior is seen as someone who can legitimately evaluate performance. It is enhanced when the superior is considered to have expertise about the employee's job and to be in a position to evaluate performance. *Power* is the extent to which the superior can control valued rewards. Ilgen and associates believe that credibility and power influence (1) how well the employee understands feedback, (2) the extent to which the feedback is seen as correct, and (3) the willingness of the employee to alter behavior as suggested by the feedback.

Cederblom (1982) found that three factors consistently contribute to effective performance appraisal interviews: the supervisor's knowledge of the subordinate's job and performance in it, the supervisor's support of the subordinate, and a welcoming of the subordinate's participation. In particular, Cawley, Keeping, and Levy (1998) found that employee participation for the sake of having one's "voice" heard was more important to the employee than participation for the purpose of influencing the end result. However, just conducting a performance appraisal interview will not resolve all problems in evaluating subordinate performance. Ilgen et al. (1981) found that even after the performance appraisal interview, subordinates and supervisors sometimes disagreed on the quality of subordinate performance, with subordinates feeling their performance was at a higher level.

In a review of performance evaluations, Greenberg (1986) identified seven characteristics that contribute to employees' accepting their evaluations and feeling they were fair:

1. Solicitation of employee input prior to the evaluation and use of it;

2. Two-way communication during the appraisal interview;

3. The opportunity to challenge/rebut the evaluation;

4. The rater's degree of familiarity with the ratee's work;

5. The consistent application of performance standards;

6. Basing of ratings on actual performance achieved; and

7. Basing of recommendations for salary/promotions on the ratings.

I fully concur with Greenberg's findings. My experience with effective performance appraisal systems underscores the importance of all these characteristics and clearly reveals there is much more to performance management than making a check mark on an appraisal instrument. Russell and Goode (1988) concluded that managers' reactions to performance appraisal systems are affected by their overall satisfaction with them (that is, their attitude toward the systems' ability to document the performance of their subordinates) and the appraisal's improvement value. Likewise, Dickinson (1993) found that the most important determinant of employee attitudes about performance appraisal is the supervisor. When the supervisor is perceived as trustworthy and supportive, then attitudes about performance appraisal are favorable. Keeping and Levy (2000) concluded that reaction criteria are almost always relevant, and an unfavorable reaction may doom the most carefully constructed appraisal system.

Concluding Comments

The conceptual standards discussed in Chapter 3 on criteria are operationally measured by performance appraisal. The prediction methods discussed in Chapter 4, when united with the topic of standards or criteria, become the basis for making the personnel decisions discussed in Chapter 5. The topic of performance appraisal has attracted strong research interest among I/O psychologists. However, the primary focus of the research has changed over time. Latham, Skarlicki, et al. (1993) noted that earlier research on performance appraisal tended to address the psychometric properties of the various types of rating instruments. Such studies included the effects of rating scales on reducing rater errors and enhancing accuracy. More recent research has addressed the broader organizational context in which performance appraisals are conducted, including user reactions, perceptions of fairness, and how evaluations can be used to develop employees. Indeed, Mayer and Davis (1999) found that employee trust in the top management of a company increased following the implementation of a more acceptable performance appraisal system. Ilgen, Barnes-Farrell, and McKellin (1993) believe that the major problems with performance appraisals are not rating scale construction or the cognitive processes raters use to make evaluations; rather, more attention should be given to the values and expectations generated by the social context in which raters find themselves. Factors such as the extent to which raters desire to be liked by ratees and beliefs about freedom to be open and honest in making evaluations are underresearched.

Hauerstein (1998) asserted that many organizations are moving toward performance management rather than performance appraisal. The performance management perspective is that performance appraisal is a formal supervisory activity embedded in the larger context of conducting performance from day to day. For example, athletic coaches do not wait until after the season to evaluate players and give feedback to them. Thus, if managers openly and regularly discuss performance issues, then the yearly evaluation becomes little more than a formality. Folger, Konovsky, and Cropanzano (1992) artfully expressed how the process of evaluating employee performance involves more than obtaining a score or grade: "Appraising people is a matter of judging them, not simply measuring them as if they were to be fitted for new clothes" (p. 171). To further elucidate how performance appraisal is embedded in a larger organizational context, Farr and Levy (2007) extended the tape measure metaphor by stating: "Indeed, even a reliable tape measure only works as well as the tailor using it and that depends on what kind of day he or she has had, the relationship he or she has with customers and organizational members, and so on" (pp. 324–325).

Case Study   What Do You Do with Poor Performers?

Anita Douglass was the regional sales manager for a national chain of fitness centers. Her job was to direct a sales force that sold fitness center franchises to operators. The salesperson's job was to recruit responsible, ambitious people who would invest their own time and money in operating a center. Each operator would pay a franchise fee to the company. The company, in turn, would lease the building, supply all the equipment, and help with the financing, if needed. Sales throughout the nation were very strong, as there was a heavy demand for fitness training. Douglass's sales territory was second best in the nation. All her salespeople were doing very well, except two. Marty Crane and Julie Forester consistently failed to meet their sales goals. Both were running out of excuses and Douglass was running out of patience. Douglass was angry and embarrassed about their poor performance. She figured the only reason her boss hadn't inquired about Crane and Forester was because she could "bury" their performance in the overall performance of her sales territory. If these two salespeople had been at the top of the pile instead of the bottom, her sales territory would be number one in the nation.

Despite their common substandard performance, Douglass viewed the two salespeople somewhat differently. After Crane's first bad performance evaluation, she undertook additional training. Even though the extra training didn't seem to help, at least she tried. Crane seemed to be working hard but getting nowhere—described in her last performance review as "an ineffectual diffusion of energy," otherwise known as "spinning your wheels." Crane had a pleasing demeanor, which may have been part of her problem. Douglass thought that perhaps Crane was more concerned with having people approve of her than making a sale. Maybe Crane would perform better for the company in a job outside of sales, she thought.

Forester, on the other hand, seemed indifferent about failing to meet her sales goals and attributed her poor performance to everyone other than herself. If Forester ever worked up a sweat, it went unnoticed by Douglass. Forester conveyed the impression that the company was lucky to have her, although the reasons for this privilege were indiscernible. None of the other salespeople wanted to have anything to do with Forester. They wouldn't trade sales territories with her, and they didn't want Forester covering for them when they went on vacation.

Douglass thumbed through the personnel files of Crane and Forester. It was becoming increasingly difficult to justify not firing them. If only one of them got the axe, Douglass decided it would be Forester. Then Douglass caught herself in midthought. The performance of both these salespeople was equally bad. How could she justify keeping one and firing the other? Douglass surmised that the only difference between Crane and Forester was that she liked one more than the other. Douglass had the reputation of being tough but fair. She couldn't understand why this was becoming a difficult decision for her, and why she was considering being more charitable to Crane than to Forester.

Questions

1. What is it about Crane that makes Douglass view her differently from Forester?
2. Are these issues relevant in judging job performance? Should they matter?
3. If you were Douglass, what would you do with Crane and Forester?
4. Do you think Douglass's boss would be critical of Douglass for tolerating poor performance, or admire her for being patient with members of her staff?
5. What other information would you like to have before deciding whether Crane and Forester should be retained or fired?

Chapter Summary

- Performance management is the process of evaluating employee behavior and using that information to enhance job performance.
- Performance appraisal is used to make important personnel decisions (such as retention and advancement) and as such is governed by fair employment laws.
- How employees are evaluated is related to how they are perceived in the workplace, which may include factors that have little to do with their performance.
- Standard sources of information about an employee's job performance are objective production data (e.g., units produced), personnel data (e.g., days absent), and judgmental data (e.g., a supervisor's rating).

- I/O psychologists have developed various types of rating scales to evaluate job performance and have identified rating errors that occur with their use.
- Individuals can be trained to make higher-quality ratings; thus the judgment of employees is a learnable skill.
- An organization may have inhibiting factors that influence a rater's decision to give accurate and honest evaluations of employees.
- Appraisals of performance can be made by peers and subordinates (as well as oneself) in addition to supervisors.
- 360-degree feedback is an approach to performance evaluation based on a confluence of ratings from people at multiple organizational levels. The technique is used for both developmental and administrative purposes.
- In some cultures it is not acceptable to solicit evaluations from any source except the supervisor.

8 Organizations and Organizational Change

Learning Objectives

- Explain two early theories of organizations.
- Understand Mintzberg's theory of organizational structure.
- Describe the components of social systems: roles, norms, and culture.
- Explain downsizing, outsourcing, offshoring, and mergers and acquisitions.
- Explain the creation of global organizations.
- Discuss the rationale for organizational change.
- Understand why employees resist change.

Many academic disciplines have contributed to the study of organizations, including I/O psychology, sociology, economics, and political science. Their contributions tend to differ in the specific constructs that are investigated. The most common I/O psychological perspective is to examine individual behaviors and attitudes within an organizational context. First, it should be noted that it is not easy to grasp the meaning of an "organization." Organizations are abstract entities, yet they are real and in fact can be considered "alive." When an organization ceases to exist (such as a company that declares bankruptcy and goes out of business), it is not unusual to refer to the "death" of this formerly living entity. Authors have tried to use metaphors to understand the meaning of an organization (Morgan, 1997). Metaphors enhance the understanding of one concept by invoking reference to a more readily understood second concept. This technique has met with limited success in explaining organizations. One metaphor is to equate an organization with a person. People have a skeletal system and a circulatory system, concepts from physiology that are useful in understanding living organisms. Organizations possess characteristics (such as size and patterns of communication) that are general analogs of these physiological concepts; however, the metaphor is not totally accurate. What defines the boundary of where a person "ends" and his or her environment begins is our skin. Organizations, unlike humans, have no such boundary-defining characteristic as skin. Organizations have loose or porous boundaries where they "end" and their environments (legal, social, political, economic, etc.) begin. If you find that organizations are rather difficult to understand as entities, you are not alone. It is a challenge to those academic disciplines that study organizations to find useful ways to explain what they are.

Recall from Chapter 1 that for its first 70 years, the field was known simply as "industrial" psychology. There was substantial agreement as to what topics defined the field, which in turn led to the field's coalescence and emergence. However, "industrial" has a decidedly blue-collar, manufacturing, factory-based image to it, which many felt retarded the field's growth. In 1973, the name was officially changed to "industrial-organizational" psychology. While linguistically awkward, the "organizational" part of the name implied that the field's scientific and practical scope extended to non-manufacturing sectors of the economy as well. The body of knowledge reflecting "organizational" psychology is multidisciplinary in origin, and does not possess as clear a boundary as does its "industrial" counterpart. Indeed, Highhouse (2007a) stated, "Documenting the history of the 'O' side of I-O psychology is made difficult by the fact that no one is really sure what constitutes organizational psychology" (p. 331). Despite its blurred origins and identity, "organizational" psychology is firmly affixed by hyphenation to its older "industrial" sibling. This chapter will explain how an organization influences and shapes the behavior of its members. The concepts that will be examined (that is, the unit of analysis) shift from the individual to larger social collectivities.

One of the dominant themes of I/O psychology today is the need to be responsive and adaptable to changing conditions. This "need" has been described at both the individual level (in terms of personal flexibility) and the job level (continually evolving jobs require new tasks to be performed). This need to respond to change is particularly acute at the organizational level. Organizations are designed or created to perform work. As will be discussed in this chapter, organizations have both structural (how work processes are arranged) and social (the pattern of interactions among employees) components.

As the work the organization performs is altered in response to external economic pressures, the organization must also change its structural and social components. Organizations are under constant pressure to change in response to their changing environment. Helping organizations change is one of the major activities of I/O psychologists who work for consulting firms and businesses. As will be seen in this chapter, it is not easy to change the way an organization functions. Before the topic of organizational change is addressed, it is necessary to discuss how organizations operate.

Two Early Theories of Organizations

Organization
A coordinated group of people who perform tasks to produce goods or services, colloquially referred to as a company.

It is probably easier to state why organizations exist than to define what they are. In their simplest form, they exist as vehicles for accomplishing goals and objectives; that is, **organizations** are collectivities of parts that cannot accomplish their goals as effectively if they operate separately. How one chooses to examine the organizing process produces the various schools of thought or theories about organizations. Two early theories provided a basis to understand organizations.

Classical Theory

Classical theory of organizations
A theory developed in the early 20th century that described the form and structure of organizations.

Classical theory, which emerged in the first few decades of the 20th century, focuses mainly on structural relationships in organizations. Classical theory begins with a statement of the basic ingredients of any organization and then addresses how the organization should best be structured to accomplish its objectives. There are four basic components to any organization:

1. *A system of differentiated activities.* All organizations are composed of the activities and functions performed in them and the relationships among these activities and functions. A formal organization emerges when these activities are linked together.

2. *People.* Although organizations are composed of activities and functions, people perform tasks and exercise authority.

3. *Cooperation toward a goal.* Cooperation must exist among the people performing their various activities to achieve a unity of purpose in pursuit of their common goals.

4. *Authority.* Authority is established through superior–subordinate relationships, and such authority is needed to ensure cooperation among people pursuing their goals.

Given that four ingredients are the basis of any organization, classical theory addresses the various structural properties by which the organization should best reach its goals. Four major structural principles are the hallmarks in the history of organizational theory.

Functional principle
The concept that organizations should be divided into units that perform similar functions.

Functional Principle.   The **functional principle** is the concept behind division of labor; that is, organizations should be divided into units that perform similar functions. Work is broken down to provide clear areas of specialization, which in turn improves the organization's overall performance. Similar work activities are often organized into departments, which enhances coordination of activities and permits more effective supervision and a more rational flow of work. It is the functional principle that accounts for the grouping of work functions into such units as production, sales, engineering, finance, and so on; these labels describe the primary nature of the work performed within each unit. The functional principle relates to the horizontal growth of the organization—that is, the formation of new functional units along the horizontal dimension.

Scalar principle
The concept that organizations are structured by a chain of command that grows with increasing levels of authority.

Scalar Principle.   The **scalar principle** deals with the organization's vertical growth and refers to the chain of command that grows with levels added to the organization. Each level has its own degree of authority and responsibility for meeting organizational goals, with higher levels having more responsibility. Each subordinate should be accountable to only one superior, a tenet referred to as the **unity of command**. Classical theorists thought the best way to overcome organizational fragmentation caused by division of labor was through a well-designed chain of command. Coordination among factions is achieved by people occupying positions of command in a hierarchy. Figure 8-1 shows a graphic representation of both the functional and scalar principles.

Unity of command
The concept that each subordinate should be accountable to only one supervisor.

Line/staff principle
The concept of differentiating organizational work into primary and support functions.

Line/Staff Principle.   One way to differentiate organizational work functions is by whether they are line or staff. **Line functions** have the primary responsibility for meeting the major goals of the organization, like the production department in a manufacturing organization. **Staff functions** support the line's activities but are regarded as subsidiary in overall importance to line functions. Typical staff functions are personnel and quality control. That is, although it is important to have good employees and to inspect products for their quality, the organization was not created to provide people with jobs or products to inspect. It was created to manufacture products (a line function), and personnel and quality control are only two staff functions designed to support this larger goal.

Line functions
Organizational work that directly meets the major goals of an organization.

Staff functions
Organizational work that supports line activities.

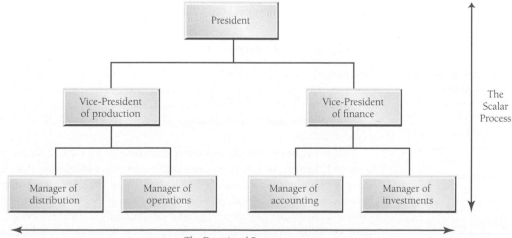

Figure 8-1   *The functional and scalar processes of an organization*

**Span-of-control
principle**
The concept that
refers to the number of
subordinates a manager
is responsible for
supervising.

Span-of-Control Principle.   The **span-of-control principle** refers to the number of subordinates a manager is responsible for supervising. A "small" span of control is 2 subordinates; a "large" span of control might be 15. Large spans of control produce flat organizations (that is, few levels between the top and bottom of the organization); small spans of control produce tall organizations (that is, many levels). Figure 8-2 is a diagram showing how the span of control affects the shape of the organization.

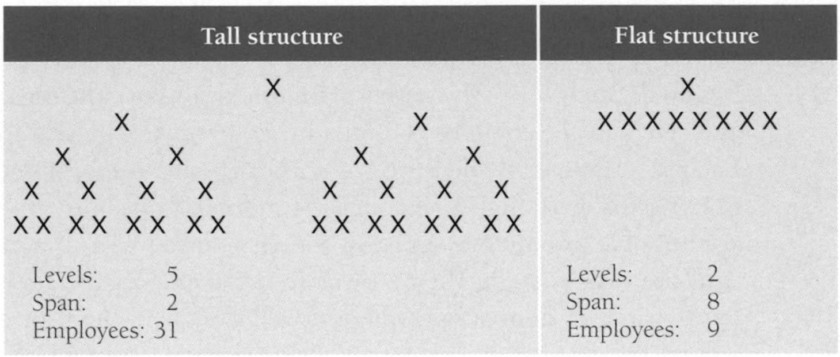

Tall structure	Flat structure
X X X X X X X X X X X X X X X XX XX XX XX XX XX XX XX	X X X X X X X X X
Levels: 5 Span: 2 Employees: 31	Levels: 2 Span: 8 Employees: 9

Figure 8-2   *Effect of span of control on organizational structure*

Classical theory is credited with providing the structural anatomy of organizations. It was the first major attempt to articulate the form and substance of organizations in a comprehensive fashion. There is little that is "psychological" about this view of organizations; indeed, none of the classical organizational theorists were psychologists. The influence of psychology became apparent in neoclassical theory, the next school of thought. Nevertheless, although current organizational researchers regard classical theory as antiquated, its four principles are deeply ingrained in the real-life structure of organizations. Problems of line/staff relationships, number of organizational levels, division of labor, coordination, and spans of control are still of major concern today. Further thinking about organizations occurred because organizations were more complex than the four classical principles suggested. This desire to add richness and realism to organizational theory gave rise to neoclassical theory.

Neoclassical Theory

**Neoclasical theory of
organizations**
A theory developed
in the 1950s that
described psychological
or behavioral issues
associated with
organizations.

Neoclassical theory was born in the 1950s, but its origins go back to the findings from the Hawthorne studies. It was identified with scholars who recognized the deficiencies in the classical school of thought. In fact, the name *neoclassical* connotes a modernization or updating of the original (classical) theory, while still acknowledging its contributions.

It is a misnomer to call neoclassical theory a "theory" because there really is no formal theory. Rather, it is a recognition of psychological and behavioral issues that question the rigidity with which the classical principles were originally stated. The neoclassicists examined the four major principles of classical theory and found evidence that challenged their apparent unassailability. This evidence was based primarily on either psychological research or an examination of real-life organizational problems.

The neoclassicists noted that while division of labor causes functional interdependence among work activities, it also depersonalizes these activities so that the individual finds little meaning in them. That is, people develop a sense of alienation from highly repetitive work, which ultimately results in dissatisfaction with their work. In turn, this dissatisfaction can result in decreased efficiency caused by lowered productivity and increased absence. In short, the neoclassicists argued for less rigid division of labor and for more "humanistic" work in which people derive a sense of value and meaning from their jobs.

The scalar principle was questioned on the grounds that other systems operate on people in organizations besides those imposed by formal superior–subordinate relationships. Individuals are influenced by interpersonal activities that extend well beyond those prescribed by the formal organizational structure. In short, although the scalar principle prescribes formal lines of authority, in reality many sources operating in an organization influence the individual.

The line/staff principle was perhaps the easiest for neoclassicists to challenge. The black-and-white theoretical distinction between line and staff functions is not always so clear in practice. Take, for example, the sales function. A manufacturing company's purpose is indeed to produce, but if it does not sell what it produces, the company cannot survive. What, then, is the sales function—a major line function or an ancillary staff function? The neoclassicists illustrated that many staff functions are critical to the success of the organization, so the value of the distinction between line and staff is not so great as originally proposed.

Finally, determining a satisfactory span of control seems far more complex than picking a number. The neoclassicists noted it depends on such issues as the supervisor's managerial ability (poor managers cannot supervise many subordinates) and the intensity of the needed supervision (one could effectively manage many more subordinates who do not require much direction than those who do require intensive direction). That is, such psychological factors as leadership style and capacity greatly influence the determination of effective spans of control.

The primary contribution of neoclassical theory was to reveal that the principles proposed by classical theory were not as universally applicable and simple as originally formulated. The neoclassicists drew heavily on behavioral research that revealed the importance of individual differences. They did not overtly reject classical theory. Rather than attempting to change the theory, they tried to make it fit the realities of human behavior in organizations.

Organizational Structure

Mintzberg (2008) greatly added to the classical and neoclassical theories by proposing a comprehensive and lucid explanation of how organizations evolve to reach a certain form and shape. We refer to these characteristics as the *structure* or formal component of an organization. Various types of structure are possible, and an organization continuously seeks to find a structure that is an optimal match to its environment. That is, the structure of an organization is an adaptive mechanism that permits the organization to function in its surroundings. Organizations that have maladaptive structures will ultimately cease to exist. Because individuals assume roles within organizations, employees feel the brunt of change caused by the continuing evolution of an organization's structure. It is in this regard that I/O psychology is involved in matters of organizational structure.

Coordinating Mechanisms

Structure
The arrangement of
work functions within an
organization designed to
achieve efficiency
and control.

Mintzberg (1983) defined the **structure** of an organization as "the sum total of the ways in which its labor is divided into distinct tasks and then its coordination is achieved among these tasks" (p. 2). Although many structures are possible for an organization, relatively few are effective structures for a particular organization. Five coordinating mechanisms have been proposed, and these mechanisms are the processes that organizations use to function.

1. *Mutual adjustment.* Mutual adjustment is the simplest coordinating mechanism and is most often achieved by individuals talking to each other to achieve a particular outcome. Mintzberg cited two people paddling a canoe as an example of the mutual adjustment between individuals needed to propel the canoe through water.

2. *Direct supervision.* When informal communication between individuals does not produce the needed coordination, one person serving in a position of authority is typically used. The person (typically a supervisor or boss) issues instructions to the workers and is ultimately responsible for their collective actions. As an organization outgrows its simplest state, it turns to this second mechanism of coordination. In effect, one brain coordinates several hands, such as the coxswain (stroke caller) of a six-person rowing crew.

3. *Standardization of work processes.* Another mechanism to achieve coordination is to standardize or specify work processes. The production assembly line of a manufacturing company is an example. A worker inserts a bolt into a holed piece of metal. There is only one action to perform, and there is no room for individual discretion in how the work is performed. The work is designed in such a way that the same process is followed no matter who is performing the job.

4. *Standardization of work output.* Yet another mechanism to achieve coordination is to standardize or specify the product of the work to be performed. The fast-food industry is an example. A hamburger ordered from a particular fast-food vendor should look and taste the same whether it was purchased in the day or at night, in July or December, in Cleveland or San Diego. The work is designed in such a way that the same output is achieved irrespective of differences in time or location.

5. *Standardization of skills and knowledge.* Finally, Mintzberg stated that coordination among work activities can be attained by specifying in advance the knowledge, skills, and training required to perform the work. In this case coordination is achieved before the work is undertaken. Organizations institute training programs for employees to standardize the skills needed to perform work, thereby controlling and coordinating the work. For example, there is rarely communication between an anesthesiologist and a surgeon while removing an appendix in an operating room. As a result of standardized medical training, the two medical specialists do not need to engage in much communication during the course of the surgical operation.

According to Mintzberg, these five coordinating mechanisms manifest themselves in a rough order. Mutual adjustment suffices as a coordinating mechanism only if the work processes are rather routine. As the work to be performed becomes more complicated, the most effective means of coordination shifts to direct supervision. As work becomes still more complex, the underlying coordinating mechanism shifts to standardization of work processes, then outputs, and finally skills. A person working alone has no need for any coordinating mechanisms. The addition of a second person requires the two individuals to adjust to each other. Mintzberg offered this description of the progression to the other coordinating mechanisms:

> As the work becomes more involved, another major transition tends to occur—toward standardization. When the tasks are simple and routine, the organization is tempted to rely on the standardization of the work processes themselves. But more complex work may preclude this, forcing the organization to turn to standardization of the outputs—specifying the results of the work but leaving the choice of the process to the worker. In very complex work, on the other hand, the outputs often cannot be standardized either, and so the organization must settle for standardizing the skills of the worker, if possible. (Mintzberg, 1983, p. 7)

It is not necessary or even feasible for an organization to achieve coordination by using a single coordinating mechanism. In reality, most organizations use all five, but to varying degrees. Irrespective of whether an organization is large or small, is engaged in complex or simple work activities, it will always be necessary to have some degree of mutual adjustment and direct supervision. Informal communication and leadership are needed in all types of organizations. Organizations often develop codified statements (company rules, policy and procedure manuals, etc.) to facilitate the standardization of work processes. The standardization of work output is evidenced by issuing standards for product specification (as in a manufacturing company) or the time needed to perform a service (as delivering a package in a shipping company). Finally, the standardization of knowledge and skills can be achieved by requiring employees to have attained a certain level of education (e.g., a Master's degree in accounting) or professional licensure (e.g., being a Certified Public Accountant—CPA).

Classical organization theory emphasized both direct supervision and standardization as coordinating mechanisms. The concepts of span of control, line/staff functions, and unity of command apply to the components of an organization's *formal structure*. Frederick Taylor sought to achieve coordination through standardization, specifying the work operations (such as body movements and when to take work breaks) of pig-iron handlers and coal shovelers. According to scholars in the beginning of the 20th century, organizational structure defined a set of official, standardized work relationships built around a tight system of formal authority.

However, neoclassical organizational theory revealed the significance of the most primary means of attaining coordination, mutual adjustment. That is, other activities take place among workers that are not in line with the official organizational structure. Thus the presence of unofficial relationships within work groups (an *informal structure*) established that mutual adjustment serves as an important coordinating mechanism in all organizations. In fact, as will be seen in Chapter 11, the mechanism of standardization, a long-standing hallmark of formal organizational structure, was actually detrimental to the psychological and physical health of the worker. It was not until the creation of modern organizational theory that a balance between the classical and neoclassical perspectives was attained and all five coordinating mechanisms were regarded as viable.

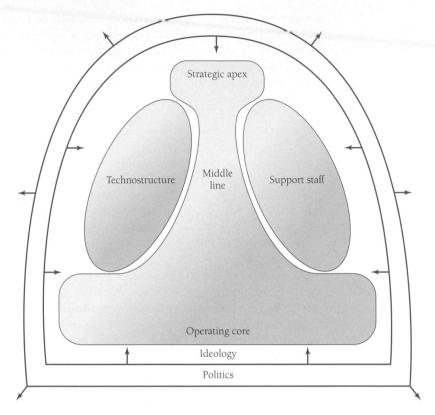

Figure 8-3 *The seven parts of an organization*

Source: From *Structuring of Organizations*, 1st ed., by H. Mintzberg. © 1979. Reprinted by permission of Pearson Education, Inc., Upper Saddle River, NJ.

The Seven Basic Parts of an Organization

Organizations are structured to define the interrelationships among their parts. Mintzberg (2008) proposed that all organizations consist of seven basic parts, as shown in Figure 8-3 above.

    1. *Operating core.* The operating core of an organization consists of those employees who are responsible for conducting the basic work duties that give the organization its defining purpose. In a manufacturing organization, it is the employees who transform raw goods (e.g., cloth) into a sellable product (e.g., apparel). In a service organization (such as a dry cleaning store), it is the employees who perform vital work functions (e.g., transform dirty clothes into clean clothes).

    2. *Strategic apex.* The strategic apex is responsible for the overall success of the entire organization. The strategic apex is associated with the executive leadership of the organization. These employees have the responsibility and authority to ensure that the larger goals of the organization are being met. Mintzberg referred to the strategic apex as the "brain" of the organization.

    3. *Middle line.* The middle line represents those employees who have the day-to-day authority for ensuring that the overall goals set by the strategic apex are

being carried out by the operating core. The middle line embodies the coordinating mechanism of direct supervision. They are mid-level bosses, ranging from senior managers down to first-level supervisors. The chain of command that starts at the strategic apex and ends at the operating core runs directly through the middle line. An organizational hierarchy is created by the various levels that separate the operating core from the strategic apex.

4. *Technostructure.* The technostructure is those employees who possess specific technical expertise that facilitates the overall operation of the organization. These employees are specialists in areas of business that influence the organization, but these people do not perform the mainstream work of the organization (the operating core) nor are they members of top management (the strategic apex). Examples include such technical areas of expertise as accounting, human resources, information technology, and law.

5. *Support staff.* The support staff provides services that aid the basic mission of the organization and typically includes the mailroom, switchboard, security, and janitorial services. Sometimes the members of the support staff and the technostructure are collectively regarded as meeting the "staff" function of an organization (vis-à-vis the line/staff distinction). However, there is a major distinction between the technostructure and the support staff. The members of the technostructure give advice to the organization, while the support staff performs services. Likewise, the technostructure and the support staff rely on different coordinating mechanisms. The technostructure relies primarily on the standardization of knowledge and skills (through education and training requirements of its members), while the support staff relies primarily on the standardization of work processes (as the uniform delivery of mail within the organization).

6. *Ideology.* All organizations are structured in response to a sixth factor that Mintzberg calls *ideology.* Ideology is a belief system that compels commitment to a particular value. Mintzberg refers to organizations that have a very strong ideology as having a "missionary" structure, but not necessarily in the religious sense. Rather, it is an organization that is singularly devoted to a particular mission, and all its actions are in pursuit of that mission. Examples include an organization that is directed to providing disaster relief for victims and an organization that is devoted to creative and innovative enterprises, such as an advertising agency or computer software designer. The ideology is the "glue" that holds the organization together. A strong ideology can produce high internal cohesion. Such organizations tend to have *few* formal rules and regulations, as they are not needed. The employees behave in accordance with their sincere conviction in the ideology of the organization, and can perform their work relatively independent of each other. All organizations have ideologies. However, in some organizations the ideology is strong enough to influence how the organization functions. In organizations with weak ideologies, its effects on individual behavior will not be pervasive. The effect of ideology within an organization is reflected in Figure 8-3 by the arrows pulling the organization together.

7. *Politics.* Mintzberg's seventh factor, *politics,* can be thought of as having the opposite effect of ideology. Ideology produces internal cohesion and provides a singular purpose to the organization; politics cause divisiveness and conflict. Politics are often the seeds of destruction within an organization. The

basis for politics is the use of power that is neither formally authorized (as by a company president) or widely accepted within the organization. The use of political power pits individuals and groups against each other for the purpose of destabilizing the legitimate power base within the organization. Destabilizing legitimate power creates opportunities for selected individuals and groups to gain illegitimate power. In highly politicized organizations there are no established coordinating mechanisms or respected boundaries between the five basic parts. Instead, the organization runs on its own highly fluid informal power bases, enacted to achieve individual objectives. Mintzberg identified the tactics of power politics to include insurgency (active resistance or passive non-compliance with organizational initiatives), professing loyalty to someone in exchange for greater power, flaunting or feigning expertise to control organizational actions, and building temporary alliances with others to advance within the organization. As such, the total organization becomes an arena or theater in which power plays at all levels are considered fair game for enhancing one's position. Mintzberg noted it is not clear how organizations degenerate into this type of structure. Given the amount of energy spent on orchestrating internal political maneuvering, the likelihood of the organization fulfilling its primary purpose is greatly reduced. All organizations contain elements of politics. In a highly politicized organization the continuous tussles for illegitimate power become the organization's consuming activity (see Field Note 3, p. 173). The effect of politics within an organization is reflected in Figure 8-3 by the arrows pulling the organization apart.

Components of Social Systems

Social system
The human components of a work organization that influence the behavior of individuals and groups.

A **social system** is a structuring of events or happenings; it has no formal structure apart from its functioning. Physical or biological systems (cars or human beings) have structures that can be identified even when they are not functioning (electrical or skeleton structures); that is, they have both an anatomy and a physiology. A social system has no anatomy in this sense. When a social system stops functioning, no identifiable structure remains. It is hard for us to think of social systems as having no tangible anatomy because it is easier to understand concepts that have concrete and simple components. Social systems do indeed have components, but they are not concrete. They are sometimes referred to as the *informal* component of an organization. We will examine three of them—roles, norms, and culture—while recognizing that they are abstract.

Roles

When an employee enters an organization, there is much for that person to learn: expected performance levels, recognition of superiors, dress codes, and time demands. Roles ease the learning process. **Roles** are usually defined as the expectations of others about appropriate behavior in a specific position. Each of us plays several roles simultaneously (parent, employee, club member, and so on), but the focus here will be on job-related roles (see The Changing Nature of Work: Jobs Versus Roles).

Role
A set of expectations about appropriate behavior in a position.

Scott et al. (1981) listed five important aspects of roles. First, they are impersonal; the position itself determines the expectations, not the individual. Second, roles are related to task behavior. An organizational role is the expected behaviors for a particular

The Changing Nature of Work: Jobs Versus Roles

The concept of a *role* is useful for understanding the diminishing value of a job as a means to explaining work. Traditionally a job was defined by a fairly static set of tasks to be performed. An employee was responsible for performing these tasks. Asking an employee to perform tasks outside of the job might be met with the response "That's not my job." The word *job* will not soon disappear from our work vocabulary, nor will its implied meaning with regard to such matters as compensation and level of authority. However, the meaning of a job in explaining what one does at work is losing its clarity. Instead of a set of tasks to be performed, employees might think of work as a series of roles they must fill simultaneously.

Consider the area of customer service. The primary responsibility for someone in this position is to tend to a customer's needs. Those needs might be met by providing information to a customer, responding to problems of a technical nature, getting the customer in touch with other parties, scheduling the customer to receive some service, and so on. One of the employee's roles is helping the customer, although the variety of ways (tasks) this might be done could be wide. Another role the employee has is to communicate back to management about the most commonly encountered customer problems and problems that are difficult to solve. Yet another role for the employee might be as a liaison to other units within the organization (such as billing or credit) who have specialized knowledge and skills in resolving certain types of issues. Thus the nature of the employee's work is to keep customers satisfied so they continue to do business with the organization. The employee must contact other individuals or units within the organization to help facilitate that outcome. The role of face-to-face customer contact may call for emotional labor skills ("service with a smile"). The role of liaison to management may call for diagnostic reasoning skills pertaining to the types of problems that repeatedly occur. Rather than thinking of work as performing a "job," another view is to think of an employee as one who helps meet the larger goals of the company by adding value through serving in different roles.

Role conflict

The product of perceptual differences regarding the content of a person's role or the relative importance of its elements.

Role overload

The conflict experienced in a role as a necessity to compromise either the quantity or quality of performance.

---

job. Third, roles can be difficult to pin down. The problem is defining who determines what is expected. Because other people define our roles, opinions differ over what our role should be. How we see our role, how others see our role, and what we actually do may differ. Fourth, roles are learned quickly and can produce major behavior changes. Fifth, roles and jobs are not the same; a person in one job might play several roles.

Role conflict refers to perceptual differences regarding the content of a person's role or the relative importance of its elements. Such differences occur between the individual and other people in a work group who do not hold the same role expectations. **Role overload** produces conflict within individuals by causing them to sacrifice quality or quantity in their duties, usually because of time pressures. Individuals often fill many roles simultaneously in life—employee, spouse, parent, friend, etc. The sense of overload is produced by not wanting to sacrifice quality of participation in a role, but feeling overwhelmed with the multiple roles to be filled. For example, consider a supervisor who says to an employee, "I want this report finished by tomorrow and I want it done well." There is conflict between the time deadline and the request for high-quality work.

Another aspect is role differentiation. This is the extent to which different roles are performed by employees in the same subgroup. One person's job might be to maintain good group relations, such as a work unit coordinator. His or her role might thus require providing emotional or interpersonal support to others. Another's role might be to set schedules, agendas, and meet deadlines; such a person is usually an administrator. When all the roles in a work group fit together like the pieces of a puzzle, the result is a smoothly running, effective group. However, all the pieces may not fit together.

Norms

Norm

A set of shared group expectations about appropriate behavior.

Norms are shared group expectations about appropriate behavior. Whereas roles define what is appropriate for a particular job, norms define acceptable group behavior. Roles differentiate positions; norms establish the behavior expected of everyone in the group, such as when employees take coffee breaks, how much they produce, when they stop for the day, and what they wear. Norms are unwritten rules that govern behavior. A company may have a formal written rule against the use of personal cell phones during work time. If employees use their cell phones at work, there is a norm that sanctions such behavior in spite of the formal rule.

Norms have several important properties. First, there is "oughtness" or "should-ness"—that is, prescriptions for behavior. Second, norms are usually more obvious for behavior judged to be important for the group. A norm might exist for the time employees stop work before lunch, but there probably is no norm about what employees eat. Third, norms are enforced by the group. Much expected behavior is monitored and enforced through formal rules and procedures. With norms, group members regulate behavior. Sometimes formal rules and group norms clash. The rule prohibiting personal cell phone use and the group norm sanctioning personal cell phone use is one such example. Unless the organization imposes sanctions on personal cell phone users (that is, rule breakers), the group norm probably prevails.

There is a three-step process for developing and communicating norms. The norm must first be defined and communicated. This can be done either explicitly ("Here is the way we do things around here") or implicitly (the desired behavior is observed). Second, the group must be able to monitor behavior and judge whether the norm is being followed. Third, the group must be able to reward conformity and punish nonconformity. Conformity enhances the predictability of behavior within the group, which in turn promotes feelings of group cohesion (Scott et al., 1981).

Compliance with norms is enforced by positive reinforcement or punishment. Positive reinforcement can be praise or inclusion in group activities. Punishment can be a dirty look, a snide remark, or actual physical abuse. Workers who exceeded the group norm for productivity in the Hawthorne studies were hit on the arm, which was called "binging." Another form of punishment is exclusion from group activities. The group often tries to convince the nonconforming employee (referred to as a *deviant*) to change his or her behavior. The group tries to alter the deviant's opinion through increased communication, verbal or nonverbal. The clearer and more important the norm and the more cohesive the group, the greater the pressure. Eventually, the deviant either changes or is rejected. If rejected, the deviant becomes an *isolate*, and the pressure to conform stops. Because the group may need the isolate to perform work tasks, they usually reach a truce; the isolate is tolerated at work but excluded from group activities and relationships. Obviously the isolate can quit the job and try to find a better match between his or her values and a group.

THE FAR SIDE®   By GARY LARSON

**"Counterclockwise, Red Eagle!
Always counterclockwise!"**

Finally, norms are not always contrary to formal organization rules or independent of them. Sometimes norms greatly promote organization goals. For example, there may be a norm against leaving for home before a certain amount of work has been done. Although quitting time is 5:00 P.M., the group may expect employees to stay until 5:15 or 5:30 to finish a certain task. In this case, the deviant is one who conforms to the formal rule (that is, leaving at 5:00 P.M.) instead of the group norm. When group norms and organization goals are complementary, high degrees of effectiveness can result.

Organizational Culture

Culture
The language, values, attitudes, beliefs, and customs of an organization.

The concept of culture was originally proposed by anthropologists to describe societies, but we have also found it useful to describe organizations. **Culture** is the languages, values, attitudes, beliefs, and customs of an organization. As can be inferred, it represents a complex pattern of variables that, when taken collectively, gives each organization its unique "flavor." Several definitions of organizational culture have been proposed, but the most straightforward was offered by Deal and Kennedy (1982): "The way we do things around here."

Ostroff, Kinicki, and Tamkins (2003) described the culture of an organization as having three layers. These three layers can be examined in any social collectivity, including a business organization, a social organization (e.g., a club), a church, or even a family.

1. *Observable artifacts.* Artifacts are the surface-level actions that can be observed from which some deeper meaning or interpretation can be drawn about the organization. Trice and Beyer (1993) identified four major categories of cultural artifacts: *symbols* (e.g., physical objects or locations); *language* (e.g., jargon, slang, gestures, humor, gossip, and rumors); *narratives* (e.g., stories, legends, and myths about the organization); and *practices* (e.g., rituals, taboos, and ceremonies). Although these artifacts are easy to observe, they are not necessarily easy to interpret or understand.

2. *Espoused values.* Espoused values are those beliefs or concepts that are specifically endorsed by management or the organization at large. Organizations per se do not possess values, but rather key individual leaders within the organization espouse these values. Two examples are "Safety is our top priority" and "We respect the opinions of all our employees." *Enacted* values are those that are converted into employee behavior. A perceived difference between espoused and enacted values can be a source of cynicism among employees. For example, despite the espoused values, actual safety efforts may be haphazard or employees may be criticized for speaking out.

3. *Basic assumptions.* Basic assumptions are unobservable and are at the core of the organization. They frequently start out as values but over time become so deeply ingrained that they are taken for granted. Basic assumptions are rarely confronted or debated and are extremely difficult to change. According to Ostroff et al., "Challenging basic assumptions produces anxiety and defensiveness because they provide security through their ability to define what employees should pay attention to, how they should react emotionally, and what actions they should take in various kinds of situations" (p. 569). Questioning a university about the value of education in society would represent a challenge to a basic assumption of academic institutions.

Culture may also be communicated through other channels, such as in-house memos, official policies, statements of corporate philosophy, and any other means of value expression (see Field Note 1).

Schein (1996) asserted that understanding the culture of an organization is critical to making sense of the behavior observed in the organization. A narrow description of behavior, divorced from the cultural context in which it occurs, is of limited value for understanding the organization. For example, Pratt and Rafaeli (1997) examined the types of clothes worn by members of a hospital staff to understand how the hospital views itself. They found that the manner of dress among the staff was symbolic of their sense of organizational identity. Furthermore, differing views among staff members

Field Note 1: A Clear Message

Organizational culture embraces the values and character of the organization. Sometimes the culture of an organization is communicated in a subtle way, and at other times the communication is loud and unambiguous. I had a client company that was founded about 90 years ago. It started through the efforts of one man who created the company when he was about 30 and served as the company's president until his death at age 80. The company manufactures world-class building supplies. Today its products are sold nationally, and the company employs about 3,000 people. The company was founded on the value of making the finest product in the market, for which it charges a high price. The marketing orientation is strictly top of the line—if you want the best, you think of this company. The culture of the organization today follows the philosophy of the founder. The founder and his philosophy are so revered that the company turned his small office into something of a shrine. Cordoned off with a thick velvet rope, the office is preserved as it was when the founder was leading the company. The office telephone, lamp, desk, chair, briefcase, and fountain pen are all period pieces. The decor of the office is not ostentatious or sumptuous but rather understated elegance, like the company's products. A 1952 calendar is hanging on the wall. Although the office is no longer in active use, it serves an extremely valuable purpose for the company. It is a constant reminder, a physical embodiment, of the person whose values continue to guide the company today, long after his death. The orientation for all new employees includes a visit to this office as a way of communicating the heritage of the company. It doesn't take long for anyone (including an outsider like me) to grasp what this company is all about. Sometimes you have to dig to unearth the culture of an organization. Not this one.

about dress were deeply felt. The authors offered the following two quotes from nurses working in the hospital:

> *Head nurse of a rehabilitation unit*: "Patients who wear pajamas and see hospital garb around them think of themselves as sick. If *they and their caretakers wear street clothes*, patients will think of themselves as moving out of the sick role and into rehabilitation. They will be ready for life outside the hospital. This is the rehab philosophy, and this is what makes this unit unique." [emphasis added]

> *Nurse on the evening shift of the same unit*: "We are medical and health professionals. We do professional work. We take care of sick patients, we deal with their bodily fluids and get their slime all over us. So we should all look like medical professionals; *we should be dressed in scrubs*." [emphasis added] (Pratt & Rafaeli, 1997, p. 862)

An organization's culture can be revealed in very subtle ways. Brown, Lawrence, and Robinson (2005) discussed territoriality in organizations through the use of nameplates on doors and family photos on desks. They serve to establish a sense of an individual belonging to that organization by the implicit marking of "turf." Baruch (2006) described a ritual among business people from different organizations who meet for the first time: the exchange of business cards. Along with the individual's name on the card is often found the organization's logo, a visual symbol of its identity. The selection of a company's logo is to send a message, coded as a symbol. The message may seek to express such values as excellence, elitism, and innovation. Anand (2006) proposed that the cartoons employees tape on their office doors not only reflect the organization's culture, but are also a production of it. The simple act of posting cartoons on doors is a message to the observer that such behavior (i.e., individual expression) is acceptable to the organization. The choice of cartoons posted by individuals were statements of their own values, as the cartoons often portrayed cynicism and sarcasm presented as satire. Anand regarded the cartoons as artifacts of the organization's culture, and they offered insight into how individuals view the organization's values. Such artifacts are not easy to decipher and they can convey different meaning to the sender and receiver of the message. Despite their subtlety, they are expressions of value and have purpose.

Schneider (1996) believes it is the people populating the organization who most define its culture. That is, people (e.g., employees) are not actors who fill predetermined roles in an established culture, but rather it is the personalities, values, and interests of these people over time that make the organization what it is. Schneider (1987) proposed what he calls the attraction–selection–attrition (ASA) cycle. The ASA cycle proposes that people with similar personalities and values are drawn to (attraction) certain organizations and hired into these organizations (selection), and people who don't fit into the pattern of shared values eventually leave the organization (attrition). This process occurs over time, however, not immediately. There can also be differences among people in the organization in values that are not important. As in the example of the two nurses and their manner of dress, if dress is a deeply held value within the hospital unit, then the ASA cycle would predict the attrition of the nurse whose view is not accepted by the rest of the unit. In support of the hypothesis that organizations attract people with relatively homogeneous personalities, Schneider et al. (1998) found that organizations differ in the modal personality types of their employees. The authors speculated that organizations with different modal personalities may well differ in their organizational cultures and structures. Further evidence of organizations staffing themselves with employees who possess similar personality characteristics was reported by Schaubroeck, Ganster, and Jones (1998), although their findings indicate various occupations (e.g., sales, clerical, etc.) also influence the ASA process. The tendency for organizations to staff themselves and socialize their members in ways that promote a monolithic culture prompted Morgan (1997) to refer to organizations as "psychic prisons."

Summary of Social System Components

Organizations have physical structures, but these alone do not define organizations. The social fabric—norms, roles, and culture—is a significant influence on the conduct of organization members. These components are not tangible entities, but they are as much attributes of an organization as its size. Organizations differ in their norms, roles, and culture. Norms influence behavior by increasing its consistency and predictability. Roles prescribe the boundaries of acceptable behavior and enhance conformity. These constructs help produce uniformity and consistency in individual behavior, which is necessary in part to ensure that all organizational members are pursuing common goals. Individuals give up some freedom when they join an organization, and these constructs represent ways through which freedom is limited. Organizations differ in culture just as individuals differ in personality. Similarly, just as certain personality types are better suited for some jobs, certain cultures foster certain behaviors. Together, these three constructs define an organization's social system; they are intangible but potent determinants of behavior.

Downsizing, Outsourcing, and Offshoring

Downsizing
The process by which an organization reduces its number of employees to achieve greater overall efficiency.

One of the most radical and tumultuous ways an organization can change in response to economic pressures is called **downsizing**. An organization may believe it has too many employees to be responsive to its environment. The most common reason for the decision to cut jobs is the organization's conclusion that it can "do more with less" (i.e., have greater efficiency with fewer employees). For most organizations the single largest expense is the wages and salaries paid to their employees. By eliminating jobs, they reduce costs. Therefore some organizations have been compelled to cut jobs just to help assure their economic survival. The work that was done by the departed employees will have to be performed by the remaining employees or through technical changes in work processes (e.g., automation). Another term given to this process of cutting jobs is *reduction-in-force*. It is not uncommon for large organizations to reduce their size by several thousand employees at one time.

Where do the eliminated jobs come from within an organization? The five core parts of the organization are targeted, with the greatest losses typically coming from the middle line, technostructure, and support staff. Jobs can also be lost in the operating core, as jobs are automated or reassigned to other countries that pay lower wages. The strategic apex may be reduced, but generally the fewest jobs are lost at this level. As noted previously, the support staff consists of such jobs as security personnel and cafeteria workers. Rather than an organization hiring its own employees to work in these jobs, organizations may contract (in effect, "rent") the services of these people through other organizations, such as a company that offers security guards or food preparers to other organizations. These jobs are said to have been outsourced.

Outsourcing
The process of eliminating jobs within the organization by having those work functions contracted to other organizations.

Outsourcing the services performed by these individuals is less costly to the organization than hiring its own employees to perform these services. Similar reductions occur in the technostructure. With fewer employees to advise (the primary function of the technostructure), there is less need for "advisers." In recent years the number of I/O psychologists working in organizations has decreased, while the number working for consulting firms has increased. In essence, organizations have reduced the number of jobs typically filled by I/O psychologists and in turn contract their services through consulting firms.

Offshoring
The process of elimination jobs within the organization by having those work functions performed in cheaper labor markets overseas (offshore).

Yet another source of job loss is **offshoring**. The work performed domestically (often jobs in the operating core) is exported to cheaper labor markets in overseas countries. Yet it is in the middle line where most of the job loss has occurred. Recall that the middle line serves as a means of direct supervision for lower-level employees. So, how can an organization survive without the middle line? The answer lies in the coordinating mechanisms. Direct supervision is one of the five coordinating mechanisms. By eliminating much of the middle line, the coordinating mechanism shifts from direct supervision to standardization. The coordination that was formerly achieved through personal contact with a supervisor is now achieved through greater standardization of the work process, the output, or employee skills.

Another manifestation of downsizing is larger spans of control. With larger spans of control, fewer managers are needed, the organizational hierarchy becomes smaller, and the shape of the organization becomes flatter. It is also common for decision making to become more decentralized following a downsizing. Figure 8-4 shows the top part of an organizational chart for a manufacturing company before downsizing. The company is structured to be organized by both function (production and sales) and location (California and Texas). There are small spans of control. Each person below the president has two subordinates. A total of 15 people are needed to staff this part of the organization with such a configuration. Figure 8-5 shows the same company following reorganization—in this case, downsizing. A total of eight jobs have been eliminated by this reorganization. The sales function has been consolidated into one job. The plant manager at each of the four locations now reports directly to the vice president. Each plant manager now also provides information directly to the sales manager (as indicated by the broken lines), but administratively the plant managers report to the vice president. The vice president now has a span of control of five. The jobs lost in this reorganization are one vice president, three sales managers, and the entire layer of (middle) managers.

What consequences might we expect from this reorganization? There would be less administrative control from the loss of managerial jobs. There would be greater pressure on the organization's parts to coordinate with each other because of the loss of direct supervision. There would probably be more stress placed on the surviving employees to work harder and find new ways to do the work of the employees whose jobs were eliminated. The organization would have fewer salary expenditures associated with the elimination of eight jobs. Eight people would be out of work.

How would you feel if you lost your job because you were fired? Probably not very well, but in all likelihood you received some signals along the way that you were not performing satisfactorily. In turn, you probably had some control over whether you would change your job behavior. How would you feel if you lost your job because it

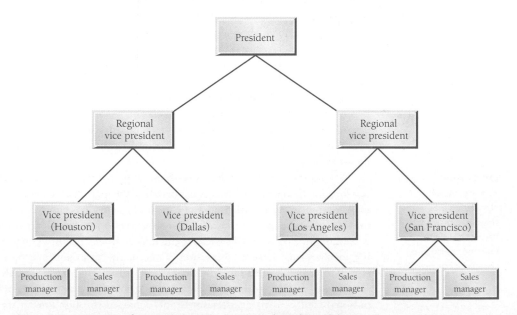

Figure 8-4   *Top part of an organizational chart before downsizing*

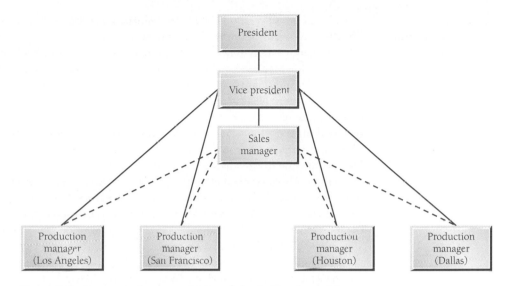

Figure 8-5   *Top part of an organizational chart after downsizing*

was eliminated? You could have been an exemplary employee, but you lost your job through no fault of your own. *You* were not released, rather the *job* you were filling was eliminated to make the organization more efficient. Chapter 11 will examine the psychological reactions to downsizing, from the perspectives of both the survivors and those whose jobs were eliminated.

When organizations are contracting in size, the overall social order of employment is altered. If, as a rule, organizations reduce the number of middle managers needed to run the business, then these displaced middle managers will not simply find new jobs as middle managers in some other companies. Rather the *job* of middle manager is being reduced in frequency, necessitating holders of middle-management jobs to enter new jobs, not new positions in the same job family. This may necessitate professional retraining, learning new skills to fill jobs that continue to exist. Thus issues of organizational structure affect not only I/O psychology but also the sociology of employment and the economics of across-occupational mobility.

Mergers and Acquisitions

One strategy organizations can use in response to environmental pressures is to become smaller—that is, to downsize. Another strategy is to become larger. But rather than just becoming a larger version of what the organization already is, organizations can choose to "marry" another organization as a way of increasing their size. The logic behind an organizational marriage is similar to that of the marriage of individuals; that is, the overall quality of life for both parties will be enhanced.

Organizational merger
The joining or combining of two organizations of approximately equal status and power.

Organizational marriages encompass both mergers and acquisitions. The technical distinction between a merger and an acquisition is slim. An **organizational merger** is the marriage or joining of two organizations of equal status and power. Their union is mutually decided. Both organizations think they will be more prosperous by their

Acquisition
The process by which one organization acquires or subsumes the resources of a second organization.

formal association with the other. An acquisition is the procurement of property (in this case, an organization) by another organization. The purchasing organization is in the dominant or more powerful role. Unlike a marriage of individuals, an acquisition can be a union between two organizations where only one party agrees to the new relationship. The dominant organization thus acquires an unwilling partner to enhance its financial status in what is called a *hostile takeover*. Other acquisitions are characterized by more friendly relations between the two organizations, but nevertheless the more powerful organization acquires the less powerful organization. The acquiring organization is referred to as the *parent*, and the organization being acquired is the *target*. For the purpose of this discussion, mergers and acquisitions will be portrayed as the combining of two companies, regardless of the difference in power between the two. There is relatively little research on this topic. What we do know applies mainly to the characteristics of the two organizations as they affect the quality of their marriage and the individual responses of employees to their organization being united with another.

Marks (2002) described three phases in the merger process: precombination, combination, and postcombination. Most of the emphasis in the precombination phase is on financial issues, such as what a target company is worth, tax implications, and expected returns on the investment. Little thought or concern is directed to psychological or cultural issues. In the combination phase individuals jockey for power and cultures clash as people focus on differences between the partners and which side won which battles. Conflict can erupt over even minor issues. Marks described this account:

> In one health care merger, the two sides could not even agree on starting times for meetings. One organization's managers began 9:00 AM meetings promptly whereas the other's managers only left their offices at the top of the hour, collected their papers, chatted with their assistants, and grabbed a cup of coffee before arriving at the conference room around 9:15. In the pre-merger culture this was no problem, because everyone knew that 9:00 AM meetings actually began at 9:15. But it infuriated counterparts from the partner organization, who described the tardiness as "disrespectful" and "undisciplined." Of course, the latecomers regarded their new partners as "uptight" and having "misplaced priorities." (p. 46)

It is in the postcombination phase that the importance of integrating the two cultures becomes acute. Declines in employee morale and customer satisfaction indicate there are other criteria of a successful merger besides initial financial appeal. Marks described the postcombination phase as steeped in concerns about implementation, and there is no predetermined date when the merger is declared to be "finalized." All parties involved in the merger must continue to understand and adapt to the new culture (and new company) that was birthed.

The International Labour Organization (2003) estimated that in the decade of the 1990s over 10 million workers lost their jobs due to mergers and acquisitions. This figure does not include job loss associated with small companies that were driven out of business because they could not compete with the new "super organizations" (such as large retail stores). As with downsizing, I/O psychologists have little experience in dealing with how individuals respond to this type of organizational activity. In the past 20 years, we have had to address new aspects of organizational behavior about which we had little knowledge. The depth and magnitude of these issues on the psychology of work have had a profound impact on the profession of I/O psychology (see Field Note 2).

Field Note 2: How Many Ways Can You Lose Your Job?

Employee turnover has been a point of great interest to I/O psychologists since the field's inception. Employees could either quit their jobs (classified as *voluntary* turnover), or be fired (classified as *involuntary* turnover). For the first 70–80 years of I/O psychology, involuntary turnover occurred primarily in one of three ways.

1. *Dismissal.* A person is fired and some other person fills the position.

2. *Automation.* Work that was performed manually is now performed by an automated process. In the late 1960s and early 1970s, computers were invented for commercial (and ultimately, personal) use. The lament of many workers of that era was, "I was replaced by a computer."

3. *Loss of company.* An entire company is dissolved, either due to financial insolvency (bankruptcy) or because the owner simply "wants to get out of the business."

Following the radical changes in the business world in the 1980s, the number of reasons for job loss grew.

4. *Downsizing or reduction-in-force (RIF).* A decision to reduce the size of the work force to reduce labor costs. For example, a company that has eight workers performing a job decides to eliminate two of the positions. The remaining six employees then have to do the work that was once performed by eight. The two workers who lost their jobs were "RIFed."

5. *Outsourcing.* Eliminating jobs by contracting with an outside company to provide a particular service at a reduced cost. Examples include security, food service, and maintenance.

6. *Mergers and acquisitions.* The elimination of jobs caused by the combination of two companies. The new, larger company does not need two sets of employees performing the same duties. Mergers and acquisitions occurred throughout the 20th century, but the decades of the 1980s and 1990s (in particular) were known as the era of "merger mania."

7. *Offshoring.* The reduction of costs by eliminating domestic jobs and having the work performed in another country at a lower wage. Examples include computer programming, manufacturing, and telephonic customer service.

When an employee is fired, another individual is hired to fill the position. There is no job loss to society as a whole. However, the remaining six reasons for job loss represent not only the basis for why people are unemployed, but also the disappearance of jobs from a national economy. From an individual perspective, people must find jobs to earn a living. From a societal perspective, for every job that is lost, a new job must be created to maintain the same overall level of employment. The term *job creation* is often associated with the development of new industries that provide jobs people can fill. Before a person can be a good fit with a job, there has to be a job that can be filled.

Global Organizations

The explosion in business being conducted on a global basis has given rise to a new type of organization—the global organization. Global organizations have all the properties of any organization (in terms of structural and social components) with the added feature that their physical locations and employees are distributed throughout the world. Global organizations are relatively new, emerging in the 1990s as a response to advances in computer technology, new trade agreements among nations, and the end of the Cold War. Chao and Moon (2005) described the magnitude of global business organizations in the contemporary workworld. There are approximately 63,000 multinational corporations that employ 90 million individuals. These companies employ a diverse array of people who differ by race, ethnicity, religion, and gender. Groups constituting a "majority" or "minority" can vary across different geographic sites of the same company. Chao and Moon believe that trying to understand culture in terms of demographics (as by race, ethnicity, etc.) is an overly simplistic way to explain the values held by people. A purely demographic description tends to promote thinking that the members of the same group hold similar values, which is often not the case. The authors believe the "cultural mosaic" reflected in multinational companies must be understood at a deeper level than by demographic membership.

For many years organizations that conducted business overseas (i.e., importing and exporting supplies to and from other countries) had a single corporate headquarters (such as in the United States) and simply engaged in international commerce. As customer sales grew in offshore locations, the parent company found it critical to establish separate divisions in other countries. Thus a single company, such as IBM, had separate multinational business units in England, France, Australia, and so on. This type of organizational structure resulted in numerous disadvantages, including duplication of internal services and poor interdivisional communication. As new computer-based technology (such as the internet) was created, people in one organization could operate on a worldwide basis as if they were (virtually) present and together. This technology created the possibility of a global organization, one that has a global organizational culture, structure, and communication process. In short, a global organization operates as if the entire world were a single entity. Thus the evolution of organizations doing business overseas has evolved from *international* to *multinational* to *global*.

Marquardt (2002) described how the diversity and differentiation created by multicultural employees can cause organizational tension that, if left unattended, can quickly lead to conflict in the global company. The key challenge is to build an organization in which there are core values that transcend specific cultures, uniform policies that are regarded as fair and reasonable, and consistent business practices that can be implemented globally but are respectful of local cultural customs. Marquardt stated, "One of the greatest powers of a global company and an important source of its competitive advantage is its diversity. Diversity provides the requisite variety. Without this inherent complexity, global organizations would not survive. They would lack the creativity, energy, and talent to develop the level of problem-solving capability necessary to be successful and thrive in the chaos of the global environment" (pp. 270–271).

The culture we grew up in causes people to see the world differently. We tend to believe that our view of the world is correct, which in turn leads us to think and act in certain ways. We can come to believe that other ways of thinking and acting are strange, bizarre, or unintelligible. Western (the United States, Canada, northern Europe, Australia, and New Zealand) and non-Western (the rest of the world) cultures reflect different sets of values that guide thinking and behavior. Table 8-1 lists some of these value differences.

Table 8-1   *Examples of Western and non-Western values*

Western Values	Non-Western Values
Individualism	Collectivism, group
Achievement	Modesty
Equality, egalitarian	Hierarchy
Winning	Collaboration, harmony
Pride	Saving face
Respect for results	Respect for status, ascription
Respect for competence	Respect for elders
Time is money	Time is life
Action, doing	Being, acceptance
Systematic, mechanistic	Humanistic
Tasks	Relationships, loyalty
Informal	Formal
Directness, assertiveness	Indirectness
Future, change	Past, tradition
Control	Fate
Specific, linear	Holistic
Verbal	Nonverbal

Source: From Marquardt, M., "Around the World: Organization Development in the International Context," in J. Waclawski and A. H. Church (eds.), *Organization Development: A Data-Driven Approach to Organizational Change* (San Francisco: Jossey-Bass, 2002). This material is used by permission of John Wiley & Sons, Inc.

Marquardt believes these differences in values can be reduced to four key dimensions that most affect the global organization:

1. *Leadership roles and expectations.* The democratic style of leadership is the hallmark of Western managers. Employees are encouraged and expected to voice their opinions to better serve the operation of the organization. Disagreements with managers are not uncommon, and employees are encouraged to challenge and question. In non-Western cultures managers are expected to make decisions rather than solicit opinions from employees. There are status differentials based on title, and lower-level employees who speak out may be considered disrespectful. Managers act in a certain formal style or else they may lose credibility.

2. *Individualism and groups.* As extensive research has indicated, the United States is the most individualistic culture in the world. As a culture we greatly value independence, and successful task completion or "getting the job done" is more important than relationships. The social interaction of different ages, genders, and races is consistent with Western values of equality and informality. Indeed, our employment laws (Civil Rights Act, Age Discrimination in Employment Act, Americans with Disabilities Act, etc.) are designed to achieve this very outcome. Non-Western cultures tend to be more group-oriented or collectivist.

Group members support each other in exchange for loyalty and acceptance in the group. Individuals identify on a personal level with the social network to which they belong. The social interaction of people of differing status may be seen as a means of subverting authority and power in the workplace and may cause embarrassment and loss of status.

3. *Communications.* Latin American, Middle Eastern, and southern European cultures value expressive communication styles. The passion with which they communicate is designed to establish and maintain social relations. Voices are raised to reflect emotions such as joy, anger, and excitement, and hugging and touching often accompany conversation. The Western style of communication places more emphasis on the factual accuracy of what is said. The primary goal is to reach an objective, unemotional conclusion that leads to actions being taken by the listener. Displays of emotion are thought to indicate a lack of professionalism and rationality. There can be extreme variability in communication styles across cultures in trying to make a point, ranging from intentional exaggeration of desire or intent in the Middle East to prolonged silence and pauses in Asian cultures. In short, there is ample opportunity for people of different cultures to misunderstand each other on the basis of their communication styles.

4. *Decision making and handling conflict.* Western cultures are highly action-oriented. We like to get work done, not waste time, and we derive pleasure from achievement. Western cultures prefer frankness and candor in dealing with conflict. We accept and expect conflict and use power to resolve our differences. Non-Western cultures are much more indirect in conveying disagreement or criticism. Greater emphasis is placed on avoiding conflict than on finding ways to resolve it. Circuitous, indirect communication is used in the desire to protect honor and avoid shame. The desire to avoid conflict is rooted in courtesy and respect. Age is often the deciding factor in determining the most important member in a group.

The American Psychological Association (2003) recognizes that organizations are now being designed that include wide cultural variability. Psychologists are formally encouraged to use culturally sensitive methods in creating these organizations, as opposed to implementing policies based on strictly Western values. Marquardt (2002) concluded that these cultural differences should be seen not as barriers but rather as sources of synergy that can help organizations become successful in a global economy (see Cross-Cultural I/O Psychology: Four Dimensions on Which Cultures Can Differ).

Organizational Change

The first part of this chapter has dealt with the concept of an organization and its constituent components. The remainder will deal with an ever-widening area of I/O psychology—the process of effecting change in organizations. It is best to begin this section by considering why organizations exist in the first place. Organizations are created to fulfill some purpose or objective. They exist in a larger environment that encompasses economic, legal, and social factors. Thus there must be a sense of fit between the organization and the environment in which it exists.

Cross-Cultural I/O Psychology: *Four Dimensions on Which Cultures Can Differ*

The concept that nations have identifiable cultures that influence the conduct of business became more salient through the research of Geert Hofstede. Hofstede worked for IBM, a multinational organization that had offices in many countries around the world. The employees in each location were administered attitude and opinion surveys as part of their employment. Hofstede analyzed the data by nation and arrived at the conclusion there were reliable and meaningful differences among the responses to the surveys. Hofstede (1980) wrote a seminal book based on his research entitled *Culture's Consequences*, and he updated his findings in a later book (Hofstede, 2001) Hofstede identified four major dimensions that are useful in understanding cross-cultural differences. The first two dimensions have already been described in this book.

1. *Power distance.* As discussed in Chapter 6, power distance refers to the extent to which less powerful members of an organization expect and accept that power is distributed unequally. The United States has a relatively small power distance (Malaysia scores highest on power distance).

2. *Individualism–collectivism.* As described in Chapter 7, individualism refers to the belief that people in a society primarily look after themselves and their family members. Collectivism is the belief that people in a society are integrated into strong, cohesive in-groups, which throughout their lifetime protect them in exchange for unquestioning loyalty. The United States has the strongest sense of individualism in the world.

3. *Masculinity–femininity.* Masculinity stands for a society in which social gender roles generally tend to be distinct. Men are supposed to be assertive, tough, and focused on material resources; women are supposed to be more modest, tender, and concerned with the quality of life. Femininity stands for a society in which social gender roles overlap; both men and women are supposed to be modest, tender, and concerned with the quality of life. The United States is more masculine than feminine (Japan scores highest on masculinity).

4. *Uncertainty avoidance.* Uncertainty avoidance is the extent to which members of a culture feel threatened by uncertain or unknown situations. The United States scores low in uncertainty avoidance (Greece scores highest on uncertain avoidance).

Thus, in the national culture of the United States, we rank very high in individualism, we do not accept large power differentials among people with varying degrees of status, we tend to see separate social roles for men and women, and we do not feel particularly threatened by conditions or events we do not know. Hofstede's research juxtaposed 50 nations on these four dimensions of culture. Critics of Hofstede's research contend that *national* culture differences do not necessarily manifest themselves in differences in *organizational* culture. There is also concern that focusing on national averages can mask variability among individuals within a nation (e.g., Oyserman, Coon, and Kemmelmeier, 2002). Nevertheless, Hofstede's research has had a major influence in how we think about culture and its consequences on business.

Organization Development

Many business organizations were founded in the first half of the 20th century. They enjoyed a period of relative stability in the environments in which they operated. Although organizations had to respond to some environmental influences, for the most

Organization development
A system of planned interventions designed to change an organization's structure and/or processes to achieve a higher level of functioning.

part the economic and social order was relatively stable until the 1980s. I/O psychology has an area of specialization devoted to the study of facilitating organizations to develop or change themselves in response to environmental influences. It is called **organization development** (OD). From the end of World War II (the mid-1940s) through the 1970s, OD was instrumental in helping those organizations that were, in effect, suffering from some "growing pains" in their own development.

For reasons discussed in Chapter 1, the business world began to change in the 1980s. Among the forces responsible for the change were the adoption and diffusion of computers into worklife, the changing cultural diversity of the workforce, the emergence of advanced communication technologies, the globalization of business, and redistributions of economic power. Using the "peg and hole" analogy, we can think of organizations as "pegs" that must fit into ever-changing business environments (the "holes"). There has always been a need for some organizations to change themselves in response to environmental pressures, but the past 30 years has witnessed an ever-growing and expanding need for all organizations to respond to the pressures placed on them by changing environmental conditions. What is different now than 30 years ago is (1) the greater strength of environmental pressures prompting change, (2) the speed at which change must occur, (3) the acceptance that responsiveness to change is a continuous organizational process, and (4) the pervasiveness of organizations caught up and affected by changing environmental conditions.

My home town has a family-owned ice cream store that still sells ice cream the way it has for seven decades. On the surface it might appear that this little store has escaped the need to adjust in response to changes in the last 70 years. To a large extent this is true, although the store has been compelled to stock low-fat and no-fat dairy products to meet changing customer preferences. For the most part, this store is an "organizational dinosaur," one of the last of a rare breed that has not had to change with the times.

I/O psychologists now fully recognize the broad-scale need for understanding organizational change. Church, Waclawski, and Berr (2002) noted that current organizational change strategies have become more grounded in business strategy, financial indicators, global trends, and customer research than interventions of a purely psychological nature. Burke (2008) candidly described what it is like to try to implement organizational change. "The implementation process is messy. Things don't proceed exactly as planned; people do things their own way, not always according to the plan; some people resist or even sabotage the process, and some people who would be predicted to support or resist the plan actually behave in just the opposite way" (p. 12).

Plowman et al. (2007) provided a vivid example of how organizational change actually occurs, including unanticipated outcomes that derived from unintended processes. The organization in question was a church. The desire for change began with some parishoners who were bored with the Sunday morning service. So instead of attending a traditional religious service, they decided to offer a free Sunday breakfast to homeless people. After five weeks of serving food, a physician in the group decided to also offer the homeless people free medical advice. This grew into the offering of eye-care, dental, and medical services. Within a few years, the church had created a separate social service organization. This organization obtained city funds to run a day care center for the homeless, serve approximately 200,000 meals per year, offer job training, and provide legal assistance. The homeless people sang in the church choir and served as ushers at the Sunday morning church service. This entire series of events started with a simple act of generosity.

This case described by Plowman et al. is not atypical in organizational change. The magnitude of the proposed intended change was small: to offer a free breakfast to some homeles people on Sunday mornings. Because there were no objections or resistance to the breakfast, the concept of accepting change got a toe-hold. Had the free breakfast idea been denied, none of the subsequent changes would have resulted. The success of the small intended change amplified the possibility for more radical changes. The entire process snow-balled, sustaining itself into continuous radical change. The sheer magnitude of the radical changes produced resistance and displeasure by other organizations. Some local businesses situated near the church objected to the amount of disruption the church's activities created in the neighborhood. However, the resistance came primarily after the new activities were fully operational.

The case provides insights into when resistance to change can best be overcome. Had the resistance emerged initially, the attempt at change may well have failed before it even could begin. After the change process produced momentum, further changes emerged, and the resistance was "too little too late" to stop it. In sum, both the process and the outcomes of organizational change could not have been envisioned at the outset, and the *timing* of events in the change process can be just as important as the nature of the events themselves.

Rousseau and Batt (2007) discussed not only the need for organizations to change, but also the need for society as a whole to change. The problems we face in the 21st century cannot necessarily be addressed with solutions that worked in the 20th century. The 21st century has produced greater life expectancy, lower job security, and major changes in how families function. There is an old saying; "We prefer the devil we know to the devil we don't know." We may know that old approaches and solutions are no longer effective, but we derive some comfort from them because they are familiar and known to us. New ideas pose a double threat: not only are we unfamiliar with them, they may be just as ineffectual as the old ideas. In short, while the need for change may be acute, there is often the temptation to stick with what is less threatening rather than venture into the more threatening (but also potentially more beneficial). Such is the paradox of organizational change and resistance to it.

Empowerment

As the workforce has become more educated and skilled, organizations need to loosen some of the constraints placed on employees to control and monitor their actions. The need for organizational control systems such as close supervision, strict channels of communication, and chains of command evolved in part because of the perceived differentiation in ability levels between management and workers. The classical perspective (emanating from the era of scientific management) was that management personnel generally had far more ability and insight into organizational issues than workers. The workers (or, in Mintzberg's terminology, the operating core) were hired to perform the basic work that needed to be done, but they required mechanisms of control, or close supervision. As time passed and the workforce became more educated, it was no longer as necessary to closely control nonmanagerial personnel. It became feasible to push some of the traditional managerial responsibilities (such as decision making) down into the lower levels of the organization. This had the combined effect of giving traditional nonmanagerial personnel managerial-type powers and requiring fewer people in traditional managerial roles. The meaning of **empowerment** comes from "power." By giving employees more power and distributing this power away from traditional managerial personnel, the downsizing or elimination of mid-level managerial jobs became possible. The power previously vested in these positions has been redistributed in part to the employees, thereby *empowering* them. Liden and Arad (1996) interpreted empowerment as the psychological outcome of structural changes in the organization designed to provide power.

Spreitzer (1997) identified four general dimensions of empowerment.

> 1. *Meaning.* An individual feels a sense of meaning when an activity "counts" in his or her own value system. Empowered individuals derive personal significance from their work. They get "energized" about a given activity and thus become connected through a sense of meaning.

> 2. *Competence.* Empowered individuals have a sense of self-effectiveness or personal competence. They believe that they have not only the needed skills and abilities but also the confidence that they can perform successfully.

> 3. *Self-determination.* Self-determination is represented by behaviors that are initiated and regulated through choices as an expression of oneself, rather than behaviors that are forced by the environment. Empowered individuals have a sense of responsibility for and ownership of their activity.

> 4. *Impact.* Impact is the individual's belief that he or she can affect or influence organizational outcomes. Empowered individuals see themselves as "making a difference"—that is, providing the intended effects of their actions.

Spreitzer asserted that empowered individuals are more likely to be innovative, exert upward influence in the organization, and be effective in their jobs. Empowered individuals are more likely to challenge and question, rather than blindly follow, traditional role expectations. Organizational change interventions are designed to enhance both effectiveness and personal satisfaction. The concept of empowerment provides a potentially useful framework for guiding the intervention. Thus one outcome of a successful change intervention is to empower the employees. However, this outcome is also dependent on the nature of the work performed by the organization and the ability levels of the employees.

Six Sigma

Six Sigma is a comprehensive approach to organizational change that is based on behavioral concepts and the use of statistical information to aid in decision making. It evolved from the principles of Total Quality Management, an earlier method designed to change organizations. The name "Six Sigma" is derived from the statistical properties of the normal distribution, presented in Chapter 2. *Sigma* is the term associated with the standard deviation, the statistical index that reveals the spread or variability of scores in a distribution. Plus or minus one sigma (or two sigmas) encompasses approximately the middle 68% of the scores in a normal distribution, plus or minus two sigmas (or four sigmas) encompasses approximately 95% of the scores, and plus

Empowerment
The process of giving employees in an organization more power and decision-making authority within a context of less managerial oversight.

Six Sigma
A method of improving business processes using statistical information to achieve greater customer satisfaction.

or minus three sigmas (or six sigmas) encompasses nearly 100% of the scores in a distribution.

The theory of Six Sigma is to understand how much variability exists in the quality of the products or services a company offers and to reduce the variability that results in customer dissatisfaction. An example is a customer waiting in line to check out at a hotel. Few travelers expect to be waited on immediately when they approach the front desk, so customer service in the hotel business does not have to be immediate. However, few customers enjoy waiting in line to check out of the hotel because it is their intent to leave the hotel and get on with their travel. There is an average time limit at which customers become dissatisfied. Let us say that time period is five minutes. If the five-minute mark is the break-point between customer satisfaction and dissatisfaction, then the hotel realizes it must modify its checkout procedure if the customer wait will exceed five minutes. Basically Six Sigma is a method of organizational change that uses statistical information (in this case, time in minutes) to execute actions (checking out hotel guests) to achieve a desired outcome (customer satisfaction). The organization's overall goal is to improve customer satisfaction by changing its practices on those matters most critical to pleasing customers. Six Sigma is thus directed toward improving the processes that organizations use to meet their customers' needs.

Eckes (2001) described the five critical phases of process improvement:

1. *Define.* The first step is to define the organization's customers, their requirements, and the key organizational processes that affect them. In the hotel business, the customers are travelers who need a place to stay while they are away from home. They value speed and quality of service.

2. *Measure.* Many variables can be measured by the hotel (e.g., the number of pieces of luggage the customer has), but the ones most critical to the customer are the ones that should be measured. Examples might include time to check in, time to check out, time to wait for a meal from room service, and the quality of the food.

3. *Analyze.* The variables measured should be analyzed to determine why the process is not performing as desired. For example, why does checkout take longer than check-in? Why is the food often delivered to a room cold?

4. *Improve.* The organization should determine the potential solutions to improve upon the processes that are causing customer dissatisfaction. For example, if checkout takes longer than check-in, should more receptionists be assigned to checking out the hotel guests? If the food is often delivered cold, can room service deliver the food faster, or could hot plates be provided to keep the food warm?

5. *Control.* The last phase is to develop, document, and implement a strategy to ensure that performance improvement remains at the desired level. Perhaps more hotel guests check out at a certain time of the day. If so, then additional receptionists might be staffed for those hours. The hotel should invest in ways to keep food warm.

The end result of the process-improvement approach is to reduce the variability in the critical measures (e.g., checkout time) and to improve the mean or average score on the index. For example, all guests should get checked out in roughly the same amount of time and that time might be three minutes (instead of eight minutes). A principle of process management is that there is always room to improve a process, no matter how good it may be. The continuous quest to reduce variability and improve the mean is the driving force behind Six Sigma. These two simple statistical indices (the mean and the standard deviation) are the foundation for assessing the quality of a process. Six Sigma advocates designating fully trained employees within the organization be devoted solely to process improvement. Their full-time job is to follow the precepts of the method (i.e., determine what is most important to customers, measure it, improve processes that affect it, and sustain those changes) as a way to get the organization to focus on what matters most—customer satisfaction (see Field Note 3).

Six Sigma was originally designed to improve product quality, but it can also save time and lower production costs. However, as Hindo (2007) described, Six Sigma is not a universal solution for all types of organizations. Much of the success of Six Sigma has been reported in companies that are heavily engaged in production or repetitive services. The method is less effective when an organization's primary goal is founded on creativity and innovation. Creativity often involves well-intentioned efforts that result in "dead ends" and "blind alleys" with no direct positive results. Many highly successful and innovative products take years to develop. Six Sigma does not facilitate an organizational culture accepting of the trial-and-error process endemic to creativity. The final phase of Six Sigma is *control*, and the creative process cannot be controlled like a production process. As an organizational intervention designed to facilitate

Field Note 3: Students as Customers?

One of the underlying principles of continuous process improvement is that the needs and preferences of the customer are of paramount importance. An organization's business strategy is directed toward satisfying the customer, which increases the likelihood of expanding the customer base as well as repeat business among current customers. For example, in the operation of a restaurant, food is prepared to the customers' specific preferences. The goal is to satisfy the customers by increasing their control over the final product. However, applying continuous process improvement principles in the field of medical practice is not so direct. A medical doctor does not regard patients as "customers," catering to their expressed needs. Rather the doctor controls the specific form of medical treatment the patient receives—for example,

with regard to medication and surgery. In the field of medicine the patients put their faith and trust in the training and experience of the doctors to provide high-quality medical treatment.

Now consider education. Are students more like "customers" (in the restaurant business) or "patients" (in the medical business)? Should educational institutions strive to please their students by giving them more control over the substance and delivery of educational programs? Or should students put their faith and trust in the training of the faculty to know what is in the students' best interests in providing high-quality education? There has been considerable interest in applying process-improvement principles to educational institutions, but there has also been controversy over how students are to be regarded.

change, Six Sigma is more effective in improving what an organization already does, rather than cultivating new ideas and concepts.

Overcoming Organizational Resistance to Change

At the core of any change effort is the desire to bring about change. However, change introduces ambiguity into the environment, with the concomitant effects of less predictability and control. Accordingly, organizational members often resist change because of the undesirable effects it has on individuals. Yet paradoxically the change is regarded as necessary for the welfare of the organization and thus its members, who are the ones resistant to it. Resistance to change is a major obstacle in any planned change effort.

Hedge and Pulakos (2002) noted that the reasons people resist change in organizations are varied. Table 8-2 presents eight reasons for resistance to organizational change. It has been my experience that all of these reasons can be powerful forces to overcome in any organization. As was noted in Chapter 1, there can be a gap between scientists who study organizational problems and practitioners who have to implement solutions to them. Muchinsky (2004b) found that in order for organizational

Table 8-2   *Reasons for resistance to organizational change*

- **Vested interest of organizational members:** Change affects the status quo and employees worry that positions may be eliminated or they may be terminated or reassigned. Not surprisingly, then, change is likely to meet with resistance.
- **Fear of uncertainty:** Employees in most jobs establish a routine; they become familiar with the expectations and responsibilities of the job. Simply put, the known is more comfortable than the unknown.
- **Misunderstandings:** Whenever situations change, misunderstandings may arise—often because of lack of clarity. Misunderstandings are especially likely between higher management and those on whom change is imposed.
- **Social disruption:** Comfortable patterns of communication and information flow are established after working with other employees over time. Changes tend to disrupt such established patterns of interaction.
- **Inconvenience:** The normal routine of performing a job is affected when new processes or procedures are introduced. If the change is merely perceived as an inconvenience, that may be enough to elicit resistance.
- **Organizational incompatibility:** Poor fit (or poor perceived fit) between the current organizational structure and the new strategy and its desired outcome may create strong resistance among organization members.
- **Lack of top-level support and commitment:** If employees perceive a lack of enthusiasm, support, or commitment from management (especially top managers), they may be less likely to embrace the change themselves.
- **Rejection of outsiders:** When change is introduced by an external change agent, there may be resistance merely because the individual is considered an outsider who cannot possibly know what is best for the organization.

Source: From Hedge, J. W., & Pulakos, E. D., "Grappling with Implementation: Some Preliminary Thoughts and Relevant Research," in J. W. Hedge & E. D. Pulakos, (Eds.), *Implementing Organizational Interventions: Steps, Processes, and Best Practices* (San Francisco: Jossey-Bass, 2002). This material is used by permission of John Wiley & Sons, Inc.

interventions to be successful, the strategies to effect the change have to be as rich and diverse as those designed to resist change. Gallagher, Joseph, and Park (2002) described how resourceful people can become when they don't want to do something:

> A group facing a significant change may resist by denying that change is necessary or by asking for unreasonable amounts of data to 'prove' that the status quo is unsatisfactory. Staff might be physically or mentally absent. They may organize to fight the change, activate their personal networks against the change, or attempt to ignore the whole thing. They may attack the credibility of the leader, turn on each other, or be passive-aggressive in the implementation of the change commitments. (p. 25)

Dirks, Cummings, and Pierce (1996) proposed a useful framework for understanding the conditions under which individuals promote and resist change. It is based on the concept of psychological ownership, which is the feeling of being psychologically tied to an object and feeling possessive of that object. In this case, the organization is the object in question.

Dirks et al. believe these concepts are critical to understanding why organizational change efforts are either accepted or resisted. The theoretical basis is a basic understanding of the self—namely, that people accept conditions that are perceived to enhance them. When employees feel a sense of psychological ownership of their organization, they have a vested interest in conditions that promote the organization and, in turn, themselves. Organizational change that is initiated from within, does not alter the fundamental identity of the relationship to the organization. It is perceived as adding to the reservoir of bonding between the individual and organization. Change that threatens fundamental psychological needs derived from organizational membership is most strongly resisted. Although it is not always possible to orchestrate how change occurs, we have some insights into why and how individuals react to change as they do.

An Example of the Need for Organizational Change

The research and writing on organizational change can appear somewhat abstract and difficult to understand in a practical sense. The following case study will help animate this material.

For more than 100 years the textile industry in the United States enjoyed economic prosperity. There was unending demand for textile products—people throughout the world need to clothe themselves. There was also a vast supply of a natural product, cotton, that was grown domestically. The raw cotton was transformed into cotton yarn, which in turn was woven into cotton fabrics (cloth). The cloth was then cut and sewn into shirts, pants, and other apparel. The United States literally "clothed the world" (or much of it) for a long time. Workers in the textile industry did not have to be highly skilled because neither the machinery for making yarn nor the looms for weaving cloth were complex. The work involved in cutting and stitching the cloth into apparel required even less technical skill. The typical wage of a textile worker in the United States in the 1980s was about $12 per hour.

Pressures on the textile industry to change began in the form of consumer demands for new types of yarn. This yarn did not grow from a natural plant but was created from a blend of cotton and synthetic fibers. The new yarn was less prone to shrink upon washing, more stain resistant, and more likely to retain its color with wear. The textile industry was forced to design a new line of manufacturing technology to produce these blended synthetic fibers. More technically competent workers were required to operate the new machinery. Some of the existing textile workers accepted the need to be trained, but others left the industry. New selection procedures had to be implemented to upgrade the skill requirements for new textile workers. This new yarn continued to be woven into cloth and then cut and sewn to create apparel.

Next came pressures from global competition. China developed a strong interest in entering the textile business. Because the yarn making process involved machinery and the Chinese could purchase this machinery as readily as any other country, large yarn producing textile companies were established in China. Because the quality of the finished yarn was comparable to yarn made in the United States, customers began to buy yarn from the Chinese because of lower costs. The lower cost was not evident in the fibers or machinery but in labor. A typical wage for a textile worker in China is approximately 90¢ per hour.

The Chinese began to flood the global market with yarn because U.S. companies could not compete with these low labor costs. Likewise, other countries built weaving operations that had lower labor costs. The third phase of the textile business, cutting and sewing cloth, was also shifted to Asia. In addition to lower wages, Asians (particularly women in Southeast Asia—Cambodia, Vietnam, and Laos) have smaller hands and fingers compared with Westerners. Their smaller features are ideally suited to the more delicate operations associated with turning cloth into apparel.

The U.S. textile industry was in dire shape. It could no longer compete with the Chinese in the manufacturing of yarn. The industry turned to political solutions to some of its problems. The textile industry lobbied the U.S. government to impose quotas and tariffs on goods made in China to give the Chinese less of a competitive edge. The U.S. government did impose quotas and tariffs on Chinese textile products but only for a limited time. The government gave the textile industry a temporary respite from its global economic problems. The textile industry is now asking the government to extend the period of quotas and tariffs. However, the government has other concerns besides the welfare of the domestic textile industry. A larger, more grave issue of a geopolitical nature is facing our nation. The United States does not want to alienate China by extending the economic sanctions on textiles because China plays a vital political role for the United States. North Korea is believed to have nuclear weapons and is antagonistic in its relations to the United States. The United States believes that China, because of its geographic and political affinity with North Korea, can be instrumental in influencing North Korea's actions. As such, the fate of the domestic textile industry must be weighed against the strategic benefit of having a favorable relationship with China.

The U.S. textile industry has not ceased to exist, but the changes facing the industry are seismic. The U.S. textile industry now makes the textiles that are not made overseas. Among its leading products are fibers used in upholstery. By federal law the U.S. military must purchase U.S.-made textile products (uniforms, tents, etc.). The cut-and-sew functions of the textile industry are now performed almost exclusively overseas. The production of yarn in the United States is limited to specialty markets that are not (currently) met overseas. There has been a massive loss of jobs in the U.S. textile industry, estimated to be in excess of 500,000. The remaining U.S. textile companies have been compelled to invent new products (e.g., sweat-resistant fibers), use the latest and most efficient computer-based manufacturing techniques, and select and train a workforce that is vastly superior to its predecessors a mere generation ago. One of the consequences of living in a global economy is that oceans no longer offer protection or insulation. Geographically a country may be half a world away, but economically it is a computer click away. The essence of organizational change is to help organizations survive in a world that is evolving at an unrelenting pace.

To compete in the new global economy, many textile companies have adopted some or all of the organizational change strategies presented here. Every U.S. company in the textile industry has had to change its culture from one of privileged position (everyone needs to wear our clothes) to the recognition that other nations can make high-quality goods cheaper. Virtually all U.S. textile companies have had to downsize to lower their costs. The remaining employees have had to find new ways to conduct their work. They have become empowered to make decisions about work problems and issues that previously were left to supervisors. Some companies implemented Six Sigma as a way to decrease the variability in their product quality and delivery times. There was massive resistance to all the changes that befell the industry. The resistance was met with an unassailable truth: either we change what we do and how we do it, or our jobs will be shipped overseas.

Case Study The Relative Value of Frogs Versus Grass

About 20 years ago a husband-and-wife team, Helen and Ted McCall, decided to start a new company, which they called The Learning Focus. The business plan was to write books for elementary school teachers that would help them teach children in kindergarten through grade 3. The books would present graphic images and ideas for explaining concepts like colors, letters of the alphabet, and numbers to children in a way they would understand. The McCalls hired former elementary school teachers to write these books because they had experience in teaching students at that level. The company prospered. Eventually the McCalls were ready to retire and found a buyer for the company. The new owner was David Nemeroff, an entrepreneur who recognized a lucrative business opportunity when he saw one. Mr. Nemeroff had never been a teacher; he was a former manufacturing executive with traditional business training. He knew The Learning Focus enjoyed an esteemed reputation in the field as a provider of high-class books for elementary school teachers. He also saw that the potential value of the company was much greater than had been realized under the first owners. The McCalls were former teachers themselves but knew little about the business functions of production, marketing, and sales. It was Nemeroff's intent to transform a "mom and pop" company into a larger scale (and more profitable) business operation. He greatly increased the sales and distribution of the existing books, hired market researchers to propose new books the teachers could use, and upgraded the production process. In a short time he increased the demand for his company's books by 80%. He set delivery dates of new books to his eager customers.

Much to his dismay, Nemeroff discovered the writers repeatedly missed production deadlines. The missed deadlines caused orders not to be filled on time, which in turn led his customers to find other books provided by his competitors. Nemeroff couldn't understand what caused the delays. He would occasionally sit in on design meetings of his writers. What he observed astounded him. At one meeting the writers actively debated for almost three hours on a good way to convey the color "green." Some writers favored the use of frogs to symbolize the color green, while others preferred grass in a lawn. The lawn proponents said some children might never have seen a frog, while the frog proponents said the idea of grass in a lawn was boring and unimaginative. The writers considered this type of debate to be enjoyable and stimulating, and they regarded it as a highlight of their work. However, it was debates about these types of issues that prolonged the production process and caused missed deadlines. Nemeroff couldn't understand how the frogs versus grass debate, for example, could consume three hours. His opinion was the book should convey the concept of the color green; how it did so was of far lesser importance. At least it was not worth a three-hour discussion and inevitable lost revenue.

Nemeroff repeatedly badgered the writers to get their work done on time. The writers said they couldn't rush quality. They believed it was precisely the passion evidenced in the frogs versus grass debate that led the company to produce such high-quality books when the McCalls ran the business. The McCalls didn't hassle the writers about production deadlines. Nemeroff would reiterate that The Learning Focus was in business to make money and that prolonged debates that led to production delays hurt the business, not helped it. The writers believed they weren't doing their work just to make money. They felt they had a noble purpose—to help educate children—which was more important than just meeting production deadlines. Nemeroff recognized that The Learning Focus did have a reputation for high-quality products, but he felt that quality would not be greatly compromised if the company ran more efficiently. He found himself repeatedly locked in confrontations with his writers, repeatedly facing missed production deadlines, and facing plummeting morale on the part of his writers. Given Nemeroff's apparent values, some writers snidely commented that the company should change its name from "The Learning Focus" to "Nemeroff's Money Machine."

Questions

1. What are some of the deeply held values by Mr. Nemeroff and the writers that in part define the organizational culture of The Learning Focus?
2. Explain how these differing values produce the conflict among the parties in this case.
3. In an attempt to bring about a change in the organization, what do you think might happen to The Learning Focus if Nemeroff fired all the existing writers and replaced them with new writers?
4. What significance does the legacy of the McCalls have on the way the writers currently view the company?
5. If you were asked to bring about change that benefited The Learning Focus, what change strategies would you follow and why?

Chapter Summary

- Organizations are complex social entities designed to achieve work-related objectives.

- Classical organizational theory defined the structure of an organization in terms of four principles: functional, scalar, line/staff, and span of control.
- Neoclassical organizational theory revealed that organizations are more complex than initially proposed by classical theory.
- Mintzberg offered a useful framework for understanding the seven basic parts of an organization: strategic apex, middle line, support staff, technostructure, operating core, ideology, and politics.
- Organizations are also defined by a social system of roles, norms, and culture.
- Downsizing, outsourcing, offshoring, and mergers and acquisitions are contemporary sources of job loss.
- The modern economy has given rise to global organizations that through electronic communication operate across time and space.
- Hofstede provided four classic dimensions useful in differentiating cultures around the world: power distance, individualism–collectivism, masculinity–femininity, and uncertainty avoidance.
- Organizations change continuously to adapt to their environments. Organizations can change suddenly and painfully, with downsizing being a major form of change.
- Empowerment and Six Sigma are two strategies that are useful in changing organizations.
- Organizations often resist change, thus it is important to understand the conditions under which change is likely to occur.

Teams and Teamwork

Learning Objectives

- Explain why the use of teams is increasing.
- Explain the concept of teamwork.
- Describe the structure and processes of teams.
- Explain how teams make decisions and share mental models.
- Explain how personnel selection, training, and performance appraisal apply to teams.

Historically, I/O psychologists have tended to make individuals the object of their attention. That is, we have been concerned with finding the right person for the job, training the individual, and subsequently monitoring his or her performance on the job. Although the existence of informal work groups was acknowledged in the Hawthorne studies, for the most part interest in groups was limited to social psychology. In recent years, however, there has been a tremendous upsurge of interest in using work groups, not just individuals, as the organizing principle through which work is accomplished. Guzzo (1995) noted that there is no real distinction between the words *groups* and *teams*. Psychology has tended to use the term *groups*, as evidenced by the study of group dynamics and group processes. Teams tend to be groups that have a more narrow focus or purpose. I/O psychologists are increasingly using the term *teams* or *work teams* in reference to groups. Some authors assert a *team* must consist of at least three members; the term *dyad* is used to describe a two-person unit.

Team
A social aggregation in which a limited number of individuals interact on a regular basis to accomplish a set of shared objectives for which they have mutual responsibility.

Teams are bounded social units that work within a larger social system—the organization. A team within an organization has identifiable memberships (that is, members and nonmembers alike clearly know who is a member and who is not) and an identifiable task or set of tasks to perform. Tasks may include monitoring, producing, serving, generating ideas, and doing other activities. The team's work requires that members interact by exchanging information, sharing resources, and coordinating with and reacting to one another in accomplishing the group task. Furthermore, there is always some degree of interdependence within the members of a team as well as interdependence among different teams in an organization. Burke et al. (2006) invoked the concept of adaptation originally proposed by the famed British biologist, Charles Darwin: "It is not the strongest of the species that survives, nor the most intelligent, but rather the most responsive to change." The authors assert that just as teams were created to deal with complex, ever-changing environments, teams themselves must find ways to adapt to the different tasks and organizational pressures they face.

Origins of Work Teams

As described in the preceding chapter, organizations are designed for a purpose. Accordingly, the traditional structure of an organization (line/staff relationships, span of control, etc.) was created to conduct and monitor the flow of work. Such traditional organizational structures were in effect and effective for most of the 20th century. In the last two decades of the 20th century, however, several forces of a technological, economic, and demographic nature reached a confluence, prompting organizations to respond. These forces were discussed in Chapter 1 and reflect the changing nature of work. Greater global economic competition and rapid advances in communication technology forced organizations to change the way they performed their work operations. Some automobile companies—Saturn, for example—developed a team approach to the production of cars compared with the traditional assembly-line approach. Products had to be developed and brought to market more quickly than in the past. Rapid changes in the business world compelled organizations to be more flexible and responsive to them. To increase flexibility, companies had to move away from tightly controlled organizational structures that often resulted in a relatively slow work pace.

There was increased emphasis on organizations' need to respond quickly in what they did and how they did it. Organizations began to change their structure in response to these environmental forces and to use work teams to accomplish the organization's work (LePine, Hanson, et al., 2000). Concurrently, the decision-making authority concerning the specific means of task accomplishment has been pushed down to these teams. The team members often must decide among themselves who will do the what, where, when, and how of work.

What is it about the contemporary world of work that underlies the creation of teams to accomplish work? Three factors are critical. The first is the burgeoning amount of information and knowledge in existence. As presented in Chapter 1, society has entered the Information Age. Scientific and technical advances have produced vast amounts of information. Information from multiple sources often has to be melded to respond to complex business issues. No one person can have technical expertise in all areas of knowledge, thus a team approach, representing a pooling of mental resources, becomes more tenable. Second, the working population is becoming increasingly more educated and trained. When the traditional organizational structures of 100 years ago were created (the tenets of classical theory discussed in Chapter 8), the workforce was relatively uneducated. A high school diploma was a level of educational attainment achieved by only a minority of the population. The members of the traditional working class were monitored by members of "management," who often possessed more education or training.

One hundred years later our working population is considerably different from its ancestors. The workers of today have achieved a much higher level of education and training. They are more qualified and willing to serve in the types of roles called for in work teams. As an employee who now works in a production team in a manufacturing organization stated, "I'm no longer expected to check my brain at the front gate when I enter the factory." The third factor is the rate of change in work activities. For many years workers had well-defined activities in their jobs that rarely changed. In fact, the static constellation of these work activities served to define the "job." The current work world contains pressures to make new products, modify services, alter processes to improve quality, and in general be in a continual state of transformation. As discussed throughout this book, rarely today are work activities static, unchanged from years past. Work teams can be responsive and adaptable to these ever-changing conditions of work. The growing conversion from individuals to teams as a means of conducting work is both a product of and a response to the confluence of forces or pressures applied to contemporary organizations. Kozlowski and Bell (2003) stated, "Increasing global competition, consolidation, and innovation create pressures that are influencing the emergence of teams as basic building blocks of organizations. These pressures drive a need for diverse skills, expertise, and experience. They necessitate more fluid, flexible, and adaptive responses. Teams enable these characteristics" (p. 333).

The evolution of teams and teamwork has compelled I/O psychology to address a host of new issues. Ilgen (1999) identified several critical constructs in understanding teams and why they are effective, including team performance and team composition. Some of what we have learned about individuals in the workplace generalizes to teams, but other issues are more specific to teams. However, teams are *not* universally superior to individuals for conducting work across all relevant performance indices. For example, teams do not necessarily produce better quality decisions than do individuals.

Naquin and Tynan (2003) asserted it is a myth that companies that use teams are more effective than those that do not. Teams are not a panacea for all work-related ills. Naquin and Tynan believe that a "team halo effect" can exist in the work world. When people seek to understand team performance, they tend to give teams credit for their success. However, individuals (as opposed to the collective group) tend to receive the blame for poor team performance. There is nothing magical about transforming individuals into work teams. Teams are merely one means of performing work. In this chapter we will examine teams as a means of accomplishing work, including the factors that lead to successful team performance.

Level of Analysis

A shift in the focus from individuals to teams as a means of conducting work also requires a shift in the conduct of I/O psychological research. Researchers can and do examine different entities as the object of their investigations. Historically I/O psychology focused on the individual with regard to such factors as desired KSAOs for employment, needed training, and standards of job performance. In such cases the *level of analysis* is the individual; that is, the conclusions drawn by the research are about individuals. However, research questions can also be posed at the team level of analysis and at the organization level of analysis. Consider an organization that has 100 employees. A researcher may be interested in assessing the relationship between the degree to which employees feel a sense of organizational identification with the company and job performance. At the individual level of analysis, the researcher would have a sample size of 100 individuals, obtain measures of organizational identification and job performance, correlate the two variables, and arrive at a conclusion regarding the relationship between them at the *individual* level of analysis. However, the 100 employees could also be organized into 25 four-person work teams. In this case the researcher would have a sample size of 25 (i.e., the 25 teams). Each team would be represented by a score reflecting its sense of organizational identification (as a team) and their work performance (as a team). The researcher would correlate these two variables and, based on a sample size of 25, arrive at a conclusion about the relationship between the two variables at the *team* level of analysis. It is also possible to study the relationship between organizational identification and performance at the organizational level of analysis. In this case the 100-employee company would be a sample size of 1. There would be one measure of organizational identification (for the entire company) and one measure of performance (for the entire company). The researcher would then have to collect data from additional organizations. The researcher would correlate these two variables, based on a sample size of however many organizations were in the study, and arrive at a conclusion about the relationship between the two variables at the *organization* level of analysis. Figure 9-1 is a diagram showing these levels of analysis.

What *is* the relationship between organizational identification and performance? The answer depends on the level of analysis under consideration. It is possible to arrive at three different conclusions, depending on whether the level of analysis is the individual, team, or organization. Furthermore, some constructs do not exist at particular levels of analysis. Size is one example. Teams and organizations can differ in their size (i.e., number of members), but individuals cannot. For the most part, I/O psychologists

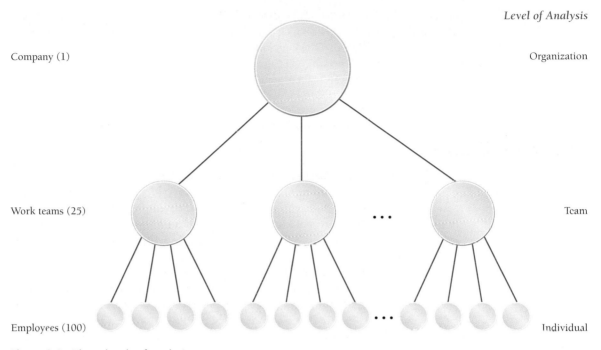

Company (1)

Organization

Work teams (25)

Team

Employees (100)

Individual

Figure 9-1 *Three levels of analysis*

have not focused their research interests on the organization level of analysis. Studying complete organizations and their relationships with other organizations is more traditionally the province of sociology. There is often a link between a particular scientific discipline and the level of analysis of its research. The field of economics examines variables at the industry (petroleum, agriculture, manufacturing, etc.) level of analysis, and the field of political science frequently examines variables at the national level of analysis.

The term *micro* is often used to describe research at the individual level of analysis, while *macro* is used to describe research at the organization level of analysis. Research at the team level of analysis is positioned somewhere between the micro and the macro. As Kozlowski and Bell (2003) stated, "Because teams occupy the intersection of the multilevel perspective, they bridge the gap between the individual and the organizational system as a whole" (p. 367). Rousseau and House (1994) proposed the term *meso* (meaning "in between," as in the word *mezzanine*) research. Meso research occurs in an organizational context where processes at two levels are examined simultaneously. Thus I/O researchers who study relationships between variables at both the individual and team levels of analysis are engaging in meso research. The entire area of multilevel research and theory is an emerging topic in our profession (e.g., Klein & Kozlowski, 2000). It addresses a fundamental dilemma in understanding human behavior in organizations; namely, we as individuals obtain employment in a larger social collectivity (an organization) and are often members of some smaller level of aggregation (such as a team, department, unit, or shift). The dilemma is to disentangle the sources of influence on our behavior from an individual, team, and organization perspective. It will also be recalled from Chapter 2 that meta-analysis is a frequently used method of research in which investigators combine the results from previously conducted research to distill a conclusion about a topic. Ostroff and Harrison (1999) cautioned that researchers must be clear about the level of analysis of their investigation. Combining findings from original studies with different levels of analysis distorts the interpretation of the findings.

Types of Teams

The term *team* has been used in many contexts to describe types of work operations, such as project teams, sales teams, new product teams, process improvement teams, cost-reduction teams, and so on. One way to differentiate teams is by their objectives. It is also possible to differentiate teams by other variables, such as the nature of their interactions (e.g., face to face vs. virtual). Larson and La Fasto (1989) proposed three basic types of teams.

Problem-resolution teams are created for the purpose of focusing on solving ongoing problems or issues. Such teams require each member of the team to expect that interactions among members will be truthful and embody a high degree of integrity. Each member must believe that the team will be consistent and mature in its approach to dealing with problems. The members must have a high degree of trust in a process of problem resolution that focuses on issues, rather than on predetermined positions or conclusions. The authors cite diagnostic teams at the Centers for Disease Control as an exemplar of this type.

Creative teams are responsible for exploring possibilities and alternatives, with the broad objective of developing a new product or service. A necessary feature of the team's structure is autonomy. For a creative team to function, it needs to have autonomy from systems and procedures as well as an atmosphere in which ideas are not prematurely quashed. Creative teams need to be insulated within the organizational structure in order to remain focused on the result to be achieved rather than on organizational processes. The IBM PC was developed by a creative team that endured many failures before arriving at a successful product. The design team needed protection from typical organizational pressures that reflect impatience with failure. The "incubation period" for the PC was many years and could not have been shortened by performance expectations imposed by others.

Tactical teams are responsible for executing a well-defined plan. To do so there must be high task clarity and unambiguous role definition. The success of tactical teams depends on a high degree of responsiveness from team members, a clear understanding of who does what, and a clear set of performance standards. An example of a tactical team is a police SWAT team or a cardiac surgical team. Each operational procedure must be well defined, and each task must be highly focused and specific. Furthermore, the standards of excellence must be clear to everyone, and ways of measuring success or failure must be understood by the entire team.

We may add a fourth type of team, which is defined primarily by its limited life span. It is sometimes called an *ad hoc* (Latin for "to this") team and is basically a hybrid cross between a problem-resolution and a tactical team. An *ad hoc* team is created for a specific purpose, addressing itself "to this" particular problem. The team members

---

Problem-resolution team
A type of team created for the purpose of focusing on solving ongoing problems or issues.

Creative team
A type of team created for the purpose of developing innovative possibilities or solutions.

Tactical team
A type of team created for the purpose of executing a well-defined plan or objective.

***Ad hoc* team**
A type of team created for a limited duration that is designed to address one particular problem.

are selected from existing employees in an organization, and after the team has completed its work, the team disbands. Thus membership in the team (and indeed the life span of the team itself) is finite and then the team no longer exists. *Ad hoc* teams are used in organizations that encounter unusual or atypical problems that require an atypical response (the creation of the *ad hoc* team). If the problem tends to recur, there may be pressure to establish the team on a longer-term basis, as a more formalized and permanent unit (see The Changing Nature of Work: Multiteam Systems, p. 292).

Principles of Teamwork

McIntyre and Salas (1995) conducted extensive research on U.S. Navy tactical teams and identified several principles of teamwork that are also relevant for other organizations that use teams. Five of the major principles are listed here.

Principle 1: Teamwork implies that members provide feedback to and accept it from one another. For teamwork to be effective, team members must feel free to provide feedback; that is, the climate within the group must be such that neither status nor power stands as an obstacle to team members providing feedback to one another. Effective teams engage in tasks with an awareness of their strengths and weaknesses. When team leaders show the ability to accept constructive criticism, they establish a norm that this type of criticism is appropriate.

Principle 2: Teamwork implies the willingness, preparedness, and proclivity to back fellow members up during operations. Better teams are distinguishable from poorer teams in that their members show a willingness to jump in and help when they are needed, and they accept help without fear of being perceived as weak. Team members must show competence not only in their own particular area but also in the areas of other team members with whom they directly interact.

Principle 3: Teamwork involves group members collectively viewing themselves as a group whose success depends on their interaction. Team members must have high awareness of themselves as a team. Each member sees the team's success as taking precedence over individual performance. Members of effective teams view themselves as connected team members, not as isolated individuals working with other isolated individuals. Successful teams consist of individuals who recognize that their effectiveness is the team's effectiveness, which depends on the sum total of all team members' performance.

Principle 4: Teamwork means fostering within-team interdependence. Fostering team interdependence means the team adopts the value that it is not only appropriate but also essential for each team member (regardless of status within the team) to depend on every other team member to carry out the team's mission. Contrary to what may take place in the rest of the organization, interdependence is seen as a virtue—as an essential characteristic of team performance—not as a weakness.

Principle 5: Team leadership makes a difference with respect to the performance of the team. Team leaders serve as models for their fellow team members. If the leaders openly engage in teamwork—that is, provide and accept feedback and supportive behaviors—other team members are likely to do the same. Team leaders are vital and have tremendous influence on teams, and when team leaders are poor, so are the teams.

McIntyre and Salas (1995) believe these principles provide a theory of teamwork. In their attempts to implement or improve team-based performance, organizations

The Changing Nature of Work: Multiteam Systems

Mathieu, Marks, and Zaccaro (2001) described how our lives are influenced by the interplay among various sets of teams operating in sequences. They are called *multiteam systems*, and they have become so ingrained in our society that we might not think of them as functioning in such a manner. Imagine there is a severe automobile accident where a life is in peril. Here is a likely sequence of actions by multiple teams: an emergency phone call reporting the accident is made to the police. The police department contacts the dispatch center of the fire department to send a crew to the scene. The police arrive at the scene to control the flow of traffic around the accident. The firefighters have the responsibility to extinguish any car fire that may have started or to apply retardant chemicals to leaking gasoline. Emergency medical technicians (EMTs), another team, work to extricate the victim from the crash. The victim is placed in an ambulance and rushed to the nearest hospital. At the hospital another team is standing by— the surgical team needed to perform a lifesaving operation. The surgical team might consist of nurses, anesthesiologists, medical technicians, and physicians. Following the surgery, the patient is admitted into the intensive care unit of the hospital and attended to by a recovery team of doctors and nurses.

Note the interconnectedness of the five teams that respond to this automobile accident and its consequences—police, fire, EMT, surgical, and recovery. Each team has a specific goal and follows a process that has beginning and ending points. Each team is specially trained to perform its tasks with great accuracy and efficiency and under severe time pressure. Furthermore, one team cannot do its work until the preceding team in the sequence has finished its work. Mathieu et al. believe this "team of teams" concept involving coordination and communication among multiple teams is fertile for advancing our understanding from both scientific and practical perspectives.

need to think specifically about how organization members can effectively serve in the capacity of team members. A theory of teamwork must be incorporated into the organization's operating philosophy. Teamwork will take place within the organization to the extent that the organization fosters it and builds upon it.

Team Structure

The structure of a team includes variables such as the number of members on the team, demographic composition, and experience of team members. A prominent theme in team structures is the diversity of its members. The term *diversity* is often associated with the gender, race, culture, and age of people. However, such is not strictly the case in describing diversity in a team. Research shows that successful teams manifest diversity in their members, where *diversity* literally means "differences." In what ways can diversity manifest itself among members on a team? Two manifestations are information diversity and value diversity. *Information diversity* refers to differences among the members in terms of what they know and what cognitive resources (e.g., factual knowledge, experiences) they can bring to the team. Successful teams often have a pooling of expertise or knowledge among their members. *Value diversity* reflects more fundamental differences among people with regard to tastes, preferences, goals, and interests. Differences in values among team members can be expressed in a wide range of issues, including the purpose of the team, the willingness to be an active team contributor, and the degree to which membership in the team is valued as a means of accomplishing work. You can think of information diversity and value diversity as the approximate team-level counterparts of the "can do" and "will do" factors described in Chapter 5. Jehn, Northcraft, and Neale (1999) reported that informational diversity positively influenced team performance, but value diversity decreased member satisfaction with the team, intent to remain on the team, and commitment to the team. The authors also found the impact of diversity on team performance was dependent on the type of task. If a task requires great speed and coordination, then information diversity may not positively influence team performance.

Some of the earliest research on team structure was conducted by Belbin (1981). Belbin proposed that diversity within a team was reflected in the members filling different roles. Belbin proposed that effective teams were composed of members who served different roles on the team, and their roles were defined by the possession of selected mental ability and personality characteristics. Belbin studied eight-person teams and arrived at the following needed roles, as shown in Figure 9-2, p. 294.

1. *A leader.* The leader of the team has to be responsible for the overall performance of the team, recognizes the team's strengths and weaknesses, and ensures that the best use is made of each team member's potential.

2. *A shaper.* A shaper influences the way in which team effort is applied, directing attention to the setting of objectives and priorities, and seeks to impose some shape or pattern on the outcome of team activities. Both the leader and shaper roles collectively define the team's direction and output.

3. *A worker.* A worker gets things done by turning concepts and plans into practical working procedures and carrying out agreed upon plans systematically and efficiently.

4. *A creator.* A creator advances new ideas and strategies with special attention to major issues and looks for possible new ways to address problems confronting the team.

5. *A resource investigator.* This role reports on ideas, developments, and resources outside of the team and creates external contacts that may be useful to the team in their actions.

6. *A monitor-evaluator.* This role requires analyzing problems and evaluating ideas and suggestions so that the team stays focused on its task. This person often functions as a critic. The more numerous and complex suggestions become, the more important is the role of the monitor-evaluator.

7. *A team facilitator.* A team facilitator supports members in their strengths, helps compensate for their weaknesses, and improves communication between members by fostering team spirit.

8. *A completer-finisher.* This role actively searches for aspects of work that need more than the usual degree of attention and maintains a sense of urgency within the team.

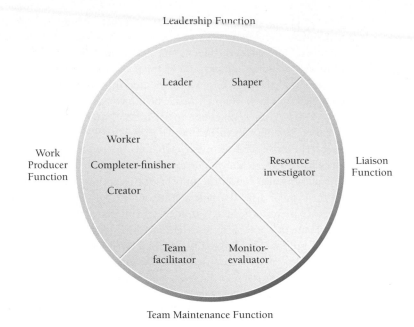

Figure 9-2   *Eight team roles distributed over four team functions*

It should be remembered, as described in Chapter 8, that these are different roles filled by individuals, and not necessarily different people. That is, although each of these roles may be critical to team success, a given individual can serve multiple roles. In teams of fewer than eight people, some team members must play more than one role. Belbin noted that a team can have more than one worker role, and some roles are more likely pairs than others. That is, one person could well serve in both the worker and completer-finisher roles. Some pairs of roles filled by the same individual are less likely, such as facilitator and monitor-evaluator. Belbin's eight roles can be further reduced to four functions within a team: (1) leadership, (2) work producers, (3) internal team maintenance, and (4) liaison to people and resources outside of the team. Fisher, Hunter, and Macrosson (1998) affirmed the validity of Belbin's team roles in teams with fewer than eight members and showed that the likelihood of individuals assuming a secondary role was based on their personalities.

Team Processes

As important as the structure of a team is to its functioning, the vast majority of research on teams has been directed to the processes that guide how teams function. *Processes* are the operations within a team that permit it to function smoothly and efficiently. There are four major team processes to consider: socialization, interpersonal, shared mental models, and decision making.

Socialization

Socialization is the process of mutual adjustment that produces changes over time in the relationship between a person and a team. It is the process a person goes through in joining a team, being on a team, and eventually leaving a team. Likewise, the team itself is affected by the arrival, presence, and departure of a team member. The socialization process can range from a formal orientation session to the team to informal one-on-one feedback between a senior team member and the newcomer. The relationship between a senior team member and a newcomer can take on many of the properties of the mentor–protégé relationship discussed in Chapter 6. New team members can be appraised by subtle observation of an older team member or by seeking feedback from the team—for example, "What does it take to be successful on this team?" and "Am I fitting in?"

Moreland and Levine (2001) proposed an explanatory framework for how socialization occurs. It is based on three psychological concepts: evaluation, commitment, and role transition. *Evaluation* involves attempts by the team and the individual to assess and maximize each other's value. This includes the team identifying the goals to which an individual can contribute, and the individual evaluating how participation on the team can satisfy his or her personal needs. Thus the evaluation process is mutual. *Commitment* is the sense of loyalty, union, and connection between the individual and the team. When the individual is committed to the team, he or she is likely to accept the team's goals, work hard to achieve them, and feel warmly toward the team. When a team is strongly committed to an individual, it is likely to accept that person's needs, work hard to satisfy them, and feel warmly toward the person. Changes in commitment transform the relationship between a team and an individual. These transformations are governed by specific levels of commitment that mark the boundaries between different membership roles the person could play in the team. Both the team and the individual try to initiate a *role transition* when commitment reaches a certain level. Figure 9-3 (p. 296) shows an individual's commitment to the team over time as he or she passes through five phases of team membership: investigation, socialization, maintenance, resocialization, and remembrance.

During the *investigation* phase, the team searches for individuals who can contribute to the achievement of team goals. Likewise, the individual, as a prospective member of the team, searches for a team that will be satisfying. If both parties achieve an initial sense of commitment, the investigation phase ends and the *socialization* phase begins. In this phase the individual assimilates into the team and the team accommodates itself to the individual. If both parties accept each other, the individual becomes a full member of the team. This acceptance marks the end of the socialization phase and the beginning of *maintenance*. Now both parties try to maximize their respective needs—the achievement of the team and the satisfaction of the individual. This phase lasts as long as both parties meet their needs. However, as commitment weakens between the team and individual, another role transition based on the divergence of commitment occurs, resulting in *resocialization*. During resocialization the team and the individual try again to influence each other so that the team's needs are more likely to be satisfied. If the resocialization process is not successful, team membership ends with a period of *remembrance*. The team recalls the individual's contributions to

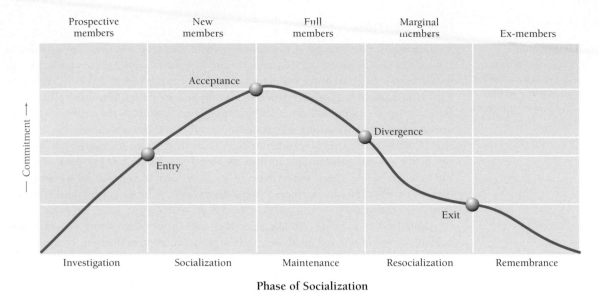

Figure 9-3   *The socialization process for team members*

Source: Adapted from "Socialization in Organizations and Work Groups," by R. L. Moreland and J. M. Levine, in *Groups at Work*, edited by M. E. Turner, pp. 69–112. Mahwah, NJ: Lawrence Erlbaum Associates, 2001.

the achievement of its goals, and the individual recalls his or her experiences with the team. Over time, feelings of commitment between the team and the individual often stabilize, usually at a low level.

The socialization process presented by Moreland and Levine reveals the subtleties and phases of group dynamics. Both the individual and the team are mutually trying to influence each other to achieve the same purpose. The socialization process occurs over time, although the length of the time period varies across individuals and teams. Teams have "lives" based on the state of socialization of their members, and this socialization process is constantly evolving.

Interpersonal Processes in Teams

The interpersonal processes in a team have been found to influence the overall performance of teams. Yeatts and Hyten (1998) identified several interpersonal characteristics that are endemic to the high-performing work teams they studied.

Communication.   Interpersonal communication in successful work teams is characterized by a consistent pattern. It is often described as open, frequent, and candid. Formal, regularly scheduled weekly meetings are held to discuss team progress. More informal communication occurs on a daily basis as team members discuss specific work issues. In high-performing groups, team members communicate problems they are having and freely solicit advice. They are not reluctant to discuss problems and concerns that might otherwise be artfully avoided. Continuous communication is regarded as not only acceptable but also desirable because it helps the team achieve results it might not attain otherwise.

Conflict.   Conflict among members is unavoidable in any team. What matters is how the conflict is dealt with in the team as well as the team's attitude about conflict. Conflict can be viewed either as something the group members actively seek to suppress or as an opportunity to learn from each other. Two types of conflict have been identified: beneficial and competitive. At the root of *beneficial conflict* is the desire of two or more members with differing ideas and interests to understand the views of the other. The team members try to understand each other's perspective and seek to fashion a mutually satisfactory decision (see Field Note 1). Such experiences tend to strengthen relationships, as members become more confident that future conflicts can also be resolved. In contrast, the basis of *competitive conflict* is the desire to win, to be judged "right" in a contest of opinions and values. The individuals in conflict regard the competition as a test of their status, power, and credibility within the organization. Although not all conflict can be framed as beneficial, Yeatts and Hyten found that high-performing work teams sought to diminish the manifestations of competitive conflict.

Cohesion.   Yeatts and Hyten (1998) defined *cohesion* as "the degree to which members of a team feel attached to their team and are compelled to stay in it" (p. 97). The attachment is posited to manifest itself in how the team performs its tasks, particularly as it relates to the accepted interdependence among team members. Team oriented

Field Note 1: Orchestrated Conflict

Conflict is often regarded as a negative influence among team members, but this is not always the case. Research reveals the positive value of beneficial conflict. Consider the following case in point. A university had a prime piece of land with an ideal location for many possible uses. An old building that stood on the property was razed, creating an opportunity for new use of the land. Many constituents of the university (students, faculty, alumni, financial supporters, etc.) held differing ideas about what use should be made of the land. The president of the university established an advisory committee to make a formal recommendation to the university on the best use of the land. However, the president did not want the ensuing land use debate to fall strictly along "party lines," such as students versus faculty. The president did not want to be perceived as favoring one party or subgroup over the rest in making the ultimate decision. The president was to select three faculty members to serve on the advisory committee. The list of possible names was reduced to four finalists, based on their expressed willingness to serve. Two strong-willed and highly opinionated professors who held similar beliefs about the land use were among the four finalists. The president chose one but not the other. When asked (privately) why both professors were not selected, the president replied, "They think too much alike. At times I believe they have two bodies but share the same brain." Here is one example where a decision was made to increase the likelihood of conflict within the group, in the belief that it would ultimately have a beneficial effect.

cohesion provides a safe environment in which members may express their opinions. Although at times some opinions may be regarded as dissenting, they are not viewed as threatening the cohesiveness of the team itself. According to Yeatts and Hyten, it is possible that once cohesive groups begin to achieve a sense of likemindedness or *group-think* (to be discussed shortly), additional information important to decision making may be rejected if it is regarded as weakening cohesion. There is also research that suggests greater team cohesion may follow from successful team performance, as opposed to causing the performance to occur. Rewards that focus on team achievements are likely to enhance cohesion, whereas individual rewards encourage competition among team members, which weakens cohesion. Other teams and individuals within an organization often take notice of cohesive teams and sometimes express the desire to be members of a cohesive unit themselves. Cohesive teams have also been found to exert more influence than less cohesive teams in the running of the organization. Still, cohesion is not critical for success in all team tasks; it appears to be most crucial in tasks that require highly efficient and synchronized member interactions (Beal et al., 2003).

Trust.   Schoorman, Mayer, and Davis (2007) identified several components to trust. Trust develops over time, it is not necessarily mutual or reciprocal between parties, and it entails a willingness to be vulnerable to actions taken by the trusted party that may be harmful. Colquitt, Scott, and LePine (2007) differentiated trust, trust propensity, and trustworthiness. *Trust* is the intention to accept vulnerability based on positive expectations of the party being trusted. Trust is earned, and people differ in their threshold to be trusting. *Trust propensity* is a personality characteristic, a willingness to rely on others, and thus be vulnerable. *Trustworthiness* is the quality (often based on perceived integrity) of a party to be trusted. Trust is fragile. Once betrayed, it is very difficult to restore. Yeatts and Hyten (1998) reported that we know less about trust than any of the other interpersonal processes in teams. Trust is defined as the belief that even though you have no control over another person's behavior toward you, that person will behave in a way that benefits you. High trust within a team permits members to direct attention to performing their respective tasks, with little time or concern devoted to questioning the actions or possible motives of others. High trust within a team also permits members to exchange roles (e.g., having a more talented team member perform a particular task) without fear of embarrassment or having a member be regarded as a slacker. In contrast, when trust is low within a team, comments and actions are regarded with suspicion because the underlying motives for them are believed to be self-serving. In general, trust develops slowly within a team, even among teams with stable memberships. It is also the most fragile of the interpersonal processes. An individual who abuses the norms within a group can quickly destroy any trust with those whose trust was violated. Dirks (1999) reported that in high-trust teams motivation was transformed into collaborative or joint efforts and hence better performance, whereas in low-trust teams motivation was translated into individual efforts. Intentional betrayal of trust is a self-serving action done with the knowledge that it is harming another person. Unintentional betrayal is the by-product of a self-serving action. Betrayal is caused by people not honoring their commitments or deceiving team members to further their individual ends. Reina and Reina (1999) described one betrayed employee who said, "It is especially painful when we are stabbed in the back by those closest to us without warning. It knocks you off your feet" (p. 35).

Yeatts and Hyten noted that these interpersonal processes are often highly inter-related in the workplace. High-performing teams often have high levels of communication, constructive means of expressing conflict, cohesion, and trust among members. Although not all high-performing teams manifest these interpersonal processes to the same degree, the processes are subtle yet enduring mechanisms for facilitating the functioning of the team.

Shared Mental Models

Shared mental model
The cognitive processes held in common by members of a team regarding how they acquire information, analyze it, and respond to it.

The concept of **shared mental models** refers to team members having some degree of similarity in how they approach problems and evaluate potential solutions. Shared mental models are posited to influence the behavior of the group. How individuals think is reflected in their behavior, and the term given to the thinking process is *cognition*. A team is a social aggregation in which a limited number of individuals interact on a regular basis to accomplish a set of shared objectives for which they have mutual responsibility. The fusion of cognition (as a psychological process) and a team (as an interacting collectivity) produces the concept of shared cognition or shared mental models, which reflects how the team acquires, stores, and uses information (Gibson, 2001).

Cannon-Bowers and Salas (2001) addressed the fundamental question of what is actually shared among team members in establishing mental models. Four broad categories were identified: task-specific information, task-related knowledge, knowledge of teammates, and shared attitudes and beliefs, as shown in Figure 9-4. Each type of knowledge has increasingly broader generalizability across differing tasks. *Task-specific*

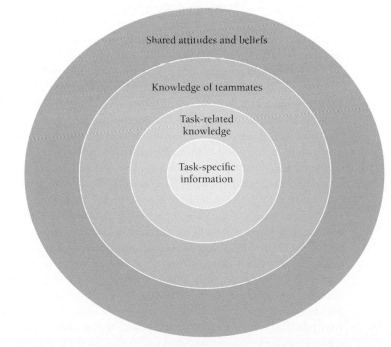

Figure 9-4   *Generalizability of four types of shared knowledge in mental models*

information is shared information among team members that allows them to act without the need to discuss it. Task-specific information involves the particular procedures, sequences, actions, and strategies necessary to perform a task. It can be generalized only to other instances of similar tasks. *Task-related knowledge* refers to common knowledge about task-related processes, but it is not limited to a single task. It is more generalizable because it is knowledge of processes that applies to many specific tasks. *Knowledge of teammates* refers to how well the members understand each other, including their performance, strengths, weaknesses, and tendencies. Thus team members must learn how the collective expertise of the team is distributed across the members. This type of shared knowledge helps teammates compensate for one another, predict each other's actions, and allocate resources according to member expertise. The final category of *shared attitudes and beliefs* permits team members to arrive at comparable interpretations of the problems they face. It enhances team cohesion, motivation, and consensus. In summary, shared mental models do not refer to a unitary concept. It appears that all the types of knowledge in these four categories needs to be shared in effective teams.

Cannon-Bowers and Salas added there is also not a singular way that knowledge can be "shared" among team members. Some common knowledge must be held by all members of a team, particularly as it relates to the specific task. Other types of knowledge are shared by being distributed or apportioned across the team members. Certain knowledge is complex or specialized, and it is unrealistic to expect all members of a team to possess this level of knowledge equally. Thus what is important is that the knowledge resides within the team as a team, not held by each team member. Shared knowledge is common in military combat teams and surgical teams. Cross-training (where team members learn to perform the tasks of others) has been found to enhance shared mental models (Marks et al., 2002).

As compelling as the evidence is for shared mental models for effective team performance, there is a potential dark side to team members "thinking alike." The phenomenon is called **groupthink**. Noted problems in history that arose from groupthink are the Bay of Pigs invasion of Cuba in the 1960s and the explosion of the Challenger space shuttle in the 1980s. Groupthink refers to a deterioration in cognitive processing caused by team members feeling threatened by external forces. The defects in decision making include incomplete consideration of options and alternatives, poor information search, and selective information processing. Groupthink is a model of thinking in which team members consider consensus to be more important than rational, independent thinking. Some symptoms are the illusion of team vulnerability, the false assumption of the team's morality, stereotyping of opposing groups, the illusion of group unanimity, and the emergence of a process that keeps opposing viewpoints from the team's consideration. The team, operating with a siege mentality, fails to perceive environments correctly and looks for confirming evidence that it is being threatened. Choi and Kim (1999) noted that the conventional interpretation of groupthink is a negative influence on performance. The term is used in reference to fiascoes like the Bay of Pigs invasion. However, although they found that some dimensions of the groupthink phenomenon (such as suppressing dissenting opinions) were related to negative team performance, some other dimensions (such as a strong sense of group identity) in fact were related to positive team performance. Turner and Horvitz (2001) concluded that groupthink is more likely found in teams that have a strong sense of social identity. In such cases team members often feel compelled to maintain and enhance their evaluation of the team and its actions. Furthermore, members become motivated to protect

Groupthink
A phenomenon associated with team decision making in which members feel threatened by forces external to the team, resulting in a deterioration in the cognitive processing of information.

the image of the team. When the image is questioned by a collective threat, the response among members is to seek concurrence about the threat and, by virtue of that, attain greater acceptance as *bona fide* team members. A threat to an individual member of a team is not as likely to engender groupthink as is a threat to the entire team.

In short, effective team performance requires members to operate on similar or complementary knowledge bases, but under conditions of perceived threat to the team, groupthink often produces the opposite effect and can drive the team to undesirable behavior.

The amount of research on shared mental models is growing, but we still have much to learn about the process of forming a "team mentality" and how the performance of a team is affected by it. Marks, Zaccaro, and Mathieu (2000) found that shared mental models provided teams with a common framework from which to perceive, interpret, and respond to novel environments. However, shared mental models were not as critical to team success in routine environments. Research by Mohammed and Dumville (2001) and Rentsch and Klimoski (2001) has expanded our understanding of the conventional statement "Great minds think alike."

Decision Making in Teams

Guzzo (1995) asserted that decision making in teams is different from individual decision making. In teams, information is often distributed unequally among members and must be integrated. Choosing among alternatives is made more complicated by having to integrate the often-differing perspectives and opinions of team members. The integration process usually includes dealing with uncertainty, with the effects of status differences among members, and with the failure of one member to appreciate the significance of the information he or she holds. Ambiguity, time pressures, heavy workloads, and other factors may become sources of stress that affect the group's ability to perform its task.

Hollenbeck, LePine, and Ilgen (1996) described the development of a multilevel theory of team decision making. The theory is called *multilevel* because effective team decision making is related to characteristics of the individuals who make up the team, pairs of people within the team, and how the team functions as a team. The theory is based on three concepts. The first is the degree to which team members are adequately informed about the issue they are evaluating. Teams can be well informed on some decisions but poorly informed on others. The general level of how well informed the team is on the issues they must address is *team informity*. Second, teams are composed of individuals who differ in their ability to make accurate decisions. That is, some individuals can make poor decisions, while others typically make very accurate decisions. The concept of *staff validity* is the average of the individual team members' abilities to make accurate decisions. The final concept is *dyadic sensitivity*. A team leader must often listen to the differing opinions or recommendations of team members. The relationship between the leader and each team member is a dyad. The leader must be sensitive to weighing each team member's recommendation in reaching an overall decision. Thus an effective decision-making team leader knows which member's opinion should be given more weight than others. The theory has been tested with computer-simulated military command-and-control scenarios in which the team is asked to decide on the level of threat posed by a series of unidentified aircraft. The results revealed that the three concepts of team informity, staff validity, and dyadic sensitivity explained more variance in team-level decision making accuracy than other concepts. The authors concluded that getting accurate information, making accurate recommendations, and ensuring that these recommendations are incorporated into the team's overall decision are the core requirements for effective decision making in teams.

Virtual Teams

Virtual team
A type of team in which the members, often geographically dispersed, interact through electronic communication and may never meet face-to-face.

Recent advances in computer technology and electronic communication networks allow for a form of social interaction that was previously unavailable. The boundaryless nature of cyberspace has resulted in a new dimension to our lives—the "virtual" environment. The definition of *virtual* is "being in essence or effect, but not in fact." A more concise definition is "almost." One application of the electronic communication technology is **virtual teams**. According to Avolio et al. (2001), virtual teams have several defining characteristics. First, communication among team members primarily takes place electronically. The electronic communication processes use multiple communication channels, which may include text, graphic, audio, and video communication. As Axtell, Fleck, and Turner (2004) reported, recent advances in electronic-based communication (such as instant messaging systems) have further encouraged the use of virtual teams. Second, the team members are usually dispersed geographically. They may be in different cities, nations, or even continents. It is not unusual for the members of a virtual team to never meet face-to-face. Third, virtual team members may interact synchronously or asynchronously. Synchronous interaction occurs when team members communicate at the same time, as in chat sessions or video conferencing (see Field Note 2). Asynchronous interaction occurs when team members communicate at different times, as through e-mail or electronic bulletin boards. Avolio et al. succinctly summarized the major differences between traditional and virtual teams as follows. "If we consider teams along a continuum, at one end of that continuum are teams that came from the same organization, same location, and interact face-to-face on a regular basis. At the other extreme end are teams of people who came from different organizations, geographical regions, cultures, and time zones, and are interacting via computer-mediated technology" (p. 340).

Virtual teams face the same challenges as face-to-face teams, including how to develop shared mental models, how to evaluate the team's results, and how to achieve greater team cohesion. The shared mental models are particularly important for providing the virtual team with a sense of coherence regarding its collective expectations and intentions. The team members must learn about each other's backgrounds, aspirations, and goals. They must also reach a mutual understanding of the perceived obstacles that face the team, what norms are acceptable and unacceptable behavior in the team, and what members expect of each other in terms of their contribution to the team's work. All of this must be accomplished without the team members ever meeting in person.

Weisband and Atwater (1999) reported that because virtual team members cannot benefit from social and nonverbal cues in getting to know each other, the process of developing cohesion is slowed. The interactions among virtual team members often deal less with relationship building and more with logistics and task requirements. There can also be cultural differences among members in the need to establish interpersonal relationships as a prerequisite to task performance (see Cross-Cultural I/O Psychology: Human Interaction in Virtual Teams, p. 304).

Field Note 2: "What's a Good Time to Get Together?"

One of the consequences of conducting business globally is a greater awareness of the time differences in cities around the world. The world is divided into 24 time zones. In the continental United States there is a three-hour time difference between the East Coast and the West Coast. This time difference can be an annoyance for conducting business across time zones during the traditional business hours of 8:00 A.M. to 5:00 P.M. However, the "annoyance" gets magnified when business is conducted around the world. The use of electronic communication permits asynchronous virtual team meetings. But sometimes virtual team members have to conduct business synchronously; that is, they all have to communicate with each other at the "same time." What time might that be?

I know of a multinational company that has offices in New York, Rio de Janeiro, Rome, and Sydney. Selecting a convenient time when team members could all talk with each other was not easy. They finally agreed upon the following schedule for a weekly conference call: 6:00 A.M. in New York; 8:00 A.M. in Rio de Janeiro; 12:00 P.M. in Rome; and 9:00 P.M. in Sydney. The New York team member didn't like the early hour, and the Sydney team member didn't like the late hour. But any other time only made matters worse for someone. The time problem was compounded by the fact that some cities change time (as from standard time to daylight savings time) while other cities are always on the same time. Also, some cities around the world have times that differ by the half-hour, not the hour. For example, when it's 9:00 A.M. in New York, it's 7:30 P.M. in Calcutta. Most people around the world work during the day and sleep at night. However, "daytime" and "nighttime" lose some of their conventional meaning in global business.

The concept of a virtual work team violates many of the tenets of traditional organizational structure. The most fundamental violation involves the control and supervision of employees. Cascio (1999) stated that managers of employees in virtual teams are asking how they can manage people that they cannot see. Wiesenfeld, Raghuram, and Garud (1999) examined various aspects of virtual teams in conducting work. They described a professional conference attended by individuals whose job responsibilities involved spearheading virtual work programs in their organizations. These virtual work team coordinators reported that the primary obstacle to the expansion of virtual work programs in their own organizations was the resistance of managers—those who must supervise virtual employees. According to the virtual work team coordinators, the resistance of middle managers lowers the rate at which employees participate in, and hinders the success of, virtual work programs. Wiesenfeld et al. also noted that the degree to which employees were satisfied and productive as virtual team members was closely related to whether or not their supervisors were also virtual. Virtual workers who were supervised by virtual managers were more likely to feel trusted, reported being more satisfied and more productive, and were less likely to feel that their virtual status would have a negative impact on their career progress. In contrast, virtual employees whose supervisors were "desked" (i.e., who worked from traditional centralized offices) were less satisfied and were more likely to expect that virtual team work would have a negative impact on their careers.

Cross-Cultural I/O Psychology: *Human Interaction in Virtual Teams*

It will be recalled from Chapter 4 that the interview is universally the most popular means of assessing an applicant's suitability for employment. No other method comes close in acceptability and frequency of use. Even though the interview is not the most accurate means of making selection decisions, there is still great appeal in seeing someone face-to-face in the conduct of human interactions. The basis for this appeal is not fully understood, but it is deeply entrenched and has become an issue in virtual teams. Virtual team members interact through a variety of electronic-based communication media—e-mail, audioconferencing, videoconferencing, and so on. However, such methods are questionable substitutes for face-to-face meetings among team members. Earley and Gibson (2002) presented the following commentary by a virtual team member from Venezuela expressing his reaction to electronic communication with his team: "Now for that particular piece I really think we're going to need to come together as a group, you know face to face and have some kind of a workshop and work on that. Because there are just some pieces that need that continuity, if you know even if it is in a room eight hours or two or

three days, you need to have that interaction, you need to get those juices flowing and not stop after a conference call. Just when you are like sort of warming up, you know the clock is ticking. Some point in time you just need that face to face" (p. 248).

Earley and Gibson stated that the most important and difficult issue in implementing a virtual team is managing the distances without losing the "humanity" and "personality" of the team itself. "There remains something quite primal and fundamental about humans when they encounter one another directly rather than through the mediated realm of e-mail, video-conferences, and other electronic means" (p. 248). Earley and Gibson believe that electronic communication can substitute for face-to-face encounters *after* the team members have first met, but they doubt that electronic communication is an adequate substitution for direct encounters. As with the employment interview, we are left with the paradoxical finding that people place great faith in meeting each other in person, yet doing so does not necessarily result in higher-quality outcomes.

It remains to be seen what role virtual technologies will play in the conduct of work in the future. Current trends indicate they will continue to be implemented, especially in global businesses. The costs of international travel alone make virtual work technologies a viable alternative. It seems likely that advances in electronic communication in the future will increase our propensity to use virtual work teams. The growing body of literature on this topic (e.g., Heneman & Greenberger, 2002; Lipnack, 2000) suggests that virtual teams are not a passing fad.

Personnel Selection for Teams

Some of what I/O psychologists have learned about the selection of individuals into organizations is not wholly transferable to the selection of teams. Traditional job analytic methods identify the KSAs needed for individual job performance, yet these methods tend to be insensitive to the social context in which work occurs. Groups or teams, by definition, are social entities that interact in a larger social context. Klimoski and Jones (1995) believe that choosing team members on the basis of individual-task KSAs alone is not enough to ensure optimal team effectiveness. For example, Guzzo and Shea (1992) indicated that considerable interest has been shown in using the Myers-Briggs Type Indicator (which assesses personality) to select team members. Salas, Burke, and Cannon-Bowers (2002) asserted that successful team members need two general types of skills. *Taskwork skills* are those needed by team members to perform the actual task. Because team members must coordinate their actions and work independently, they must also possess *teamwork skills*. These are behaviorial, cognitive, and attitudinal skills. "Although taskwork skills are the foundation for the operational side of performance, teamwork skills are the foundation for the necessary synchronization, integration, and social interaction that must occur between members for the team to complete the assigned goal" (p. 240).

Successful selection of team members requires identifying the best mix of personnel for effective team performance. Thus the selection requirements for particular individuals may involve complementing the abilities that other individuals will bring to the task. Creating the right mix can also mean considering those factors that account for interpersonal comparability. Establishing team requirements involves identifying and assessing the congruence among members with regard to personality and values. Prieto (1993) asserted that five social skills are particularly critical for an individual to enhance the performance of the group:

1. Gain the group acceptance.
2. Increase group solidarity.
3. Be aware of the group consciousness.
4. Share the group identification.
5. Manage others' impressions of him or her.

We are also learning about the relationship between personality variables and team effectiveness. Barry and Stewart (1997) reported that extraverts were perceived by other team members as having greater effect than introverts on group outcomes. Thus individuals with more reserved personalities may be less successful in getting the team to accept their ideas and suggestions. A related finding was reported by Janz, Colquitt, and Noe (1997) pertaining to ability. They concluded that especially talented team members are likely to feel frustrated when they must work with lower-ability individuals on interdependent tasks. The introverted team member with high ability may feel particularly vexed in influencing team processes and outcomes. Barrick et al. (1998) reported that extraversion and emotional stability are predictive of team performance and viability (the capacity of the team to maintain itself over time). Neuman and Wright (1999) extended the validity of the Big 5 personality factors to the prediction of team performance. They found that Conscientiousness and Agreeableness predicted various dimensions of team performance, while Agreeableness predicted ratings of the interpersonal skills of team members. Finally, Stevens and Campion (1999) developed a paper-and-pencil selection test for staffing work teams. The KSAs measured by the test included conflict resolution, collaborative problem solving, communication, and planning. Test scores were found to predict supervisory and peer ratings of teamwork and overall job performance. An unexpected finding was that the teamwork test exhibited a high correlation with traditional aptitude tests, suggesting that the new teamwork test had a substantial general mental ability component. Thus individuals judged to be effective team members also manifested high levels of general mental ability. This finding, established at the team level, corroborates the findings at the individual level, as discussed in Chapter 4.

In general, research results suggest that individuals with outgoing and somewhat dominant personalities strongly influence the functioning of teams, yet a team composed of only those personality types may be thwarted by its own internal dynamics. Although this stream of research suggests that the "will do" factors of personality are critical for team success, the "can do" factors of ability cannot be dismissed or minimized. Cognitive and technical skills are also needed. Locke et al. (2001) quoted a leading business executive, who said, "A collaboration of incompetents, no matter how diligent or well-meaning, cannot be successful" (p. 503).

THE FAR SIDE®   BY GARY LARSON

**"I've got it too, Omar ... a strange feeling like
we've just been going in circles."**

Recent research on teams has revealed other aspects of team performance that highlight the need for selected interpersonal skills. LePine, Colquitt, and Erez (2000) noted that teams often face situations that are not what they had anticipated. Then their success depends on their ability to adapt to these changing contexts. LePine (2003) reported that the most adaptable team members have the same profile of attributes identified in Chapter 5 as high individual performers. These team members were characterized by high cognitive ability, strong need for achievement, and openness to new experiences. Porter et al. (2003) described the importance of "backing up" team members. Team members should be willing to provide help to others when their own tasks demand less than their full attention and resources. The legitimacy of the need to back up team members often derives from an uneven workload distribution—some tasks in a team context are more demanding than others. Three personality factors predicted willingness to back up teammates: conscientiousness, emotional stability, and extraversion. Chapter 7 explained the concept of contextual performance as it applies to individuals. It is the propensity of individuals to go beyond their specific job duties to help the organization succeed. Bell (2007) and Morgeson, Reider, and Campion (2005) also identified a contextual performance dimension to teamwork. Effective individual team members go beyond their prescribed roles to do the little things that facilitate the performance of the entire team.

Training for Teams

The logic of team training is the same as the logic of individual training, although the mechanisms are somewhat different. The process begins with a job or task analysis, but one aimed at the functioning of teams. Salas and Cannon-Bowers (1997) described a team task analysis as an extension of traditional task analysis to tasks that require coordination. SMEs are asked to provide information (e.g., ratings of difficulty, importance) on each task in which there is interdependency. The information obtained is then used to specify team training objectives and to develop realistic scenarios for practice.

The results of a team task analysis provide information about the knowledge, skills, and attitudes the team members must possess to be successful. Salas and Cannon-Bowers referred to these three as the *thinking, doing*, and *feeling* needed for the structure of team training, as shown in Figure 9-5. Identifying the criteria for team effectiveness serves to guide instructional activities in team training. The instructional

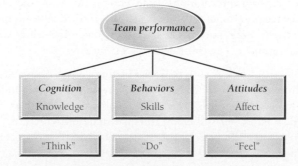

Figure 9-5 *The structure of team training*

Source: Adapted from "Methods, Tools, and Strategies for Team Training," by E. Salas and J. A. Cannon-Bowers, 1997, in *Training for a Rapidly Changing Workplace*, edited by M. A. Quinones and A. Ehrenstein. Washington, DC: American Psychological Association.

activities focus on providing team members with shared mental models and knowledge structures. These activities are designed to foster common ways for team members to analyze information and make decisions. Cannon-Bowers and Salas (1997) postulated that the next decade will witness rapid growth in computer networking capabilities for team training purposes. Such technologies as video teleconferencing (or distance learning) permit team members who are physically dispersed to receive feedback on their performance.

Much of what we know about team training has come, directly or indirectly, from military applications. The military has been responsible primarily for advanced training technologies (such as intelligent tutoring systems) as well as strategies in team training, such as cross-training. The rationale behind cross-training is that exposure to and practice on other teammates' tasks should result in better team member knowledge about task responsibilities and coordination requirements. I/O psychologists who work in military support roles have provided much of our knowledge of team training.

Performance Appraisal in Teams

Chapter 7 addressed the topic of performance appraisal, primarily as it applies to individual employees. The same issues identified at the individual level of analysis have their counterpart at the team level of analysis. Moreover, the team level of analysis includes some additional factors not evidenced at the individual level.

Jackson and LePine (2003) identified different responses of team members to the "weakest link" in their team. Team members tend to feel high levels of sympathy for a member who exhibits low performance for reasons that are beyond his or her control. Likewise, members feel low levels of sympathy for a team member who performs poorly because of factors under his or her control. If the group feels sympathy, they are more willing to train the poor performer or assist the individual by doing a portion of his or her tasks. But if the group feels little sympathy, they may attempt to motivate the low performer (perhaps with veiled threats) or to simply reject the individual.

A major issue in team performance appraisal is the extent to which individuals slacken their performance within the team. A team member may assume that individual slacking will not be noticed within the larger social context of a team, or that other members will elevate their performance within the team to achieve a satisfactory team level of performance. The term given to this phenomenon of slacking is **social loafing**, and it refers to the demotivating effect on individuals of working in a group or team context. When team outcomes are emphasized, individuals see less connection between their own contributions (time, effort, and skills) and the recognition and rewards they receive (Karau & Williams, 2001). Individual team members feel they have less incentive to work hard. Locke et al. (2001) identified three ways in which a lack of individual incentives can contribute to social loafing.

Social loafing
A phenomenon identified in groups or teams in which certain individuals withhold effort or contributions to the collective outcome.

- *Free riding.* In some situations, social loafing derives from a desire to benefit (or free ride) from the efforts of others. When a team task makes individual contributions anonymous and rewards are shared equally, team members can reduce their own individual effort but still enjoy an equal share of the results. Thus social loafing is more likely to occur when team members believe their own contributions cannot be identified.

- *The "sucker" effect.* When conditions allow team members to take a free ride, some team members may assume that other group members will do so. Rather than be a "sucker" who contributes more than others, people reduce their effort to match the low level they expect from others. Mulvey and Klein (1998) observed the sucker effect in a study of college students working on team-level academic tasks.

- *Felt dispensability.* In some cases social loafing results from the feeling of being dispensable. Team members may feel dispensable when more able team members are available to accomplish the task or when they believe their efforts are redundant because they duplicate the contributions of others. When team members feel dispensable, they often reduce their effort.

Locke et al. observed that these three forms of social loafing share the following characteristics: (1) individual team members are concerned with the impact of their personal contributions on team performance; (2) team members expect some return on their effort; and (3) teamwork can weaken the links among individual effort, contributions to team success, and individual outcomes (see Field Note 3). Therefore, although effective team processes (e.g., interaction, trust, cohesion) are important to achieve team success, it is individuals who make up teams and many organizational rewards (such as salary and career progression) are administered at the individual level.

Not all the research on team performance appraisal is limited to social loafing. Peer appraisals have been found to be effective at the individual level, and they also

Field Note 3: Teams in Education

Have you ever been in a class where one of the course requirements was some sort of team project or team presentation? How did you feel about the experience? Did you find it difficult to arrange a time when all the team members could meet? How did you decide who would be responsible for what within the group? Did you think everyone on the team "pulled their own weight" in the collective effort? Did you detect any social loafing among your team members? Did each member in the team have to evaluate every other team member's contribution to the final product? Did everyone on the team receive the same grade for the product of the team's work?

The use of teams in society is escalating (a phenomenon Locke et al. refer to as "groupism"), and their use in education as a learning mechanism for students is increasing as well. If you have ever participated in a team project for a class, your particular team members were probably specific to that class. However, there is a new approach to graduate education in business where students go through the entire degree program (not just in a class) as a team. The name given to this group of students is a "cohort." Each year the admitted students are regarded as a cohort; they all take the same classes in the same sequence and they all graduate at the same time as a group. It is expected that the students will stay in touch with each other after they graduate, as they share how they applied their graduate education in their respective careers. The concept of a cohort in education is designed to promote students learning from each other as students and continuing their education of each other after they graduate.

appear to have a positive influence at the team level. Druskat and Wolff (1999) found that developmental peer appraisals in work teams had a positive impact on team communication, task focus, and member relationships. As the volume of research on team performance appraisal grows, we will have a firmer basis on which to examine the generalizability of findings previously established in appraising individuals.

Concluding Comments

Salas, Stagl, and Burke (2004) are of the opinion that the migration of work performed by individuals to teams will not abate. "Travelers seeking refuge from the accelerating storm of team research and practice and its associated roller coaster of complexities will not find sanctuary. In fact, as expressed by the second law of thermodynamics, chaos is always increasing" (p. 76). As the world becomes increasingly complex, organizations must find new ways to adapt to this complexity. Teams are viewed as one means of doing so. The conversion from an individual to a team perspective of work requires that we reexamine our knowledge about many facets of I/O psychology. Furthermore, although some of our concepts might generalize directly from individuals to teams, some procedures might be incompatible (e.g., Campion, Papper, & Medsker, 1996). It will be recalled from Chapter 7 that one purpose of performance appraisal is to identify performance differences across individuals and to reward them differentially. If we strive for teamwork and a sense of unity across team members, we should then *not* differentially reward the "best" individual team members. We will have to develop appraisal and reward processes that treat all members of a group as a single entity, not as individuals. Organizations get what they reward. If they choose to appraise and reward individual job performance, then they should not decry a lack of teamwork and cooperation among their employees (Kerr, 1995). I believe I/O psychology should gird itself for the journey of understanding how work performed by teams requires insight into new psychological concepts and existing concepts with unknown validity when generalized to teams. Salas et al. (2007) regard the growing use of teams to conduct work as an organizational response to a changing world. The past 25 years provided the strongest catalyst for I/O psychologists to understand teams and how teamwork functions. However, the actual use of teams as a means of accomplishing work has been with us since long before the birth of I/O psychology. What is new about teams is our growing reliance on them to accomplish work that was once performed by individuals. Salas et al. stated, "It seems clear that after we compile all the lessons we have learned over the last century, one message is clear: industries, governments, and organizations count on teams . . . Teams have proven to be beneficial and will continue to proliferate as the complexity of our world increases. Teams always have and always will exist" (p. 432).

Case Study   The Grenoble Marketing Company

It had been a financially tight year for the Grenoble Marketing Company. The company designed printed advertisements and television commercials for its clients. However, with a sagging business economy, more and more clients were cutting back on how much they would spend to advertise their products. Grenoble was split fairly evenly between the print medium and the electronic (television) medium sides of the business. The print medium team was known as the "Ink Crowd," and the electronic medium team went by the nickname "TV Land." In fact, the employees in the two teams rarely interacted with each other. Each side of the advertising business required very different skills. Each team had separately lobbied the company's vice president, Anthony Prizzio, to hire someone who would solicit new accounts, a generator of new business. Prizzio knew that getting a new position authorized by the president of Grenoble wouldn't be easy given the company's financial position. However, Prizzio was delighted to hear from his boss that Grenoble would approve adding one new position. Prizzio convened the members of the two teams in a rare joint meeting. He told the respective team members that the president had just authorized adding one new person to the company; that person would be responsible for generating new business. Because the print and electronic media were so different, however, it was extremely unlikely that one person could be found who was qualified in both areas. In short, in all likelihood one team would get a new position and the other wouldn't. Prizzio decided to foster what he called "healthy competition" between the two teams. Each team would recruit and recommend for hire its top candidate. Prizzio would then have the ultimate authority and responsibility to select the better of the two candidates. It thus behooved each team to put forth as strong a candidate as it could find.

Each team went about its search for the new person. The position was advertised, leads were followed, and the recruitment process was pursued in earnest. In a brief time TV Land settled on its top candidate. The individual was a proven veteran in the field of television advertising, a person who worked for a competitor of Grenoble and was ready for a career move. Everyone in TV Land was very pleased with the choice and felt reasonably confident Prizzio would likewise be impressed. The Ink Crowd was not so quick to announce its top candidate. In fact, two candidates emerged who split the team with regard to its preference. One was established in the field of print advertising and had the reputation of being a consistent revenue producer. The other was younger and less experienced but designed extraordinarily creative and powerful advertising copy. A recipient of an industry award for innovation in printing advertising, this was a "can't miss" candidate.

Prizzio asked the Ink Crowd for its decision, but neither half would back down from its enthusiastic preference. The Ink Crowd was deeply divided. Each side accused the other of using pressure tactics, being blind to the obvious talents of the other's choice, and "sabotaging" their chances in the overall competition with TV Land. The members of the Ink Crowd realized they were embroiled in two competitions—one within their team and one with TV Land. Someone suggested the Ink Crowd put forth both candidates for Prizzio's consideration. This idea was rebuked by those who said, "If we can't even make up our own minds about who we like, why wouldn't Prizzio go with TV Land? They know who they like." Another suggestion was to ask Prizzio to hire both candidates from the Ink Crowd because both were so good in their own way. This idea brought further criticism. One team member said, "Why not propose that Prizzio hire all three candidates since they are all so terrific? I'll tell you why not—it's because we don't have the money to hire but one of them!" TV Land got word of the conflict going on in the Ink Crowd. TV Land was delighted, believing the conflict only increased the chances for their own candidate. A similar sentiment was expressed by a senior member of the Ink Crowd. "TV Land doesn't have to beat us. We are killing ourselves." Meanwhile, Prizzio awaited their response.

Questions

1. Do you believe that Prizzio's concept of "healthy competition" can be beneficial for Grenoble, or does deliberately pitting teams against each other inevitably produce a divisive outcome? Why do you feel as you do?
2. Should the Ink Crowd unite behind one of its two candidates "for the good of the team," or is there a way the within-team conflict might benefit Grenoble?
3. Consider the concept of the level of analysis. Can a team "win" and the organization "lose" (or vice versa) in this case? Why?
4. What evidence is there of groupthink operating in this case, and what organizational factors are present that foster its occurrence?
5. If you were an adviser to the president of the Grenoble Marketing Company, what advice would you give to enhance the long-term success of the company?

Chapter Summary

- Work teams are an adaptive response of organizations to the changing business world.
- Teams exist at a level of analysis that is in between the individual and the organization.
- What distinguishes a team from several individuals working together are five core principles pertaining to the processes that operate within the team.
- Teams have a definable structure as indexed by the roles members assume within a team.
- Teams function through important processes pertaining to communication, conflict, cohesion, and trust.
- Teams must learn to make decisions that affect every member and result in the emergence of a team mentality.
- Some teams, known as virtual teams, consist of members around the world who may have never met each other face-to-face, yet they function through electronic communication.
- Issues such as personnel selection, training, and performance appraisal apply to teams, just as they do to individuals.
- The social processes that hold teams together and allow them to function are influenced by the cultural backgrounds of their members.

10 Organizational Attitudes and Behavior

Learning Objectives

- Explain the organizational attitudes of job satisfaction, job involvement, and organizational commitment.

- Understand the concept of organizational justice.

- Understand the concept of organizational citizenship behavior and its relationship to other concepts.

- Understand the concept of the psychological contract in employment and its changing nature.

- Understand the basis of antisocial behavior in the workplace.

The preceding chapters examined several conceptual approaches to organizations and teams, including their structure and configuration and the social mechanisms that enable them to function. This chapter will examine various psychological concepts that have emerged within organizations. In particular, the focus will be on concepts that not only have theoretical value but also have been found to influence a wide array of practical matters relating to work behavior.

The chapter will begin with an examination of three important attitudes employees hold about their work: how satisfied they are with their jobs, how involved they are with their jobs, and how committed they are to their organizations. Subsequent topics will expand on the psychological constructs that represent the domain of organizational attitudes and behavior.

Job Satisfaction

Job satisfaction
The degree of pleasure an employee derives from his or her job.

Job satisfaction is the degree of pleasure an employee derives from his or her job. Hulin and Judge (2003) asserted that an employee's affective reaction to a job is based on a comparison of the actual outcomes derived from the job with those outcomes that are expected. Dawis (2004) added that feelings of job satisfaction can change with time and circumstances. People differ in what is important to them, and this may also change for the same person. Because work is one of our major life activities, I/O psychologists have had a long-standing interest in job satisfaction.

One hundred years ago employment conditions were, by today's standards, unacceptable. Work was often performed under unsafe conditions, work hours were very long, offices were not air-conditioned, and benefits we often take for granted today, such as paid vacations, medical insurance, and retirement contributions, did not exist. You might think that the employees of today, who enjoy more favorable working conditions, would be highly satisfied with their jobs; however, that is not the case. Although some employees derive great pleasure and meaning from their work, many others regard work as drudgery.

Why is this so? The answer lies in individual differences in expectations and, in particular, the degree to which a job meets one's expectations. There are broad differences in what people expect from their jobs and thus broad reactions to them. As Hulin (1991) stated, "Jobs with responsibility may be dissatisfying to some because of the stress and problems that are associated with responsibility; others may find responsibility a source of positive affect. Challenging jobs may be satisfying to some because of how they feel about themselves after completing difficult job assignments; others may find such self-administered rewards irrelevant" (p. 460). Why people differ in their preferences for job outcomes is posited to be related to their developmental experiences and levels of aspiration.

Research has revealed that people develop overall feelings about their jobs as well as about selected dimensions or facets of their jobs, such as their supervisor, coworkers, promotional opportunities, pay, and so on. I/O psychologists differentiate these two levels of feelings as *global job satisfaction* and *job facet satisfaction*, respectively. Considerable research has been devoted over the years to the measurement of job satisfaction. The Job Descriptive Index (Smith, Kendall, & Hulin, 1969) has been used to measure job satisfaction for more than 35 years, and it is regarded with professional esteem within I/O psychology (Kinicki et al., 2002). Likewise, the Minnesota Satisfaction

Questionnaire (Weiss et al., 1967) is highly regarded within the profession. A version of the Minnesota Satisfaction Questionnaire is shown in Figure 10-1.

Thoresen et al. (2003) stated, "For 50 years, people's attitudes about their jobs were thought to largely be a function of their work environment. However, the last two decades have witnessed an 'affective revolution' in organizational psychology" (p. 914). The concept of *affect* refers to a fundamental difference in how people view

---

Ask yourself: How satisfied am I with this aspect of my job?

Very Sat. means I am very satisfied with this aspect of my job.

Sat. means I am satisfied with this aspect of my job.

N means I can't decide whether I am satisfied or not with this aspect of my job.

Dissat. means I am dissatisfied with this aspect of my job.

Very Dissat. means I am very dissatisfied with this aspect of my job.

On my present job, this is how I feel about . . .	Very Dissat.	Dissat.	N	Sat.	Very Sat.
1. Being able to keep busy all the time	❏	❏	❏	❏	❏
2. The chance to work alone on the job	❏	❏	❏	❏	❏
3. The chance to do different things from time to time	❏	❏	❏	❏	❏
4. The chance to be "somebody" in the community	❏	❏	❏	❏	❏
5. The way my boss handles subordinates	❏	❏	❏	❏	❏
6. The competence of my supervisor in making decisions	❏	❏	❏	❏	❏
7. Being able to do things that don't go against my conscience	❏	❏	❏	❏	❏
8. The way my job provides for steady employment	❏	❏	❏	❏	❏
9. The chance to do things for other people	❏	❏	❏	❏	❏
10. The chance to tell people what to do	❏	❏	❏	❏	❏
11. The chance to do something that makes use of my abilities	❏	❏	❏	❏	❏
12. The way company policies are put into practice	❏	❏	❏	❏	❏
13. My pay and the amount of work I do	❏	❏	❏	❏	❏
14. The chances for advancement on this job	❏	❏	❏	❏	❏
15. The freedom to use my own judgment	❏	❏	❏	❏	❏
16. The chance to try my own methods of doing the job	❏	❏	❏	❏	❏
17. The working conditions	❏	❏	❏	❏	❏
18. The way my coworkers get along with each other	❏	❏	❏	❏	❏
19. The praise I get for doing a good job	❏	❏	❏	❏	❏
20. The feeling of accomplishment I get from the job	❏	❏	❏	❏	❏

Figure 10-1 *Minnesota Satisfaction Questionnaire (short form)*

Source: From *Manual for the Minnesota Satisfaction Questionnaire*, by D. J. Weiss, R. V. Dawis, G. W. England, and L. H. Lofquist, © 1967. Minneapolis: Industrial Relations Center, University of Minnesota. Used by permission of Vocational Psychology Research, University of Minnesota. http://www.psych.umn.edu/psylabs/vpr

life, their general disposition, and attitude. Affect is typically described along a positive–negative continuum. People who are high in positive affect tend to be active, alert, enthusiastic, inspired, and interested. They are optimistic about life. Such people tend to interpret failure as a temporary setback caused by external circumstances and are likely to persevere. People who are high in negative affect are pessimistic about life and "see the glass as half-empty rather than half-full." Over the past two decades we have grown to understand that how satisfied a person feels about his or her job is related to affect as much as to objective job conditions. These are the more factual bases of one's job, including level of pay, hours of work, and physical working conditions.

Brief (1998) proposed a model of job satisfaction (as depicted in Figure 10-2) based on these two components (affect and objective job conditions), which lead to an assessment or interpretation of the job circumstances. The interpretation is based on many considerations, including the perceived adequacy of the pay for the work performed, the level of stress on the job, and the match of the job to the person's skills and abilities. Recent research has confirmed the validity of affect in influencing one's job satisfaction. Affect is considered to be a component of personality, which in turn is posited to have a genetic basis. Judge, Heller, and Mount (2002) established a linkage between personality traits and job satisfaction. Job satisfaction was found to correlate .29 with Neuroticism, .25 with Extraversion, .02 with Openness to experience, .17 with Agreeableness, and .26 with Conscientiousness. As a set these Big 5 personality traits had a multiple correlation coefficient of .41 with job satisfaction. Similarly Ilies and Judge (2003) proposed that feelings of job satisfaction are inheritable, based on a study of identical twins reared apart. In short, feelings of job satisfaction are related both to the objective conditions of work (that are under the control of the organization) and to the personality of the worker.

Bowling et al. (2005) proposed a theory of job satisfaction based on original research in sensation and perception. In a classic study from over 60 years ago, individuals were asked to judge the heaviness of several weights. Prior to judging the weights, the individuals lifted either a heavier or lighter weight relative to the weight of the

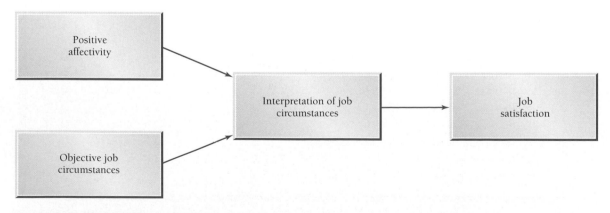

Figure 10-2　*Model of job satisfaction*

Source: Adapted from *Attitudes in and Around Organizations*, by A. P. Brief, p. 97. Copyright © 1998, Sage Publications, Inc. Adapted with permission of Sage Publications, Inc.

target item. The judgment of the target item was found to be influenced by the weight of the previous item. Individuals adjusted their judgment of the target item by what they experienced before. As such, our judgments are embedded in a relative context, and cannot be made independently of that context. The authors believe that how people feel about their jobs is also a contextual judgment. Individuals differ in their underlying personalities, and their sensitivity to positive and negative workplace events (i.e., the analogue of lighter and heavier weights). The theory suggests that organizational efforts to improve long-term job satisfaction in employees are probably futile. Improvements in job satisfaction are possible, but their effects are likely to be short-lived, as the employees re-calibrate or re-adapt themselves to the new environment in which they find themselves.

Recent research has introduced another component to job attitudes: emotions (Lord, Klimoski, & Kanter, 2002). For the most part I/O psychology has not addressed the emotional dimensions of work life, historically being more interested in cognitive issues (as witnessed by the amount of research on *g*). However, moods and emotions play an undeniable role in how we feel about life, including work. Fisher (2000) proposed that even though moods may not be directly controllable given their somewhat vague and diffuse causes, organizations may be more successful in elevating employees' moods than in raising their overall level of job satisfaction. For example, organizations could concentrate on providing a work environment free of minor irritations and hassles that produce frequent, if mild, feelings of frustration and annoyance. Muchinsky (2000), drawing upon the research of Lazarus and Lazarus (1994), identified five categories of emotions, all of which are (or can be) manifested in the workplace. These five categories are presented in Table 10-1. In summary, moods and emotions are related but not identical to attitudes. It is possible that intense but short-lived emotional reactions

Table 10-1 *Five categories of human emotions*

Category	Emotion
1. Positive	Happiness Love Pride
2. Negative	Sadness Hopelessness Despair
3. Existential	Anxiety Guilt Shame
4. "Nasty"	Anger Envy Jealousy
5. Empathetic	Gratitude Compassion Sympathy

Source: Adapted from *Passion and Reason: Making Sense of Our Emotions*, by R. S. Lazarus and B. N. Lazarus, 1994. New York: Oxford.

to workplace incidents have an enduring effect on job satisfaction. Bono et al. (2007) found that supervisors exert substantial influence on the moods of their employees. The authors reported that employees experience more negative and fewer positive emotions when interacting with supervisors than when interacting with clients, customers, or co-workers. Employees who felt compelled to regulate their emotions (conceal negative emotions and fake positive emotions) experienced more stress and lower satisfaction on their jobs compared to employees who did not feel compelled to engage in emotion regulation. Fisher and Ashkanasy (2000) concluded that "the study of emotions in the workplace has the potential to add an understanding of behavior in organizations" (p. 123). I/O psychologists have much to learn about how emotions influence organizational attitudes and behaviors (see The Changing Nature of Work: Emotions in the Workplace).

The relationship between job satisfaction and important job-related criteria has been examined extensively. Three criteria will be presented: performance, turnover, and absence. The relationship between job satisfaction and job performance has been researched for more than 40 years. The reason is obvious—ideally we would like to be both productive and happy in our work. However, the relationship between satisfaction and performance is not very strong. Iaffaldano and Muchinsky (1985) conducted a meta-analysis of studies that examined this relationship and reported the best estimate of their correlation to be .17. A more recent study by Judge, Thoresen,

The Changing Nature of Work: Emotions in the Workplace

Only recently have I/O psychologists begun to study emotions as they apply to the work world. Understanding emotions helps us to better understand other concepts, such as the role they play in teams. West (2001) described how several emotions can operate in the functioning of a work team. Three of these emotions are negative in nature. *Jealousy* is a consequence of the threat or experience of being excluded by the group. Team members are likely to be jealous when they feel less favored than a particular powerful or influential team member. Jealousy may also manifest itself when team members feel that others are more accepted and included in the team. Perceptions of inclusion or exclusion by the team leader are likely to strongly influence feelings of jealousy. *Guilt* can cause some individuals to exert more effort to maintain their relationships in the group by spending more time or paying more attention to other team members. Within a team, some members may induce guilt when they feel that inadequate concern is being shown for the well-being of their team members. West believes guilt-inducing signals are likely to be directed toward the team leader because he or she carries a greater share of the responsibility for group cohesion. *Grief* can occur within a team over the departure of a team member. This is especially likely when the departing team member was instrumental to the well-being of other team members or was effective in reducing within-team conflict. Likewise, the departing team member may feel grief over the loss of the entire team. George (2002) described the phenomenon of *emotional contagion* within a team—a tendency to mimic and synchronize facial expressions, vocalizations, and postures—which creates emotional convergence among the members. Although our knowledge of emotions in the workplace is not extensive, I/O psychologists regard them as offering a useful explanation of organizational attitudes and behavior.

et al. (2001) estimated the satisfaction–performance correlation to be .30. Based on this study the percentage of variance shared between these two concepts (r^2) is 9%, meaning 91% of the variance in one concept is *not* explained by the other. This correlation is not nearly as high as some scholars and practitioners would intuitively believe. Its implication is that organizational attempts to enhance both worker satisfaction and performance *simultaneously* will likely be unsuccessful. The reason is that the two concepts are only mildly related. In fact, some organizational attempts to increase productivity (for example, cracking down on employees through tough supervisory practices) may decrease job satisfaction.

As discussed in Chapter 2, it is difficult to determine causality in I/O research. Using sophisticated analytic methods, Schneider et al. (2003) concluded there is no single causal relationship between satisfaction and performance. It appears some dimensions of performance are caused by having satisfied workers, while some employee attitudes are caused by the financial performance of the organization. Furthermore, the relationship between satisfaction and performance need not always be positive. Zhou and George (2001) reported that feelings of job dissatisfaction were associated with workers being more creative on the job; they used creativity as an outlet for their dissatisfaction. Finally, Lucas and Diener (2003) offered the possibility that the changing nature of our work world may influence the future relationship between satisfaction and performance. As our economy has moved from manufacturing to service jobs, there is a greater reliance on teamwork, the sharing of information, and interpersonal activity among workers. Therefore we may find a different pattern of relationships between satisfaction and performance than was found in our earlier manufacturing-based economy.

Turnover and absence are often referred to as *withdrawal behavior* because they reflect the employee withdrawing from a noxious employment condition, either temporarily (absence) or permanently (turnover). The relationship between how much you like your job and whether you withdraw from it has attracted considerable interest among I/O psychologists. In general, the research shows that the more people dislike their job, the more likely they are to quit. The magnitude of the satisfaction–turnover correlation, on average, is about −.40. However, this relationship is influenced by several factors, including the availability of other work. People would rather endure a dissatisfying job than be unemployed (Hom & Kinicki, 2001). Conversely, when alternative employment is readily available, workers are more likely to leave unsatisfying jobs (Carsten & Spector, 1987).

The correlation between job satisfaction and absence is considerably smaller, approximately −.25 (Johns, 1997). Absence from work can be caused by many factors that have nothing to do with how much you like your job, including transportation problems and family responsibilities. However, when researchers control for methodological issues in the design of research addressing this relationship (including whether the absence from work is paid or unpaid, and whether organizational sanctions are imposed on absent workers), a mild but consistent negative relationship emerges between the two. A practical implication of the finding is that if you like your job, you are more likely to make the extra effort needed to get to work (as when you have a cold) than if you are dissatisfied with your job. How people feel about their jobs is also related to how they feel about their life in general. The link between work and family lives will be discussed in Chapter 11.

Job Involvement

Job involvement
The degree to which a person identifies psychologically with his or her work and the importance of work to one's self-image.

Job involvement refers to the degree to which a person identifies psychologically with his or her work and the importance of work to one's self-image. Brown (1996) asserted that people may be stimulated by and drawn deeply into their work, or they may be alienated from it mentally and emotionally. As others have noted, the quality of one's entire life can be greatly affected by one's degree of involvement in, or alienation from, work. Brown stated: "A state of involvement implies a positive and relatively complete state of engagement of core aspects of the self in the job, whereas a state of alienation implies a loss of individuality and separation of the self from the work environment" (p. 235). Some items from a job involvement questionnaire (Kanungo, 1982) are listed in Figure 10-3.

I consider my job to be very critical to my existence.

I am very much involved personally in my job.

Most of my personal life goals are job-oriented.

The most important things that happen in my life involve work.

Work should be considered central to life.

Life is worth living only when people get absorbed in work.

Figure 10-3   *Sample items from a job involvement questionnaire*

Source: From "Measurement of Job and Work Involvement," by R. N. Kanungo, 1982, *Journal of Applied Psychology, 67,* pp. 341–349.

Research has shown a wide range of correlations between job involvement and other work-related constructs. Brown (1996) conducted a meta-analysis of studies that examined job involvement and reported an average correlation of .45 with overall job satisfaction, .09 with performance, −.13 with turnover, and .53 with a personality dimension related to conscientiousness. These results suggest that job involvement is more strongly related to how people view their work and their approach to it and less related to how well they perform their jobs.

Organizational Commitment

Organizational commitment
The extent to which an employee feels a sense of allegiance to his or her employer.

Organizational commitment is the extent to which an employee feels a sense of allegiance to his or her employer. Allen and Meyer (1990) proposed three components to this construct. The *affective* component refers to the employee's emotional attachment to, and identification with, the organization. The *continuance* component refers to commitment based on the costs that the employee associates with leaving the organization. The *normative* component refers to the employee's feelings of obligation to remain with the organization. In essence, affective commitment reflects allegiance based on liking the organization, continuance commitment reflects allegiance because it is unlikely the person could get a better job elsewhere, and normative commitment reflects allegiance to the organization out of a sense of loyalty.

Meyer (1997) asserted that organizational commitment reflects the employee's relationship with the organization and that it has implications for his or her decision to continue membership in the organization. Committed employees are more likely to remain in the organization than are uncommitted employees. Sample items from a questionnaire (Dunham, Grube, & Castaneda, 1994) measuring organizational commitment are listed in Figure 10-4.

> I really feel as if this organization's problems are my own.
>
> This organization has a great deal of personal meaning for me.
>
> Too much in my life would be disrupted if I decided I wanted to leave my organization now.
>
> One of the major reasons I continue to work for this company is that leaving would require considerable sacrifice; another organization may not match the overall benefits I have here.
>
> I think that people these days move from company to company too often.
>
> I was taught to believe in the value of remaining loyal to one organization.

Figure 10-4 *Sample Items from an organizational commitment questionnaire*

Source: From "Organizational Commitment: The Utility of an Integrated Definition," by R. B. Dunham, J. A. Grube, and M. B. Castaneda, 1994, *Journal of Applied Psychology, 79*, pp. 370–380.

Morrow (1993) proposed that an individual can be committed to different focal points in work—one's job, one's organization, and one's occupation. An occupation represents a constellation of requisite skills, knowledge, and duties that are different from other occupations and are transferable across organizations within an occupation. Occupational commitment is an emotional connection that the person feels with the occupation. Organizational commitment reflects a sense of loyalty to one's particular employer. Finally, job involvement represents the narrowest focal point of commitment, loyalty to one's own job. It would therefore be possible for a person to have high occupational commitment (for example, to nursing) but low organizational commitment. In such a case a person might readily change employers within the larger nursing occupation. Alternatively, a person could have high organizational commitment and low job involvement, indicating the person would be receptive to moving across jobs within the same organization.

Morrow developed a model that illustrates the various forms of commitment through a series of concentric circles, as shown in Figure 10-5 (p. 322). At the center of the model is one's work ethic, a personality dimension reflecting how important and central work is to one's life. Working outward from the center of the model is occupational commitment, followed by the continuance dimension of organizational commitment, followed by the affective dimension of organizational commitment, and lastly job involvement. According to Morrow, the innermost forms of commitment are more dispositional in nature, whereas those in the outer circles are determined more by situational factors. Although Cohen (2003) questioned the accuracy of Morrow's conception of work commitment (particularly the relationships among the circles),

Figure 10-5   *Concentric circle model of work commitment*

Source: Adapted from *The Theory and Measurement of Work Commitment*. P. C. Morrow, p. 163. Copyright © 1993 JAI Press. Adapted with permission from Elsevier Science.

Lee, Carswell, and Allen (2000) supported the importance of occupational commitment for understanding various aspects of organizational behavior. Meyer and Allen (1997) concluded that employees can feel varying levels of commitment to the different identifications with work (job, organization, occupation), and we must gain a better understanding of what is meant by "work commitment."

Cooper-Hakim and Viswesvaran (2005) described two theoretical approaches often adopted by researchers of work commitment. The first is grounded in *conflict* between the employee's organization versus his or her occupation. Some occupations (e.g., medicine) exert strong role pressures on their members' behavior by having a professional code of conduct. However, employees must behave in ways that are supportive of the larger goals of the organization. Legitimate conflict can ensue between these two sources of influence that threatens loyalty to either the organization or the occupation.

The second theoretical basis is *social exchange*, which is the concept that there are benefits and costs associated with all relationships. Work life consists of multiple commitments; to the organization, the occupation, one's work group, customers or clients, and so on. The pattern of interrelated social exchanges provides the basis for the different commitments employees feel. The loss of job security in the contemporary workplace threatens the basis of why employees would commit to their organization. Through downsizing, outsourcing, mergers, offshoring, etc., employees can lose their jobs through no fault of their own, thus weakening the basis of the social exchange with the organization.

Based on a meta-analysis by Brown (1996), the average correlations between organizational commitment and other work-related constructs are similar to the pattern found for job involvement, only stronger. The average correlations were .53 with overall job satisfaction, −.28 with turnover, and .67 with a personality construct similar to conscientiousness. Brown also estimated a correlation of .50 between job involvement and organizational commitment. Riketta (2002) estimated a correlation of .20 between organizational commitment and job performance based on a meta-analytic study. The general pattern of results reveals that job satisfaction, job involvement, and organizational commitment are substantially correlated with each other but only modestly correlated with performance and turnover. Thus organizational attitudes tend to be substantially intercorrelated. Performance is determined by ability, motivation, and situational constraints, whereas turnover is determined in part by external economic variables. The linkage between organizational attitudes and behavior is thus moderated by factors beyond the control of the individual.

Historically, managerial and professional workers have exhibited a high degree of job involvement and organizational commitment. However, as seen in Chapter 8, it is these workers who often lose their jobs during downsizing, outsourcing, and offshoring. The loss of work for these people is particularly painful because so much of their personal identity is defined by their work. The reactions of people who lose their jobs will be discussed later in this chapter.

Organizational Justice

Organizational justice
The theoretical concept pertaining to the fair treatment of people in organizations. The three types of organizational justice are distributive, procedural, and interactional.

Organizational justice is concerned with the fair treatment of people in organizations. It can be thought of as a more limited application of social justice, a concept that has been debated by philosophers for hundreds of years. All organizational contexts have competing goals and objectives. A case in point is personnel selection. Job applicants seek employment with an organization. The organization, in turn, offers employment to some applicants and denies the opportunity to others. Both the outcome of the selection decision (who is offered employment and who isn't) and the process (whether the assessment is rendered via a psychological test, interview, etc.) can be questioned in terms of fairness. That is, was a just and fair outcome reached through the use of just and fair methods? Organizational justice is a useful concept to examine a wide range of important organizational issues. Justice has been claimed to be "the first virtue of social institutions" (Rawls, 1971, p. 3).

Various configurations or typologies of organizational justice have been proposed over the years (e.g., Greenberg, 1993). However, the most current research and thinking on the topic have yielded the typology shown in Figure 10-6 (Colquitt et al., 2001), p. 324. Work organizations are highly sensitized to the issue of fairness and have developed mechanisms to ensure that conditions in the workplace are fair (training employees for dealing with interpersonal conflict, training managers in how to conduct performance appraisals, soliciting employee suggestions and ideas to improve the workplace, and so on). As such, some scholars have proposed that more formal mechanisms are in place to ensure justice at work than in other forms of social collectivity, like families and civic groups. Colquitt et al. believe that organizational justice has been among the most frequently researched topics in I/O psychology in

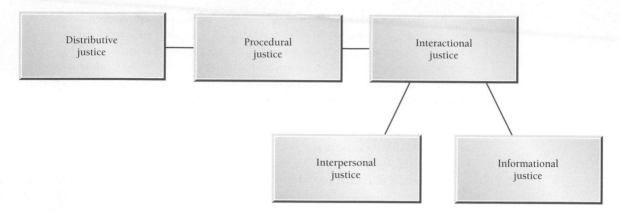

Figure 10-6 *Categories of organizational justice*

the last two decades. This conclusion is justified because organizational justice has been found to be associated with many of the topics studied in I/O psychology, including performance, turnover, absenteeism, trust, job satisfaction, and organizational commitment.

Distributive Justice

Distributive justice
The fairness with which the outcomes or results are distributed among members of an organization.

Distributive justice refers to the fairness of the outcomes, results, or ends achieved. Distributive justice, like all forms of justice, is heavily predicated upon values. These values are the rules or standards by which judgments of fairness are rendered. Three such rules have been identified as the basis for distributive justice: equity, equality, and need.

Equity.   The equity distribution rule suggests that people should receive rewards that are consistent with the contributions they make or bring to a situation. Consider a company that is willing to send two of its managers to an expensive and professionally valuable management development program. Using the equity distribution rule, the company decides to send the two managers judged most deserving on the basis of their high job performance. These two individuals are judged to contribute the most to the company in terms of their ability, effort, and potential to advance in the company, so they are selected to attend the program. In this case it is "fair" that the two most competent and promising managers are offered the development training.

Equality.   The equality distribution rule suggests that all individuals should have an equal chance of receiving the outcome or reward, regardless of differentiating characteristics such as ability. In its purest sense, the equality rule suggests the developmental training recipients should be selected randomly. Because organizations don't make selection decisions randomly, however, a modified equality rule must be used. In this example there are two openings for participation in the training, so the managers are divided into two categories—for example, by gender. The company then selects the most qualified male manager and the most qualified female manager to attend the program. The "most qualified" consideration is derived from the equity rule, and the one male/one female consideration is derived from the equality rule. In this case it is "fair" that one person from each gender is offered the training program.

Need.   The need distribution rule suggests that rewards should be distributed on the basis of individual need. The special consideration that the needy individual receives is thus perceived as fair. The company therefore selects two managers who are most in need of having their professional skills enhanced by the training (irrespective of gender). In this case it is "fair" that the two managers most in need of training are selected to participate.

As you might imagine, there can be legitimate differences of opinion about which is the "fairest" rule to use in selecting two managers. One possible resolution might be to segment the recipients—that is, to offer one based on merit performance and the other based on need. If the most professionally competent manager is a woman, then the other selection could be awarded to the male manager most in need of the training. With such a distribution the training recipients are chosen (in part) on the basis of equity, equality, and need. However, some people might say that it is *unfair* to weigh equity and need the same and that both training recipients should be chosen solely on the basis of need (or equity). Arguments could be made that the top performing managers obviously don't need the training; they are already performing very well. Alternatively, the beneficial professional training could be regarded as a reward for being the top two managers in the company, thereby increasing the likelihood that the two best will become even better.

These types of disagreements regarding what is fair (and unfair) about distributions are not at all uncommon. Because distribution rules are based on values, no rule is inherently right or wrong. Organizations typically address differences of opinion regarding distribution rules by seeking to gain consensus on which rule is the "fairest" to follow or by distributing different rewards by different rules. Leung (1997) reported a relationship between cultural orientations and reward allocation preferences. Some cultures, as typified by North America, tend to value *individualism* and are concerned more with individual interests, needs, and goals. Other cultures, as typified by Asia, tend to value *collectivism* and are concerned more with the interests, needs, and goals of in-group members. Individualistic cultures prefer the equity rule because of the emphasis on competition and self-gain. Collectivist cultures prefer the equality rule because of the emphasis on solidarity, harmony, and cohesion. Kabanoff (1997) proposed that nations differ in their collective preferences for reward allocation strategies based on the individualism–collectivism orientation. It is often difficult to reach a consensus on fairness, and there can be far-reaching implications for organizations from differing views on what constitutes fairness in their practices (see Field Note 1, p. 326).

Procedural Justice

Procedural justice
The fairness by which means are used to achieve results in an organization.

The second major type of justice is **procedural justice**, which is the fairness of the means used to achieve the results. As the name suggests, it deals with the perceived fairness of the policies and procedures used to make decisions. In essence, the distinction between distributive and procedural justice is the difference between content and process that is basic to many philosophical approaches to the study of justice.

Field Note 1: What Is "Fair"?

What does it mean to be "fair"? Most certainly there are many ways to consider fairness, and I was party to one situation that evoked these multiple perspectives. A wealthy individual died and bequeathed $3,000,000 to a university to support students who attended the school. The university invested the $3,000,000 such that it earned 6% interest, or $180,000, per year. Thus every year the university could grant $180,000 to students to support their education, without having to use the original $3,000,000 gift. The university formed a committee to determine the most fair way of dispersing the $180,000 per year. I was a member of that committee. Three distinct schools of thought emerged as to what constituted the "most fair" disbursement of money.

The first school of thought was to grant a financial award to the most academically talented applicants. As indexed by high school grades and standardized test scores, the "best" applicants were to receive the financial support. This university had highly reputable programs in engineering and agriculture, majors that typically attract more men than women. Because these programs attracted many of the most highly qualified applicants to the university, and because the vast majority of these applicants were men, the financial award recipients would be very heavily represented by men.

Proponents of the second perspective pointed out that the university sought to embrace all groups in society—across genders, racial groups, age groups, the physically disabled, and so on. Therefore the financial support should be intentionally allocated to individual students who represent the various groups. In this way the university would show its support for recruiting a diverse student body.

The third perspective was to allocate the money based on financial need. It was proposed that the best use of the money would be to pay for students to obtain a college education who could not otherwise afford it. Therefore the recipients of the financial support would be the financially neediest students.

These were the three basic schools of thought on what was a "fair" strategy to disburse the money. I was struck not only by how different the recipients would be depending upon which strategy was followed, but also by the inherent plausibility of each strategy. That is, I felt each position had some intuitive appeal; each one made some sense to me. The three groups argued over such matters as the difference between a scholarship and financial aid, and what the intentions of the deceased benefactor were in disbursing his money. The final decision by the committee reflected a compromise—a (fair) resolution of conflicting standards of fairness. A portion of the funds was set aside to be allocated on the basis of need. The rest would be allocated on the basis of academic ability, with members of all the various groups represented. It was not a decision the committee enthusiastically endorsed, but one it could live with.

If you had been on that committee, what position would you have taken in allocating the funds? Why do you think your position is the "most fair" one?

According to Folger and Greenberg (1985), there are two dimensions to conceptualizing procedural justice. One emphasizes the role of the individual's "voice" in the process. Procedures are perceived to be more fair when affected individuals have an opportunity to either influence the decision process or offer input. Indeed, Schminke, Ambrose, and Cropanzano (2000) found that higher levels of participation in decision making by employees within an organization were associated with higher levels of perceived procedural fairness. Gilliland and Chan (2001) reported that giving workers the opportunity to respond to their own performance evaluations, including the possibility of modifying them, is one of the most influential factors in their acceptability. The second dimension emphasizes the structural components of the process, whereby procedural justice is a function of the extent to which procedural rules are satisfied or violated. These procedural rules suggest that decisions should be made consistently, without personal biases, with as much accurate information as possible, and with an outcome that could be modified.

In applying the concept of procedural justice to a personnel selection system, for example, one could posit several components of what constitutes a "fair" selection process (Gilliland, 1993). Ideally the selection test should be job-related (or more precisely from the applicant's view, face valid), allow the candidate to demonstrate his or her proficiency, and be scored consistently across applicants. Furthermore, candidates should receive timely feedback on their application for employment, be told the truth, and be treated respectfully in the assessment process. Note that these procedural justice issues pertain to the selection process, not the outcome of whether the applicant is accepted or rejected (which is a matter of distributive justice). Leventhal (1980) proposed six criteria by which procedures can be judged as fair: (1) consistent, (2) bias free, (3) accurate, (4) correctable in case of an error, (5) representative of all concerned, and (6) based on prevailing ethical standards. Folger and Cropanzano (1998) asserted that Leventhal's criteria for procedural justice have been supported by subsequent research.

Interactional Justice

Interactional justice
The fairness with which people are treated within an organization and the timeliness, completeness, and accuracy of the information received in an organization.

A third major type of organizational justice has been identified, referred to as **interactional justice**. In turn, interactional justice has two components: interpersonal and informational. *Interpersonal justice* is manifested by showing concern for individuals and respecting them as people who have dignity. Ostensible displays of politeness and respect for citizens' rights enhance their perceptions of fair treatment by authorities, such as the police and the courts. Similarly, apologies demonstrate interpersonal justice because they express remorse and serve to distance individuals from the negative effects of their actions. As Folger and Skarlicki (2001) stated, it rarely costs anything to be polite. The lack of politeness, sensitivity, and caring for the emotional pain inflicted by organizations on employees only adds insult to injury. As will be discussed in the section on workplace violence, employees who seek to physically harm their manager or coworkers often have their vengefulness abetted by a perceived lack of politeness and fairness. Folger and Skarlicki concisely summarized this point: "Politeness costs less than you think, and it stands to reap greater benefits than you might have realized. Paraphrased and shortened, politeness pays" (p. 116). Greenberg (2007) believes that many positive organizational outcomes can be derived from strongly promoting interactional justice: "The key is that being far more dignified and respectful to people than they expect cannot help but result in positive reactions . . . Importantly, these reactions are likely to be 'contagious' insofar as they contribute to a culture in which such positive acts are openly encouraged and in which violations are critically discouraged" (p. 172).

Informational justice is manifested by providing knowledge about procedures that demonstrate regard for people's concerns. People are given adequate accounts and explanations of the procedures used to determine desired outcomes. For explanations to be perceived as fair, they must also be recognized as genuine in intent (without any ulterior motives) and based on sound reasoning. Because it is typically the open sharing of information that promotes this form of organizational justice, the term *information* is used to identify it.

A study by Greenberg (1994) illustrates interpersonal and informational justice. Two announcements of a work site smoking ban were made to employees of a large company. The announcements differed in the amount of information they gave about the need for the ban and the degree of interpersonal sensitivity shown for the personal impact of the ban. Some employees received a great deal of information about the reason for the smoking ban, while others received only the most cursory information. Furthermore, some employees received a personally sensitive message ("We realize that this new policy will be very hard on those of you who smoke. Smoking is an addiction, and it's very tough to stop. We are quite aware of this, and we do not want you to suffer"), while other employees received a message showing less personal concern ("I realize that it's tough to stop smoking, but it's in the best interest of our business to implement the smoking ban. And, of course, business must come first"). Immediately after the announcement, employees completed surveys on their acceptance of the ban. Although heavy smokers were least accepting of the ban, they showed the greatest incremental gain in acceptance after they received thorough information presented in a highly sensitive manner. Regardless of how much they smoked, all smokers recognized the procedural fairness associated with giving thorough information in a socially sensitive manner. By contrast, all nonsmokers' acceptance of the ban was uniformly unaffected by the way it was presented to them.

A major meta-analytic review of 25 years of organizational justice research by Colquitt et al. (2001) concluded that distributive justice, procedural justice, and the two types of interactional justice (interpersonal and informational) each contribute incremental variance to perceptions of fairness in the workplace. Although the different justice dimensions are not totally distinct, each reflects a facet of "what is fair." Greenberg (2007) observed that much of what is known about organizational justice has been discovered from its violation; that is, organizational injustice. Greenberg offered that because justice is expected as the norm, it is more informative to examine deviations from the norm (i.e., injustice) than behavior consistent with the norm (i.e., justice). Simons and Roberson (2003) concluded that the fair treatment of employees by organizations has important effects on individual employee attitudes, such as satisfaction and commitment, and on individual behaviors, such as absenteeism and citizenship behavior. Cohen-Charash and Spector (2001) reported that of the three major types of justice, procedural justice was most closely related to organizational attitudes and behaviors.

Organizational Citizenship Behavior

Organizational citizenship behavior
The contributions that employees make to the overall welfare of the organization that go beyond the required duties of their job.

The classic approach to thinking about a job is in terms of the tasks that comprise it. In fact, one purpose of job analysis (as described in Chapter 3) is to identify these tasks. In turn, performance appraisal (as discussed in Chapter 7) is concerned with assessing how well employees perform the tasks that make up their jobs. However, organizational researchers have discovered that some employees contribute to the welfare or effectiveness of their organization by going beyond the duties prescribed in their jobs. That is, they give extra discretionary contributions that are neither required nor expected. The most frequently used term for this phenomenon is **organizational citizenship behavior**. It is also referred to as *prosocial behavior, extra-role behavior*, and *contextual behavior*. We first mentioned contextual behavior in Chapter 3 on criteria and again in Chapter 5 on personnel decisions. Organ (1994) referred to a person who engages in organizational citizenship behavior as a "good soldier."

Five dimensions to citizenship behavior have been supported by empirical research (LePine, Erez, & Johnson, 2002):

1. *Altruism* (also called *helping behavior*) reflects willfully helping specific people with an organizationally relevant task or problem.

2. *Conscientiousness* refers to being punctual, having attendance better than the group norm, and judiciously following company rules, regulations, and procedures.

3. *Courtesy* is being mindful and respectful of other people's rights.

4. *Sportsmanship* refers to avoiding complaints, petty grievances, gossiping, and falsely magnifying problems.

5. *Civic virtue* is responsible participation in the political life of the organization. Civic virtue reflects keeping abreast of not only current organizational issues but also more mundane issues, such as attending meetings, attending to in-house communications, and speaking up on issues. It has been suggested that civic virtue is the most admirable manifestation of organizational citizenship behavior because it often entails some sacrifice of individual productive efficiency.

Employees who exhibit prosocial behavior are highly valued by their managers. Indeed, they should be because they contribute above and beyond the normal requirements and expectations of the job. However, Bolino (1999) raised the possibility that employees who are judged to exhibit prosocial behavior may be "good actors" as well as "good soldiers." Good soldiers act selflessly on behalf of their organizations, whereas good actors may engage in such prosocial behaviors for the self-serving reason of enhancing their image within the organization. Indeed, Hui, Lam, and Law (2000) demonstrated the strategic value of prosocial behavior for employees. Employees who perceived prosocial behavior as instrumental to getting a promotion and who were promoted were more likely to decrease their prosocial behavior after the promotion. Thus prosocial behavior has instrumental value for increasing the likelihood of a promotion, but after the promotion its instrumental value decreases.

An empirical study of performance evaluation revealed the degree to which citizenship behavior influences judgments of job performance. MacKenzie, Podsakoff, and Fetter (1991) examined three objective measures of weekly productivity relating to sales volume for a sample of insurance agents. Also obtained for these agents was an evaluation of their dimensions of organizational citizenship behavior, as well as a managerial assessment of their overall job performance. The results indicated that the managers' subjective evaluations of the agents' job performance were determined as much by the agents' altruism and civic virtue as by their objective productivity levels. Podsakoff, Ahearne, and MacKenzie (1997) reported that altruism and sportsmanship had substantial effects on the overall quantity of performance of machine crews working in a paper mill, whereas altruism was related to the quality of performance. Allen and Rush (1998) demonstrated that students gave higher evaluations to teachers who exhibited high organizational citizenship behavior than to teachers who exhibited low organizational citizenship behavior, while controlling for the level of the teachers' task performance. Heilman and Chen (2005) examined the extent to which the altruism dimension of organizational citizenship behavior influenced the evaluations of male and female employees. Men who engaged in altruistic behavior on the job received higher evaluations than men who did not engage in altruistic behavior. Conversely, women who did not engage in altruistic behavior had lower evaluations than men who did not engage in altruistic behavior. The authors concluded that assisting others with tasks and going the "extra mile" (i.e., being a helper) is central to a female gender stereotype perception. Men who engage in helping others exceed the male gender stereotype perception, while women who help others are simply eliciting typical female behavior. In turn, these gender-based stereotypes influence the evaluations received by men and women on the job.

Are manifestations of such prosocial behavior a product of our individual dispositions (which are fairly immutable), or can organizations conduct themselves in ways that bring out such behavior in their employees? Research supports both the dispositional and situational antecedents of organizational citizenship behavior.

Support for dispositional antecedents comes from the Big 5 model of personality (as discussed in Chapter 4). Two of the Big 5 dimensions appear relevant to organizational citizenship behavior. One, Agreeableness, pertains to the ease or difficulty one has in getting along with people, or how good-natured one is in interpersonal relationships. The second, Conscientiousness, pertains to reliability, dependability, punctuality, and discipline. Evidence indicates that some people, given selected aspects of their personality, are more likely to engage in organizational citizenship behaviors than others. As McNeely and Meglino (1994) noted, organizations can promote prosocial behavior by selecting applicants who have high scores on Agreeableness and Conscientiousness. Likewise, additional research (Lee & Allen, 2002; Rioux & Penner, 2001) found that individual personality characteristics and motives were associated with the willingness to help other employees with their jobs in the organization.

The second explanation for organizational citizenship behavior—situational antecedents—has at its basis the concept of organizational justice. It is proposed that if employees believe they are treated fairly, then they are more likely to hold positive attitudes about their work. Organ (1988) hypothesized that fairness perceptions may influence prosocial behavior by prompting employees to define their relationship with the organization as a social exchange. In exchange for being treated fairly, it is proposed that employees would engage in discretionary gestures of organizational citizenship behavior. However, to the extent that unfairness is perceived in the relationship, the tendency would be to recast the relationship as a more rigidly defined exchange. Thus, in a trusting relationship with the organization, the employee contributes more to the exchange than is formally required. However, to the degree the organization is perceived as lacking fairness, the employee retreats to contributing to the exchange only what he or she is obligated.

In a test of this proposition, Moorman (1991) examined the relationship between forms of organizational justice (distributive and procedural) and organizational citizenship behavior. It was proposed that employees engage in citizenship behavior because they perceive the organization to be fair (both distributively and procedurally). Moorman discovered that organizational citizenship behavior was related to perceptions of procedural justice but *not* distributive justice. Furthermore, the courtesy dimension of citizenship behavior was most strongly related to procedural justice. Employees who believed that their supervisors personally treated them fairly appeared to be more likely to exhibit citizenship behaviors.

The major implication of the study is that supervisors can directly influence employees' citizenship behavior. Employees' perception of justice was based on whether supervisors used procedures designed to promote fairness. Moorman concluded that if supervisors want to increase citizenship behavior among their employees, they should work to increase the fairness of their interactions with employees. Subsequent research has strengthened the finding of a reciprocal exchange between the employee and the organization. Organizations that are perceived as being equitable and that recognize desirable behavior in their employees reap the benefits of having employees engage in more citizenship behavior. Zellers and Tepper (2003) concluded: "Organizations that successfully attract and hire individuals with strong self-concepts comprised in part by values reflecting the importance of being a 'good citizen' may be able to reduce costly amounts of supervision since the individual is intrinsically motivated to be a 'good citizen'" (p. 415).

The Psychological Contract

Psychological contract
The implied exchange relationship that exists between an employee and the organization.

Rousseau (1995) described the **psychological contract** as the exchange relationship between the individual employee and the organization. It is not a formal written contract between the two parties but an implied relationship based on mutual contributions. The psychological contract is the employee's perception of the reciprocal obligations that exist within the organization. The employees have beliefs about the organization's obligations to them as well as their obligations to the organization. Thus employees may believe the organization has agreed to provide job security and promotional opportunities in exchange for hard work and loyalty by the employee. The psychological contract is oriented toward the future. Without the promise of future exchange, neither party has incentive to contribute anything to the other and the relationship may not endure. The contract is composed of a belief that some form of a promise has been made and that the terms and conditions of the contract have been accepted by both parties.

Beliefs or perceptions about implied promises and acceptance are the basis of the psychological contract. Each party believes that both parties have made promises and that both parties have accepted the same contract terms (Rousseau, 1989). However, this does not necessarily mean that both parties share a common understanding of all contract terms. Each party believes only that they share the same interpretation of the contract. Dabos and Rousseau (2004) asserted that the psychological contract is founded on two principles: *mutuality* (the extent to which workers and employees share beliefs about specific terms of the exchange) and *reciprocity* (their commitments to each). Dabos and Rousseau believe mutuality may be more easily achieved than reciprocity because there is no stated time frame in which the reciprocal commitments are to be made. For instance, an employer may indicate a willingness to develop a worker and support his or her career advancement. However, it may not be clear how and over what time period the worker is to make a reciprocal contribution to the employer. The psychological contract is made not once but is revised throughout the employee's tenure in the organization. The longer the relationship endures and the two parties interact, the broader the array of contributions that might be included in the contract. Rousseau and Parks (1993) found that employment itself is perceived as a promise (i.e., the implied contract of continued future employment) and that an employee's performance is perceived as a contribution (a way of paying for the promise). Robinson, Kraatz, and Rousseau (1994) examined how psychological contracts change over time. They found that during the first two years of employment, employees came to perceive that they owed less to their employers, while the employers owed them more.

Rousseau suggested that psychological contracts lie along a continuum from the transactional to the relational. *Transactional contracts* are characterized by short time frames and specific obligations. Financial resources are the primary vehicle of exchange. *Relational contracts* are characterized by long-term relationships with diffuse obligations. Transactional contracts are predicated on total self-interest, whereas relational contracts implicitly acknowledge the value of the relationship itself, in which one party may put the immediate interests of the other party ahead of his or her own. At the relational end of the continuum, obligations are ambiguous and constantly evolving. These contracts are long term and exchange not only financial resources but also socioemotional resources such as loyalty and affiliation. Figure 10-7 shows the continuum of psychological contracts and the range of social behaviors within an organization.

There is an element of power in all contracts. Power can be distributed either equally (i.e., symmetrically) between the two parties or unequally (i.e., asymmetrically). Asymmetrical power is most common in employment relationships. Power asymmetries affect the perceived voluntariness of the exchange relationship, dividing the two parties into contract makers (relatively powerful) and contract takers (relatively powerless). As contract takers, employees cannot easily influence the employment relationship. This may result in a perceived loss of control in the relationship, which is likely to intensify feelings of mistreatment and injustice when violations are perceived. As the more powerful party, the employer can dictate terms of the contract to the less powerful employee, who must either accept them or exit the relationship.

Nature of Psychological Contract

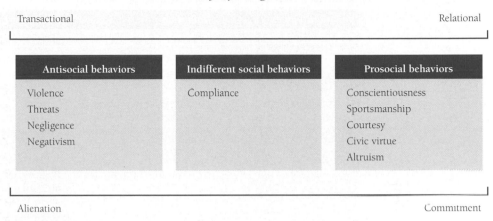

Figure 10-7   *Relationship between the psychological contract and the range of social behaviors*

Source: Adapted from "'Till Death Do Us Part . . .': Changing Work Relationships in the 1990s" by J. M. Parks and D. L. Kidder, 1994, in *Trends in Organizational Behavior*, Vol. 1 (p. 120), edited by C. L. Cooper and D. M. Rousseau, New York: Wiley.

Violations of the Psychological Contract

The psychological contract is violated when one party in a relationship perceives that another has failed to fulfill the promised obligations. Table 10-2, p. 334, lists typical organizational violations of the psychological contract and related example quotes from employees. The failure of one party to meet its obligations to another can be expected to erode both the relationship and the affected party's belief in the reciprocal obligations of the two parties. Violations by an employer may affect not only what an employee feels he or she is owed by the employer but also what an employee feels obligated to offer in return. Violation of a psychological contract undermines the very factors (e.g., trust) that led to the emergence of a relationship. If the employer reneges on an implied promise, the employer's integrity is questioned. A violation signals that the employer's original motives to build and maintain a mutually beneficial relationship have changed or were false from the beginning. Cavanaugh and Noe (1999) and Turnley and Feldman (2000) found that violations of the psychological contract negatively influenced employees' intent to remain with the employer and job satisfaction. The psychological contract binds the employee and employer—a form of guarantee that if each does his or her part, then the relationship will be mutually beneficial. Thus violations weaken the bond.

What is the typical employee response to violations of the psychological contract? Robinson et al. (1994) found that psychological contracts become less relational and more transactional following violations. Employees turn away from the socioemotional aspects of work and focus on the monetary benefits of the relationship. This has the effect of increasing the psychological distance between the employee and the employer, making the contract more transactional. A sequential pattern of five employee

Table 10-2 *Types of violations of the psychological contract*

Violation Type	Definition	Examples
Training/development	Absence of training or training experience not as promised	"Sales training was promised as an integral part of marketing training. It never materialized."
Compensation	Discrepancies in promised and realized pay, benefits, and bonuses	"Specific compensation benefits were promised. Either they were not given to me, or I had to fight for them."
Promotion	Promotion or advancement schedule not as promised	"I perceived a promise that I had a good chance of promotion to manager in one year. While I received excellent performance ratings, I was not promoted in my first year."
Job security	Promises not met regarding the degree of job security one could expect	"The company promised that no one would be fired out of the training program, that all of us were safe until placement. In return for this security we accepted lower pay. The company subsequently fired four people from the training program."
Feedback	Feedback and reviews inadequate compared with what was promised	"I did not receive performance reviews as promised."
People	Employer perceived as having misrepresented the type of people at the firm, in terms of things such as their expertise, work style, or reputation	"It was promised as dynamic and as having a challenging environment . . . rubbing elbows with some of the brightest people in the business . . . a lie. The true picture started to come out after the initial hype of working at one of the best 100 companies in the country had worn off."

Source: Adapted from "Violating the Psychological Contract: Not the Exception but the Norm" by S. L. Robinson and D. M. Rousseau, 1994, *Journal of Organizational Behavior*, 15, pp. 245–259.

responses to violations has been identified. The first is *voice*: employees voice their concerns over the violations and seek to reinstate the contract. Dulebohn (1997) found that employees are somewhat reluctant to use formal mechanisms of voice because they fear subsequent reprisal by management. People who use formal voice mechanisms (grievance or appeal systems) are often labeled as organizational dissenters and experience retaliation. Instead, employees are more likely to use subtle influence tactics to affect procedural justice. If unsuccessful, voice is followed by *silence*. Silence connotes compliance with the organization, but a loss of commitment. Silence is followed by *retreat*, as indicated by passivity, negligence, and shirking of responsibility. *Destruction* may then occur, whereby employees retaliate against the employer through theft, threats, sabotage, and in extreme cases homicide. The topic of workplace violence will be discussed in greater detail later in this chapter. Finally, in the *exit* stage, employees quit the organization or provoke the organization to dismiss them. Research has shown that justice perceptions play a role in responses to violations of the psychological contract. In particular, procedural justice is of primary importance to employees whose relational contract was violated. The use of fair and equitable procedures by organizations can lessen the impact of the contract violation on employees (see Field Note 2)

Zhao et al. (2007) conducted a meta-analysis of breaches to the psychological contract; that is, employee perceptions regarding the extent to which an organization has failed to fulfill its promises or obligations. Breaches of the psychological contract were associated with higher mistrust, lower job satisfaction, lower organizational commitment, lower prosocial behavior, and lower job performance compared with the perceptions by employees that their psychological contract was not breached. Downsizing, outsourcing, and offshoring produce lower job security for employees. Individuals can lose something vital to their welfare—gainful employment—even if the employees are performing their jobs satisfactorily. Control over our own lives is vital for our sense of well-being (a topic addressed in the next chapter). The perceived loss of control

Field Note 2: Mutual Expectations

The concept of the psychological contract can be extended from employees in a work organization to students in an educational organization. The psychological contract involves a set of mutual expectations that both parties in a relationship have for each other. What expectations do students have for their professors? Reasonable expectations might include that the professors are qualified to teach the subject matter, will fairly evaluate the students' performance in class, and harbor no personal bias toward any student. Have you ever been in a class where one or more of these expectations were, in your opinion, unmet? If so, how did it affect your attitude toward the professor, the class, the school? If you felt the basic psychological contract between the students and the professor was violated, it is reasonable that your attitude and perhaps behavior (e.g., attendance, performance in class) were adversely affected. However, the psychological contract consists of *mutual* expectations—in this case, expectations the professors have of students. What expectations do professors have for their students? Reasonable expectations might include that the students want to learn, will complete assignments on time, and respect the institution of higher learning. Have you ever been in a class where it seemed the professor felt these expectations were violated by the students? If so, how did the professor respond to these perceived violations? The psychological contract applies to both parties in a relationship, but we know less about organizational expectations of their members than vice versa.

over our own job security compels employees to move down the continuum toward a more transactional relationship with their employer, with the resulting effect of less employee commitment and loyalty toward the employer. To what degree are employers aware of the effects of the changing psychological contract in the workplace? Spitzer (1995) reported a survey of major U.S. employers revealed the following:

- 50% of employees expend only enough effort to avoid being fired.
- 73% of employees are perceived to be less motivated than they used to be.
- 84% of employees could be more productive if they wanted.

In short, the changing psychological contract has produced corrosive effects for both employees and employers. These effects are the consequences of rupturing a long-standing relationship between the two parties: loyalty and effort in exchange for steady employment.

Based on a multinational analysis, Rousseau and Schalk (2000) concluded that the psychological contract as a promise-based exchange is widely generalizable to a variety of societies. Given the rise of global business, cultural differences in the psychological contract will most likely continue to evolve. For example, traditionally Asians prefer to first establish a relationship between parties and then carry out business transactions, whereas Westerners prefer to create a relationship through repeated business transactions. In the future it is likely that both styles will manifest themselves in new and varied forms (see Cross-Cultural I/O Psychology: Cross-Cultural Influences on Organizational Attitudes and Behavior).

Next the chapter will examine one of the most fundamental violations of a psychological contract—the organization's decision to reduce employment through layoffs or downsizing. Such decisions demonstrate huge power differentials between employer and employee and involve the complete loss of control by the employee. As noted in Chapter 8, downsizing affects thousands of employees annually and is changing the nature of the psychological contract as we know it.

Individual Responses to Job Loss

As discussed in Chapter 8, organizational downsizing, outsourcing, and offshoring has targeted middle-level managers and professional staffs as well as blue-collar employees. These developments are harbingers of fundamental change in the evolution and nature of organizational behavior. This section will examine downsizing from the perspective of individual employees, both those who have lost their jobs and the survivors (Kozlowski et al., 1993).

Terminated Personnel

The individuals most directly affected by downsizing are those who lose their jobs. Downsized employees face the immediate prospect of a loss of income. The amount of time employees have between hearing their jobs have been eliminated and the date of their termination is often a matter of weeks and sometimes days. There is often little time to search for a new job. Buss and Redburn (1987) reported that eight years after a plant closing, 27% of the affected workforce were still unemployed. Furthermore,

Cross-Cultural I/O Psychology: *Cross-Cultural Influences on Organizational Attitudes and Behavior*

Organizational attitudes and behaviors are strongly affected by cross-cultural influences. Research on many of the topics addressed in this chapter revealed culture-specific interpretations and applications. Lam, Hui, and Law (1999) found that employees in Hong Kong and Japan were more likely to regard some facets of *organizational citizenship behavior* as an expected or defined part of the job than were employees in the United States and Australia. Thus what employees in some cultures consider extra-role (discretionary) behavior, employees in other cultures consider in-role (expected) behavior. Judge, Parker, et al. (2001) reported cross-cultural differences in *job satisfaction* that are consistent with the individualism–collectivism dimension. Workers in collectivist cultures derive more satisfaction from the social, collegial aspects of work, whereas workers in individualistic cultures derive more satisfaction from opportunities for advancement and achievement. Glazer (2002) reported cultural differences in *organizational justice* as pertaining to preferences for the distribution of resources. In collectivist cultures greater justice is achieved by distributing resources

equally because it helps to preserve harmony. In individualistic cultures greater justice is achieved by distributing resources on the basis of merit, such as differential pay raises on the basis of job performance. Finally, the scope of *psychological contracts* also differs by culture. Schalk and Rousseau (2001) described how societal and cultural beliefs influence the kind of exchanges that are negotiable between an employee and employer. A manager in the United States might avoid hiring close friends or family members because of possible allegations of conflict of interest. In other cultures hiring family members or friends might be viewed as desirable because the person is not unknown to the hiring manager. In some countries employment relationships are formally specified or "spelled out" so there is little room for discretionary give-and-take. In other countries there may be much more room for individual negotiation between the two parties, with the associated problem of fewer institutional and guaranteed protections afforded by the lack of formal employment policies. There is ample variability in manifestations of organizational attitudes and behavior in cultures throughout the world.

DILBERT   by Scott Adams

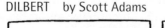

Dilbert: © Scott Adams/Dist. by United Feature Syndicate, Inc. Reprinted with permission.

those who do find some employment may be able to obtain only less attractive and lower-paying jobs. Individuals with skills that do not readily transfer outside of the organization and those with less education suffer greater financial losses.

Employment has a number of psychological benefits that are lost when an individual becomes unemployed. Individuals who lose their job suffer physical symptoms caused by the strain of unemployment. Some indicators of the stress of unemployment are headaches, stomach problems, and high blood pressure. Unemployed individuals have been found to exhibit patterns of learned helplessness, lower feelings of self-worth, and increased depression. Older, white-collar employees experience particularly acute feelings of betrayal by their organization, demoralization, and cynicism. Issues of stress and well-being will be discussed in greater detail in the next chapter.

Surviving Personnel

Although downsizing has more direct implications for the individuals who lose their jobs, employees who remain with the organization are also affected by downsizing strategies intended to make the organization run more efficiently. Survivors often respond with reduced trust and commitment because the organization broke its psychological contract with them (see Field Note 3). The reactions of these survivors to the downsizing process, as well as their reactions to the organization's treatment of terminated employees, can adversely affect the future effectiveness of the organization.

Field Note 3: The Loss of Resources

To understand the impact of downsizing on the surviving members of an organization, consider an analogy: the employees of an organization are one of its resources (which is why they are often referred to as "human resources"). The organization uses these employees to accomplish its objectives. Individuals have resources as well. One resource that we all have in common is time. Every person has 24 hours in each day to accomplish his or her objectives. Organizational downsizing that results in the loss of 20% of the workforce is not unusual. How would you deal with a 20% reduction in your time resources? That is, instead of a 24-hour day, your day has been "downsized" by 20% (or 5 hours) to become a 19-hour day. You still have to do everything you did before: but you now have 5 fewer hours in which to do it. How would you live your life differently? If you normally sleep 8 hours, would you now sleep only 3 hours? If you need 8 hours of sleep and have to continue working an 8-hour day, that leaves only 3 hours for everything else, including eating, transportation time, and recreation. Do you think you would feel stressed under these conditions? Do you think you might not be as fully committed to your activities under these conditions? Although we all probably waste some time each day, it is questionable whether we waste 20% of it. Therefore eliminating 20% of our day would not necessarily make us more efficient. It might compel us to use our time more wisely, but it would also have a cost to us; that is, we would probably have to "give" on some other aspects of life. Such is the predicament faced by the survivors of organizational downsizing. They face increased pressure to perform the work that was once performed by a larger workforce.

Antisocial Behavior in the Workplace

Surviving employees are still employed by the organization, but their conditions of employment may be different from before. In order to remain with the organization, some individuals may have to be demoted to lower-level jobs. They may have to take a salary reduction as well. Other downsizing strategies targeted to reduce costs include job sharing, part-time schedules, and reduced hours. Although affected employees may experience a reduction in income, the experience is still less painful than the total loss of employment.

Rather than staffing permanent employees, many organizations are making greater use of contingent (temporary) workers (Smither, 1995). Contingent workers perform particular tasks for a specific time period. The need for their services varies as a function of the organization's work flow. Contingent workers may work through temporary employment agencies that allocate their services to organizational clients that need them. They are the modern organizational equivalent of migrant farm workers, people who obtain temporary employment by following the harvesting of crops across the nation. Contingent workers receive lower salaries than if they were permanent employees performing the same work, and they rarely receive benefits, such as medical insurance or pensions. Contingent workers are disproportionately young, female, and minority, those who exemplify the transactional psychological contract. They have a short-term outlook on their involvement with an organization because the future holds no promise for them. Although contingent workers may increase organizational flexibility and decrease labor costs, there is a price. Contingent workers exhibit fewer prosocial behaviors or, worse, engage in antisocial behaviors.

Downsizing has forced both organizations and individuals to reassess the nature of the employment relationship. One consequence has been an apparent increase in transactional psychological contracts, with the accompanying decrease in employees' sense of loyalty and commitment to their employer. It has been argued that downsizing is a necessary response to organizational structures that have become bloated and economically inefficient. Organizations that resist downsizing as a means of addressing their imperiled conditions risk their total demise (and the loss of even more jobs). However, downsizing has become bitter medicine for individuals as a treatment for organizational maladies. Its presence and frequency of use have prompted a major reassessment by I/O psychologists on long-held tenets regarding the nature of the employment relationship.

Antisocial Behavior in the Workplace

Antisocial behavior
Any behavior that brings harm or is intended to bring harm to an organization or its members.

Antisocial behavior in the workplace refers to a range of employee behaviors aimed at exacting revenge against the organization or fellow workers for some perceived injustice. Antisocial behavior includes insults, threats, lies, theft, sabotage, physical violence, and occupational homicide. The phenomenon has also been called *organizational deviance* (Bennett & Robinson, 2000) and *workplace incivility* (Pearson, Andersson, & Porath, 2000). It represents one of the more recent areas of research in I/O psychology.

Andersson and Pearson (1999) proposed a spiraling effect of incivility in the workplace. Workplace incivility is low-intensity deviant behavior with ambiguous intent to harm the target individual, in violation of workplace norms for mutual respect. Uncivil behaviors are characteristically rude and discourteous, displaying a lack of regard for others. The spiraling effect refers to the prospects that incivility can escalate into intense aggressive behavior. Glomb, Steele, and Arvey (2002) stated, "[M]ildly aggressive acts can have great impact when they are experienced in quantity. . . . These overlapping effects build on each other, augmenting their impact. Eventually, repeated mild aggression can create considerable distress and oppression itself, such as that seen after periods of prolonged provocation or threat" (p. 229). Andersson and Pearson stated that the spiral of incivility often begins with a thoughtless act or a rude comment. This can be followed by a maligning insult, which prompts a counterinsult. If the spiral of escalation continues, threats of physical attack can follow, ultimately leading to violence. The authors believe there is a "tipping point" in the spiral where the accumulation of minor affronts escalates into coercive action. In a meta-analysis of workplace aggression, Hershcovis et al. (2007) found that co-workers were more likely than supervisors to be targets of workplace aggression. This finding may be attributable to co-workers having less retaliatory power than supervisors, as well as their greater representation within an organization.

Bies, Tripp, and Kramer (1997) described what they call the "thermodynamics of revenge" in organizations. It is predicated on the violation of two underlying concepts previously examined in this chapter: the psychological contract and organizational justice. There is typically a sparking event of one of two types. One is a violation of rules, norms, or promises by the organization. An organizational agent changes the rules or criteria of decision making after the fact to justify a self-serving judgment. The second is status or power derogation, such as destructive criticism or public ridicule intended to embarrass the employee. The employee then "heats up" and experiences anger and bitterness, often feeling a need to satisfy a burning desire for revenge. This is followed by a "cooling down" phase, which can take several forms. One is *venting*, in which the employee talks heatedly and animatedly to friends, "blows off steam," and has little or no intention of acting out his or her feelings. A second is *dissipation*, where the employee gives the harm-doer the benefit of the doubt and searches for plausible explanations for the harm-doer's behavior. A third form is *fatigue*, in which employees maintain their negative feelings for long periods of time. These people do not forgive, forget, and let go. They often obsessively ruminate and express regret about not getting even with the harm-doer. The final form is *explosion*, which can manifest itself in the employee working harder to prove the critic wrong, mobilizing opposition to the harm-doer, or engaging in physical violence.

Skarlicki and Folger (1997) asserted that organizational agents, particularly managers and supervisors, can play prominent roles in reducing employee desires to seek revenge. When managers and supervisors showed sensitivity and concern for employees, treating them with dignity and respect, the employees were willing to tolerate organizational violations of justice that would otherwise lead to retaliatory tendencies (Skarlicki, Folger, & Tesluk, 1999). Such retaliatory behaviors included deliberately damaging equipment or work processes, taking supplies home without permission, and wasting company material. Cropanzano and Greenberg (1997) discovered that workers who were treated in a disrespectful manner by their supervisor stole objects that were of no value to themselves but were valuable to their employer. Disrespectful treatment, adding insult to the injury of unfair treatment, encouraged people to retaliate against their employers. The employees sought to harm employers in exchange for being harmed, even if doing so did nothing more than even the score between them symbolically.

Violence in the Workplace

As Bies et al. (1997) noted, one of the responses to perceived violations of organizational justice is physical violence. Physical violence in the workplace is a growing epidemic. Prior to 1980 such terms as "violence in the workplace" and "occupational homicide" did not exist. In 1998 the U.S. Department of Justice reported the following statistics about workplace violence. Workplace violence costs U.S. businesses approximately $4.2 billion per year. One out of every six violent crimes experienced in the United States occurs in the workplace. Nearly 1,000 workers are murdered and 1.5 million workers are assaulted each year. Homicide is the second leading cause of fatal occupational injuries in the nation. Bulatao and VandenBos (1996) reported that homicide is the leading cause of fatal occupational injuries in the retail trade, sales, service, managerial, and clerical occupations. Reporting statistics on crime has the subtle effect of making them seem dry and impersonal. Here are descriptions of specific acts of violence in the workplace (Mantell, 1994, pp. 2–4):

- A Tampa, Florida, man returned to his former workplace and shot three of his supervisors as they sat eating their lunches. He wounded two others before killing himself.

- A Sunnyvale, California, worker at a defense contractor shot and killed seven people in the office after a female coworker turned down his romantic advances.

- A woman in a Corona, California, hospital opened fire with a .38-calibre handgun, wounding a nurse and spraying the infant nursery with bullets.

- A man in Atlanta who lost $400,000 in bad investments killed 9 people and wounded 13 others at a brokerage office before killing himself.

- A Wakefield, Massachusetts, employee upset with his employer's decision to withhold his wages to pay back taxes killed seven coworkers with a semiautomatic rifle.

It may be tempting to dismiss these accounts as sensationalized reporting of isolated events. However, it appears that the frequency and severity of workplace violence are escalating, both nationally and internationally. Kelleher (1996) described the breadth of the problem: "If you are a gas station attendant, government employee, or retail store clerk, you have a higher probability of being murdered on the job than a police officer in your own community. If you are a secretary or clerk in an office, you are more likely to be murdered at work than a West Virginia miner is likely to be accidentally killed in an industry-related accident" (p. xi). Furthermore, Barling (1996) noted there are both primary and secondary victims of workplace violence—family members of primary victims plus coworkers who themselves were not violated but whose perceptions, fears, and expectations are changed as a result of being exposed to the violence.

A starting point in understanding the psychology of workplace violence is with the topic of aggression. Cox and Leather (1994) stated, "Human aggression is typically the product of interpersonal interactions wherein two or more persons become involved in a sequence of escalating moves and countermoves, each of which successively modifies the probability of subsequent aggression" (p. 222). Thus aggressive acts are frequently retaliatory responses to a previous act or acts by the aggressor. A violent act is therefore conceptualized as a step in an integrated series of social acts. The retaliatory response can be understood in part by the concepts of organizational justice and the psychological contract.

Perpetrators of workplace violence often see themselves as victims of some injustice in the workplace (Steensma, 2002). They may be particularly inclined to perceive the organization as having violated the principles of procedural justice. In fact, Johnson and Indvik (1994) posited that violation of the psychological contract is one of the leading causes of workplace violence. A term frequently associated with perpetrators of workplace violence is "disgruntled." Mantell (1994) reported that acts of physical violence are invariably preceded by indications of anger or betrayal, such as verbal threats or sullenness. Actual violence is often preceded by verbal assaults or stalking of the victim. In most cases of workplace hostility, however, the verbal assaults and stalking do not escalate to homicide (Schouten, 2003). That is, there is a continuum of hostile workplace behaviors, with homicide (or attempted homicide) being the extreme point (Neuman & Baron, 1998). Perpetrators seemingly want more from the organization in terms of personal identity and purpose than the organization can provide, and in turn they personalize a sense of rejection when their needs are unmet. They tend to see themselves as having their relationship (contract) with the organization violated, while accepting little or no responsibility for their own behavior. It also appears that perpetrators of violent workplace crimes often have maladaptive personalities and have experienced interpersonal conflict in other aspects of their lives.

The search for systematic patterns among perpetrators of workplace violence has led to the identification of some consistent characteristics. A problem with this profile approach is that even though it may indeed describe perpetrators, the identified characteristics may also describe many other individuals. That is, many employees may "fit" the profile but in fact do *not* engage in workplace violence. For example, most employees whose jobs were downsized feel a sense of rejection and injustice, yet they do not commit violent acts. Hindsight or "postdiction" may give the impression that perpetrators were obvious candidates to commit such crimes and therefore should have been identified and deterred from their actions. Despite the prevalence of workplace violence, its occurrence is still relatively rare in the total constellation of employed individuals. Therefore the correct prediction of such events is far more problematic than "looking backward" after their occurrence.

Aggression is the product of both individual and situational factors. Among the situational factors identified are population density, noise, heat, and alcohol use. Both laboratory and field research on aggression (e.g., Geen, 1990) indicates that it becomes increasingly likely under conditions of perceived crowding, uncontrollable noise, and high ambient temperatures. However, the research on the relationship between alcohol use and aggression is most declarative (Greenberg & Barling, 1999). Pernanen (1991) posited that alcohol completely modifies one's ability to understand a social situation. Alcohol leads to both a narrowing of the situation at hand and a dampening of intellectual and verbal ability. Alcohol encourages an overinflated evaluation of one's sense of control, power, and mastery over the world. The inebriated individual may be led into aggression by both a biased interpretation of the situation and increased confidence in being able to cope by largely physical means (Cox & Leather, 1994).

Many perpetrators of workplace violence were found to have consumed alcohol prior to their action.

Recent research on workplace aggression has examined institutional characteristics that induce aggressive behaviors in addition to the characteristics of employees who are prone to elicit such behaviors (Bowling & Beehr, 2006). Inness, Barling, and Turner (2005) examined a sample of people who worked two jobs. The authors discovered that organizational factors were more predictive of aggression toward supervisors than characteristics of the employee. Employees in high stress jobs and employees with abusive supervisors were more likely to act aggressively in those jobs than the same employees in their other jobs. Judge, Scott, and Ilies (2006) identified differences between people who exhibit consistent hostile attitudes and people who have momentary bursts of hostility. Even if a selection test were to screen out the most consistently hostile employees, over half of organizationally deviant behavior (e.g., devoting work time to personal matters, tardiness, working slowly, etc.) would still occur from employees who only engage in it sporadically. Bing et al. (2007) noted that, in general, organizations desire employees with low levels of aggressive tendencies and high levels of prosocial behavior. However, some jobs (such as manager) may best be performed by individuals who are willing to assertively confront poorly performing employees and counsel them. Such a managerial style is preferable to conflict avoidance, where problems are dealt with by ignoring them. Other jobs (such as bodyguard, bill collector, and soldier) might best be filled by individuals who can manifest aggression, as long as their aggressive tendencies can be controlled in situations where aggressive behavior is not desirable or necessary.

Companies are often reluctant to participate in research on workplace violence because it is such a sensitive and volatile subject. Fox and Spector (1999) described a research study addressing workplace violence in which some companies declined to participate. The authors reported, "The primary reason given by companies in declining to participate was that they did not want to 'unsettle' their employees. Employees in precisely such companies might provide the richest information about counterproductive behavioral responses to aversive work environments" (p. 929). Antisocial behavior in the workplace is a complex phenomenon. Baron, Hoffman, and Merrill (2000) asserted there are close parallels between violence at work and violence in nonwork areas of life. Like drug use in the workplace, violence spills over into other areas traditionally removed from I/O psychology. It remains to be seen how big a role I/O psychology will play in addressing this topic. If primary emphasis is placed on the act (criminal violence) rather than on its location, then the role of I/O psychology will probably not be large. However, if such violence is examined primarily in terms of its location (the workplace), I anticipate that I/O psychology will be called upon to help understand and control this serious problem.

Case Study ⟲   Where Should the Axe Fall?

Ted Simmons stared pensively at two personnel files. Simmons was the vice president of finance for Savannah Mills, a long-time business leader in the textile industry. Savannah Mills had endured another difficult year, as sales and profits were again lower than projected. Simmons had just returned from a staff meeting where he was told the company would be downsizing its staff as a way to reduce expenses. Simmons had to eliminate one of his two financial manager positions, and other job losses were to follow down the line in his department. In fact, all the major departments at Savannah Mills would face job losses, some more than others.

Simmons had the pleasure of working with two exemplary managers, and eliminating one of these jobs from the company would be extremely difficult and unpleasant. Warren Davis had been with the company for almost 25 years. He had devoted his entire career to Savannah Mills; he started working there after high school. His dedication and commitment to the company were almost legendary. He had earned a college degree on a part-time basis while holding a job at Savannah Mills, getting a bachelor's degree in general business. Whatever the company asked Davis to do, he did with vigor and good cheer. He willingly accepted assignments where the company needed him and always expressed sincere gratitude for the chance to be with Savannah Mills. His father had been an employee of the company for over 40 years when he retired, and the Davis children grew up playing on company-sponsored recreational teams. Warren Davis was also very active in the community, representing Savannah Mills on various civic projects. Davis was once referred to as a "walking billboard" for the company, so deep was his loyalty to the company that meant so much to him and his family.

The other manager was Barry Steele. Steele had a very different history from Davis. Steele was 29 and had been with Savannah Mills for five years. He had earned an MBA degree from a highly prestigious university in New England. Upon graduation, Steele had many job offers but chose Savannah Mills because of its expressed intent to more strongly professionalize the financial operations at the company and to give Steele the opportunity to put his talents to work. Steele delivered on all the expectations of him and in fact exceeded these expectations. He revolutionized the company's system of managing financial assets through the use of automated control principles he had learned in graduate school. It was through Steele's shrewd assessments that Savannah Mills avoided even bigger financial losses, and he positioned the company to return to profitability. Steele was known as "the wonder kid" because of his accomplishments, but he never acted arrogant or pompous. He was not active in company or civic affairs but quietly went about his business. If there was ever a young employee who seemed destined for a highly successful future with Savannah Mills, it was Steele.

Simmons faced a dreadful choice. He didn't have to fire one of his managers because poor job performance was not the issue. Rather, he had to choose to eliminate the job of a person whose contributions to the company were very positive. Simmons argued to the company president on the merits of keeping both managers. His arguments were to no avail because the issue was to reduce expenses, and all departments had to suffer the loss of good employees. Simmons felt this was one of the toughest calls he ever had to make, and no matter which way it went, the decision would speak loudly about what type of employee Savannah Mills valued the most.

Questions

1. Recall the concept of the psychological contract. What aspects of the contract are at issue in this case?
2. If Davis's position is eliminated, what message will that send to the other employees at Savannah Mills?

3. If Steele's position is eliminated, what message will that send to the other employees at Savannah Mills?
4. Recall the concept of organizational citizenship behavior. To what degree does this concept influence your thoughts about a just decision in this case?
5. If you were Simmons, whose position would you eliminate, and why?

Chapter Summary

- Individuals in an organizational context develop attitudes and exhibit behaviors associated with their participation in the organization.
- Job satisfaction is one of the most frequently studied organizational attitudes. How much people like their jobs is associated with both their individual personalities and the objective characteristics of the work they perform.
- The concept of organizational justice explains why employees want a sense of fairness associated with their employment. Organizational justice manifests itself in three forms: distributive, procedural, and interactional.
- The actions of employees in going beyond their formal job duties and responsibilities to contribute to the welfare of the organization are called organizational citizenship behaviors.
- The psychological contract is the exchange relationship between the individual and the organization. Although unwritten, it is based on the expectations each party has of itself and of the other party.
- Violations of the psychological contract (i.e., when one party has not lived up to the expectations of the other) result in a wide range of behaviors that often distance the two parties in the relationship.
- Organizational actions pertaining to downsizing have been found to produce strong reactions among employees affected by such actions.
- Antisocial behavior in the workplace includes insults, threats, lies, theft, sabotage, physical violence, and occupational homicide.
- Occupational homicide, the most severe form of antisocial behavior, results in nearly 1,000 murders of workers in the United States every year.

The Origins of Occupational Health

It will be recalled from Chapter 1 that early in the 20th century the principles of scientific management determined how work was performed. Work was broken down into specific discrete tasks. Performing one task (like attaching a nut to a bolt) might be an entire job for a worker. By using many workers in sequence, each one performing a task, an organization made a complete product. Such production methods were efficient, training time was minimal, little skill was required, and a departed worker could easily be replaced. Scientific management principles intentionally tried to separate "thinking" from "doing" on the part of the worker. No consideration was given to employee emotions at work because it was assumed that emotions interfered with productive work. Designing work that involved repetitive actions, perhaps performing the same task once every ten seconds, led to mind-numbing boredom and fatigue. However, in the early years of the 20th century, that was the price a worker paid for having a production job. This model of work persisted for much of the century.

Over time the workforce became more educated. Having a high school diploma, which was relatively rare in the early 1900s, became a traditional standard of educational achievement by mid-century. Proportionately fewer workers were willing to accept jobs that were so divorced from the human component. By the 1930s a topic began to emerge (commonly referred to as "mental hygiene") that addressed the affective and emotional issues associated with work. The profession of counseling psychology recognized that many life-related adjustment problems had some connection to people's worklives. Nevertheless, there was still a wide gap between industrial psychology (which was concerned primarily with work productivity issues) and counseling psychology (which was concerned with adjustment and health-related issues). By the mid-20th century the discipline of **occupational health** began to crystallize, with its focus on improving the health and well-being of people in relation to their conditions of their employment.

Occupational health
A broad-based concept that refers to the mental, emotional, and physical well-being of employees in relation to the conduct of their work.

The acceptability and legitimacy of occupational health to I/O psychologists were facilitated by the publication of a book in 1965 by Arthur Kornhauser entitled *Mental Health of the Industrial Worker*. Kornhauser (an I/O psychologist) interviewed 400 Detroit auto workers about their work (which was still performed under the principles of scientific management). Zickar (2003) credited the emergence of the field of occupational health psychology to Kornhauser's landmark book. Since that time the field has begun investigating questions related to occupational health and to work/family conflict. According to Zickar, Kornhauser's research helped pave the way for other I/O psychologists interested in worker well-being. As Barling and Griffiths (2003) noted, by the end of the 20th century occupational health psychology was embracing the very opposite beliefs to those proposed by scientific management at the start of the 20th century. In short, it took approximately one hundred years to reach the conclusion that a productive workforce depends on (and thus is not independent of) the health of the workforce. In Chapter 1 the major fields of interest to I/O psychology were presented. Occupational health is directed toward one of those fields, the quality of worklife.

Because work is a defining characteristic of many people's lives, it is recognized that individuals should have a safe and healthy work environment. Tetrick and Quick (2003) stated, "The purpose of occupational health psychology is to develop, maintain, and promote the health of employees directly and the health of their families. The primary focus of occupational health psychology is the prevention of illness or injury by creating safe and healthy working environments" (p. 4). Perhaps the most pressing health-related issue in the workplace today is stress. Levi (2003) reported that work-related stress is endemic to all industrialized nations. Levi found that more than half of the 160 million workers in the European Union report working at a high speed and under tight deadlines. Hart and Cooper (2001) believe that if efforts to reduce occupational stress are going to be successful, they cannot be portrayed as being primarily concerned with general health issues. Although no one will argue against health, business organizations are principally designed to be profitable. Therefore the big issue is to demonstrate the link between organizational profitability and worker health. It thus might be more useful to think of "organizational health" rather than "occupational health." As Hart and Cooper explained:

> A fundamental requirement for most organizations that wish to improve their "bottom line," however, is the need to develop appropriate structures and processes that will reduce occupational stress and, at the same time, enhance employee satisfaction and performance. From this viewpoint, the organizational health perspective recognizes the fact that having happy and satisfied employees is of little value to an organization unless employees are also performing efficiently and productively. Likewise, having an efficient and productive organization is of little value if this is achieved at the expense of employee well-being. (p. 99)

Sigmund Freud was once asked what he thought a "normal" person should be able to do well. He is reported to have said "Lieben und Arbeiten" ("to love and to work"; Erickson, 1963, p. 265). Freud believed that it is through one's family that love-related needs are gratified and that work has a more powerful effect than any other aspect of human life in binding a person to reality. Therefore Freud's call for a normal person to love and to work can be interpreted as an emphasis on both work and family for healthy psychological functioning (Quick et al., 1992). Work and the role it plays in our lives have been a subject of interest and controversy down through recorded history (see Field Note 1). Opinions about work are highly varied, as reflected in the following three quotations:

- "Work consists of whatever a body is obligated to do. Play consists of whatever a body is not obligated to do."—Mark Twain
- "The world is full of willing people; some willing to work, the rest willing to let them."—Robert Frost
- "The first sign of a nervous breakdown is when you start thinking your work is terribly important."—Milo Bloom

A person's work and occupational stature play a critical role in an individual's sense of identity, self-esteem, and psychological well-being. Work is the central and defining characteristic of life for most individuals. Work may have intrinsic value, instrumental value, or both. The intrinsic value of work is the value an individual finds in performing the work, in and of itself. The instrumental value of work is in providing the necessities of life and serving as a channel for the individual's talents, abilities, and knowledge. It has been suggested that the split in a person's work and home identities dates back to the Industrial Revolution of the mid 19th century. It was then that it became necessary for a person to leave the home and "go to work."

Field Note 1: The Meaning of Work

Why do people work? This seemingly simple question has been debated for centuries from many perspectives, including religion, economics, psychology, and philosophy. Some religious doctrine teaches that work is a form of punishment for our original sin. Work is an obligation or duty toward building God's kingdom. Work is thus good, and hard work even better. Work is noble because of its taxing nature and because it is a hardship that strengthens our character. Religious teachings also emphasized work as a means of controlling and restraining our passions. Lack of work, or idleness, fosters unhealthy impulses, which deflect us from more admirable pursuits. Thus work is thought of as an arduous process, deliberately filled with hardships, a means of facilitating our personal development. The view from an economic perspective is that work provides us with the financial resources to sustain life and the aspiration to improve the quality of our material life. The most commonly accepted definition of *work*—the exchange of labor services for pay—clearly reflects an economic viewpoint. Work has psychological meaning as well, giving us a source of identity and union with other individuals, in addition to being a source of personal accomplishment. Work also has the effect of providing a temporal rhythm to our lives. Our work gives us our time structure—when we have to leave for work and when we are off work to pursue other activities. Finally, work even provides a philosophical explanation of our mission in life: to derive meaning from creating and giving service to others. As can be inferred, there is no one answer to the question of why we work, but its multiple meanings provide a basis to understand why work is so important.

Positive psychology
The study of the factors and conditions in life that lead to pleasurable and satisfying outcomes for individuals.

Recently there has been a call among psychologists to address what is called **positive psychology**. According to Seligman and Csikszentmihalyi (2000), for the past 60 years psychology has become a science largely about healing. They proposed that psychologists should come to understand what makes life worth living, not just how to cope with and heal from negative life events. Wright and Cropanzano (2007) stated that psychological research manifests a decided emphasis on the negative aspects of human behavior, often to the neglect of positive aspects. In support of their position, they cited a recent computer search of contemporary literature on psychology. Over 375,000 articles were found on negative concepts such as mental illness, fear, and anger, but only about 1,000 articles on positive concepts as hope, flourishing, and enthusiasm. By any reasonable standard, a ratio of 375/1 indicates a strong imbalance in our relative interest in negative and positive psychology. Diener (2000) believes that society is caught up with materialism, yet the acquisition of material goods is only mildly related to how happy we feel in life. Diener recommended that nations should measure and monitor how frequently and intensely people feel satisfied and happy in various life circumstances and across situations. As long as national indicators focus on the production of goods and services (like the Gross National Product—GNP), it is those factors that national leaders are likely to consider. If a national indicator of well-being were available, policies could be judged by how they influence happiness. Csikszentmihalyi (1999) posed the question, "If we are so rich, why aren't we happy?" It is because material rewards alone are not sufficient to make us happy. Other conditions, such as a satisfying family life, intimate friends, and time to reflect and pursue diverse interests, have been shown to be related to happiness. In theory, there is no reason these two sets of rewards—the material and the socioemotional—should be mutually exclusive. Lyubomirsky, King, and Diener (2005) concluded that happy people are successful across multiple life domains, including marriage, friendship, income, work performance, and health. The authors proposed that positive affect, the hallmark of well-being, may be the underlying cause of many of the desirable human qualities and experiences associated with happiness. In practice, however, it is very difficult to reconcile their conflicting demands. Time is the ultimate scarce resource, and the allocation of time presents difficult choices that eventually determine the content and quality of our lives. Csikszentmihalyi stated, "This is why professional and business persons find it so difficult to balance the demands of work and family, and why they so rarely feel that they have not shortchanged one of these vital aspects of their lives" (p. 823). As will be seen in this chapter, the fundamental need to balance work and nonwork activities in life often produces stress in people, and the means of striving for balance between the two is often at the core of issues pertaining to occupational health.

Environmental Influences on Mental Health

Warr (2007b) proposed that a sense of well-being from work must first be understood in terms of the general environmental determinants of mental health. Warr identified nine of these determinants that can be viewed as the bases for psychological well-being.

1. *Opportunity for control.* The first determinant of mental health is an environment in which people are in control of the major events or activities in their lives. Personal control over one's life is associated with better mental health. Warr asserted that control has two dimensions. The first pertains to the opportunity to choose your own behavior; to conduct yourself as you wish. The second dimension relates to understanding the relationship between your behavior and the consequences that follow from it. The inability to control the outcome of one's chosen behavior defeats the purpose of engaging in the behavior in the first place. Theorell (2003) reported that the combination of small decision latitude and a high level of psychological demands produces a large risk for mental illness.

2. *Opportunity for skill use.* A second feature is the capacity of the environment to facilitate or retard skill use. The inability to use one's skills may be due to two reasons. One reason pertains to a lack of opportunity to use the skills a person has already developed, while the second is the lack of opportunity to develop new skills. This latter condition compels the individual to rely on a diminished skill set, with the associated negative consequences to the person.

3. *Externally generated goals.* An environment that provides the opportunity to create challenges and goals for the individual is the third dimension. The opportunity to set goals and channel behavior in pursuit of these goals enhances

mental health. An environment that offers no challenges provides no stimulation. The lack of stimulation promotes apathy, which in turn diminishes striving for achievement. The mere pursuit of goals, quite apart from their full attainment, is conducive to mental health.

4. *Environmental variety.* This dimension refers to the benefits associated with an environment that provides choices and options. An environment that lacks variety leads to a corresponding reduction in the array of skills needed to function in it. Highly repetitive activity produces monotony and poorer mental health.

5. *Environmental clarity.* The fifth dimension associated with mental health is the degree to which it is clear what the environment demands of the individual. Clarity is provided in two ways. First, there are unambiguous rules and standards for acceptable behavior. Second, the individual receives accurate feedback regarding the appropriateness of the exhibited behaviors.

6. *Availability of money.* The presence of money does not ensure mental health, but the absence of money (poverty) increases the likelihood of mental, physical, and emotional impairment. A lack of money impairs mental health by decreasing the amount of control and the number of choices a person has when making life decisions.

7. *Physical security.* It is difficult, if not impossible, to be mentally healthy if your physical security is in jeopardy. The environment must provide a continuous sense of assurance that the basics of life (freedom from harm, sleeping, and eating) are secure. The absence of this security threatens the foundation of mental health.

8. *Opportunity for interpersonal contact.* A mentally healthy person is one who experiences positive relationships with other people, for both social and emotional fulfillment. An environment that precludes such interpersonal contact, in effect placing the person in social isolation, can greatly harm mental health. The isolated individual is compelled to complete tasks alone that could more efficiently be performed by several people working together. The individual must likewise live without the advice and suggestions provided by others.

9. *Valued social position.* The ninth environmental determinant of mental health is a position in society that is held in high esteem. People derive self-esteem from the value placed on the contributions they make to society. Holding a job provides a sense of social purpose to one's life. Conversely, the loss of employment can be associated with poorer mental health among individuals who feel diminished in such a role.

Warr recognized some overlap among these nine dimensions but thought that a recognition of each was necessary to understand how environments affect mental health. The importance of these nine dimensions to mental health can be seen by looking at their pronounced absence. People who are convicted of crimes may be sentenced to lengthy prison terms. One ostensible purpose of their incarceration is to rehabilitate them. The environment experienced in prison life provides few (if any) of these nine determinants of mental health, however. Thus many individuals are not in good mental health when they are released from prison. This poor mental health is posited to be a cause of *recidivism*, which is the pattern of ex-convicts committing new crimes and being sentenced to additional prison terms. The environment provided by a prison can achieve the opposite effect of rehabilitation by adversely affecting the mental health of the inmates.

The Concept of Mental Health

Although the nine environmental factors that contribute to mental health have been examined, the concept itself has not yet been defined. This is in part because no single definition exists; it is easier to understand the meaning of mental health by referencing its determinants. Societal standards contribute to the meaning of mental health (with many derived from contemporary Western society) as well as standards proposed by the medical profession regarding mental illness. We will not explore the varied contributions of these sources in conceptualizing mental health. Rather, we will take an overall view of mental health as proposed by Warr (2007b) and focus on its five major components.

1. *Affective well-being*. Warr (2007b) stipulated that affective well-being has two dimensions: pleasure and arousal. It is thus possible for a level of pleasure to be associated with lethargy (low arousal) or excitement (high arousal). Likewise, arousal can be associated with feelings ranging from pleasurable to unpleasurable. Figure 11-1 portrays this two-dimensional model of affective well-being. A feeling of well-being derives from both dimensions. For example, the lower left section of Figure 11-1 reveals terms such as *sad* and *gloomy*, reflecting both low pleasure and low arousal. The highest levels of affective well-being are presented in the upper right section of the figure. Terms such as *full of energy* and *delighted* indicate both high pleasure and high arousal. In general, a person's affective well-being can be described in terms of the proportion of time spent in each of the four sections of Figure 11-1. Warr noted the word *happiness* is typically avoided by psychologists in their professional lives. Instead, terms like *well-being* or *positive affect* are typically used. Warr believes that happiness would be a more useful explanatory construct. "People are fascinated by the presence or absence of happiness, recognizing a strong personal relevance and wishing better to understand the experience" (p. 17). Warr cited a study that surveyed college students in 47 countries. Of all personal values; including wealth, health, and love, happiness was overwhelmingly rated the most important. Accordingly, Warr asserted that research on people in work organizations would have greater impact on a wider population if it were presented in terms of happiness or unhappiness, rather than the more technical terms frequently used by scientists.

2. *Competence*. Good mental health is evidenced by being successful in various sectors of life's activities, such as relationships with others, gainful employment, and adaptability. The competent person has adequate psychological resources to deal with life's problems. It has been suggested that dealing with adversity in life provides a strong test of one's mental health. A successful response to adversity requires a mixture of adaptive skills as well as beliefs and opinions that are consistent with reality.

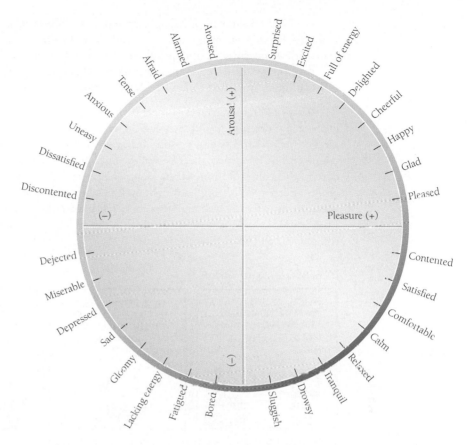

Figure 11-1 *Two-dimensional model of subjective well-being*

Source: From *Work, Happiness, and Unhappiness*, by P. Warr, 2007, Erlbaum.

3. *Autonomy.* Autonomy is the freedom to choose the path of one's own behavior. Mentally healthy people have the capacity to express their values and preferences when choosing their actions. This contrasts sharply with the feeling of being helpless when one is confronted with life's difficulties. The contribution of autonomy to mental health appears to be given greater importance in Western than in Eastern cultures.

4. *Aspiration.* A mentally healthy person is always striving to achieve a more desirable outcome. It is this sense of striving, being focused, and having a strong goal orientation that invigorates people to channel their energies. In striving to achieve personal goals, one may face stressful situations, and indeed one may create them by pursuing difficult challenges. Low levels of aspiration are associated with a sense of resignation and acceptance of one's current conditions, no matter how unsatisfying they may be.

5. *Integrated functioning.* The capstone dimension of mental health is the most difficult to define and is most unlike the other four. Warr stated, "Integrated functioning concerns the person as a whole. People who are mentally healthy

exhibit several forms of balance, harmony, and inner relatedness" (p. 59). Consider Freud's statement about love and work. Integrated functioning is the hallmark of mentally healthy people in that they have found a way to balance the two. Integrated functioning is the most difficult goal to achieve as our lives are continuously pushed and pulled in competing directions.

Warr's (2007b) portrayal of mental health represents a comprehensive assessment of the major dimensions of psychological well-being. Competence, autonomy, and aspiration reflect aspects of a person's behavior in relation to the environment and often determine a person's affective well-being. For example, an inability to cope with current difficulties (a form of low competence) may give rise to distress (an aspect of low affective well-being). Affective well-being has its roots in medical criteria; the person reports feeling well and also not being impaired psychologically or physically. Integrated functioning, however, deals with the multiple relationships among the four components and covers broader issues.

DILBERT   by Scott Adams

Dilbert: © Scott Adams/Dist. by United Features Syndicate, Inc. Reprinted with permission.

Work/Family Conflict

Work/family conflict
The dilemma of trying to balance the conflicting demands of work and family responsibilities.

Work/family conflict is the dilemma of trying to balance the conflicting demands of work and family responsibilities. As Thomas and Ganster (1995) described, over the past three decades the American family has undergone significant structural and functional changes. These changes have not been accompanied by equally dramatic shifts in organizational policies. Although there are fewer families in which the father works outside the home while the mother stays home to care for the house and the children, many companies continue to be guided by traditional workplace policies that were fashioned when that was the predominant pattern. Today's diverse workplace is increasingly populated with women, single parents, and dual-career couples. The potential for conflict and stress increases as most workers struggle with the demands of balancing paid employment and home responsibilities.

Jones, Burke, and Westrum (2006) noted that people typically put more time, energy, and commitment into work than other areas of life. We often measure ourselves by our work-related achievements. Our dedication to work affords us an opportunity to avoid emotional intimacy with others, which can serve to balance out the demands of work. As such, the difficulties of trying to balance work and family can be avoided rather than solved or accepted. Workplaces are governed by rules and institutionalized procedures that provide mechanisms for control. Family life can be far more unstructured and thus less controllable, thus enhancing the appeal of the workplace. "While ultimately less fulfilling and likely to lead to long-term problems, colluding with the pressure to dedicate all one's time and energy to work may often seem the easiest option" (Jones et al., p. 292). Easiest perhaps, but not the best, as illustrated by the following quote of uncertain origin: "Nobody on his or her deathbed ever said, 'I wish I had spent more time at the office'."

Interest in family-related issues by I/O psychologists has manifested itself primarily in the past 30 years. For many years we tended to limit our focus to work-related issues (e.g., tasks, jobs, occupations, organizations) and left the subject of domestic matters (e.g., family) to other areas of professional study. However, I/O psychologists began to see legitimate linkages or connections between the two spheres of work and family and thus have expanded our areas of inquiry. Spector et al. (2004) conducted a major cross-cultural study of work/family conduct among managers. The research was done in three culturally distinct regions of the world: Anglo (Australia, Canada, England, New Zealand, and the United States); China (Hong Kong, People's Republic of China, and Taiwan); and Latin America (seven countries). The average numbers of hours worked per week by managers in the three cultures were similar: 49 (Anglo), 47 (China), and 50 (Latin America). However, Spector et al. found a stronger relationship between number of hours worked and work/family pressures in individualistic regions (Anglo) than in collectivist regions (China and Latin America). Anglos may view working extra hours as taking away from their families, which may create feelings of guilt and more work/family conflict. The researchers proposed that the economies in the Anglo countries tend to be stronger than those in China and Latin America, resulting in higher average household incomes. Therefore working longer hours in the Anglo world may appear to be less necessary for family survival. Where making a living is more difficult, family members may be more accepting of longer work hours. There may also be greater extended family support for child care in collectivist countries, so it would be easier for families to manage with one or even both parents working long hours.

Zedeck (1992) described the following three topics as targets of research in work/family conflict.

- *The effect of work on family.* This area examines what impact work factors have on family matters. To express this relationship in terms of research design, *work* is regarded as the independent variable and *family* is the dependent variable. This perspective is most typical of I/O psychological research. For example, Major, Klein, and Ehrhart (2002) found that the hours spent at work predicted interference with family life, which in turn predicted psychological distress (see The Changing Nature of Work: Occupational Health and National Policy, p. 356).

- *The effect of family on work.* This perspective is the opposite of the former and generally focuses on how structural or developmental aspects of the family have an impact on work behavior. For example, some researchers have viewed family life as a "shock absorber": if home life is positive, it blocks disappointment at work. Others view family responsibility as a major determinant of work absenteeism and tardiness.

- *The family–work interaction.* This third perspective views work and family as interacting and concludes that there is no simple or direct causal link between work and

The Changing Nature of Work: Occupational Health and National Policy

One standard for judging the impact of scientific research is the degree to which it affects policy making; that is, to what degree are changes in federal laws attributable to a body of scientific research conducted on a topic? A vast amount of research has been conducted on work stress, occupational health, and well-being in employment. In the United States, the changes in response to this research have been primarily at the organizational level. For example, employee assistance programs were created to help with problems such as alcoholism. However, very few national policies in the United States have flowed from occupational health research. One exception is the Family and Medical Leave Act, which was enacted to help abate work/family conflict.

However, in the European Union the entire matter of worker well-being has risen to become a significant political issue. Article 152 of the European Treaty of Amsterdam states that "a high level of human health protection shall be ensured in the definition and implementation of all Community policies and activities" (Levi, 2003, p. *x*). Thus some programs can be created to treat the effects of stress, while other initiatives are to be directed at changing the conditions that produce stress in the first place. As a matter of national policy, workers in some European countries get six weeks of paid vacation per year. In the United States, two weeks is more common. Many European countries have liberal policies on absence days, believing that an occasional day off can be therapeutic for the worker. There are even policies that deter employees from never being absent—the opposite of a "perfect attendance" policy. The length of a workweek also varies across nations. While the standard workweek in the United States is 40 hours, it is 36 hours in many European countries. There is no evidence that work in Europe is less stressful than in the United States, but many European nations have enacted laws that allow their workers more time to deal with the consequences of work-related stress. It is unknown whether the United States will change its policies to give workers more time away from work.

family matters. One view of the family–work interaction concerns the compatibility or incompatibility of family–work relationships and their impact on other processes, such as the transition between roles.

Regardless of which of these three perspectives is emphasized, researchers have offered conceptual models to explain the relationship between work and family. Three basic types of models have been proposed, and they represent different perspectives on how we fill both work and family roles.

- *Spillover model.* The spillover model asserts that there is similarity between what occurs in the work environment and what occurs in the family environment. It also proposes that a person's work experiences influence what he or she does away from work. It is assumed that attitudes at work become ingrained and carried over into home life, affecting a basic orientation toward the self and family members. In general, spillover is a notion of positive relationships between work and family variables such that an individual's satisfaction with work enhances family life.

- *Compensation model.* The compensation model is most often contrasted with the spillover model. It proposes an *inverse* relationship between work and family. It further assumes that individuals make differential investments of themselves in the two settings so that what is provided by one makes up for what is missing in the other. Thus deprivations experienced in work are made up or compensated for in nonwork activities.

- *Segmentation model.* The segmentation model proposes that the work and nonwork spheres are distinct so that an individual can be successful in one without any influence on the other. The two spheres exist side by side and for all practical purposes are separated. This separation, in type, space, or function, allows one to effectively compartmentalize one's life. The dominant view is that the family is the realm of intimacy and empathy, whereas the work world is impersonal and instrumental.

Barling (1990) observed a historical trend in when each of these three models was proposed. Barling concluded: (1) the suggestion that work and family affect each other had emerged by the 1930s; (2) the pervasive assumption during the 1950s was that work and family were independent; (3) by the 1970s the assumption was that work and family roles were intertwined; and (4) today there is considerable empirical evidence attesting to the overlap between work and family for most individuals.

MacDermid, Seery, and Weiss (2002) noted that psychologists tend to study enduring characteristics of people (such as cognitive ability and personality) when it may be short-term phenomena that best explain feelings of work/family conflict. They noted: "[A]lthough we cognitively recognize the presence of conflict most of the time, we feel it only some of the time" (pp. 402–403). MacDermid et al. believe that a better understanding of our emotions may help explain the causes of work/family conflict because the transfer of emotions (e.g., anger) across situations tends to occur over very short intervals, such as a few hours or days.

Zedeck (1992) believes that reactions to work and nonwork are not totally stable but vary over time and conditions. Furthermore, the relationship is not the same across families. Friedman et al. (1996) offered this description of how the effects of domestic violence do not stay at home: "The battered woman who receives threatening calls or visits by her abuser at work, or who is suffering from the mental and physical bruises of the night before, is likely to have difficulty fulfilling her employer's expectations" (p. 153). There also appear to be meaningful differences between men and women in the effect of work/family conflict on job and life satisfaction. Kossek and Ozeki (1998) reported a stronger correlation between work/family conflict and job satisfaction for women (.35) than for men (.29). Likewise, the correlation between work/family conflict and life satisfaction was stronger for women (.42) than for men (.32). Thus women have a greater association than men between resolving work/family conflict and feeling satisfaction. Ford, Heinen, and Langkamer (2007) concluded that families with children experienced a stronger negative relationship between hours of work per week and family satisfaction. Employees without children were better able to sustain a satisfactory family life despite long work hours. Finally, based on a broad national survey of employees, Frone (2000) reported that employees who reported experiencing work/family conflict were up to 30 times more likely to experience a clinically significant mental health problem than were employees who reported no work/family conflict.

Friedman and Galinsky (1992) noted some of the major changes in the labor force and how organizational efforts have had to change in order to recruit and retain a productive workforce. By 2000 about two-thirds of the new entrants into the workforce were women, and about three-fourths of them became pregnant at some point during their working years. More than half of these women returned to work before their child's first birthday. An estimated 20% of workers—mostly women—will be responsible for their aging parents. Although women still perform most family tasks, 60% of men have wives who work. Casper et al. (2007) concluded that most of our knowledge about work/family conflict is based upon the traditional concept of a family, and employees working in managerial and professional jobs. We know far less about single-parent families and members of other types of occupations.

The pressures of work and family are accelerating, and families, which already have borne the greater burden of conflicts experienced between home and work, can do little more to achieve a balance. Baltes and Heydens-Gahir (2003) reported that additional skills besides time management (making "to do" lists and "trying harder") are needed to reduce work/family conflict. Changes in the social pattern of worker participation have forced companies to make accommodations to their workers. These accommodations are directed toward reducing the conflict between work and family, which if ignored, ultimately lead to lower efficiency in the workplace. Such inefficiency is reflected in more tardiness, absenteeism, turnover, and stress-related reductions in job performance. Frone (2003) cited flexible work hours, compressed workweeks, working at home, and leaves of absence as examples of organizational initiatives to reduce work/family conflict (see Field Note 2).

On-site or near-site child-care centers have been developed to reduce work/family conflict. Companies may develop such centers exclusively for their own employees or in a consortium with other employees for use by several participating companies. Approximately 1,400 on-site or near-site child-care centers are sponsored by employers in

Field Note 2: Artificial Energy

An adage from clinical psychology is, "Some disorders are best detected by their disguise." A parallel statement from I/O psychology might be, "Some work-related problems are best detected by our attempts to address them." In the on-going battle to fulfill the demands on our time, including trying to balance work/family conflict, one of the resources we sacrifice is sleep time. While individuals differ in the amount of sleep needed to feel rested and rejuvenated, the average is about 8 hours. The time needed to complete all our self-imposed duties often requires a sacrifice of something else, and often what is sacrificed is the seemingly unproductive time we devote to sleep. So we "cheat", trading an hour or two of sleep for another hour or two for performing work or personal tasks. What is the consequence? We are often sleepy, fatigued, and inattentive. Recognizing this widespread condition, many artificial stimulant products have been created to combat chronic tiredness. These products include highly caffeinated beverages that are touted to "provide energy" or "boost stamina". Products designed to achieve the same effect also are marketed in the form of food or over-the-counter medications. It is questionable what the consumer demand would be for these products if we felt less sleep-deprived. In short, tampering with the normal rhythm of our lives produces unwanted side effects. Many of the currently available products used to address these side effects were not commercially available one generation ago.

the United States. Although their number is growing, many companies are too small to have the resources to provide such a center. Spector et al. (2007) reported findings of particular relevance to global organizations. The creation of flexible working hours and organization-based child care were created in response to lowering work/family conflict. However, these interventions were based upon the needs of employees in predominately Western cultures. The authors found that in Asian, Eastern European, and Latin American countries, parents of employees often live in close proximity to their children and grand-children. This older generation is a resource not as readily available to employees in Western cultures. Accordingly, there would be less of a need for organizations to provide means of reducing work/family conflict in these parts of the world.

Another type of assistance to employees is family leave. In 1993 President William Jefferson Clinton signed into law the Family and Medical Leave Act, whereby employees can withdraw from the workforce to attend to family needs without risking the loss of their jobs. The law gives workers up to 12 weeks of unpaid leave each year for the birth, adoption, or foster care of a child; care for a spouse, parent, or child with a serious health condition; or the employee's own serious health condition. The law is designed to be of particular value to parents of newborn children. Research has shown that the single most important predictor of job retention following childbirth is the availability of job-guaranteed maternity leave. One company with an excellent leave policy found that only 5% of new mothers did not return to their jobs. Grover and Crooker (1995) reported from a national survey of workers that in organizations offering family-responsive human resource policies such as child-care assistance, employees showed significantly higher organizational commitment and expressed less intention to quit their jobs. The same findings were evidenced for employees without children, which the authors interpreted as supporting the theory that offering assistance to employees in need symbolizes concern for employees and positively influences attachment to the organization.

Major and Germano (2006) commented on the relationship between an ever-changing workworld and the unchanging responsibility to achieve balance between our work and family lives. "It is rather ironic that in this discussion of the changing nature of work the one thing that has not changed is the notion that work-family behavior is the employee's problem to solve. Until social and political movements aimed at reducing work hours and protecting personal time gain momentum, it is up to individual employees to be their own best advocates in pursuing accomodations that create a desirable work-family interface" (p. 32).

Dual-Career Families

Dual-career family
A family in which both adults have their own individual careers and try to balance their respective careers.

Balancing the demands of work and family can be an arduous task. Issues of adjustment are further compounded in **dual-career families**. It is estimated that mothers with young children work an average of 77 hours per week in the home. Adding a career to that workload can create extraordinary pressures on both women and men seeking to have fulfilling work and home lives.

Silberstein (1992) concluded that most dual-career couples have a work-oriented lifestyle prior to the birth of children. Once there are children, however, the dual-career system undergoes a profound shift. The pragmatic demands of home life increase dramatically and cannot be postponed, rescheduled, or ignored. Both men and women attest that the arrival of children creates the greatest conflict between work and family.

For the majority of both men and women, having children translates into fewer hours at work. However, the extent to which this occurred and the meanings of this shift differed for men and women. Karambayya and Reilly (1992), for example, reported that more women than men accommodated their careers to fit their families. The felt need to make an accommodation influenced the women's choice of a career (e.g., assuring a flexible schedule) or a work site. Many women reported that their work environments were not willing or able to bend to the demands of family. Additionally, some women have described hostile reactions from work colleagues to pregnancies.

Men, on the other hand, tend to differentiate their feelings of conflict over family and career from their wives' feelings. This difference between husbands and wives stems from expectations in men that work is primarily for men and family is primarily for women. Silberstein (1992) offered the following statement from a man in his mid-30s:

> I have the suspicion that it's more difficult for a woman. If you're a traditional, career-oriented man, you're supposed to spend a lot of time in the office, and bring work home, and commute long distances. And the man has less time for the family, which is not a good thing, but that's how it is traditionally. Whereas for a woman, there's always the other side of the mirror, which is the woman who is at home, spending hours and hours with her children, and is always there when they need her. And that imposes some degree of guilt on a woman who is successful in her career. (p. 100)

Silberstein (1992) reported that the difference in the degree that wives and husbands accommodate their careers for children has become a central marital tension. Differential investment in career and family is the recurrent issue in arguments, and it demands constant renegotiation. In the dual-career marriage, both spouses arrive at their own definition of what is required for work success and what level of involvement in the family feels right. Each partner therefore argues from personal experience about the appropriate balance of work and family, whereas in the one-career marriage, the spheres of wife and husband are less comparable.

Dual-career couples often cite a lack of temporal control over their lives. There appears to be insufficient time to fulfill the obligations of both work and family. The creation of time schedules to coordinate activities can be helpful, but adherence to the schedules can be a source of tension in itself. Other time-related issues pertain to the lack of personal time for individual activity (such as exercise or leisure) and coordinated social activities. Time constraints are also associated with reformulating role activities in the marriage, such as the division of domestic labor. The lack of time contributes to a couple's decision to seek external support services such as child care and assistance with household chores.

In examining the benefits and costs of dual-career marriages, Silberstein (1992) reported that most marriages are aided by the self-fulfillment each spouse derives from the pursuit of a career. Each spouse experiences an independent source of self-esteem, and they benefit as a couple from the combined stimulation of each partner's worklife. Both partners are also likely to feel that each is contributing in a similar fashion to the welfare of the marriage. However, the costs of dual careers are also considerable, with most sacrifices associated with losses of time and energy. In particular, dual-career couples are likely to save the least amount of time and energy for their own personal relationship, after attending to the demands of work, children, and the managerial aspects of domestic life. This sentiment was expressed by a woman in her early 40s:

"I hesitate to use the analogy, but right now I feel we are more business partners than husband and wife. It's like we operate this small corporation together, but the intimate aspect is somewhat lacking." (Silberstein, 1992, p. 147)

Stress from work can also originate from the schedules we must follow on our jobs. The next section will examine what I/O psychologists have learned about how work schedules influence our attitudes and behaviors.

Work Schedules

Shift Work

Not all employees work from 8:00 A.M. to 5:00 P.M., Monday through Friday. The nature of the services performed may necessitate other schedules. Police officers, firefighters, and telephone operators provide 24-hour-a-day service. In industrial manufacturing, some technology requires constant monitoring and operation. It isn't practical to shut off furnaces, boilers, and chemical process operations at 5:00 P.M. just because workers go home. In those cases it is advantageous to have different shifts work around the clock. About 20% of all working hours in the United States are estimated to be "nontraditional." Psychologists have become interested in how different hours (or **shift work**) affect occupational health.

Shift work
A non-traditional work pattern in which an operation functions 24 hours per day. Typical employee shifts are 7:00 A.M. to 3:00 P.M., 3:00 P.M. to 11:00 P.M., and 11:00 P.M. to 7:00 A.M.

There are no uniform shift-work hours; companies use different shifts. Usually a 24-hour day is divided into three 8-hour work shifts, like 7:00 A.M.–3:00 P.M. (day shift), 3:00 P.M.–11:00 P.M. (swing or afternoon shift), and 11:00 P.M.–7:00 A.M. (night shift). Some companies have employees work just one shift, but workers generally don't like the swing and night shifts, so many firms rotate the shifts. Employees may work two weeks on the day shift, two weeks on the swing shift, and then two weeks on the night shift. A shift workweek need not be Monday through Friday. Also, there may be an uneven number of days off between shifts, like two days off after the swing shift and three after the night shift.

Shift workers experience many problems in physiological and social adjustment. Most physiological problems are associated with interruptions of the circadian rhythm. Smith, Folkard, and Fuller (2003) explained that the circadian rhythm has an evolutionary basis:

> Life on earth has evolved in an environment subject to regular and pronounced changes produced by planetary movements. The rotation of the earth on its own axis results in the 24-hour light/dark cycle, whereas its rotation around the sun gives rise to seasonal changes in light and temperature. During the process of evolution, these periodic changes have become internalized, and it is now widely accepted that living organisms possess a "body clock," such that organisms do not merely respond to environmental changes but actively anticipate them. (p. 164)

Because most people work during the day and sleep at night, shift workers also have social problems. They often experience difficulties with children, marital relationships, and recreation. The World Health Organization (2007) concluded that working the night shift is a cause of cancer. It is estimated that 20% of the workers in the Western world work non-traditional hours. Our bodies respond to light and dark cycles through production of melatonin, a hormone that regulates sleep cycles and bolsters the immune system. Artificial light cannot make up for the qualities of natural light, nor can sleeping during the day make up for the darkness of night time sleep. Frost and Jamal (1979) reported that shift workers experienced less need fulfillment, were more likely to quit their jobs, and participated in fewer voluntary organizations. Jamal (1981) reported similar findings: workers on fixed work schedules were better off than workers on rotating schedules in terms of mental health, job satisfaction, and social participation. Smith et al. (2003) found that divorces and separations were 50% more frequent in night-shift workers than in any other group of workers.

Shift workers make up a relatively small proportion of the population; they are thus forced to fit their schedules to the rest of society. Ironically, some have suggested that many social problems would be alleviated by *increasing* shift work. Society would then make more concessions to the needs of shift workers. Changes might be made in such things as restaurant service, recreational services, and hours of business operation (banks, supermarkets, gas stations, and the like). In fact, convenience food stores and automated bank machines derive much of their business from employees who work nontraditional hours.

Research indicates that shift work has a strong influence on the lives of people who perform it. As long as certain industries require 24-hour-a-day operations, psychologists will continue searching for ways to improve this particularly difficult person/environment fit. Social problems may be lessened by changing some existing patterns in the community; however, physiological problems will be more difficult to overcome. Monk, Folkard, and Wedderburn (1996) noted that shift workers must face three enduring conditions of *biochronology*: (1) human beings and society are diurnal (awake in the day, asleep in the night), (2) daylight has a cueing effect to initiate wakefulness, and (3) the circadian system is slow to adjust to night work. Any organizational or social policy designed to assist shift workers must address these conditions.

At least one major source of physiological difficulty is the rotation of workers across shifts. If workers were assigned to a fixed shift (day, swing, or night), their behavior would be consistent, which would help them adjust to the circadian rhythms. Some people prefer to work afternoons or nights, so part of the solution may be personnel selection. Workers could choose a shift; if enough workers of the appropriate skill level were placed in the shift of their choice, that would meet both individual and organizational needs. Barton (1994) found that the physical and psychological health of nurses was better when they worked a fixed night shift than when they engaged in night work as part of a rotating-shift schedule. However, fixed shifts are not without their own problems. Bohle and Tulley (1998) found that the night shift was most related to sleep disturbance and work/family conflict. Smith, Reilly, and Midkiff (1989) developed a scale based on circadian rhythms. They concluded that the scale could be used to select workers for the night shift based on their preference for evening activities. Indeed, Jamal and Jamal (1982) found that employees who worked a fixed shift had better mental and physical health than employees on a rotating shift. Using a sample of medical technicians, Blau and Lunz (1999) found that fixed-shift day employees experienced a greater variety of work activities and sources of stimulation than did employees on evening, night, or rotating shifts. Rotating shift work seems particularly difficult to adjust to. There is also evidence (Knauth, 1996) that backward rotation (from day to night to afternoon shifts) is more difficult to adjust to than forward rotation (from day to afternoon to night). Totterdell et al. (1995) reported that nurses felt worse (on such measures as alertness, calmness, and moodiness) on a rest day following a night shift than after a day shift.

The findings attest to the costs of fatigue and adjustment to and from a nocturnal work routine. In fact, Freese and Okonek (1984) reported that some people who have reached the emotional, mental, and physical breaking point because of rotating shift work are told by their physicians to find jobs with traditional work hours. Costa (1996) estimated that 20% of workers have to leave shift work in a short time because of serious disturbances; those who remain show different and varying levels of adaptation and tolerance. Tepas (1993) concluded that organizations should design educational programs for shift workers and their families to better prepare them for the demands imposed by this work schedule.

Flexible Working Hours

Flextime

A schedule of work hours that permits employees flexibility in when they arrive at and leave work.

One variation in work schedules is flexible working hours, popularly known as **flextime**. According to Gottleib, Kelloway, and Barham (1998), 73% of U.S. employers offer flextime to their workers. The main objective of flextime is to create an alternative to the traditional fixed working schedule by giving workers some choice in arrival and departure times. The system is usually arranged so that everyone must be present during certain designated hours ("coretime"), but there is latitude in other hours ("flexband"). For example, coretime may be 9:00 A.M. to 3:00 P.M. and flexband may be 6:00 A.M. to 6:00 P.M. Some employees may start working at 9:00 A.M. and work until 6:00 P.M.; some may end at 3:00 P.M. by starting at 6:00 A.M.; others work any combination in between. Flexible working hours may alleviate problems with family commitments, recreation, second jobs, commuting, and stress. Lateness is virtually eliminated because the workday begins with arrival. Workers can be late only if they arrive after coretime has begun.

In general, the findings on flextime appear quite positive; at least no very adverse effects have yet been reported. The variables examined include satisfaction, productivity, absence, and turnover. Some studies reported more positive results than others. Golembiewski and Proehl (1978) summarized the findings of several studies on flextime; they reported that worker support for adoption or continuation of flextime across nine samples of workers ranged from 80% to 100%. It thus appears that most employees favor the plan. Hicks and Klimoski (1981) found that employees did not become more satisfied with their work after flextime was adopted. Nevertheless, they reported other benefits like easier travel and parking, less interrole conflict, more feelings of control in the work setting, and more time for leisure activities.

Narayanan and Nath (1982) examined the impact of flextime at two organizational levels: lower-level and professional employees. They concluded that flextime primarily benefited lower-level employees by giving them more flexibility in their schedules. For professional employees, the flextime system merely formalized the already existing informal system they had with the company. Ralston (1989) found that flextime was especially helpful for working mothers and dual-career couples, two growing segments of the workforce. In a six-year study of flextime, Dalton and Mesch (1990) reported large reductions in employee absenteeism compared with a control group that had regular work hours. However, the rates of turnover in the two groups were the same.

Although there is ample evidence that flextime benefits individuals (Gottleib et al., 1998), it is likely to be detrimental to the functioning of teams. If employees must work as a team, the individualized schedules that flextime permits may limit the continuity of the team. However, we need additional research to address this issue. For the present, flextime appears to be highly beneficial in accommodating the scheduling needs of individual employees.

Compressed Workweek

Employees traditionally have worked 8 hours a day, five days a week, for a 40-hour workweek. Some employees work 10 hours a day for four days, popularly known as the "4/40." Gottleib et al. (1998) reported that 21% of U.S. employers have **compressed workweeks**.

There are several obvious advantages to a compressed workweek for both the individual and the organization. Individuals have a three-day weekend, which gives them more recreation time, the chance to work a second job, more time for family life, and so on. Organizations have fewer overhead costs because they are open one day less per week. However, the possible drawbacks include worker fatigue, fewer productive hours, and more accidents.

In a major review of the 4/40, Ronen and Primps (1981) reached some conclusions based on many studies. The plan had a positive effect on home and family life as well as on leisure and recreation. There appeared to be no change in employee job performance, however. There were mixed results with regard to absenteeism, and worker fatigue definitely increased.

A few studies have been reported on reactions to a 12-hour shift, typically noon to midnight and then midnight to noon. The results are mixed. Breaugh (1983) reported that nurses on 12-hour shifts experienced substantial fatigue associated with the longer hours. However, the midnight-to-noon shift felt more out of phase with physiological and social rhythms than did the noon-to-midnight shift. Pierce and Dunham (1992) reported significant improvements in attitudes toward the work schedule, general affect, and fatigue in a sample of police officers who switched from a rotating 8-hour-shift work schedule to a fixed 12-hour schedule. Duchon, Keran, and Smith (1994) examined underground miners who switched from an 8-hour to a 12-hour schedule. The miners reported improved sleep quality with the new schedule, but fatigue had either no change or only slight improvement. The findings from such studies may be influenced by the variety of jobs examined in the research.

Conversion to a compressed workweek is not simply a matter of worker preference. Organizations are limited in altering their work schedules by the services they provide and other factors. For example, a compressed workweek is not viable if customer service must be provided five days a week. The success of organizations that provide services depends partially on accessibility. Dunham, Pierce, and Castaneda (1987) cautioned against blanket support for the 4/40; its success depends on the type of organization and the people in it. Baltes et al. (1999) concluded on the basis of a meta-analysis that there are mixed effects of the compressed workweek related to the specific outcome criterion in question. For example, compressed workweeks seem to increase job satisfaction, but they do not lead to reductions in absences.

Compressed workweek
A schedule of work hours that typically involves more hours per day and fewer days per week.

Alcoholism and Drug Abuse in the Workplace

Alcoholism and drug abuse are global problems affecting all arenas of life. Moore (1994) offered this concise statement: "Alcohol and work. This has always been an uneasy relationship. Genius may be fired by wine. More commonplace talent is often fired because of it" (p. 75). Due to the sensitivity and confidentiality of substance abuse, we do not have a very strong research foundation on which to base our knowledge. That is, it is difficult to collect reliable and valid data on substance abuse, given the delicacy of the issue. What follows is a brief overview of some of the major dimensions of this complex social problem.

Substance abuse
The ingestion of a broad array of substances (such as alcohol, tobacco, or drugs) that are deemed to have a harmful effect on the individual.

The term **substance abuse** covers a broad array of substances but usually includes alcohol, prescription drugs, and illegal drugs. Some people include tobacco (both smoking and chewing). Most of our knowledge is limited to alcoholism and illegal drugs. It has been estimated that there are more than 10 million alcoholic American workers. Tyson and Vaughn (1987) reported that approximately two-thirds of the people who enter the workforce have used illegal drugs. Four to five million people in the United States use cocaine monthly. The frequency of marijuana use is much higher (Schwenk, 1999). Every year $50 billion is spent on cocaine in the United States—the same amount that companies spend annually on substance abuse programs for their employees. The Americans with Disabilities Act (ADA) regards former drug use as a disability and thus provides legal protection to former drug users. However, current drug users are not covered by the law. By any reasonable standard, substance abuse is a major problem in industry today. Furthermore, substance abuse has long-term negative relationships to work adjustment, both as a cause and as an effect. Galaif, Newcomb, and Carmona (2001) conducted a longitudinal study of polydrug use (alcohol, marijuana, and cocaine). They found that polydrug use predicted lower job satisfaction four years later and that job instability (i.e., being fired or laid off) predicted subsequent substance abuse.

Although I/O psychologists may approach the topic of substance abuse from several perspectives, a primary area of concern is performance impairment—that is, the extent to which substance abuse contributes to lower job performance. Experts in employee assistance programs estimate that as much as 50% of absenteeism and on-the-job accidents are related to drugs and alcohol use. Drug addiction also contributes to employee theft to support a habit. Thus we have some knowledge about how substance abuse affects the more global performance criteria of absence, accidents, and theft. Our knowledge of the effects of substance abuse on skill decay is more tentative. Much of what we know is based on industrial accidents in which alcohol or drug use was confirmed. It is also very difficult to make categorical statements about "drugs" in general because of their variety, duration of effects, and interactive properties with other substances. We do know that cognitive skills such as vigilance, monitoring, reaction time, and decision making are adversely affected by many kinds of drugs. We do not know whether these drugs simply lengthen the amount of time needed to perform these cognitive functions, or whether they cause attention to be focused on irrelevant or competing stimuli. Jobs that involve the use of these skills in areas like the transportation industry (for example, pilots and railroad engineers) have regrettably contributed to our knowledge through tragic accidents. Some drugs (such as anabolic steroids) have been found to enhance aspects of physical performance (most notably, strength and speed), but their long-term effects can be very harmful to the user.

Hollinger (1988) concluded that the employees most likely to work under the influence of alcohol or other drugs are men younger than 30 and that the likelihood of their (or other employees) doing so increases when they feel unhappy about their jobs and socialize frequently with coworkers off the job. Trice and Sonnenstuhl (1988) found not only that employees seek relief from the effects of job stress with alcohol, but also that organizational subcultures establish norms for alcohol use. That is, employees may be expected to consume alcohol after work with their coworkers if there is a norm that encourages such behavior. Bacharach, Bamberger, and Sonnenstuhl (2002) found that problem drinking was based on a permissive norm that was part of the workplace culture. Individuals who wanted to be accepted by coworkers matched or exceeded the drinking level of the referent group. Harris and Trusty (1997) reported that international cultural norms are less disparaging of alcohol use in work contexts than U.S. norms are, asserting that alcohol use is "part and parcel of business life" (p. 309). Alcohol abuse is an epidemic among workers in the former Soviet Union.

Frone (2006) reported the results of a telephone survey of approximately 3,000 U.S. workers about illicit drug use. Professional telephone interviewers received four weeks of training in how to ask questions about a highly sensitive topic: the use of marijuana and cocaine. Based upon the results from the sample generalized to the entire population, it was estimated that 18 million workers nationally (14% of employed adults) use drugs. Furthermore, 4 million workers nationally (3% of employed adults) use illicit drugs within two hours of coming to work, during lunch breaks, during other breaks, or while working. Certain segments of the U.S. workforce had much higher usage rates than the national average. For example, 56% of men aged 18-30 used illicit drugs, and 28% of them used them in the workplace. Bruno (1994) reported that in Italy drug dependence does not limit a person's right to keep a job, even if employees perform tasks dangerous to their own or others' safety. To safeguard others, federal laws require employers to reassign such employees to other tasks. The introduction of drug testing in the workplace in Italy has been delayed because it appears to create a conflict between the organization's right to safeguard its interests and the individual's right to privacy.

Economic issues are also salient to drug use. Bennett, Blum, and Roman (1994) noted that organizations typically address the problem of drug use at work in two ways. The first is drug testing, designed to exclude drug users from the workplace. The second is employee assistance programs (EAPs). EAPs started mostly after World War II to rehabilitate veterans who came home with alcohol abuse problems. Drug abuse treatment was added to the EAPs mainly after the Vietnam War for veterans returning with drug problems. Currently EAPs address all kinds of adjustment, stress, and family problems faced by workers. Such programs are mandated by the federal government for all employers who receive more than a specified amount of federal funding. Bennett et al. found that organizations in geographic areas with high unemployment rates are more likely to use pre-employment drug testing, whereas work sites with low turnover more often provide an EAP. Cooper, Dewe, and O'Driscoll (2003) believe the role of EAPs in organizations will expand in the future to include issues of work/family conflict. Such programs will be expected to support the investment organizations make in their employees and the value they place on a healthy workforce.

Finally, Normand, Lempert, and O'Brien (1994) offered some staggering estimates of the annual financial costs of alcohol and drug abuse to society. Estimates were based on four factors: the costs of treatment, lowered work productivity, the lost income that would have been earned by individuals who die prematurely from substance abuse, and crime-related costs. The total estimated cost of alcohol abuse is $70 billion; the total estimated cost of drug abuse is $44 billion.

It is difficult for I/O psychologists to conduct high-quality research on substance abuse. Given ethical concerns, alcohol or drugs can be administered in an experimental setting only under the most restrictive conditions. Reliance on self-report measures are problematic, given the factors of social desirability and accuracy. Civil and legal issues are also associated with drug testing, both in this country and internationally, particularly pertaining to the constitutional rights of individuals to refuse to submit to drug testing. As with most complex social problems, researchers and scholars from many professions (such as pharmacology, toxicology, law, and genetics) must take an interdisciplinary approach to addressing these issues. Although I/O psychologists will contribute only a small piece of the total picture, I envision our efforts as concentrated in two traditional areas: individual assessment and performance measurement. Perhaps in 20 years an evaluation of working conditions may also include the propensity of certain jobs to induce substance abuse and the likelihood your coworker is under the influence of drugs or alcohol. Whether we are ready for it or not, I believe society will expect I/O psychologists to provide information on problems our predecessors could scarcely have imagined.

The Psychological Effects of Unemployment

As was discussed in Chapter 8, the possibility of job loss is a major concern for the contemporary worker. Thousands of employees lose their jobs annually through downsizing, outsourcing, offshoring, and mergers and acquisitions. Perilous economic conditions have resulted in large-scale job loss both domestically and globally (see Cross-Cultural I/O Psychology: Unemployment in China, p. 368). What have we learned about the meaning of work to individuals as a result of involuntary unemployment? This section will address the primarily negative psychological effects of unemployment.

Jahoda (1981) asserted that being employed has both intended and unintended consequences for the individual. Earning a living is the most obvious intended consequence of employment, but the primary psychological meaning of work derives from the unintended or latent consequences. The five important latent consequences of employment are: (1) imposition of a time structure on the waking day, (2) regular shared experiences and contacts with people outside the nuclear family, (3) the linking of individuals to goals and purposes, (4) the definition of aspects of personal status and identity, and (5) the enforcement of activity. Jahoda claimed that these unintended consequences of employment "meet human needs of an enduring kind." Accordingly, when one is unemployed and is deprived of these functions, one's enduring human needs are unsatisfied. It is thus argued that employment is the major institution in society that reliably and effectively provides these supports to psychological well-being.

Cross-Cultural I/O Psychology: *Unemployment in China*

With the growing influence of China in the global economy, researchers are beginning to understand work-related issues in this previously closed nation. Wanberg, Kammeyer-Meuller, and Shi (2001) described the experience of unemployment in China. Before the period of economic reform in China that began in the 1970s, business organizations were primarily owned by the government and were called "state enterprises." These state enterprises did not compete with one another or with companies from other nations. Workers at state enterprises were provided with lifetime jobs. These lifetime jobs were provided by law, and the state enterprises were also responsible for providing much of the workers' food, clothing, housing, and medical care. Under new Chinese leadership, China began an intense period of opening itself to the outside world. As the nation moved to a market economy, state enterprises were compelled to become more competitive and to use their human resources more productively. The change in national economic policy coupled with economic hardship led to massive layoffs in the state enterprises (more than 6 million workers per year in 1997, 1998, and 1999). The actual level of unemployment was estimated to greatly exceed reported statistics because the official tally included only urban workers. The statistics excluded individuals who did not register with the employment bureau and individuals who were laid off but

who believed they would be called back. Some of the Chinese population relocated from rural to urban centers seeking employment. For example, although 1 million people from across the country came to Beijing and found jobs, more than 100,000 Beijing natives could not find work.

Psychological research on unemployment in China is just emerging. One study revealed that many workers who lost their jobs waited for the government to solve their unemployment problems instead of seeking work on their own. Some workers did not think they were laid off but still considered themselves part of their former state enterprise. The emotions of laid-off workers followed a shock–optimistic–hopeless pattern. At first they were shocked to discover they had lost their lifetime employment. This was followed by a strong sense of optimism that new work would be found. Because many were older, had few skills, and were not experienced in becoming re-employed, however, they felt hopeless as they repeatedly could not find work.

The research by Wanberg et al. is a rare glimpse at I/O psychology topics in China that have long been studied elsewhere. As organizational downsizing is new to China, so too is the experience of large-scale unemployment. It is unknown the degree to which Western research on unemployment will generalize to a culture that is in the midst of great economic and social changes.

Fryer and Payne (1986) offered a different explanation for why unemployment is psychologically devastating based upon a loss of discretionary control. Their explanation is heavily tied to the loss of income associated with unemployment. Financial problems are an outstanding worry for most unemployed people, and lack of money is one of the underlying causes of problems in maintaining relationships. While the loss of adequate income is certain for most unemployed people, there is also uncertainty about how long the low income will persist. The poor resources of the unemployed cause them to have much less discretion or freedom to pursue various decision options, such as food or clothes to purchase. The act of choosing is severely restricted by unemployment. Attempting to solve problems with limited resources frequently means that the quality of the solution is poorer, which can engender a sense of failure and lowered self-esteem. Thus the loss of financial resources limits choices, thereby enhancing feelings of limited control over one's life. In turn, lowered psychological health follows from this condition.

The explanations offered by both Jahoda (1981) and Fryer and Payne (1986) are represented in Warr's (2007b) nine environmental factors needed for mental health (listed at the beginning of this chapter). A loss of employment has been found to trigger changes in eight of the nine environmental determinants of psychological well-being.

Wanberg (1997) reported that the act of job seeking can have a negative effect on mental health. Job search involves putting oneself on the line and dealing with feelings about being judged harshly, evaluated critically, and ultimately rejected. Wanberg believes the best intervention programs for unemployed individuals incorporate exercises that promote feelings of self-esteem, optimism, and control as well as job-seeking skills. Gowan, Riordan, and Gatewood (1999) concluded that individuals who can manage the negative emotions associated with job loss may appear to be stable and confident in interviews and thus improve their chances of receiving job offers. Finally, Wanberg, Kanfer, and Banas (2000) reported that individual actions directed toward contacting friends, acquaintances, and referrals to get information, leads, or advice on getting a job (i.e., what is popularly referenced as "networking") did not result in greater or faster re-employment. Although networking is a useful re-employment strategy, it is not superior to traditional job-search techniques.

An individual's opportunity for control is clearly lessened by unemployment. Lack of success in job seeking, the inability to influence employers, and increased dependence on social welfare programs all reduce people's ability to control what happens to them. The opportunity to use skills is also likely to be reduced during unemployment. Occupational skills are generally not used during unemployment, although there may be opportunities to use certain skills in domestic activities. People who become unemployed from jobs that demand a high level of skill are likely to suffer a greater reduction in this feature than people whose previous employment required only limited skill. Unemployment reduces externally generated goals because fewer demands are placed on the individual. Because external demands are often linked to particular times (such as family meal times or the start of a workday), a general reduction in demands is often accompanied by a loss of temporal differentiation. Time markers that break up the day or week and indicate one's position in it are no longer as frequent or urgent.

An unemployed person loses variety by having to leave the house less often and also lacks the contrast between job and nonjob activities. Those domestic demands that impinge on the person are likely to be similar and unchanging from day to day, with standard routines and little novelty. Environmental clarity is also likely to be reduced during unemployment. Information relating to the future permits planning within predictable time schedules and reduces the anxiety typically generated by uncertainty. Planning for the future is difficult in view of uncertainty about one's occupational or financial position in the months to come. Payment for work is at the heart of the employment contract, and the standard of living of almost all adults below retirement age is principally determined by income received from a job. Unemployment removes that income and in almost all cases has a serious and wide-ranging impact on the availability of money.

Physical security is usually associated with the availability of money. There appears to be a general need for some personal and private territory that contributes to a stable self-concept and enhanced well-being. Reduced income can give rise to loss of adequate housing or the threat that this will happen. The only determinant of mental health that appears primarily unaffected by unemployment is the opportunity for interpersonal contact. Younger and middle-aged unemployed individuals typically report no change in the amounts of interpersonal contact they have before and after job loss. Some research findings (e.g., Warr & Payne, 1983) indicated that social contacts even *increase* in frequency for these groups during unemployment. Unemployed persons report spending more time with neighbors and family members. However, older individuals (particularly women) report a reduction in social contacts after becoming unemployed, typically spending their days alone at home. On becoming unemployed, a person loses a socially approved role and the positive self-evaluations that go with it. The new position is widely felt to be of lower prestige, deviant, second-rate, or not providing full membership in society. Even when social welfare benefits remove the worst financial hardships, there may be shame attached to receiving funds from public sources and a seeming failure to provide for one's family. McKee-Ryan et al. (2005) conducted a meta-analytic study of psychological and physical well-being during unemployment. The authors concluded, "In cross-sectional studies unemployed individuals had lower well-being than employed individuals. In longitudinal studies well-being declines as individuals move from employment to unemployment, but improves as individuals move from unemployment to re-employment" (p. 67). Job loss and unemployment produced a cascade of worry, uncertainty, and financial, family, and marital difficulties.

Based on these assessments provided by Warr (2007b), there is a strong linkage between unemployment and mental health. Indeed, Murphy and Athanasou (1999) conducted a meta-analysis of longitudinal studies examining how employment affects one's mental health. The results revealed an average correlation coefficient of .54 between gaining employment and improved mental well-being, and an average correlation of .36 between losing employment and decreased mental health. Work provides a sense of meaning and purpose to life, and the removal of that purpose lowers the quality of life.

Child Labor and Exploitation

We will conclude this chapter with a facet of occupational health that is rarely addressed by I/O psychologists. It pertains to the health of children who are compelled to work. Our awareness of child labor, a disturbing and deplorable aspect of worklife, comes from increased interest in global business practices (Piotrkowski & Carrubha, 1999). Although child labor is relatively rare (and illegal in most circumstances) in the United States, it is not in many other countries, and some U.S. companies utilize child labor in developing countries to make their products (see Field Note 3).

Child labor
The pattern of compelling children under the age of 15 throughout the world to perform labor that is harmful to their overall health and psychological well-being.

Child labor refers to economic activities carried out by persons under 15 years of age. The International Labour Organization (ILO) established in 1996 that 250 million children worldwide, 5–14 years old, are working, half of them full-time. Child labor is most common in developing countries, particularly in Asia, Africa, and Latin America. But it occurs in wealthy countries as well. Child workers typically are found in agriculture, working long hours, sometimes under inhumane and hazardous

Field Note 3: Child Labor by U.S. Companies

In 1909 my maternal grandmother was orphaned as a result of an outbreak of tuberculosis. She was 14 years old at the time. Her mother had taught her how to crochet, a form of knitting. My grandmother found work in a sweatshop in New York City, making doilies, working 14 hours and earning 25¢ *per day.* She endured abysmal working conditions but ultimately prevailed through this very difficult period of her life. In 1938 a federal law was passed (the Fair Labor Standards Act, FLSA) that prohibited many of the types of conditions my grandmother faced in 1909. A standard workweek (40 hours) was established, as was a minimum hourly wage. As of July, 2008 the minimum wage is $6.55 per hour, and as of July, 2009, $7.25 per hour. The law was passed in part to eliminate the use of child labor in the United States. As a nation we place a very high value on our children, and we have passed other laws over the years to protect their welfare and safety.

It has now been 100 years since my grandmother toiled in a sweatshop for 25¢ per day. You might think the use of child labor by U.S. companies ended long ago. Not exactly. The FLSA applies to companies operating in the United States. As a means of reducing labor costs (defined in part by the minimum wage), some U.S. companies have sent jobs formerly held by U.S. workers offshore to developing nations with cheaper labor markets. These nations do not have the same restrictions on employment that are found in the United States. In some countries it is acceptable for children to hold full-time jobs and to be paid a wage that is consistent with the standards of that country. That wage may be, for example, 80¢ per hour. Furthermore, workers in such nations may be grateful to secure steady employment that pays 80¢ per hour. It might be concluded the situation appears equitable for all parties concerned. That is, the company lowers its labor costs by not having to pay the U.S. minimum wage, the overseas workers get paid what is to them a fair wage by their standards, and the use of child labor is not illegal.

Some people and advocacy groups have decried this business practice by U.S. companies. Even though it is economically feasible, it can be perceived as violating the ethical standards of fair treatment of workers. How do you feel about this issue? Should U.S. companies be prohibited from using child labor overseas to make products for very low wages (by U.S. standards) because it is morally corruptive and defeats the underlying purpose of the FLSA? Or is this an equitable exchange of labor for money, and "everyone wins"?

conditions for little or no pay. In Zimbabwe some children work 60 hours per week picking cotton or coffee. In Nepal children work on tea estates, some for up to 14 hours per day. In its most extreme form, the exploitation of working children takes the form of slavery or forced labor, still practiced in parts of Asia and Africa. Children's work may be pledged by parents for payment of a debt, the children may be kidnapped and imprisoned in brothels or sweatshops, or they may be given away or sold by families. Child labor is evidenced in the United States by children trafficking drugs in inner-city neighborhoods.

The ILO (2004) estimated that 10 million children worldwide are forced to work in slavelike conditions as domestic servants in private homes. In parts of Africa, Central America, and Asia, girls as young as 8 work 15 hours a day, every day, for little or no pay. The ILO report found that South Africa had the highest number of children working as servants, more than 2 million. Other countries with high numbers were Indonesia, Brazil, and Pakistan. The child workers, who are employed in homes where having servants is a sign of social status, are sometimes sexually abused. The study found that some children forget their own names after simply being called "girl" or "boy" for years. When they are considered too old, many children are evicted by their employers and live on the streets because they have no idea where or how to find their families.

The U.S. Department of Labor (2006) issued a report examining the use of child labor in 137 nations. The study revealed that child labor is common throughout much of the world. The study limited itself only to the *worst forms* of child labor, as these are universally regarded as the most offensive and objectionable forms of work, even for adults. The worst forms of child labor were specifically described as follows:

A. All forms of slavery or practices similar to slavery, such as the sale or trafficking of children, debt bondage, serfdom, or forced or compulsory recruitment of children for use in armed conflict;

B. The use, procuring, or offering of a child for prostitution, for the production of pornography or for pornographic purposes;

C. The use, procuring or offering of a child for illicit activity in the production or trafficking of drugs; and

D. Work by its nature or the circumstances in which it is carried out, is likely to harm the health, safety, or morals of children (p. 1).

Girls are primarily trafficked for commercial sexual exploitation, domestic services, or forced marriage. Boys are trafficked mostly for the purpose of exploitative labor in agriculture, mining, manufacturing, organized begging, and armed conflict. The massive earthquake and tsunami in December, 2004 resulted in the deaths of thousands of parents whose surviving children became at great risk to exploitative labor. The tsunami destroyed many schools that provided an alternative venue for children other than work. The report concluded: "The creation of good new jobs for adults can increase the chances that children will be able to stay in school rather than engage in hazardous work to help support their families . . . When governments pressure the elimination of the worst forms of child labor and the promotion of basic education as national priorities, they make an important investment in their country's children and in the potential of their national economies" (p. 9).

According to Piotrkowski and Carrubha (1999), child labor is harmful when it interferes with healthy development by imposing inappropriate physical and social demands on children, directly exposes children to noxious conditions that harm them physically or psychologically, and is detrimental to children's full social and psychological development. Children are especially vulnerable to dangerous or stressful working conditions because they are emotionally, physically, and cognitively immature. Child laborers are too young to understand the physical and psychological hazards they face and are too powerless to escape them. The plight of children around the world confronted with extreme family poverty and crime as precursors to forced labor has been the subject of major initiatives by the United Nations.

Piotrkowski and Carrubha summarized their review of child labor with the following sober conclusion:

> The economic exploitation and maltreatment of defenseless young children are violations of their basic human rights. Even when permitted by law, child labor may be harmful. Insofar as child labor abuses are tied to family poverty, they cannot be tackled alone, without regard for the economic needs of these families. The idea that children are primarily of sentimental value, rather than of economic value, is a fairly recent historical development. Parents may not understand the harms associated with child labor, believing instead that they have a right to make use of all their human resources. Although child labor may help individual families in their day-to-day efforts to survive, ultimately it perpetuates the cycle of poverty. As such, it has enormous social costs. In depriving children of their rights and subjecting them to harm, exploitative child labor has enormous human costs. (p. 151)

I doubt the subject of child labor will become a dominant issue among I/O psychologists, in part because of its inherent social repulsiveness. However, it underscores one of the major reasons we work: our services have economic and instrumental value. As adults we have the free will to decide how and where we will offer our services to enhance our economic standing in life. Children, on the other hand, do not possess this free will. They are compelled to work to enhance the economic standing of others. Such actions violate the basic tenets of social justice referenced in Chapter 10.

Concluding Comments

Work/family conflict not only is a frequent problem for employees but also appears to be more and more accepted as part of the price individuals pay for employment. The fact that stress management programs are directed not at making work less stressful but at increasing our capacity to deal with stress suggests that few people believe stress can be eliminated or drastically reduced from work. As discussed in Chapter 8, one of the consequences of organizational downsizing is that fewer employees now must do the work that was once performed by a greater number of employees. The prevailing sentiment is that organizations are expected to do more (work) with less (resources). Technological advances (particularly relating to computer-based operations) have also accelerated the speed at which work is performed. These changes have the potential to diminish overall mental health by reducing autonomy or control and thus worker self-esteem (Locke, McClear, & Knight, 1996). In the evolution of work design, employees are becoming increasingly controlled by situational factors, as opposed to exerting control over their own work environments. As research on mental health and stress has revealed, the reduction in self-regulation (i.e., feeling "out of control") impairs psychological well-being (Murphy, Hurrell, & Quick, 1992). Rather than denying the reality of work stress or assuming no responsibility for it, organizations are becoming increasingly committed to addressing it. Annual health care costs in this country alone exceed $1.3 trillion, with business paying about half the cost. It is simply cheaper to promote healthful behavior than to pay the costs associated with not promoting it.

Case Study 🌀 Two Siblings, Two Lifestyles

Joe Vesco rarely got to see his older sister, Rita. Although they lived only 70 miles apart, their visits seemed limited to family holidays. Rita was 31, married, and had two boys, ages 6 and 3. She was a supervisor for a telemarketing company, overseeing the work of 15 sales agents. Rita put in long hours, typically 50 to 60 hours per week. She frequently worked until 8:00 P.M. because many sales calls were made in the early evening. She had a departmental sales quota to reach and also had to monitor the individual sales quotas of each of her agents. Work was very stressful. She experienced considerable guilt and anxiety over how her worklife was affecting her family. Her husband picked the children up from day care and fed them dinner. The younger child was often asleep before Rita arrived home. She and her husband had discussed at length whether Rita should look for another job with more conventional hours. It always seemed to come down to money. They needed both incomes to maintain their family, and Rita's job paid particularly well. She was paid partly on commission, and because she frequently exceeded her department's sales quota, Rita received about 20% additional income over her base salary. No other job would pay so well.

Joe had a very different life. He was single, 24, and worked as a surveyor for the county. He had his own apartment, just recently purchased his first new car, and loved his independence. His job didn't pay very well, but the hours were stable. He left work every day at 4:30. Joe didn't worry about being fired or losing his job. The county employed only a few surveyors, and no one could remember anyone in his department ever being fired or laid off. It was a highly secure job but not very challenging. Joe didn't think he would make a career out of the job, but for the present it suited him very well.

Joe and Rita got together at their parents' anniversary party. Joe hadn't seen Rita for quite some time and was surprised at how stressed out she looked. He remembered his sister as being a stabilizing influence on him while they were growing up. She always seemed to be in control of her life. That apparent control, whether real or just imagined by Joe, was no longer evident. Rita complained about not being able to leave her work problems at work; she worried about her children while at work. She acknowledged taking medication to help her get to sleep, which had never been a problem before. Rita also talked about going back to smoking, after having given up cigarettes for almost seven years.

Joe reflected on his own life in comparison to his sister's. He didn't make nearly the money she did, but his biggest concern in life seemed to be which sporting event he would watch on TV when he came home from work. And car payments. Joe remembered his own mother always being home when he got back from school. He wondered how his nephews would respond to their mother's absence after school. Joe concluded that Rita was wondering the same thing.

Questions

1. What are the primary sources of work/family conflict in Rita's life?
2. To what degree does gender play a role in Rita's work/family conflict? Why?
3. What are the rewards and drawbacks for both Rita and Joe in the jobs they hold?
4. To what do you attribute the difference in lifestyle between Joe and Rita: age, gender, marital status, children, income?

5. Do you think Rita made a conscious choice to pursue her lifestyle, or do you think she was subtly drawn into it over time? What does your answer suggest about the nature of work/family conflict?

Chapter Summary

- The topic of occupational health emerged in I/O psychology as we came to understand that both work and family issues contribute to our overall welfare.
- There are nine determinants of psychological well-being at work and each contributes to our mental health.
- Understanding the conflict between the work and family spheres of our lives is a major activity of I/O psychologists.
- Organizations try to alleviate work/family conflict by providing flexible work hours and on-site day care centers.
- Some work operations must be performed continuously. Employees who work non-traditional work shifts are generally less healthy than traditional day workers.
- The psychological effects of unemployment can be severe, especially over a prolonged time period. Unemployment is a problem of global proportions.
- The illicit exploitation of child labor around the world is estimated to involve more than 250 million children between the ages of 5 and 14.

Chapter Outline

Learning Objectives

- Explain five critical concepts central to work motivation.
- Understand the conceptual basis and degree of empirical support for these work motivation theories: expectancy, goal setting, self-regulation, and work design.
- Provide an overview and synthesis of the work motivation theories.
- Give practical examples of applying motivational strategies.

Have you ever known a person who appears "driven" to perform well or succeed? Perhaps you would describe yourself in that way. Such people may or may not have more ability than others, but it appears they are willing to work harder or expend more effort. Psychologists refer to this attribute or trait as ambition, or being motivated. Motivation is not directly observable; it must be inferred from an analysis of a continuous stream of behaviors. As Mitchell and Daniels (2003a) stated, "Motivation is a core construct. To understand why people behave the way they do in organizations, one must know something about motivation" (p. 225).

Work motivation refers to the domain of motivational processes directed to the realm of work. Pinder (1998) offered this definition:

> Work motivation is a set of energetic forces that originate both within as well as beyond an individual's being, to initiate work-related behavior, and to determine its form, direction, intensity, and duration. (p. 11)

There are three noteworthy components to this definition. First, *direction* addresses the choice of activities we make in expending effort. That is, we might choose to work diligently at some tasks and not at others. Second, *intensity* implies we have the potential to exert various levels of effort, depending on how much we need to expend. Third, *persistence* reflects duration of motivation over time, as opposed to a one-time choice between courses of action (direction) or high levels of effort aimed at a single task (intensity). A comprehensive understanding of work motivation requires an integration of these concepts. Each dimension has its associated issues and concerns. In an employment context, each dimension is highly relevant to both the organization and the individual. *Direction* pertains to those activities in life to which you direct your energy. Organizations want employees who will direct themselves to their work responsibilities, and many employees want jobs that will inspire their motivation and commitment. *Intensity* pertains to the amount of motivation that is expended in pursuit of an activity. Organizations want employees who will exhibit high levels of energy. Such people are often referred to as "self-starters" or "self-motivated" individuals, implying that they bring a high level of energy to the job and do not require organizational inducements to work hard. Likewise, many employees hope to find jobs that are sufficiently appealing to invite large commitments of energy. The third dimension, *persistence*, pertains to sustained energy over time. It is concerned with how long the energy will be expended. Researchers know the least about this dimension, but it is the focus of more recent motivational theories. You can think of a career as an interrelated series of jobs through which individuals manifest their energies over a working lifetime. Organizations want employees who will persevere through good times and bad. Likewise, employees want jobs that will sustain their interests over the long haul. Each of the three dimensions of motivation has direct implications for both organizations and individuals (see The Changing Nature of Work: The Work Motivation of Older Employees, p. 378).

Klehe and Anderson (2007) identified a distinction between the upper limit of what people can do (maximum performance) versus what they will do (typical performance). One conception of motivation is that it accounts for the difference between typical and maximum performance. Individuals with high ability may be able to sustain an acceptable level of typical performance, but they would be capable of much greater (i.e., maximum) performance if they were sufficiently motivated to perform at this higher level. They stand in sharp contrast with other individuals who have to

The Changing Nature of Work: The Work Motivation of Older Employees

It has been emphasized that the world of work is changing rapidly. Smith and Dickson (2003) questioned the degree to which societal changes challenge what we know about motivation as it applies to the need to adapt, continuous learning, the movement toward team structures, and so on. While our work world is certainly changing, so too are population demographics. Kanfer and Ackerman (2004) noted by the year 2010 nearly half the U.S. labor force will be composed of individuals 45 years and older. The demographics in most other developed countries will be similar. The prevalence of midlife and older persons in the U.S. workforce has resulted from the aging of the baby boom generation (those born between 1946 and 1960) and recent economic conditions that discourage workers from retiring. Kanfer and Ackerman believe that much of what we know about work motivation is predicated upon a younger workforce. There is ample evidence from developmental psychology that individuals change across their life-span, including what motivates them. For example, younger workers have relatively less economic security and social status, so they are more strongly motivated by financial rewards and opportunities for advancement (compared with older workers). From personality research we have learned that older workers are less open to new experiences but are more conscientious than their younger counterparts. In terms of ability, younger individuals succeed in jobs because of their ability to learn them, whereas older workers have a larger reservoir of knowledge to draw upon in guiding their behavior. Older workers are often more willing to share their knowledge with younger workers who are receptive to learning, which is the basis for mentoring (as discussed in Chapter 6).

Kanfer and Ackerman (2004) stated that work motivation theories frequently emphasize time and effort rather than knowledge as a personal resource that an individual allocates to performing tasks. For older workers, knowledge is typically in far greater supply than time and cognitive effort. For younger workers, the reverse is true. From an organizational perspective the most useful strategies for motivating older workers might target their strongest resources—knowledge and experience. Kanfer and Ackerman made the following proposition: "If theories of work motivation suggest that older workers are as a group less motivated, perhaps the problem lies in limitations of our current theories and organization practices, rather than with the class of individuals" (p. 456).

work very hard to be successful because they lack high ability. The degree to which greater effort can compensate for lesser ability in attaining satisfactory performance varies across jobs. Individuals with high ability can also seek out jobs that don't require high effort if averse to working hard.

Five Critical Concepts in Motivation

It is relatively easy to misunderstand or confuse several concepts critical to work motivation. The distinctions among these concepts are not always discernible, or at the least they can become blurred. To help you differentiate them throughout the chapter, five critical concepts will be articulated next.

- *Behavior.* Behavior is the action from which we infer motivation. The behavior in question may be typing speed, firing a rifle at a target, or engaging in any of a broad constellation of human activities.

- *Performance.* Performance entails some evaluation of behavior. The basic unit of observation is behavior, but coupled with the behavior is an assessment of the behavior as judged against some standard. If the behavior is typing 60 words per minute, a judgment can be made as to whether this *level of performance* is adequate or inadequate to hold a job. Thus the behavior is appraised within some organizational context, and 60 words per minute might represent adequate performance in some jobs and inadequate performance in others. Many organizational theories tend to be concerned with performance, not just behavior. Performance, however, is determined by factors that transcend behavior.

- *Ability.* Ability is one of three determinants of behavior. It is generally regarded as fairly stable within individuals and may be represented by a broad construct like intelligence or a more specific construct like physical coordination.

- *Situational factors.* Situational factors are the second determinant of behavior. They are environmental influences and opportunities that facilitate or constrain behavior (and ultimately performance). Examples include tools, equipment, procedures, and the like, which if present, facilitate behavior, and if absent, diminish it. If no situational constraints are present, it is possible to maximize behavior. Individual behavior manifests itself in some environmental or situational context that influences the conduct of behavior but is beyond the control of the individual.

- *Motivation.* Motivation is the third determinant of behavior. You can think of ability as reflecting what you *can* do, motivation as what you *will* do (given your ability), and the situational factors as what you are *allowed* to do.

Each of the three determinants is critical to the manifestation of behavior. Behavior is at a maximum when a person has high ability, exhibits high motivation, and is in an environment that is supportive of such behavior. The judgment of "poor performance" could be attributed to four factors. First, the organization in which the behavior occurs may have high standards; the same behavior in another organization may receive a more positive evaluation. Second, the individual may lack the needed ability to exhibit the desired behavior. (I was never very good at catching fly balls in baseball.) Third, the individual may lack the motivation to exhibit the desired behavior. (Countless hours of practice didn't seem to enhance my ball-catching behavior.) Fourth, the individual may lack the needed equipment or opportunity to exhibit the behavior. (An expensive new baseball glove didn't help either.)

Work Motivation Theories

Over the past 40 years there has been a profusion of work motivation theories. In the past 10 to 20 years, however, attempts have been made to identify consistency in the psychological constructs that underlie the theories. As will be witnessed, certain psychological constructs coalesce more readily across theories than others.

Four different theories of work motivation will be presented here. They differ markedly in the psychological constructs that are hypothesized to account for

FRANK AND ERNEST   by Bob Thaves

I THINK OF MYSELF AS BEING IN MOTIVATION RESEARCH -- EVERY MORNING I WONDER WHY I GO TO WORK.

Frank & Ernest: © Thaves/Dist. by Newspaper Enterprise Association, Inc. Reprinted with permission.

motivation. Each theory will be presented in three sections: a statement of the theory, empirical tests, and an evaluation (see Field Note 1). At the conclusion of this presentation, there will be a discussion of points of convergence among the theories and the fundamental perspectives that have been taken in addressing work motivation.

Expectancy Theory

Statement of the Theory.   **Expectancy theory** originated in the 1930s, but at that time it was not related to work motivation. Vroom (1964) brought expectancy theory into the arena of work motivation. In the past 40 years, expectancy theory has been one of the most popular and prominent motivation theories in I/O psychology. Since Vroom's formulation, several other researchers have proposed modifications. This section will not examine all variations but instead focus on key elements.

This is a cognitive theory. Each person is assumed to be a rational decision maker who will expend effort on activities that lead to desired rewards. Individuals are thought to know what they want from work and understand that their performance will determine whether they get the rewards they desire. A relationship between effort expended and performance on the job is also assumed.

The theory has five major parts: job outcomes, valence, instrumentality, expectancy, and force.

1. *Job outcomes* are the results an employee can experience by working for the organization, such as pay, promotions, and vacation time. Theoretically there is no limit to the number of outcomes. They are usually thought of as rewards or positive experiences, but they need not be. Getting fired or being transferred to a new location could be an outcome. Outcomes can also be intangibles like feelings of recognition or accomplishment.

2. *Valences* are the employee's feelings about the outcomes and are usually defined in terms of attractiveness or anticipated satisfaction. The employee can indicate whether an outcome has positive or negative valence. If the employee anticipates that all outcomes will lead to satisfaction, then varying degrees of positive valence are given. If the employee anticipates that an outcome will lead to dissatisfaction, then that outcome will have a negative valence. Last, if the employee

Field Note 1: Sensemaking

Weick (2001) proposed a concept he called *sensemaking*. It is not directly a theory of motivation, but it explains many facets of human behavior. The term "sensemaking" should be interpreted literally: it is the process by which we make sense of our lives and the world around us. We are driven (i.e., motivated) to understand phenomena in our lives, and the lack of making sense of something is often troubling to us. For example, how often have you thought or said these words about something you experienced in your life?

"It just doesn't make sense to me."

"If only I could figure it out."

"Why would someone do something like that?"

"It just doesn't add up."

"I don't understand that at all."

Each statement addresses Weick's fundamental concept of sensemaking. We feel compelled to derive meaning and understanding from experiences in our lives—understanding, not necessarily approval or disapproval. Sensemaking implies there is no single objective truth we are searching for (as a combination to a lock or safe), but rather something personal that allows us the comfort of understanding a problem or issue that may initially seem unfathomable. Fay (1990) has portrayed life as a puzzling terrain and "there is nobody here but us scratching around trying to make our experience and our world as comprehensible to ourselves in the best way we can" (p. 38). The terrain we seek to understand is continuously changing, a condition no more evident than that witnessed by the seismic changes in the business world over the past 25 years. As explained in Chapter 10, the rupturing of the traditional psychological contract of employment "just doesn't make any sense" to the generation that entered the workworld prior to the current turbulent period in society. Why would an organization *not* value loyalty and hard work in exchange for job security? All that employees can ever give to their employer is "100% of the brains and hearts", but even that no longer guarantees continued employment. Society was compelled to understand that the traditional psychological contract made sense under one set of economic conditions (i.e., relative stability, immunity from economic problems in other parts of the world, primarily local competition for goods, etc.). Under a different set of economic conditions (i.e., high instability, global economic interdependence, and the availability of cheaper goods a computer click away), the traditional psychological contract no longer made sense. Now employees have become expendable, regardless of their job proficiency and organizational loyalty. The cost of employees (i.e., labor costs) are often the single largest expense item in a corporate budget. Organizations found they had to cut back on their expenses to compete in the global economy, and in so doing the prevailing model of employment was cut with it.

Weick's conception of sensemaking is grounded in philosophy as well as psychology. Informational justice (as discussed in Chapter 10) is fundamentally about providing information to employees in a fair and equitable manner. Its overall goal is to help people make sense of events in their organization. The quest to make sense of our world is an unending process. We are probably more sensitized to when things don't make sense to us than when they do. It is the absence of understanding that motivates us to try to comprehend our world. We often feel relieved when we finally make sense out of something and can remain disquieted when we don't.

feels indifferent about an outcome, that outcome would have a valence of zero. Every outcome has a corresponding valence as perceived by the employee.

3. *Instrumentality* is defined as the perceived degree of relationship between performance and outcome attainment. This perception exists in the employee's mind. Instrumentality is equivalent to the word *conditional* and literally means the degree to which the attainment of a certain outcome is conditional on the individual's performance on the job. For example, if a person thinks that pay increases are highly conditional on performance, then the instrumentality associated with that outcome (a pay raise) is very high. If an employee thinks that being transferred is highly unrelated to job performance, then the instrumentality associated with that outcome (a transfer) is zero. Like valences, instrumentalities are perceived by the individual. He or she perceives the degree of relationship between performance and outcome attainment on the job. Instrumentalities are usually thought of as probabilities (which therefore range from 0 to 1). An instrumentality of 0 means the attainment of that outcome is completely unrelated to job performance; an instrumentality of 1 means the attainment of that outcome is completely conditional on job performance. An alternative conceptualization of instrumentality is as a correlation, which ranges from -1.0 to $+1.0$. The significance of the correlational conception of instrumentality is that it permits the possibility that increases in performance are, in fact, negatively related to outcome attainment. An example might be when increased job performance *decreases* the likelihood of a promotion: an organization might be reluctant to advance an employee out of a job in which he or she excels. Just as there are as many valences as there are outcomes, there are as many instrumentalities as there are outcomes.

4. *Expectancy* is the perceived relationship between effort and performance. In some jobs there may seem to be no relationship between how hard you try and how well you do. In others there may be a very clear relationship: the harder you try, the better you do. Expectancy is scaled as a probability. An expectancy of 0 means there is no probability that an increase in effort will result in an increase in performance. An expectancy of 1 means that an increase in effort will be followed by a corresponding increase in performance. After thinking about the relationship between effort and performance on the job, the individual renders an assessment of that relationship. Unlike valences and instrumentalities, usually only *one* expectancy value is perceived by the employee to reflect the effort–performance relationship in his or her job.

5. *Force*, the last component, is the amount of effort or pressure within the employee to be motivated. The larger the force, the greater the hypothesized motivation. Mathematically, force is the product of valence, instrumentality, and expectancy, as expressed by this formula:

$$\text{Force} = E\left(\sum_{i=1}^{n} V_i I_i\right) \qquad \text{[Formula 12-1]}$$

The formula can be explained better with the aid of the information in Figure 12-1. The components that constitute expectancy theory—job outcomes (O), rated valences, instrumentalities, and expectancy—are presented for a hypothetical employee. To

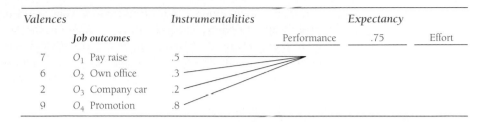

Valences		Instrumentalities	Expectancy		
	Job outcomes		Performance	.75	Effort
7	O_1 Pay raise	.5			
6	O_2 Own office	.3			
2	O_3 Company car	.2			
9	O_4 Promotion	.8			

Figure 12-1 *An example of Vroom's expectancy theory*

compute this individual's force, we multiply the valence for an outcome by its corresponding instrumentality and then sum these numbers. Therefore

$$(7 \times .5) + (6 \times .3) + (2 \times .2) + (9 \times .8) = \sum_{i=1}^{4} V_i I_i = 12.9 \quad \text{[Formula 12-2]}$$

We then multiply 12.9 by the listed expectancy of .75, which yields a force score of

$$E\left(\sum_{i=1}^{4} V_i I_i\right) = .75(12.9) = 9.7 \quad \text{[Formula 12-3]}$$

This product—9.7—represents the amount of force within the person to be motivated. It is the end product of the information on the valences, instrumentalities, and expectancy.

Now that we have this force score, what do we do with it? Think of it as a predictor of how motivated a person is. As with any predictor, the next step is to assess its validity in forecasting a criterion. Because the force score predicts effort, the criterion must also measure effort. The most common measure of effort is a subjective assessment, usually a rating: the individual renders a self-assessment of his or her effort, the individual's supervisor makes the judgment, or peer assessments are used. For example, the number of hours spent studying each week has been used to predict the motivation of students. In one type of validation paradigm of expectancy theory, force scores and criterion measures of effort are calculated for a group of people. If the theory is valid, then the higher the person's force score, the greater the effort should be. The theory's validity is typically assessed by correlating the force scores with the criterion of effort. High correlations between the two variables would substantiate the theory; low correlations would disconfirm it. The validation process will be examined more closely in the next section.

Expectancy theory provides a rich rational basis for understanding motivation in a given job. Each component is a framework for analyzing the motivation process. First, we should consider the outcomes and their perceived valences. If a person perceives little value associated with the outcomes (a low valence), there is no reason to work hard to attain them. According to expectancy theory, therefore, the first ingredient for motivation is valued outcomes. Second, the person must believe that there is some relationship between job performance and attainment of outcomes (instrumentalities must be high). If a person values the outcomes but does not see performance as a means of getting them, there is no link between what is done and what is valued. Reward practices and the supervisor are crucial in establishing high instrumentalities. If a supervisor says, "Your performance has been very good lately; therefore, I will reward you with a raise (or promotion)," the individual will see that the attainment of a pay raise or a promotion is conditional on (instrumental to) good performance. Conversely, if a supervisor says, "We don't give pay raises or promotions on the basis of performance; we grant them only on the basis of seniority," the individual will not be motivated to perform well to attain these outcomes. Perhaps the only motivation is to work hard enough not to be fired, so these outcomes would eventually be attained through longer service with the organization. When outcomes are made contingent on performance and the individual understands this relationship, expectancy theory predicts that job performance will be enhanced.

Finally, the notion of expectancy is crucial. People must see a relationship (an expectancy) between how hard they try and how well they perform. If expectancy is low, it will make no difference to them whether they work hard because effort and performance seem unrelated. When I first started college, I was a chemistry major. I desired certain outcomes (for example, good grades, a sense of accomplishment). I also realized that attaining these outcomes was conditional on my performance in classes. I had high valences for both the outcomes and the perceived high instrumentalities. However, after three agonizing semesters, my expectancy was near zero. It did not seem to matter how hard I tried; I just could not alter my (low) performance in chemistry classes. My overall motivation fell dramatically along with my performance, and I eventually chose a new major. In retrospect, I realize I lacked the abilities to perform well as a chemist. All the motivation I could muster would not lead to good performance.

The idea of expectancy also explains why work motivation can be very high in jobs where employees perceive very high expectancies. On assembly lines, the group performance level is determined by the speed of the line. No matter how hard a person works, he or she cannot produce any more until the next object moves down the line. The employee soon learns that he or she need only keep pace with the line. Thus there is no relationship between individual effort and performance. Alternatively, sales jobs are characterized by high expectancy. Salespeople who are paid on commission realize that the harder they try (the more sales calls they make), the better their performance (sales volume) is. Expectancy theory predicts that motivation is highest in jobs that have high expectancies.

In summary, expectancy theory is very insightful in understanding the components of motivation. It provides a rational basis on which to assess people's expenditure of effort.

Empirical Tests of the Theory.   Research has focused on the specific predictions the theory tries to make. One approach assumes the theory tries to distinguish the "most motivated" from the "least motivated" people in a group. With one force score derived for each person, the person with the highest score should be the most motivated and the person with the lowest score the least motivated. This type of approach is called an *across-subjects design* because predictions are made across people.

The second approach tests the theory differently. Here the theory assumes that each person is confronted with many tasks and then predicts on which tasks the person will work the hardest and on which he or she will expend the least effort. The theory is expanded to derive a force score for each task under consideration, and a criterion of effort is obtained for each. For each person, a correlation is computed between predictions of effort made by the theory and actual amounts of effort expended on the tasks. This type of approach is called a *within-subjects design*; predictions are made for each individual separately.

Validation studies generally find better predictions for the within-subjects design than the across-subjects design. Average validity coefficients for the across-subjects design are usually in the .30–.50 range, whereas average validity coefficients for within-subjects designs are usually .50–.70. The theory seems better at predicting the levels of effort an individual will expend on different tasks than at predicting gradations of motivation across different people (Kennedy, Fossum, & White, 1983). These validity coefficients are impressive; they are generally higher than those reported for other motivation theories.

In a major study on incentive motivation techniques, Pritchard, DeLeo, and Von Bergen (1976) reported that a properly designed, successful program for motivating employees will have many of the attributes proposed by expectancy theory. Among the conditions they recommend for a program to be successful are the following:

- Incentives (outcomes) must be provided and identified as highly attractive.
- The rules (behaviors) for attaining the incentives must be clear to both those administering the system and those actually in it.
- People in the system must perceive that variations in controllable aspects of their behavior will result in variations in their level of performance and ultimately their rewards.

In somewhat different words, these three conditions for an effective incentive motivation program reflect the concepts of valence, instrumentality, and expectancy, respectively. The importance of having desired incentives is another way of stating that the outcomes should have high valence. The clarity of the behaviors needed to attain the incentives reflects the strength or magnitude of the instrumentalities. The ability to control performance through different expenditures of effort is indicative of the concept of expectancy. In short, expectancy theory contains the key elements of a successful incentive system as derived through empirical research. Although not all research on expectancy theory is totally supportive, the results have tended to confirm its predictions.

Evaluation of the Theory.   Expectancy theory is a highly rational and conscious explanation of human motivation. The theory has also been used to predict other contexts that involve decisions besides choosing levels of effort. Also included are how people choose an occupation and how they choose to engage in one particular task over others. People are assumed to behave in a way that will maximize their expected gains (attainment of outcomes) from exhibiting certain job behaviors and expending certain levels of effort. To the extent that behavior is not directed toward maximizing gains in a rational, systematic way, the theory will not be upheld. Whenever unconscious motives deflect behavior from what a knowledge of conscious processes would predict, expectancy theory will not be predictive. Research suggests that people differ in the extent to which their behavior is motivated by rational processes. This was apparent in one of my own studies (Muchinsky, 1977). I examined the extent to which expectancy theory predicted the amount of effort college students put into each of their courses. In a within-subjects design, the average validity of the theory for all students was .52; however, for individual students it ranged from −.08 to .92. Thus the theory accurately predicted the expenditure of effort by some students but was unable to predict it for others. This supports the idea that some people have a very rational basis for their behavior, and thus the theory works well for them; others appear to be motivated more by unconscious factors, and for them the theory does not work well (Stahl & Harrell, 1981).

Van Eerde and Thierry (1996) conducted a meta-analysis of the expectancy theory of motivation. They concluded that reduced conceptualization of the theory (not involving the measurement of all the components) resulted in superior predictions of effort compared with the complete Valence-Instrumentality-Expectancy (VIE) model. On a practical level people do not go through life calculating VIE-based force scores, and at a conceptual level it appears equally untenable. However, the underlying concepts of expectancy theory provide one of the dominant explanations of work motivation in I/O psychology. As Pinder (1998) concluded, "At the very least [expectancy theory] is probably an accurate representation of how people form work-related intentions" (p. 359).

Goal-Setting Theory

Goal-setting theory of motivation
A theory of motivation based on directing one's effort toward the attainment of specific goals that have been set or established.

Statement of the Theory.   **Goal-setting theory** is a theory of motivation based on directing one's effort toward the attainment of specific goals that have been set or established. The theory is based on the assumption that people behave rationally. The crux of the theory is the relationship among goals, intentions, and task performance. Its basic premise is that conscious ideas regulate a person's actions. Goals are what the individual is consciously trying to attain, particularly as they relate to future objectives.

According to Locke and Latham (1990), goals have two major functions: they are a basis for motivation and they direct behavior. A goal provides guidelines for a person in deciding how much effort to put into work. Goals are intended behaviors; in turn, they influence task performance. However, two conditions must be met before goals can positively influence performance. First, the individual must be aware of the goal and know what must be accomplished. Second, the individual must accept the goal as something he or she is willing to work for. Goals can be rejected because they are seen as too difficult or too easy or because the person does not know what behaviors are needed to attain them. Acceptance of the goal implies the individual intends to engage in the behavior needed to attain it.

Locke and Latham's theory of goal setting states that more difficult goals lead to higher levels of job performance. The authors believe that commitment to a goal is proportional to its difficulty. Thus more difficult goals engender more commitment to their attainment. Goals also vary in specificity. Some goals are general (for example, to be a good biology student), and others are more specific (to get an A on the next biology test). The more specific the goal, the more concentrated the individual's effort in its pursuit and the more directed the behavior. It is also important for the person to receive feedback about task performance; this guides whether he or she should work harder or continue at the same pace.

Therefore, according to goal-setting theory, the following factors and conditions induce high motivation and task performance. Goals are behavioral intentions that channel our energies in certain directions. The more difficult and specific the goal, the greater is our motivation to attain it. Feedback on our performance in pursuit of the goal tells us whether our efforts are "on target." The source of motivation, according to goal setting, is the desire and intention to attain the goal; this must be coupled with the individual's acceptance of the goal. Goal-setting theory assumes people set acceptable target objectives and then channel their efforts in pursuit of them. In particular, the emphasis in goal-setting theory is on the direction of behavior.

Empirical Tests of the Theory.   For the most part, empirical tests of the theory are supportive. As an example, Latham and Baldes (1975) studied truck drivers hauling logs to lumber mills. The drivers' performance was studied under two conditions. First, drivers were told only to "do their best" in loading the trucks. After a time, they were told to set a specific, difficult goal of loading their trucks up to 94% of the legal weight limit. (The closer to the legal limit, the fewer trips were needed.) Each truck driver got feedback from a loading scale that indicated tonnage. Figure 12-2 shows the drivers' performance over a 48-week period. At the onset of goal setting, performance improved greatly; however, the cause is not clear-cut. One explanation may be the effects of goal setting. Another could be a sense of competition among the drivers as to who could load the truck closest to the legal limit. (The decline in performance between the fourth and fifth blocks was due to the truck drivers' "testing" of management to gauge its reaction.) In any case, the study clearly showed that performance under goal setting was superior to the "do your best" condition.

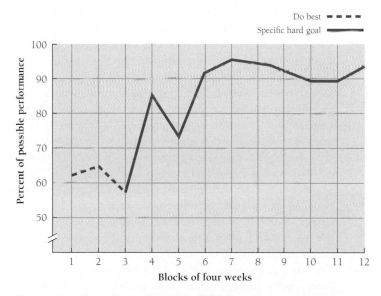

Figure 12-2   *The effect of specific, difficult goals on productivity*

Source: From "The Practical Significance of Locke's Theory of Goal Setting," by G. P. Latham and J. J. Baldes, 1975, *Journal of Applied Psychology, 60*, p. 123.

Wright (1990), however, concluded that assigned goals produce greater increases in performance than self-set goals. Also, Hollenbeck, Williams, and Klein (1989) reported that commitment to difficult goals is greater when goals are stated publicly rather than privately. Although the task behaviors and acceptance of goal setting vary, research indicates that goal setting produces better performance than the absence of goals or very general goals. As Latham and Marshall (1982) stated, the key issue appears to be not how a goal is set but *whether* the goal is set.

Evaluation of the Theory.   You should be struck by the elegance and simplicity of goal-setting theory. As Latham and Locke (1991) observed, goal-setting theory lies within the domain of purposefully directed action. The theory focuses on why some people perform better on work tasks than others. If the people are equal in ability and situational conditions, then the cause must be motivational. The theory states that the simplest and most direct motivational explanation of why some people perform better than others is that they have different performance goals. The difficulty and specificity of the goal influence performance, as do the amount and nature of feedback. There are some differences in performance between goals that are assigned and those that are self-selected. Different types of people also prefer different types of goals, but it is clear that goal setting elicits better performance.

Why is goal setting an effective motivational strategy? Pinder (1998) offered several reasons. Goals direct attention and action. They identify the target of intended behavior, and if they are stated specifically (as is recommended), the focus of the person's effort becomes well defined. Similarly, the condition that goals be made difficult relates directly to the intensity and persistence components of the motivation concept. If a goal is difficult, it normally requires more effort, over a longer period of time, to be attained. One element of persistence is tenacity, which is the refusal to quit trying, despite obstacles, until the goal is achieved. Commitment is one factor that contributes to tenacity, as does the sheer difficulty of the goal itself. Goal setting requires the development of a task-related strategy. When people contemplate a goal, they must also consider the means for its attainment, especially when the goal is seen as difficult. It may be that harder tasks are more likely to stimulate more strategy development than are easy tasks. Pinder believes the more specific the task goal, the more likely it is that people devise specific techniques to achieve it. Rousseau (1997) posited that goal setting is a form of self-management, where people can set their own goals and translate them into action. The acceptance of goals, when they are not self-set, is critical to their attainment. Thus goal setting puts people in control of their own behavior, which can itself serve as an incentive. Donovan and Williams (2003) reported that when people's behavior falls short of their stated goals, under certain conditions they may revise their goals. If the cause of the discrepancy is perceived to be a lack of ability, then individuals may revise their goals to be less difficult to attain. However, if the cause of the discrepancy is attributed to luck or unstable causes (e.g., an unusual combination of events that is unlikely to reoccur), goals are less likely to be revised.

Goal setting is not limited to highly rational people, although it does assume that people follow through with their intentions. The theory has a cognitive basis: employees must think about the goals they want to pursue; they must decide whether the goals are acceptable; they must understand what behaviors they have to exhibit to attain the goal; and they must know how to evaluate feedback on their progress. Research on feedback has shown that it is critical for optimal performance, but that people differ in their ability to use the information provided. There is also evidence that goal setting is effective for groups. Thus a work group can set a goal to decrease the scrap rate, for example, or to increase productive output. Group goals can be more difficult to attain, however, because in many cases the success of the overall group depends on more than just the success of individual members. A basketball team may set a goal of winning a certain number of games in a season, but its success is determined by more than just the number of points each player scores. Player coordination and integration must also be considered. One player might help the team by passing, another by rebounding, and the others by shooting.

Locke et al. (1981) reviewed 12 years of goal-setting research studies and came to the following conclusion: 90% of the studies show that specific and challenging goals lead to higher performance than easy goals, "do your best" goals, or no goals. Goal setting was found to improve task performance when (1) subjects have sufficient ability, (2) feedback is provided on progress relative to goals, (3) rewards are given for goal attainment, (4) management is supportive, and (5) individuals accept assigned goals.

Pritchard et al. (1988) noted that most research on improving productivity through goal setting has studied relatively simple jobs with the individual as the unit of analysis. Because most jobs are more complex and given the interdependencies in work, they think that group-level intervention studies are needed. The authors studied work group productivity for nine months. They introduced a group-level intervention designed to enhance group productivity consisting of three parts: feedback, group goal setting, and incentives (time off from work). Group-level feedback was found to increase productivity by 50% over the baseline, and goal setting plus feedback increased productivity by 75% over the baseline. The combined effect of feedback, goal setting, and incentives increased productivity by 76% over the baseline. The study showed that the principles of goal setting, proven useful with individual performance, also hold for group performance.

Locke and Latham (2002) asserted that the principles of goal setting theory generalize widely. Setting specific, difficult goals has been shown to increase performance on a wide range of variables, including quantity, quality, and time spent. The effects of goal setting have lasted as long as 25 years, and the theory is applicable to individuals, groups, and entire organizations. Locke and Latham concluded: "goal-setting theory is among the most valid and practiced theories of employee motivation in organizational psychology" (p. 714).

Self-Regulation Theory

Statement of the Theory.   There is not a single theory of self-regulation. Rather, a family of theories share some basic commonalities. A complete description of all the theories and an examination of the specific formulations by which they differ are beyond the scope of this book. Some of the more notable specific theories from this family of theories are self-efficacy theory and control theory. What follows is an explanation of the basic concepts of **self-regulation theory**.

Self-regulation theory of motivation A theory of motivation based on the setting of goals and the receipt of accurate feedback that is monitored to enhance the likelihood of goal attainment.

At the core of the theory is the idea of goals. It is presumed that people consciously set goals for themselves that guide and direct their behavior toward the attainment of these goals. Furthermore, individuals engage in a process of self-monitoring or self-evaluation; that is, they are aware of their progress in pursuit of the goals they have set. Their awareness of their progress is facilitated by receiving feedback. Feedback is information about how successful or "on target" the individual is in progressing toward the goal attainment. The feedback can and often does produce a discrepancy between the individual's current status in pursuing a goal and the desired or needed status to attain the goal. In essence, the feedback can provide an "error message" that the individual is off-track in pursuit of the goal. It is at this point that the individual responds to the information provided by the feedback. The individual's response can be in the form of altering behavior so as to reduce the magnitude of the discrepancy between the current progress toward attaining the goal and the needed progress toward goal attainment. Alternatively, the feedback received by the individual can show little or no discrepancy between the actual and desired status in the path toward goal attainment. If the discrepancy is small, the individual has enhanced self-efficacy, a sense of personal control and mastering of the environment, resulting in greater self-confidence that the goal can and will be attained. However, large discrepancies result in a loss of self-efficacy, which decreases the individual's sense of confidence that the goal will be attained. When the discrepancies are large, the individual may engage in goal revision, a process of readjusting or modifying the initial goal to a less difficult or ambitious level. Finally, life is a process of repeatedly pursuing goals in one form or another. With each success we experience in attaining the goals we set, we gain a greater collective sense of self-efficacy. Goal attainment acquires a degree of perceived generalizability, meaning the individual thinks that future goals are more likely to be attained because of his or her success in attaining past goals. The name of this family of theories, *self-regulation* theory, implies that individuals play an active role in monitoring their own behavior, seeking feedback, responding to the feedback, and forming opinions regarding their likelihood of success in future endeavors.

Ilies and Judge (2005) found evidence of self-regulation in goal setting. Goals are initially set, but following negative feedback goal levels were adjusted downward and raised following positive feedback. Thus the nature of the feedback received becomes a mechanism for the self-regulation of behavior. For example, assume an individual sets a goal of losing 30 pounds by dieting and exercising. The 30-pound weight loss is scheduled to occur over a 10-week period, with a loss of 3 pounds per week for 10 weeks. The feedback comes from weighing on a scale. If after 2 weeks, for example, the individual had not lost 6 pounds, a different pattern of eating and exercising may follow. If the individual continued not to meet the weight-loss goal over the ensuing weeks, the individual may revise the stated goal to perhaps 20 pounds over the 10-week period, or extend the 30-pound weight loss over a longer period of time, as perhaps 20 weeks. To the extent the individual is successful in meeting the weight-loss goal, the individual's self-efficacy about personal weight loss is enhanced to seek possible additional weight loss in the future. Furthermore, the sense of self-efficacy regarding the weight loss could generalize to other goals in other aspects of life.

Empirical Tests of the Theory.   Self-regulation theory has been tested in a wide variety of contexts as diversified as the various conceptualizations of the theory. Examples include how children learn in school (Zimmerman, 1995), career choice and development (Hackett, 1995), and treatment of addictive behaviors (Marlatt, Baer, & Quigley, 1995). The general pattern of results is very positive. Among the more supportive findings is the perceived importance of personal causation and control over goal pursuit. Self-regulation theory clearly positions the individual as the agent responsible for striving to attain the goal. We are continuing to learn the conditions under which individuals will remain committed to a goal (e.g., Klein et al., 1999) even when they perceive discrepancies from the feedback regarding their progress in goal attainment. VandeWalle and Cummings (1997) demonstrated some of the conditions under which individuals seek out feedback. In many cases there are few mechanisms for giving immediate and precise feedback to individuals on the state of their progress, like the scale for providing feedback regarding weight loss.

VandeWalle et al. (1999) confirmed a difference between a *learning* goal orientation and a *performance* goal orientation in a study of salespeople. A learning goal orientation is one in which the individual is committed to acquiring new skills and mastering new situations. A performance goal orientation is one in which the individual is committed to demonstrating his or her competence by seeking favorable judgments from others. VandeWalle et al. found that commitment to a learning goal orientation led to increased self-regulation tactics (i.e., seeking feedback, self-monitoring performance, planning future actions) and better on-the-job sales performance than just wanting to appear to others to have high ability. A practical implication of the findings is that organizations should assess the learning goal orientation of job applicants. When the job involves more than the conduct of rote and unchanging job duties, possession of a learning goal orientation will allow employees to learn new duties and responsibilities as the conduct of their work changes. Bell and Kozlowski (2002) reported that the goal orientation of employees to learning was influenced by their cognitive ability. Individuals with high cognitive ability pursued more challenging tasks and used more complex learning strategies than individuals with low cognitive ability. In short, self-regulation theory provides a rich conceptual basis to understand how individuals become motivated to pursue various goals and why they persevere in their pursuit of the goals.

Evaluation of the Theory.   Although some components of self-regulation theory have not been expressed in earlier theories of motivation, self-regulation theory has several concepts associated with other theories. The importance of setting goals and consciously focusing on their attainment is supported by early research on goal-setting theory. The association between expending effort in pursuit of a goal and ultimately attaining the goal is reflected in the concept of expectancy from expectancy theory. Furthermore, repeated success in goal attainment results in higher self-efficacy, which is the analog in expectancy theory of perceiving a strong relationship between effort and performance. The research on self-regulation theory reveals that we are more likely to be committed to goals that we regard as particularly significant and important to us than to trivial goals.

Self-efficacy is the belief in one's capabilities and capacity to attain the goals that have been set. In short, much of self-regulation theory is a distillation of previous motivational theories buttressed with new concepts (most notably the feedback/expectation discrepancy; Kluger, 2001) not found in other theories. Furthermore, it emphasizes how cognitive processes become translated or activated in behavior (e.g., Lord & Levy, 1994).

As was stated at the beginning of the description of this theory, there are multiple manifestations of self-regulation theory. Not all of the manifestations make identical predictions of behavior in specific circumstances (e.g., Phillips, Hollenbeck, & Ilgen, 1996). Nevertheless, the theory reaches the following conclusions about people (Bandura & Locke, 2003):

- They form intentions that include plans and strategies for attaining them.
- They set goals for themselves and anticipate the likely outcomes of possible actions to guide and motivate their efforts.

- They adapt personal standards and monitor and regulate their actions by self-reactive influences.
- They reflect on their efficiency, the soundness of their thoughts and actions, and the meaning of their pursuits and make corrective adjustments if necessary.

The concept of self-efficacy does indeed appear to be a useful and insightful way for us to understand our participation, performance, and persistence in a wide range of human endeavors (see Field Note 2).

Field Note 2: We Measure What We Treasure

Measurement is the process of assigning numbers to something in order to enhance our understanding of it. Some measurements are very basic, as the percentage of females and males in a particular group (class, organization, occupation). Other measurements are very precise. In chemistry, the concentration of a liquid is measured in "parts per million". What characteristics of *you* have been measured? Three examples might be your grade point average, your body weight, and your financial indebtedness. Why are these measurements taken? Because they serve some larger purpose, as for example, your grade point average is used to determine whether or not you will graduate.

We measure what is important to us, or to express it in rhyme, "we measure what we treasure." We may seek out activities in life to help us improve in what is important to us; a tutor to help improve our grade point average, a diet to help us lose weight, and a second job to help us pay our bills. But all that is important in life cannot be measured precisely. The best example of something that does not lend itself to precise measurement is quality. Interpersonal relationships are very important to us, yet their quality has long defied measurement.

Organizations that value quality (and virtually all do) often attempt to measure it. That which becomes measured is not always the same as the underlying issue that is treasured. I know of a medical clinic that measured the quality of its doctor-patient relationships by the average amount of time the doctor spent with a patient. The clinic reported that attempts to improve quality were successful, because the average amount of doctor-patient time increased from 8 minutes to 11 minutes. When you hear a voice message that states, "This call may be monitored for quality assurance," have you ever wondered what exactly is being *monitored* and what exactly is being *assured*?

We live in a society that is dominated by the measurement process. Many things in life can be measured with high precision. However, the precision of a measurement does not guarantee its relevance. Organizational attempts to "improve their numbers" are relevant only to the extent the numbers truly reflect what is treasured. However, our limited ability to quantify quality can lead us to false conclusions regarding the success of efforts to improve.

Work Design Theory

Statement of the Theory.   The **work design theory** of motivation is based on the presence of dimensions or characteristics of jobs that foster the expenditure of effort. This theory proposes that, for the most part, the locus of control for motivation is not individuals but the environment where work is performed. This theory proposes that, given the proper design of jobs, work can facilitate motivation in individuals. All people can be highly motivated given a work environment that fosters the expenditure of effort. The theory proposes there are characteristics or attributes of jobs that facilitate motivation. The number of these attributes and their identification have been the subject of extensive research. Early research (i.e., Turner & Lawrence, 1965) identified a set of attributes of job structure that affected motivation. However, the authors also found that not all individuals responded in the same way to the job attitudes. That is, there appeared to be individual differences across people that explain why some individuals respond favorably to a job with a high motivating potential. The process of designing jobs to possess these attributes is called **job enrichment**.

In 1976 Hackman and Oldham proposed the job characteristics model that best exemplifies this approach to motivation. It is among the most heavily researched theories in the history of I/O psychology. The model consists of four major parts. The first part is the specification of the particular *job characteristics* (also called *core job dimensions*) that induce motivation:

1. *Skill variety*—the number of different activities, skills, and talents the job requires;

2. *Task identity*—the degree to which a job requires completion of a whole, identifiable piece of work—that is, doing a job from beginning to end, with visible results;

3. *Task significance*—the job's impact on the lives or work of other people, whether within or outside the organization;

4. *Autonomy*—the degree of freedom, independence, and discretion in scheduling work and determining procedures that the job provides; and

5. *Task feedback*—the degree to which carrying out the activities required results in direct and clear information about the effectiveness of performance.

The second part of the model deals with the effect of the core job dimensions on the individual. They are said to influence three critical psychological states. The *experienced meaningfulness of work* is high when the job involves skill variety, task identity, and significance. The *experienced responsibility for work outcomes* is influenced mainly by the amount of autonomy. *Knowledge of results of work activities* is a function of feedback. According to the theory, high levels of the critical psychological states will lead to favorable personal and work outcomes, including high internal work motivation, work performance, and satisfaction, and low absenteeism and turnover.

The third part of the job characteristics model is a personality variable called growth need strength (GNS), which reflects a desire to be psychologically challenged by work. Like others before them, Hackman and Oldham felt that people with high needs for personal growth and development should respond more positively to jobs high on the core dimensions. Only people with high GNS should strongly experience the critical psychological states associated with such jobs. The entire job characteristics model is portrayed in Figure 12-3.

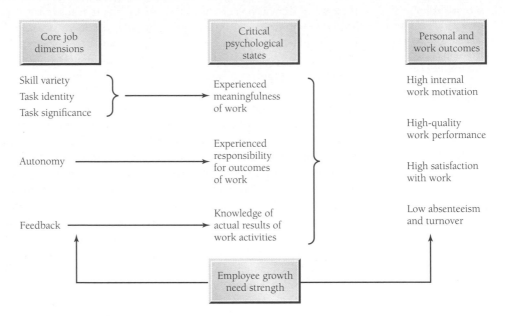

Figure 12-3   *The job characteristics model*

Source: From "Motivation Through the Design of Work: Test of a Theory," by J. R. Hackman and G. R. Oldham, 1976, *Organizational Behavior and Human Performance*, p. 256.

Hackman and Oldham then proposed the fourth part of the model, an equation for indexing the potential of a job to motivate its holder. The equation is based on the five core dimensions. The authors refer to their index as the *motivating potential score* (MPS) and define it as

$$\text{MPS} = \frac{\text{Skill variety} + \text{Task identity} + \text{Task significance}}{3} \times \text{Autonomy} \times \text{Feedback}$$

The first three core dimensions are averaged because they all contribute to the experienced meaningfulness of work, the first critical psychological state. The other two dimensions, autonomy and feedback, reflect the remaining critical states and thus are not averaged.

The job's motivating potential is very high when each factor in the equation is high. Because the factors are multiplied, low scores on any one yield a low motivating potential score. A score of zero on any of the major components (for example, a job completely lacking in autonomy) reduces the MPS to zero; the job has no potential for motivating incumbents.

Finally, as shown in Figure 12-3, the entire effect of the job characteristics model is moderated by the growth need strength. Only employees who are trying to satisfy the need for personal growth will respond favorably to a job high in motivating potential.

In summary, the theory posits that individuals who possess high growth need strength will exhibit high motivation in jobs characterized by having high motivation potential. It is also proposed that people in such jobs will experience high job satisfaction, another hypothesized outcome of the model.

Empirical Tests of the Theory.   Many studies have tested the relationships and predictions of the model. The empirical support is mixed; certain parts of the model are substantiated more than others.

Hackman and Oldham (1976) provided validation evidence for their own theory. In general, the overall results were moderately supportive:

- The core job dimensions related to the critical psychological states. Skill variety, task identity, and task significance combined to predict the level of perceived meaningfulness. The authors were thus able to identify those factors that contributed to "meaningful work," a frequent desire of employees.

- Individual differences in GNS have a moderating effect, as Hackman and Oldham suggested. In particular, high-GNS employees were more likely to have favorable personal and work outcomes after experiencing the critical psychological states.

- The core dimensions of autonomy and feedback were not as strongly supported with the corresponding critical psychological states of experienced responsibility and knowledge of results. Some of the other dimensions predicted these states as well or better.

In general, the results showed that jobs high on the core job dimensions were associated with high levels of motivation. Individuals with high GNS responded most favorably to these types of jobs. The importance of the intervening critical psychological states was not strongly supported.

Based on a review of more than 200 studies that tested the model, Fried and Ferris (1987) reached three conclusions. First, research suggests the existence of multiple job characteristics, but it is not clear how many there are. Second, the linkage between the job characteristics and the critical psychological states is not as strong as originally hypothesized. Third, the level of individual motivation specified in the model is indeed related to the job characteristics.

Humphrey, Nahrgang, and Morgeson (2007) conducted a meta-analysis of research that examined the five core job dimensions. The authors found the five motivational characteristics of work explained 25% of the variance in job performance, 34% in job satisfaction, and 24% in organizational commitment. They concluded that the motivating properties of work (and thus how work can be designed to increase motivation) have meaningful implications for important constructs in I/O psychology. Campion and Berger (1990) reported that jobs characterized by higher scores on the core job dimensions were associated with higher aptitudes and higher pay. Thus, when organizations want to make jobs more motivating, they should realize that they will need people with more ability, and should be prepared to pay them accordingly.

Evaluation of the Theory.   Work design theory, as represented by the job characteristics model, is one of the most heavily researched theories in I/O psychology. The meta-analytic review of the theory by Fried and Ferris (1987) was based on more than 200 studies that tested the model. What does the model offer us as a theory of motivation? The job characteristics model asserts that it is properties of the job or the workplace that foster motivation in people. In short, motivation is not a durable personal attribute or a trait that some people possess more of than others, but rather a variable attribute that can be enhanced if properly and intentionally designed within a work environment. However, research reveals that some jobs cannot be designed to enhance worker stimulation or motivation because of the inherent nature of the tasks performed on the job (see Field Note 3).

Research on the model has been criticized by some because assessments of the job characteristics are subjective, not objective. That is, the level of the job characteristics present in a job is measured by how people perceive and judge the job. They are not objective properties of the work environment, such as the number of hours in a workday or the air temperature at which work is performed. With a crucial reliance on subjective evaluations, the validity of the model is threatened by many of the rating issues discussed in Chapter 7. That is, two people performing the same job may differ (perhaps markedly) in their assessment of how much autonomy (for example) the job offers. Likewise, over time people with high GNS might tend to gravitate toward more complex jobs, while people with low GNS might tend to gravitate toward more simple jobs. Thus the "type of job" and "type of person" performing the job in real life are

Field Note 3: Packing Lightbulbs

As the research on work design has revealed, some jobs cannot be designed to be stimulating, motivating, and challenging. Some jobs are very routine, involving highly repetitive actions, and not much can be done to enhance their appeal. Yet, unglamorous as they may be, these jobs may be vital to an organization.

A company manufactured a special type of light bulb used primarily by commercial photographers. The bulbs were very delicate and fragile, and had a relatively brief life-span. It was imperative that the bulbs be packed in pre-formed casing, one bulb per pack. Four individually packed light bulbs would be placed in a larger case for shipping to retail stores. The company tried an automated packing system, but the breakage rate of the fragile bulbs was unacceptably high. It then tried packing the light bulbs by hand, but the employee turnover rate was excessive and attributed to the tedious nature of the work. The company decided it needed people to pack the light bulbs, but needed to find workers who would not want more intel-

lectual stimulation from the job than it could possibly provide. A facility for mentally handicapped people was contacted by the company. One of the goals of the facility was to find work their members could perform. The company hired six individuals with limited mental capability. The new workers found the job of packing light bulbs to be within their range of capability. In the first 8 years of staffing the job with mentally handicapped workers, the company incurred turnover of only one packer; a much lower rate of turnover than for any other area of the company. The light bulb packers are very proud of their contributions to the company and the company is equally proud of the packers. The packers acquired the status of heroes within the company, and represent a success story of the employ-ability of handicapped workers. This was a case of *not* redesigning a job to make it more stimulating, but rather finding employees who were sufficiently challenged by the job to perform it successfully and to continue performing it.

often confounded. Nevertheless, research on the job characteristics model has revealed some important findings about the concept of motivation. Rather than just trying to identify and select highly motivated job applicants, organizations can also design work in a way that fosters or facilitates motivation. The implication is that organizations need not be passive in their desire to identify motivated employees. By the way they design work, organizations can help achieve the very outcomes they strive to attain. Morgeson and Humphrey (2006) concluded that the motivational characteristics of work reflect the underlying mental demands of work. While some jobs can be redesigned to enhance worker motivation to perform them, other jobs cannot be altered in any meaningful way. For example, the job of parking lot attendant is monotonous because it involves little information processing. As such, this job would best be staffed with employees who are content with the lack of stimulation inherent in the highly repetitive nature of the tasks performed. Other jobs, as an air traffic controller, already have a very high level of information processing, and adding to it would only increase stress.

An Emerging Theory of Motivation

Many of the theories of motivation were originally developed in the 1960s and 1970s, before radical changes in society were brought about through globalization, information technology, downsizing, and teamwork (Steers, Mowday, & Shapiro, 2004). As Capelli (1999) stated, "Most observers of the corporate world believe that the traditional relationship between employer and employee is gone, but there is little understanding of why it ended and even less about what is replacing that relationship" (p. 1). To what degree do these changing relationships necessitate a new theory of work motivation? Latham and Budworth (2007) believe that theories of motivation must address themselves to how people adapt to their rapidly changing work worlds.

Stajkovic (2006) proposed a motivational construct called *core confidence*. This theory is based on a mix of personality factors and personal affect, similar to the characteristics of a mentally healthy person (as discussed in Chapter 11). The term "core confidence" connotes an enduring ability to effectively deal with uncertainty. The new demands of a rapidly changing workplace may readily induce worries over the possibility of job loss and substantial job changes. Core confidence represents the needed attributes to succeed in such a dynamic environment. Stajkovic proposed four dimensions to core confidence:

- *Active hope*—the person knows what needs to be done and is determined to do it. Active hope requires initiative by the person, as opposed to passive hope for the attainment of some outcome beyond the person's control (e.g., "I hope to win the lottery").
- *Self-efficacy*—the belief in one's abilities to perform well in the new work environment, whatever it may be.
- *Optimism*—the expectation that success will result from diligently applying yourself.
- *Resilience*—the capacity to bounce back from hardship; the acceptance that setbacks are temporary and can be overcome.

It should be noted that Stajkovic's conception of a motivated person is similar to Warr's (2007b) conception of a mentally healthy person. This similarity is not coincidental. Motivation and mental health share the same fundamental premise of being able to control one's life, as opposed to being a passive recipient of control by external forces. If Stajkovic's theory is representative of other motivational theories born in the 21st century, such theories will manifest an integration of psychological concepts that 20th century theories segregated. Latham and Budworth stated, "At the dawn of this new millenium, it would appear that cognitive theories of motivation will likely be integrated with affective processes as well as personality" (p. 375). The core confidence construct proposed by Stajkovic clearly embodies affective processes and personality, while other recent theories (e.g., De Shon & Gillespie, 2005) are more cognitive in nature. The primary issue facing researchers is to understand what psychological constructs are most useful in explaining human behavior in an era unlike we have witnessed before.

Overview and Synthesis of Work Motivation Theories

After studying the four theories of work motivation presented, one can reasonably ask whether any unifying themes run through them. Kanfer (1992) proposed that the theories can be examined along a continuum of their conceptual proximity to action. The endpoints of the continuum are distal (i.e., distant) and proximal (i.e., near) constructs. *Distal* constructs such as personality exert indirect effects on behavior. *Proximal* constructs begin with the individual's goals and characteristics of the workplace that directly influence behavior. Figure 12-4 portrays the motivation constructs

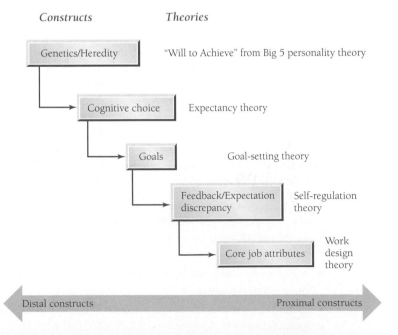

Figure 12-4   *A framework of motivation constructs and theories*

Source: Adapted from "Work Motivation: New Directions in Theory and Research," by R. Kanfer, 1992, *International Review of Industrial and Organizational Psychology*, C. L. Cooper and I. T. Robertson (eds.), p. 4, London: Wiley.

and associated theories arrayed along the distal/proximal continuum proposed by Kanfer.

As illustrated by the arrangement of the motivational theories in Kanfer's framework, the array of explanations for motivation range from genetic predisposition to the characteristics of jobs.

At the extreme distal end is the construct of genetics/heredity. Ilies, Arvey, and Bouchard (2006) provided comprehensive empirical evidence to support the proposition that genetic factors influence work motivation. This chapter has not formally examined a genetics-based theory of motivation, but we are familiar with it from another area. It will be recalled that a contemporary interpretation of personality is represented in the Big 5 theory. One personality factor of considerable interest to I/O psychologists is Conscientiousness. Another name for conscientiousness is "will to achieve" (Digman & Takemoto-Chock, 1981). This name implies that individuals who are attentive to detail, rule abiding, and honest also exhibit high ambition. Accordingly this view of motivation is that the capacity to be motivated is genetically determined, is an enduring component of one's personality, and can be assessed with a paper-and-pencil personality inventory. Indeed, Kanfer and Ackerman (2000) developed such a measure, the Motivational Trait Questionnaire. Mitchell and Daniels (2003a) concluded that the fastest-growing area of research in motivation pertains to personality-based or dispositional approaches. For example, Van Eerde (2000) found that procrastination is a stable personality characteristic. Likewise, Erez and Isen (2002) found that people with positive affect performed better and exhibited more persistence than people with negative affect. This area of research indicates that our willingness to expend effort is a defining component of our personality. Kanfer and Heggestad (1997) refer to this personality factor as "trait achievement."

As we continue down the continuum toward proximal constructs, there is increasing reliance on the assumption that people make conscious, deliberate, controllable choices about how much effort they choose to expend. This is the antithesis of a genetic/dispositional orientation toward motivation. Proximal theories are heavily predicated upon a cognitive explanation for motivation. Expectancy theory postulates that individuals are consciously aware of the results or outcomes they wish to attain, perceive relationships between their behavior and attaining those outcomes, and also perceive a relationship between their effort and their behavior. The theory elevates motivation to a conscious choice made by the individual. Goal-setting theory is another example of this orientation and offers motivation as an opportunity to engage in self-control or self-regulation. The capacity to control one's own life was noted in the preceding chapter as one of the determinants of mental health. Goal-setting theory postulates that one way we can take some control over our life is to decide how hard we are willing to work. Locke (1991) offered this description of how important individual choice or volition is in our lives:

> For example, people can choose . . . what their needs are and how to satisfy them; what values they should pursue and the validity of the values other people have told them to pursue; whether and how to apply their values to a specific situation; what goals to set, how to develop plans to reach them, and whether to commit to the goals and plans; what their performance capacity is for a specific task and how to raise it; what their performance means and who is responsible for it; the adequacy of their

rewards and the relation of these rewards to their values; the causes of their affective reactions to their performance and rewards; and how to modify these reactions (e.g., by changing their performance or changing their value standards). (pp. 297–298)

The self-regulation theory of motivation is an extension and modification of goal-setting theory. Self-regulation theory also involves consciously setting goals, then obtaining feedback on the degree to which the individual is on target in pursuit of the goal, and then using that feedback to modify or maintain the chosen paths of action to goal attainment. The process of self-monitoring or self-evaluation clearly is predicated upon a conscious, rational, deliberate strategy of using information to guide behavior. Finally, work design theory specifies there are dimensions or components of the job itself that induce motivation. Although there are individual differences with regard to how people will respond to these job characteristics, it is the properties of the work environment itself that facilitate energized behavior. Work design theory contains the most proximal constructs, constructs that in fact can be designed or structured by the organization to induce motivation. A general summary of the major theories of work motivation discussed in this chapter is presented in Table 12-1.

Table 12-1 *Summary and evaluation of work motivation theories*

Theory	Source of Motivation	Empirical Support	Organizational Applicability
Expectancy theory	Relationship among desired outcomes, performance–reward, and effort–performance variables	Moderate–strong: More strongly supported in within-subjects than across-subjects experiments.	Strong: Theory provides a rational basis for why people expend effort, although not all behavior is consciously determined as postulated.
Goal-setting theory	Intention to direct behavior in pursuit of acceptable goals	Moderate–strong: Performance under goal-setting conditions is usually superior to conditions in which no goals are set.	Strong: Ability to set goals is not restricted to certain types of people or jobs.
Self-regulation theory	Self-monitoring of feedback designed to enhance goal attainment	Moderate–strong: Feedback can provide direction for behavior if monitored and acted upon.	Strong: Organizations can provide directive feedback to individuals to facilitate goal attainment.
Work design theory	Attributes of jobs that can facilitate motivation among people with a strong need to achieve	Moderate–strong: Clear support for the validity of the job characteristics but less support for the critical psychological states	Moderate: Not all jobs can be designed to be stimulating and motivating.

A few researchers (e.g., Erez & Earley, 1993) proposed motivational concepts that originated in non-Western cultures but may be universally applicable. For example, Earley (1997) discussed the concept of *face* (as in "saving face") as a basis of social motivation. Face has been considered a predominantly Asian concept. Earley defined *face* as the evaluation of a person based on self and external social judgments. Face does not lie completely within or outside the individual because face is both given (by others) and claimed (by the self). Thus the concept of face is grounded in a social exchange process involving self-presentation. It is proposed that our behavior is guided by efforts to regulate and enhance our self-image. Examples include deriving a sense of prestige from a job title, living in an affluent neighborhood, and maintaining a certain physical appearance (e.g., "power dressing"). The loss of face is associated with shame and weakens the network of social relations of which we are all a part. Earley believes the concept of face is a useful framework for understanding our behavior within a social context. We are motivated to enhance face, and our actions can be judged as being instrumental for doing so. This perspective takes a decidedly social view of motivation. Although it remains to be seen what role such concepts as face will play in the evolution of motivation theories, Earley's theory presents a cross-culturally based explanation for what is a timeless and boundaryless phenomenon—an understanding of our behavior (see Cross-Cultural I/O Psychology: Cross-Cultural Differences in Incentives).

The subject of human motivation is also being addressed from a genetic basis. This view is in marked contrast to considering motivation as a product of job or social influences. Rather, the search is inward to the cellular and genetic levels for the biochemical determinants of human behavior. Ridley (1999) described the mapping of the human genome, particularly with reference to the gene *D4DR*, which is a component of chromosome 11. This gene determines how receptive neurons are to dopamine,

Cross-Cultural I/O Psychology: *Cross-Cultural Differences in Incentives*

Given the documented differences across cultures with regard to values and attitudes, it is not surprising that workers around the world have different preferences for incentives and rewards. Sanchez-Runde and Steers (2003) described some of these differences identified through cross-cultural research. Individual-based incentive pay (e.g., financial bonuses for meritorious performance) is commonly used in the United States. It is designed to accentuate and reward differences among workers. A study found that Asian companies that adopted this Western strategy for motivation met with substantial problems. A merit-based reward system that would reduce the pay of less productive workers would also cause them to lose face and disrupt group harmony. Giving all employees the same bonus irrespective of merit defeated the intent of the incentive system and substantially escalated labor costs. Another form of incentive pay is compensation-at-risk. Instead of a fixed salary, managers can opt to place a portion of their salary "at risk." The practical implication is if the managers perform well, their total pay will be greater than what they would have earned with a fixed salary. The converse is also true, however, with poorer performance resulting in less pay. One study found that American managers were more risk-oriented; some were willing to convert 100% of their pay to at-risk compensation. European managers were much more risk-averse; they would seldom commit more than 10% of their pay to at-risk compensation.

Another study reported that Swedes typically preferred additional time off for superior performance instead of additional income, whereas if given a choice, Japanese workers prefer financial incentives (with a strong preference for group-based incentives). Japanese workers tend to take only about half of their paid holidays because taking all the time available may show a lack of commitment to the group. Sanchez-Runde and Steers stated that Japanese workers who take their full vacations or refuse to work overtime are labeled *wagamama* ("selfish"). "As a result, *karoshi* (death by overwork) is a serious concern in Japan, while Swedes see taking time off as part of an inherent right to a healthy and happy life" (p. 366).

which in turn controls neural electrical discharge and regulates the flow of blood to the brain. Ridley stated, "To simplify grossly, dopamine is perhaps the brain's motivational chemical. Too little and the person lacks initiative and motivation. Too much and the person is easily bored and frequently seeks new adventures. Here perhaps lies the root of a difference in 'personality'" (p. 163). Erez and Eden (2001) succinctly summarized this orientation toward the origins of human behavior: "Although for us as psychologists the jump from chemicals to motivation to personality is a bit abrupt, the trend is clear: We are drawing nearer to the dream—or nightmare—of chemistry-based motivation" (p. 7).

The Application of Motivational Strategies

After four approaches to work motivation have been presented, it is almost inevitable to ask which theory has the greatest practical value or, perhaps more to the point, which theory will "work" for you. There is no simple answer to this question, but some practical guidelines are available to assist in the decision. Mitchell (1997) referred to this process as "matching" motivational strategies with varying organizational contexts.

Mitchell stated that we must begin with a general assessment of the situation we face and then systematically narrow our focus. There are three major determinants to human behavior: ability, motivation, and situational factors (including constraints). The most obvious beginning point for our assessment is constraints. Constraints are obstacles or impediments that limit the range of our behavior. It would be our initial goal to remove the constraints, or at the least reduce their limiting effect on our behavior. The lack of a needed piece of equipment (e.g., a computer) is an example of a situational constraint. Gaining access to a computer might readily improve your behavior in a way that "trying harder" might not.

If your behavior is not constrained or limited, the next step is to examine whether you have sufficient skills and abilities to engage in the desired behavior. Perhaps you have a computer, but you don't have the knowledge, ability, or sufficient training to use it. If lack of ability does not appear to be a major issue, the problem may have a large motivational component. In short, there is nothing preventing you from engaging in the behavior and you have the ability to engage in the behavior, but you are unwilling to or uninterested in doing so. However, there are several types of motivational issues to consider. If you feel bored or indifferent, the motivational issue is one of arousal. If you are interested and try to succeed but your efforts result in failure, perhaps your energies are being channeled in the wrong direction. If you are going in the wrong direction to achieve your goal, trying harder will not result in success. Alternatively, some successful behaviors require a high intensity of motivation. In this context "trying harder" would be an appropriate strategy because moderate levels of effort may not be adequate to attain the desired outcome.

Finally, there is also a persistence dimension to motivation. Some outcomes can be achieved by engaging in short but intense bursts of energy (e.g., getting a good grade by "cramming" the night before the exam). Other outcomes can be achieved only by persistence and dedicated effort over the long haul, not by a sudden burst of motivation. Becoming physically fit through proper exercise and diet is an example of an outcome that can be achieved only through persistence.

Thus, motivation is a product of arousal, direction, intensity, and persistence. Mitchell recommended finding the best "match" between the motivational strategy and the work context you face. Work contexts differ in many ways—for example, the clarity of the performance criteria by which you will be judged, the frequency and nature of the feedback you receive about your behavior, whether your performance is judged on an individual or group basis, and so on. Although goal setting and self-regulation are the most supportable and adaptable motivational strategies, they require accurate and timely feedback. For example, if you set the goal of earning an A in a class but your grade is determined by one comprehensive exam at the end of the course, you will have received no formal feedback on your performance throughout the semester. Instead, you will have to rely on informal feedback for an internal sense of how well you are understanding the course material, which may be inaccurate. Expectancy theory can provide guidance on issues of direction and intensity, such as the perceived degree of association between how hard you try in a class and how well you perform. If the level of association is not high, do you have any insights about factors that determine the low level of association? That is, could you seek the assistance of the professor or a teaching assistant outside of class? Finally, if the class utilizes team projects, can team goals and team rewards be created? The various theories of motivation are differentially applicable depending on the time frame in question and characteristics of the individual.

Donovan (2001) concluded that it is not possible to integrate all the theories of motivation into a single universal theory of motivation. However, Mitchell and Daniels (2003b) summarized the entire body of findings on motivation as follows:

> First, goals are a major factor on the motivational landscape. Almost every approach to this topic includes goals. Humans are goal setters and goal seekers. People also prefer pleasure to pain and will seek positive outcomes and states and avoid negative ones. Third, we prefer mastery and control to uncertainty and ambiguity. Mastery and control are direct antecedents of our explanations, confidence, and efficiency. We also prefer interesting, stimulating, and satisfying to boring, stressful, and repetitious activities. In addition, we are consistently involved in social interactions and social comparison. We want to have a positive view of ourselves and be liked by others and treated fairly. The social context is a major source of such information. And finally, we are all unique with genetic and personal backgrounds that shape our wants, desires, and reactions to events. These individual differences play a crucial role in understanding motivation and variation in motivation. (p. 38)

The length and breadth of issues addressed in this concluding paragraph reflect the inherent complexity of work motivation.

Case Study What to Do with Harry?

Joe Collins, Production Manager of York Tool and Die Company, tapped Harry Simpson on the shoulder. "Harry," Collins said, "I'd like to talk to you in my office."

"Right now?" asked Simpson.

"Right now," Collins replied.

Simpson took off his safety goggles and put them on the rack. He was a line foreman, and it was unusual to be called away from his line. He figured it had to be something big; otherwise, Collins would have waited until break.

"Hey, Willie," Simpson yelled at his lead man, "cover for me, will you? I've got to talk to Joe."

Simpson walked into Collins's office and sat down. The look on Collins's face told him it wasn't going to be good news.

"Harry, I've known you for eight years," Collins began. "You've always kept your nose to the grindstone. You've been conscientious and diligent. I've had fewer problems with you than with most of the other foremen. But lately things have been different. You've come to work late five times in the past month. You've been late turning in your weekly production sheets. The scrap rate of your line has been going up, too. I was also told that Willie had to spend a lot of time breaking in the two new guys. That's your job. What's going on, Harry?"

Simpson shuffled his feet and cleared his throat. "I didn't realize these things were happening."

"You didn't know you were late?" Collins was incredulous. "You've been coming to work at seven-thirty for eight years. When you punch in at seven-forty-five, you're late, and you know it."

"I don't know, Joe. I just haven't felt with it lately," Simpson explained. "Doris says I've been moping around the house a lot lately, too."

"I'm not here to chew you out, Harry," Collins replied. "You're a valuable man. I want to find a way to get you back in gear. Anything been bugging you lately?"

"Well, I've finally figured out I'm not going to make it to supervisor. At least not in the near future. That's what I've been working for all along. Maybe I've hit my peak. When Coleman made it to supervisor, I figured I'd be the next one up. But it never happened. I'm not sore—Coleman is a good man and he deserved it. I just feel kind of deflated."

"You're well respected by management, Harry, and your line thinks you're great, too. You've set a tough example to live up to. I want you to keep it up—we need people like you."

"I know I have an important job," said Simpson, "but I figure I can't get ahead anymore, at least not on how well I do my job. I guess it boils down to luck or something."

"What if I give you a new line to run?" Collins asked. "Would that give you a new challenge?"

"No, I wouldn't want that, Joe," replied Simpson. "I like my line, and I don't want to leave them."

"All right, Harry, but here's the deal," Collins stated. "I want you to cut back on the lateness, pronto. Get your production reports in on time, and watch the scrap. With the price of copper going up, we've got to play it tight. Oh, and give Willie a break. He's got enough to do. Does this sound okay to you?"

"Yeah," Simpson said. "You're only telling me to do what I'm supposed to be doing."

"Keep at it, Harry," Collins said with a smile. "In two more years, you'll get a ten-year pin."

Simpson got up to leave. "It won't pay the rent, but I'd like to have it."

Simpson walked back to the line. Willie looked up and saw him coming. "What'd Joe want?" Willie asked.

"Oh, nothing much," Simpson replied.

Willie knew Simpson was hiding something, and Simpson figured Willie knew what it was.

Questions

1. In terms of expectancy theory, how would you describe Simpson's valence for a promotion and its instrumentality?
2. What goals did Collins set for Simpson? Should Simpson have set these goals for himself? Why or why not?
3. What specific types of feedback might Simpson seek to ensure the goals were being met?
4. How might Simpson's job be re-designed to make it more challenging for him?
5. Do you think Simpson has become lazy or unmotivated, or is just going through a temporary slump in his performance? What does your answer suggest about the stability or endurance of motivation over time?

Chapter Summary

- Work motivation is one of the most fundamental and critical issues in understanding the way people behave in organizations.
- Motivation is a very complex topic, and many theories have been proposed to explain why people behave as they do.
- One set of theories posits that people differ in their motivation because of innate personality differences, perhaps of a genetic origin.
- The expectancy theory of motivation posits that individuals establish a linkage between what they want to attain, how well they must perform to get what they want, and how hard they must work to perform at that level.
- The goal-setting theory of motivation states that people intentionally set goals for themselves and then direct their behavior to attain the desired goal.
- A set of theories pertaining to the self-regulation theory of motivation asserts that people set goals for themselves and then engage in a process of self-monitoring. The feedback they receive tells them whether they are "on target" in achieving their goals, and then they will adjust their effort and behavior accordingly.
- The work design theory of motivation posits that the capacity for motivation lies not within people but within the work environment. Jobs can be designed in a way that motivates the people who perform them.
- The various theories of work motivation offer practical techniques that can be applied to enhance motivation.
- Recent research on motivation is directed toward understanding the process by which people adapt to their ever-changing jobs.

Learning Objectives

- Explain the major topics of interest among leadership researchers.

- Describe the major theoretical approaches to the study of leadership: trait, behavioral, power and influence, transformational and charismatic leadership, implicit leadership, and substitutes for leadership.

- Understand the points of convergence among the leadership approaches.

- Understand cross-cultural leadership issues.

- Understand the concept of entrepreneurship.

- Understand diversity issues in leadership.

When you think of leadership, many ideas might come to mind. Your thoughts might relate to power, authority, and influence. Maybe you think of actual people—Washington, Lincoln, Kennedy, King—or what effective leaders do. In short, the concept of leadership evokes a multitude of thoughts, all of which in some way address the causes, symptoms, or effects of leadership. Bennis (2007) framed the concept of leadership in terms of three factors. "Leadership is grounded in a relationship. In its simplest form, it is a tripod—a leader or leaders, followers, and the common goal they want to achieve. None of these three elements can survive without the others" (pp. 3–4).

This chapter will examine how I/O psychologists have tried to grapple with the multifaceted concept of leadership, particularly as it relates to behavior in the world of work. Research on leadership has been varied because investigators have approached the concept from different perspectives. Some research has examined what strong leaders are like as people by looking at demographic variables, personality traits, skills, and so on. Without followers, there can be no leaders; accordingly, some research has examined leader–follower relationships. Presumably "strong" leaders accomplish things that "weak" leaders do not; thus other research focuses on the effects of leadership. An interesting question addresses contextual effects in leadership—for example, is leadership of a prison more demanding than leadership of a business organization? Thus the situation in which leadership occurs has attracted much attention. Although the diversity of interests in the domain of leadership research expands our basis of understanding, it also creates ambiguity as to exactly what leadership is all about.

It is also a matter of scientific debate whether "leadership" is different from "management" or "administration." Historically and practically, these terms have been used interchangeably. For example, one might readily encounter this sentence: "The leaders of the company manage its resources and are responsible for its administration." A slight variation would be: "The management of the company administers its operations by providing leadership." Are these terms really synonymous? Some researchers think not, believing that management requires administrative oversight but not necessarily the manifestation of leadership. Leadership implies providing a vision of the future and inspiring others to make that vision a reality. As such, a large component of leadership is implicitly future-oriented. In contrast, management and administration refer more to present-oriented activities. According to some scholars, leadership has a heroic, larger-than-life quality that differentiates it from related concepts. Some people believe that many people can be trained to be managers, but leaders possess unique qualities that may not be developed in all individuals. This particular view of leadership is evidenced in some of the theories presented here.

The scientific study of leadership also embodies two methodological research issues previously discussed in this book. The first is the use of qualitative research methods and the second is differing levels of analysis. Lowe and Gardner (2000) conducted a major review of leadership research done in the past decade. Unlike many areas of research in I/O psychology, the use of qualitative research methods in the study of leadership is fairly common. Lowe and Gardner estimated that about one-third of all leadership research conducted in the past decade utilized qualitative methods. Also, the examination of differing levels of analysis is common in leadership research. As will shortly be discussed, the study of leadership can involve the characteristics of leaders, the characteristics of the group that is led, the situation in which leadership occurs, and the interaction of these factors (e.g., certain types of leaders in certain types of situations). Lowe and Gardner asserted that all these differing levels of analysis are evident in leadership research.

Leadership is of interest to the I/O practitioner as well as to the scientist. In fact, leadership is one of the richer areas of interplay between the two; it has had a healthy influx of ideas from both camps. Identifying and developing leaders are major concerns of organizations today. Companies often train their higher-level personnel in skill areas (interpersonal relations, decision making, planning, etc.) that directly affect their performance as leaders. In Greensboro, North Carolina, there is an organization called the Center for Creative Leadership whose purpose is to enhance, through training, the leadership skills of key business personnel. Not surprisingly, the military is also greatly concerned with leadership. It sponsors a wide variety of research projects that have the potential for enhancing our understanding of this subject. In summary, the balance between the theory and practice of leadership is fairly even as a result of this dual infusion of interest.

Major Topics in Leadership Research

Because of the many facets of leadership, researchers have focused on selected areas. Six major categories of studies will be presented next.

Positional Power

Some investigators view leadership as the exercise of *positional power*: the higher the position in the organizational hierarchy, the more power the position has. In the leadership context, we are most concerned with *legitimate power*: the formal power given to a position. The positional power of a company president exceeds that of a manager; in turn, the manager has more power than a secretary. Viewing leadership in terms of positional power separates the person from the role. Little attention is given to the individual's attributes; most is aimed at the use of positional power. Organizational theorists use such terms as the "power of the presidency" and "administrative clout;" issues not really related to the people in such positions. Sometimes history judges leaders on their inability to use all the power their positions give them. Other leaders try to exceed the power granted their positions. In some countries leaders emerge by seizing power through military or political coups. According to this perspective, leadership is inherent in an organizational position based on the concept of power.

In the total spectrum of leadership research, a relatively small number of studies have been done on positional power. Many I/O psychology researchers find it hard to separate leadership itself from the characteristics of people in leadership positions. But research on positional power has shown that some leadership issues transcend individual differences.

The Leader

Characteristics of individual leaders have been one of the most researched areas of leadership. Most leadership theories are based on understanding the differences among personal traits and behaviors. This is almost the opposite of the emphasis on positional power, which minimizes individual differences. Many early studies considered demographic and personality variables. Others examined what behaviors individual leaders exhibit that influence the judgment of whether they are strong or weak leaders. Statements like "Strong leaders radiate confidence" and "Weak leaders are indecisive" reflect the school of thought that emphasizes the importance of the leader in the leadership process. Research has been done on the selection of people into leadership positions; other research has been devoted to training people to enhance their leadership skills. The significance here is the focus on leader characteristics or behavior and their influence on others. This is a classic I/O psychology perspective, and it is the most popular in leadership research literature.

The Led

Another area of interest is the characteristics of the followers, or the led. This is a shift in emphasis from the preceding area, in that leadership is construed more in terms of who is led than who does the leading. Casual observation suggests that some people are easier for leaders to work with than others. Military leaders have long known that some groups of recruits are more responsive, cohesive, or productive. Teachers have noted variations among student classes. Organizational training directors have found differences among trainee groups. We thus have evidence that a leader's performance is not the same across different groups of followers. We might label this class of studies "followership" research.

As an example, consider the case of a high school science teacher. The material may remain fairly constant over time, but the teacher's behavior may vary depending on the students. One year the teacher may have a class of bright, motivated students who quickly grasp the material. The teacher may respond by offering the class more advanced topics, laboratory experiments, or field trips. Another year the teacher could have students who have difficulty learning the material. The teacher may have to instruct at a slower pace, use more examples, and offer help sessions. Other variables are class size, disciplinary problems, and student backgrounds. Thus attributes of the led (the students) as indexed by their intelligence, motivation, number, interpersonal harmony, and background would be examined as factors affecting the behavior of the leader (the teacher).

The Influence Process

Rather than focusing on either the leaders or the led, some researchers have found it instructive to examine the relationship or link between the two parties, particularly as they influence each other. Here researchers give their attention to the dynamics of this relationship, although they may also consider characteristics of both the leaders and the followers. In a general sense, what leaders "do" to a group is influence its members in the pursuit of some goal. Research on the influence process examines how this process is enacted.

The concept of influence entails how one person's actions affect another's. There are several methods of influence, including coercion, manipulation, authority, and persuasion. *Coercion* involves modifying behavior by force. *Manipulation* is a controlled distortion of reality, as seen by those affected. People are allowed to see only those things that will evoke the kind of reaction desired. In the case of *authority*, agents appeal to a mutual decision giving them the right to influence. *Persuasion* means displaying judgment in such a way that those exposed to it accept its value. Researchers study how these methods are used in leader–follower relationships. As an example, Greene and Schriesheim (1980) studied two types of leader behavior: instrumental and supportive. In *instrumental* leadership a leader clarifies the group's goals. A *supportive* leader is friendly and considerate of others' needs. Greene and Schriesheim classified various work groups by size. The results showed that relatively small groups are most influenced by a supportive leader and that instrumental leadership works better in larger groups (perhaps because it brings order and structure to the group).

The Situation

Leadership research has also focused on the situation or context in which leader–group relationships occur. The situation can greatly affect the types of behaviors a leader has to exhibit to be effective. Imagine the leader of a Boy Scout troop, the supervisor of a production crew, and the warden of a prison. Each faces a different situation. Research on situational factors has tried to identify how contexts differ and what effect they have on leader behavior.

The context in which leadership occurs influences which type of leader behavior is called for. As an example, Green and Nebeker (1977) studied two types of leadership situations: one favorable and one unfavorable. In the favorable situation leaders emphasized interpersonal relations and were supportive of the group members. In the unfavorable situation the leaders became more task-oriented and more concerned with goal accomplishment than with interpersonal relations. Green and Nebeker were able to show that different situations evoke different styles of leadership behavior.

Leader Emergence Versus Leader Effectiveness

The final category considered here is emergence versus effectiveness of leaders. Some leadership researchers are interested in the dynamics of what causes leaders to emerge within a group. This emergence process can either be formal (that is, a person is designated to be the leader) or informal (that is, a person evolves as the leader of a group without having been so designated). Researchers examine such characteristics as the leader's age, gender, and physical appearance, or they consider verbal and nonverbal behaviors associated with the subsequent emergence. Also of interest might be the characteristics of the group from which the leader emerges. For example, Goktepe and Schneier (1989) reported in a study no difference in the proportion of men and women who emerged as leaders. However, group members with masculine gender-role characteristics emerged as leaders significantly more than those with feminine gender-role characteristics. In short, leader emergence is concerned with the process that results in someone being regarded as the leader of a group.

Research on leader effectiveness is concerned with the performance of the leader. In this line of research, the characteristics of the leader (or the group) that are associated with evaluations of leader quality and the criteria for effective leaders are of interest. In the former case, effective leaders might be identified as possessing certain characteristics, such as verbal fluency, sensitivity, decisiveness, and so on. In the latter case, effective leadership might be regarded as success in task completion (that is, an effective leader gets the job done) or acceptance by the group (that is, an effective leader has group support). Taggar, Hackett, and Saha (1999) found that individuals who emerged as leaders were characterized as having high general mental ability, followed by the Big 5 personality characteristics of Conscientiousness, Extraversion, and Emotional Stability. Issues associated with both leader emergence and leader acceptance have long been of interest to I/O psychologists.

Overview

Leadership researchers do not limit their studies or theories to just one of these six areas. A researcher interested in influence processes might consider in which situations influence attempts will be successful. Interest in leader traits may also include consideration of follower traits. The purpose in describing these areas is to highlight the major categories of leadership research and acknowledge their different units of analysis while realizing that the areas are not mutually exclusive. Table 13-1 summarizes the six major research areas and lists the types of topics and questions each area tends to address.

Table 13-1 *Research topics and assorted issues in leadership research*

Research Topic	Unit of Analysis	Variables of Interest	Research Questions
Positional power	Organizational roles and positions	Influence tactics; use of power	Under what conditions will organizations resort to strong influence attempts?
The leader	Individual leaders	Personality characteristics; leader behaviors	What traits and behaviors differentiate effective and ineffective leaders?
The led	Work groups and subordinates	Group size; experience of subordinates	What types of subordinates desire close supervision?
Influence process	Superior–subordinate interface	Receptivity to influence; nature of influence attempts	Under what conditions are leaders most susceptible to subordinate influence attempts?
The situation	Environment or context in which leadership occurs	Situational effects on leader behavior; factors defining favorable situations	How do various situations modify leader behavior?
Leader emergence versus effectiveness	Individual and/or groups	Group dynamics and individual characteristics	How do individuals become recognized as leaders?

Theoretical Approaches to Leadership

Several theoretical approaches have been developed to explain leadership. These orientations will be presented in terms of their dominant focus and contribution to the study of leadership.

The Trait Approach

The **trait approach** is the oldest conception of leadership. Zaccaro, Kemp, and Bader (2004) defined leader traits as "relatively stable and coherent integration of personality characteristics that foster a consistent pattern of leadership performance across a variety of group and organizational situations. These characteristics reflect a range of stable individual differences, including personality, temperament, motives, cognitive abilities, skills, and expertise" (p. 104). Day and Zaccaro (2007) added that personality traits do not "cause" behavior, but are labels or terms used to make sense of behaviors. In this view of leadership, effective leaders are described as possessing characteristics (traits) that are associated with leadership talents. The list of such traits is extensive and often includes personality characteristics such as being decisive, dynamic, outgoing, assertive, strong, bold, and persuasive. Various other traits have also been proposed as related to the acceptance of a leader, including being tall, good-looking, poised, articulate, confident, and authoritative. The constellation of traits in a person can prompt others to regard the person as a "natural leader." Research by Kirkpatrick and Locke (1991) revealed that although the presence of such traits is associated with people in leadership positions, their presence does not guarantee success.

An extension of the trait approach to leadership is that certain traits are more (or less) important for success depending upon the leadership situation. That is, some leadership situations call for a leader who possesses such traits as emotional empathy, tolerance for stress, and the capacity to provide a calming influence on others. Other situations might call for a leader with a very high energy level, an unrelenting need to advance and achieve, and an unwillingness to accept failure or setbacks. The classic research of McClelland and his colleagues (e.g., McClelland & Boyatzis, 1982) identified three motives or needs that drive the behavior of leaders. They are the need for power, the need for achievement, and the need for affiliation. In this sense requisite leadership traits are represented not as attributes that people possess, but as the underlying basis for why they behave as they do. The need for power is reflected in the desire to influence other people, to control events, and to function in a position of formal authority. The need for achievement is evidenced in the desire to solve problems, attain results, and accomplish objectives. The need for affiliation is manifested in the desire to associate or affiliate with other people in a social context, to provide guidance and support for them, and to derive gratification from helping others to succeed. These three needs are classics in the field of personality, where one's personality is defined from the perspective of the dominant needs that drive leader behavior.

Other research on personality as a basis for explaining leadership has also been conducted. Using the Big 5 theory of personality as a conceptual framework, Judge, Bono, et al. (2002) reported a multiple correlation coefficient of .48 between the five personality factors and success as a leader. The two strongest individual personality dimensions were Extraversion ($r = .31$) and Conscientiousness ($r = .38$). Clearly there is a personality basis to effective leadership.

A related line of research addresses leader skills, as opposed to personality traits, in the belief that skill is required to implement the traits in leadership roles. Three basic categories of skills have been proposed: technical, conceptual, and interpersonal. *Technical skills* include knowledge of work operations; procedures and equipment; and markets, clients, and competitors. *Conceptual skills* include the ability to analyze complex events and perceive trends, recognize changes, and identify problems. *Interpersonal skills* include an understanding of interpersonal and group processes, the ability to maintain cooperative relationships with people, and persuasive ability. In general, the research supports the conclusion that technical, conceptual, and interpersonal skills are necessary in most leadership positions. However, the relative importance of most specific skills probably varies greatly depending on the situation.

In general, the trait approach was dominant in the early days of leadership research, then fell out of favor for a long time, and only lately has regained some credibility through the recent advances in personality assessment. Traits offer the potential to explain why people seek leadership positions and why they act the way they do when they occupy these positions. It is now evident that some traits and skills increase the likelihood of leadership success, even though they do not ensure it. Despite this progress, the utility of the trait approach for understanding leadership is limited by the elusive nature of traits. Traits interact with situational demands and constraints to influence a leader's behavior, and this behavior interacts with other situational variables to influence group process variables, which in turn affect group performance. It is therefore difficult to understand how leader traits can affect subordinate motivation or group performance unless we examine how traits are expressed in the actual behavior of leaders. Emphasis on leadership behavior ushers in the next era of research on leadership.

The Behavioral Approach

Behavioral approach to leadership
A conception that leadership is best understood in terms of the actions taken by an individual in the conduct of leading a group.

The **behavioral approach** to leadership shifts the focus from traits that leaders possess to specific behaviors or actions in which leaders engage. One might think of the trait approach as attempting to ascertain the causes of leadership, whereas the behavioral approach attempted to establish the symptoms of leadership. The behavioral approach thus tries to understand leadership more in terms of "doing" than "having."

A major contribution to the behavioral approach to leadership was made in the 1950s by researchers at Ohio State University. Their research is regarded as classic among efforts to understand the phenomenon of leadership. The researchers asked workers to describe the actions of their supervisors in leadership situations. Based on the results, two critical leadership factors were identified. One relates to how the leader gets work accomplished. This factor was named *initiation of structure* and addresses the means by which leaders provide direction or structure to get workers to accomplish tasks. The second factor addresses how the leader interacts on a personal level with workers. This factor was named *consideration* and concerns the people-oriented aspects of leadership (i.e., being considerate of others). The researchers developed a questionnaire used to assess leaders based on these two factors. This questionnaire—the *Leader Behavior Description Questionnaire* (LBDQ)—is regarded as one of the most influential assessment techniques developed by I/O psychologists. Fifty years after its original development, researchers are still reporting evidence of its value. Judge, Piccolo, and Ilies (2004) conducted a meta-analysis of studies that examined the validity of initiation of structure and consideration. Initiation of structure was highly correlated with leader effectiveness, while consideration was predictive of workers being satisfied with their leader.

Over the years the behavioral approach was expanded to include other dimensions of leadership besides those originally identified in the Ohio State studies. Likewise, other assessment methods have been designed, such as the *Leadership Practices Inventory* developed by Kouzes and Posner (1995).

Research from the behavioral approach identified specific leader behaviors that are associated with effective leadership. Two such behaviors are monitoring the employees' work and providing clarification on ambiguous issues. Researchers discovered that although monitoring is an important leadership behavior, it alone does not account for effective leadership. Monitoring an employee's work may identify a problem, but it is also necessary to find a solution to the problem. Likewise, clarifying a work problem by delegating assignments to different employees will be effective only if the employees accept their assignments and have the skills needed to perform them. It became evident that the behavioral approach (i.e., the identification of specific leader behaviors) interacted in complex ways with other factors, such as the skill level of the employees. In short, although the behavioral approach identified critical leader behaviors, the process of being an effective leader was more complicated than simply eliciting those behaviors. In particular, it was concluded that how a leader exercises power and influence with subordinates is particularly important to understand. This realization led to the next phase of leadership research.

The Power and Influence Approach

Power and influence approach to leadership
A conception that leadership is best understood by the use of the power and influence exercised by a person with a group.

The **power and influence approach** is yet another way of conceptualizing leadership. The trait approach focused on what attributes a leader possesses; the behavioral approach focused on what a leader does. The power and influence approach asserts that leadership is an exercise of power by one person (the leader) over other people (the subordinates). Furthermore, how the leader exercises power is by influencing the subordinates to behave in certain ways. As such, this approach to leadership attempts to understand the meaning of power and the tactics of influence.

DILBERT   by Scott Adams

Dilbert: © Scott Adams/Dist. by United Feature Syndicate, Inc. Reprinted with permission.

Power and Leader Effectiveness.   Power manifests in many ways. French and Raven (1960) developed a classic taxonomy that proposed five types of power: reward, coercive, legitimate, expert, and referent.

1. *Reward power.* This is the capacity of an organization (or a member in a specified role) to offer positive incentives for desirable behavior. Incentives include promotions, raises, vacations, good work assignments, and so on. Power to reward an employee is defined by the formal authority inherent in a superior's role.

2. *Coercive power.* The organization can punish an employee for undesirable behavior. Dismissal, docking of pay, reprimands, and unpleasant work assignments are examples. This capacity to punish is also defined by formal sanctions inherent in the organization.

3. *Legitimate power.* Sometimes referred to as *authority,* this means that the employee believes the organization's power over him or her is legitimate. Norms and expectations help define the degree of legitimate power. If a boss asks an individual to work overtime, this would likely be seen as legitimate, given the boss's authority. However, if a coworker makes the same request, it might be turned down. The coworker has no legitimate authority to make the request, although the individual might agree out of friendship.

4. *Expert power.* The employee believes that some other individual has expertise in a given area and that he or she should defer to the expert's judgment. Consultants are called on for help in handling problems because they are seen as experts in certain areas. The source of expert power is the perceived experience, knowledge, or ability of a person. It is not formally sanctioned in the organization. There are also differences in the perceived boundaries of expertise. One employee may be seen as the expert on using tools and equipment; others turn to him or her for help with technical problems. However, that expertise may not be seen as extending to other areas, like interpersonal relations.

5. *Referent power.* This is the most abstract type of power. One employee might admire another, want to be like that person, and want to be approved of by him or her. The other worker is a *referent,* someone the employee refers to. The source of referent power is the referent's personal qualities. Cultural factors may contribute to these qualities. Younger people will often defer to an older person partly because age, *per se,* is a personal quality that engenders deference. Norms can also generate referent power. An employee may wish to identify with a particular group and will bow to the group's expectations.

Yukl (1994) noted that the success of an influence attempt is a matter of degree. It produces three qualitatively distinct outcomes. *Commitment* describes an outcome in which an individual (the target) enthusiastically accepts a request from another individual (the agent) and makes a great effort to carry out the request effectively. *Compliance* describes an outcome in which the target is willing to do what the agent asks but is apathetic rather than enthusiastic about it and makes only a minimal effort. *Resistance* describes an outcome in which the target person is opposed to the request, rather than merely indifferent about it, and actively tries to avoid carrying it out.

Research on legitimate power indicates that it is a daily influence on routine matters for managers in formal organizations (Yukl & Falbe, 1991). Research on positive reward behavior, which is based on reward power, finds that it has beneficial effects on subordinate satisfaction. Punishment, which is based on coercive power, can be used to influence the behavior of individuals who jeopardize the mission of the organization or threaten the leader's legitimate authority. Referent and expert power are used to make nonroutine requests and motivate commitment to tasks that require great effort, initiative, and persistence.

Some researchers have proposed that the manner in which power is exercised largely determines whether it results in enthusiastic commitment, passive compliance, or stubborn resistance. Effective leaders use combinations of power in a subtle fashion that minimizes status differentials and avoids threats to the self-esteem of subordinates. In contrast, leaders who exercise power in an arrogant and manipulative manner are likely to engender resistance.

Organizations differ in the extent to which they use the various bases of power. Authoritarian managers rely on reward and coercive power. Managers with a participative style rely on expert and referent power. The military relies heavily on the legitimate power inherent in military rank. Stahelski, Frost, and Patch (1989) reported that university administrators use referent and expert power more than legitimate, reward, or coercive power to influence professors.

Ragins and Sundstrom (1989) examined gender differences in the path to power within organizations. They concluded that power seems to grow incrementally through the accumulation of multiple resources over the span of a career. For women, the path to power contains many impediments and barriers that create an obstacle course. The path to power for men contains fewer obstacles that derive from their gender and may actually have sources of support unavailable to their female counterparts.

Leader–Member Exchange Theory.   Graen and his associates (e.g., Dansereau, Graen, & Haga, 1975) proposed a theory of leadership based on mutual influence, called **leader–member exchange (LMX) theory**. The theory postulates that leaders differentiate their subordinates in terms of (1) their competence and skill, (2) the extent to which they can be trusted (especially when not being watched by the leader), and (3) their motivation to assume greater responsibility within the unit. Subordinates with these attributes become members of what Graen calls the *in-group*. In-group members go beyond their formal job duties and take responsibility for completing tasks that are most critical to the success of the work group. In return, they receive more attention, support, and sensitivity from their leaders (see Field Note 1). Subordinates who do not have these attributes are called the *out-group*; they do the more routine, mundane tasks and have a more formal relationship with the leader. Leaders influence out-group members by using formal authority, but this is not necessary with in-group members. Thus leaders and subordinates use different types and degrees of influence depending on whether the subordinate is in the in- or out-group. As expressed by Liden, Sparrowe, and Wayne (1997): "Quite simply, members who receive more information and support from the leader and who engage in tasks that require challenge and responsibility are expected to have more positive job attitudes and engage in more positive behaviors than members whose support is limited to what is required by the employment contract" (p. 60).

Leader–member exchange theory
A theory of leadership based on the nature of the relationship between a leader and members of the group he or she leads.

Transformational and Charismatic Leadership

Transformational leadership
A conception that leadership is the process of inspiring a group to pursue goals and attain results.

Transformational leadership refers to the process of influencing major changes in the attitudes and assumptions of organization members and building commitment for major changes in the organization's objectives and strategies. Transformational leadership involves influence by a leader over subordinates, but the effect of the influence is to empower subordinates who also become leaders in the process of transforming the organization. Thus transformational leadership is usually viewed as a shared process, involving the actions of leaders at different levels and in different subunits of an organization.

Field Note 1: Participation as Shared Power

One leader style is to allow subordinates to participate in the decision-making process. I/O psychologists have had considerable difficulty figuring out the conditions under which this style is effective. Many factors seem to contribute to its success. We can start with the leader. Some individuals like to retain the decision-making authority inherent in their leadership roles. One basis for their feelings is that as leaders, they have more expertise than their subordinates, so why dilute the quality of the decision by delegating it to others? Some leaders solve this problem by giving subordinates the authority to make trivial decisions, or what is sometimes called "throwing them a bone."

Another factor is the subordinates. Most of us like to have our feelings solicited in matters that pertain to us, but there are wide individual differences. Some subordinates like to get involved in the fine details of decisions, and others do not. Some subordinates resent having to make all sorts of decisions. If they are going to be burdened with the responsibility for making administrative decisions, then they want the salary and title that traditionally come with it. When invited by the boss to participate in certain decisions, they are inclined to think "That's your job, not mine." Willingness to participate is also moderated by the nature of the decision problem. Some problems are fair game for employee involvement, and others are not.

Finally, there are cross-cultural differences in the acceptance of participative leadership. A leading U.S. company once opened a production plant in Latin America. Using the latest leadership ideas from the United States, company officials invited the local employees to participate in a wide range of work-related decisions. Within a short period, turnover became exceedingly high. When the company investigated the cause of the turnover, it was shocked to learn its own management practices were primarily responsible. The employees interpreted management's participative style as evidence of its ignorance about running the plant. The employees were saying, in effect, "We're the workers, not management. If you don't know how to run your own plant, how do you expect us to know?"

In a review of the theory, Dienesch and Liden (1986) concluded that there are three psychological bases for the "exchange" between the superior and subordinate. *Personal contribution* refers to the perception of the amount, direction, and quality of work-oriented activity each member puts forth toward the mutual goals of the dyad. *Loyalty* is the expression of public support for the goals and personal character of the other member. *Affect* is the degree of liking members of the dyad have for each other. The authors refer to these three dimensions as the "currencies of exchange" within the dyad. Liden and Maslyn (1998) identified a fourth dimension of exchange, the level of *professional respect* the parties have for each other. Based on a meta-analytic review of LMX theory, Gerstner and Day (1997) concluded that the relationship an employee has with his or her supervisor is "a lens through which the entire work experience is viewed" (p. 840) and is not limited to leader–subordinate relationships. Indeed, the theory has been expanded to include exchanges between coworkers (CWX; Sherony & Green, 2002) and team members (TMX; Liden, Wayne, & Sparrowe, 2000).

Charismatic leadership
A conception that leadership is the product of charisma, a trait that inspires confidence in others to support the ideas and beliefs of an individual who possesses this trait.

Charismatic leadership is defined more narrowly and refers to follower perception that a leader possesses a divinely inspired gift and is somehow unique and larger than life. Followers not only trust and respect the leader but also idolize or worship the leader as a superhuman hero or spiritual figure (Bass, 1985). The indicators of charismatic leadership include a follower's trust in the correctness of the leader's beliefs, unquestioning acceptance of the leader, affection for the leader, and willing obedience. Leaders who engender these feelings among followers are often associated with attributions of morality (Turner et al., 2002) and spirituality (Pfeffer, 2003). Thus, with charismatic leadership the focus is on an individual leader rather than on a leadership process that may be shared among multiple leaders.

Transformational Leadership.   Transformational leadership derives its name from the process hypothesized to account for the success of the group. A successful leader transforms the members into believing in themselves, generating confidence in their respective abilities, and elevating their self-expectations. In short, a transformational leader's success is indexed by the group's capacity to function at a much higher level of performance than previously evidenced. A transformational leader unleashes the power and harnesses the talent within a group to help it be successful. Understanding this conversion process is the object of research on transformational leadership.

Bass (1998) suggested that transformational leaders make followers feel more aware of their own importance and value to the success of the group. Followers are expected to sublimate their self-interests for the overall benefit of the group. The desire to be trusted and respected by the leader prompts the group to respond with greater effort and commitment to achieve a common goal. Kark, Shamir, and Chang (2003) found that followers socially identify with transformational leaders and feel empowered to take action as a result of their relationship to the leader.

Transformational leaders do more with colleagues and followers than set up simple exchanges or agreements. They behave in ways to achieve superior results by using one or more of the four components of transformational leadership (Bass, 1998).

- *Idealized influence.* Transformational leaders behave in ways that make them role models for their followers. The leaders are admired, respected, and trusted. Followers identify with the leaders and want to emulate them; leaders are endowed by their followers with extraordinary capabilities, persistence, and determination.

- *Inspirational motivation.* Transformational leaders behave in ways that motivate and inspire those around them by providing meaning and challenge to their followers' work. Leaders get followers involved in envisioning attractive future states; they create clearly communicated expectations that followers want to meet.

- *Intellectual stimulation.* Transformational leaders stimulate their followers' efforts to be innovative and creative by questioning assumptions, reframing problems, and approaching old situations in new ways. New ideas and creative problem solutions are solicited from followers, who are included in the process of addressing problems and finding solutions.

- *Individualized consideration.* Transformational leaders pay special attention to each individual follower's needs for advancement and growth by acting as a coach or mentor. Followers and colleagues are developed to successively higher levels of potential. Individual differences in needs and desires are recognized, and the leader's own behavior demonstrates acceptance of these differences.

A leadership scale has been developed (the *Multifactor Leadership Questionnaire*) that assesses these components of transformational leadership. Research (e.g., Lowe, Kroeck, & Sivasubramaniam, 1996) has supported the construct validity of these components and has revealed that transformational leadership is strongly associated with work unit effectiveness. In particular, the idealized influence component is most strongly related to overall effectiveness. Bass (1997) asserted that these four components of transformational leadership transcend organizational and national boundaries and speak to the "universality of leadership."

Charismatic Leadership.   Charismatic leadership may be considered a subset of transformational leadership because it focuses on a unique characteristic of the leader who transforms the group. In a sense, charismatic leadership can be thought of as a return to the oldest approach to leadership, the trait approach. However, in this case, only one trait is involved. That trait is extremely elusive and almost mystical in quality—charisma.

Charismatic leaders give their followers a vision of the future that promises a better and more meaningful life. Conger and Kanungo (1987) believe charismatic leaders are regarded as "heroes" who exhibit unconventional behaviors and transform people to share the radical changes they advocate. Manz and Sims (1991) added that such leaders should also be viewed as hero makers, and the spotlight should be on the achievements of the followers as well as the leaders. House, Spangler, and Woycke (1991) examined the personality and charisma of U.S. presidents and their effectiveness as leaders. The authors concluded that personality and charisma did make a difference in the effectiveness of the presidents. Towler (2003) found some support that charismatic leadership behavior can be developed through training; thus people are not necessarily born with charisma. Gardner and Avolio (1998) identified the effective use of "staging" by charismatic leaders. Staging involves attention to the development and manipulation of symbols, including physical appearances, settings, props, and other artifactual displays. For example, a leader may stage a presentation by giving a speech in front of a building that has symbolic significance for the followers (see Field Note 2, p. 420).

Yorges, Weiss, and Strickland (1999) proposed that leaders who appeared willing to endure hardship for the expression of their beliefs would enhance their influence over followers, whereas leaders who appeared to achieve personal gain would reduce their influence over others. Research results confirmed their hypotheses. Waldman et al. (2001) found that charismatic leaders were particularly effective in conditions of high situational uncertainty but not effective in conditions of low uncertainty. The results indicated that charismatic leaders provide a sense of direction to the organization when it most needs it—that is, when the organization has no clear path to follow. However, the effectiveness of a charismatic leader is diminished when the organization is positioned in a system of high situational predictability.

Hogan, Raskin, and Fazzini (1990) cautioned that there can be a "dark side" to charismatic leaders. Because they have excellent social skills, sometimes to the point of being charming, they are readily liked by their followers. But sometimes lurking behind the mask of likability is a person with pronounced adjustment problems. Only

Field Note 2: Use of Props by Leaders

Current research has studied the use of props by leaders and the "staging" of activities designed to enhance communication effectiveness. Several examples of props have been used by U.S. political leaders. When Richard Nixon was Vice President of the United States, he was accused of inappropriately accepting gifts from people who wanted Nixon to use his influence on their behalf. In his defense Nixon appeared on television holding a cocker spaniel puppy named "Checkers." Nixon explained that he returned all the gifts he had received, except the dog, which he noted had become the family pet. The talk by Nixon while holding the dog became long remembered as "Nixon's Checkers speech."

When Dwight Eisenhower was President, he gave a speech on television to outline his philosophy of leadership. A camera was mounted above Eisenhower's head pointing downward at the top of his desk. Eisenhower took a piece of string out of his pocket and then demonstrated that if he pulled the string, it would follow his fingers. But if he pushed the string, it would go nowhere. Equating the nation with the string, Eisenhower conveyed that he wanted to lead the nation to prosperity, not push it from behind.

Earl Butz was Secretary of Agriculture under President Nixon. Butz appeared before a congressional committee to explain the financial budget of the Department of Agriculture. While seated before the committee, Butz pulled a loaf of sliced bread out of a paper bag. He proceeded to stack the slices in various sized piles, demonstrating symbolically how the Department of Agriculture budget was allocated to various directives.

In these examples leaders used a dog, a piece of string, and a loaf of bread as props to explain issues of considerable complexity. The props were remembered long after people had forgotten the content of the speeches. Dunham and Freeman (2000) suggested that business leaders should learn to utilize some of the techniques of theater directors in show business to enhance their impact through the use of staging.

after these people fail in their leadership roles do we ever learn of their maladjustment, which was cleverly concealed by their ability to manipulate people to like them. Babiak and Hare (2006) described such individuals as "snakes in suits" and referred to them by their clinical designation: psychopaths. The authors explained how psychopaths can work their way into leadership roles and thus are positioned to cause immeasurable harm within the organization because of their destructive personalities. "Some companies quite innocently recruit individuals with psychopathic tendencies, because some hiring managers may mistakenly attribute leadership labels to what are, in actuality, psychopathic behaviors. For example, taking charge, making decisions, and getting others to do what you want are classic features of leadership and management, yet they can also be well-packaged forms of coercion, domination, and manipulation" (p. *xi*).

In conclusion, both transformational and charismatic leadership theories identify the importance of leaders having a profound influence over their followers. Charismatic leadership theory tends to emphasize the characteristics of the leader, whereas transformational leadership theory tends to emphasize the processes by which the work group is transformed or developed.

The Implicit Leadership Theory

Implicit leadership theory
A conception that leadership is a perceived phenomenon as attributed to an individual by others.

The previous theories of leadership presume that leadership is something that is really "out there," and the various theories are merely different ways to explain what it is. A radically different view is that leadership exists only in the mind of the beholder, usually the follower. It may be that "leadership" is nothing more than a label we attach to a set of outcomes; that is, we observe a set of conditions and events and make the attribution that leadership has occurred or exists. **Implicit leadership theory** regards leadership as a subjectively perceived construct rather than an objective construct. Implicit leadership theory is also referred to as the *attribution theory of leadership* or *social information processing theory.*

Lord and his associates have made the greatest contribution to this view of leadership. For example, Lord, Foti, and Phillips (1982) concluded that individuals hold conceptions of prototypical leaders (that is, what they think leaders are like) and then evaluate actual leaders according to their conceptions. People judged as "good" leaders are likely to be those whose actions and demeanors conform to the conception we hold. Thus "effectiveness" in leadership is determined not objectively but through the confirmation of expectations. Phillips and Lord (1981) discovered that individuals develop global impressions of leader effectiveness and then use those global impressions to describe specific dimensions of leader behavior. Thus individuals make confident judgments of behavior they have had no opportunity to observe, in much the same way halo error operates in performance appraisal. Meindl and Ehrlich (1987) discussed what they called "the romance of leadership" as it relates to assessments of organizational performance. In their study, subjects gave better evaluations to performance outcomes attributed to leadership factors than they gave to the same outcomes when they were attributed to nonleadership factors. The authors concluded that leadership has assumed a heroic, larger-than-life quality in people's minds. Meindl and Ehrlich believe leadership may serve a symbolic role, causing people to feel assured and confident that the fate and fortune of an organization are in good hands. Thus the authors contended that leadership may not account for as much of an organization's success as we believe, but "leadership" has a symbolic value in producing subordinate support, which may then paradoxically produce organizational effectiveness.

Lord and Brown (2004) asserted leadership is best understood from the perspective of followers. Leadership is viewed as a process through which one person, the leader, changes the way followers envision themselves. A follower-centered perspective of leadership is deemed most insightful because it is through followers' reactions and behaviors that leadership attempts succeed or fail. It is proposed that followers regulate their own behavior as a result of the meaning derived from leadership acts. Thus a useful way to gauge the effectiveness of leaders is through the self-identity of followers. Epitropaki and Martin (2004) believe leaders should be made aware of how followers conceptualize effective leadership. Followers tend to regard effective leaders as sensitive, intelligent, dedicated, and dynamic (and not manipulative, domineering, or pushy).

Epitropaki and Martin stated that leaders should be trained to present themselves as followers want to see them.

Substitutes for Leadership

Kerr and Jermier (1978) asked what it is that organization members need to maximize in seeking organizational and personal outcomes. They concluded that employees seek both guidance and good feelings from their work settings. Guidance usually comes from role or task structuring; good feelings may stem from any type of recognition. The authors feel that although these factors must be present, they do not necessarily have to come from a superior. Other sources may provide guidance and recognition as well. In these cases the need for formal leadership is lessened. The authors reference **substitutes for leadership** and highlight the point that a leader is merely one vehicle for providing these services. Indeed, some organizations have abandoned formal supervisory positions as increasingly more work is performed by employees organized into teams (as discussed in Chapter 9). Podsakoff, MacKenzie, and Bommer (1996) reported that leaders and substitutes for leadership can simultaneously affect work groups. For example, leaders can create less need for formal supervision by carefully selecting employees who can function relatively independently. The authors concluded that such substitutes have very important effects on the work group, but they do not diminish the role of the leader. Dionne et al. (2002) reached a similar conclusion—that substitutes for leadership cannot fully replace the role of the leader.

There is evidence that the concept of leadership does not have to be vested in a formal position. Howell and Dorfman (1981) tested whether leader substitution can replace or "act in the place of" a specific leader. They examined whether having a closely knit cohesive work group and tasks that provide feedback concerning performance can take the place of a formal leader. The authors found partial support for the substitution of leadership, giving some credence to the idea that leadership need not always reside in a person. Pierce, Dunham, and Cummings (1984) provided further support for leader substitutes. They examined four environmental sources from which employees get structure and direction in how to perform their work: the job itself, technology, the work unit, and the leader. The authors found that only when the first three sources of structure were weak did the influence of the leader strongly affect employees. It seems that employees can derive typical leader qualities (that is, structure and direction) from inanimate sources in their environments and that leadership functions need not be associated with someone in authority. It is thus possible to envision a successfully operating leaderless group in which the job itself provides direction in what to do (initiating structure) and the work group members support and tend to one another (consideration).

There is also evidence that some individuals are capable of directing themselves, a concept called *self-leadership*. Manz (1986) found that some employees could lead themselves if their values and beliefs were congruent with those of the organization. In summary, the research on substitutes for leadership suggests that leadership can be thought of as a series of processes or functions that facilitate organizational and personal effectiveness. These processes or functions need not necessarily emanate from a

Substitutes for leadership
The conception that there are sources of influence in an environment that can serve to act in place of, or be substitutes for, formal leadership.

person in a formal leadership role, but may be derived from characteristics of the work being performed by the group members.

Points of Convergence Among Approaches

Despite the profusion of leadership approaches and related empirical findings, Yukl (1994) noted there is some convergence in the findings from different lines of leadership research. Yukl identified three consistent themes.

Importance of Influencing and Motivating.   Influence is the essence of leadership. Yukl stated that leaders are heavily involved in influencing the attitudes and behaviors of people, including subordinates, peers, and outsiders. The array of influence tactics available to a leader are all designed to induce followers to pursue selected goals and objectives. Charismatic leadership is a pronounced example of the use of influence to motivate. The result is to have followers embrace a vision, inspire commitment to its attainment, and feel a sense of ownership for the accomplishment. Situational factors exert a strong influence on the need for leaders to motivate their employees. When the tasks to be performed are stimulating and enjoyable, the need for an inspirational and influential leader is minimal. When the tasks to be performed are frustrating and ambiguous, the need for a leader to inspire motivation is great. How leaders use power and their own personal needs affect the type of influence attempts they make. Skillful leaders provide an appealing vision for the future and inspire people to pursue it.

Importance of Maintaining Effective Relationships.   Yukl asserted that leaders recognize the importance of cooperative relationships among people and are skillful in achieving that outcome. Organizations operate more effectively when employees work within an environment of trust, loyalty, and mutual respect. Employees are more satisfied with leaders who demonstrate concern for their needs and values. A leader who exhibits diplomacy, social sensitivity, and professionalism is likely to engender those same qualities among employees. The capacity of a leader to make employees feel good about themselves and affirm their worth as contributors to the organization will likely be both well received and regarded as instrumental for the success of the company. Alternatively, leaders who regard organizations as simply arenas for their own self-enhancement are likely to alienate the very people who can make the organization be successful.

Importance of Making Decisions.   Decisions are made in the present but their consequences occur in the future. A leader who makes good decisions is skillful in shaping the future. Such talent is the hallmark of a good leader. Increases in power and influence within an organization often follow demonstrated proficiency in decision making. However, group commitment to a decision is enhanced by giving group members input into the decision-making process. Some decisions are made under conditions of urgency and demand high technical expertise. Other decisions can be the product of a more deliberate analysis of information and data. Furthermore, many decisions are sequential or conditional; the decisions made at one point in time will affect the decision options available at a later time. It is typically impossible for one leader to possess all the information needed to make an informed decision. Consequently, the ability to obtain relevant information, the skill to know the differential importance of the information as it relates to a given decision, and the capacity to weigh various decision options are all critical leadership skills. Great leaders are skilled decision makers, or they know how to delegate the responsibility for decision making to others within the organization (which is a form of decision making in itself).

Several of the traits and skills that predict leadership effectiveness are relevant for decision making. Leaders with extensive technical knowledge and cognitive skills are more likely to make high-quality decisions. These skills are important for analyzing problems, identifying causal patterns and trends, and forecasting likely outcomes of different strategies for attaining objectives. Self-confidence and tolerance for ambiguity and stress help leaders cope with the responsibility for making major decisions on the basis of incomplete information.

Zaccaro and Klimoski (2001) presented some additional requirements for successful leaders in the new economy. Among them are proficiency with political, financial, and technical matters. As was described in Chapter 5, all organizations exist in a political environment where conflicting motives and goals operate. Leaders must be skilled in understanding their resource bases within the organization and can ill afford to alienate key constituents. A successful leader is required to weld together the diverse interests and values of multiple functions (sales, human resources, finance, information technology, etc.) into a cohesive organization. Financial proficiency is often reflected in balancing short-term versus long-term economic objectives. Under constant pressure to achieve positive financial results for the organization, the leader may be tempted to select short-term courses of action that will show immediate financial results. However, the sustained economic success of the organization is achieved in the long term (years, not months). If the leader adopts a strictly long-term orientation for the company and in so doing experiences repeated short-term financial results that are judged unacceptable, the leader may be replaced. Finally, the Information Age has revolutionized the way business is conducted. Leaders must change the structure and decision-making authority of the company to be responsive to the urgency and timeliness of new information (customer needs, price changes, and so on). As McKenna and McKenna (2002) noted, "There are organizations that have chosen to ignore, avoid, or minimize the impact of the Internet and digital technology in their business [see The Changing Nature of Work: e-Leadership]. Many of these organizations will die protecting . . . business models that worked in a pre-Internet business environment" (p. 279).

Cross-Cultural Leadership Issues

For many years most of what we knew about cross-cultural leadership issues derived from international business. For example, one company might conduct business in two countries (such as the United States and Japan). Research findings indicated what leadership practices would and would not generalize across the two nations. However, we are now in the era of global business, where commerce is conducted on a worldwide basis (see Field Note 3, p. 426). A major study was completed on leadership and

The Changing Nature of Work: e-Leadership

The powerful influence of electronic technology on work has given rise to new types of required leadership skills. Avolio et al. (2003) referred to this as "e-leadership," the fusion of leadership and information technology. Successful leaders in the new economy must be skilled in getting their organizations to adopt information technology systems and not resist or reject them. They must be adept at getting those new systems integrated into the existing norms and culture of their organization. In a survey of chief information officers, Oz and Sosik (2000) reported that passive leadership was the main factor contributing to the failure of implementing information technology systems. Leadership can restrict the adoption and use of new information systems to such an extent that they have little impact on organizational effectiveness. Some reluctance on the part of leaders to adopt these systems may be understandable given there is no recent precedent in business. In the 1960s, when computers were first available for widespread commercial use, some companies were slow to shift away from manual systems of record keeping. However, that era was more than a generation ago, and few leaders today grew up in a computerless environment. Furthermore, the sheer speed of technological change today is greater than at any time in the past. Thus the adoption of information technology is an ongoing process, with each new iteration in technical capability. One perspective for thinking of business is supply chain management. Every business is linked to suppliers and customers; that is, every organization is both a customer of some other company and a supplier to yet another. The connection of suppliers and customers creates a chain, and each organization is a link in the chain that adds value to some product or service. Entire information systems have been developed to help connect suppliers and customers in this chain. The successful e-leader is one who solidifies an organization's position in the chain and is consistently attuned to changes that occur "upstream" and "downstream" in the chain.

culture. It is called *GLOBE*, an acronym for Global Leadership and Organizational Behavior Effectiveness. The goal of the massive research project was to address how culture is related to societal, organizational, and leadership effectiveness. The researchers measured the practices and values of managers in different industries (financial services, food processing, telecommunications, etc.) and organizations (951 of them) within 62 societies representing 59 nations (alphabetically from Albania to Zimbabwe). The initial product of their work is a book (House et al., 2004) that represents our best understanding of cross-cultural issues in leadership.

House et al. drew upon the research of Hofstede (2001) in establishing major cultural dimensions (such as power distance, individualism–collectivism, and uncertainty avoidance) as well as proposing some additional dimensions. Understandably, the results of the research are complex and multifaceted; however, here are some of the major findings:

- In some cultures the concept of leadership is denigrated. Members of the culture are highly suspicious of individuals who are in positions of authority for fear they will acquire and abuse power. In these cultures substantial constraints are placed on what individuals in positions of authority can and cannot do. Alternatively, in some

Field Note 3: One CEO's Office

A description of one chief executive officer's (CEO) office gives a glimpse into how the business world has changed. This CEO is head of one of the largest textile companies in the United States. Fifteen years ago the office of his predecessor had a map of the United States hanging on the wall. Inserted into the map were colored push-pins. The blue pin was the site of the corporate headquarters of the company where his office was located. Red pins indicated eight manufacturing facilities located in a three-state area, all in the southeastern United States. Green pins represented regional warehouses, and yellow pins showed the locations of major customers. That was fifteen years ago.

Today there is a new CEO and two new maps hang on the wall. The first is a map of the world, showing the various local times compared to 12:00 P.M. at the corporate headquarters. The company now has business operations in Brazil, Honduras, Ireland, Israel, South Africa, Hong Kong, and Thailand. The second map is of China. China will be the location for many future business dealings, currently in various stages of negotiation and development. The company is now as familiar with such major cities in China as Beijing, Guangzhou, and Shanghai as it is with New York, Chicago, and Los Angeles. The map of China highlights railroad lines, major highways, and rivers that can be used to transport goods to airports and deep-water ports for ultimate distribution around the world. Fifteen years ago the focus and field of vision of the company was the United States, as embodied in the map of the United States. Today the company has a global perspective; it thinks globally and views the world as one big marketplace. China will soon be the epicenter of its global business operations. Gone are the different colored push-pins, and conspicuously absent from the wall is the map of the United States. Whereas the previous CEO was not concerned with global business, the current CEO cannot be concerned with only domestic business.

cultures the concept of leadership is romanticized and leaders are given exceptional privileges and status and are held in great esteem.

- Twenty-two leadership traits were identified as being universally desirable. Two examples are decisiveness and foresight.
- Eight leadership traits were identified as being universally undesirable. Two examples are irritability and ruthlessness.
- Many leadership traits were culturally contingent, being desirable in some cultures and undesirable in others. Two examples are ambition and elitism.
- Members of different cultures share common observations and values about what constitutes effective and ineffective leadership. Six styles of leadership were identified: charismatic, team-oriented, participative, autonomous, humane-oriented, and self-protective. Although all cultures recognized these six leadership styles, they were seen as differentially contributing to outstanding leadership. Anglo and Nordic

European cultures, for example, tend to see charismatic and participative leadership styles as being particularly effective. Asian and Sub-Saharan African cultures are more favorably disposed to humane-oriented and self-protective leadership styles. Middle Eastern cultures do not place great value on team-oriented and participative styles for achieving success.

The researchers found clear cultural underpinnings to the way societies generate and distribute wealth and take care of their people. The findings indicate that decisions designed to change the way governments operate or the way societies allocate their resources must take into consideration cultural issues. House et al. found that certain leadership traits (such as integrity) were universally endorsed, but they question whether the leader behaviors associated with this trait would be common across cultures. For example, in one culture a leader with high integrity might be regarded as someone who gives great thought and consideration to an issue before making a decision. In another culture high integrity by a leader might be manifested by soliciting a wide range of opinions from others before making a decision.

The manifestation of specific behaviors from culturally endorsed traits awaits further research in the GLOBE project. The myriad of findings from the GLOBE study will provide us with a much better understanding of how cultural issues influence a wide range of human behavior. As Lowe and Gardner (2000) stated, most leadership research has had a technological, modern, and U.S. bias. The GLOBE project will help us understand leadership from other perspectives from around the world (see Cross-Cultural I/O Psychology: Self-Protective Leadership Style, p. 428).

Entrepreneurship

Entrepreneurship
The process by which individuals pursue opportunities and organize resources that can lead to new job creation and business growth.

The topic of **entrepreneurship** has been addressed for over 100 years. *Entrepreneurs* and *entrepreneurial* are other terms often used in its discussion. There has been a re-birth of interest in entrepreneurship associated with the emergence of global business. The traditional business model was based on stability and continuity. For example, a particular organization was created to provide a service or make a product. The organization hired employees to achieve the goals of the organization, and in so doing provided stable employment for the workers. However, the emergence of information technology and global business has greatly reduced the luxury that stability in business provided for employees and customers. The business world is now very unstable and thus less predictable. Jobs can disappear quickly due to outsourcing, downsizing, and offshoring. Revolution grips the entire social order of commerce. It became evident that new solutions were needed for the problems facing the new era of business.

One approach is to re-examine how businesses are created in the first place. All business organizations were created by individuals who at some point in time thought they had a "good idea." Such individuals who started these businesses are called *entrepreneurs*, and *entrepreneurship* is the underlying concept of business creation. It is believed that a greater understanding of how businesses are created will lead to the development of new organizations (often called "start-up" companies) that will grow and prosper. Such organizations would not only add value to society by the products and services they offer, but also as a source of employment.

Cross-Cultural I/O Psychology: *Self-Protective Leadership Style*

As identified in the GLOBE project, one of the leadership styles is self-protective. Based on previous research (mostly of Western origin), we know the least about this style. This style of leadership behavior focuses on ensuring the safety and security of the individual and the group through status enhancement and face saving. Self-protective leadership is characterized by self-centeredness, elitism, status consciousness, and a tendency to induce conflict with others. Leaders who engage in self-protective behavior in Albania, Taiwan, Egypt, Iran, and Kuwait reported the style as being slightly effective in achieving results. In contrast, self-protective behavior was reported to be an impediment to highly effective leadership in all other nations. Self-protective leadership is more likely to be used in cultures that have large power distance, collectivism, and uncertainty avoidance. It is also used in cultures where men and women assume very different roles in society (i.e., low gender egalitarianism). It will be recalled from Hofstede's research presented earlier that Anglo cultures are characterized by small power distance, high individualism, and low uncertainty avoidance. Thus it should not be too surprising that organizations that espouse typical Anglo values find it difficult to relate to the self-protective leadership behaviors found in some other cultures. Yet in these cultures such a style of leader behavior is regarded as acceptable and perhaps imminently plausible. One of the strongest findings from the GLOBE project was that self-protective leadership behaviors were not seen as highly effective in most cultures of the world. Its usage, particularly as it relates to the tendency to induce conflict, may be interpreted that leadership is not about seeking compromise or unity (a typical Western view) but rather establishing differences (as in what is mine versus yours). Knowing the tendency for some countries to regard this style of leadership behavior as acceptable may help us better understand the strategic intent of their leaders.

Entrepreneurship is more deeply rooted in business than psychology. However, a close examination of entrepreneurship reveals it has many psychological components. In fact, it is argued that entrepreneurship cannot be understood apart from its psychological basis. I/O psychologists have recently become drawn into the study of entrepreneurship because of its growing emergence in society, and because I/O psychology has much to offer in understanding entrepreneurship. Successful entrepreneurs have much in common with successful leaders, although they are not identical.

In its simplest formulation, entrepreneurship can best be thought of as an interaction between a person and a situation. Situations differ in the extent to which they provide opportunities for business creation. People differ in the extent to which they correctly perceive these opportunities, and have the KSAOs needed to transform the opportunity into the creation of value. The interaction between a person and a situation is the fundamental basis for understanding many facets of human behavior, especially leadership.

Shane (2003) describes a six-step process that is the basis for entrepreneurship:

1. *Existence of opportunity.* There must be an opportunity to provide a new product or service that is desired, or to improve upon an existing one.

2. *Discovery of opportunity.* A person must perceive this opportunity to exist. Not perceived, the opportunity is "missed." When a person perceives an opportunity when in fact there is none, the perception is an "illusion."

3. *Decision to pursue the opportunity.* A person must decide whether the opportunity is of sufficient magnitude to warrant the expenditure of time, money, and skill needed to pursue it.

4. *Resource acquisition.* Once the decision is made to pursue the opportunity, a person has to marshal the resources needed for its pursuit.

5. *Entrepreneurial strategy.* Strategy is the process by which a person can convert or transform the opportunity, upon application of the resources, into a product or service valued by others.

6. *Organizing process.* The organizing process is the means by which the entrepreneurial strategy is enacted. It may involve the founding of a new organization, or some other process of pursuing the opportunity that previously did not exist.

As such, at the heart of entrepreneurship is innovation; thinking of new ways or methods to extract value out of an opportunity that presents itself.

With the exception of the existence of an objective opportunity (which naturally occurs in the environment), the remaining five steps all involve a human component. That is, each requires a person who: sees the opportunity; decides to act upon it; obtains the needed resources; develops a strategy; and develops an organizing process to create the new product or services. It is this strong human component to entrepreneurship that interests I/O psychologists. Entrepreneurship is highly interdisciplinary. Reliance on one scientific discipline to understand a topic that cuts across disciplines is rarely effective. For example, the 4th step (resource acquisition) entails the procurement of money needed to pursue the opportunity. This step is typically the domain of investment management. There are individuals who will provide the needed money for some entrepreneurial activity. Such people are called "venture capitalists," and it is their goal to identify a potentially lucrative opportunity, invest their money (capital) in it, and share in the success of the venture. As noted by Shane, research that focuses only on the financial dimension of entrepreneurship fails to understand the importance of the individual entrepreneur whose idea is being supported. Likewise, an examination of the psychological profile (e.g., intelligence, personality, values, etc.) of successful entrepreneurs fails to understand the situations in which they operate. We might think of entrepreneurship as a special case of the "peg and the hole", where the criterion of fit is successful innovation.

There is disagreement within I/O psychology about whether entrepreneurship is truly different from leadership (Antonakis & Autio, 2007). Vecchio (2003) believes that entrepreneurship is nothing more than leadership embedded within an entrepreneurial organization. However, there is evidence that highly creative individuals who inspire innovation are not necessarily skilled in other leadership dimensions, such as interpersonal skills. Two major psychological constructs are associated with entrepreneurship. The first derives from experimental psychology and is called *pattern perception*. Baron, Frese, and Baum (2007) stated: "When an entrepreneur identifies an opportunity . . . this implies there is 'something' out there to notice—some kind of stimulus or stimulus configuration that is perceived or noticed" (p. 356). Thus, the second step in Shane's six-step process is for a person to perceive something of value hidden within distracting clutter. The authors propose various ways that successful entrepreneurs "look for" opportunities (i.e., patterns) that others do not see. The third step in the process pertains to the willingness or inclination to pursue the opportunity upon its detection. Zhao and Seibert (2006) conducted a meta-analysis of personality factors that differentiated entrepreneurs compared to a sample of traditional business managers. Entrepreneurs were found to score higher on conscientiousness and openness to experience.

A compelling finding from the study of entrepreneurs is their high rate of failure. Shane reported that nearly half of all entrepreneurs fail to even complete their organizing efforts (step 6). In the United States, 750,000 new businesses are founded and fail every year. Approximately 64% fail to survive five years. The goal of all businesses is to grow and prosper. However, the initial goal is just to survive, and research indicates organizational survival is more the exception than the rule. The reasons for failure rest in each of the steps proposed by Shane. While I/O psychology cannot contribute to understanding entrepreneurship from a financial perspective, it can contribute from a human perspective. A blending of knowledge from different fields is necessary to understand entrepreneurship. Baron et al. concluded: "In sum, it seems clear that the benefits of closer ties between I/O psychology and entrepreneurship are indeed reciprocal in nature. Both fields can gain measurably from such links" (p. 369).

Diversity Issues in Leadership

Hogan, Curphy, and Hogan (1994) questioned the role of leadership within organizations in the 21st century. They made the following observations. Historically, the typical American worker has been a White man with a high school education employed in a manufacturing job. Our knowledge of leadership largely focuses on how to lead that kind of person in those kinds of jobs in those kinds of organizations. Demographic trends suggest, however, that the national economy is shifting from manufacturing to service jobs and that the workforce is becoming older, more diverse, and more female (Offerman & Gowing, 1990). The labor market for skilled workers will tighten, and there will be increased competition for talented personnel. As noted in Chapter 8, as organizations shrink, fewer middle managers will be needed and the responsibilities of first-line managers will expand.

Chemers and Murphy (1995) noted that one explanation for gender differences in leadership is cultural. This view holds that because of their roles as family caretakers, women are socialized to be sensitive, nurturing, and caring. When they carry that socialization over into organizational roles, women are likely to be warm, considerate, and democratic leaders. An alternative explanation proposed that observed differences in leadership styles between men and women are more a function of biases in the observation process than the result of true differences. If we are more likely to notice and remember behaviors that are consistent with our categorical stereotypes, our observation of male and female leaders may be biased in attention, selection, memory, or recall. Although differences in leadership styles between men and women may be minor, our biases exaggerate the perception of these differences.

Lyness and Heilman (2006) noted that one explanation often put forth as to why there are relatively few women in top-level managerial jobs is "lack of fit". Men are stereotypically viewed as forceful, achievement-oriented, and tough. Women are stereotypically viewed as caring, relationship-oriented, and kind. Accordingly, men are often perceived as a better fit. The authors compared performance evaluations and promotions for men and women. Those women who were promoted had higher performance ratings than men, suggesting stricter standards for promotion were applied to women. There appears to be no empirical basis for the disproportionately small representation of women in top leadership jobs in the United States. Eagly, Johannesen-Schmidt, and van Engen (2003) found only small male–female differences in leadership. Furthermore, women's typical leadership styles tend to be more transformational than those of men, which has been found to be predictive of effectiveness. Lyness (2002) documented reasons why women and racial minorities experience difficulties with participating in leadership development activities, including being slotted into jobs that don't facilitate advancement, having problems obtaining influential mentors or sponsors, and being excluded from informal networks where critical information and career opportunities are shared. Lyness commented, "I have been struck by how much more we seem to know about barriers for women and people of color than about how best to overcome the barriers" (p. 265).

Concluding Comments

As was discussed earlier, sometimes research investigations meld major topics of interest to I/O psychologists. A notable example by Chan and Drasgow (2001) combined motivation and leadership in a study that addressed the motivation to lead. Chan and Drasgow proposed the existence of a personality construct that explains why some people seek leadership positions. Using sophisticated analytic methods, the authors identified three types of people who desire to lead others. The first type sees themselves as having leadership qualities: they are outgoing and sociable (i.e., extraverts), they value competition and achievement, and they are confident in their own leadership abilities. The second type does not expect rewards or privileges to flow from leading but consents to do so because of their agreeable disposition. They value harmony in the group, irrespective of their own leadership experience or self-efficacy. The third type does not necessarily see themselves as having leadership qualities but is motivated to lead by a sense of social duty and obligation. The study revealed that the motivation to lead is not a unidimensional construct, but rather people can be drawn to leadership roles for different types of reasons.

Hackman and Wageman (2007) believe that leadership research has been adversely affected by seeking answers to simplistic questions that belie the inherent complexity of leadership. They believe the answers researchers get about leadership depend upon the questions asked, and the right questions need to be asked. For example, we should not ask what are the traits of leaders, but instead how do leaders' personal attributes interact with situational properties to shape outcomes. The most useful and insightful questions are based upon the simultaneous consideration of the multiple components of leadership, not just any one component in isolation of the others. Although several approaches have been taken to understand leadership, all reach the same conclusion that leadership is a vital process in directing work within organizations. There appear to be boundary conditions regarding when formal leadership is most effective as well as the processes leaders use to galvanize the members of their organizations. It is also insightful that current thinking about leadership considers leaders as not only heroes but also as hero makers. Thus leadership need not be a phenomenon vested exclusively in upper-level positions but rather is a contagious process that can manifest itself throughout all levels of an organization. It is concluded that people not only need leaders but also want them in their lives. We feel comforted by the presence of strong, effective, yet approachable leaders, and we place our trust in them (Dirks & Ferrin, 2002). The breadth of topics addressed in this chapter attests to the complexity of leadership; it is a phenomenon that has intrigued us throughout the history of civilization.

Case Study   Which Direction Should We Follow?

Wayne LaPoe, President of Americom, studied his notes in preparation for the company's annual business planning and strategy meeting. It was at this meeting that most of the major goals for the next year would be set. As a diversified company in the communications field, Americom could go in several different directions. However, they basically boiled down to two possible avenues. One was to develop a wider range of products in anticipation of changing market needs. The other was to increase the sales and marketing of existing products. Each direction had its own champion within the company, and the decision of which path the company should take would be decided at the meeting where two executive vice presidents would state their cases.

Brandon McQuaid, Vice President of Sales and Marketing, was a dominant force within the company. McQuaid stood 6 feet 4 inches tall, was perfectly trim, always appeared slightly tanned, and had an engaging smile and a resonant voice. He was impeccably dressed in the latest styles. He inspired tremendous loyalty among his staff. Always warm and gregarious, McQuaid was liked by everyone. It would be difficult not to like McQuaid, thought LaPoe. McQuaid had a knack for making everyone feel good about themselves, and he usually got a great deal of support for his ideas.

Ralph Pursell was Vice President of Research and Development. An engineer by training, Pursell was about as different from McQuaid as night from day. Pursell was 5 feet 7 inches tall, at least 30 pounds overweight, and often appeared unkempt. No one ever accused Pursell of making a fashion statement. Although his interpersonal skills were minimal, lurking behind his chubby face was the mind of a brilliant product designer. It was under his guidance in product development that Americom captured a huge share of the market in fiber optics. He was the most highly respected employee in the company. Some made snide remarks behind his back about his physical appearance, but many employees realized they owed their jobs to Pursell's genius.

LaPoe anticipated how the planning meeting would go. He had seen it unfold the same way in past years. Pursell would make a pitch for developing some new products, using language that only he understood. The other executives in the room would simply take it on faith that Pursell knew what he was talking about. Then McQuaid would have his turn. Radiating confidence and optimism, McQuaid would soon have just about everyone eating out of his hand. He would argue that the company hadn't begun to scratch the surface in marketing Pursell's current trendsetting products. After 15 minutes of this charm, there would be a lot of smiling and head nodding in the room. When all was said and done, it was usually McQuaid's position that the management staff voted to adopt. Pursell would go back to his lab and wonder why the rest of the company didn't see things his way.

LaPoe questioned whether his management staff responded more to McQuaid's form than to Pursell's substance. He didn't want to alienate his staff by overturning their approval of McQuaid's position, yet LaPoe wondered how much longer Pursell would continue to live with losing battles to McQuaid. LaPoe felt somewhat trapped himself. He needed the loyalty and commitment inspired by McQuaid, yet it was Pursell's ideas that McQuaid sold. LaPoe concluded that if it were possible to combine Pursell's technical ability with McQuaid's interpersonal skills, Americom would probably have a new president.

Questions

1. Is the management staff blinded by McQuaid's engaging leadership style, or is charm a legitimate component of leadership?
2. Should all leaders have strong interpersonal skills, or is someone like Pursell entitled to a leadership position on the basis of technical expertise?
3. If you were LaPoe, would you recommend that Pursell get some training in interpersonal skills and communication to enhance his credibility? Why, or why not?
4. Why are so many people at Americom "taken" with McQuaid? What does this suggest about why we accept people as leaders?
5. Is there a difference between having influence and being a leader? In what ways are these concepts related and unrelated?

Chapter Summary

- Leadership is a topic that has intrigued humankind since antiquity.
- Leadership has been examined from many perspectives, including power, characteristics of the leader, characteristics of the led, and shared influence.
- The trait approach to leadership posits that effective leaders possess certain personality attributes that make them effective.
- The behavioral approach to leadership posits that leadership is a learned skill and that demonstrating key behaviors is the basis of effective leadership.
- Power and influence theories of leadership assert that leadership is a process that stems from the shared relationship between parties, and leadership is associated with effectively managing that relationship.
- Transformational and charismatic leadership theories assert that effective leaders offer their followers visions of a better life, are charming and engaging, and are regarded by their followers as heroes.
- Implicit leadership theory asserts that the concept of leadership exists primarily in the minds of followers. As such, "leadership" is not so much real as implied by a set of actions that are taken or decisions that are made. It is proposed that people are comforted by the idea of having powerful leaders who will protect and help them, thus legitimating their existence.

- The concept of substitutes for leadership is that the functions provided by leadership need not be vested in a person. Characteristics of the work can substitute for the need to have a leader.
- Entrepreneurship represents a context in which leadership can be examined as a means of creating new jobs through innovation.
- There are vast cross-cultural differences in what people want from their leaders and what styles of leadership are acceptable.

Over the years I/O psychologists have studied a broad range of topics relating to work. Strangely enough, one not often addressed is union/management relations. This area cannot be dismissed as "tangential" to work; for many organizations, union-related issues are among the most crucial. Many authors have observed that there is a great imbalance in I/O psychologists' interest between union and management problems. The two are not mutually exclusive, but I/O psychology seems more aligned with management. A listing of some of the professional activities of I/O psychologists testifies to this: managerial consulting, management development, use of assessment centers to identify those with management ability, and cross-cultural managerial issues. However, it is not as if I/O psychologists have spurned advances from unions. Shostak (1964) described the relationship as "mutual indifference." Unions appear reluctant to approach I/O psychologists for help in solving their problems. Rosen and Stagner (1980) think this is caused partly by the belief that I/O psychologists are not truly impartial and partly by reluctance to give outsiders access to union data.

The reasons for the unions' attitudes are numerous. One explanation is that the development of industrial psychology is closely tied to the work of Frederick Taylor. Criticisms of "Taylorism" have been raised by union workers; they see it as exploiting workers to increase company profits. There can be an adversarial relationship between unions and management, a "we/they" perspective. Unions may still see I/O psychologists as a partner of "them." Also, some factors may appear to place I/O psychologists more in the management camp. I/O psychologists are often placed in management-level positions. Management invariably sees the need for, explains the problems to, and pays the consultant. In short, I/O psychology has been more involved with management than with unions (to the point that some authors refer to I/O psychology as a "management tool"). This is most apparent in the conspicuous absence of psychological research on unions. However, another reason was recently presented by Zickar (2001). One of the major contributions of I/O psychology to employment has been the development and use of psychological assessments of job candidates, the results of which are used to make personnel selection decision. One notable type of psychological assessment is the personality test. Zickar described an unethical application of personality testing: **union-busting**. The author noted "that management, in collaboration with some I/O psychologists, initially used personality inventories, not to predict job performance, but to screen potential employees who might be likely to affiliate with unions" (p. 149). Zickar added, "Regardless of the genesis of this practice, it is clear that by the late 1930s psychologists . . . were marketing these [personality] scales for union busting. This alliance with management helped fuel labor's suspicion of social scientists . . . This partisanship made it difficult for psychologists who wished to implement policies that would ease the tensions between labor and management. Labor unions became suspicious of even the best intentioned psychologists" (p. 161). A list of the major reasons unions distrust I/O psychologists was offered by Huszczo, Wiggins, and Currie (1984) and is presented in Table 14-1.

In the state of New York psychologists became unionized. Verdi (2000) posed this question: "Why are highly trained, certified, licensed, and well-compensated in-

Union-busting
A derogatory term used to describe actions taken to prevent a labor union from representing employees.

Table 14-1   *Reasons unions distrust I/O psychologists*

They are associated with management.

They are associated with F. W. Taylor's scientific management (i.e., emphasis on efficiency, time, and motion studies).

Unions are ignored in textbooks and journals of I/O psychology.

They are moralistic intellectuals who want social reform.

Methods (e.g., attitude surveys) have been used to avoid or beat union organizing attempts or to lower pay demands.

They are associated with job enrichment techniques that interfere with job classification and standards systems.

Methods of psychological testing emphasize differentiation among workers (hence, anti-solidarity and antiseniority systems).

Many psychologists have not had work experience similar to union members', which causes suspicion and communication barriers.

Source: From "The Relationship Between Psychology and Organized Labor: Past, Present, and Future," by G. E. Huszczo, J. G. Wiggins, and J. S. Currie, 1984, *American Psychologist, 39*, pp. 432–440.

dividuals who have earned the right to work in their chosen specialties as entrepreneurs seeking to unionize" (p. 31)? The answer is that the 3,200 members of the New York State Psychological Association were frustrated by their lack of power in dealing with managed health care. The psychologists became members of a powerful labor union, the American Federation of Teachers, which has more than 400,000 members. As members of a large union, they now have a stronger voice in negotiating issues regarding their employment, one of the classic reasons workers join unions. Yet Verdi reported that psychologists had some stereotypical concerns about unions: "There is the loss of status—people view union members as individuals who work with their hands and not their heads for a living" (p. 32). Yet even professions that historically have not been aligned with unions turn to them for help with employment-related matters.

Bownas (2000) described the fundamental similarity in the motives of both the union and management:

> The kinds of motives that drive union spokespeople in organizations are no different from those that motivate corporate management. Sometimes the different vantage points from which the two groups operate cause them to reach different conclusions about specific outcomes, but the underlying motives are the same [see Field Note 1, p. 438]. We all try to maximize personal outcomes (such as power, prestige, and influence) and to maximize the outcomes of constituents and other loyal followers. (p. 197)

This chapter will examine the nature of unions, the factors that influence union/management relations, recent research on unions, and how unionization affects many topics discussed earlier.

Field Note 1: Why Study Unions?

I believe that unions have been given inadequate attention by educators. When the topic of labor unions comes up, students are more likely to have heard of Jimmy Hoffa (a union leader with reputed criminal connections) than Walter Reuther (a major contributor to organized labor). Why? There are probably many reasons, but one seems fundamental. Schools, colleges, and higher education in general are founded on scholarly intellectual values. They produce learned people, many of whom rise to become business leaders. Unions, on the other hand, got their start representing less educated workers, rank-and-file employees, rather than business leaders. Rightly or wrongly, unions have had the image of representing the "common man" in labor over the "privileged intellectuals." Some union leaders become suspicious and skeptical of the motives of formally educated people, feeling they are more likely to share values held by management.

Few textbooks in this country offer more than a passing look at organized labor. It seems the "we/they" dichotomy between labor and management has filtered down into textbook writing; unions simply are infrequently discussed in books. This book, in fact, is one of the few I/O psychology textbooks that devotes a chapter to union/management issues. However, the anti-intellectual attitude that some unions hold is costing them in ways beyond exposure in education. Unions rarely hire outside professionals; they generally promote from within their own ranks. If you were an I/O psychologist who wanted to work full time for a union, I doubt you would have many employment possibilities. Furthermore, unions are currently experiencing a decline in membership, an unprecedented number of unions are being decertified, and unions are losing their effectiveness in negotiating for desired employment conditions. In short, I think unions need some fresh ideas. They could benefit from organizational change interventions. But unless they are willing to look beyond their own ranks for expertise, I doubt that they (like any organization) will have sufficient internal strength to pull themselves up by the bootstraps. The paradoxical split between I/O psychology (the study of people at work) and labor unions (which represent a large portion of workers) has been detrimental to both parties.

What Is a Union?

Union
A labor organization with defined members whose purpose is to enhance the welfare of its members in their employment relationship with the company.

Unions are organizations designed to promote and enhance the social and economic welfare of their members. Basically, unions were created to protect workers from exploitation. Unions originally sprang from the abysmal working conditions in this country more than 100 years ago. Workers got little pay, had almost no job security, had no benefits, and, perhaps most important, worked in degrading and unsafe conditions. Unions gave unity and power to employees. This power forced employers to deal with workers as a group. Certain federal laws compelled employers to stop certain activities (such as employing children) and engage in others (such as making Social Security contributions). Collectively, labor unions and labor laws brought about many changes in the workplace. Although the problems facing the North American worker today are not as severe as they were 75 to 100 years ago, unions continue to give a sense of security and increased welfare to their members (see Field Note 2).

Why do workers join unions? What can unions accomplish? According to several authors, unions have consistently contributed to the attainment of certain outcomes. Based upon labor research, unions have made these contributions to worker welfare:

- They have increased wages; in turn, employers have raised the wages of some non-union workers.

- They have bargained for and gotten benefits such as pensions, insurance, vacations, and rest periods.

- They have provided formal rules and procedures for discipline, promotion, wage differentials, and other important job-related factors. This has led to less arbitrary treatment of employees.

There are other reasons as well: unions can provide better communication with management, better working conditions, increased employee unity, and higher morale. Other authors cite social reasons, like belonging to a group with whom workers can share common experiences and fellowship. Schiavone (2008) advocated that unions make social justice issues, such as bargaining for better child care, primary negotiating concerns. Unions that pursued social justice issues were found to attract more members than unions that bargained over traditional economic issues. Matters of social justice have an appeal to a wide constituency, which is the base from which unions derive power. Thus there are both economic and personal reasons for joining unions.

Field Note 2: Is History Repeating Itself?

In the early years of the 20th century, the use of child labor was prevalent in the United States, particularly in large cities. Children toiled for long hours (10–12 hours per day) in unsafe conditions (poor air to breathe, no heating or cooling) and for minuscule wages (pennies per hour) in what were called "sweat shops." Eventually state and federal labor laws were enacted to prohibit child labor. Then 80–90 years later some U.S. companies moved their production facilities to foreign countries that had no child labor laws. In some factories children again work long hours in unsafe conditions for minuscule wages (less than $1 per hour). How do you feel about this practice?

Should U.S. companies follow U.S. labor laws in foreign countries where the laws are much different, particularly with regard to child labor? Should social pressure (e.g., economic boycotts) be exerted against companies that use child labor? Some companies argue that the reduced costs they incur by using child labor are passed on to consumers in the form of lower costs of the products. How should companies in particular and our society as a whole balance economic gain and social conscience? We are finding that history is repeating itself; the conditions that spawned labor laws in this country many years ago are now being exploited by some companies in foreign countries.

Unions as Organizations

Approximately 12 million U.S. citizens belong to labor unions, representing about 15% of the workforce. The largest labor union is the American Federation of Labor–Congress of Industrial Organizations (AFL-CIO). Other large unions are the United Auto Workers and the United Mine Workers. Historically unions were strongest among blue-collar employees, but now white-collar workers (particularly government employees and teachers) are the dominant union base. In recent years there has been a decline in unionization as the number of service jobs has increased and the number of manufacturing jobs (a traditional union stronghold) has decreased.

Each union has a headquarters, but its strength is its many locals. A local may represent members in a geographic area (for example, all tollbooth collectors in Philadelphia) or a particular plant (for example, Amalgamated Beef Packers at Armour's Dubuque, Iowa, slaughterhouse). The local elects officials. If it is large enough, it affords some officials full-time jobs. Other officials are full-time company employees who may get time off for union activities. The shop, or union, steward has a union position equivalent to that of a company supervisor. The steward represents the union on the job site; he or she handles grievances and discipline. Usually the steward is elected by union members for a one-year term.

A union represents an organization (for example, a labor organization) within another organization (the company). The local depends on the company for its existence. Large companies often have a multiunion labor force and thus multiple organizations within themselves. In this case the employer must deal with several collectively organized groups—for example, production workers, clerical workers, and truck drivers. Each union negotiates separately, trying to improve the welfare of its members. A large, multiunion employer is a good example of how organizations are composed of interdependent parts. Each union has a certain degree of power, which can influence the behavior of the total organization.

Union members pay dues, which are the union's chief resource. The union can also collect money for a strike fund, a pool members can draw from if they are on strike and do not get paid. (Strikes will be discussed in more detail shortly.) Unions use their funds to offer members such things as special group automobile insurance rates or union-owned vacation facilities. Unions are highly dependent on their members. Increased membership gives a union more bargaining clout, generates more revenue, and provides a greater range of services for members. Without members, a union cannot exist; indeed, declining membership can threaten its very survival. Figure 14-1 is a graphic representation of the relationship between the company, the union, and the employees.

The Formation of a Union

When employees want to consider being represented by a labor union, they follow a standard procedure. First, they invite representatives to solicit union membership. Federal law allows organizers to solicit membership as long as this does not endanger employees' safety or performance. Solicitations usually occur over lunch or at break time. It is illegal for employers to threaten physically, interfere with, or harass organizers. It is also illegal to fire employees for prounion sentiments.

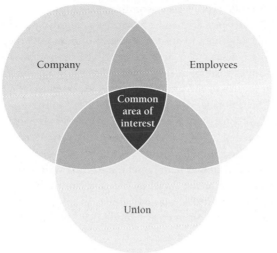

Figure 14-1 *Management/ employee/union relationships*

Source: Fom *Managing Change in a Union- ized Workplace*, by K. Blackard. Figure 5.2, p. 65. Copyright © 2000 Quorum. Reprinted by permission of Greenwood Publishing Group, Inc., Westport, CT.

National Labor Relations Board
An agency of the federal government that has oversight responsibility for enforcing laws pertaining to union/ management relations.

Authorization card
A card employees sign authorizing an election to determine whether a union will represent employees in the collective bargaining process.

Certification election
An election in which employees vote to determine whether a union will represent them in the collective bargaining process.

Both the union and the company typically mount campaigns on behalf of their positions. The union emphasizes how it can improve the workers' lot. The company's countercampaign stresses how well off the employees already are, the costs of union membership, and the loss of freedom. Then a federal agency, the **National Labor Relations Board (NLRB)**, becomes involved. The NLRB sends a hearing officer to over- see the union campaign and monitor developments.

Employees are asked to sign cards authorizing a union election. If fewer than 30% sign the **authorization cards**, the process ends. If 30% or more sign, an election is held to determine whether a union will represent the employees. The NLRB officer must determine which employees are eligible to be in the union and thus eligible to vote. Management personnel (supervisors, superintendents, and managers) are excluded. The hearing officer schedules the election, provides secret ballots and ballot boxes, counts the votes, and certifies the election. This expression of voter preference is termed a **certification election**. If more than 50% of the voters approve, the union is voted in. If the union loses the election, it can repeat the entire process at a later date. A union that loses a close election will probably do so. Hepburn and Barling (2001) reported that employees who abstained from voting in a union representation election possessed less extreme work and union attitudes and believed less in the ability of their vote to af- fect the election outcome, compared with employees who did vote in the election.

Brief and Rude (1981) proposed that the decision to accept or reject a union is not unlike other choices facing an individual. Employees will support a union to the extent that it will obtain outcomes important to them without prohibitive costs. More than 60 years ago Bakke (1945) stated this most eloquently:

> The worker reacts favorably to union membership in proportion to the strength of his belief that this step will reduce his frustrations and anxieties and will further his opportunities relevant to the achievement of his standards of successful living. He reacts unfavorably in proportion to the strength of his belief that this step will increase his frustrations and anxieties and will reduce his opportunities relevant to the achieve- ment of such standards. (p. 38)

Tetrick et al. (2007) proposed an explanation of why workers join unions (See Figure 14-2). The process begins by workers regarding a labor union as being instrumental in helping them to attain the results or outcomes they desire. If such union instrumentality is accepted, a labor union will be supported. To the extent that the labor union continues to remain instrumental in attaining the desired outcomes, workers will exhibit loyalty to the union. Tetrick et al. extended the concept of organizational citizenship behaviors (as discussed in Chapter 10) to become "union citizenship behaviors". The two constructs are composed of similar dimensions, including active participation, exerting a voice, and demonstrating civic virtue. The difference is that the behaviors are directed to the union as a means of contributing to its effectiveness. The workers view the union as being essential to their well-being, and thus they contribute to the maintenance of the social exchange relationship with management. Buttigieg, Deery, and Iverson (2007) reported similar findings regarding the instrumentality of unions to help achieve greater procedural justice within the organization.

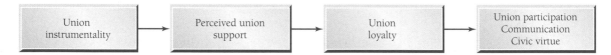

Figure 14-2   *A model of union participation*

Source: From L. E. Tetrick, L. M. Shore, L. N. McClung, and R. J. Vandenberg, 2007. "A Model of Union Participation: The Impact of Perceived Union Support, Union Instrumentality, and Union Loyalty." *Journal of Applied Psychology, 92*, 820–828.

Summers, Betton, and DeCotiis (1986) found that union instrumentality can be lowered when different unions are competing for the right to represent employees. They discovered that employees are likely to take antiunion information more seriously if its source is another union rather than management. Premack and Hunter (1988) carefully studied the unionization decision by means of elaborate statistical methods. They concluded that some employees hold strong attitudes about unions, both pro and con, and their attitudes are usually not altered one way or the other during the organizing campaign. However, other employees are uncertain about their attitudes toward unions, and their attitudes can be altered by the behavior of both parties during the organizing campaign. Premack and Hunter noted that these employees' votes are critical to the outcome of the election because most union representation elections are decided by a small number of votes.

The Labor Contract

Labor contract
A formal agreement between labor and management that specifies the terms and conditions of employment.

Once a union is recognized, its officials are authorized to negotiate a **labor contract**. This is a formal agreement between union and management that specifies the conditions of employment over a set period.

Both sides prepare a preliminary list of what they want included; the union presents its *demands* and the employer its *offers*. The union tends to ask for more than it knows it can get; management tends to offer less. While both sides seek a satisfactory agreement, they often resort to bombast, which is a hallmark of such negotiations.

Impasse
A point in the collective bargaining process at which both the union and management conclude they are unable to reach an agreement in the formation of a labor contract.

Union officials may allege that management is making huge profits and taking advantage of workers. Management may allege that malicious union leaders have duped the good workers and that their policies may force the company into bankruptcy. Over time, both sides usually come to an agreement; the union often gets less than it wanted and management gives more. When agreement is not reached (an **impasse**), other steps are taken, as will be discussed.

Contract negotiations take place between two teams of negotiators. The union side typically consists of local union officials, shop stewards, and perhaps a representative of the national union. Management usually fields a team of a few personnel and production managers, who follow preset guidelines. The contract contains many articles; there are also many issues to bargain over. The issues can generally be classified into five categories: compensation and working conditions, employee security, union security, management rights, and contract duration. Table 14-2 gives examples of these issues and the positions typically taken by each side.

In the process each bargaining team checks with its members to see whether they will compromise on the initial positions. Each side may be willing to yield on some points but not others. Eventually they reach a tentative agreement. Union members then vote on the contract. If they approve it, the contract is ratified and remains in effect for the agreed-on time (typically two to three years). If members reject the contract, further negotiation is necessary.

Both sides will use whatever external factors are available to influence the contract in their favor. If there is high unemployment and the company can easily replace workers who go on strike, management has an advantage. If the company does much of its business around Christmas, the union may choose that time to negotiate a contract, knowing the company can ill afford a strike then. Each side looks for factors that will bolster its position.

Table 14-2 *Typical bargaining issues and positions taken by union and management*

Issue	Union's Position	Management's Position
Compensation	Higher pay, more benefits, cost-of-living adjustments	Lower company expenditures, not yielding to all union demands
Employee security	Seniority is the basis for promotions, layoffs, and recall decisions	Merit or job performance is the basis for these decisions
Union security	A union shop in which employees must join the union when hired	An open shop in which employees can choose to join the union
Management rights	Union wants more voice in setting policies and making decisions that affect employees	Management feels certain decisions are its inherent right and does not want to share them with the union
Contract duration	Shorter contracts	Longer contracts

Collective Bargaining and Impasse Resolution

Collective bargaining
The process by which labor and management negotiate a labor contract.

Whether the **collective bargaining** process runs smoothly often depends on the parties' approaches. Pruitt (1993) distinguished between distributive and integrative bargaining postures. *Distributive bargaining* is predominant in the United States. This assumes a win/lose relationship; whatever the employer gives the union, the employer loses, and vice versa. Because both sides are trying to minimize losses, movement toward a compromise is often painful and slow. The alternative is *integrative bargaining*. Both sides work to improve the relationship while the present contract is in effect. Contract renewal is not seen as the time and place for confrontation. Instead, both parties seek to identify common problems and propose acceptable solutions that can be adopted when the contract expires. Labor and management collaboratively seek "win-win" situations to the issues they face. Although it is not always a strict either/or decision, distributive bargaining is far more characteristic of union/management relations than is integrative bargaining.

What happens if the two parties cannot reach an agreement? In some cases the labor contract may stipulate what will be done if an impasse is reached. In other cases union and management must jointly determine how to break the impasse. In either case there are three options, all involving third parties: mediation, fact-finding, and arbitration.

Mediation
A method of dispute settlement in which a neutral third party offers advice to the union and management to help them agree on a labor contract.

Mediation.   **Mediation** is the most used yet the most informal third-party option. A neutral third party (a mediator) assists union and management in reaching voluntary agreement. A mediator has no power to impose a settlement; rather, he or she facilitates bringing both parties together.

Where do mediators come from? The Federal Mediation and Conciliation Service (FMCS) has a staff of qualified mediators. An organization may contact FMCS for the services of such a person. The mediator need not be affiliated with FMCS; any third party acceptable to labor and management may serve. Generally, however, both parties prefer someone who has training and experience in labor disputes, so FMCS is often used.

How a mediator intervenes is not clear-cut. Mediation is voluntary; thus no mediator can function without the trust, cooperation, and acceptance of both parties. Acceptance is important because an effective mediator obtains confidential information that the parties have withheld from each other. If the information is used indiscriminately, the parties' bargaining strategy and leverage could be weakened. The mediator tries to reduce the number of disputed issues; ideally, he or she reaches a point where there are no disputes at all. The mediator encourages information sharing to break the deadlock. Without a mediator, it is often difficult for parties to "open up" after assuming adversarial roles. The mediator facilitates the flow of information and progress toward compromise. If the mediator is unsuccessful, both parties may engage in the next phase: fact-finding.

Fact-finding
A method of dispute settlement in which a neutral third party makes public the respective positions of labor and management with the intention that the public will influence the two sides to resolve their disputes in establishing a labor contract.

Fact-Finding.   **Fact-finding** is more formal than mediation. A qualified mediator may also serve as a fact finder, but his or her role is different. In fact-finding the third party reviews the facts, makes a formal recommendation to resolve the dispute, and makes the recommendation public. It is presumed that if the recommendation is public, the parties will be pressured to accept it or use it for a negotiated settlement.

Arbitration
A method of dispute settlement in which a neutral third party resolves the dispute between labor and management by using a decision that is typically final and binding on both parties.

Interest arbitration
A type of arbitration used to resolve disputes between labor and management in the formation of a labor contract.

Conventional arbitration
A form of arbitration in which the arbitrator is free to fashion whatever decision is deemed most fair in resolving a dispute.

Final-offer arbitration
A form of arbitration in which the arbitrator is obligated to accept the final offer of either the union or management in their dispute.

Total-package arbitration
A form of final-offer arbitration in which the arbitrator is obligated to accept either the union's position or management's position on every issue in dispute between the parties.

Issue-by-issue arbitration
A form of final-offer arbitration in which the arbitrator is obligated to accept either the union's position or management's position on an issue-by-issue basis in disputes between the parties.

However, fact-finding has typically not produced the desired pressure. Public interest is apparently aroused only when a strike threatens or actually imposes direct hardship on the public.

Fact-finding may be most useful when one party faces internal differences and needs recommendations from an expert to overcome opposition to a settlement. There appears to be a difference in the effectiveness of fact-finding between private- and public-sector employers. In the public sector fact-finding has met with limited success. Parties learn that rejecting a fact-finding recommendation is not politically or economically costly, so they are unlikely to value the opinion of the fact finder. In the private sector, fact-finding can be helpful primarily because the final technique of settlement (arbitration) is strongly opposed by unions and management. However, fact-finding is not used very often in the private sector.

Arbitration.   **Arbitration** is the final and most formal settlement technique. Both parties must abide by the decision of the neutral third party. "Final and binding" is usually associated with arbitration. The use of arbitration may be stipulated in the labor contract; it may also be agreed on informally. This is called **interest arbitration** because it involves the interests of both parties in negotiating a new contract.

Arbitrators must have extensive experience in labor relations. The American Arbitration Association (AAA) maintains the standards and keeps a list of qualified arbitrators. Arbitrators listed by AAA can also serve as mediators listed by FMCS. Effective mediators, fact finders, and arbitrators all need the same skills. What distinguishes the services is the clout of the third party.

There are many forms of interest arbitration. With voluntary arbitration, the parties agree to the process. It is most common in the private sector to settle disputes that arise while a contract is still in effect. Compulsory arbitration is legally required. It is most common in the public sector.

There are other types of arbitration. With **conventional arbitration**, the arbitrator creates the settlement he or she deems appropriate. In **final-offer arbitration**, the arbitrator must select the proposal of either union or management; no compromise is possible. For example, suppose the union demands $12 per hour and the company offers $8. In conventional arbitration the arbitrator could decide on any wage but would probably split the difference and decide on $10. In final-offer arbitration the arbitrator must choose the $8 or the $12. An additional variation also holds for final-offer arbitration: the arbitrator may make the decision with **total-package arbitration**: he or she chooses the complete proposal of either the employer or the union on all issues. The decision may also be made with **issue-by-issue arbitration**: the arbitrator might choose the employer wage offer but select the union demand on vacation days. Decisions on voluntary versus compulsory arbitration, conventional versus final-offer arbitration, and total-package versus issue-by-issue arbitration are determined by law for public-sector employers and by mutual agreement in the private sector (see Field Note 3, p. 446).

Interest arbitration is more common in the public sector. Historically, the private sector has been opposed to outside interference in resolving labor problems that are "private" affairs. Thus private-sector employers will readily seek the advice of a mediator but shun strategies that require certain courses of action. The public sector, however, is quite different. Strikes in the public sector (for example, police) can have devastating effects on the general public. Because they are often prohibited by law, other

Field Note 3: Overuse of Arbitration?

Interest arbitration can be a seductively simple means of resolving impasses—so simple, in fact, that some people fear it is overused. Let us say the union wants a $1-per-hour pay increase and management offers 40¢ per hour. Both sides believe from past experience that an arbitrator will likely split the difference between the two, settling on 70¢ per hour. It has been suggested that the more arbitration is used to resolve impasses and the more splitting that occurs, the more likely it is that parties will not bargain seriously between themselves; that is, they will opt for the effortless remedy, arbitration. Thus the parties will disregard the mediation and fact-finding stages and go directly to arbitration. Arbitration becomes an addictive response to impasse; this phenomenon has been labeled the "narcotic effect" of arbitration.

How do you weaken the narcotic effect of arbitration? Arbitrators are free to fashion whatever decisions they think are fair. Splitting the difference is often perceived as the fairest thing to do, and it increases the acceptability of the arbitrator for future cases because neither party will have received preferential treatment.

Thus, with each split decision, the narcotic effect becomes stronger. One way to weaken the narcotic effect is to prohibit split decisions, which is what happens in final-offer arbitration. Here, the arbitrator is bound to accept either the $1 or 40¢ position and not any figure over, under, or in between. Given this, it has been hypothesized that negotiators will offer more serious, reasonable proposals if they know the alternative is to have an arbitrator choose one position over the other. An absurd offer would never get chosen. In total-package, final-offer arbitration the arbitrator must choose the entire package of either the union or management, which tends to drive both parties to compromise. The alternative version of issue-by-issue, final-offer arbitration produces its own type of split decisions; that is, because there can be no within-issue splits, the arbitrator splits between issues. Thus the union position is accepted on one issue and management's position on another. The creation of total-package, final-offer arbitration is presumed to have greatly decreased reliance on arbitration for impasse resolution.

means of settlement (fact-finding, arbitration) are used. Some public-sector employees have gone on strike (sometimes legally but usually illegally), but strikes are more often the outcome of impasses in the private sector.

Responses to Impasse

Consider the situation in which union and management cannot resolve their disputes. They may or may not have used a mediator. Assume the private sector is involved because mediation, fact-finding, and arbitration might be required in the public sector. What happens if the two parties cannot agree?

In collective bargaining both sides can take actions if they are not pleased with the outcome. These actions are tactics with which to bring about favorable settlements.

Labor strike
A cessation of work activities by unionized employees as a means of influencing management to accept the union position in a dispute over the labor contract.

The union can call for a **labor strike**. Union members must vote for a strike. If members support a strike and no settlement is reached, they will stop work at a particular time. That point is typically the day after the current contract expires. Taking a strike vote during negotiations brings pressure on management to agree to union demands.

The right to strike is a very powerful tool. A company's losses from a long strike may be greater than the concessions made in a new contract. Also, unions are skilled in scheduling their strikes (or threatening to do so) when the company is particularly vulnerable (such as around Christmas for the airline industry). If employees do strike, the company is usually closed down completely. There may be limited production if management performs some jobs. It is also possible to hire workers to replace those on strike. These replacements are called "scabs." Given the time it takes to recruit, hire, and train new workers, replacements will not be hired unless a long strike is predicted.

The Wizard Of ID

By permission of John L. Hart FLP and Creators Syndicate, Inc.

Although a strike hurts management, it is unpleasant for the workers as well. Because they are not working, they do not get paid. The employees may have contributed to a strike fund, but such funds usually pay only a fraction of regular wages. A strike is the price employees pay to get their demands. It sometimes also limits their demands. By the time a union faces a strike, it is usually confronted with two unpalatable options. One is to accept a contract it does not like; the other is to strike. Employees may seek temporary employment while they are on strike, but such jobs are not always available. On the basis of labor economists' studies of the costs of strikes to both employees and employers, it is safe to say that strikes rarely benefit either party. Sometimes the company suffers the most; in other cases the union does. There are rarely any "winners" in a strike.

One study examined some of the dynamics associated with strikes. Stagner and Effal (1982) looked at the attitudes of unionized automobile workers at several times, including when contracts were being negotiated, during an ensuing strike, and seven months after the strike ended. The authors found that union members on strike (1) had a higher opinion of the union and its leadership than before the strike, (2) evaluated the benefit package more highly after the strike, (3) became more militant toward the employer during the strike, and (4) reported more willingness to engage in union activities. The results of this study support predictions based on theories of conflict and attitude formation.

Management is not totally defenseless in the case of a strike. If it anticipates a strike, it might boost production beforehand to stockpile goods. Most public-sector employees, on the other hand, perform services, and services cannot be stockpiled. This is one reason strikes are illegal in some parts of the public sector. Sometimes a strike uncovers information about the quality of the workforce. When one company replaced strikers with temporary help, new production records were set. In this case the strike revealed a weakness in the employees.

A strike is not the only option available to the union. **Work slowdowns** have also been used in which workers operate at lower levels of efficiency. They may simply put out less effort and thus produce less, or they may be absent to reduce productivity. Because strikes are illegal in the police force, police officers who are dissatisfied with their contracts may call in sick en masse with what has become known as the "blue flu." Such tactics can exert great pressure on management to yield to union demands.

Sabotage is another response to impasse in negotiations. Stagner and Rosen (1965) described a situation in which factory production was increased from 2,000 to 3,000 units per day by modifying a drill press. Wages were not raised, however, and workers resented it. They found that bumping the sheet metal against the drill would eventually break the drill. Then the employee handling the drill would have to wait idly for a replacement. By some curious accident, average production continued at around 2,000 units per day. Management got the "message." Although sabotage is not a sanctioned union activity like a strike, it is a way of putting pressure on management to accept demands.

Management also has a major tactic to get the union to acquiesce. It is called a **lockout** and is considered the employer's equivalent of a strike. The company threatens to close if the union does not accept its offer. Employees cannot work and thus "pay" for rejecting the employer's offer. A threatened lockout may cause a majority of workers to pressure a minority holding out against a contract issue. Like strikes, lockouts are costly to both the company and the union, and they are not undertaken lightly. They are management's ultimate response to an impasse.

Before this section ends, note that strikes, slowdowns, sabotage, and lockouts represent failures in the collective bargaining process. These actions are taken because a settlement was not reached. Like most responses to frustration, they are rarely beneficial in the long run. Some unions may want to "teach the company a lesson"; some companies want to break a union. But the two parties have a symbiotic relationship. A company cannot exist without employees; without a company, employees have no jobs. Collective bargaining reflects the continual tussle for power, but neither side can afford to be totally victorious. If a union exacts so many concessions that the company goes bankrupt, it will have accomplished nothing. As Estey (1981) put it, "Labor does not seek to kill the goose that lays the golden eggs; it wants it to lay more golden eggs, and wants more eggs for itself" (p. 83). If management drives employees away by not making enough concessions, it will not have a qualified workforce. Industrial peace is far more desirable for all parties than warfare. Conflict can provide opportunities for change and development; if conflict gets out of hand, it can be devastating.

Union/management relations are not all infighting and power plays. Nothing unites opposing factions faster than a common enemy. Because the United States was losing some economic battles to foreign competition, some union/management relations became far more integrative. For example, unions in the auto industry have given up some concessions they gained before the current contract expired. The industry, in turn, used the money saved to become more competitive. By remaining solvent, the

---

Work slowdown
A tactic used by some employees to influence the outcome of union/management negotiations in which the usual pace of work is intentionally reduced.

Sabotage
A tactic used by some employees to influence the outcome of union/management negotiations in which company equipment is intentionally damaged to reduce work productivity.

Lockout
Action taken by management against unionized employees to prevent them from entering their place of work as a means of influencing the union to accept the management position in a dispute over the labor contract.

industry continued to provide jobs. Both management and labor could pursue some common goals. Collective bargaining is a delicate process. Neither side should lose sight of the total economic and social environment, even though short-term, narrow issues are often at the heart of disputes.

Grievances

Collective bargaining is mainly directed toward resolving disputes over new labor contracts; however, disputes also occur over contracts that are in effect. No matter how clearly a labor contract is written, disagreements can arise over its meaning. Developing a clear and precise contract involves writing skills in their highest form. Despite the best intentions of those involved, events occur that are not covered clearly in a labor contract. For example, companies often include a contract clause stating that sleeping on the job is grounds for dismissal. A supervisor notices that an employee's head is resting on his arms and his eyes are closed. The supervisor infers the employee is asleep and fires him. The employee says he was not sleeping but felt dizzy and chose to rest for a moment rather than risk falling down. Who is right?

Grievance
A formal complaint made by an employee against management alleging a violation of the labor contract in effect.

If the supervisor dismissed the employee, the employee would probably file a **grievance**, or formal complaint. The firing decision can be appealed through a grievance procedure, which is usually a provision of a labor contract. First, the employee and supervisor try to reach an understanding. If they do not, the shop steward represents the employee in negotiating with the supervisor. This is often done whether or not the steward thinks the employee has a "case"; above all, the steward's job is to represent union members. If it is not resolved, the case may then be taken to the company's director of industrial relations, who hears testimony from both sides and issues a verdict. This may be a compromise—such as the employee keeps his or her job but is put on probation. The final step is to call in an arbitrator. He or she examines the labor contract, hears testimony, and renders an opinion. This process is called rights or **grievance arbitration**; it involves the rights of the employee. The labor contract usually specifies that union and management share the cost of arbitration, which may be $2,000 per hearing. This is done to prevent all grievances from being routinely pushed to arbitration. Each side must believe it has a strong case before calling in an arbitrator.

Grievance arbitration
A type of arbitration used in resolving disputes between labor and management in interpretation of an existing labor contract. Also called rights arbitration.

The arbitrator must be acceptable to both sides; this means he or she must be seen as neither prounion nor promanagement. The arbitrator may decide in favor of one side or issue a compromise decision. The decision is final and binding. If an arbitrator hears many cases in the same company and repeatedly decides in favor of one side, he or she may become unacceptable to the side that always loses. Articles of the labor contract that are repeated subjects of grievance (due mainly to ambiguous language) become prime candidates for revision in the next contract.

Think of grievances as a somewhat contaminated index of the quality of union/management relations. In general, when the working relationship is good, there are fewer grievances. However, as Gordon and Miller (1984) noted, in some organizations work problems are resolved informally between the conflicting parties and never develop into formal grievances. Although formal grievances are usually indicative of conflict, their absence does not always reflect a problem-free work environment. Also, the more ambiguous the labor contract, the more likely conflicts will ensue. A poorly written or inconsistently interpreted contract invites grievances. There can be much grievance activity in a recently unionized organization; employees use grievances to "test" management's knowledge of the labor contract (Muchinsky & Maassarani, 1981). Particularly in the public sector, where collective bargaining is relatively new, government employees are expected to act as "management" even though they have little or no training in dealing with labor. This can contribute to errors in contract administration. Gordon and Bowlby (1989) found that employees were more likely to file a grievance when management actions against them were perceived as a threat and when the employees attributed the discipline to a manager's personal disposition (animus toward a worker). Employees were less likely to file a grievance when they perceived managers as simply following rules that required punishment for the specific worker behavior.

Employee concern over capricious management decisions is one of the major reasons employees opt for union representation. Fryxell and Gordon (1989) reported that the amount of procedural justice afforded by a grievance system was the strongest predictor of employee satisfaction with a union. Gordon and Bowlby (1988) also challenged the assertion that grievances are best resolved at the lowest step of the grievance process. Grievants who won their cases at higher levels of the grievance process showed greater faith in the fairness and perceived justice of the dispute resolution process. Klaas (1989) reported that at higher levels in the grievance process managers were influenced by the grievant's work history as documented in performance appraisals, even when that history was not relevant to evaluating the merits of the grievance. Olson-Buchanan (1996) found that, consistent with procedural justice, employees who had access to a grievance system were more willing to continue working for the organization.

There is also a growing use of arbitration to resolve disputes in nonunion companies. Richey et al. (2001) reported that in the past 20 years there has been a 400% increase in employment litigation and a 2,200% increase in discrimination lawsuits, with a corresponding increase in company costs and negative publicity. With the increased number of lawsuits in the courts, there has been growing support for *alternative dispute resolution* procedures among employees, legislators, and the courts. Arbitration is being proposed as a means of resolving disputes between employees and employers. The arbitration process may be voluntary (i.e., the employee has the option to submit the dispute to an impartial arbitrator) or mandatory (i.e., the employee is required to submit any dispute to an impartial arbitrator as a condition of employment at the company). Likewise, the outcome of the arbitration process can be nonbinding (meaning if the arbitrator's judgment does not satisfy the employee, the employee can choose to pursue the dispute in court) or binding (meaning the outcome of the arbitration process is final and binding and may not be pursued in court). Richey et al. found that job applicants were more inclined to view an employer negatively if they used either mandatory or binding arbitration as a means of resolving disputes. The finding was interpreted as limiting avenues of procedural justice for employees.

In conclusion, although there is much publicity about strike-related issues, union members think the union's highest priority should be enhancing their welfare. Unions serve many purposes; however, the most pressing need they fill seems to be ensuring fair treatment in employment. Of course, this is a primary reason that unions appeal to workers.

Influence of Unions on Nonunionized Companies

Even if they do not have unionized employees, companies are still sensitive to union influence. Companies that are unresponsive to employees' needs invite unionization. A nonunion company that wants to remain so must be receptive to its workers' ideas and complaints. If a company can satisfy its employees' needs, a union is unnecessary; that is, if the company does voluntarily what a labor union would force it to do. A given community or industry often has a mix of union and nonunion companies. If unionized employees get concessions from management on wages, benefits, hours, and so on, these become reference points for nonunionized employees. Thus, for example, a nonunion company may feel compelled to raise wages to remain competitive. If a labor contract calls for formal grievance procedures, a nonunion company may well follow suit. Workers are aware of employment conditions in other companies, which gives them a frame of reference for judging their own. If a company does not offer comparable conditions, employees may see a union as a means of improving their welfare. This is not to say that nonunion companies must offer identical conditions. There are costs associated with a union (for example, dues); a nonunion company might set wages slightly lower than those paid in a unionized company so the net effect (higher wages minus dues) is comparable. What economists call the **union/nonunion wage differential** has been the subject of extensive research. Jarrell and Stanley (1990) reported that the union/nonunion wage differential varied with the national unemployment rate and ranged from 8.9% to 12.4%.

Union/nonunion wage differential
The average difference in wages paid to union versus nonunion employees across an industry or geographic area for performing the same jobs.

Although a prudent nonunion employer keeps abreast of employment conditions in the community and the industry, a company cannot act to keep a union out "at all costs." There is powerful labor relations legislation. Many laws (like the National Labor Relations Act) were enacted to prohibit unfair practices on both sides. For example, an employer cannot fire a worker just because he or she supports a union. The history of labor relations is full of cases of worker harassment by unions or management to influence attitudes toward unionization. But both sides can suffer for breaking the law.

Behavioral Research on Union/Management Relations

Thus far this chapter has examined the structure of unions, collective bargaining, and various issues in union/management relations. For the most part, psychological issues have not been discussed. With the exception of grievances, there is little behavioral research on union/management relations. However, over the past few decades, interest in this area has increased. We are beginning to see an interdisciplinary approach to topics that historically were treated with parochialism (Brett, 1980). This section will examine research on union/management relations with a strong behavioral thrust.

Employee Support for Unions

Numerous studies have examined why employees support a union, particularly with regard to personal needs and job satisfaction. Feuille and Blandin (1974) sampled the attitudes toward unionization of more than 400 college professors at a university experiencing many financial and resource cutbacks. The items measured satisfaction with areas like fairness of the university's personnel decisions, adequacy of financial support, representation of faculty interests in the state legislature, and salary. The professors were also asked to rate their inclination to accept a union. Professors who were dissatisfied with employment conditions were much more likely to support a union. Respondents also were consistent in their attitudes toward a union and their perceptions of its impact and effectiveness. Proponents of a union saw it as an effective way to protect employment interests and as having a positive impact. In general, results indicated that unionization is more attractive as employment conditions deteriorate.

Using a similar research design and sample, Bigoness (1978) correlated measures of job satisfaction and job involvement with disposition to accept unionization. Bigoness found that feelings of dissatisfaction correlated with acceptance of unionization. In particular, dissatisfaction with work, pay, and promotions each correlated at .35 with attitude toward unionization. Additionally, unionization was more appealing to people who were less involved in their jobs. Combining all independent variables in a multiple regression equation, Bigoness accounted for more than 27% of the variance in attitudes toward unionization.

Hamner and Smith (1978) examined union activity in 250 units of a large organization. In half the units there had been some union activity; the other half had no activity. Using an immense sample of more than 80,000 employees, the authors found that employee attitudes predicted the level of unionization activity. The strongest predictor was dissatisfaction with supervision. Schriesheim (1978) found that prounion voting in a certification election was positively correlated with dissatisfaction; also, dissatisfaction with economic issues was more predictive than dissatisfaction with noneconomic factors. Furthermore, research by Youngblood et al. (1984) and Zalesny (1985) showed the importance of two other factors in union support. The first factor is attitude toward collective bargaining in general. The more acceptable unions in general are to a person, the more likely he or she will vote for unionization. The second factor is attitude toward unions as being instrumental in enhancing worker welfare. Employees may not be satisfied with their employment conditions, but they may feel that unions can do little to aid them.

These studies show that dissatisfaction with employment conditions is predictive of support for unionization. The more satisfied workers are, the less likely they are to think a union is necessary or that it can improve their welfare. These results are not surprising. They reveal the types of dissatisfaction associated with a disposition toward unions. Some authors tout the social benefits of unions (for example, association with similar people), but it is mainly the perceived economic advantages that give unions their appeal. Not all support for unions, however, is based on dissatisfaction with economic conditions. Hammer and Berman (1981) found that the faculty at one college wanted a union mainly because they distrusted administrative decision making and were dissatisfied with work content. Prounion voting was motivated by the faculty's desire to have more power in dealing with the administration. The decision to support a union is grounded in theories of organizational justice. Aryee and Chay (2001) found that perceived union support and union instrumentality were closely linked to workers' desire for procedural justice. Similarly, Fuller and Hester (2001) reported support for unionization on the basis of interactional justice—in this case, higher-quality interactions between employees and management.

Union Influence

What influence do unions have on enhancing employee welfare? Various studies have produced different conclusions. Gomez-Mejia and Balkin (1984) found that samples of unionized and nonunionized college teachers were equally satisfied with all job facets except pay; unionized faculty were more satisfied with their wages. Carillon and Sutton (1982) found a strong positive relationship between union effectiveness in representing teachers and their reported quality of worklife. Allegedly, college administrators fear that faculty unionization will affect organization effectiveness. Cameron (1982) examined this in 41 colleges; faculty were unionized in 18 colleges and nonunionized in 23. Cameron proposed nine indices of effectiveness for a college, including student academic development, faculty and administrator satisfaction, and ability to acquire resources. Nonunionized colleges were significantly more effective on three of the nine indices; unionized colleges were not significantly more effective on any. Cameron also collected attitude data from faculty members on four factors relating to their work. These results are presented in Figure 14-3. Faculty power and "red tape" were seen as increasing since unionization; collegiality was seen as decreasing. The study revealed some major differences in the effectiveness of union and nonunion colleges; however, the cause was not determined. Unionization may cause colleges to be less effective, which would be a strong argument against unions. However, less effective colleges may turn to unions for improvement, which is obviously an argument supporting unionization. As discussed in Chapter 2, causality is difficult to determine. Raelin (1989) suggested that the literature on this topic indicates that less effective colleges turn to unions in an attempt to restore their professional status.

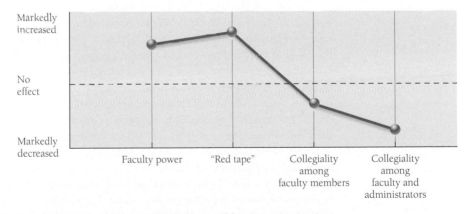

Figure 14-3   *Perceptions of the effects of faculty unionization*

From "The Relationship Between Faculty Unionism and Organizational Effectiveness" by K. Cameron, 1982, *Academy of Management Journal, 25,* p. 13.

Fullagar et al. (1995) tested the proposition that new organizational members are socialized to consider joining a union. There are two types of socialization. The first is *institutional*, which refers to the collective and formal practices organizations use to provide newcomers with a common set of experiences and information to elicit standardized responses. In contrast, *individual* socialization practices are idiosyncratic and informal. Individual socialization is informal in that learning takes place on the job through interactions with other organizational members. Fullagar et al. found that individual socialization practices had a positive impact on both affective and behavioral involvement in the union. Institutional socialization practices were shown to be either ineffective or counterproductive. The practical implications are that important interactions occur between union officials and new members in developing new members' affective attachment to the union and later participation in union activities. Informal and individual socialization tactics may be undertaken by active or interested rank-and-file members and not necessarily by union stewards. Institutional socialization efforts (e.g., an orientation program to the union) seemingly are more effective in increasing awareness, whereas individual socialization efforts are more effective in producing involvement (Fullagar et al., 1994).

Dispute Settlement

I/O psychologists have examined the process by which disputes are settled in both laboratory and field settings. As in some other areas of I/O research, the generalizability of laboratory findings in this area is somewhat limited. Gordon, Schmitt, and Schneider (1984) think the value of laboratory studies is to prepare people for undertaking actual collective bargaining in the future and to help develop questionnaires for later field use in dispute settlement. They noted that the limitations of laboratory and field research on dispute settlement are the classic ones discussed in Chapter 2. There is questionable generalizability from laboratory studies, and field studies fail to identify causal relationships.

Several studies have looked at mediation and arbitration as means of settling disputes. Bazerman and Neale (1982) asked whether strategies of personnel selection and training can improve negotiating effectiveness. They proposed selecting negotiators on the basis of their ability to take a broad perspective on problems and training them not to be overconfident about effecting a resolution. The authors found that training increased the number of concessions negotiators were willing to make and concluded that it may be a useful tool in dispute settlement. Neale (1984) determined that when the costs of arbitration are high, negotiators are more likely to reach a resolution on their own before they resort to arbitration. However, when cost is not much of an issue, they are more likely to accept arbitration. Researchers have also discovered the behavioral implications of the different types of arbitration. Starke and Notz (1981) reported that subjects who anticipated final-offer arbitration were closer to agreement at the conclusion of their bargaining than subjects who anticipated conventional arbitration. In fact, Grigsby and Bigoness (1982) concluded that final-offer, conventional, total-package, and issue-by-issue arbitration all produced different bargaining outcomes even though they are all variations of the same resolution process (arbitration). These behavioral studies on dispute settlement have enhanced our understanding in ways that traditional labor economic research has been unable to do. In fact, Brett, Goldberg, and Ury (1990) discussed how I/O psychologists can be used to resolve disputes. They proposed that a dispute-system designer organize procedures in a low- to high-cost sequence and work with parties to help them acquire new motivation, negotiation skills, and recourses to new procedures. The individual may even recommend changes in the broader organization that will facilitate the success of a dispute resolution system. Brett et al. (2007) found that the words people use in on-line dispute resolution affected the likelihood of settlement. The authors studied disputes between buyers and sellers on eBay, an on-line auction service. Settlement was more likely when parties engaged in face-saving gestures, as by providing a possible causal account for the misunderstanding between the two parties. Conversely, settlement was less likely when parties felt attacked by verbal expressions of negative emotions or by making demands.

Conlon, Moon, and Ng (2002) have experimented with hybrid means of dispute settlement. The criteria for dispute resolution include getting the two parties to resolve their own differences and having both parties feel some measure of satisfaction in the resulting outcome. Conlon et al. noted that mediation is generally more effective as a means of dispute settlement when it is followed by binding arbitration (compared with mediation alone). That is, when both parties know (and have agreed in advance) that a settlement will be made for them by a third party (an arbitrator), they are more likely to reach a voluntary agreement on their own. Conlon et al. proposed a hybrid means of dispute settlement where arbitration *precedes* (not follows) mediation. The three-phase process worked as follows. In phase one the two parties present their cases to an arbitrator, who then makes a ruling. The ruling is sealed in an envelope and is not revealed to the two parties. In the second phase the two parties engage in traditional mediation with no third party present. A precise time period is set for the two parties to reach an agreement. Conlon et al. (2007) noted that with a fixed time period set for the mediation phase, neither party can afford to engage in posturing or delays. Any wasted time in the mediation phase increases the likelihood a settlement will not be reached, thereby placing control of the settlement in the hands of the arbitrator. If the two sides reach an agreement, the dispute is settled and the arbitrator's (unknown) ruling is rendered moot. However, if the two parties do not resolve their dispute in mediation, the third phase of the process is to make the arbitrator's ruling known to both parties, and they are both obligated to accept it. It was reported that this hybrid method of "putting the cart before the horse" did result in successful voluntary agreements in the mediation phase, and was often used in highly contested disputes.

Commitment to the Union

The concept of employee commitment to a union addresses the notion of dual allegiance: can a person be loyal to both a labor union and the employing company? Researchers have examined the antecedents of both union and company commitment.

Union commitment
The sense of identity and support unionized employees feel for their labor union.

Our understanding of **union commitment** was enhanced through a major study by Gordon et al. (1980). These authors developed a questionnaire for measuring commitment that was completed by more than 1,800 union members. Responses were statistically analyzed, and union commitment was found to be composed of four dimensions: loyalty, responsibility to the union, willingness to work for the union, and belief in unionism. The research had at least two major benefits for unions. First, unions could use the questionnaires to assess the effect of their actions and estimate solidarity, especially before negotiations. Second, the research revealed the importance of socialization to new union members. The authors found that union commitment increases when both formal and informal efforts are made to involve a member in union activities soon after joining. Coworker attitudes and willingness to help are crucial to the socialization process. Improving the socialization of new members improves their commitment, which is one index of union strength. In a follow-up study by Ladd et al. (1982), the questionnaire was administered to nonprofessional and professional members of a white-collar union. The results were the same as those from the original study despite the sample differences, although other researchers arrived at somewhat different conclusions (Friedman & Harvey, 1986). Klandermans (1989) found the scale useful for understanding unionism in the Netherlands (see Cross-Cultural I/O Psychology: Cross-National Labor Unions?).

Cross-Cultural I/O Psychology: *Cross-National Labor Unions?*

What impact does the U.S. economy moving from a manufacturing base to a service base have on labor unions? Although experts are not in full agreement, the impact appears to be substantial. The percentage of workers in the United States who are represented by a labor union (known as "union density") is half of what it was 40 years ago. Rubery and Grimshaw (2003) estimate 15% of U.S. workers are unionized, one of the lowest union densities in the developed world. Scandinavian countries are among the most heavily unionized, about 75% of the workforce. Approximately one-fourth of the workforce is unionized in Japan and about one-third in Australia. Countries also differ in the extent to which employment conditions bargained for by labor unions extend to non-union companies.

In the 1930s labor unions in the United States were at their peak of influence. They exerted a strong influence in political elections, with unions invariably endorsing candidates from the Democratic Party. Today the political influence of U.S. labor unions is relatively weak as organized labor has become a progressively smaller portion of the workforce. In an attempt to revitalize U.S. unions, consideration is being given to labor unions "going global" just as business has done so. Is it possible to have cross-border solidarity of workers, the primary appeal of labor unions? Although money may flow across borders in pursuit of new business ventures, the structure of organized labor is not so fluid. The reasons for the difficulty include the following. First, there are still lingering vestiges of the Cold War, when the world was divided between communist and anticommunist nations. Countries that were formerly adversaries (or at least not allies) are reluctant to join forces through organized labor. Second, there is not a single type of labor union but rather many types and roles across nations. Some are heavily dependent on their governments and in effect have a partnership with them. In other nations labor unions have a more independent relationship with their governments. Third, the shrinking state of many U.S. unions makes them relatively unattractive to unions in other countries. Solidarity is based on common cause, and it is difficult to find commonality across cultures that have different values. Finally, throughout history the existence of labor unions has been associated with social classes. Labor unions in the United States traditionally viewed themselves as representing blue-collar working class people. As we move into the Information Age, there is less of a class divide in the United States, although such class distinctions still exist in other cultures.

Nissen (2002) believes U.S. labor unions will have to evolve into a different structure if they are going to be successful in achieving cross-border labor solidarity. One example would be alliances among workers in multinational or global businesses. Just as the Information Age compelled businesses to derive creative solutions to conducting global commerce, so too will labor unions if they are to remain a viable force in the economy.

Mellor (1990) studied membership decline in 20 unions. The unions with the greatest decline in membership showed the strongest commitment to the union by the surviving members. Members in locals with more severe losses expressed a greater willingness to participate in future strikes. Fullagar and Barling (1989) reported that union loyalty was best predicted by union instrumentality, extrinsic job dissatisfaction, and early socialization experiences with unions. The authors proposed that greater union loyalty resulted in more formal participation in union activities. In a study of dual allegiance, Margenau, Martin, and Peterson (1988) found that satisfied workers felt allegiance to both the company and the union, whereas dissatisfied workers showed allegiance only to the union.

Tetrick (1995) proposed that union commitment occurs in a context of organizational rights that are provided by the union as well as organizational citizenship behaviors on the part of union members. Tetrick stated that the degree of commitment to the union can be understood in terms of the psychological contract between the employee and the organization, and the role the union plays in maintaining this relationship. Sverke and Kuruvilla (1995) identified two dimensions that explain why employees are committed to a union. The first is *instrumentality*, the perceived value or usefulness associated with union membership. The second is *ideology*, the individual's acceptance and support of the ideals or principles upon which labor unions are based.

Sverke and Sjoberg (1995) developed a typology of union members' commitment to the union based on these two dimensions, as shown in Figure 14-4. Each dimension (instrumentality and ideology) is divided into two levels, high and low, resulting in a four-cell classification model. As shown in Figure 14-4, the *alienated member* is the noncommitted member who is likely to be nonparticipative and who might intend to withdraw membership. The *instrumental member* can be expected to retain membership and to support union activities directed at improving wages and working conditions. Members committed primarily because of their prounion ideology (*ideological members*) support and take part in union activities, such as attending meetings. The *devoted member* category, representing members with high degrees of commitment on both dimensions, is postulated to contain the most active union members. Other forms of union participation activities include holding office, serving on union committees, and voting in elections (Kelloway, Catano, & Carroll, 1995).

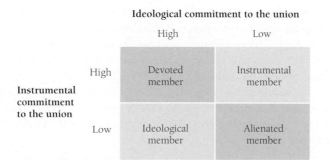

Figure 14-4   *Typology of union commitment*

Source: Adapted from "Union Membership Behavior: The Influence of Instrumental and Value-Based Commitment" by M. Sverke and A. Sjoberg, 1995, in *Changing Employment Relations* (pp. 229–254), edited by L. E. Tetrick and J. Barling. Washington, DC: American Psychological Association.

Finally, Gordon and Ladd (1990) provided a cautionary note about professional ethics to researchers studying dual allegiance. They said researchers should be fully aware of the reasons that either the union or the company would encourage research on allegiance. I/O psychologists should not allow themselves to be "used" by either side to further their own aims by conducting such research. A similar point was raised by Zickar (2001) regarding how I/O psychologists were involved in union-busting by using personality tests to detect "prounion" job candidates.

I/O Psychology and Industrial Relations

Hartley (1992) proposed that there are many areas where I/O psychology might contribute to the field of industrial relations. These include many of the issues already examined, including why workers join unions, dispute settlement, and dual commitment. Five traditional I/O topics will be examined from a labor union perspective: personnel selection, training, leadership development, employee involvement, and organizational change.

Personnel Selection and Promotion.   In both union and nonunion companies, management determines the knowledge, skills, and abilities needed to fill jobs. The human resources office usually determines fitness for employment in lower-level jobs. For higher-level jobs, responsibility is spread through various units of the company. However, in a union company the labor contract may stipulate that those hired for jobs represented by the union must join the union after a probationary period. This is a **union shop**; the employee has no choice about joining.[1] In other unionized companies the employee has the choice of joining a union; these are agency or **open shops**. However, considerable pressure can be put on an employee to join. In many cases it is to the employee's advantage to join the union for the benefits and protection it affords.

Union influence in personnel selection can affect both applicants and companies. Those who do not endorse unions (or who are uncertain about them) might not apply for jobs in unionized companies. Obviously, the applicant pool for unionized companies is smaller if such feelings are widespread. The extent of this problem varies with antiunion sentiment and availability of other jobs.

Union influence can also work in reverse. One company I know of prides itself on remaining nonunionized. It believes unionization is encouraged by employees who have prior union experience, and therefore it carefully screens job applicants for union membership. Those who have been members are not considered (however, they are not told why). The company wants applicants who have the talent needed, but it places a higher priority on avoiding unions. Whether the company can continue this practice without adversely affecting the quality of its workforce will depend on the job openings and the number of applicants for employment with the company. Thus, from the perspectives of both the applicants and the company, unions can and do ultimately influence who gets hired.

Union shop
A provision of employment stipulating that new employees must join the union that represents employees following a probationary period.

Open shop
A provision of employment stipulating that, although new employees need not join the union that represents employees, in lieu of union dues they must pay a fee for their representation.

---

[1] Currently 22 states have "right to work" laws prohibiting compulsory union membership as a condition of continued employment.

One of the classic differences between unions and management is their preference for determining how employees will be promoted or advanced to higher jobs. The clear preference of management is merit, as determined by an assessment of current job performance. It will be recalled from Chapter 7 that performance appraisals are conducted for use in making promotion decisions. Unions, in contrast, prefer seniority as the basis for subsequent job moves. Bownas (2000) described the basis for the preference as follows:

> Once an employee becomes a dues-paying member of a union, the union generally prefers seniority as the sole criterion for subsequent job moves. Seniority has two attractive features for its proponents: it's completely objective and it comes to all members who have the patience to wait for it. Union representatives can argue for one member and against another on the basis of seniority without disparaging or offending either of them, and unions will go to extreme lengths to avoid being put in the position of articulating disparities between the value of two of their members. (p. 204)

A compromise position between merit and seniority is "qualified seniority." The employees must first meet some standard of proficiency (such as passing a job knowledge test), and among those who pass, the employee with the most seniority is promoted into the job (see the Changing Nature of Work: Union Influence on Personnel Selection, p. 461).

Personnel Training.   One area in which unions have significant influence is personnel training. One of the oldest forms is **apprentice training**, and unions have a long history of this kind of training, especially in trades and crafts. Apprenticeship is governed by law; at the national level it is administered by the Department of Labor. The Office of Apprenticeship Training, Employer and Labor Services (OATELS) works closely with unions, vocational schools, state agencies, and others. According to the U.S. Department of Labor (2004), there are more than 30,000 apprentice programs employing over 488,000 apprentices. Apprentices go through a formal program of training and experience. They are supervised on the job and are given the facilities needed for instruction. There is a progressive wage schedule over the course of apprenticeship, and the individual is well versed in all aspects of the trade.

Most apprentice programs are in heavily unionized occupations (such as construction, manufacturing, and transportation); thus unions work closely with OATELS. For example, Figure 14-5, p. 460, shows the cooperation among various organizations and agencies in the carpentry trade. Although not all unions are involved in apprentice programs, the linkage between unions and apprenticeship is one of the oldest in the history of American labor.

Leadership Development.   Often employees elected to leadership roles within their unions (e.g., shop stewards) or within the organization (e.g., supervisors) have had little developmental instruction in how to behave in a position of leadership. Several studies used the tenets of procedural justice as a basis to explain the concept of organizational fairness. Cole and Latham (1997) used a development exercise to teach supervisors to take effective disciplinary action with employees. The supervisors were placed into either a training group or a control group. Following simulated role-playing exercises derived from organizational incidents, both unionized employees and

Apprentice training
A method of training in which the trainee learns to perform a job by serving under the supervision of an experienced worker who provides guidance, direction, and support.

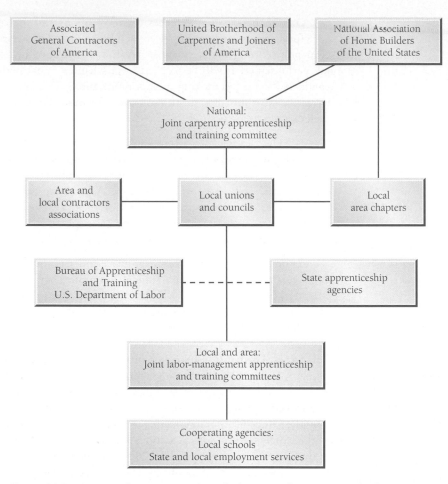

Figure 14-5   *Cooperation among unions, industry, and government in the apprenticeship system of the carpentry trade*

Source: From *Apprenticeship: Past and Present* (p. 25) by U.S. Department of Labor, 1994. Washington, DC: U.S. Government Printing Office.

disciplinary subject matter experts (managers, union officials, and attorneys) rated the trained supervisors higher on disciplinary fairness than the supervisors in the control group. Skarlicki and Latham (1996) examined whether training union officers in the skills necessary for implementing principles of organizational justice would increase citizenship behaviors on the part of members of a labor union. The results showed that three months after training, the perceptions of union fairness among members whose leaders were in the training group were higher than among members whose leaders were in the control group. Skarlicki and Latham (1997) taught shop stewards methods of procedural justice using cases based on organizational incidents. The training improved knowledge of what constitutes fairness and may result in fewer grievances among employees regarding alleged unfairness in work. These examples illustrate how concepts such as procedural justice and organizational citizenship behavior can be used to improve the quality of leadership in organizations with labor unions.

The Changing Nature of Work: Union Influence on Personnel Selection

As discussed in Chapter 5, I/O psychologists are deeply concerned about predictive accuracy in making personnel selection decisions. We strive to ensure that the inferences we draw from tests are valid and that we use professionally acceptable standards in guiding our work. The most current theory on personnel selection from a scientific standpoint deals with the construct level. That is, I/O psychologists believe behavior is best explained and understood in terms of abstract constructs, such as general mental ability and conscientiousness. Accordingly, selection tests are designed to measure these constructs. In a unionized company, however, it is important for the labor unions to support the means of selecting workers. The company selects the employees, and the union represents them in their employment relationship with the company. Bownas (2000) reported that unions greatly prefer highly job-related methods of personnel selection (e.g., work samples), which are the opposite of paper-and-pencil tests designed to assess abstract constructs.

Union leaders have suggested using the ultimate measure of a person's suitability for employment, the job tryout, for *all* jobs. From the union perspective this method affords equal opportunity for all members, with final retention based on documented performance in the tryout period. As Bownas noted, job tryouts are usually too costly and impractical in terms of training, development, and performance management. However, the logic of such a selection method is unassailable in theory: there is no need to predict (by use of a test, interview, work sample, etc.) behavior on the job when you can actually insert people into jobs and see how they perform. In practice this idea ignores the problem of having multiple applicants for few openings as well as the consequences of making errors in the tryout period.

Bownas advised companies to use selection methods that are highly face valid (as well as construct valid) in selecting unionized employees. As described previously, however, it is often difficult for companies to identify construct valid tests, let alone tests that manifest both construct *and* face validity. Because unions distrust tests that measure abstract constructs, Bownas reported that attempts to validate such tests (e.g., an integrity test) will likely fail "because the union instructs its members not to take the test honestly" (p. 208). As reported by Muchinsky (2004b), the implementation of new selection procedures (that are, in effect, an attempt at organizational change) is likely to be met with resistance. I/O psychologists must respond in a way that fairly addresses the basis of the resistance (i.e., unions don't like abstract employment tests) yet remains faithful to the scientific principles of our profession.

Employee Involvement.   Employee involvement embraces some of the newer management concepts such as employee ownership of companies, employee profit-sharing plans, and self-managed work teams. It is reasonable to question whether the increased interest in workers' participation in management has resulted in a reduction of "we/they" attitudes on the part of employees. Kelly and Kelly (1991) concluded that employees express positive attitudes toward particular innovations (self-managed work groups) but these attitudes are specific to the innovation and do not generalize to broader "we/they" attitudes and the industrial relations climate. Kelly and Kelly believe that the conditions have not been right for fostering broader cooperative attitudes. They noted that attitudes are more likely to change where there is a perception of personal choice and control, but economic conditions and management directives have not provided the conditions that encourage employee perceptions of choice and control. That is, there is a perception among workers that management has been compelled because of economic pressures to try new concepts that reduce the power differential between workers and management. Therefore, the amount of sincere trust between workers and management is insufficient to increase the cooperation between parties in some companies.

In a related vein, Fields and Thacker (1992) examined changes in union and organizational commitment after the implementation of a joint union–management quality-of-worklife program. The results indicated that company commitment among unionized workers increased only when participants perceived the program as successful, but union commitment increased irrespective of the perception of the program's success. In general, it appears that unionized employees recognize the benefits of employee involvement programs, but participation in them does not mean the boundaries between union and management are less well defined.

Organizational Change.   As was discussed in Chapter 8, it is difficult to bring about change in any organization. It is even more difficult to bring about change in an organization whose employees are represented by a labor union. Blackard (2000) offered this assessment of the process of managing change in a unionized workplace:

1. Labor/management relationships have evolved over time and fall somewhere on a continuum between open warfare and efforts to create labor/management partnerships. Even those relationships near the partnership end of the continuum, however, usually manifest some discord.

2. Management in a unionized workplace is governed by laws that do not apply in a nonunion environment. These laws, particularly those relating to bargaining and labor contracts, are a major factor in the management of change.

3. Management faces more sources of resistance, more reasons for resistance, and a greater ability to resist in a unionized than a nonunion workplace. (p. 6)

Blackard noted that the need for organizations to change in response to changing environmental conditions (international competition, increasing costs, etc.) is greater today than ever before, a theme identified throughout this book. However, in a unionized company change must take place at two levels. First, management must make all the business changes that are necessary to remain competitive in the rapidly changing world. Second, it needs to change its relationship with its union. A union is in a position to delay, prevent, or make such changes more difficult, and what it elects to do will be largely determined by its relationship with management. According to Blackard, if that relationship is less than positive, management must improve it before the company can effectively make the many business changes that are required. Typically business changes lead to fewer jobs, different roles and responsibilities for existing jobs, new or revised work rules, and changes in pay, benefits, and work hours. Employees will resist much of the change, both individually and through their elected union representatives. This resistance will confirm their union as a legitimate force in the change process and require management to work not only with employees but also with the union that represents them.

A union may refuse to discuss a company proposal that affects an issue covered by a previously negotiated labor contract, such as wages, hours, or conditions of work. In such a case, the matter is closed to discussion and the union could exercise its right to have a "deal be a deal" until the scheduled termination of the labor contract in effect, which might be several years in the future. When the contract expires, the company may, after appropriate bargaining, implement planned changes at the risk of other union resistance tactics. The psychology of union resistance to change is predicated, in part, upon the union not wanting to appear irrelevant in the relationship between employees and the company (see Figure 14-1, p. 441). Individuals are often reluctant to change because the change represents some loss (or perceived loss) of control over their lives.

The union, therefore, can become an instrument for increasing employee control, even to the possible long-term detriment of the employees. If the union shows little resistance to proposed management changes, the very viability of the union as an agent of the employees can be questioned. Blackard contends there is a gap in our knowledge about organizational change in unionized companies: such knowledge is based on understanding both organizational change methods (as discussed in Chapter 8) and labor unions (as presented in this chapter). Consider Figure 14-6. It is a badge made by a labor union (the United Steelworkers of America) expressing protest against a safety program initiated by management. The name given to the program was "Behavioral Safety"; the program was designed to encourage workers to behave safely in steel factories. The union badge represents a defiant statement against the Behavioral Safety program ("No B.S."). While the labor union was in favor of reducing work-related injuries to their members, the union resented the assumption that the behavior of their members was responsible for the injuries ("Don't Blame Workers"). The union's explanation for the work-related injuries incurred by their members pertained to factors under the control of management ("Eliminate Hazards"). This badge is symbolic of what Blackard described as unions offering resistance to proposed management changes (i.e., a safety program designed to reduce work-related injuries), even if the change was for the

Figure 14-6 *A badge worn by union members expressing contempt for a management program on behavioral safety.*

workers' benefit. If the union supported the safety program, the instrumental value of the union as an agent of the employees could be questioned.

Concluding Comments

The role of labor unions in the service and industry sectors of the U.S. economy has changed over the years. The high-water mark of union influence and power was in the 1930s and 1940s. American labor unions have steadily lost membership and influence since the 1970s. Bronfenbrenner (2005) found that women are grossly under-represented in staff and leadership positions within unions. Even sectors of the economy where women predominate, such as insurance and retailing, typically have very low levels of union representation. Masters (1997) believes unions are at a cross-roads in their evolution. One path of the crossroads leads to rejuvenation; the other leads to irrelevance. Masters noted that unions pursue three traditional objectives. The first is to bargain collectively with employers, gaining favorable wages and job conditions for unionized workers. The second is political activity, which is regarded by some scholars as the main objective of European labor unions. Political activity is intended to lead to laws favorable to unions and their members. As such, some labor scholars contend that unions have been more influential in Europe than in the United States because of their greater political and ideological orientation. The third objective is organization activities that generate new members and increased revenues in the form of dues. Each objective adds to the overall strength of the union. Masters asserted that unions must devote more financial and human resources to strengthen their own organizations and reaffirm their value in society.

As a science, I/O psychology can benefit from examining topics from a union perspective in addition to the more traditional management perspective. A case in point is violence in the workplace. The management perspective tends to emphasize detecting workers who are likely candidates to exhibit antisocial behavior. The union perspective, according to King and Alexander (1996), is to place the issue of workplace violence in the total context of workplace safety and health. The workers identify precursors to violence at the work site, such as production pressures, stress, long hours, forced overtime, and fears of plant shutdown or job loss. Furthermore, they are often evidence regarding what needs to be done to alleviate the problems that lead to outbreaks of fights and threats on the job site. Unions claim that management is unwilling to respond to the work conditions that are precursors to violence, whereas the management perspective is to weed out those job candidates who will respond negatively to those conditions. In my opinion, both perspectives have merit, and it is this type of creative interplay between the two views that increases our chances of better understanding the issue of workplace violence.

Case Study   Should We Let in a Labor Union?

Carl Dwyer and Ann Stovos were faculty members at Springdale College. The college had been in existence for about 30 years, and Dwyer had been on the staff almost since the beginning. Stovos was a relative newcomer, just completing her third year as a faculty member. For the past two years, there had been talk about unionizing the faculty. Much of the interest was sparked by two events. First, the college had experienced financial cutbacks due to low enrollment. Without adequate tuition revenues, it was facing hardships paying the faculty. As a result, six teaching positions had been eliminated. The faculty understood the college's financial situation, but they felt cutbacks should be made in other areas, like some administrative positions. The faculty was also critical of how the college determined which teaching positions were eliminated. The other event was that for the third year in a row, the faculty were given only a 5% raise. Other colleges in the state were giving bigger raises, and some of the Springdale faculty thought they were getting the short end of the stick.

Various union representatives had been on campus; there was enough support for a representation election to be held in about a month. The faculty really seemed divided. Some openly supported a union, some were openly opposed, but the majority did not voice their sentiments. Dwyer was opposed to the idea of collective bargaining; Stovos supported it. Because they were officemates, the topic came up quite often. On this particular day, they were discussing whether the goals of unions were compatible with the goals of higher education.

Dwyer began the conversation: "I just don't think there is any place in a college for burly picketers carrying placards and threatening to beat up anyone who crosses the picket line. A college is a place for quiet, scholarly thought, an opportunity to teach interested students and to contemplate some of the deeper values. I've been here since we had only five buildings and a staff of twenty. I don't want to see this place turned into a playground for skull crushers."

"You've been watching too many movies, Carl," Stovos replied. "No one is going to turn Springdale into a battlefield. I want the same things you do. I didn't come here to be physically intimidated. I wouldn't like that any more than you do. But I also want to be treated fairly by the administration. I'd like some security from arbitrary decisions. There's nothing immoral about that, is there?"

"Do you think a union can prevent layoffs and get us 25% yearly raises?" Dwyer asked facetiously.

"No, I don't," Stovos countered, "but a union can force the drafting of fair and equitable policies if layoffs have to occur. And if everyone else is getting 10% raises, maybe they can help us there, too. A union won't work miracles, but it can help prevent injustice."

"You don't understand, Ann. A college is not a factory. Different ideals run a college. It's not profit but scholarship. We have to foster a climate for inquisitive minds, learning, and personal growth. If I were interested only in making a buck, I wouldn't have become a college professor," Dwyer replied.

"Whether you like it or not, Carl, we are employees like all other working people. What's wrong with trying to ensure fair treatment at work? We have bills to pay and families to support just like everyone else. I don't understand why a college is somehow *different* from all other employers."

"That's the problem in a nutshell," Dwyer rejoined. "A college is not just an employer, and we don't just have jobs. We have careers, and the success of our careers depends on an environment that supports what we are trying to do. Union organizers, picket lines, labor contracts, and mediators have no place in a college."

"I don't see why a college is somehow immune from having to treat its employees fairly like every other employer. What makes a college so special?" Stovos asked.

"Twenty years ago—ten years ago, even—the very thought of a union would have been absurd. The fact that we're now considering one is just proof the quality of education in this country is going downhill. I can just see it now: 'Sorry, class, this is our last meeting. I'm going on strike Monday,'" Dwyer fumed. He got up from his desk, grabbed his coat and hat, and headed off for a meeting.

Stovos shot back, "I suppose you'd feel better if you met your class for the last time because you were one of the ones whose position got eliminated."

Dwyer didn't answer, but he slammed the door on the way out.

Questions

1. Do you think Dwyer is correct in believing a union would interfere with the goals of higher education?
2. What benefits does Stovos see from unionization?
3. Do you believe that some organizations, because of their purpose and goals, should not have unionized employees? If so, which ones, and why?
4. Do you think the respective lengths of time that Dwyer and Stovos have spent at the college are related to their attitudes? Why, or why not?
5. When you think of unions, what thoughts come to mind? Why do you feel as you do?

Chapter Summary

- Labor unions were created to improve the quality of worklife.
- I/O psychology does not have a favorable or positive image in the eyes of labor unions.
- Labor unions are found throughout the world. Countries differ greatly in the extent to which their respective workforces are represented by labor unions.
- Labor unions appeal to workers to the extent the unions are perceived as being instrumental in achieving desired outcomes.
- A labor contract specifies the terms and conditions of the employment relationship.
- Mediation, fact-finding, and arbitration are means of resolving disputes between the parties in a labor contract.
- Strikes and lockouts are the responses both sides can use to put pressure on the other to accept the terms of a labor contract.
- Grievances are complaints filed by workers alleging a violation of the labor contract by management.
- Employees differ in the strength of their commitment to a labor union.
- Labor unions typically have represented manufacturing employees. As our economy moves toward a service economy, union influence has declined in the United States. However, with the emergence of global businesses composed of unionized employees in their own respective countries, it is possible the future will witness new forms and types of labor unions that stretch across national boundaries.

Glossary

Acquisition The process by which one organization acquires or subsumes the resources of a second organization.

Actionable knowledge Knowledge produced from research that helps formulate policies or action to address a particular issue.

Actual criterion The operational or actual standard that researchers measure or assess. Often contrasted with conceptual criterion. For example, academic grade point average is often the actual criterion for assessing the conceptual criterion of learning.

Ad hoc **team** A type of team created for a limited duration that is designed to address one particular problem.

Adverse impact A type of unfair discrimination in which the result of using a particular personnel selection method has a negative effect on protected group members compared with majority group members. Often contrasted with disparate treatment.

Affirmative action A social policy that advocates members of protected groups will be actively recruited and considered for selection in employment.

Antisocial behavior Any behavior that brings harm or is intended to bring harm to an organization or its members.

Apprentice training A method of training in which the trainee learns to perform a job by serving under the supervision of an experienced worker who provides guidance, direction, and support.

Arbitration A method of dispute settlement in which a neutral third party resolves the dispute between labor and management by using a decision that is typically final and binding on both parties.

Armed Services Vocational Aptitude Battery (ASVAB) A test developed in the 1980s by I/O psychologists for the selection and placement of military personnel.

Army Alpha Test An intelligence test developed during World War I by I/O psychologists for the selection and placement of military personnel.

Army Beta Test A nonverbal intelligence test developed during World War I by I/O psychologists to assess illiterate recruits.

Army General Classification Test (AGCT) A test developed during World War II by I/O psychologists for the selection and placement of military personnel.

Assessment center A technique for assessing job candidates in a specific location using a series of structured, group-oriented exercises that are evaluated by raters.

Authorization card A card employees sign authorizing an election to determine whether a union will represent employees in the collective bargaining process.

Banding A method of interpreting test scores such that scores of different magnitude in a numeric range or band (e.g., 90–95) are regarded as being equivalent.

Behaviorally anchored rating scale (BARS) A type of performance appraisal rating scale in which the points or values are descriptions of behavior.

Base rate The percentage of current employees in a job who are judged to be performing their jobs satisfactorily.

Behavior modeling A method of training that makes use of imitative learning and reinforcement to modify human behavior.

Behavioral approach to leadership A conception that leadership is best understood in terms of the actions taken by an individual in the conduct of leading a group.

Behavioral criteria A standard for judging the effectiveness of training that refers to changes in performance that are exhibited on the job as a result of training.

Benchmarking The process of comparing a company's products or procedures with those of the leading companies in an industry.

Big 5 personality theory A theory that defines personality in terms of five major factors: Neuroticism, Extraversion, Openness to experience, Agreeableness, and Conscientiousness. Also called the "Five-Factor" theory of personality.

Biographical information A method of assessing individuals in which information pertaining to past activities, interests, and behaviors in their lives is considered.

Business games A method of training that simulates a business environment with specific objectives to achieve and rules for trainees to follow.

Categorical variables Objects of study that do not inherently have numerical values associated with them, as gender. Often contrasted with quantitative variables.

Central-tendency error A type of rating error in which the rater assesses a disproportionately large number of ratees as performing in the middle or central part of a distribution of rated performance in contrast to their true level of performance.

Certification election An election in which employees vote to determine whether a union will represent them in the collective bargaining process.

Charismatic leadership A conception that leadership is the product of charisma, a trait that inspires confidence in others to support the ideas and beliefs of an individual who possesses this trait.

Child labor The pattern of compelling children under the age of 15 throughout the world to perform labor that is harmful to their overall health and psychological well-being.

Classical theory of organizations A theory developed in the early 20th century that described the form and structure of organizations.

Classification The process of assigning individuals to jobs based on two or more test scores.

Collective bargaining The process by which labor and management negotiate a labor contract.

Competency modeling A process for determining the human characteristics (i.e., competencies) needed to perform successfully within an organization.

Compressed workweek A schedule of work hours that typically involves more hours per day and fewer days per week. An example is 10 hours per day and 4 days per week.

Computer-based training A method of training that utilizes computer technology (such as CD-ROM) to enhance the acquisition of knowledge and skills.

Computerized adaptive testing (CAT) A form of assessment using a computer in which the questions have been precalibrated in terms of difficulty, and the examinee's response (i.e., right or wrong) to one question determines the selection of the next question.

Conceptual criterion The theoretical standard that researchers seek to understand.

Conditional reasoning test A type of personality assessment that appears to be measuring reasoning.

Confidentiality A condition associated with testing pertaining to which parties have access to test results.

Construct validity The degree to which a test is an accurate and faithful measure of the construct it purports to measure.

Content validity The degree to which subject matter experts agree that the items in a test are a representative sample of the domain of knowledge the test purports to measure.

Contextual performance Behavior exhibited by an employee that contributes to the welfare of the organization but is not a formal component of an employee's job duties. Also called prosocial behavior and extra-role behavior.

Conventional arbitration A form of arbitration in which the arbitrator is free to fashion whatever decision is deemed most fair in resolving a dispute. Often contrasted with final-offer arbitration.

Correlation coefficient A statistical index that reflects the degree of relationship between two variables.

Creative team A type of team created for the purpose of developing innovative possibilities or solutions.

Criteria Standards used to help make evaluative judgments.

Criterion contamination The part of the actual criterion that is unrelated to the conceptual criterion.

Criterion deficiency The part of the conceptual criterion that is not measured by the actual criterion.

Criterion-related validity The degree to which a test forecasts or is statistically related to a criterion.

Criterion relevance The degree of overlap or similarity between the actual criterion and the conceptual criterion.

Criterion variable A variable that is a primary object of a research study; it is forecasted by a predictor variable. Usually used in the context of nonexperimental research. Similar to a dependent variable. Often contrasted with a predictor variable.

Cross-cultural psychology An area of research that examines the degree to which psychological concepts and findings generalize to people in other cultures and societies.

Cultural diversity training A method of training directed at improving interpersonal sensitivity and awareness of cultural differences among employees.

Culture The language, values, attitudes, beliefs, and customs of an organization.

Declarative knowledge A body of knowledge about facts and things. Often compared with procedural knowledge.

Deductive method A research process in which conclusions are drawn about a specific member of a class of objects or people based on knowledge of the general class under investigation. Often contrasted with the inductive method.

Dependent variable A variable whose values are influenced by the independent variable. Usually used in the context of experimental research. Similar to a criterion variable. Often contrasted with an independent variable.

Descriptive statistics A class of statistical analyses that describe the variables under investigation. Typical descriptive statistics are indices of central tendency and variation.

Disparate treatment A type of unfair discrimination in which protected group members are afforded differential procedures in consideration for employment compared with majority group members. Often contrasted with adverse impact.

Distributive justice The fairness with which the outcomes or results are distributed among members of an organization.

Downsizing The process by which an organization reduces its number of employees to achieve greater overall efficiency.

Drug testing A method of assessment typically based on an analysis of urine that is used to detect illicit drug use by the candidate.

Dual-career family A family in which both adults have their own individual careers and try to balance their respective careers.

Dynamic performance criteria Aspects of job performance that change (increase or decrease) over time.

Emic An approach to researching phenomena that emphasizes knowledge derived from the participants' awareness and understanding of their own culture. Often contrasted with etic.

Emotional intelligence A construct that reflects a person's capacity to manage emotional responses in social situations.

Emotional labor The requirement in some jobs that employees express emotions to customers or clients that are associated with enhanced performance in the job.

Empowerment The process of giving employees in an organization more power and decision-making authority within a context of less managerial oversight.

Entrepreneurship The process by which individuals pursue opportunities and organize resources that can lead to new job creation and business growth.

Equivalent-form reliability A type of reliability that reveals the equivalence of test scores between two versions or forms of the test.

Error management training A system of training in which employees are encouraged to make errors and then learn from their mistakes.

Ethnography A research method that utilizes field observation to study a society's culture.

Etic An approach to researching phenomena that emphasizes knowledge derived from the perspective of a detached objective investigator in understanding a culture. Often contrasted with emic.

Executive coaching An individualized developmental process for business leaders provided by a trained professional (the coach).

Expatriate A person native to one country who serves a period of employment in another country.

Expectancy theory of motivation A theory of motivation based on the perceived degree of relationship between how much effort a person expends and the performance that results from that effort.

External validity The degree to which the relationships evidenced among variables in a particular research study are generalizable or accurate in other contexts.

Face validity The appearance that items in a test are appropriate for the intended use of the test by the individuals who take the test.

Fact-finding A method of dispute settlement in which a neutral third party makes public the respective positions of labor and management with the intention that the public will influence the two sides to resolve their disputes in establishing a labor contract.

False negatives A term to describe individuals who were incorrectly rejected for employment because they would have been successful employees.

False positives A term to describe individuals who were incorrectly accepted for employment because they were unsuccessful employees.

Final-offer arbitration A form of arbitration in which the arbitrator is obligated to accept the final offer of either the union or management in their dispute. Often contrasted with conventional arbitration.

Flextime A schedule of work hours that permits employees flexibility in when they arrive at and leave work.

Functional job analysis (FJA) A method of job analysis that describes the content of jobs in terms of People, Data, and Things.

Functional principle The concept that organizations should be divided into units that perform similar functions.

g The symbol for "general mental ability," which has been found to be predictive of success in most jobs.

Generalizability The extent to which conclusions drawn from one research study spread or apply to a larger population.

Goal-setting theory of motivation A theory of motivation based on directing one's effort toward the attainment of specific goals that have been set or established.

Graphology A method of assessment in which characteristics of a person's handwriting are evaluated and interpreted.

Grievance A formal complaint made by an employee against management alleging a violation of the labor contract in effect.

Grievance arbitration A type of arbitration used in resolving disputes between labor and management in interpretation of an existing labor contract. Also called rights arbitration.

Group test A type of test that is administered to more than one test taker at a time. Often contrasted with an individual test.

Groupthink A phenomenon associated with team decision making in which members feel threatened by forces external to the team, resulting in a deterioration in the cognitive processing of information.

Halo error A type of rating error in which the rater assesses the ratee as performing well on a variety of performance dimensions, despite having credible knowledge of only a limited number of performance dimensions.

Hawthorne effect A positive change in behavior that occurs at the onset of an intervention followed by a gradual decline, often to the original level of the behavior prior to the intervention. First identified in the Hawthorne studies, which is why it is so named.

Hawthorne studies A series of research studies that began in the late 1920s at the Western Electric Company and ultimately refocused the interests of I/O psychologists on how work behavior manifests itself in an organizational context.

Hostile environment sexual harassment A legal classification of sexual harassment in which individuals regard conditions in the workplace (such as unwanted touching or off-color jokes) as offensive. Often compared with *quid pro quo* sexual harassment.

I/O psychology An area of scientific study and professional practice that addresses psychological concepts and principles in the work world.

Impasse A point in the collective bargaining process at which both the union and management conclude they are unable to reach an agreement in the formation of a labor contract. Impasse (literally meaning "blockage") triggers the use of other means (besides negotiation) to resolve the dispute between the parties.

Implicit leadership theory A conception that leadership is a perceived phenomenon as attributed to an individual by others.

Independent variable A variable that can be manipulated to influence the values of the dependent variable. Usually used in the context of experimental research. Similar to a predictor variable. Often contrasted with a dependent variable.

Individual test A type of test that is administered to one individual test taker at a time. Often contrasted with a group test.

Inductive method A research process in which conclusions are drawn about a general class of objects or people based on knowledge of a specific member of the class under investigation. Often contrasted with the deductive method.

Integrity test A type of test that purports to assess a candidate's honesty or character.

Intelligent tutoring systems A sophisticated type of computer-based training that uses artificial intelligence to customize learning to the individual.

Interactional justice The fairness with which people are treated within an organization and the timeliness, completeness, and accuracy of the information received in an organization.

Interactive multimedia training A type of computer-based training that combines visual and auditory information to create a realistic but nonthreatening environment.

Interest arbitration A type of arbitration used to resolve disputes between labor and management in the formation of a labor contract.

Internal-consistency reliability A type of reliability that reveals the homogeneity of the items in a test.

Internal validity The degree to which the relationships evidenced among variables in a particular research study are accurate or true. Often contrasted with external validity.

Inter-rater reliability A type of reliability that reveals the degree of agreement among the assessments of two or more raters.

Invasion of privacy A condition pertaining to the asking of questions that are unrelated to the assessment's intent or are inherently intrusive.

Inventory A method of assessment in which the responses to questions are recorded and interpreted but are not evaluated in terms of their correctness, as in a vocational interest inventory.

Issue-by-issue arbitration A form of final-offer arbitration in which the arbitrator is obligated to accept either the union's position or management's position on an issue-by-issue basis in disputes between the parties. Often contrasted with total-package final-offer arbitration.

Job A set of similar positions in an organization. For example, similar secretarial positions in an organization make up the job of a secretary.

Job analysis A formal procedure by which the content of a job is defined in terms of tasks performed and human qualifications needed to perform the job.

Job enrichment The process of designing work so as to enhance individual motivation to perform the work.

Job family A grouping of similar jobs in an organization. For example, the jobs of secretary, data entry, and receptionist make up the clerical job family.

Job involvement The degree to which a person identifies psychologically with his or her work and the importance of work to one's self-image.

Job satisfaction The degree of pleasure an employee derives from his or her job.

Knowledge compilation The body of knowledge acquired as a result of learning.

KSAOs An abbreviation for "knowledge, skills, abilities, and other" characteristics. Often used in the context of job analysis.

Labor contract A formal agreement between labor and management that specifies the terms and conditions of employment.

Labor strike A cessation of work activities by unionized employees as a means of influencing management to accept the union position in a dispute over the labor contract.

Laboratory experiment A type of research method in which the investigator manipulates independent variables and assigns subjects to experimental and control conditions.

Leader member exchange theory A theory of leadership based on the nature of the relationship between a leader and members of the group he or she leads.

Learning The process by which change in knowledge or skills is acquired through education or experience.

Learning criteria A standard for judging the effectiveness of training that refers to the amount of new knowledge and skills acquired through training.

Leniency error A type of rating error in which the rater assesses a disproportionately large number of ratees as performing well (positive leniency) or poorly (negative leniency) in contrast to their true level of performance.

Level of analysis The unit or level (individuals, teams, organizations, nations, etc.) that is the object of the researchers' interest and about which conclusions are drawn from the research.

Licensure The process by which a professional practice is regulated by law to ensure quality standards are met to protect the public.

Line functions Organizational work that directly meets the major goals of an organization.

Line/staff principle The concept of differentiating organizational work into primary and support functions.

Linkage analysis A technique in job analysis that establishes the connection between the tasks performed and the human attributes needed to perform them.

Lockout Action taken by management against unionized employees to prevent them from entering their place of work as a means of influencing the union to accept the management position in a dispute over the labor contract.

Management development The process by which individuals serving in management or leadership positions are trained to better perform the job.

Mean The arithmetic average of a distribution of numbers.

Median The midpoint of all the numbers in a distribution.

Mediation A method of dispute settlement in which a neutral third party offers advice to the union and management to help them agree on a labor contract.

Melting pot conception A concept behind facilitating relationships among people of different cultures based on them relinquishing their individual cultural identities to form a new, unified culture as a means of coexisting. Often contrasted with multicultural conception.

Mental Measurements Yearbooks (MMY) A classic set of reference books in psychology that provide reviews and critiques of published tests in the public domain.

Mentor Typically an older and more experienced person who helps to professionally develop a less experienced person.

Meta-analysis A quantitative secondary research method for summarizing and integrating the findings from original empirical research studies.

Mode The most frequently occurring number in a distribution.

Multicultural conception A concept behind facilitating relationships among people of different cultures based on them retaining their individual cultural identities as a means of coexisting. Often contrasted with melting pot conception.

Multiple correlation A statistical index used to indicate the degree of predictability (ranging from 0 to 1.00) in forecasting one variable on the basis of two or more other variables. Often expressed in conjunction with multiple regression analysis.

Multiple regression analysis A statistical procedure used to predict one variable on the basis of two or more other variables.

National Labor Relations Board An agency of the federal government that has oversight responsibility for enforcing laws pertaining to union/management relations.

Neoclassical theory of organizations A theory developed in the 1950s that described psychological or behavioral issues associated with organizations.

Norm A set of shared group expectations about appropriate behavior.

Objective performance criteria A set of factors used to assess job performance that are (relatively) factual in character. Examples are days absent, units of production, and sales volume.

Observation A type of research method in which the investigator observes subjects for the purpose of understanding their behavior and culture.

Occupational health A broad-based concept that refers to the mental, emotional, and physical well-being of employees in relation to the conduct of their work.

Occupational Information Network (O*NET) An online computer-based source of information about jobs.

Offshoring The process of eliminating jobs within the organization by having those work functions performed in cheaper labor markets overseas (offshore).

Open shop A provision of employment stipulating that, although new employees need not join the union that represents employees, in lieu of union dues they must pay a fee for their representation. Often contrasted with a union shop.

Organization A coordinated group of people who perform tasks to produce goods or services, colloquially referred to as a company.

Organization development A system of planned interventions designed to change an organization's structure and/or processes to achieve a higher level of functioning.

Organizational analysis A phase of training needs analysis directed at determining whether training is a viable solution to organizational problems, and if so, where in the organization training should be directed.

Organizational citizenship behavior The contributions that employees make to the overall welfare of the organization that go beyond the required duties of their job.

Organizational commitment The extent to which an employee feels a sense of allegiance to his or her employer.

Organizational justice The theoretical concept pertaining to the fair treatment of people in organizations. The three types of organizational justice are distributive, procedural, and interactional.

Organizational merger The joining or combining of two organizations of approximately equal status and power.

Outsourcing The process of eliminating jobs within the organization by having those work functions contracted to other organizations.

Paper-and-pencil test A method of assessment in which the responses to questions are recorded on a piece of paper.

Peer assessment A technique of performance appraisal in which individuals assess the behavior of their peers or coworkers. Peer assessments include nominations, ratings, and rankings.

Peer nomination A technique of appraising the performance of coworkers by nominating them for membership in a group.

Peer ranking A technique of appraising the performance of coworkers by ranking them on a dimension of their job behavior.

Peer rating A technique of appraising the performance of coworkers by rating them on a dimension of their job behavior.

Performance test A type of test that requires the test taker to exhibit physical skill in the manipulation of objects, as in a typing test.

Person analysis A phase of training needs analysis directed at identifying which individuals within an organization should receive training.

Person-organization fit A criterion for employment with an organization that reflects the belief the candidate exhibits attributes and values consistent with those held by the organization.

Person perception A theory that how we evaluate other people in various contexts is related to how we acquire, process, and categorize information.

Personnel selection The process of determining those applicants who are selected for hire versus those who are rejected.

Physical fidelity The degree of similarity between the physical characteristics of the training environment and the work environment. Often compared with psychological fidelity.

Placement The process of assigning individuals to jobs based on one test score.

Polygraph An instrument that assesses responses of an individual's central nervous system (heart rate, breathing, perspiration, etc.) that supposedly indicate giving false responses to questions.

Position A set of tasks performed by a single employee. For example, the position of a secretary is often represented by the tasks of typing, filing, and scheduling. There are usually as many positions in an organization as there are employees.

Position Analysis Questionnaire (PAQ) A method of job analysis that assesses the content of jobs on the basis of approximately 200 items in the questionnaire.

Positive psychology The study of the factors and conditions in life that lead to pleasurable and satisfying outcomes for individuals.

Power and influence approach to leadership A conception that leadership is best understood by the use of the power and influence exercised by a person with a group.

Power test A type of test that usually does not have a precise time limit; a person's score on the test is the number of items answered correctly. Often contrasted with a speed test.

Predictor cutoff A score on a test that differentiates those who passed the test from those who failed; often equated with the passing score on a test.

Predictor variable A variable used to predict or forecast a criterion variable. Usually used in the context of nonexperimental research. Similar to an independent variable. Often contrasted with a criterion variable.

Primary research methods A class of research methods that generates new information on a particular research question.

Problem resolution team A type of team created for the purpose of focusing on solving ongoing problems or issues.

Procedural justice The fairness by which means are used to achieve results in an organization.

Procedural knowledge A body of knowledge about how to use information to address issues and solve problems. Often compared with declarative knowledge.

Programmed instruction The most basic computer-based training that provides for self-paced learning.

Prosocial behavior Behavior by an individual that goes beyond the formal requirements of the job. Also referred to as extra-role behavior and organizational citizenship behavior.

Protected group A designation for members of society who are granted legal status by virtue of a demographic characteristic, such as race, gender, national origin, color, religion, age, and disability.

Protégé Typically a younger and less experienced person who is helped and developed in job training by a more experienced person.

Psychological contract The implied exchange relationship that exists between an employee and the organization.

Psychological fidelity A concept from training pertaining to the degree of similarity between the knowledge, skills, and abilities (KSAs) learned in training and the KSAs needed to perform the job. Often contrasted with physical fidelity.

Psychometric Literally, the measurement ("metric") of properties of the mind (from the Greek word "psyche"). The standard used to measure the quality of psychological assessments.

Qualitative research A class of research methods in which the investigator takes an active role in interacting with the subjects he or she wishes to study. Often contrasted with quantitative research methods.

Quantitative variables Objects of study that inherently have numerical values associated with them, such as weight. Often contrasted with categorical variables.

Quasi-experiment A type of research method for conducting studies in field situations where the researcher may be able to manipulate some independent variables.

Questionnaire A type of research method in which subjects respond to written questions posed by the investigator.

Quid pro quo sexual harassment A legal classification of harassment in which specified organizational rewards are offered in exchange for sexual favors. Often compared with hostile environment sexual harassment.

Range A descriptive statistical index that reflects the dispersion in a set of scores; arithmetically, the difference between the highest score and the lowest score.

Rater motivation A concept that refers to organizationally induced pressures that compel raters to evaluate ratees positively.

Rater training The process of educating raters to make more accurate assessments of performance, typically by reducing the frequency of halo, leniency, and central-tendency errors.

Reaction criteria A standard for judging the effectiveness of training that refers to the reactions or feelings of individuals about the training they received.

Recruitment The process by which individuals are solicited to apply for jobs.

Regression analysis A statistical procedure used to predict one variable on the basis of another variable.

Reliability A standard for evaluating tests that refers to the consistency, stability, or equivalence of test scores. Often contrasted with validity.

Research A formal process by which knowledge is produced and understood.

Research design A plan for conducting scientific research for the purpose of learning about a phenomenon of interest.

Results criteria A standard for judging the effectiveness of training that refers to the economic value that accrues to the organization as a function of the new behaviors exhibited on the job.

Role A set of expectations about appropriate behavior in a position.

Role conflict The product of perceptual differences regarding the content of a person's role or the relative importance of its elements.

Role overload The conflict experienced in a role as a necessity to compromise either the quantity or quality of performance.

Role playing A training method directed primarily at enhancing interpersonal skills in which training participants adopt various roles in a group exercise.

Sabotage A tactic used by some employees to influence the outcome of union/management negotiations in which company equipment is intentionally damaged to reduce work productivity.

Scalar principle The concept that organizations are structured by a chain of command that grows with increasing levels of authority.

Schema A cognitive approach to processing information that results in making sense of events and actions that in turn influence how decisions are made on the basis of that information.

Scientist–practitioner model A model or framework for education in an academic discipline based on understanding the scientific principles and findings evidenced in the discipline and how they provide the basis for the professional practice.

Secondary research methods A class of research methods that examines existing information from research studies that used primary methods.

Selection ratio A numeric index ranging between 0 and 1 that reflects the selectivity of the hiring organization in filling jobs; the number of job openings divided by the number of job applicants.

Self-assessment A technique of performance appraisal in which individuals assess their own behavior.

Self-efficacy A sense of personal control and being able to master one's environment.

Self-regulation theory of motivation A theory of motivation based on the setting of goals and the receipt of accurate feedback that is monitored to enhance the likelihood of goal attainment.

Sexual harassment Unwelcome sexual advances, requests for sexual favors, and other verbal or physical conduct of a sexual nature that creates an intimidating, hostile, or offensive work environment.

Shared mental model The cognitive processes held in common by members of a team regarding how they acquire information, analyze it, and respond to it.

Shift work A non-traditional work pattern in which an operation functions 24 hours per day. Typical employee shifts are 7:00 A.M. to 3:00 P.M., 3:00 P.M. to 11:00 P.M., and 11:00 P.M. to 7:00 A.M.

Situational exercise A method of assessment in which examinees are presented with a problem and asked how they would respond to it.

Situational interview A type of job interview in which candidates are presented with a problem and asked how they would respond to it.

Situational judgment test A type of test that describes a problem to the test taker and requires the test taker to rate various possible solutions in terms of their feasibility or applicability.

Six Sigma A method of improving business processes using statistical information to achieve greater customer satisfaction.

Social loafing A phenomenon identified in groups or teams in which certain individuals withhold effort or contributions to the collective outcome.

Social system The human components of a work organization that influence the behavior of individuals and groups.

Socialization The process of mutual adjustment between the team and its members, especially new members.

Society for Industrial and Organizational Psychology (SIOP) The professional organization that represents I/O psychologists in the United States.

Span-of-control principle The concept that refers to the number of subordinates a manager is responsible for supervising.

Speed test A type of test that has a precise time limit; a person's score on the test is the number of items attempted in the time period. Often contrasted with a power test.

Staff functions Organizational work that supports line activities.

Standard deviation A statistic that shows the spread or dispersion of scores around the mean in a distribution of scores.

Structure The arrangement of work functions within an organization designed to achieve efficiency and control.

Structured interview A format for the job interview in which the questions are consistent across all candidates. Often contrasted with the unstructured interview.

Subject matter expert (SME) A person knowledgeable about a topic who can serve as a qualified information source. Often associated with individuals who provide job analysis information.

Subjective performance criteria A set of factors used to assess job performance that are the product of someone's (e.g., supervisor, peer, customer) judgment of these factors.

Substance abuse The ingestion of a broad array of substances (such as alcohol, tobacco, or drugs) that are deemed to have a harmful effect on the individual.

Substitutes for leadership The conception that there are sources of influence in an environment that can serve to act in place of, or be substitutes for, formal leadership.

Tactical team A type of team created for the purpose of executing a well-defined plan or objective.

Task The lowest level of analysis in the study of work; a basic component of work (such as typing for a secretary).

Task analysis A phase of training needs analysis directed at identifying which tasks in a job should be targeted for improved performance.

Task-oriented procedure A procedure or set of operations in job analysis designed to identify important or frequently performed tasks as a means of understanding the work performed. Often contrasted with worker-oriented procedure.

Taxonomy A classification of objects designed to enhance understanding of the objects being classified.

Team A social aggregation in which a limited number of individuals interact on a regular basis to accomplish a set of shared objectives for which they have mutual responsibility.

Test–retest reliability A type of reliability that reveals the stability of test scores upon repeated applications of the test.

Theory A statement that proposes to explain relationships among phenomena of interest.

360-degree feedback A process of evaluating employees from multiple rating sources, usually including supervisor, peer, subordinate, and self. Also called multisource feedback.

Top grading A method of performance management whereby employees are graded on their overall contribution to the organization, and each year the bottom 10% of the employees are dismissed.

Total-package arbitration A form of final-offer arbitration in which the arbitrator is obligated to accept either the union's position or management's position on every issue in dispute between the parties. Often contrasted with issue-by-issue final-offer arbitration.

Training The process through which the knowledge and skills of employees are enhanced.

Trait approach to leadership A conception that leadership is best understood in terms of traits or dispositions held by an individual that are accountable for the observed leadership.

Transfer of training The degree of generalizability of the behaviors learned in training to those behaviors evidenced on the job that enhance performance.

Transformational leadership A conception that leadership is the process of inspiring a group to pursue goals and attain results.

True negatives A term to describe individuals who were correctly rejected for employment because they would have been unsuccessful employees.

True positives A term to describe individuals who were correctly selected for hire because they became successful employees.

Union A labor organization with defined members whose purpose is to enhance the welfare of its members in their employment relationship with the company.

Union-busting A derogatory term used to describe actions taken to prevent a labor union from representing employees.

Union commitment The sense of identity and support unionized employees feel for their labor union.

Union/nonunion wage differential The average difference in wages paid to union versus nonunion employees across an industry or geographic area for performing the same jobs.

Union shop A provision of employment stipulating that new employees must join the union that represents employees following a probationary period. Often contrasted with an open shop.

Unity of command The concept that each subordinate should be accountable to only one supervisor.

Unstructured interview A format for the job interview in which the questions are different across all candidates. Often contrasted with the structured interview.

Utility A concept reflecting the economic value (expressed in monetary terms) of making personnel decisions.

Validity A standard for evaluating tests that refers to the accuracy or appropriateness of drawing inferences from test scores. Often contrasted with reliability.

Validity coefficient A statistical index (often expressed as a correlation coefficient) that reveals the degree of association between two variables. Often used in the context of prediction.

Validity generalization A concept that reflects the degree to which a predictive relationship empirically established in one context spreads to other populations or contexts.

Variability The dispersion of numerical values evidenced in the measurement of an object or concept.

Variable An object of study whose measurement can take on two or more values.

Virtual reality training A type of computer-based training that uses three-dimensional computer-generated imagery.

Virtual team A type of team in which the members, often geographically dispersed, interact through electronic communication and may never meet face-to-face.

Work design theory of motivation A theory of motivation based on the presence of dimensions or characteristics of jobs that foster the expenditure of effort.

Work/family conflict The dilemma of trying to balance the conflicting demands of work and family responsibilities.

Work samples A type of personnel selection test in which the candidate demonstrates proficiency on a task representative of the work performed in the job.

Work slowdown A tactic used by some employees to influence the outcome of union/management negotiations in which the usual pace of work is intentionally reduced.

Worker-oriented procedure A procedure or set of operations in job analysis designed to identify important or frequently utilized human attributes as a means of understanding the work performed. Often contrasted with task-oriented procedure.

References

Ackerman, P. L. (1987). Individual differences in skill learning: An integration of psychometric and information processing perspectives. *Psychological Bulletin, 102,* 3–27.

Ackerman, P. L. (1992). Predicting individual differences in complex skill acquisition: Dynamics of ability determinants. *Journal of Applied Psychology, 77,* 598–614.

Ackerman, P. L., & Heggestad, E. D. (1997). Intelligence, personality, and interests: Evidence of overlapping traits. *Psychological Bulletin, 121,* 219–245.

Ackerman, P. L., & Kanfer, R. (1993). Integrating laboratory and field study for improving selection: Development of a battery for predicting air traffic controller success. *Journal of Applied Psychology, 78,* 413–432.

Adair, J. G. (1984). The Hawthorne effect: A reconsideration of the methodological artifact. *Journal of Applied Psychology, 69,* 334–345.

Aguinis, H., & Henle, C. A. (2002). Ethics in research. In S. G. Rogelberg (Ed.), *Handbook of research methods in industrial and organizational psychology* (pp. 34–56). Malden, MA: Blackwell.

Allen, N. J., & Meyer, J. P. (1990). The measurement and antecedents of affective, continuance, and normative commitment to the organization. *Journal of Occupational Psychology, 63,* 1–18.

Allen, T. D., Eby, L. T., Poteet, M. L., Lentz, E., & Lima, L. (2004). Career benefits associated with mentoring for protégés: A meta-analysis. *Journal of Applied Psychology, 89,* 127–136.

Allen, T.D., Eby, L.T., & Lentz, E. (2006a). Mentorship behaviors and mentorship quality associated with formal mentoring programs: Closing the gap between research and practice. *Journal of Applied Psychology, 91,* 56–78.

Allen, T.D., Eby, L.T., & Lentz, E. (2006b). The relationship between formal mentoring program characteristics and perceived program effectiveness. *Personnel Psychology, 59,* 125–153.

Allen, T. D., & Rush, M. C. (1998). The effects of organizational citizenship behavior on performance judgments: A field study and a laboratory experiment. *Journal of Applied Psychology, 83,* 247–260.

Alley, W. E. (1994). Recent advances in classification theory and practice. In M. G. Rumsey, C. B. Walker, & J. H. Harris (Eds.), *Personnel selection and classification* (pp. 431–442). Hillsdale, NJ: Erlbaum.

Alliger, G. M., & Janak, E. A. (1989). Kirkpatrick's levels of training criteria: Thirty years later. *Personnel Psychology, 42,* 331–342.

Alliger, G. M., Lilienfield, S. O., & Mitchell, K. E. (1995). The susceptibility of overt and covert integrity tests to coaching and faking. *Psychological Science, 7,* 32–39.

Alliger, G. M., Tannenbaum, S. I., Bennett, W., Traver, H., & Shotland, A. (1997). A meta-analysis of the relations among training criteria. *Personnel Psychology, 50,* 341–358.

American Educational Research Association, American Psychological Association, & National Council on Measurement in Education. (1999). *Standards for educational and psychological testing.* Washington, DC: American Educational Research Association.

American Psychological Association. (2002). Ethical principles of psychologists and code of conduct. *American Psychologist, 57,* 1060–1073.

American Psychological Association. (2003). Guidelines on multicultural education, training, research, practice, and organizational change for psychologists. *American Psychologist, 58,* 377–402.

Americans with Disabilities Act. (1990). P.L. 101–336, 104 Statute 327, 26 July.

Anand, N. (2006). Cartoon displays as autoproduction of organizational culture. In A. Rafaeli & M.G. Pratt (Eds.), *Artifacts and organizations* (pp. 85–100). Mahwah, NJ: Erlbaum.

Anderson, C. C., Warner, J. L., & Spencer, C. C. (1984). Inflation bias in self-assessment examinations: Implications for valid employee selection. *Journal of Applied Psychology, 69,* 574–580.

Anderson, J. R. (1985). *Cognitive psychology and its implications* (2nd ed.). New York: Freeman.

Anderson, L., & Wilson, S. (1997). Critical incident technique. In D. L. Whetzel & G. R. Wheaton (Eds.), *Applied measurement methods in industrial psychology* (pp. 89–112). Palo Alto, CA: Consulting Psychologists Press.

Andersson, L. M., & Pearson, C. M. (1999). Tit for tat? The spiraling effect of incivility in the workplace. *Academy of Management Review, 24,* 452–471.

Antonakis, J., & Autio, E. (2007). Entrepreneurship and leadership. In J.R. Baum, M. Frese, & R.A. Baron (Eds.), *The psychology of entrepreneurship* (pp. 189–208). Mahwah, NJ: Erlbaum.

Argyris, C. (1996). Actionable knowledge: Design causality in the service of consequential theory. *Journal of Applied Behavioral Science, 32*, 390–406.

Arnold, D. W. (2001). Seventh circuit rules favorably regarding use of banding. *The Industrial-Organizational Psychologist, 39(1)*, 153.

Arthur, W., & Bennett, W. (1995). The international assignee: The relative importance of factors perceived to contribute to success. *Personnel Psychology, 48*, 99–114.

Arthur, W., Bennett, W., Edens, P. S., & Bell, S. T. (2003). Effectiveness of training in organizations: A meta-analysis of design and evaluation features. *Journal of Applied Psychology, 88*, 234–245.

Arthur, W., Jr., Bell, S.T., Villado, A.J., & Doverspike, D. (2006). The use of person-organization fit in employment decision making: An assessment of its criterion-related validity. *Journal of Applied Psychology, 91*, 786–801.

Arvey, R. D., & Campion, J. E. (1982). The employment interview: A summary and review of recent research. *Personnel Psychology, 35*, 281–322.

Arvey, R. D., Landon, T. E., Nutting, S. M., & Maxwell, S. E. (1992). Development of physical ability tests for police officers: A construct validation approach. *Journal of Applied Psychology, 77*, 996–1009.

Aryee, S., & Chay, Y. W. (2001). Workplace justice, citizenship behavior, and turnover intentions in a union context: Examining the mediating role of perceived union support and union instrumentality. *Journal of Applied Psychology, 86*, 154–160.

Atwater, L. E. (1998). The advantages and pitfalls of self-assessment in organizations. In J. W. Smither (Ed.), *Performance appraisal* (pp. 331–369). San Francisco: Jossey-Bass.

Austin, J. T., Scherbaum, C. A., & Mahlman, R. A. (2002). History of research methods in industrial and organizational psychology: Measurement, design, analysis. In S. G. Rogelberg (Ed.), *Handbook of research methods in industrial and organizational psychology* (pp. 3–33). Malden, MA: Blackwell.

Austin, J. T., & Villanova, P. (1992). The criterion problem: 1917–1992. *Journal of Applied Psychology, 77*, 836–874.

Author. (1999). Test security: Protecting the integrity of tests. *American Psychologist, 54*, 1078.

Author. (2002). JAIOP: The Japanese Association of I-O Psychology. *The Industrial-Organizational Psychologist, 40(2)*, 117.

Avery, D. R. (2003). Reactions to diversity in recruitment advertising: Are differences black and white? *Journal of Applied Psychology, 88*, 672–679.

Avolio, B. J., Kahai, S., Dumdum, R., & Sivasubramaniam, N. (2001). Virtual teams: Implications for e-leadership and team development. In M. London (Ed.), *How people evaluate others in organizations* (pp. 337–358). Mahwah, NJ: Erlbaum.

Avolio, B. J., Sosik, J. J., Jung, D. I., & Bierson, Y. (2003). Leadership models, methods, and applications. In W. C. Borman, D. R. Ilgen, & R. J. Klimoski (Eds.), *Handbook of psychology* (Vol. 12, pp. 277–307). *Industrial and organizational psychology*. Hoboken, NJ: Wiley.

Axtell, C. M., Fleck, S. J., & Turner, N. (2004). Virtual teams: Collaborating across distance. In C. L. Cooper & I. T. Robertson (Eds.), *International review of industrial and organizational psychology 2004* (Vol. 19, pp. 205–249). West Sussex: Wiley.

Aycan, Z., & Kanungo, R. N. (2001). Cross-cultural industrial and organizational psychology: A critical appraisal of the field and future directions. In N. Anderson, D. S. Ones, H. K. Sinangil, & C. Viswesvaran (Eds.), *Handbook of industrial, work, and organizational psychology* (Vol. 1, pp. 385–408). London: Sage.

Babiak, P., & Hare, R.D. (2006). *Snakes in suits: When psychopaths go to work*. New York: ReganBooks.

Bacharach, S. B., Bamberger, P. A., & Sonnenstuhl, W. J. (2002). Driven to drink: Managerial control, work-related risk factors, and employee problem drinking. *Academy of Management Journal, 45*, 637–658.

Bakke, E. W. (1945). Why workers join unions. *Personnel, 22*, 37–46.

Baldwin, T. T., & Ford, J. K. (1988). Transfer of training: A review and directions for future research. *Personnel Psychology, 41*, 63–105.

Baldwin, T. T., & Magjuka, R. J. (1991). Organizational training and signals of importance: Effects of pre-training perceptions on intentions to transfer. *Human Resource Development, 2(1)*, 25–36.

Baldwin, T. T., & Padgett, M. Y. (1993). Management development: A review and commentary. In C. L. Cooper & I. T. Robertson (Eds.), *International review of industrial and organizational psychology* (Vol. 8, pp. 35–85). London: Wiley.

Baltes, B. B., Briggs, T. E., Huff, J. W., Wright, J. A., & Neuman, G. A. (1999). Flexible and compressed workweek schedules: A meta-analysis of their effects on work-related criteria. *Journal of Applied Psychology, 84*, 496–513.

Baltes, B. B., & Heydens-Gahir, H. A. (2003). Reduction of work-family conflict through the use of selection, optimization, and compensation behaviors. *Journal of Applied Psychology, 88*, 1005–1018.

Balzer, W. K., & Sulsky, L. M. (1992). Halo and performance appraisal research. *Journal of Applied Psychology, 77*, 975–985.

Balzer, W. K., Greguras, G. J., & Raymark, P. H. (2004). Multisource feedback. In J. C. Thomas (Ed.), *Comprehensive handbook of psychological assessment* (Vol. 4, pp. 390–411). Hoboken, NJ: Wiley.

Bandura, A., & Locke, E. A. (2003). Negative self-efficacy and goal effects revisited. *Journal of Applied Psychology, 87,* 87–99.

Baranowski, L.E., & Anderson, L.E. (2006). Examining rating source variation in work behavior and KSA linkages. *Personnel Psychology, 58,* 1041–1054.

Barling, J. (1990). *Employment, stress and family functioning.* Chicester: Wiley.

Barling, J. (1996). The prediction, experience, and consequence of workplace violence. In G. R. VandenBos & E. Q. Bulatao (Eds.), *Violence on the job* (pp. 29–50). Washington, DC: American Psychological Association.

Barling, J., & Griffiths, A. (2003). A history of occupational health psychology. In J. C. Quick & L. E. Tetrick (Eds.), *Handbook of organizational health psychology* (pp. 19–34). Washington, DC: American Psychological Association.

Barnes-Farrell, J. L. (2001). Performance appraisal: Person perception processes and challenges. In M. London (Ed.), *How people evaluate others in organizations* (pp. 135–154). Mahwah, NJ: Erlbaum.

Baron, R.A., Frese, M., & Baum, J.R. (2007). Research gains: Benefits of closer links between I/O psychology and entrepreneurship. In J.R. Baum, M. Frese, & R. A. Baron (Eds.), *The psychology of entrepreneurship* (pp. 347–373). Mahwah, NJ: Erlbaum.

Baron, S. A., Hoffman, S. J., & Merrill, J. G. (2000). *When work equals life: The next stage of workplace violence.* Oxnard, CA: Pathfinder.

Barrick, M. R., & Mount, M. K. (1991). The Big Five personality dimensions and job performance: A meta-analysis. *Personnel Psychology, 44,* 1–26.

Barrick, M. R., Stewart, G. L., Neubert, M. J., & Mount, M. K. (1998). Relating member ability and personality to work-team processes and team effectiveness. *Journal of Applied Psychology, 83,* 377–391.

Barry, B., & Stewart, G. L. (1997). Composition, process, and performance in self-managed groups: The role of personality. *Journal of Applied Psychology, 82,* 62–78.

Bartlett, C. J. (1983). What's the difference between valid and invalid halo? Forced-choice measurement without forcing a choice. *Journal of Applied Psychology, 68,* 218–226.

Barton, J. (1994). Choosing to work at night: A moderating influence on individual tolerance to shiftwork. *Journal of Applied Psychology, 79,* 449–454.

Bartram, D. (2005). The great eight competencies: A criterion-centric approach to validation. *Journal of Applied Psychology, 90,* 1185–1203.

Bartunek, J. M., & Seo, M. G. (2002). Qualitative research can add new meanings to quantitative research. *Journal of Organizational Behavior, 23,* 237–242.

Baruch, Y. (2006). On logos and business cards: The case of UK universities. In A. Rafaeli, & M.G. Pratt (Eds.), *Artifacts and organizations* (pp. 181–198). Mahwah, NJ: Erlbaum.

Bashore, T. R., & Rapp, P. E. (1993). Are there alternatives to traditional polygraph procedures? *Psychological Bulletin, 113,* 3–22.

Bass, B. M. (1985). *Leadership and performance beyond expectations.* New York: Free Press.

Bass, B. M. (1997). Does the transactional-transformational leadership paradigm transcend organizational and national boundaries? *American Psychologist, 52,* 130–139.

Bass, B. M. (1998). *Transformational leadership.* Mahwah, NJ: Erlbaum.

Bauer, T. N., Truxillo, D. M., & Paronto, M. E. (2004). The measurement of applicant reactions to selection. In J. C. Thomas (Ed.), *Comprehensive handbook of psychological assessment* (Vol. 4, pp. 482–506). Hoboken, NJ: Wiley.

Bazerman, M. H. (2005). Conducting influential research: The need for prescriptive implications. *Academy of Management Research, 30,* 25–31.

Bazerman, M.H., & Neale, M. A. (1982). Improving negotiation effectiveness under final offer arbitration: The role of selection and training. *Journal of Applied Psychology, 67,* 543–548.

Beal, D. J., Cohen, R. R., Burke, M. J., & McLendon, C. L. (2003). Cohesion and performance in groups: A meta-analytic clarification of construct relations. *Journal of Applied Psychology, 88,* 989–1004.

Beal, D. J., Trougakos, J.P., Weiss, H.M., & Green, S.G. (2006). Episodic processes in emotional labor: Perceptions of affective delivery and regulation strategies. *Journal of Applied Psychology, 91,* 1053–1065.

Beal, D.J., Weiss, H.M., Barros, E., & MacDermid, S.M. (2005). An episodic process model of affective influences in performance. *Journal of Applied Psychology, 90,* 1054–1068.

Becker, T. E., & Colquitt, A. L. (1992). Potential versus actual faking of a biodata form: An analysis along several dimensions of item type. *Personnel Psychology, 45,* 389–406.

Beehr, T. A., Ivanitskaya, L., Hansen, C. P., Erofeev, D., & Gudanowski, D. M. (2001). Evaluation of 360 degree feedback ratings: Relationships with each other and with performance and selection predictors. *Journal of Organizational Behavior, 22,* 775–788.

Belbin, R. M. (1981). *Management teams.* New York: Wiley.

Bell, B. S., & Kozlowski, S. W. (2002). Goal orientation and ability: Interactive effects in self-efficiency, performance, and knowledge. *Journal of Applied Psychology*, *87*, 497–505.

Bell, S.T. (2007). Deep-level composition variables as predictors of team performance: A meta-analysis. *Journal of Applied Psychology*, *92*, 595–615.

Benjamin, L. T., Jr. (1997). Organized industrial psychology before Division 14: The ACP and the AAAP (1930–1945). *Journal of Applied Psychology*, *82*, 459–466.

Benjamin, L.T., Jr. (2006). Hugo Münsterberg's attack on the application of scientific psychology. *Journal of Applied Psychology*, *91*, 414–425.

Bennett, G. K. (1980). *Test of mechanical comprehension.* New York: Psychological Corporation.

Bennett, N., Blum, T. C., & Roman, P. M. (1994). Pressure of drug screening and employee assistance programs: Exclusive and inclusive human resource management practices. *Journal of Organizational Behavior*, *15*, 549–560.

Bennett, R. J., & Robinson, S. L. (2000). Development of a measure of workplace deviance. *Journal of Applied Psychology*, *85*, 349–360.

Bennis, W. (2007). The challenges of leadership in the modern world. *American Psychologist*, *62*, 2–5.

Ben-Shakhar, G., Bar-Hillel, M., Bilu, Y., Ben-Abba, E., & Flug, A. (1986). Can graphology predict occupational success? Two empirical studies and some methodological ruminations. *Journal of Applied Psychology*, *71*, 645–653.

Berdahl, J.L. (2007). The sexual harassment of uppity women. *Journal of Applied Psychology*, *92*, 425–437.

Bernardin, H. J., Cooke, D. K., & Villanova, P. (2000). Conscientiousness and agreeableness as predictors of rating leniency. *Journal of Applied Psychology*, *85*, 232–236.

Bernardin, H. J., Hagan, C. M., Kane, J. S., & Villanova, P. (1998). Effective performance management. In J. W. Smither (Ed.), *Performance appraisal* (pp. 3–48). San Francisco: Jossey-Bass.

Bernardin, H. J., & Pence, E. C. (1980). Effects of rater training: Creating new response sets and decreasing accuracy. *Journal of Applied Psychology*, *65*, 60–66.

Berry, C.M., Ones, D.S., & Sackett, P.R. (2007). Interpersonal deviance, organizational deviance, and their common correlates: A review and meta-analysis. *Journal of Applied Psychology*, *92*, 410–424.

Berry, C.M., Sackett, P.R., & Wiemann, S. (2007). A review of recent developments in integrity test research. *Personnel Psychology*, *60*, 271–301.

Bersoff, D. N. (1999). *Ethical conflicts in psychology* (2nd ed.). Washington, DC: American Psychological Association.

Bies, R. J., Tripp, T. M., & Kramer, R. M. (1997). At the breaking point. In R. A. Giacalone & J. Greenberg (Eds.), *Antisocial behavior in organizations* (pp. 18–36). Thousand Oaks, CA: Sage.

Bigoness, W. J. (1978). Correlates of faculty attitudes toward collective bargaining. *Journal of Applied Psychology*, *63*, 228–233.

Bing, M.N., Stewart, S,M., Davison, H.K., Green, P.D., McIntyre, M.D., & James, L.R. (2007). An integrative typology of personality assessment for aggression: Implications for predicting counterproductive workplace behavior. *Journal of Applied Psychology*, *92*, 722–744.

Bingham, W. V. (1917). Mentality testing of college students. *Journal of Applied Psychology*, *1*, 38–45.

Binning, J. F., & Barrett, G. V. (1989). Validity of personnel decisions: A conceptual analysis of the inferential and evidential bases. *Journal of Applied Psychology*, *74*, 478–494.

Blackard, K. (2000). *Managing change in a unionized workplace.* Westport, CT: Quorum.

Blanchard, P. M., & Thacker, J. W. (2004). *Effective training: Systems, strategies, and practices* (2nd ed.). Upper Saddle River, NJ: Prentice Hall.

Blau, G., & Lunz, M. (1999). Testing the impact of shift schedules on organizational variables. *Journal of Organizational Behavior*, *20*, 933–942.

Blum, M. L., & Naylor, J. C. (1968). *Industrial psychology: Its theoretical and social foundations.* New York: Harper & Row.

Bobko, P. (1994). Issues in operational selection and classification systems: Comments and commonalities. In M. G. Rumsey, C. B. Walker, & J. H. Harris (Eds.), *Personnel selection and classification* (pp. 443–456). Hillsdale, NJ: Erlbaum.

Boehm, V. R. (1980). Research in the "real world"—A conceptual model. *Personnel Psychology*, *33*, 495–504.

Bohle, P., & Tulley, A. J. (1998). Early experience of shift-working: Influences on attitudes. *Journal of Occupational & Organizational Psychology*, *71*, 61–79.

Bolino, M. C. (1999). Citizenship and impression management: Good soldiers or good actors? *Academy of Management Review*, *24*, 82–98.

Bommer, W. H., Johnson, J., Rich, G. A., Podsakoff, P. M., & MacKenzie, S. B. (1995). On the interchangeability of objective and subjective measures of employee performance: A meta-analysis. *Personnel Psychology*, *48*, 587–605.

Bono, J.E., Foldes, H.J., Vinson, G., & Muros, J.P. (2007). Workplace emotions: The role of supervision and leadership. *Journal of Applied Psychology*, *92*, 1357–1367.

Borman, W. C. (1974). The rating of individuals in organizations: An alternative approach. *Organizational Behavior and Human Performance*, *12*, 105–124.

Borman, W. C. (1978). Exploring upper limits of reliability and validity in performance ratings. *Journal of Applied Psychology, 63*, 135–144.

Borman, W. C. (1991). Job behavior, performance, and effectiveness. In M. D. Dunnette & L. M. Hough (Eds.), *Handbook of industrial and organizational psychology* (2nd ed., Vol. 2, pp. 271–326). Palo Alto, CA: Consulting Psychologists Press.

Borman, W. C., Hedge, J. W., Fierstl, K. L., Kaufman, J. D., Farmer, W. L., & Bearden, R. M. (2003). Current directions and issues in personnel selection and classification. In J. J. Martocchio & G. R. Ferris (Eds.), *Research in personnel and human resources management* (Vol. 22, pp. 287–355). Kidlington, UK: Elsevier.

Borman, W. C., & Motowidlo, S. J. (1993). Expanding the criterion domain to include elements of contextual performance. In N. Schmitt & W. C. Borman (Eds.), *Personnel selection in organizations* (pp. 71–98). San Francisco: Jossey-Bass.

Borman, W. C., White, L. A., & Dorsey, D. W. (1995). Effects of ratee task performance and interpersonal factors on supervisor and peer performance in ratings. *Journal of Applied Psychology, 80*, 168–177.

Boutelle, C. (2004). New Principles encourage greater accountability for test users and developers. *The Industrial-Organizational Psychologist, 41(3)*, 20–21.

Bowling, N.A., & Beehr, T.A. (2006). Workplace harassment from the victim's perspective: A theoretical model and meta-analysis. *Journal of Applied Psychology, 91*, 998–1012.

Bowling, N.A., Beehr, T.A., Wagner, S.H., & Libkuman, T.M. (2005). Adaptation-level theory, opponent process theory, and dispositions: An integrated approach to the stability of job satisfaction. *Journal of Applied Psychology, 90*, 1044–1053.

Bownas, D. A. (2000). Selection programs in a union environment: A commentary. In J. F. Kehoe (Ed.), *Managing selection in changing organizations* (pp. 197–209). San Francisco: Jossey-Bass.

Bracken, D. W., Dalton, M. A., Jako, R. A., McCauley, C. D., & Pollman, V. A. (1997). *Should 360-degree feedback be used only for developmental purposes?* Greensboro, NC: Center for Creative Leadership.

Bramel, D., & Friend, R. (1981). Hawthorne, the myth of the docile worker, and class bias in psychology. *American Psychologist, 36*, 867–878.

Brand, C. (1987). The importance of general intelligence. In S. Modgil & C. Modgil (Eds.), *Arthur Jensen: Consensus and controversy.* New York: Falmer.

Brannick, M. T., & Levine, E. L. (2002). *Job analysis.* Thousand Oaks, CA: Sage.

Brannick, M.T., Levine, E.L., & Morgeson, F.P. (2007). *Job and work analysis* (2nd ed.). Thousand Oaks, CA: Sage.

Breaugh, J. A. (1983). The 12-hour work day: Differing employee reactions. *Personnel Psychology, 36*, 277–288.

Brett, J. M. (1980). Behavioral research on unions and union management systems. In B. M. Staw & L. L. Cummings (Eds.), *Research in organizational behavior* (Vol. 2). Greenwich, CT: JAI Press.

Brett, J. M., Goldberg, S. B., & Ury, W. L. (1990). Designing systems for resolving disputes in organizations. *American Psychologist, 45*, 162–170.

Brett, J.M., Olekalns, M., Friedman, R., Goates, N., Anderson, C., & Lisco, C.C. (2007). Sticks and stones: Language, face, and online dispute resolution. *Academy of Management Journal, 50*, 85–99.

Brett, J. M., & Stroh, L. K. (2003). Working 60 plus hours a week: Why do managers do it? *Journal of Applied Psychology, 88*, 67–78.

Brett, J. M., Tinsley, C. H., Janssens, M., Barsness, Z. I., & Lytle, A. L. (1997). New approaches to the study of culture in industrial/organizational psychology. In P. C. Earley & M. Erez (Eds.), *New perspectives on international industrial/organizational psychology* (pp. 75–129). San Francisco: New Lexington Press.

Brief, A. P. (1998). *Attitudes in and around organizations.* Thousand Oaks, CA: Sage.

Brief, A. P., & Barsky, A. (2000). Establishing a climate for diversity: The inhibition of prejudiced reactions in the workplace. In G. R. Ferris (Ed.), *Research in personnel and human resources management* (Vol. 19, pp. 91–129). New York: Elsevier.

Brief, A. P., & Motowidlo, S. J. (1986). Prosocial organizational behavior. *Academy of Management Review, 11*, 710–725.

Brief, A. P., & Rude, D. E. (1981). Voting in a union certification election: A conceptual analysis. *Academy of Management Review, 6*, 261–267.

Bronfenbrenner, K. (2005). Organizing women: The nature and process of union-organizing efforts among U.S. women workers since the mid-1990s. *Work and Occupations, 32*, 441–463.

Brooks, M. E., Grauer, E., Thornbury, E. E., & Highhouse, S. (2003). Value differences between scientists and practitioners: A survey of SIOP members. *The Industrial-Organizational Psychologist, 40(4)*, 17–23.

Brooks, M.E., & Highhouse, S. (2006). Can good judgment be measured? In J.A. Weekley & R.E. Ployhart (Eds.), *Situational judgment tests* (pp. 39–56). Mahwah, NJ: Erlbaum.

Brown, G., Lawrence, T.B., & Robinson, S.L. (2005). Territoriality in organizations. *Academy of Management Review, 30*, 577–594.

Brown, K. G., & Ford, J. K. (2002). Using computer technology in training: Building an infrastructure for active learning. In K. Kraiger (Ed.), *Creating, implementing, and managing effective training and development* (pp. 192–233). San Francisco: Jossey-Bass.

Brown, S. P. (1996). A meta-analysis and review of organizational research in job involvement. *Psychological Bulletin*, *120*, 235–255.

Bruno, F. (1994). Drug and alcohol problems in the workplace in Italy. *Journal of Drug Issues*, *24*, 697–713.

Bryan, W. L. (1904). Theory and practice. *Psychological Review*, *11*, 71–82.

Bryan, W. L., & Harter, N. (1897). Studies in the physiology and psychology of the telegraphic language. *Psychological Review*, *4*, 27–53.

Bryan, W. L., & Harter, N. (1899). Studies of the telegraphic language. *Psychological Review*, *6*, 345–375.

Bulatao, E. Q., & VandenBos, G. R. (1996). Workplace violence: Its scope and the issues. In G. R. VandenBos & E. Q. Bulatao (Eds.), *Violence on the job* (pp. 1–24). Washington, DC: American Psychological Association.

Burke, C.S., Stagl, K.C., Salas, E., Pierce, L., & Kendall, D. (2006). Understanding team adaptation: A conceptual analysis and model. *Journal of Applied Psychology*, *91*, 1189–1207.

Burke, W.W. (2008). *Organizational change: Theory and practice* (2nd ed.): Thousand Oaks, CA: Sage.

Buss, T. F., & Redburn, F. S. (1987). Plant closings: Impacts and responses. *Economic Development Quarterly*, *1*, 170–177.

Buster, M.A., Roth, P.L., & Bobko, P. (2005). A process for content validation of education and experienced-based minimum qualifications: An approach resulting in federal court approval. *Personnel Psychology*, *58*, 771–799.

Buttigieg, D.M., Deery, S.J., & Iverson, R.D. (2007). An event history analysis of union joining and union leaving. *Journal of Applied Psychology*, *92*, 829–839.

Callinan, M., & Robertson, I. T. (2000). Work sample testing. *International Journal of Selection and Assessment*, *8*, 248–260.

Camara, W. J., & Schneider, D. L. (1994). Integrity tests: Facts and unresolved issues. *American Psychologist*, *49*, 112–119.

Cameron, K. (1982). The relationship between faculty unionism and organizational effectiveness. *Academy of Management Journal*, *25*, 6–24.

Campbell, J.E., & Campbell, D.E. (2005). Eco-I-O psychology? Expanding our goals to include sustainability. *The Industrial-Organizational Psychologist*, *43*(2), 23–28.

Campbell, J. P. (1990a). An overview of the Army selection and classification project. *Personnel Psychology*, *43*, 231–240.

Campbell, J. P. (1990b). The role of theory in industrial and organizational psychology. In M. D. Dunnette & L. M. Hough (Eds.), *Handbook of industrial and organizational psychology* (2nd ed., Vol. 1, pp. 39–74). Palo Alto, CA: Consulting Psychologists Press.

Campbell, J. P. (1996). Group differences and personnel decisions: Validity, fairness, and affirmative action. *Journal of Vocational Behavior*, *49*, 122–158.

Campbell, J. P. (1999). The definition and measurement of performance in the New Age. In D. R. Ilgen & E. D. Pulakos (Eds.), *The changing nature of performance* (pp. 399–429). San Francisco: Jossey-Bass.

Campbell, J.P. (2007). Profiting from history. In L.L. Koppes (Ed.), *Historical perspectives in industrial and organizational psychology* (pp. 441–457). Mahwah, NJ: Erlbaum.

Campbell, J. P., Harris, J. H., & Knapp, D. J. (2001). The Army selection and classification research program: Goals, overall design, and organization. In J. P. Campbell & D. J. Knapp (Eds.), *Exploring the limits in personnel selection and classification* (pp. 31–52). Mahwah, NJ: Erlbaum.

Campbell, J. P., McCloy, R. A., Oppler, S. H., & Sager, C. E. (1993). A theory of performance. In N. Schmitt & W. C. Borman (Eds.), *Personnel selection in organizations* (pp. 35–70). San Francisco: Jossey-Bass.

Campbell, W. J., & Reilly, M. E. (2000). Accommodation for persons with disabilities. In J. F. Kehoe (Ed.), *Managing selection in changing organizations* (pp. 319–367). San Francisco: Jossey-Bass.

Campion, J. E. (1972). Work sampling for personnel selection. *Journal of Applied Psychology*, *56*, 40–44.

Campion, M. A. (1991). Meaning and measurement of turnover: Comparison of alternative measures and recommendations for research. *Journal of Applied Psychology*, *76*, 199–212.

Campion, M. A., & Berger, C. J. (1990). Conceptual integration and empirical test of job design and compensation relationships. *Personnel Psychology*, *43*, 525–554.

Campion, M. A., & Campion, J. E. (1987). Evaluation of an interviewee skills training program in a natural field experiment. *Personnel Psychology*, *40*, 675–691.

Campion, M. A., Outtz, J. L., Zedeck, S., Schmidt, F. L., Kehoe, J. F., Murphy, K. R., & Guion, R. M. (2001). The controversy over score banding in personnel selection: Answers to 10 key questions. *Personnel Psychology*, *54*, 149–185.

Campion, M. A., Palmer, D. K., & Campion, J. E. (1997). A review of structure in the selection interview. *Personnel Psychology*, *50*, 655–702.

Campion, M. A., Papper, E. M., & Medsker, G. J. (1996). Relations between work team characteristics and effectiveness: A replication and extension. *Personnel Psychology*, *49*, 429–452.

Cannon-Bowers, J. A., & Salas, E. (1997). A framework for developing team performance measures in training. In M. T. Brannick, E. Salas, & C. Prince (Eds.), *Team performance assessment and measurement: Theory, methods, and applications* (pp. 45–62). Mahwah, NJ: Erlbaum.

Cannon-Bowers, J. A., & Salas, E. (2001). Reflections on shared cognition. *Journal of Organizational Behavior*, *22*, 195–202.

Capelli, P. (1999). *The new deal at work*. Boston: Harvard Business School.

Cardy, R. L. (1998). Performance appraisal in a quality context: A new look at an old problem. In J. W. Smither (Ed.), *Performance appraisal* (pp. 132–162). San Francisco: Jossey-Bass.

Carillon, J. W., & Sutton, R. I. (1982). The relationship between union effectiveness and the quality of members' worklife. *Journal of Occupational Behavior*, *3*, 171–179.

Carling, P. (1994). Reasonable accommodations in the workplace for persons with psychiatric disabilities. In S. M. Bruyere & J. O'Keeffe (Eds.), *Implications of the Americans with Disabilities Act for psychology* (pp. 103–136). New York: Springer.

Carretta, T. R., & Ree, M. J. (2000). General and specific cognitive and psychomotor abilities in personnel selection: The prediction of training and job performance. *International Journal of Selection and Assessment*, *8*, 227–236.

Carson, K. P., Becker, J. S., & Henderson, J. A. (1998). Is utility really futile? A failure to replicate and an extension. *Journal of Applied Psychology*, *83*, 84–96.

Carsten, J. M., & Spector, P. E. (1987). Unemployment, job satisfaction, and employee turnover: A meta-analytic test of the Muchinsky model. *Journal of Applied Psychology*, *72*, 374–381.

Cascio, W. F. (1982). *Applied psychology in personnel management* (2nd ed.). Reston, VA: Reston.

Cascio, W. F. (1989). Using utility analyses to assess training outcomes. In I. L. Goldstein (Ed.), *Training and development in organizations* (pp. 63–88). San Francisco: Jossey-Bass.

Cascio, W. F. (1999). Virtual workplaces: Implications for organizational behavior. In C. L. Cooper & D. M. Rousseau (Eds.), *Trends in organizational behavior: The virtual organization* (Vol. 6, pp. 1–14). New York: Wiley.

Cascio, W. F., Alexander, R. A., & Barrett, G. V. (1988). Setting cutoff scores: Legal, psychometric, and professional issues and guidelines. *Personnel Psychology*, *41*, 1–24.

Casper, W.J., Eby, L.T., Bordeaux, C., Lockwood, A., & Lambert, D. (2007). A review of research methods in IO/OB work-family research. *Journal of Applied Psychology*, *92*, 28–41.

Catano, V.M., Darr, W., & Campbell, C.A. (2007). Performance appraisal of behavior-based competencies: A reliable and valid procedure. *Personnel Psychology*, *60*, 201–230.

Cavanaugh, M. A., & Noe, R. A. (1999). Antecedents and consequences of relational components of the new psychological contract. *Journal of Organizational Behavior*, *20*, 323–340.

Cawley, B. D., Keeping, L. M., & Levy, P. E. (1998). Participation in the performance appraisal process and employee reactions: A meta-analytic review of field investigations. *Journal of Applied Psychology*, *83*, 615–633.

Cederblom, D. (1982). The performance appraisal interview: A review, implications and suggestions. *Academy of Management Review*, *7*, 219–227.

Cederblom, D., & Lounsbury, J. W. (1980). An investigation of user acceptance of peer evaluations. *Personnel Psychology*, *33*, 567–580.

Chan, K. Y., & Drasgow, F. (2001). Toward a theory of individual differences and leadership: Understanding the motivation to lead. *Journal of Applied Psychology*, *86*, 481–498.

Chan, K. Y., Drasgow, F., & Sawin, L. L. (1999). What is the shelf life of a test? The effect of time on the psychometrics of a cognitive ability test battery. *Journal of Applied Psychology*, *84*, 610–619.

Chao, G.T., & Moon, H. (2005). The cultural mosaic: A metatheory for understanding the complexity of culture. *Journal of Applied Psychology*, *90*, 1128–1140.

Chapanis, A., Garner, W. R., & Morgan, C. T. (1949). *Applied experimental psychology*. New York: Wiley.

Chapman, D.S., Uggerslev, K.L., Carroll, S.A., Piasentin, K.A., & Jones, D.A. (2005). Applicant attraction to organizations and job choice: A meta-analytic review of the correlates of recruiting outcomes. *Journal of Applied Psychology*, *90*, 928–944.

Chemers, M. M., & Murphy, S. E. (1995). Leadership and diversity in groups and organizations. In M. M. Chemers, S. Oskamp, & M. A. Costanzo (Eds.), *Diversity in organizations: New perspectives for a changing workforce* (pp. 157–188). Thousand Oaks, CA: Sage.

Chen, G., Gully, S. M., Whiteman, J. A., & Kilcullen, R. N. (2000). Examination of relationships among trait-like individual differences, state-like individual differences, and learning performance. *Journal of Applied Psychology*, *85*, 835–847.

Choi, J. N., & Kim, M. U. (1999). The organizational applications of groupthink and its limitations in organizations. *Journal of Applied Psychology, 84,* 297–306.

Chrobot-Mason, D., & Quinones, M. A. (2002). Training for a diverse workplace. In K. Kraiger (Ed.), *Creating, implementing, and managing effective training and development* (pp. 117–159). San Francisco: Jossey-Bass.

Church, A. H. (2001). Is there a method to our madness? The impact of data collection methodology on organizational survey results. *Personnel Psychology, 54,* 937–969.

Church, A. J., Waclawski, J., & Berr, S. A. (2002). Voices from the field: Future directions for organization development. In. J. Waclawski & A. H. Church (Eds.), *Organization development* (pp. 321–336). San Francisco: Jossey-Bass.

Ciarrochi, J., & Mayer, J.D. (2007). Introduction. In Ciarrochi & J.D. Mayer (Eds.), *Applying emotional intelligence* (pp. *xii-xiv*). New York: Taylor and Francis.

Clause, C. S., Mullins, M. E., Nee, M. T., Pulakos, E., & Schmitt, N. (1998). Parallel test form development: A procedure for alternative predictors and an example. *Personnel Psychology, 51,* 193–208.

Cleveland, J. N., & Kerst, M. E. (1993). Sexual harassment and perceptions of power: An under-articulated relationship. *Journal of Vocational Behavior, 42,* 49–67.

Clifford, J. P. (1994). Job analysis: Why do it, and how should it be done? *Public Personnel Management, 23,* 321–338.

Cohen, A. (2003). *Multiple commitments in the workplace.* Mahwah, NJ: Erlbaum.

Cohen, D. J. (1990, November). What motivates trainees? *Training and Development Journal,* 91–93.

Cohen-Charash, Y., & Spector, P. E. (2001). The role of justice in organizations: A meta-analysis. *Organizational Behavior and Human Decision Processes, 86,* 278–321.

Cohn, L. D., & Becker, B. J. (2003). How meta-analysis increases statistical power. *Psychological Methods, 8,* 243–253.

Colarelli, S. M. (1998). Psychological interventions in organizations: An evolutionary perspective. *American Psychologist, 53,* 1044–1056.

Cole, N. D., & Latham, G. P. (1997). Effects of training in procedural justice on perceptions of disciplinary fairness by unionized employees and disciplinary subject matter experts. *Journal of Applied Psychology, 82,* 699–705.

Collins, J. M., & Gleaves, D. H. (1998). Race, job applicants, and the five-factor model of personality: Implications for black psychology, industrial/organizational psychology, and the five-factor theory. *Journal of Applied Psychology, 83,* 531–544.

Collins, J. M., & Schmidt, F. L. (1993). Personality, integrity, and white collar crime: A construct validity study. *Personnel Psychology, 46,* 295–311.

Colquitt, J. A., Conlon, D. E., Wesson, M. J., Porter, C. O., & Ng, K. Y. (2001). Justice at the millennium: A meta-analytic review of 25 years of organizational justice research. *Journal of Applied Psychology, 86,* 425–445.

Colquitt, J.A., Scott, B.A., & LePine, J.A. (2007). Trust, trustworthiness, and trust propensity: A meta-analytic test of their unique relationships with risk taking and job performance. *Journal of Applied Psychology, 92,* 909–927.

Conger, J. A., & Kanungo, R. N. (1987). Toward a behavioral theory of charismatic leadership in organizational settings. *Academy of Management Review, 12,* 637–647.

Conlon, D.E., Meyer, C.J., Lytle, A.L., & Willaby, H.W. (2007). Third party interventions across cultures: No "one best choice." In J.J. Martocchio (Ed.), *Research in personnel and human resources management* (pp. 309–349). Oxford, UK: JAI.

Conlon, D. E., Moon, H., & Ng, K. Y. (2002). Putting the cart before the horse: The benefits of arbitrating before mediating. *Journal of Applied Psychology, 87,* 978–984.

Conway, J. M. (1999). Distinguishing contextual performance from task performance for managerial jobs. *Journal of Applied Psychology, 84,* 3–13.

Cooper, C. L., Dewe, P., & O'Driscoll, M. (2003). Employee assistance programs. In J. C. Quick & L. E. Tetrick (Eds.), *Handbook of organizational health psychology* (pp. 289–304). Washington, DC: American Psychological Association.

Cooper, W. H. (1981). Ubiquitous halo. *Psychological Bulletin, 90,* 218–244.

Cooper-Hakim, A., & Viswesvaran, C. (2005). The construct of work commitment: Testing an integrative framework. *Psychological Bulletin, 131,* 241–259.

Cortina, J. M., Goldstein, N. B., Payne, S. C., Davison, H. K., & Gilliland, S. W. (2000). The incremental validity of interview scores over and above cognitive ability and conscientiousness scores. *Personnel Psychology, 53,* 325–351.

Costa, G. (1996). The impact of shift and night work on health. *Applied Ergonomics, 27,* 9–16.

Costa, P. T. (1996). Work and personality: Use of the NEO-PI-R in industrial/organizational psychology. *Applied Psychology: An International Review, 45,* 225–241.

Cox, T., & Leather, P. (1994). The prevention of violence at work: Application of a cognitive behavioral theory. In C. L. Cooper & I. T. Robertson (Eds.), *International review of industrial and organizational psychology* (Vol. 9, pp. 213–245). London: Wiley.

Cropanzano, R., & Greenberg, J. (1997). Progress in organizational justice: Tunneling through the maze. In C. L. Cooper & I. T. Robertson (Eds.), *International* review of industrial and organizational psychology (Vol. 12, pp. 317–372). Chichester: Wiley.

Crosby, F. J., Iyer, A., Clayton, S., & Downing, R. A. (2003). Affirmative action: Psychological data and policy debates. *American Psychologist*, 58, 93–115.

Crosby, F. J., & VanDeVeer, C. (Eds.). (2000). *Sex, race, & merit*. Ann Arbor: University of Michigan Press.

Csikszentmihalyi, M. (1999). If we are so rich, why aren't we happy? *American Psychologist*, 54, 821–827.

Cullen, M. J., & Sackett, P. R. (2003). Personality and counterproductive workplace behavior. In M. R. Barrick & A. M. Ryan (Eds.), *Personality and work: Reconsidering the role of personality in organizations* (pp. 150–182). San Francisco: Jossey-Bass.

Cullen, M. J., & Sackett, P. R. (2004). Integrity testing in the workplace. In J. C. Thomas (Ed.), *Comprehensive handbook of psychological assessment* (Vol. 4, pp. 149–165). Hoboken, NJ: Wiley

Cunningham, M. R., Wong, D. T., & Barbee, A. P. (1994). Self-presentation dynamics on overt integrity tests: Experimental studies of the Reid Report. *Journal of Applied Psychology*, 79, 643–658.

D'Adamo, P. J. (1996). *4 blood types, 4 diets: Eat right for your type*. New York: Putnam.

Dabos, G. E., & Rousseau, D. M. (2004). Mutuality and reciprocity in the psychological contracts of employees and employers. *Journal of Applied Psychology*, 89, 52–72.

Daft, R. L. (1983). Learning the craft of organizational research. *Academy of Management Review*, 8, 539–546.

Dalton, D. R., & Mesch, D. J. (1990). The impact of flexible scheduling on employee attendance and turnover. *Administrative Science Quarterly*, 35, 370–387.

Daniel, M. H. (1997). Intelligence testing. *American Psychologist*, 52, 1038–1045.

Danielson, C. C., & Wiggenhorn, W. (2003). The strategic challenge for transfer: Chief learning officers speak out. In E. F. Holton & T. T. Baldwin (Eds.), *Improving learning transfer in organizations* (pp. 16–38). San Francisco: Jossey-Bass.

Dansereau, F., Graen, G., & Haga, W. (1975). A vertical dyad linkage approach to leadership in formal organizations. *Organizational Behavior and Human Performance*, 13, 46–78.

Dawis, R. V. (2004). Job satisfaction. In J. C. Thomas (Ed.), *Comprehensive handbook of psychological assessment* (Vol. 4, pp. 470–481). Hoboken, NJ: Wiley.

Day, D. V., & Sulsky, L. M. (1995). Effects of frame-of-reference training and information configuration on memory organization and rater accuracy. *Journal of Applied Psychology*, 80, 158–167.

Day, D.V., & Zaccaro, S.J. (2007). Leadership; A critical historical analysis of the influence of leader traits. In L.L. Koppes (Ed.), *Historical perspectives in industrial and organizational psychology* (pp. 383–405). Mahwah, NJ: Erlbaum.

De Corte, W. (1999). Weighing job performance predictors to both maximize the quality of the selected workforce and control the level of adverse impact. *Journal of Applied Psychology*, 84, 695–702.

De Corte, W., Lievens, F., & Sackett, P.R. (2007). Combining predictors to achieve optimal trade-offs between selection quality and adverse impact. *Journal of Applied Psychology*, 92, 1380–1393.

De Shon, R.P., & Gillespie, J.Z. (2005). A motivational action theory account of goal orientation. *Journal of Applied Psychology*, 90, 1096–1127.

Deal, T., & Kennedy, A. (1982). *Corporate cultures*. Reading, MA: Addison-Wesley.

DeGroot, T., & Motowidlo, S. J. (1999). Why visual and vocal interview cues can affect interviewers' judgments and predict job performance. *Journal of Applied Psychology*, 84, 986–993.

DeNisi, A. S., & Peters, L. H. (1996). Organization of information in memory and the performance appraisal process: Evidence from the field. *Journal of Applied Psychology*, 81, 717–737.

Dickinson, T. L. (1993). Attitudes about performance appraisal. In H. Schuler, J. L. Farr, & M. Smith (Eds.), *Personnel selection and assessment* (pp. 141–162). Hillsdale, NJ: Erlbaum.

Diener, E. (2000). Subjective well-being: The science of happiness and a proposal for a national index. *American Psychologist*, 54, 34–43.

Dienesch, R. M., & Liden, R. C. (1986). Leader-member exchange model of leadership: A critique and further development. *Academy of Management Review*, 11, 618–634.

Dierdorff, E.C., & Surface, E.A. (2007). Placing peer ratings in context: Systematic influences beyond ratee performance. *Personnel Psychology*, 60, 93–126.

Digman, J. M., & Takemoto-Chock, N. K. (1981). Factors in the natural language of personality: Re-analysis and comparison of six major studies. *Multivariate Behavioral Research*, 16, 149–170.

Dionne, S. D., Yammarino, F. J., Atwater, L. E., & James, L. R. (2002). Neutralizing substitutes for leadership theory: Leadership effects and common-source bias. *Journal of Applied Psychology*, 87, 454–464.

Dipboye, R. L. (1990). Laboratory vs. field research in industrial and organizational psychology. In C. L. Cooper & I. T. Robertson (Eds.), *International review of industrial and organizational psychology* (Vol. 5, pp. 1–34). London: Wiley.

Dipboye, R. L. (1997). Structured selection interviews: Why do they work? Why are they underutilized? In N. Anderson & P. Herriot (Eds.), *International handbook of selection and assessment* (pp. 455–473). Chichester: Wiley.

Dirks, K. T. (1999). The effects of interpersonal trust on work group performance. *Journal of Applied Psychology, 84*, 445–455.

Dirks, K. T., Cummings, L. L., & Pierce, J. L. (1996). Psychological ownership in organizations: Conditions under which individuals promote and resist change. In R. W. Woodman & W. A. Pasmore (Eds.), *Research in organizational change and development* (Vol. 9, pp. 1–24). Greenwich, CT: JAI Press.

Dirks, K. T., & Ferrin, D. L. (2002). Trust in leadership: Meta-analytic findings and implications for research and practice. *Journal of Applied Psychology, 87*, 611–628.

Donovan, J. J. (2001). Work motivation. In N. Anderson, D. S. Ones, H. K. Sinangil, & C. Viswesvaran (Eds.), *Handbook of industrial, work, and organisational psychology* (Vol. 2, pp. 53–76). London: Sage.

Donovan, J. J., & Williams, K. J. (2003). Missing the mark: Effects of time and causal attribution on goal revision in response to goal-setting discrepancies. *Journal of Applied Psychology, 88*, 379–390.

Dotlich, D. L. (1982, October). International and intracultural management development. *Training and Development Journal, 36*, 26–31.

Dovidio, J. F., & Gaertner, S. L. (1996). Affirmative action, unintentional racial biases, and intergroup relations. *Journal of Social Issues, 52*, 51–75.

Dreher, G. F., Ash, R. A., & Hancock, P. (1988). The role of the traditional research design in underestimating the validity of the employment interview. *Personnel Psychology, 41*, 315–328.

Druskat, V. A., & Wolff, S. B. (1999). Effects and timing of developmental peer appraisals in self-managing work groups. *Journal of Applied Psychology, 84*, 58–74.

DuBois, D. A. (2002). Leveraging hidden expertise: Why, when, and how to use cognitive task analysis. In K. Kraiger (Ed.), *Creating, implementing, and managing effective training and development* (pp. 80–114). San Francisco: Jossey-Bass.

Duchon, J. C., Keran, C. M., & Smith, T. J. (1994). Extended workdays in an underground mine: A work performance analysis. *Human Factors, 36*, 258–268.

Dulebohn, J. H. (1997). Social influences in justice evaluations of human resources systems. In G. R. Ferris (Ed.), *Research in personnel and human resources management* (Vol. 15, pp. 241–292). Greenwich, CT: JAI Press.

Dunham, L., & Freeman, R. E. (2000). There is business like show business: Leadership lessons from the theatre. *Organizational Dynamics, 29*, 108–122.

Dunham, R. B., Grube, J. A., & Castaneda, M. B. (1994). Organizational commitment: The utility of an integrated definition. *Journal of Applied Psychology, 79*, 370–380.

Dunham, R. B., Pierce, J. L., & Castaneda, M. B. (1987). Alternative work schedules: Two field quasi-experiments. *Personnel Psychology, 40*, 215–242.

Eagly, A. H., Johannesen-Schmidt, M. C., & van Engen, M. L. (2003). Transformation, transactional, and laissez-faire leadership styles: A meta-analysis comparing women and men. *Psychological Bulletin, 129*, 569–591.

Earley, P. C. (1997). Doing an about-face: Social motivation and cross-cultural currents. In P. C. Earley & M. Erez (Eds.), *New perspectives on international industrial/organizational psychology* (pp. 243–255). San Francisco: New Lexington Press.

Earley, P. C., & Gibson, C. B. (2002). *Multinational work teams.* Mahwah, NJ: Erlbaum.

Ebel, R. L. (1972). *Essentials of educational measurement.* Englewood Cliffs, NJ: Prentice Hall.

Eby, L.T., Butts, M., Lockwood, A., & Simon, S.A. (2004). Protégés negative mentoring experiences: Construct development and nomological validation. *Personnel Psychology, 57*, 411–447.

Eckes, G. (2001). *The Six Sigma revolution.* New York: Wiley.

Edwards, J. R., & Bagozzi, R. P. (2000). On the nature and direction of relationships between constructs and measure. *Psychological Methods, 5*, 155–174.

Ellis, S., Mendel, R., & Nir, M. (2006). Learning from successful and failed experience: The moderating role of kind of after-event review. *Journal of Applied Psychology, 91*, 669–680.

Epitropaki, O., & Martin, R. (2004). Implicit leadership theories in applied settings: Factor structure, generalizability, and stability over time. *Journal of Applied Psychology, 89*, 293–310.

Equal Employment Opportunity Commission. (1980). Discrimination because of sex under Title VII of the Civil Rights Act of 1964, as amended; adoption of interim interpretive guidelines. *Federal Register, 45*, 25024–25025.

Erez, A., & Isen, A. M. (2002). The influence of positive affect on the components of expectancy motivation. *Journal of Applied Psychology, 87*, 1055–1067.

Erez, M., & Earley, P. C. (1993). *Culture, self-identity, and work.* New York: Oxford University Press.

Erez, M., & Eden, D. (2001). Introduction: Trends reflected in work motivation. In M. Erez, U. Kleinbeck, &

H. Thierry (Eds.), *Work motivation in the context of a globalizing economy* (pp. 1–8). Mahwah, NJ: Erlbaum.

Erickson, E. H. (1963). *Childhood and society* (2nd ed.). New York: Norton.

Estey, M. (1981). *The unions: Structure, development, and management* (3rd ed.). New York: Harcourt Brace Jovanovich.

Evans, D. C. (2003). A comparison of other-directed stigmatization produced by legal and illegal forms of affirmative action. *Journal of Applied Psychology, 88*, 121–130.

Facteau, J. D., & Craig, S. B. (2001). Are performance appraisal ratings from different rating sources comparable? *Journal of Applied Psychology, 86*, 215–227.

Farr, J.L., & Levy, P.E. (2007). Performance appraisal. In L.L. Koppes (Ed.), *Historical perspectives in industrial and organizational psychology* (pp. 311–327). Mahwah, NJ: Erlbaum.

Farr, J. L., & Tesluk, P. E. (1997). Bruce V. Moore: First president of Division 14. *Journal of Applied Psychology, 82*, 478–485.

Farrell, J. N., & McDaniel, M. A. (2001). The stability of validity coefficients over time: Ackerman's (1988) model and the general aptitude test battery. *Journal of Applied Psychology, 86*, 60–79.

Fay, B. (1990). Critical realism? *Journal for the Theory of Social Behaviour, 20*, 33–41.

Ferdman, B. M. (1992). The dynamics of ethnic diversity in organizations: Toward integrative models. In K. Kelly (Ed.), *Issues, theory, and research in industrial/organization psychology* (pp. 339–384). Amsterdam: North Holland.

Fetterman, D. M. (1998). Ethnography. In L. Bickman & D. J. Rog (Eds.), *Handbook of applied social research methods* (pp. 473–504). Thousand Oaks, CA: Sage.

Feuille, P., & Blandin, J. (1974). Faculty job satisfaction and bargaining sentiment: A case study. *Academy of Management Journal, 17*, 678–692.

Fields, M. W., & Thacker, J. W. (1992). Influence of quality of work life on company and union commitment. *Academy of Management Journal, 35*, 439–450.

Fine, S.A., & Cronshaw, S.F. (1999). *Functional job analysis.* Mahwah, NJ: Erlbaum.

Fisher, C. D. (2000). Mood and emotions while working: Missing pieces of job satisfaction? *Journal of Organizational Behavior, 21*, 185–202.

Fisher, C. D., & Ashkanasy, N. M. (2000). The emerging role of emotions in work life: An introduction. *Journal of Organizational Behavior, 21*, 123–129.

Fisher, S. G., Hunter, T. A., & Macrosson, W. D. (1998). The structure of Belbin's team roles. *Journal of Occupational & Organizational Psychology, 71*, 283–288.

Flanagan, M. F., & Dipboye, R. L. (1981). Research settings in industrial and organizational psychology: Facts, fallacies, and the future. *Personnel Psychology, 34*, 37–47.

Fleishman, E. A., & Quaintance, M. K. (1984). *Taxonomies of human performance.* Orlando, FL: Academic Press.

Fletcher, C. (2001). Performance appraisal and management: The developing research agenda. *Journal of Occupational & Organizational Psychology, 74*, 473–487.

Fletcher, D., & Perry, E. L. (2001). Performance appraisal and feedback: A consideration of national culture and a review of contemporary research of future trends. In N. Anderson, D. S. Ones, H. J. Sinangil, & C. Viswesvaran (Eds.), *Handbook of industrial, work, and organizational psychology* (Vol. 1, pp. 127–144). London: Sage.

Folger, R., & Cropanzano, R. (1998). *Organizational justice and human resource management.* Thousand Oaks, CA: Sage.

Folger, R., & Greenberg, J. (1985). Procedural justice: An interpretive analysis of personnel systems. In K. Rowland & G. Ferris (Eds.), *Research in personnel and human resources management* (Vol. 3, pp. 141–183). Greenwich, CT: JAI Press.

Folger, R., Konovsky, M., & Cropanzano, R. (1992). A due process metaphor for performance appraisal. In B. Staw & L. Cummings (Eds.), *Research in organizational behavior* (Vol. 14) (pp. 129–177). Greenwich, CT: JAI.

Folger, R., & Skarlicki, D. P. (2001). Fairness as a dependent variable: Why tough times can lead to bad management. In R. Cropanzano (Ed.), *Justice in the workplace* (Vol. 2, pp. 97–120). Mahwah, NJ: Erlbaum.

Ford, J. K., & Kraiger, K. (1995). The application of cognitive constructs and principles to the instructional systems model of training: Implications for needs assessment, design, and transfer. In C. L. Cooper & I. T. Robertson (Eds.), *International review of industrial and organizational psychology* (Vol. 10, pp. 1–48). New York: Wiley.

Ford, J. K., Quinones, M., Sego, D., & Speer, J. (1991). *Factors affecting the opportunity to use trained skills on the job.* Paper presented at the 6th annual conference of the Society for Industrial and Organizational Psychology, St. Louis.

Ford, J. K., Smith, E. M., Weissbein, D. A., Gully, S. M., & Salas, E. (1998). Relationships of goal orientation, metacognitive activity and practice strategies with learning outcomes and transfer. *Journal of Applied Psychology, 83*, 218–233.

Ford, M.T., Heinen, B.A., & Langkamer, K.L. (2007). Work and family satisfaction and conflict: A meta-analysis of cross-domain relations. *Journal of Applied Psychology, 92*, 57–80.

Fox, S., & Spector, P. E. (1999). A model of work frustration—aggression. *Journal of Organizational Behavior, 20*, 915–932.

Freese, M., & Okonek, K. (1984). Reasons to leave shiftwork and psychological and psychosomatic complaints of former shiftworkers. *Journal of Applied Psychology, 69*, 509–514.

French, J. R. P., & Raven, B. (1960). The basis of social power. In D. Cartwright & A. F. Zander (Eds.), *Group dynamics* (2nd ed.). Evanston, IL: Row & Peterson.

Fried, Y., & Ferris, G. R. (1987). The validity of the job characteristics model: A review and meta-analysis. *Personnel Psychology, 40*, 287–322.

Friedman, D. E., & Galinsky, E. (1992). Work and family issues: A legitimate business concern. In S. Zedeck (Ed.), *Work, families, and organizations* (pp. 168–207). San Francisco: Jossey-Bass.

Friedman, L., & Harvey, R. J. (1986). Factors of union commitment: The case for a lower dimensionality. *Journal of Applied Psychology, 71*, 371–376.

Friedman, L. N., Tucker, S. B., Neville, P. R., & Imperial, M. (1996). The impact of domestic violence on the workplace. In G. R. VandenBos & E. Q. Bulatao (Eds.), *Violence on the job* (pp. 153–162). Washington, DC: American Psychological Association.

Frisch, M. H. (1998). Designing the individual assessment process. In R. Jeanneret & R. Silzer (Eds.), *Individual psychological assessment* (pp. 135–177). San Francisco: Jossey-Bass.

Frone, M. R. (2000). Work-family conflict and employee psychiatric disorders: The national comorbidity survey. *Journal of Applied Psychology, 85*, 888–895.

Frone, M. R. (2003). Work-family balance. In J. C. Quick & L. E. Tetrick (Eds.), *Handbook of organizational health psychology* (pp. 143–162). Washington, DC: American Psychological Association.

Frone, M.R. (2006). Prevalence and distribution of illicit drug use in the workforce and in the workplace: Findings and implications from a U.S. national survey. *Journal of Applied Psychology, 61*, 856–869.

Frost, P. J., & Jamal, M. (1979). Shift work, attitudes and reported behaviors: Some association between individual characteristics and hours of work and leisure. *Journal of Applied Psychology, 64*, 77–81.

Fryer, D., & Payne, R. (1986). Being unemployed: A review of the literature on the psychological experience of unemployment. In C. L. Cooper & I. Robertson (Eds.), *International review of industrial and organizational psychology* (Vol. 1, pp. 235–278). London: Wiley.

Fryxell, G. E., & Gordon, M. E. (1989). Workplace justice and job satisfaction as predictors of satisfaction with union and management. *Academy of Management Journal, 32*, 851–866.

Fullagar, C., & Barling, J. (1989). A longitudinal test of a model of the antecedents and consequences of union loyalty. *Journal of Applied Psychology, 74*, 213–227.

Fullagar, C., Clark, P. F., Gallagher, D. G., & Gordon, M. E. (1994). A model of the antecedents of early union commitment: The role of socialization experiences and steward characteristics. *Journal of Organizational Behavior, 15*, 517–533.

Fullagar, C., Gallagher, D. G., Gordon, M. E., & Clark, P. F. (1995). Impact of early socialization on union commitment and participation: A longitudinal study. *Journal of Applied Psychology, 80*, 147–157.

Fuller, J. B., Jr., & Hester, K. (2001). A closer look at the relationship between justice perceptions and union participation. *Journal of Applied Psychology, 86*, 1096–1106.

Galaif, E. R., Newcomb, M. D., & Carmona, J. V. (2001). Prospective relationships between drug problems and work adjustment in a community sample of adults. *Journal of Applied Psychology, 86*, 337–350.

Gallagher, C. A., Joseph, L. E., & Park, M. V. (2002). Implementing organizational change. In J. W. Hedge & E. D. Pulakos (Eds.), *Implementing organizational interventions: Steps, processes, and best practices* (pp. 12–42). San Francisco: Jossey-Bass.

Gardner, W. L., & Avolio, B. J. (1998). The charismatic relationship: A dramaturgical perspective. *Academy of Management Review, 23*, 32–58.

Geen, R. G. (1990). *Human aggression.* London: Open University Press.

Geisinger, K.F., Spies, R.A., Carlson, J.F., & Plake, B.S. (Eds.) (2007). *The seventeenth mental measurements yearbook.* Lincoln, NE: University of Nebraska Press.

Gelfand, M.J., Nishii, L.H., & Raver, J.L. (2006). On the nature and importance of cultural tightness–looseness. *Journal of Applied Psychology, 91*, 1225–1244.

Gelfand, M. J., Raver, J. L., & Ehrhart, K. H. (2002). Methodological issues in cross-cultural organizational research. In S. G. Rogelberg (Ed.), *Handbook of research methods in industrial and organizational psychology* (pp. 216–246). Malden, MA: Blackwell.

George, J. M. (2002). Affective regulation in groups and teams. In R. G. Lord, R. J. Klimoski, & R. Kanfer (Eds.), *Emotions in the workplace* (pp. 183–217). San Francisco: Jossey-Bass.

Gerstner, C. R., & Day, D. V. (1997). Meta-analytic review of leader–member exchange theory: Correlations and construct issues. *Journal of Applied Psychology, 82*, 827–844.

Gettman, H.J., & Gelfand, M.J. (2007). When the customer shouldn't be king: Antecedents and consequences of sexual harassment by clients and customers. *Journal of Applied Psychology, 62*, 757–770.

Ghiselli, E. E., & Brown, C. W. (1955). *Personnel and industrial psychology.* New York: McGraw-Hill.

Gibson, C. B. (2001). From knowledge accumulation to accommodation: Cycles of collective cognition in work groups. *Journal of Organizational Behavior, 22*, 121–134.

Gilliland, S. W. (1993). The perceived fairness of selection systems: An organizational justice perspective. *Academy of Management Review, 18*, 694–734.

Gilliland, S. W., & Chan, D. (2001). Justice in organizations: Theory, methods, and applications. In N. Anderson, D. S. Ones, H. K. Sinangil, & C. Viswesvaran (Eds.), *Handbook of industrial, work, and organisational psychology* (Vol. 2, pp. 143–165). London: Sage.

Glazer, S. (2002). Past, present and future of cross-cultural studies in industrial and organizational psychology. In C. L. Cooper & I. T. Robertson (Eds.), *International review of industrial and organizational psychology* (Vol. 17, pp. 145–185). West Sussex: Wiley.

Glomb, T. M., Steele, P. D., & Arvey, R. D. (2002). Office sneers, snipes, and stab wounds: Antecedents, consequences, and implications of workplace violence and aggression. In R. G. Lord, R. J. Klimoski, & R. Kanfer (Eds.), *Emotions in the workplace* (pp. 227–259). San Francisco: Jossey-Bass.

Goktepe, J. R., & Schneier, C. E. (1989). Role of sex, gender roles, and attraction in predicting emergent leaders. *Journal of Applied Psychology, 74*, 165–167.

Goldstein, I. L. (1991). Training in work organizations. In M. D. Dunnette & L.M. Hough (Eds.), *Handbook of industrial and organizational psychology* (2nd ed., Vol. 2, pp. 507–619). Palo Alto, CA: Consulting Psychologists Press.

Goldstein, I. L. & Ford, J.K. (2002). *Training in organizations* (4th ed.). Belmont, CA: Wadsworth.

Goldstein, I. L., Zedeck, S., & Schneider, B. (1993). An exploration of the job analysis–content validity process. In N. Schmitt & W. C. Borman (Eds.), *Personnel selection in organizations* (pp. 3–34). San Francisco: Jossey-Bass.

Goleman, D. (1995). *Emotional intelligence.* New York: Bantam.

Golembiewski, R. T., & Proehl, C. W. (1978). A survey of the empirical literature on flexible workhours: Character and consequences of a major innovation. *Academy of Management Review, 3*, 837–853.

Gomez-Mejia, L. R., & Balkin, D. B. (1984). Faculty satisfaction with pay and other job dimensions under union and nonunion conditions. *Academy of Management Journal, 27*, 591–602.

Gordon, M. E., & Bowlby, R. L. (1988). Propositions about grievance settlements: Finally, consultation with grievants. *Personnel Psychology, 41*, 107–124.

Gordon, M. E., & Bowlby, R. L. (1989). Reactance and intentionality attributions as determinants of the intent to file a grievance. *Personnel Psychology, 42*, 309–330.

Gordon, M. E., & Ladd, R. T. (1990). Dual allegiance: Renewal, reconsideration, and recantation. *Personnel Psychology, 43*, 37–69.

Gordon, M. E., & Miller, S. J. (1984). Grievances: A review of research and practice. *Personnel Psychology, 37*, 117–146.

Gordon, M. E., Philpot, J. W., Burt, R. E., Thompson, C. A., & Spiller, W. E. (1980). Commitment to the union: Development of a measure and an examination of its correlates. *Journal of Applied Psychology, 65*, 479–499.

Gordon, M. E., Schmitt, N., & Schneider, W. G. (1984). Laboratory research on bargaining and negotiations: An evaluation. *Industrial Relations, 23*, 281–233.

Gottfredson, L. S. (1994). The science and politics of race norming. *American Psychologist, 49*, 955–963.

Gottlieb, B. H., Kelloway, E. K., & Barham, E. (1998). *Flexible work arrangements.* Chichester: Wiley.

Gowan, M. A., Riordan, C. M., & Gatewood, K. D. (1999). Test of a model of coping with involuntary job loss following a company closing. *Journal of Applied Psychology, 84*, 75–86.

Grandey, A.A., Fisk, G.M., & Steiner, D.D. (2005). Must "service with a smile" be stressful? The moderating role of personal control for American and French employees. *Journal of Applied Psychology, 90*, 893–904.

Green, S. G., & Nebeker, D. M. (1977). The effects of situational factors and leadership style on leader behavior. *Organizational Behavior and Human Performance, 19*, 368–377.

Greenberg, J. (1986). Determinants of perceived fairness of performance evaluations. *Journal of Applied Psychology, 71*, 340–342.

Greenberg, J. (1993). The social side of fairness: Interpersonal and informational classes of organizational justice. In R. Cropanzano (Ed.), *Justice in the workplace: Approaching fairness in human resource management* (pp. 79–103). Hillsdale, NJ: Erlbaum.

Greenberg, J. (1994). Using socially fair treatment to promote acceptance of a work site smoking ban. *Journal of Applied Psychology, 79*, 288–297.

Greenberg, J. (2007). Positive organizational justice: From fair to fairer—and beyond. In J.E. Dutton & B.R. Ragins (Eds.), *Exploring positive relationships at work* (pp. 159–178). Mahwah, NJ: Erlbaum.

Greenberg, J., & Scott, K. S. (1996). Why do workers bite the hands that feed them? Employee theft as a social exchange process. In B. M. Staw & L. L. Cummings (Eds.), *Research in organizational behavior* (Vol. 18, pp. 111–156). Greenwich, CT: JAI.

Greenberg, L., & Barling, J. (1999). Predicting employee aggression against coworkers, subordinates, and supervisors: The roles of person behaviors and perceived workplace factors. *Journal of Organizational Behavior, 20,* 897–913.

Greene, C. N., & Schriesheim, C. A. (1980). Leader–group interactions: A longitudinal field investigation. *Journal of Applied Psychology, 65,* 50–59.

Greguras, G. J., & Robie, C. (1998). A new look at within-source interrater reliability of 360-degree feedback ratings. *Journal of Applied Psychology, 83,* 960–968.

Greguras, G. J., Robie, C., Schleichea, D. J., & Goff, M. (2003). A field study of the effects of rating purpose on the quality of multisource ratings. *Personnel Psychology, 56,* 1–22.

Grigsby, D. M., & Bigoness, W. J. (1982). Effects of mediation and alternative forms of arbitration on bargaining behavior: A laboratory study. *Journal of Applied Psychology, 67,* 549–554.

Grover, S. L., & Crooker, K. J. (1995). Who appreciates family-responsive human resource policies: The impact of family-friendly policies on the organizational attachment of parents and non-parents. *Personnel Psychology, 48,* 271–288.

Guion, R. M. (1998a). *Assessment, measurement, and prediction for personnel decisions.* Mahwah, NJ: Erlbaum.

Guion, R. M. (1998b). Some virtues of dissatisfaction in the science and practice of personnel selection. *Human Resource Management Review, 8,* 351–366.

Gutek, B. A. (1985). *Sex and the workplace.* San Francisco: Jossey-Bass.

Gutman, A. (2002). Implications of 9/11 for the workplace. *The Industrial-Organizational Psychologist, 39(3),* 35–40.

Gutman, A. (2003). The *Grutter, Gratz, & Costa* rulings. *The Industrial-Organizational Psychologist, 41(2),* 117–127.

Gutman, A. (2004). Ground rules for adverse impact. *The Industrial-Organizational Psychologist, 41(3),* 109–119.

Guzzo, R. A. (1995). Introduction: At the intersection of team effectiveness and decision making. In R. A. Guzzo & E. Salas (Eds.), *Team effectiveness and decision making in organizations* (pp. 1–8). San Francisco: Jossey-Bass.

Guzzo, R. A., & Shea, G. P. (1992). Group performance and intergroup relations in organizations. In M. D. Dunnette & L. M. Hough (Eds.), *Handbook of industrial and orga-*

nizational psychology (2nd ed., Vol. 3, pp. 269–313). Palo Alto, CA: Consulting Psychologists Press.

Hackett, G. (1995). Self-efficacy in career choice and development. In A. Bandura (Ed.), *Self-efficacy in changing societies* (pp. 232–258). New York: Cambridge.

Hackman, J.P., & Wageman, R. (2007). Asking the right questions about leadership. *American Psychologist, 62,* 43–47.

Hackman, J. R., & Oldham, G. R. (1976). Motivation through the design of work: Test of a theory. *Organizational Behavior and Human Performance, 16,* 250–279.

Haladyna, T. M. (1999). *Developing and validating multiple-choice test items* (2nd ed.). Mahwah, NJ: Erlbaum.

Hall, G. S. (1917). Practical relations between psychology and the war. *Journal of Applied Psychology, 1,* 9–16.

Hall, G. S., Baird, J. W., & Geissler, L. R. (1917). Foreword. *Journal of Applied Psychology, 1,* 5–7.

Hammer, T. H., & Berman, M. (1981). The role of noneconomic factors in faculty union voting. *Journal of Applied Psychology, 66,* 415–421.

Hamner, W. C., & Smith, F. J. (1978). Work attitudes as predictors of unionization activity. *Journal of Applied Psychology, 63,* 415–421.

Handbook of human engineering data. (1949). Medford, MA: Tufts College and United States Naval Training Devices Center.

Haney, W. (1981). Validity, vaudeville, and values: A short history of social concerns over standardized testing. *American Psychologist, 36,* 1021–1034.

Harrell, T. W. (1992). Some history of the Army General Classification Test. *Journal of Applied Psychology, 77,* 875–878.

Harris, L. (2000). Procedural justice and perceptions of fairness in selection practice. *International Journal of Selection and Assessment, 8,* 148–157.

Harris, M. M. (2003). The Internet and I-O psychology: Lifeless mummy or sleeping giant? *The Industrial-Organizational Psychologist, 40(3),* 75–79.

Harris, M. M., Smith, D. E., & Champagne, D. (1995). A field study of performance appraisal purpose: Research- versus administrative-based ratings. *Personnel Psychology, 48,* 151–160.

Harris, M. M., & Trusty, M. L. (1997). Drug and alcohol programs in the workplace: A review of recent literature. In C. L. Cooper & I. T. Robertson (Eds.), *International review of industrial and organizational psychology* (Vol. 12, pp. 289–316). New York: Wiley.

Harrison, D.A., Kravitz, D.A., Mayer, D.M., Leslie, L.M., & Lev-Arey, D. (2006). Understanding attitudes toward affirmitive action programs in employment: Survey and meta-analysis of 35 years of research. *Journal of Applied Psychology, 91,* 1013–1036.

Hart, P. M., & Cooper, C. L. (2001). Occupational stress: Toward a more integrated framework. In N. Anderson, D. S. Ones, H. K. Sinangil, & C. Viswesvaran (Eds.), *Handbook of industrial, work, and organisational psychology* (Vol. 2, pp. 93–114). London: Sage.

Hartley, J. F. (1992). The psychology of industrial relations. In C. L. Cooper & I. T. Robertson (Eds.), *International review of industrial and organizational psychology* (Vol. 7, pp. 201–243). London: Wiley.

Harvey, R. J. (1991). Job analysis. In M. D. Dunnette & L. M. Hough (Eds.), *Handbook of industrial and organizational psychology* (2nd ed., Vol. 2, pp. 71–163). Palo Alto, CA: Consulting Psychologists Press.

Harvey, R. J., & Lozada-Larsen, S. R. (1988). Influence of amount of job descriptive information on job analysis rating accuracy. *Journal of Applied Psychology, 73,* 457–461.

Hattrup, K., Rock, J., & Scalia, C. (1997). The effects of varying conceptualizations of job performance on adverse impact, minority hiring, and predicted performance. *Journal of Applied Psychology, 82,* 656–664.

Hauerstein, N. M. (1998). Training raters to increase the accuracy of appraisals and the usefulness of feedback. In J. W. Smither (Ed.), *Performance appraisal* (pp. 404–444). San Francisco: Jossey-Bass.

Hausknecht, J.P., Halpert, J.A., Di Paolo, N.T., & Gerrard, M.O. (2007). Retesting in selection: A meta-analysis of coaching and practice effects for tests of cognitive ability. *Journal of Applied Psychology, 92,* 373–385.

Hedge, J. W., & Kavanagh, M. J. (1988). Improving the accuracy of performance evaluations: Comparison of three methods of performance appraisal training. *Journal of Applied Psychology, 73,* 68–73.

Hedge, J. W., & Pulakos, E. D. (2002). Grappling with implementation: Some preliminary thoughts and relevant research. In J. W. Hedge & E. D. Pulakos (Eds.), *Implementing organizational interventions: Steps, processes, and best practices* (pp. 1–11). San Francisco: Jossey-Bass.

Hedlund, J., & Sternberg, R. J. (2000). Practical intelligence: Implications for human resources research. In G. R. Ferris (Ed.), *Research in personnel and human resources management* (Vol. 19, pp. 1–52). New York: Elsevier.

Heilman, M. E. (1996). Affirmative actions' contradictory consequences. *Journal of Social Issues, 52(4),* 105–109.

Heilman, M. E., & Alcott, V. B. (2001). What I think you think of me: Women's reactions to being viewed as beneficiaries of preferential selection. *Journal of Applied Psychology, 86,* 574–582.

Heilman, M. E., Block, C. J., & Lucas, J. A. (1992). Presumed incompetent? Stigmatization and affirmative action efforts. *Journal of Applied Psychology, 77,* 536–544.

Heilman, M.E., & Chen, J.J. (2005). Same behavior, different consequences: Reactions to men's and women's altruistic citizenship behavior. *Journal of Applied Psychology, 90,* 431–441.

Hemphill, H., & Haines, R. (1997). *Discrimination, harassment, and the failure of diversity training.* Westport, CT: Quorum.

Heneman, R. L., & Greenberger, D. B. (Eds.). (2002). *Human resource management in virtual organizations.* Greenwich, CT: Information Age.

Hepburn, C. G., & Barling, J. (2001). To vote or not to vote: Abstaining from voting in union representation elections. *Journal of Organizational Behavior, 22,* 569–591.

Hershcovis, M.S., Turner, N. Barling, J., Arnold, K.A., Dupre, K.E., Inness, M., LeBlanc, M.M., & Sivanathan, N. (2007). Predicting workplace aggression: A meta-analysis. *Journal of Applied Psychology, 92,* 228–238.

Hesketh, B. (2001). Adapting vocational psychology to cope with change. *Journal of Vocational Behavior, 59,* 203–212.

Heslin, P.A., Latham, G.P., & VandeWalle, D. (2005). The effect of implicit person theory on performance appraisals. *Journal of Applied Psychology, 90,* 842–856.

Hicks, W. D., & Klimoski, R. J. (1981). The impact of flexitime on employee attitudes. *Academy of Management Journal, 24,* 333–341.

Highhouse, S. (1999). The brief history of personnel counseling in industrial-organizational psychology. *Journal of Vocational Behavior, 55,* 318–336.

Highhouse, S. (2007a). Applications of organizational psychology: Learning through failure or failure to learn? In L.L. Koppes (Ed.), *Historical perspectives in industrial and organizational psychology* (pp. 331–352). Mahwah, NJ: Erlbaum.

Highhouse, S. (2007b). Where did this name come from anyway? A brief history of the I-O label. *The Industrial-Organizational Psychologist, 45(1),* 53–56.

Highhouse, S., Stierwalt, S., Bachiochi, P., Elder, A. E., & Fisher, G. (1999). Effects of advertised human resource management practices on attraction of African American applicants. *Personnel Psychology, 52,* 425–442.

Hindo, B. (2007). At 3M, a struggle between efficiency and creativity. *Businessweek,* June 11, 8–14.

Hoffman, C. C. (1999). Generalizing physical ability test validity: A case study using test transportability, validity generalization, and construct-related validation evidence. *Personnel Psychology, 52,* 1019–1041.

Hoffman, C. C., Holden, L. M., & Gale, K. (2000). So many jobs, so little "N": Applying expanded validation methods to support generalization of cognitive test validity. *Personnel Psychology, 53*, 955–991.

Hoffman, C. C., & McPhail, S. M. (1998). Exploring options for supporting test use in situations precluding local validation. *Personnel Psychology, 51*, 987–1003.

Hoffman, C. C., & Thornton, G. C. (1997). Examining selection utility where competing predictors differ in adverse impact. *Personnel Psychology, 50*, 455–470.

Hofstede, G. (1980). *Culture's consequences: International differences in work-related values.* Beverly Hills, CA: Sage.

Hofstede, G. (2001). *Culture's consequences* (2nd ed.): *Comparing values, behaviors, institutions, and organizations across nations.* Thousand Oaks, CA: Sage.

Hofstee, W. K. (2001). Intelligence and personality: Do they mix? In J. M. Collis & S. Messick (Eds.), *Intelligence and personality: Bridging the gap in theory and measurement* (pp. 43–60). Mahwah, NJ: Erlbaum.

Hogan, J. (1991). Structure of physical performance in organizational tasks. *Journal of Applied Psychology, 76*, 495–507.

Hogan, J., Barrett, P., & Hogan, R. (2007). Personality measurement, faking, and employment selection. *Journal of Applied Psychology, 92*, 1270–1285.

Hogan, J., & Brinkmeyer, K. (1997). Bridging the gap between overt and personality-based integrity tests. *Personnel Psychology, 50*, 587–600.

Hogan, R. T. (1991). Personality and personality measurement. In M. D. Dunnette & L. M. Hough (Eds.), *Handbook of industrial and organizational psychology* (2nd ed., Vol. 2, pp. 873–919). Palo Alto, CA: Consulting Psychologists Press.

Hogan, R. T., Curphy, G. J., & Hogan, J. (1994). What we know about leadership: Effectiveness and personality. *American Psychologist, 49*, 493–504.

Hogan, R. T., & Hogan, J. (1992). *Hogan Personality Inventory.* Tulsa, OK: Hogan Assessment Systems.

Hogan, R. T., Hogan, J., & Roberts, B. W. (1996). Personality measurement and employment decisions: Questions and answers. *American Psychologist, 51*, 469–477.

Hogan, R. T., Raskin, R., & Fazzini, D. (1990). The dark side of charisma. In K. E. Clark & M. B. Clark (Eds.), *Measures of leadership.* West Orange, NJ: Leadership Library of America.

Hollenbeck, J. R., LePine, J. A., & Ilgen, D. R. (1996). Adapting to roles in decision-making teams. In K. R. Murphy (Ed.), *Individual differences and behaviors in organizations* (pp. 300–333). San Francisco: Jossey-Bass.

Hollenbeck, J. R., Williams, C. R., & Klein, H. J. (1989). An empirical examination of the antecedents of commitment to difficult goals. *Journal of Applied Psychology, 74*, 18–23.

Hollinger, R. C. (1988). Working under the influence (WUI): Correlates of employees' use of alcohol and other drugs. *Journal of Applied Behavioral Science, 24*, 439–454.

Hollinger, R., & Clark, J. (1983). *Theft by employees.* Lexington, MA: Lexington Books.

Holton, E. F., & Baldwin, T. T. (2003). Making transfer happen: An active perspective on learning transfer systems. In E. F. Holton & T. T. Baldwin (Eds.), *Improving learning transfer in organizations* (pp. 3–15). San Francisco: Jossey-Bass.

Holzbach, R. L. (1978). Rater bias in performance ratings: Superior, self-, and peer assessments. *Journal of Applied Psychology, 63*, 579–588.

Hom, P. W., & Griffeth, R. W. (1995). *Employee turnover.* Cincinnati, OH: South-Western.

Hom, P. W., & Kinicki, A. J. (2001). Toward a greater understanding of how dissatisfaction drives employee turnover. *Academy of Management Journal, 44*, 975–987.

Honts, C. R. (1991). The emperor's new clothes: Application of polygraph tests in the American workplace. *Forensic Reports, 4*, 91–116.

Honts, C. R., & Amato, S. L. (2002). Countermeasures. In M. Kleiner (Ed.), *Handbook of polygraph testing* (pp. 251–264). San Diego: Academic Press.

House, R. J., Hanges, P. J., Javidan, M., Dorman, P. W., & Gupta, V. (Eds.). (2004). *Culture, leadership, and organizations: The GLOBE study of 62 societies.* Thousand Oaks, CA: Sage.

House, R. J., Spangler, W. D., & Woycke, J. (1991). Personality and charisma in the U.S. presidency: A psychological theory of leader effectiveness. *Administrative Science Quarterly, 36*, 364–396.

Howard, A., & Lowman, R. L. (1985). Should industrial/organizational psychologists be licensed? *American Psychologist, 40*, 40–47.

Howell, J. P., & Dorfman, P. W. (1981). Substitutes for leadership: Test of a construct. *Academy of Management Journal, 24*, 714–728.

Howell, W. C., & Cooke, N. J. (1989). Training the human information processor: A review of cognitive models. In I. L. Goldstein (Ed.), *Training and development in organizations* (pp. 121–182). San Francisco: Jossey-Bass.

Huffcutt, A. I., Conway, J. M., Ruth, P. L., & Stone, N. J. (2001). Identification and meta-analytic assessment of psychological constructs measured in employment interviews. *Journal of Applied Psychology, 86*, 897–913.

Huffcutt, A. I., & Roth, P. L. (1998). Racial group differences in employment interview evaluations. *Journal of Applied Psychology, 83*, 179–189.

Hui, C., Lam, S. S., & Law, K. S. (2000). Instrumental values of organizational citizenship behavior for promotion: A field quasi-experiment. *Journal of Applied Psychology, 85*, 822–828.

Hulin, C. (1991). Adaptation, persistence, and commitment in organizations. In M. D. Dunnette & L. M. Hough (Eds.), *Handbook of industrial and organizational psychology* (2nd ed., Vol. 2, pp. 445–505). Palo Alto, CA: Consulting Psychologists Press.

Hulin, C. (2001). Applied psychology and science: Differences between research and practice. *Applied Psychology: An International Review, 50*, 225–234.

Hulin, C. L., & Judge, T. A. (2003). Job attitudes. In W. C. Borman, D. R. Ilgen, & R. J. Klimoski (Eds.), *Handbook of psychology* (Vol. 12): *Industrial and organizational psychology* (pp. 255–276). Hoboken, NJ: Wiley.

Humphrey, S.E., Nahrgang, J.D., & Morgeson, F.P. (2007). Integrating motivational, social, and contextual work design features: A meta-analytic summary of theoretical extensions of the work design literature. *Journal of Applied Psychology, 92*, 1332–1356.

Hunt, D. M., & Michael, C. (1983). Mentorship: A career training and development tool. *Academy of Management Review, 8*, 475–485.

Hunter, J. E., & Schmidt, F. L. (1990). *Method of meta-analysis: Correcting error and bias in research findings.* Newbury Park, CA: Sage.

Hunter, J. E., & Schmidt, F. L. (1996). Cumulative research knowledge and social policy formation: The critical role of meta-analysis. *Psychology, Public Policy, and Law, 2*, 324–347.

Hurtz, G. M., & Donovan, J. J. (2000). Personality and job performance: The big five revisited. *Journal of Applied Psychology, 85*, 869–879.

Huszczo, G. E., Wiggins, J. G., & Currie, J. S. (1984). The relationship between psychology and organized labor: Past, present and future. *American Psychologist, 39*, 432–440.

Iaffaldano, M. T., & Muchinsky, P. M. (1985). Job satisfaction and performance: A meta-analysis. *Psychological Bulletin, 97*, 251–273.

Ilgen, D. R. (1999). Teams embedded in organizations: Some implications. *American Psychologist, 54*, 129–139.

Ilgen, D. R., Barnes-Farrell, J. L., & McKellin, D. B. (1993). Performance appraisal process research in the 1980s: What has it contributed to appraisals in use? *Organizational Behavior and Human Decision Processes, 54*, 321–368.

Ilgen, D. R., Fisher, C. D., & Taylor, M. S. (1979). Motivational consequences of individual feedback on behavior in organizations. *Journal of Applied Psychology, 64*, 349–371.

Ilgen, D. R., Peterson, R. B., Martin, B. A., & Boeschen, D. A. (1981). Supervisor and subordinate reactions to performance appraisal sessions. *Organizational Behavior and Human Performance, 28*, 311–330.

Ilgen, D. R., & Pulakos, E. D. (1999). Employee performance in today's organizations. In D. R. Ilgen & E. D. Pulakos (Eds.), *The changing nature of performance* (pp. 1–18). San Francisco: Jossey-Bass.

Ilies, R., Arvey, R.D., & Bouchard, T.J. (2006). Darwinism, behavioral genetics, and organizational behavior: A review and agenda for future research. *Journal of Organizational Behavior, 27*, 121–141.

Ilies, R., & Judge, T. A. (2003). On the heritability of job satisfaction: The mediating role of personality. *Journal of Applied Psychology, 88*, 750–759.

Ilies, R., & Judge, T.A. (2005). Goal regulation across time: The effects of feedback and affect. *Journal of Applied Psychology, 90*, 453–467.

Inness, M., Barling, J., & Turner, N. (2005). Understanding supervisor-targeted aggression: A within person, between-jobs design. *Journal of Applied Psychology, 90*, 731–739.

International Labour Organization (2003). *The employment effects of mergers and acquisitions in commerce.* Geneva: Author.

International Labour Organization. (2004). *Helping hands or shackled lives? Understanding child domestic labour and responses to it.* Geneva: Author.

Jackson, C. L., & LePine, J. A. (2003). Peer responses to a team's weakest link: A test and extension of LePine and Van Dyne's model. *Journal of Applied Psychology, 88*, 459–475.

Jahoda, M. (1981). Work, employment, and unemployment: Values, theories and approaches in social research. *American Psychologist, 36*, 184–191.

Jamal, M. (1981). Shift work related to job attitudes, social participation, and withdrawal behavior. A study of nurses and industrial workers. *Personnel Psychology, 34*, 535–548.

Jamal, M., & Jamal, S. M. (1982). Work and nonwork experiences of employees on fixed and rotating shifts: An empirical assessment. *Journal of Vocational Behavior, 20*, 282–293.

James, L.R. (1998). Measurement of personality by conditional reasoning tests. *Organizational Behavior Research, 1*, 131–163.

Janz, B. D., Colquitt, J. A., & Noe, R. A. (1997). Knowledge worker team effectiveness: The role of autonomy, interdependence, team development, and contextual support variables. *Personnel Psychology, 50*, 877–904.

Jarrell, S. B., & Stanley, T. D. (1990). A meta-analysis of the union–nonunion wage gap. *Industrial and Labor Relations Review, 44*, 54–67.

Jawahar, I. M., & Williams, C. R. (1997). Where all the children are above average: The performance appraisal purpose effect. *Personnel Psychology, 50*, 905–925.

Jayne, M. E., & Rauschenberger, J. M. (2000). Demonstrating the value of selection in organizations. In J. F. Kehoe (Ed.), *Managing selection in changing organizations* (pp. 123–157). San Francisco: Jossey-Bass.

Jeanneret, P. R., D'Egidio, E. L., & Hanson, M. A. (2004). Assessment and development opportunities using the Occupational Information Network (O*NET). In J. C. Thomas (Ed.), *Comprehensive handbook of psychological assessment* (Vol. 4, pp. 192–202). Hoboken, NJ: Wiley.

Jehn, K. A., Northcraft, G. B., & Neale, M. A. (1999). Why differences make a difference: A field study of diversity, conflict, and performance in workgroups. *Administrative Science Quarterly, 44*, 741–763.

Jelley, R. B., & Goffin, R. D. (2001). Can performance-feedback accuracy be improved? Effects of rater priming and rating-scale format on rating accuracy. *Journal of Applied Psychology, 86*, 134–144.

Jenkins, J. G. (1946). Validity for what? *Journal of Consulting Psychology, 10*, 93–98.

Johns, G. (1994). How often were you absent? A review of the use of self-reported absence data. *Journal of Applied Psychology, 79*, 574–591.

Johns, G. (1997). Contemporary research on absence from work: Correlates, causes, and consequences. In C. L. Cooper & I. T. Robertson (Eds.), *International review of industrial and organizational psychology* (Vol. 12, pp. 115–173). Chichester: Wiley.

Johnson, J. W. (2001). The relative importance of task and contextual performance dimensions to supervisor judgments of overall performance. *Journal of Applied Psychology, 86*, 984–996.

Johnson, J. W. (2003). Toward a better understanding of the relationship between personality and individual job performance. In M. R. Barrick & A. M. Ryan (Eds.), *Personality and work: Reconsidering the role of personality in organizations* (pp. 83–120). San Francisco: Jossey-Bass.

Johnson, P. R., & Indvik, J. (1994). Workplace violence: An issue of the nineties. *Public Personnel Management, 23*, 515–523.

Jones, F., Burke, R.J., & Westman, M. (2006). Work and life: The road ahead. In F. Jones, R.J. Burke, & M. Westman (Eds.), *Work-life balance: A psychological perspective.* Hove, UK: Taylor & Francis.

Jones, N. (1994). The alcohol and drug provisions of the ADA: Implications for employers and employees.

In S. M. Bruyere & J. O'Keeffe (Eds.), *Implications of the Americans with Disabilities Act for psychology* (pp. 151–168). New York: Springer.

Jonson, J. L., & Plake, B. S. (1998). A historical comparison of validity standards and validity practices. *Educational and Psychological Measurement, 58*, 736–753.

Judge, T. A., Bono, J. E., Ilies, R., & Gerhardt, M. W. (2002). Personality and leadership: A qualitative and quantitative review. *Journal of Applied Psychology, 87*, 765–780.

Judge, T. A., Heller, D., & Mount, M. K. (2002). Five-factor model of personality and job satisfaction: A meta-analysis. *Journal of Applied Psychology, 87*, 530–541.

Judge, T. A., Higgins, C. A., & Cable, D. M. (2000). The employment interview: A review of recent research and recommendations for future research. *Human Resource Management Review, 10*, 383–406.

Judge, T. A., Higgins, C. A., Thoresen, C. J., & Barrick, M. R. (1999). The big five personality traits, general mental ability, and career success across the life span. *Personnel Psychology, 52*, 621–652.

Judge, T. A., Parker, S. K., Colbert, A. E., Heller, D., & Ilies, R. (2001). Job satisfaction: A cross-cultural review. In N. Anderson, D. S. Ones, H. K. Sinangil, & C. Viswesvaran (Eds.), *Handbook of industrial, work, and organisational psychology* (Vol. 2, pp. 25–52). London: Sage.

Judge, T. A., Piccolo, R. F., & Ilies, R. (2004). The forgotten ones? The validity of consideration and initiating structure in leadership research. *Journal of Applied Psychology, 89*, 36–51.

Judge, T.A., Scott, B.A., & Ilies, R. (2006). Hostility, job attitudes, and workplace deviance: Test of a multilevel model. *Journal of Applied Psychology, 91*, 126–138.

Judge, T. A., Thoresen, C. J., Bono, J. E., & Patton, G. K. (2001). The job satisfaction–job performance relationship: A qualitative and quantitative review. *Psychological Bulletin, 127*, 376–407.

Kabanoff, B. (1997). Organizational justice across cultures: Integrating organization-level and culture-level perspectives. In P. C. Earley & M. Erez (Eds.), *New perspectives on international industrial/organizational psychology* (pp. 676–712). San Francisco: New Lexington Press.

Kagitcibasi, C., & Berry, J. W. (1989). Cross-cultural psychology: Current research and trends. *Annual Review of Psychology, 40*, 493–531.

Kane, J. S., Bernardin, H. J., Villanova, P., & Peyrefitte, J. (1995). Stability of rater leniency: Three studies. *Academy of Management Journal, 38*, 1036–1051.

Kanfer, R. (1992). Work motivation: New directions in theory and research. In C. L. Cooper & I. T. Robertson

(Eds.), *International review of industrial and organizational psychology* (Vol. 7, pp. 1–53). London: Wiley.

Kanfer, R., & Ackerman, P. L. (1989). Motivation and cognitive abilities: An integrative/aptitude–treatment interaction approach to skill acquisition. *Journal of Applied Psychology, 74,* 657–690.

Kanfer, R., & Ackerman, P. L. (2000). Individual differences in work motivation: Further explorations of a trait framework. *Applied Psychology: An International Review, 49,* 470–482.

Kanfer, R., & Ackerman, P. L. (2004). Aging, adult development and work motivation. *Academy of Management Review, 29,* 440–458.

Kanfer, R., & Heggestad, E. D. (1997). Motivational traits and skills: A person-centered approach to work motivation. In B. M. Staw & L. L. Cummings (Eds.), *Research in organizational behavior* (Vol. 19, pp. 1–56). Greenwich, CT: JAI Press.

Kanungo, R. N. (1982). Measurement of job and work involvement. *Journal of Applied Psychology, 67,* 341–349.

Karambayya, R., & Reilly, A. H. (1992). Dual earner couples: Attitudes and actions restructuring work for family. *Journal of Organizational Behavior, 13,* 585–601.

Karau, S. J., & Williams, K. D. (2001). Understanding individual motivation in groups: The collective effort model. In M. E. Turner (Ed.), *Groups at work* (pp. 113–142). Mahwah, NJ: Erlbaum.

Kark, R., Shamir, B., & Chang, G. (2003). The two faces of transformational leadership: Empowerment and dependency. *Journal of Applied Psychology, 88,* 246–255.

Katzell, R. A., & Austin, J. T. (1992). From then to now: The development of industrial-organizational psychology in the United States. *Journal of Applied Psychology, 77,* 803–835.

Keeping, L. M., & Levy, P. E. (2000). Performance appraisal reaction: Measurement, modeling, and method bias. *Journal of Applied Psychology, 85,* 708–723.

Kehoe, J. F. (2000). Research and practice in selection. In J. F. Kehoe (Ed.), *Managing selection in changing organizations* (pp. 397–437). San Francisco: Jossey-Bass.

Kehoe, J. F. (2002). General mental ability and selection in private sector organizations. A commentary. *Human Performance, 15,* 96–106.

Keinan, G., & Eilat-Greenberg, S. (1993). Can stress be measured by handwriting analysis? The effectiveness of the analytic method. *Applied Psychology: An International Review, 42,* 153–170.

Kelleher, M. D. (1996). *New arenas for violence: Homicide in the American workplace.* Westport, CT: Praeger.

Kelloway, E. K., Catano, V. M., & Carroll, A. E. (1995). The nature of member participation in local union activities. In L. E. Tetrick & J. Barling (Eds.), *Changing employment relations* (pp. 333–348). Washington, DC: American Psychological Association.

Kelly, J. E., & Kelly, C. (1991). "Them and us": Social psychology and "The new industrial relations." *British Journal of Industrial Relations, 29,* 25–48.

Kennedy, C. W., Fossum, J. A., & White, B. J. (1983). An empirical comparison of within-subjects and between-subjects expectancy theory models. *Organizational Behavior and Human Performance, 32,* 124–143.

Kerr, S. (1995). On the folly of rewarding A, while hoping for B. *Academy of Management Executive, 9,* 7–14.

Kerr, S., & Jermier, J. M. (1978). Substitutes for leadership: Their meaning and measurement. *Organizational Behavior and Human Performance, 22,* 375–403.

Khanna, C., & Medsker, G.J. (2007). 2006 income and employment survey results for the Society for Industrial and Organizational Psychology. *The Industrial-Organizational Psychologist, 45(1),* 17–32.

Kidd, S. A. (2002). The role of qualitative research in psychological journals. *Psychological Methods, 7,* 126–138.

Kilburg, R. R. (2000). *Executive coaching: Developing managerial wisdom in a world of chaos.* Washington, DC: American Psychological Association.

King, J. L., & Alexander, D. G. (1996). Unions respond to violence on the job. In G. R. VandenBos & E. Q. Bulatao (Eds.), *Violence on the job* (pp. 315–326). Washington, DC: American Psychological Association.

Kinicki, A. J., McKee-Ryan, F. M., Schriesheim, C. A., & Carson, K. P. (2002). Assessing the construct validity of the Job Descriptive Index: A review and meta-analysis. *Journal of Applied Psychology, 87,* 14–32.

Kirk, R. E. (1996). Practical significance: A concept whose time has come. *Educational and Psychological Measurement, 56,* 746–759.

Kirkpatrick, S. A., & Locke, E. A. (1991). Leadership: Do traits matter? *Academy of Management Executive, 5(2),* 48–60.

Klaas, B. S. (1989). Managerial decision making about employee grievances: The impact of the grievant's work history. *Personnel Psychology, 42,* 53–68.

Klahr, D., & Simon, H. A. (1999). Studies of scientific discovery: Complementary approaches and convergent findings. *Psychological Bulletin, 125,* 524–543.

Klandermans, B. (1989). Union commitment: Replications and tests in the Dutch context. *Journal of Applied Psychology, 74,* 869–875.

Klehe, U-C., & Anderson, N. (2007). Working hard and working smart: Motivation and ability during typical and maximum performance. *Journal of Applied Psychology, 92,* 978–992.

Klein, H. J., Wesson, M. J., Hollenbeck, J. R., & Alge, B. J. (1999). Goal commitment and the goal-setting process: Conceptual clarification and empirical synthesis. *Journal of Applied Psychology, 84*, 885–896.

Klein, K. J., & Kozlowski, S. W. (2000). *Multilevel theory, research, and methods in organizations.* San Francisco: Jossey-Bass.

Klimoski, R. J., & Donahue, L. M. (2001). Person perception in organizations: An overview of the field. In M. London (Ed.), *How people evaluate others in organizations* (pp. 5–44). Mahwah, NJ: Erlbaum.

Klimoski, R. J., & Inks, L. (1990). Accountability forces in performance appraisal. *Organizational Behavior and Human Decision Processes, 45*, 194–208.

Klimoski, R. J., & Jones, R. G. (1995). Staffing for effective group decision making: Key issues in marketing people and teams. In R. A. Guzzo & E. Salas (Eds.), *Team effectiveness and decision making in organizations* (pp. 291–332). San Francisco: Jossey-Bass.

Klimoski, R. J., & Palmer, S. N. (1994). The ADA and the hiring process in organizations. In S. M. Bruyere & J. O'Keeffe (Eds.), *Implications of the Americans with Disabilities Act for psychology* (pp. 37–84). New York: Springer.

Klimoski, R. J., & Strickland, W. J. (1977). Assessment centers—Valid or merely prescient? *Personnel Psychology, 30*, 353–361.

Kluger, A. N. (2001). Feedback-expectation discrepancy, arousal and locus of cognition. In M. Erez, U. Kleinbeck, & H. Thierry (Eds.), *Work motivation in the context of a globalizing economy* (pp. 111–120). Mahwah, NJ: Erlbaum.

Kluger, A. N., & DeNisi, A. (1996). The effects of feedback interventions on performance: A historical review, a meta-analysis, and a preliminary feedback intervention theory. *Psychological Bulletin, 119*, 254–284.

Kluger, A. N., Reilly, R. R., & Russell, C. J. (1991). Faking biodata tests: Are option-keyed instruments more resistant? *Journal of Applied Psychology, 76*, 889–896.

Knauth, P. (1996). Designing better shift systems. *Applied Ergonomics, 27*, 39–44.

Kohn, L. S., & Dipboye, R. L. (1998). The effects of interview structure on recruiting outcomes. *Journal of Applied Social Psychology, 28*, 821–843.

Kolmstetter, E. (2003). I-O's making an impact: TSA transportation security screener skill standards, selection system, and hiring process. *The Industrial-Organizational Psychologist, 40(4)*, 39–46.

Komaki, J. L. (1986). Toward effective supervision: An operant analysis and comparison of managers at work. *Journal of Applied Psychology, 71*, 270–279.

Komaki, J. L. (1998). When performance improvement is the goal: A new set of criteria for criteria. *Journal of Applied Behavior Analysis, 31*, 263–280.

Koppes, L. L. (1997). American female pioneers of industrial and organizational psychology during the early years. *Journal of Applied Psychology, 82*, 500–515.

Koppes, L. L. (2002). The rise of industrial-organizational psychology: A confluence of dynamic forces. In D. K. Freedheim (Ed.), *History of Psychology* (pp. 367–389). New York: Wiley.

Koppes, L.L. (Ed.) (2007). *Historical perspectives in industrial and organizational psychology.* Mahwah, NJ: Erlbaum.

Koppes, L.L., & Pickren, W. (2007). Industrial and organizational psychology: An evolving science and practice. In L.L. Koppes (Ed.), *Historical perspectives in industrial and organizational psychology* (pp. 3–35). Mahwah, NJ: Erlbaum.

Kornhauser, A. W. (1965). *Mental health of the industrial worker: A Detroit study.* New York: Wiley.

Kossek, E. E., & Ozeki, C. (1998). Work–family conflict, policies, and the job–life satisfaction relationship: A review and directions for organizational behavior–human resources research. *Journal of Applied Psychology, 83*, 139–149.

Kotter, J. P. (1988). *The leadership factor.* New York: Free Press.

Kouzes, J. M., & Posner, B. Z. (1995). *The leadership challenge.* San Francisco: Jossey-Bass.

Kozlowski, S. W., & Bell, B. S. (2003). Work groups and teams in organizations. In W. C. Borman, D. R. Ilgen, & R. J. Klimoski (Eds.), *Handbook of psychology* (Vol. 12): *Industrial and organizational psychology* (pp. 333–375). Hoboken, NJ: Wiley.

Kozlowski, S. W., Chao, G. T., & Morrison, R. F. (1998). Games raters play: Politics, strategies, and impression management in performance appraisal. In J. W. Smither (Ed.), *Performance appraisal* (pp. 163–208). San Francisco: Jossey-Bass.

Kraiger, K. (2003). Perspective on training and development. In W. C. Borman, D. R. Ilgen, & R. K. Klimoski (Eds.), *Handbook of psychology* (Vol. 12): *Industrial and organizational psychology* (pp. 171–192). Hoboken, NJ: Wiley.

Kraiger, K., & Aguinis, H. (2001). Training effectiveness: Assessing training needs, motivation, and accomplishments. In M. London (Ed.), *How people evaluate others in organizations* (pp. 203–220). Mahwah, NJ: Erlbaum.

Kraiger, K., & Ford, J.K. (2007). The expanding role of workplace training: Themes and trends influencing training research and practice. In L.L. Koppes (Ed.),

Historical perspectives in industrial and organizational psychology (pp. 281–309). Mahwah, NJ: Erlbaum.

Kraiger, K., & Jung, K. M. (1997). Linking training objectives to evaluation criteria. In M. A. Quinones & A. Ehrenstein (Eds.), *Training for a rapidly changing workplace* (pp. 151–176). Washington, DC: American Psychological Association.

Kram, K. E., & Isabella, L. A. (1985). Alternatives to mentoring: The role of peer relationships in career development. *Academy of Management Journal, 28,* 110–132.

Krapohl, D. J. (2002). The polygraph in personnel screening. In M. Kleiner (Ed.), *Handbook of polygraph testing* (pp. 217–236). San Diego: Academic Press.

Kravitz, D. A., & Klineberg, S. L. (2000). Reactions to two versions of affirmative action among Whites, Blacks, and Hispanics. *Journal of Applied Psychology, 85,* 597–611.

Kristof-Brown, A.L., & Jansen, K.J. (2007). Issues of person-organization fit. In C. Ostroff & T.A. Judge (Eds.), *Perspectives on organizational fit* (pp. 123–153). Mahwah, NJ: Erlbaum.

Kuncel, N.R., & Klieger, D.M. (2007). Application patterns when applicants know the odds: Implications for selection research and practice. *Journal of Applied Psychology, 92,* 586–593.

Ladd, R. T., Gordon, M. E., Beauvais, L. L., & Morgan, R. L. (1982). Union commitment: Replication and extension. *Journal of Applied Psychology, 67,* 640–644.

Lam, S. S., Hui, C., & Law, K. S. (1999). Organizational citizenship behavior: Comparing perspectives of supervisors and subordinates across four international samples. *Journal of Applied Psychology, 84,* 594–601.

Lance, C. E., LaPointe, J. A., & Fisicaro, S. A. (1994). Tests of three causal models of halo rater error. *Organizational Behavior and Human Decision Processes, 57,* 83–96.

Landy, F. J. (1992). Hugo Münsterberg: Victim or visionary? *Journal of Applied Psychology, 77,* 787–802.

Landy, F. J. (1997). Early influences on the development of industrial and organizational psychology. *Journal of Applied Psychology, 82,* 467–477.

Landy, F. J., & Vasey, J. (1991). Job analysis: The composition of SME samples. *Personnel Psychology, 44,* 27–50.

Larson, C. E., & La Fasto, F. M. (1989). *Teamwork.* Newbury Park, CA: Sage.

Latham, G. P. (1986). Job performance and appraisal. In C. L. Cooper & I. T. Robertson (Eds.), *International review of industrial and organizational psychology* (Vol. 1, pp. 117–155). London: Wiley.

Latham, G. P. (2001). The reciprocal transfer of learning from journals to practice. *Applied Psychology: An International Review, 50,* 201–211.

Latham, G. P., & Baldes, J. J. (1975). The practical significance of Locke's theory of goal setting. *Journal of Applied Psychology, 60,* 122–124.

Latham, G.P., & Budworth, M-H. (2007). The study of work motivation in the 20th century. In L.L. Koppes (Ed.), *Historical perspectives in industrial and organizational psychology* (pp. 353–381). Mahwah, NJ: Erlbaum.

Latham, G. P., & Finnegan, B. J. (1993). Perceived practicality of instructional, patterned, and situational interviews. In H. Schuler, J. L. Farr, & M. Smith (Eds.), *Personnel selection and assessment* (pp. 41–56). Hillsdale, NJ: Erlbaum.

Latham, G. P., & Kinne, S. B. (1974). Improving job performance through training in goal setting. *Journal of Applied Psychology, 59,* 187–191.

Latham, G. P., & Locke, E. A. (1991). Self-regulation through goal-setting. *Organizational Behavior and Human Decision Processes, 50,* 212–247.

Latham, G. P., & Marshall, H. A. (1982). The effects of self-set, participatively set, and assigned goals on the performance of government employees. *Personnel Psychology, 35,* 399–404.

Latham, G. P., Skarlicki, D., Irvine, D., & Siegel, J. P. (1993). The increasing importance of performance appraisals to employee effectiveness in organizational settings in North America. In C. L. Cooper & I. T. Robertson (Eds.), *International review of industrial and organizational psychology* (Vol. 8, pp. 87–132). London: Wiley.

Latham, G. P., Wexley, K. N., & Pursell, E. D. (1975). Training managers to minimize rating errors in the observation of behavior. *Journal of Applied Psychology, 60,* 550–555.

Law, K. S., Wong, C-S., & Song, L. J. (2004). The construct and criterion validity of emotional intelligence and its potential utility for management studies. *Journal of Applied Psychology, 89,* 483–496.

Lazarus, R. S., & Lazarus, B. N. (1994). *Passion and reason: Making sense of our emotions.* New York: Oxford.

LeBreton, J.M., Barksdale, C.D. Robin, J.D., & James, L.R. (2007). Measurement issues associated with conditional reasoning tests: Indirect measurement and test faking. *Journal of Applied Psychology, 92,* 1–16.

Lee, K., & Allen, N. J. (2002). Organizational citizenship behavior and workplace violence: The role of affect and cognitions. *Journal of Applied Psychology, 87,* 131–142.

Lee, K., Carswell, J. J., & Allen, N. J. (2000). A meta-analytic review of organizational commitment: Relations with person- and work-related variables. *Journal of Applied Psychology, 85,* 799–811.

Lee, T. W., Mitchell, T. R., & Sablynski, C. J. (1999). Qualitative research in organizational and vocational psychology, 1979–1999. *Journal of Vocational Behavior, 55,* 161–187.

Lefkowitz, J. (2003). *Ethics and values in industrial-organizational psychology.* Mahwah, NJ: Erlbaum.

LePine, J. A. (2003). Team adaptation and postchange performance: Effects of team composition in terms of members' cognitive ability and personality. *Journal of Applied Psychology, 88,* 27–39.

LePine, J. A., Colquitt, J. A., & Erez, A. (2000). Adaptability to changing task contexts: Effects of general cognitive ability, conscientiousness, and openness to experience. *Personnel Psychology, 53,* 563–593.

LePine, J. A., Erez, A., & Johnson, D. E. (2002). The nature and dimensionality of organizational citizenship behavior: A critical review and meta-analysis. *Journal of Applied Psychology, 87,* 52–65.

LePine, J. A., Hansom, M. A., Borman, W. C., & Motowidlo, S. J. (2000). Contextual performance and teamwork: Implications for staffing. In G. R. Ferris (Ed.), *Research in personnel and human resources management* (Vol. 19, pp. 53–90). New York: Elsevier.

Leung, K. (1997). Negotiation and reward allocations across cultures. In P. C. Earley & M. Erez (Eds.), *New perspectives on international industrial/organizational psychology* (pp. 640–675). San Francisco: New Lexington Press.

Levashina, J., & Campion, M.A. (2007). Measuring faking in the employment interview: Development and validation of an interview faking behavior scale. *Journal of Applied Psychology, 92,* 1638–1656.

Levi, L. (2003). Foreward. In J. C. Quick & L. E. Tetrick (Eds.), *Handbook of organizational health psychology* (pp. *ix–xiii*). Washington, DC: American Psychological Association.

Levine, E. L., Ash, R. A., & Levine, J. D. (2004). Judgmental assessment of job-related experience, training, and education for use in human resource staffing. In J. C. Thomas (Ed.), *Comprehensive handbook of psychological assessment* (Vol. 4, pp. 269–296). Hoboken, NJ: Wiley.

Levine, E. L., Ash, R. A., Hall, H., & Sistrunk, F. (1983). Evaluation of job analysis methods by experienced job analysts. *Academy of Management Journal, 26,* 339–347.

Levine, E. L., Sistrunk, F., McNutt, K. J., & Gael, S. (1988). Exploring job analysis systems in selected organizations: A description of process and outcomes. *Journal of Business and Psychology, 3,* 3–21.

Liden, R. C., & Arad, S. (1996). A power perspective of empowerment and work groups: Implications for human resources management research. In G. R. Ferris (Ed.),

Research in personnel and human resources management (Vol. 14, pp. 205–251). Greenwich, CT: JAI Press.

Liden, R. C., & Maslyn, J. M. (1998). Multidimensionality of leader-member exchange: An empirical assessment through scale development. *Journal of Management, 24,* 43–72.

Liden, R. C., Sparrowe, R. T., & Wayne, S. J. (1997). Leader–member exchange theory: The past and potential for the future. In G. R. Ferris (Ed.), *Research in personnel and human resources management* (Vol. 15, pp. 47–120). Greenwich, CT: JAI Press.

Liden, R. C., Wayne, S. J., & Sparrowe, R. T. (2000). An examination of the mediating role of psychological empowerment on the relations between the job, interpersonal relationships, and work outcomes. *Journal of Applied Psychology, 85,* 407–416.

Lievens, F. (2006). International situational judgment tests. In J.A. Weekley & R.E. Ployhart (Eds.), *Situational judgment tests* (pp. 279–300). Mahwah, NJ: Erlbaum.

Lievens, F., Chasteen, C.S., Day, E.A., & Christiansen, N.D. (2006). Large-scale investigation of the role of trait activation theory for understanding assessment center convergent and discriminant validity. *Journal of Applied Psychology, 91,* 247–258.

Lievens, F., & Klimoski, R. J. (2001). Understanding the assessment centre process: Where are we now? In C. L. Cooper & I. T. Robertson (Eds.), *International review of industrial and organizational psychology* (Vol. 16, pp. 245–286). West Sussex, England: Wiley.

Lipnack, J. (2000). *Virtual teams: People working across boundaries with technology* (2nd ed.). New York: Wiley.

Lobel, S. A. (1993). Sexuality at work: Where do we go from here? *Journal of Vocational Behavior, 42,* 136–152.

Locke, E. A. (1991). The motivation sequence, the motivation hub, and the motivation core. *Organizational Behavior and Human Decision Processes, 50,* 288–299.

Locke, E. A. (Ed.). (1985). *The generalizability of laboratory experiments: An inductive study.* Lexington, MA: D.C. Heath.

Locke, E. A., Jirnauer, D., Roberson, Q., Goldman, B., Latham, M. E., & Weldon, E. (2001). The importance of the individual in an age of groupism. In M. E. Turner (Ed.), *Groups at work* (pp. 501–528). Mahwah, NJ: Erlbaum.

Locke, E. A., & Latham, G. P. (1990). *A theory of goal setting and task performance.* Englewood Cliffs, NJ: Prentice Hall.

Locke, E. A., & Latham, G. P. (2002). Building a practically useful theory of goal setting and task motivation: A 35-year odyssey. *American Psychologist, 57,* 705–717.

Locke, E. A., McClear, K., & Knight, D. (1996). Self-esteem and work. In C. L. Cooper & I. T. Robertson (Eds.), *International review of industrial and organizational psychology* (Vol. 11, pp. 1–32). Chichester, England: Wiley.

Locke, E. A., Shaw, K. N., Saari, L. M., & Latham, G. P. (1981). Goal setting and task performance: 1969–1980. *Psychological Bulletin, 90,* 125–152.

Locke, K., & Golden-Biddle, K. (2002). An introduction to qualitative research: Its potential for industrial and organizational psychology. In S. G. Rogelberg (Ed.), *Handbook of research methods in industrial and organizational psychology* (pp. 99–118). Malden, MA: Blackwell.

Lombardo, M. M., & McCauley, C. D. (1988). *The dynamics of management derailment* (Tech. Report No. 134). Greensboro, NC: Center for Creative Leadership.

London, M. (2001). Social cognition and person perception. In M. London (Ed.), *How people evaluate others in organizations* (pp. 1–3). Mahwah, NJ: Erlbaum.

London, M., Smither, J. W., & Adsit, D. J. (1997). Accountability: The Achilles' heel of multisource feedback. *Group & Organization Management, 22,* 162–184.

Lord, R. G., & Brown, D. L. (2004). *Leadership processes and follower self-identity.* Mahwah, NJ: Erlbaum.

Lord, R. G., Foti, R. J., & Phillips, J. S. (1982). A theory of leadership organization. In J. G. Hunt, U. Sekaran, & C. Schriesheim (Eds.), *Leadership: Beyond establishment views.* Carbondale, IL: Southern Illinois University.

Lord, R. G., Klimoski, R. J., & Kanfer, R. (Eds.). (2002). *Emotions in the workplace.* San Francisco: Jossey-Bass.

Lord, R. G., & Levy, P. E. (1994). Moving from cognition to action: A control theory perspective. *Applied Psychology: An International Review, 43,* 335–367.

Lowe, K. B., & Gardner, W. L. (2000). Ten years of the Leadership Quarterly: Contributions and challenges for the future. *Leadership Quarterly, 11,* 459–514.

Lowe, K. B., Kroeck, K. G., & Sivasubramaniam, N. (1996). Effectiveness correlates of transformational and transactional leadership: A meta-analytic review of the MLQ literature. *Leadership Quarterly, 7,* 385–425.

Lowman, R. L. (1999). *The ethical practice of psychology in organizations.* Washington, DC: American Psychological Association.

Lubinski, D., & Dawis, R. V. (1992). Aptitudes, skills, and proficiencies. In M. D. Dunnette & L. M. Hough (Eds.), *Handbook of industrial and organizational psychology* (2nd ed., Vol. 3, pp. 1–59). Palo Alto, CA: Consulting Psychologists Press.

Lucas, R. E., & Diener, E. (2003). The happy worker: Hypotheses about the role of positive affect in worker productivity. In M. R. Barrick & A. M. Ryan (Eds.), *Personality and work: Reconsidering the role of personality in organizations* (pp. 30–59). San Francisco: Jossey-Bass.

Lund, J. (1992). Electronic performance monitoring: A review of research issues. *Applied Ergonomics, 23,* 54–58.

Lyness, K. S. (2002). Finding the key to the executive suite: Challenges for women and people of color. In R. Silzer (Ed.), *The 21 century executive* (pp. 229–273). San Francisco: Jossey-Bass.

Lyness, K.S., & Heilman, M.E. (2006). When fit is fundamental: Performance evaluations and promotions of upper level female and male managers. *Journal of Applied Psychology, 91,* 777–785.

Lyness, K. S., & Thompson, D. E. (1997). Above the glass ceiling: A comparison of matched samples of female and male executives. *Journal of Applied Psychology, 82,* 359–375.

Lyubomirsky, S., King, L., & Diener, E. (2005). The benefits of frequent positive affect: Does happiness lead to success? *Psychological Bulletin, 131,* 803–855.

MacDermid, S. M., Seery, B. L., & Weiss, H. M. (2002). An emotional examination of the work-family interface. In R. G. Lord, R. J. Klimoski, & R. Kanfer (Eds.), *Emotions in the workplace* (pp. 402–427). San Francisco: Jossey-Bass.

Macey, B. (2002). The licensing of I-O psychologists. *The Industrial-Organizational Psychologist, 39(3),* 11–13.

Machin, M. A. (2002). Planning, managing, and optimizing transfer of training. In K. Kraiger (Ed.), *Creating, implementing, and managing effective training and development* (pp. 263–301). San Francisco: Jossey-Bass.

MacKenzie, S. B., Podsakoff, P. M., & Fetter, R. (1991). Organizational citizenship behavior and objective productivity as determinants of managerial evaluations of salespersons' performance. *Organizational Behavior and Human Decision Processes, 50,* 123–150.

Mael, F. A. (1991). A conceptual rationale for the domain and attributes of biodata items. *Personnel Psychology, 44,* 763–792.

Mael, F. A., Connerly, M., & Morath, R. A. (1996). None of your business: Parameters of biodata invasiveness. *Personnel Psychology, 49,* 613–650.

Mager, R. F. (1984). *Preparing instructional objectives.* Belmont, CA: Pitman Learning.

Major, D.A., & Germano, L.M. (2006). The changing nature of work and its impact on the work-home interface. In F. Jones, R.J. Burke, & M. Westman (Eds.), *Work-life balance: A psychological perspective* (pp. 13–38). Hove, UK: Taylor & Francis.

Major, V. S., Klein, K. J., & Ehrhart, M. G. (2002). Work time, work interference with family, and psychological distress. *Journal of Applied Psychology, 87,* 427–436.

Malos, S. B. (1998). Current legal issues in performance appraisal. In J. W. Smither (Ed.), *Performance appraisal* (pp. 49–94). San Francisco: Jossey-Bass.

Mantell, M. (1994). *Ticking bombs: Defusing violence in the workplace.* Burr Ridge, IL: Irwin.

Manz, C. C. (1986). Self-leadership: Toward an expanded theory of self-influence. *Academy of Management Review, 11,* 585–600.

Manz, C. C., & Sims, H. P. (1991). Superleadership: Beyond the myth of heroic leadership. *Organizational Dynamics, 19(4),* 18–35.

Marchant, G., & Robinson, J. (1999). Is knowing the tax code all it takes to be a tax expert? On the development of legal expertise. In R. J. Sternberg & J. A. Howath (Eds.), *Tacit knowledge in professional practice* (pp. 3–20). Mahwah, NJ: Erlbaum.

Margenau, J. M., Martin, J. E., & Peterson, M. M. (1988). Dual and unilateral commitment among stewards and rank-and-file union members. *Academy of Management Journal, 31,* 359–376.

Marks, M. A., Sabella, M. J., Burke, C. S., & Zaccaro, S. J. (2002). The impact of cross-training on team effectiveness. *Journal of Applied Psychology, 87,* 3–13.

Marks, M. A., Zaccaro, S. J., & Mathieu, J. E. (2000). Performance implications of leader briefings and team-interaction training for team adaptation to novel environments. *Journal of Applied Psychology, 85,* 971–986.

Marks, M. L. (2002). Mergers and acquisitions. In J. W. Hedge & E. D. Pulakos (Eds.), *Implementing organizational interventions: Steps, processes, and best practices* (pp. 43–77). San Francisco: Jossey-Bass.

Marlatt, G. A., Baer, J. S., & Quigley, L. A. (1995). Self-efficacy and addictive behavior. In A. Bandura (Ed.), *Self-efficacy in changing societies* (pp. 289–315). New York: Cambridge.

Marquardt, M. (2002). Around the world: Organization development in the international context. In J. Waclawski & A. H. Church (Eds.), *Organization development: A data-driven approach to organizational change* (pp. 266–285). San Francisco: Jossey-Bass.

Martin, S. L., & Terris, W. (1991). Predicting infrequent behavior: Clarifying the impact on false-positive rates. *Journal of Applied Psychology, 76,* 484–487.

Martocchio, J. J., & Harrison, D. A. (1993). To be there or not to be there: Questions, theories, and methods in absenteeism research. In G. R. Ferris (Ed.), *Research in personnel and human resources management* (Vol. 11, pp. 259–329). Greenwich, CT: JAI Press.

Marx, R. D. (1982). Relapse prevention for managerial training: A model for maintenance of behavior change. *Academy of Management Review, 7,* 433–441.

Marx, R. D., & Karren, R. K. (1988). *The effects of relapse prevention training and interactive follow-up on positive transfer of training.* Paper presented at the National Academy of Management Meeting, Anaheim, CA.

Masters, M. F. (1997). *Unions at the crossroads: Strategic membership, financial, and political perspectives.* Westport, CT: Quorum.

Mateer, F. (1917). The moron as a war problem. *Journal of Applied Psychology, 1,* 317–320.

Mathieu, J. E., Marks, M. A., & Zaccaro, S. J. (2001). Multiteam systems. In N. Anderson, D. S. Ones, H. K. Sinangil, & C. Viswesvaran (Eds.), *Handbook of industrial, work, & organizational psychology* (Vol. 2, pp. 289–313). London: Sage.

Mathieu, J. E., Tannenbaum, S. I., & Salas, E. (1990). *A causal model of individual and situational influences on training effectiveness measures.* Paper presented at the 5th annual conference of the Society for Industrial and Organizational Psychology, Miami.

Maurer, T. J., Raju, N. J., & Collins, W. C. (1998). Peer and subordinate performance appraisal measurement equivalence. *Journal of Applied Psychology, 83,* 693–702.

Maurer, T.J., & Solamon, J.M. (2006). The science and practice of a structured employment interview coaching program. *Personnel Psychology, 59,* 433–456.

Maxwell, J. A. (1998). Designing a qualitative study. In L. Bickman & D. J. Rog (Eds.), *Handbook of applied social research methods* (pp. 69–100). Thousand Oaks, CA: Sage.

Mayer, J. D., Salovey, P., & Caruso, D. R. (2002). *Mayer-Salovey-Caruso Emotional Intelligence Test (MSCEIT)* User's manual. Toronto: MHS Publishers.

Mayer, R. C., & Davis, J. H. (1999). The effect of the performance appraisal system on trust for management: A field quasi-experiment. *Journal of Applied Psychology, 84,* 123–136.

McCall, M. W., & Bobko, P. (1990). Research methods in the service of discovery. In M. D. Dunnette & L. M. Hough (Eds.), *Handbook of industrial and organizational psychology* (2nd ed., Vol. 1, pp. 381–418). Palo Alto, CA: Consulting Psychologists Press.

McCarthy, J. M., & Goffin, R. D. (2001). Improving the validity of letters of recommendation: An investigation of three standardized reference forms. *Military Psychology, 13,* 199–222.

McClelland, D. C., & Boyatzis, R. E. (1982). Leadership motive pattern and long term success in management. *Journal of Applied Psychology, 67,* 737–743.

McCormick, E. J., & Jeanneret, P. R. (1988). Position analysis questionnaire (PAQ). In S. Gael (Ed.), *The job analysis handbook for business, industry, and government* (Vol. 2, pp. 825–842). New York: Wiley.

McCrae, R. R., & Costa, P. T. (1987). Validation of the five-factor model of personality across instruments and observers. *Journal of Personality & Social Psychology, 56,* 586–595.

McCrae, R. R., & Costa, P. T. (1997). Personality trait structure as a human universal. *American Psychologist, 52,* 509–516.

McDaniel, M.A., Hartman, N.S., Whetzel, D.L., & Grubb, W.L., III. (2007). Situational judgment tests, response instructions, and validity: A meta-analysis. *Personnel Psychology, 60,* 63–91.

McDaniel, M. A., Morgeson, F. P., Finnegan, E. B., Campion, M. A., & Brauerman, E. P. (2001). Use of situational judgment tests to predict job performance: A clarification of the literature. *Journal of Applied Psychology, 86,* 730–740.

McDaniel, M.A., Rothstein, H.R., & Whetzel, D.L. (2006). Publication bias: A case study of four test vendors. *Personnel Psychology, 59,* 927–953.

McDaniel, M. A., Whetzel, D. L., Schmidt, F. L., & Maurer, S. D. (1994). The validity of employment interviews: A comprehensive review and meta-analysis. *Journal of Applied Psychology, 79,* 599–616.

McIntyre, R. M., & Salas, E. (1995). Measuring and managing for team performance: Lessons from complex environments. In R. A. Guzzo & E. Salas (Eds.), *Team effectiveness and decision making in organizations* (pp. 9–45). San Francisco: Jossey-Bass.

McKee-Ryan, F.M., Song, Z., Wanberg, C.R., & Kinicki, A.J. (2005). Psychological and physical well-being during unemployment: A meta-analytic study. *Journal of Applied Psychology, 90,* 53–76.

McKenna, D. D., & McKenna, R. B. (2002). E-executives: Leadership priorities for the new economy. In R. Silzer (Ed.), *The 21 century executive* (pp. 274–299). San Francisco: Jossey-Bass.

McNeely, B. L., & Meglino, B. M. (1994). The role of dispositional and situational antecedents in prosocial organizational behavior: An examination of the intended beneficiaries of prosocial behavior. *Journal of Applied Psychology, 79,* 836–844.

Meijer, R. R., & Nering, M. L. (1999). Computerized adaptive testing: Overview and introduction. *Applied Psychological Measurement, 23,* 187–194.

Meindl, J. R., & Ehrlich, S. B. (1987). The romance of leadership and the evaluation of organizational performance. *Academy of Management Journal, 30,* 91–109.

Mellor, S. (1990). The relationship between membership decline and union commitment: A field study of local unions in crisis. *Journal of Applied Psychology, 75,* 258–267.

Mero, N. P., & Motowidlo, S. J. (1995). Effects of rater accountability on the accuracy and the favorability of performance ratings. *Journal of Applied Psychology, 80,* 517–524.

Messick, S. (1995). Validity of psychological assessment: Validation of inferences from persons' responses and performances as scientific inquiry into score meaning. *American Psychologist, 50,* 741–749.

Meyer, G. J., Finn, S. E., Eyde, L. D., Kay, G. G., Moreland, K. L., Dies, R. R., Eisman, E. J., Kubiszyn, T. W., & Reed, G. M. (2001). Psychological testing and psychological assessment: A review of evidence and issues. *American Psychologist, 56,* 128–165.

Meyer, H. H. (1980). Self-appraisal of job performance. *Personnel Psychology, 33,* 291–296.

Meyer, H. H., Kay, E., & French, J. R. P., Jr. (1965). Split roles in performance appraisal. *Harvard Business Review, 43,* 123–129.

Meyer, J. P. (1997). Organizational commitment. In C. L. Cooper & I. T. Robertson (Eds.), *International review of industrial and organizational psychology* (Vol. 12, pp. 175–228). Chichester, England: Wiley.

Meyer, J. P., & Allen, N. J. (1997). *Commitment in the workplace: Theory, research, and application.* Thousand Oaks, CA: Sage.

Mintzberg, H. (1979). *Structuring of organizations.* Upper Saddle River, N.J.: Pearson Education.

Mintzberg, H. (1983). *Structure in fives: Designing effective organizations.* Englewood Cliffs, NJ: Prentice Hall.

Mintzberg, H. (2008). *Structure in sevens.* Upper Saddle Ridge, NJ: Prentice-Hall.

Mirvis, P. H., & Seashore, S. E. (1979). Being ethical in organizational research. *American Psychologist, 34,* 766–780.

Mitchell, J. L., & McCormick, E. J. (1990). *Professional and managerial position questionnaire.* Logan, UT: PAQ Services.

Mitchell, T. R. (1985). An evaluation of the validity of correlation research conducted in organizations. *Academy of Management Review, 10,* 192–205.

Mitchell, T. R. (1997). Matching motivational strategies with organizational contexts. In B. M. Staw & L. L. Cummings (Eds.), *Research in organizational behavior* (Vol. 19, pp. 57–149). Greenwich, CT: JAI Press.

Mitchell, T. R., & Daniels, D. (2003a). Motivation. In W. C. Borman, D. R. Ilgen, & R. J. Klimoski (Eds.), *Handbook of psychology* (Vol. 12): *Industrial and organizational psychology* (pp. 225–254). Hoboken, NJ: Wiley.

Mitchell, T. R., & Daniels, D. (2003b). Observation and commentary on recent research in work motivation. In L. W. Porter, G. A. Bigley, & R. M. Steers (Eds.), *Motivation and work behavior* (7th ed., pp. 26–44). Boston: McGraw-Hill Irwin.

Moghaddam, F.M. (2005). The staircase to terrorism: A psychological exploration. *American Psychologist, 60*, 161–169.

Mohammed, S., & Dumville, B. C. (2001). Team mental models in a team knowledge framework: Expanding theory and measurement across disciplinary boundaries. *Journal of Organizational Behavior, 22*, 89–106.

Monk, T. H., Folkard, S., & Wedderburn, A. I. (1996). Maintaining safety and high performance on shiftwork. *Applied Ergonomics, 27*, 17–23.

Mook, D. G. (1983). In defense of external invalidity. *American Psychologist, 38*, 379–387.

Moore, D. A. (1994). Company alcohol policies: Practicalities and problems. In C. L. Cooper & S. Williams (Eds.), *Creating healthy work organizations* (pp. 75–96). Chichester, England: Wiley.

Moorman, R. H. (1991). Relationship between organizational justice and organizational citizenship behaviors: Do fairness perceptions influence employee citizenship? *Journal of Applied Psychology, 76*, 845–855.

Moreland, J. L., Eyde, L. D., Robertson, G. J., Primoff, E. S., & Most, R. B. (1995). Assessment of test user qualifications. *American Psychologist, 50*, 14–23.

Moreland, R. L., & Levine, J. M. (2001). Socialization in organizations and work groups. In M. E. Turner (Ed.), *Groups at work* (pp. 69–112). Mahwah, NJ: Erlbaum.

Morgan, G. (1997). *Images of organizations.* Thousand Oaks, CA: Sage.

Morgeson, F. P., & Campion, M. A. (2003). Work design. In W. C. Borman, D. R. Ilgen, & R. J. Klimoski (Eds.), *Handbook of psychology* (Vol. 12): *Industrial and organizational psychology* (pp. 423–452). Hoboken, NJ: Wiley.

Morgeson, F.P., Campion, M.A., Dipboye, R.L., Hollenbeck, J.R., Murphy, K., & Schmitt, N. (2007). Reconsidering the use of personality tests in personnel selection contexts. *Personnel Psychology, 60*, 683–729.

Morgeson, F.P., & Humphrey, S.E. (2006). The work design questionnaire (WDQ): Developing and validating a comprehensive measure for assessing job design and the nature of work. *Journal of Applied Psychology, 91*, 1321–1339.

Morgeson, F.P., Reider, M.H., & Campion, M.A. (2005). Selecting individuals in team settings: The importance of social skills, personality characteristics, and teamwork. *Personnel Psychology, 58*, 583–612.

Morrison, R. F., & Brantner, T. M. (1992). What enhances or inhibits learning a new job? A basic career issue. *Journal of Applied Psychology, 77*, 926–940.

Morrow, P. C. (1993). *The theory and measurement of work commitment.* Greenwich, CT: JAI.

Moscoso, S. (2000). Selection interview: A review of validity evidence, adverse impact, and applicant reactions. *International Journal of Selection and Assessment, 8*, 237–247.

Motowidlo, S. J., Hanson, M. A., & Crafts, J. L. (1997). Low-fidelity simulations. In D. L. Whetzel & G. R. Wheaton (Eds.), *Applied measurement methods in industrial psychology* (pp. 241–260). Palo Alto, CA: Consulting Psychologists Press.

Motowidlo, S. J., & Van Scotter, J. R. (1994). Evidence that task performance should be distinguished from contextual performance. *Journal of Applied Psychology, 79*, 475–480.

Mount, M. K. (1984). Psychometric properties of subordinate ratings of managerial performance. *Personnel Psychology, 37*, 687–702.

Mount, M. K., & Scullen, S. E. (2001). Multisource feedback ratings: What do they really measure? In M. London (Ed.), *How people evaluate others in organizations* (pp. 155–180). Mahwah, NJ: Erlbaum.

Muchinsky, P. M. (1977). A comparison of within- and across-subjects analyses of the expectancy-valence model for predicting effort. *Academy of Management Journal, 20*, 154–158.

Muchinsky, P. M. (2000). Emotions in the workplace: The neglect of organizational behavior. *Journal of Organizational Behavior, 21*, 801–805.

Muchinsky, P. M. (2004a). Mechanical aptitude and spatial ability testing. *Comprehensive handbook of psychological assessment* (Vol. 4, pp. 21–34). Hoboken, NJ: Wiley.

Muchinsky, P. M. (2004b). When the psychometrics of test development meet organizational realities: A conceptual framework for organizational change, examples, and recommendations. *Personnel Psychology, 57*, 175–209.

Muchinsky, P. M., & Maassarani, M. A. (1981). Public sector grievances in Iowa. *Journal of Collective Negotiations, 10*, 55–62.

Mulvey, P. W., & Klein, H. J. (1998). The impact of perceived loafing and collective efficacy in group goal processes and group performance. *Organizational Behavior & Human Decision Processes, 74*, 62–87.

Mumford, M. D., & Stokes, G. S. (1992). Developmental determinants of individual action: Theory and practice in applying background measures. In M. D. Dunnette & L. M. Hough (Eds.), *Handbook of industrial and organizational psychology* (2nd ed., Vol. 3, pp. 61–138). Palo Alto, CA: Consulting Psychologists Press.

Münsterberg, H. (1913). *Psychology and industrial efficiency.* Boston: Houghton Mifflin.

Murphy, G. C., & Athanasou, J. A. (1999). The effect of unemployment on mental health. *Journal of Occupational & Organizational Psychology, 72,* 83–99.

Murphy, K. R. (1996). Individual differences and behavior in organizations: Much more than *g*. In K. R. Murphy (Ed.), *Individual differences and behavior in organizations* (pp. 3–30). San Francisco: Jossey-Bass.

Murphy, K. R. (1997). Meta-analysis and validity generalization. In N. Anderson & P. Herriot (Eds.), *International handbook of selection and assessment* (pp. 323–342). Chichester, England: Wiley.

Murphy, K. R. (1999). The challenge of staffing a postindustrial workplace. In D. R. Ilgen & E. D. Pulakos (Eds.), *The changing nature of performance* (pp. 295–324). San Francisco: Jossey-Bass.

Murphy, K. R. (2000). Impact of assessments of validity generalization and situational specificity on the science and practice of personnel selection. *International Journal of Selection and Assessment, 8,* 194–206.

Murphy, K. R. (2003). The logic of validity generalization. In K. R. Murphy (Ed.), *Validity generalization: A critical review* (pp. 1–30). Mahwah, NJ: Erlbaum.

Murphy, K.R. (Ed.) (2006). *A critique of emotional intelligence: What are the problems and how can they be fixed?* Mahwah, NJ: Erlbaum.

Murphy, K. R., & Anhalt, R. L. (1992). Is halo error a property of the rater, ratees, or the specific behaviors observed? *Journal of Applied Psychology, 77,* 494–500.

Murphy, K. R., & Cleveland, J. N. (1995). *Understanding performance appraisal: Social, organizational, and goal-based perspectives.* Thousand Oaks, CA: Sage.

Murphy, K. R., Cronin, B. E., & Tam, A. P. (2003). Controversy and consensus regarding the use of cognitive ability testing in organizations. *Journal of Applied Psychology, 88,* 660–671.

Murphy, K. R., & De Shon, R. (2000). Progress in psychometrics: Can industrial and organizational psychology catch up? *Personnel Psychology, 53,* 913–924.

Murphy, K. R., Osten, K., & Myors, B. (1995). Modeling the effects of banding in personnel selection. *Personnel Psychology, 48,* 61–84.

Murphy, K. R., Thornton, G. C., & Prue, K. (1991). Influence of job characteristics on the acceptability of employee drug testing. *Journal of Applied Psychology, 76,* 447–453.

Murphy, L.L., Spies, R.A., & Plake, B.S. (Eds.) (2006) *Tests in print VII.* Lincoln, NE: Buros Institute of Mental Measurements.

Murphy, L. R., Hurrell, J. J., & Quick, J. C. (1992). Work and well-being: Where do we go from here? In J. C. Quick, L. R. Murphy, & J. J. Hurrell (Eds.), *Stress and well-being at work* (pp. 331–347). Washington, DC: American Psychological Association.

Murray, H. A., & MacKinnon, D. W. (1946). Assessment of OSS personnel. *Journal of Consulting Psychology, 10,* 76–80.

Murrell, A. J., & Jones, R. (1996). Assessing affirmative action: Past, present, and future. *Journal of Social Issues, 52(4),* 77–92.

Naglieri, J. A., Drasgow, F., Schmit, M., Handler, L., Prifitera, A., Margolis, A., & Velasquez, R. (2004). Psychological testing on the Internet: New problems, old issues. *American Psychologist, 59,* 150–162.

Naquin, C. E., & Tynan, R. O. (2003). The team halo effect: Why teams are not blamed for their failures. *Journal of Applied Psychology, 88,* 332–340.

Narayanan, V. K., & Nath, R. (1982). Hierarchical level and the impact of flextime. *Industrial Relations, 21,* 216–230.

Neale, M. A. (1984). The effects of negotiation and arbitration cost salience on bargainer behavior: The role of the arbiter and constituency in negotiator judgment. *Organizational Behavior and Human Performance, 34,* 97–111.

Neuman, G. A., & Wright, J. (1999). Team effectiveness: Beyond skills and cognitive ability. *Journal of Applied Psychology, 84,* 376–389.

Neuman, J. H., & Baron, R. A. (1998). Workplace violence and workplace aggression: Evidence concerning specific forms, potential causes, and preferred targets. *Journal of Management, 24,* 391–419.

Newell, S., & Tansley, C. (2001). International uses of selection methods. In C. L. Cooper & I. T. Robertson (Eds.), *International review of industrial and organizational psychology* (Vol. 16, pp. 195–213). Chichester, England: Wiley.

Newman, D.A., Jacobs, R.R., & Bartram, D. (2007). Choosing the best method for local validity estimation: Relative accuracy of meta-analysis versus a local study versus Bayes-analysis. *Journal of Applied Psychology, 92,* 1394–1413.

Nickels, B. J. (1994). The nature of biodata. In G. S. Stokes, M. D. Mumford, & W. A. Owens (Eds.), *Biodata handbook: Theory, research, and use of biographical information in selection and performance prediction* (pp. 1–16). Palo Alto, CA: Consulting Psychologists Press.

Nilsen, D., & Campbell, D. P. (1993). Self-observer rating discrepancies: Once an overrater, always an overrater? *Human Resource Management, 32,* 265–282.

Nissen, B. (Ed.). (2002). *Unions in a globalized environment: Changing borders, organizational boundaries, and social roles.* Armonk, NY: M. E. Sharpe.

Noe, R., & Ford, J. K. (1992). Emerging issues and new directions for training research. In K. Rowland & G. Ferris (Eds.), *Research in personnel and human resource management* (Vol. 10, pp. 345–384). Greenwich, CT: JAI Press.

Normand, J., Lempert, R. O., & O'Brien, C. P. (Eds.). (1994). *Under the influence? Drugs and the American workforce.* Washington, DC: National Academy Press.

Normand, J., Salyards, S. D., & Mahoney, J. J. (1990). An evaluation of preemployment drug testing. *Journal of Applied Psychology, 75,* 629–639.

Nyfield, G., & Baron, H. (2000). Cultural context in adopting selection practices across borders. In J. F. Kehoe (Ed.), *Managing selection in changing organizations* (pp. 242–268). San Francisco: Jossey-Bass.

O'Keeffe, J. (1994). Disability, discrimination, and the Americans with Disabilities Act. In S. M. Bruyere & J. O'Keeffe (Eds.), *Implications of the Americans with Disabilities Act for psychology* (pp. 1–14). New York: Springer.

Offerman, L. R., & Gowing, M. K. (1990). Organizations of the future. *American Psychologist, 45,* 95–108.

Olson-Buchanan, J. B. (1996). Voicing discontent: What happens to the grievance filer after the grievance? *Journal of Applied Psychology, 81,* 52–63.

Ones, D. S., Viswesvaran, C., & Schmidt, F. L. (1993). Comprehensive meta-analysis of integrity test validities: Findings and implications for personnel selection and theories of job performance. *Journal of Applied Psychology, 78,* 679–703.

Organ, D. W. (1988). *Organizational citizenship behavior: The good soldier syndrome.* Lexington, MA: Lexington Books.

Organ, D. W. (1994). Organizational citizenship behavior and the good soldier. In M. G. Rumsey, C. B. Walker, & J. H. Harris (Eds.), *Personnel selection and classification* (pp. 53–68). Hillsdale, NJ: Erlbaum.

Ostroff, C., & Ford, J. K. (1989). Assessing training needs: Critical levels of analysis. In I. L. Goldstein (Ed.), *Training and development in organizations* (pp. 25–62). San Francisco: Jossey-Bass.

Ostroff, C., & Harrison, D. A. (1999). Meta-analysis, level of analysis, and best estimates of population correlations: Cautions for interpreting meta-analytic results in organizational behavior. *Journal of Applied Psychology, 84,* 260–270.

Ostroff, C., Kinicki, A. J., & Tamkins, M. M. (2003). Organizational culture and climate. In W. C. Borman, D. R. Ilgen, & R. J. Klimoski (Eds.), *Handbook of psychology* (Vol. 12): *Industrial and organizational psychology* (pp. 565–593). Hoboken, NJ: Wiley.

Overton, R. C., Harms, H. J., Taylor, L. R., & Zickar, M. J. (1997). Adapting to adaptive testing. *Personnel Psychology, 50,* 171–185.

Overton, R. C., Taylor, L. R., Zickar, M. J., & Harms, H. J. (1996). The pen-based computer as an alternative platform for test administration. *Personnel Psychology, 49,* 455–464.

Oyserman, D., Coon, H. M., & Kemmelmeier, M. (2002). Rethinking individualism and collectiveness: Evaluation of theoretical assumptions and meta-analyses. *Psychological Bulletin, 128,* 3–72.

Oz, E., & Sosick, J. J. (2000). Why information system projects are abandoned: A leadership and communication theory exploratory study. *Journal of Computer Information Systems, 41,* 66–78.

Patenaude, A. F., Guttmacher, A. E., & Collins, F. S. (2002). Genetics testing and psychology. *American Psychologist, 57,* 271–282.

Payne, S.C., & Pariyothorn, M.M. (2007). I-O psychology in introductory psychology textbooks: A survey of authors. *The Industrial-Organizational Psychologist, 44*(4), 37–42.

Pearlman, K., & Barney, M. F. (2000). Selection for a changing workplace. In J. F. Kehoe (Ed.), *Managing selection in changing organizations* (pp. 3–72). San Francisco: Jossey-Bass.

Pearson, C. M., Andersson, L. M., & Porath, C. L. (2000). Assessing and attacking workplace incivility. *Organizational Dynamics, 29,* 123–137.

Pernanen, K. (1991). *Alcohol in human violence.* London: Guilford Press.

Perrewe, P. L., & Spector, P. E. (2002). Personality research in the organizational sciences. In G. R. Ferris & J. J. Martocchio (Eds.), *Research in personnel and human resources management* (Vol. 21, pp. 1–63). Kidlington, UK: Elsevier.

Peterson, D. B. (2002). Management development: Coaching and mentoring programs. In K. Kraiger (Ed.), *Creating, implementing, and managing effective training and development* (pp. 160–191). San Francisco: Jossey-Bass.

Peterson, N. G., & Jeanneret, P. R. (1997). Job analysis. In D. L. Whetzel & G. R. Wheaton (Eds.), *Applied measurement methods in industrial psychology* (pp. 13–50). Palo Alto, CA: Consulting Psychologists Press.

Peterson, N. G., Mumford, M. D., Borman, W. C., Jeanneret, P. R., & Fleishman, E. A. (Eds.). (1999). *An occupational information system for the 21st century: The development of the O*NET.* Washington, DC: American Psychological Association.

Peterson, N. G., Mumford, M. D., Borman, W. C., Jeanneret, P. R., Fleishman, E. A., Campion, M. A., Mayfield, M. S., Morgeson, F. P., Pearlman, K., Gowing, M. K., Lancaster, A., & Dye, D. (2001). Understanding work using the Occupational Information Network (O*NET): Implications for research and practice. *Personnel Psychology, 54*, 451–492.

Peterson, N. G., Wise, L. L., Arabian, J., & Hoffman, R. G. (2001). Synthetic validation and validity generalization: When empirical validation is not possible. In J. P. Campbell & D. J. Knapp (Eds.), *Exploring the limits in personnel selection and classification* (pp. 411–452). Mahwah, NJ: Erlbaum.

Pfeffer, J, (2003). Business and the spirit: Management practices that sustain values. In R. A. Giacalone & C. L. Jurkiewicz (Eds.), *Handbook of workplace spirituality and organizational performance* (pp. 29–45). Armonk, NY: M. E. Sharpe.

Phillips, J. M., Hollenbeck, J. R., & Ilgen, D. R. (1996). Prevalence and prediction of positive discrepancy creation: Examining a discrepancy between two self-regulation theories. *Journal of Applied Psychology, 81*, 498–511.

Phillips, J. S., & Lord, R. G. (1981). Causal attribution and prescriptions of leadership. *Organizational Behavior and Human Performance, 28*, 143–163.

Pierce, C. A., Byrne, D., & Aguinis, H. (1996). Attraction in organizations: A model of workplace romance. *Journal of Organizational Behavior, 17*, 5–32.

Pierce, J. L., & Dunham, R. B. (1992). The 12-hour work day: A 48-hour, four-day week. *Academy of Management Journal, 35*, 1086–1098.

Pierce, J. L., Dunham, R. B., & Cummings, L. L. (1984). Sources of environmental structuring and participant responses. *Organizational Behavior and Human Performance, 33*, 214–242.

Pinder, C. C. (1998). *Work motivation in organizational behavior.* Upper Saddle River, NJ: Prentice Hall.

Piotrkowski, C. S., & Carrubba, J. (1999). Child labor and exploitation. In J. Barling & E. K. Kelloway (Eds.), *Young workers: Varieties of experience* (pp. 129–157). Washington, DC: American Psychological Association.

Plowman, D.A., Baker, L.T., Beck, T.E., Kulkari, M., Solansky, S.T., & Travis, D.V. (2007). Radical change accidentally: The emergence and amplification of small change. *Academy of Management Journal, 50*, 515–543.

Ployhart, R. E., & Ryan, A. M. (1998). Applicants' reactions to the fairness of selection procedures: The effects of positive rule violations and time of measurement. *Journal of Applied Psychology, 83*, 3–16.

Ployhart, R. E., Weekley, J. A., Holtz, B. C., & Kemp, C. (2003). Web-based and pencil-and-paper testing of applicants in a proctored setting: Are personality, biodata, and situational judgment tests comparable? *Personnel Psychology, 56*, 733–752.

Podlesny, J. A., & Truslow, C. M. (1993). Validity of an expanded-issue (Modified General Question) polygraph technique in a simulated distributed-crime-roles context. *Journal of Applied Psychology, 78*, 788–797.

Podsakoff, P. M., Ahearne, M., & MacKenzie, S. B. (1997). Organizational citizenship behavior and the quantity and quality of work group performance. *Journal of Applied Psychology, 82*, 262–270.

Podsakoff, P. M., MacKenzie, S. B., & Bommer, W. H. (1996). Meta-analysis of the relationship between Kerr and Jermier's substitutes for leadership and employee job attitudes, role perceptions, and performance. *Journal of Applied Psychology, 81*, 380–399.

Porter, C. O., Hollenbeck, J. R., Ilgen, D. R., Ellis, A. P., West, B. J., & Moon, H. (2003). Backing up behaviors in teams: The role of personality and legitimacy of need. *Journal of Applied Psychology, 88*, 391–403.

Posthuma, R. A., Morgeson, F. P., & Campion, M. A. (2002). Beyond employment interview validity: A comprehensive narrative review of recent research and trends over time. *Personnel Psychology, 55*, 1–81.

Posthuma, R.A., Roehling, M.V., & Campion, M.A. (2006). Applying U.S. employment discrimination laws to international employees: Advice for scientists and practitioners. *Personnel Psychology, 59*, 705–739.

Potosky, D., & Bobko, P. (2004). Selection testing via the internet: Practical considerations and exploratory empirical findings. *Personnel Psychology, 57*, 1003–1034.

Pratt, M. G., & Rafaeli, A. (1997). Organizational dress as a symbol of multilayered social identities. *Academy of Management Journal, 40*, 862–898.

Premack, S. L., & Hunter, J. E. (1988). Individual unionization decisions. *Psychological Bulletin, 103*, 223–234.

Prieto, J. M. (1993). The team perspective in selection and assessment. In H. Schuler, J. L. Farr, & M. Smith (Eds.), *Personnel selection and assessment* (pp. 221–234). Hillsdale, NJ: Erlbaum.

Pritchard, R. D., DeLeo, P. J., & Von Bergen, C. W. (1976). A field experimental test of expectancy-valence incentive motivation techniques. *Organizational Behavior and Human Performance, 15*, 355–406.

Pritchard, R. D., Jones, S. D., Roth, P. L., Stuebing, K. K., & Ekeberg, S. E. (1988). Effects of group feedback, goal setting, and incentives on organizational productivity. *Journal of Applied Psychology, 73*, 337–358.

Pruitt, D. G. (1993). *Negotiation in social conflict.* Pacific Grove, CA: Brooks/Cole.

Pulakos, E. D. (1997). Ratings of job performance. In D. L. Whetzel & G. R. Wheaton (Eds.), *Applied measurement methods in industrial psychology* (pp. 291–318). Palo Alto, CA: Consulting Psychologists Press.

Pulakos, E. D., Borman, W. C., & Hough, L. M. (1988). Test validation for scientific understanding: Two demonstrations of an approach to studying predictor–criterion linkages. *Personnel Psychology, 41,* 703–716.

Pulakos, E. D., & Schmitt, N. (1995). Experience-based and structured interview questions: Studies of validity. *Personnel Psychology, 48,* 289–308.

Quick, J. C., Murphy, L. R., Hurrell, J. J., & Orman, D. (1992). The value of work in the risk of distress and the power of prevention. In J. C. Quick, L. R. Murphy, & J. J. Hurrell (Eds.), *Stress and well-being at work* (pp. 3–13). Washington, DC: American Psychological Association.

Quinones, M. A., Ford, J. K., & Teachout, M. S. (1995). The relationship between work experience and job performance: A conceptual and meta-analytic review. *Personnel Psychology, 48,* 485–509.

Raelin, J. A. (1989). Unionization and deprofessionalization: Which comes first? *Journal of Organizational Behavior, 10,* 101–115.

Rafaeli, A., & Klimoski, R. J. (1983). Predicting sales success through handwriting analysis: An evaluation of the effects of training and handwriting sample content. *Journal of Applied Psychology, 68,* 212–217.

Ragins, B. R., & Sundstrom, E. (1989). Gender and power in organizations: A longitudinal perspective. *Psychological Bulletin, 105,* 51–88.

Raju, N. S., Burke, M. J., Normand, J., & Langlois, G. M. (1991). A new meta-analytic approach. *Journal of Applied Psychology, 76,* 432–446.

Ralston, D. A. (1989). The benefits of flextime: Real or imagined? *Journal of Organizational Behavior, 10,* 369–374.

Rawls, J. (1971). *A theory of justice.* Cambridge, MA: Harvard University Press.

Raymark, P. H., Schmit, M. J., & Guion, R. M. (1997). Identifying potentially useful personality constructs for employee selection. *Personnel Psychology, 50,* 723–736.

Ree, M. J., Earles, J. A., & Teachout, M. S. (1994). Predicting job performance: Not much more than g. *Journal of Applied Psychology, 79,* 518–524.

Reeve, C. L., & Hakel, M. D. (2002). Asking the right questions about g. *Human Performance, 15,* 47–74.

Reina, D. S., & Reina, M. L. (1999). *Trust & betrayal in the workplace.* San Francisco: Barrett-Koehler.

Rentsch, J. R., & Klimoski, R. J. (2001). Why do "great minds" think alike?: Antecedents of team member schema agreement. *Journal of Organizational Behavior, 22,* 107–120.

Rhodes, S. R., & Steers, R. M. (1990). *Managing employee absenteeism.* Reading, MA: Addison-Wesley.

Richey, B., Bernardin, H. J., Tyler, C. L., & McKinney, N. (2001). The effect of arbitration program characteristics on applicants' intentions toward potential employees. *Journal of Applied Psychology, 86,* 1006–1013.

Ridley, M. (1999). *Genome: The autobiography of a species in 23 chapters.* New York: Harper Collins.

Riketta, M. (2002). Attitudinal organizational commitment and job performance: A meta-analysis. *Journal of Organizational Behavior, 23,* 257–266.

Rioux, S. M., & Penner, L. A. (2001). The causes of organizational citizenship behavior: A motivational analysis. *Journal of Applied Psychology, 86,* 1306–1314.

Robinson, S. L., Kraatz, M. S., & Rousseau, D. M. (1994). Changing obligations and the psychology contract: A longitudinal study. *Academy of Management Journal, 37,* 137–152.

Robinson, S. L., & Rousseau, D. M. (1994). Violating the psychological contract: Not the exception but the norm. *Journal of Organizational Behavior, 15,* 245–259.

Roethlisberger, F. J., & Dickson, W. J. (1939). *Management and the worker.* Cambridge, MA: Harvard University Press.

Rogelberg, S. G., & Brooks-Laber, M. E. (2002). Securing our collective future: Challenges facing those designing and doing research in industrial and organizational psychology. In S. G. Rogelberg (Ed.), *Handbook of research methods in industrial and organizational psychology* (pp. 479–485). Malden, MA: Blackwell.

Rogelberg, S. G., Luong, A., Sederburg, M. E., & Cristol, D. S. (2000). Employee attitude surveys: Examining the attitudes of noncompliant employees. *Journal of Applied Psychology, 85,* 284–293.

Ronen, S. (1989). Training the international assignee. In I. L. Goldstein (Ed.), *Training and development in organizations* (pp. 417–454). San Francisco: Jossey-Bass.

Ronen, S., & Primps, S. B. (1981). The compressed work week as organizational change: Behavioral and attitudinal outcomes. *Academy of Management Review, 6,* 61–74.

Rosen, H., & Stagner, R. (1980). Industrial/organizational psychology and unions: A viable relationship? *Professional Psychology, 11,* 477–483.

Rosenthal, R. (1991). *Meta-analytic procedures for social research* (2nd ed.). Newbury Park, CA: Sage.

Rosse, R. L., Campbell, J. P., & Peterson, N. G. (2001). Personnel classification and differential job assignments: Estimating classification gains. In J. P. Campbell & D. J. Knapp (Eds.), *Exploring the limits in personnel* selection and classification (pp. 453–506). Mahwah, NJ: Erlbaum.

Rotchford, N. L. (2002). Performance management. In J. W. Hedge & E. D. Pulakos (Eds.), *Implementing organizational interventions: Steps, processes, and best practices* (pp. 167–197). San Francisco: Jossey-Bass.

Roth, P. L., & BeVier, C. A. (1998). Response rates in HRM/OB survey research: Norms and correlates, 1990–1994. *Journal of Management, 24*, 97–117.

Roth, P.L., Bobko, P., & McFarland, L.A. (2005). A meta-analysis of work sample test validity: Updating and integrating some classic literature. *Personnel Psychology, 58*, 1009–1037.

Rotundo, M., Nguyen, D-H., & Sackett, P. R. (2001). A meta-analytic review of gender differences is perceptions of sexual harassment. *Journal of Applied Psychology, 86*, 914–922.

Rousseau, D. M. (1989). Psychological and implied contracts in organizations. *Employee Responsibilities and Rights Journal, 2*, 121–139.

Rousseau, D. M. (1995). *Psycholological contracts in organizations*. Thousand Oaks, CA: Sage.

Rousseau, D. M. (1997). Organizational behavior in the new organizational era. *Annual Review of Psychology, 48*, 515–546.

Rousseau, D.M., & Batt, R. (2007). Global competition's perfect storm: Why business and labor cannot solve their problems alone. *Academy of Management Perspectives, 21*(2), 16–23.

Rousseau, D. M., & House, R. J. (1994). Meso organizational behavior: Avoiding three fundamental biases. In C. L. Cooper & D. M. Rousseau (Eds.), *Trends in organizational behavior* (Vol. 1, pp. 13–30). New York: Wiley.

Rousseau, D. M., & Parks, J. M. (1993). The contracts of individuals and organizations. In B. M. Staw & L. L. Cummings (Eds.), *Research in organizational behavior* (Vol. 15, pp. 1–43). Greenwich, CT: JAI.

Rousseau, D. M., & Schalk, R. (2000). Learning from cross-national perspectives on psychological contracts. In D. M. Rousseau & R. Schalk (Eds.), *Psychological contracts in employment: Cross-national perspectives* (pp. 283–304). Thousand Oaks, CA: Sage.

Roznowski, M., Dickter, D. N., Hong, S., Sawin, L. L., & Shute, V. J. (2000). Validity of measures of cognitive processes and general ability for learning and performance on highly complex computerized tutors: Is the *g* factor of intelligence even more general? *Journal of Applied Psychology, 85*, 940–955.

Ruback, R. B., & Innes, C. A. (1988). The relevance and irrelevance of psychological research. *American Psychologist, 43*, 683–693.

Rubery, J., & Grimshaw, D. (2003). *The organization of employment: An international perspective*. New York: Palgrave MacMillan.

Rupp, D.E., & Spencer, S. (2006). When customers lash out: The effects of customer interactional justice on emotional labor and the mediating role of discrete emotions. *Journal of Applied Psychology, 91*, 971–978.

Russell, J. S., & Goode, D. L. (1988). An analysis of managers' reactions to their own performance appraisal feedback. *Journal of Applied Psychology, 73*, 63–67.

Ryan, A. M., & Ployhart, R. E. (2003). Customer service behavior. In W. C. Borman, D. R. Ilgen, & R. J. Klimoski (Eds.), *Handbook of psychology* (Vol. 12): *Industrial and organizational psychology* (pp. 377–397). Hoboken, NJ: Wiley.

Ryan, A. M., Ployhart, R. E., & Friedel, L. A. (1998). Using personality testing to reduce adverse impact: A cautionary note. *Journal of Applied Psychology, 83*, 298–307.

Rynes, S., & Rosen, B. (1995). A field survey of factors affecting the adoption and perceived success of diversity training. *Personnel Psychology, 48*, 247–270.

Rynes, S. L. (1993). Who's selecting whom? Effects of selection practices on applicant attitudes and behavior. In N. Schmitt & W. C. Borman (Eds.), *Personnel selection in organizations* (pp. 240–274). San Francisco: Jossey-Bass.

Rynes, S.L., Brown, K.G., & Colbert, A.E. (2002). Seven common misconceptions about human resource practices: Research findings versus practitioner beliefs. *Academy of Management Executive, 16*(3), 92–103.

Rynes, S. L., & Cable, D. M. (2003). Recruitment research in the twenty-first century. In W. C. Borman, D. R. Ilgen, & R. J. Klimoski (Eds.), *Handbook of psychology* (Vol. 12): *Industrial and organizational psychology* (pp. 55–76). Hoboken, NJ: Wiley.

Rynes, S. L., McNatt, D. B., & Bretz, R. D. (1999). Academic research inside organizations: Inputs, processes, and outcomes. *Personnel Psychology, 52*, 869–898.

Saal, F. E., Downey, R. G., & Lahey, M. A. (1980). Rating the ratings: Assessing the psychometric quality of rating data. *Psychological Bulletin, 88*, 413–428.

Sackett, P. R., & Laczo, R. M. (2003). Job and work analysis. In W. C. Borman, D. R. Ilgen, & R. J. Klimoski (Eds.), *Handbook of psychology* (Vol. 12): *Industrial and organizational psychology* (pp. 21–37). Hoboken, NJ: Wiley.

Sackett, P. R., & Wanek, J. E. (1996). New developments in the use of measures of honesty, integrity, conscientiousness, dependability, trustworthiness, and reliability for personnel selection. *Personnel Psychology, 49*, 787–829.

Sackett, P. R., & Wilk, S. L. (1994). Within-group norming and other forms of score adjustment in psychological testing. *American Psychologist, 49*, 929–954.

Sackett, P. R., Schmitt, N., Ellingson, J. E., & Kabin, M. B. (2001). High-stakes testing in employment, credentialing, and higher education: Prospects in a post-affirmative-action world. *American Psychologist, 56,* 302–318.

Salas, E., Burke, C. S., & Cannon-Bowers, J. A. (2002). What we know about designing and delivering team training: Tips and guidelines. In K. Kraiger (Ed.), *Creating, implementing, and managing effective training and development* (pp. 234–259). San Francisco: Jossey-Bass.

Salas, E., & Cannon-Bowers, J. A. (1997). Methods, tools, and strategies for team training. In M. A. Quinones & A. Ehrenstein (Eds.), *Training for a rapidly changing workplace* (pp. 249–280). Washington, DC: American Psychological Association.

Salas, E., DeRouin, R.E., & Gade, P.A. (2007). The military's contribution to our science and practice: People, places, and findings. In L.L. Koppes (Ed.), *Historical perspectives in industrial and organizational psychology* (pp. 169–189). Mahwah, NJ: Erlbaum.

Salas, E. Priest, H.A., Stagl, K.C., Sims, D.E., & Burke, C.S. (2007). Work teams in organizations: A historical reflection and lessons learned. In L.L. Koppes (Ed.), *Historical perspectives in industrial and organizational psychology* (pp. 407–438). Mahwah, NJ: Erlbaum.

Salas, E., Stagl, K. C., & Burke, C. S. (2004). 25 years of team effectiveness in organizations: Research, themes, and emerging needs. In C. L. Cooper & I. T. Robertson (Eds.), *International review of industrial and organizational psychology* (Vol. 19, pp. 47–91). West Sussex: Wiley.

Salgado, J. F. (1997). The five factor model of personality and job performance in the European Community. *Journal of Applied Psychology, 82,* 30–43.

Salgado, J. F. (1998). Sample size in validity studies of personnel selection. *Journal of Occupational & Organizational Psychology, 71,* 161–164.

Salgado, J. F. (2000). Personnel selection at the beginning of the new millennium. *International Journal of Selection and Assessment, 8,* 191–193.

Salgado, J. F., Anderson, N., Moscoso, S., Bertua, C., & de Fruyt, F. (2003). International validity generalization of GMA and cognitive abilities: A European community meta-analysis. *Personnel Psychology, 56,* 573–605.

Salovey, P., & Mayer, J. D. (1990). Emotional intelligence. *Imagination, Cognition, and Personality, 9,* 185–211.

Sanchez, J. I. (2000). Adopting work analysis to a fast-paced and electronic business world. *International Journal of Selection and Assessment, 8,* 207–215.

Sanchez, J. I., & Levine, E. L. (2001). The analysis of work in the 20th and 21st centuries. In N. Anderson, D. S. Ones, H. K. Sinangil, & C. Viswesvaran (Eds.), *Handbook of industrial, work, and organisational psychology* (Vol. 1, pp. 71–89). London: Sage.

Sanchez-Runde, C. J., & Steers, R. M. (2003). Cultural influences in work motivation and performance. In L. W. Porter, G. A. Bigley, & R. M. Steers (Eds.), *Motivation and work behavior* (7th ed., pp. 357–398). Boston: McGraw-Hill Irwin.

Schalk, K., & Rousseau, D. M. (2001). Psychological contracts in employment. In N. Anderson, D. S. Ones, H. K. Sinangil, & C. Viswesvaran (Eds.), *Handbook of industrial, work, and organisational psychology* (Vol. 2, pp. 133–142). London: Sage.

Schaubroeck, J., Ganster, D. C., & Jones, J. R. (1998). Organization and occupation influences in the attraction-selection-attrition process. *Journal of Applied Psychology, 83,* 869–891.

Schein, E. H. (1996). Culture: The missing concept in organizational studies. *Administrative Science Quarterly, 41,* 229–240.

Schiavone, M. (2008). *Unions in crisis?* London: Praeger.

Schippmann, J. S. (1999). *Strategic job modeling: Working at the core of integrated human resources.* Mahwah, NJ: Erlbaum.

Schippmann, J. S., Ash, R. A., Battista, M., Carr, L., Eyde, L. D., Hesketh, B., Kehoe, J., Pearlman, K., Prien, E. P., & Sanchez, J. I. (2000). The practice of competency modeling. *Personnel Psychology, 53,* 703–740.

Schippmann, J. S., Prien, E. P., & Katz, J. A. (1990). Reliability and validity of in-basket performance measures. *Personnel Psychology, 43,* 837–859.

Schleicher, D.J., Venkataraman, V., Morgeson, F.P., & Campion, M.A. (2006). So you didn't get the job . . . *now* what do you think? Examining opportunity-to-perform fairness perceptions. *Personnel Psychology, 59,* 559–590.

Schmidt, F. L. (1991). Why all banding procedures in personnel selection are logically flawed. *Human Performance, 4,* 265–278.

Schmidt, F. L., & Hunter, J. E. (1978). Moderator research and the law of small numbers. *Personnel Psychology, 31,* 215–232.

Schmidt, F. L., & Hunter, J. E. (1980). The future of criterion-related validity. *Personnel Psychology, 33,* 41–60.

Schmidt, F. L., & Hunter, J. E. (1981). Employment testing: Old theories and new research findings. *American Psychologist, 36,* 1128–1137.

Schmidt, F. L., & Hunter, J. E. (1995). The fatal internal contradiction in banding: Its statistical rational is logically inconsistent with its operational procedures. *Human Performance, 8,* 203–214.

Schmidt, F. L., & Hunter, J. E. (1998). The validity and utility of selection methods in personnel psychology:

Practical and theoretical implications of 85 years of research findings. *Psychological Bulletin, 124,* 437–454.

Schmidt, F. L., & Hunter, J. E. (2001). Meta-analysis. In N. Anderson, D. S. Ones, H. K. Sinangil, & C. Viswesvaran (Eds.), *Handbook of industrial, work, and organisational psychology* (Vol. 1, pp. 51–70). London: Sage.

Schmidt, F. L., Hunter, J. E., McKenzie, R. C., & Muldrow, T. W. (1979). Impact of valid selection procedures on work-force productivity. *Journal of Applied Psychology, 64,* 609–626.

Schmidt, F. L., & Rader, M. (1999). Exploring the boundary conditions for interview validity: Meta-analytic findings for a new interview type. *Personnel Psychology, 52,* 445–464.

Schminke, M., Ambrose, M. L., & Cropanzano, R. S. (2000). The effect of organizational structure on perceptions of procedural fairness. *Journal of Applied Psychology, 85,* 294–304.

Schmitt, N., & Landy, F. J. (1993). The concept of validity. In N. Schmitt & W. C. Borman (Eds.) *Personnel selection in organizations* (pp. 275–309). San Francisco: Jossey-Bass.

Schmitt, N., & Oswald, F.L. (2006). The impact of corrections for faking on the validity of noncognitive measures in selection settings. *Journal of Applied Psychology, 91,* 613–621.

Schneider, B. (1987). The people make the place. *Personnel Psychology, 40,* 437–454.

Schneider, B. (1996). When individual differences aren't. In K. R. Murphy (Ed.), *Individual differences and behaviors in organizations* (pp. 548–572). San Francisco: Jossey-Bass.

Schneider, B., Hanges, P. J., Smith, D. B., & Salvaggio, A. N. (2003). Which comes first: Employee attitudes or organizational, financial and market performance? *Journal of Applied Psychology, 88,* 836–851.

Schneider, B., Smith, D. B., Taylor, S., & Fleenor, J. (1998). Personality and organizations: A test of the homogeneity of personality hypothesis. *Journal of Applied Psychology, 83,* 462–470.

Schneider, K. T., Hitlan, R. T., & Radhakrishnan, P. (2000). An examination of the nature and correlates of ethnic harassment experiences in multiple contexts. *Journal of Applied Psychology, 85,* 3–12.

Schneider, K. T., Swan, S., & Fitzgerald, L. F. (1997). Job-related and psychological effects of sexual harassment in the workplace: Empirical evidence from two organizations. *Journal of Applied Psychology, 82,* 401–415.

Schoenfeldt, L. F. (1999). From dust bowl empiricism to rational constructs in biographical data. *Human Resource Management Review, 9,* 147–167.

Schoorman, F.D., Mayer, R.C., & Davis, J.H. (2007). An integrative model of organizational trust: Past, present, and future. *Academy of Management Review, 35,* 344–354.

Schouten, R. (2003). Violence in the workplace. In J. P. Kahn & A. M. Langleib (Eds.), *Mental health and productivity in the workplace: A handbook for organizations and clinicians* (pp. 314–328). San Francisco: Jossey-Bass.

Schriesheim, C. A. (1978). Job satisfaction, attitudes toward unions, and voting in a union representation election. *Journal of Applied Psychology, 63,* 548–552.

Schuler, H. (1993). Social validity of selection situations: A concept and some empirical results. In H. Schuler, J. L. Farr, & M. Smith (Eds.), *Personnel selection and assessment* (pp. 11–26). Hillsdale, NJ: Erlbaum.

Schwenk, C. (1999). *Marijuana and the workplace.* Westport: Quorum.

Scott, W. D. (1903). *The theory of advertising.* Boston: Small, Maynard.

Scott, W. D. (1908). *The psychology of advertising.* New York: Arno Press.

Scott, W. D. (1911a). *Increasing human efficiency in business.* New York: Macmillan.

Scott, W. D. (1911b). *Influencing men in business.* New York: Ronald Press.

Scott, W. G., Mitchell, T. R., & Birnbaum, P. H. (1981). *Organization theory: A structural and behavioral analysis.* Homewood, IL: Richard D. Irwin.

Scullen, S.E., Bergey, P.K., & Aiman-Smith, L. (2005). Forced distribution rating systems and the improvement of workplace potential: A baseline simulation. *Personnel Psychology, 58,* 1–32.

Scullen, S. W., Mount, M. K., & Goff, M. (2000). Understanding the latent structure of job performance ratings. *Journal of Applied Psychology, 85,* 956–970.

Seashore, S. E., Indik, B. P., & Georgopoulos, B. S. (1960). Relationship among criteria of job performance. *Journal of Applied Psychology, 44,* 195–202.

Seligman, M. E., & Csikszentmihalyi, M. (2000). Positive psychology: An introduction. *American Psychologist, 55,* 5–14.

Senders, J. W., & Moray, N. P. (1991). *Human error: Cause, prediction, and reduction.* Hillsdale, NJ: Erlbaum.

Shadish, W. R. (1996). Meta-analyses and the explanation of causal mediating processes: A primer of examples, methods, and issues. *Psychological Methods, 1,* 47–65.

Shadish, W. R. (2002). Revisiting field experimentation: Field notes for the future. *Psychological Methods, 7,* 3–18.

Shaffer, M. A., & Harrison, D. A. (2001). Forgotten partners of international assignments: Development and test of a model of spouse adjustment. *Journal of Applied Psychology, 86,* 238–254.

Shane, S. (2003). *A general theory of entrepreneurship*. Cheltenham, UK: Edward Elgar.

Shapiro, D.L., Kirkman, B.L., & Coutney, H.G. (2007). Perceived causes and solutions of the translation problems in management research. *Academy of Management Journal, 50*, 249–266.

Sharf, J. C., & Jones, D. P. (2000). Employment risk management. In J. F. Kehoe (Ed.), *Managing selection in changing organizations* (pp. 271–318). San Francisco: Jossey-Bass.

Sherony, K. M., & Green, S. G. (2002). Coworker exchange: Relationships between coworkers, leader-member exchange, and work attitudes. *Journal of Applied Psychology, 87*, 542–548.

Shore, T. H., Shore, L. M., & Thornton, G. C. (1992). Construct validity of self- and peer evaluations of performance dimensions in an assessment center. *Journal of Applied Psychology, 77*, 42–54.

Shostak, A. B. (1964). Industrial psychology and the trade unions: A matter of mutual indifference. In G. Fisk (Ed.), *The frontiers of management psychology*. New York: Harper & Row.

Silberstein, L. R. (1992). *Dual-career marriage: A system in transition*. Hillsdale, NJ: Erlbaum.

Silvester, J., & Chapman, A. J. (1997). Asking "why" in the workplace. In C. L. Cooper & D. M. Rousseau (Eds.), *Trends in organizational behavior* (Vol. 4, pp. 1–14). London: Wiley.

Simons, T., & Roberson, Q. (2003). Why managers should care about fairness: The effects of aggregate justice perceptions on organizational outcomes. *Journal of Applied Psychology, 88*, 432–443.

Siskin, B. R. (1995). Relation between performance and banding. *Human Performance, 8*, 215–226.

Sitzman, T., Kraiger, K., Stewart, D., & Wisher, R. (2006). The comparative effectiveness of web-based and classroom instruction: A meta-analysis. *Personnel Psychology, 59*, 623–664.

Skarlicki, D. P., & Folger, A. (1997). Retaliation in the workplace: The roles of distributive, procedural, and interactional justice. *Journal of Applied Psychology, 82*, 434–443.

Skarlicki, D. P., Folger, R., & Tesluk, P. (1999). Personality as a moderator in the relationship between fairness and retaliation. *Academy of Management Journal, 42*, 100–108.

Skarlicki, D. P., & Latham, G. P. (1996). Increasing citizenship behavior within a labor union: A test of organizational justice theory. *Journal of Applied Psychology, 81*, 161–169.

Skarlicki, D. P., & Latham, G. P. (1997). Leadership training in organizational justice to increase citizenship behavior within a labor union: A replication. *Personnel Psychology, 50*, 617–654.

Slaughter, J. E., Sinar, E. F., & Bachiochi, P. D. (2002). Black applicants' reactions to affirmative action plans: Effects of plan content and previous experience with discrimination. *Journal of Applied Psychology, 87*, 333–344.

Smart, B. (2005). *Topgrading: How leading companies win by hiring, coaching, and keeping the best people*. New York: Penguin.

Smith, C. S., Folkard, S., & Fuller, J. A. (2003). Shiftwork and working hours. In J. C. Quick & L. E. Tetrick (Eds.), *Handbook of organizational health psychology* (pp. 163–184). Washington, DC: American Psychological Association.

Smith, C. S., Reilly, C., & Midkiff, K. (1989). Evaluation of three circadian rhythm questionnaires with suggestions for an improved measure of morningness. *Journal of Applied Psychology, 74*, 728–738.

Smith, D. B., & Dickson, M. W. (2003). Staffing the dynamic organization: Rethinking selection and motivation in the context of continuous change. In R. S. Peterson & E. A. Mannix (Eds.), *Leading and managing people in the dynamic organization* (pp. 41–64). Mahwah, NJ: Erlbaum.

Smith, E. M., Ford, J. K., & Kozlowski, S. W. (1997). Building adaptive expertise: Implications for training design strategies. In M. A. Quinones & A. Ehrenstein (Eds.), *Training for a rapidly changing workplace* (pp. 89–118). Washington, DC: American Psychological Association.

Smith, P. B., Fisher, R., & Sale, N. (2001). Cross-cultural industrial/organizational psychology. In C. L. Cooper & I. T. Robertson (Eds.), *International review of industrial and organizational psychology* (Vol. 16, pp. 147–193). West Sussex, England: Wiley.

Smith, P. C., Kendall, L., & Hulin, C. L. (1969). *The measurement of satisfaction in work and retirement*. Chicago: Rand McNally.

Smither, J. W. (1995). Creating an internal contingent workforce: Managing the resource link. In M. London (Ed.), *Employees, careers, and job creation* (pp. 142–164). San Francisco: Jossey-Bass.

Smither, J.W., London, M., & Reilly, R.R. (2005). Does performance improve following multisource feedback? A theoretical model, meta-analysis, and review of empirical findings. *Personnel Psychology, 58*, 1–32.

Smither, J. W., Reilly, R. R., Millsap, R. E., & Pearlman, K. (1993). Applicant reactions to selection procedures. *Personnel Psychology, 46*, 49–76.

Society for Industrial and Organizational Psychology (2003). *Principles for the validation and use of personnel selection procedures* (4th ed.). Bowling Green, OH: Author.

Solomonson, A. L., & Lance, C. E. (1997). Examination of the relationship between true halo and halo error in performance ratings. *Journal of Applied Psychology, 82,* 665–674.

Spector, P.E., Allen, T.D., Poelmans, S.A., Lapierre, L.M., Cooper, C.L., O'Driscoll, M., Sanchez, J.I., Abarca, N., Alexandrova, M., Beham, B., Brough, P., Ferreiro, P., Fraile, G., Lu, C-Q, Lu, L., Moreno-Velazquez, I., Pagon, M., Pitariu, H., Salamatov, V., Shima, S., Simoni, A.S., Siu, O.L., & Widerszal-Bazyl, M. (2007). Cross-national differences in relationships of work demands, job satisfaction, and turnover intentions with work-family conflict. *Personnel Psychology, 60,* 805–835.

Spector, P. E., Cooper, C. L., Poelmans, S., Allen, T. D., O'Driscoll, M., Sanchez, J. I., Siu, O. L., Dewe, P., Hart, P., Lu, L., De Moraes, L. F., Ostrognay, G. M., Sparks, K., Wong, P., & Yu, S. (2004). A cross-national comparative study of work-family stressors, work hours, and well-being. China and Latin America versus the Anglo world. *Personnel Psychology, 57,* 119–142.

Spitzer, D. R. (1995). *Super-motivation: A blue-print for energizing your organization from top to bottom.* New York: American Management Association.

Spreitzer, G. M. (1997). Toward a common ground in defining empowerment. In W. A. Pasmore & R. W. Woodman (Eds.), *Research in organizational change and development* (Vol. 10, pp. 31–62). Greenwich, CT: JAI Press.

Spreitzer, G. M., McCall, M. M., & Mahoney, J. D. (1997). Early identification of international executive potential. *Journal of Applied Psychology, 82,* 6–29.

Stagner, R., & Effal, B. (1982). Internal union dynamics during a strike: A quasi-experimental study. *Journal of Applied Psychology, 67,* 37–44.

Stagner, R., & Rosen, H. (1965). *Psychology of union-management relations.* Belmont, CA: Wadsworth.

Stahelski, A. J., Frost, D. E., & Patch, M. E. (1989). Use of socially dependent bases of power: French and Raven's theory applied to workgroup leadership. *Journal of Applied Psychology, 19,* 283–297.

Stahl, G.K., & Caligiuri, P. (2005). The effectiveness of expatriate coping strategies: The moderating role of cultural distance, position level, and time on the international assignment. *Journal of Applied Psychology, 90,* 603–615.

Stahl, M. J., & Harrell, A. M. (1981). Modeling effort decisions with behavioral decision theory: Toward an individual differences model of expectancy theory. *Organizational Behavior and Human Performance, 27,* 303–325.

Stajkovic, A.D. (2006). Development of a core confidence—higher order construct. *Journal of Applied Psychology, 91,* 1208–1234.

Stanton, J. M. (1998). An empirical assessment of data collection using the Internet. *Personnel Psychology, 51,* 709–725.

Stanton, J. M., & Rogelberg, S. G. (2002). Beyond online surveys: Internet research opportunities for industrial-organizational psychology. In S. G. Rogelberg (Ed.), *Handbook of research methods in industrial and organizational psychology* (pp. 275–294). Malden, MA: Blackwell.

Starke, F. A., & Notz, W. W. (1981). Pre and post-intervention effects of conventional versus final offer arbitration. *Academy of Management Journal, 24,* 832–850.

Steele-Johnson, D., Osburn, H. G., & Pieper, K. F. (2000). A review and extension of current models of dynamic criteria. *International Journal of Selection and Assessment, 8,* 110–136.

Steensma, H. (2002). Violence in the workplace: The explanatory strength of social (in)justice theories. In M. Ross & D. T. Miller (Eds.), *The justice motive in everyday life* (pp. 149–167). New York: Cambridge University Press.

Steers, R.M., Mowday, R.T., & Shapiro, D.L. (2004). The future of work motivation theory. *Academy of Management Review, 29,* 379–387.

Steiner, D. D., & Gilliland, S. W. (1996). Fairness reactions to personnel selection techniques in France and the United States. *Journal of Applied Psychology, 81,* 134–141.

Sternberg, R. J. (1997). The concept of intelligence and its role in lifelong learning and success. *American Psychologist, 52,* 1030–1057.

Stevens, M. J., & Campion, M. A. (1999). Staffing work teams: Development and validation of a selection test for teamwork settings. *Journal of Management, 25,* 207–228.

Stokes, G. S., & Cooper, L. A. (2004). Biodata. In J.C. Thomas (Ed.), *Comprehensive handbook of psychological assessment* (Vol. 4, pp. 243–268). Hoboken, NJ: Wiley.

Strasser, S., & Bateman, T. S. (1984). What we should study, problems we should solve: Perspectives of two constituencies. *Personnel Psychology, 37,* 77–92.

Streufert, S., Pogash, R. M., Roache, J., Gingrich, D., Landis, R., Severs, W., Lonardi, L., & Kantner, A. (1992). Effects of alcohol intoxication on risk taking, strategy, and error rate in visuomotor performance. *Journal of Applied Psychology, 77,* 515–524.

Strickler, L. J. (2000). Using just noticeable differences to interpret test scores. *Psychological Methods*, 5, 415–424.

Sturman, M.C. (2007). The past, present, and future of dynamic performance research. In J.J. Martocchio (Ed.), *Research in personnel and human resources management* (pp. 49–110). Oxford, UK: JAI.

Sulsky, L. M., & Balzer, W. K. (1988). Meaning and measurement of performance rating accuracy: Some methodological and theoretical concerns. *Journal of Applied Psychology*, 73, 497–506.

Sulsky, L. M., & Day, D. V. (1992). Frame-of-reference training and cognitive categorization: An empirical investigation of rater memory issues. *Journal of Applied Psychology*, 77, 501–510.

Summers, T. P., Betton, J. H., & DeCotiis, T. A. (1986). Voting for and against unions: A decision model. *Academy of Management Review*, 11, 643–655.

Sverke, M., & Kuruvilla, S. (1995). A new conceptualization of union commitment: Development and test of an integrated theory. *Journal of Organizational Behavior*, 16, 505–532.

Sverke, M., & Sjoberg, A. (1995). Union membership behavior: The influence of instrumental and value-based commitment. In L. E. Tetrick & J. Barling (Eds.), *Changing employment relations* (pp. 229–254). Washington, DC: American Psychological Association.

Taggar, S., Hackett, R., & Saha S. (1999). Leadership emergence in autonomous work teams: Antecedents and outcomes. *Personnel Psychology*, 52, 899–926.

Tannenbaum, S. I. (2002). A strategic view of organizational training and learning. In K. Kraiger (Ed.), *Creating, implementing, and managing effective training and development* (pp. 10–52). San Francisco: Jossey-Bass.

Tannenbaum, S. I., & Yukl, G. (1992). Training and development in work organizations. *Annual Review of Psychology*, 43, 399–441.

Taylor, F. W. (1911). *The principles of scientific management.* New York: Harper.

Taylor, P.J., Pajo, K., Cheung, G.W., & Stringfield, P. (2004). Dimensionality and validity of a structured telephone reference check procedure. *Personnel Psychology*, 57, 745–772.

Taylor, P.J., Russ-Eft, D.F., & Chen, D.W. (2005). A meta-analytic review of behavior modeling training. *Journal of Applied Psychology*, 90, 692–709.

Tenopyr, M. L. (1996). The complex interactions between measurement and national employment policy. *Psychology, Public Policy, and Law*, 2, 348–362.

Tenopyr, M. L. (1998). Measure me not: The test taker's new bill of rights. In M. D. Hakel (Ed.), *Beyond multiple choice: Evaluating alternatives to traditional testing for selection* (pp. 17–22). Mahwah, NJ: Erlbaum.

Tepas, D. I. (1993). Educational programmes for shiftworkers, their families, and prospective shiftworkers. *Ergonomics*, 36, 199–209.

Tesluk, P. E., & Jacobs, R. R. (1998). Toward an integrated model of work experience. *Personnel Psychology*, 51, 321–355.

Tetrick, L. E. (1995). Developing and maintaining union commitment: A theoretical framework. *Journal of Organizational Behavior*, 16, 583–595.

Tetrick, L. E., & Quick, J. C. (2003). Prevention at work: Public health in occupational settings. In J. C. Quick & L. E. Tetrick (Eds.), *Handbook of organizational health psychology* (pp. 3–18). Washington, DC: American Psychological Association.

Tetrick, L.E., Shore, L.M., McClurg, L.N., & Vandenberg, R.J. (2007). A model of union participation: The impact of perceived union support, union instrumentality, and union loyalty. *Journal of Applied Psychology*, 92, 820–828.

Tharenou, P. (1997). Managerial career advancement. In C. L. Cooper & I. T. Robertson (Eds.), *International review of industrial and organizational psychology* (Vol. 12, pp. 39–94). New York: Wiley.

Tharenou, P., Latimer, S., & Conroy, D. (1994). How do you make it to the top? An examination of influences on women's and men's managerial advancement. *Academy of Management Journal*, 37, 899–931.

Theorell, T. (2003). To be able to exert control over one's own situation: A necessary condition for coping with stressors. In J. C. Quick & L. E. Tetrick (Eds.), *Handbook of organizational health psychology* (pp. 201–220). Washington, DC: American Psychological Association.

Thomas, L. T., & Ganster, D. C. (1995). Impact of family-supportive work variables on work–family conflict and strain: A control perspective. *Journal of Applied Psychology*, 80, 6–15.

Thompson, D. E., & Thompson, T. A. (1982). Court standards for job analysis in test validation. *Personnel Psychology*, 35, 865–874.

Thompson, L. F., Surface, E. A., Martin, D. L., & Sanders, M. G. (2003). From paper to pixels: Moving personnel surveys to the Web. *Personnel Psychology*, 56, 197–227.

Thoresen, C. J., Kaplan, S. A., Barsky, A. P., Warren, C. R., & de Charmont, K. (2003). The affective underpinnings of job perceptions and attitudes: A meta-analytic review and interpretation. *Psychological Bulletin*, 129, 914–945.

Thornton, G. C., III. (1980). Psychometric properties of self-appraisals of job performance. *Personnel Psychology*, 33, 263–272.

Tippins, N.T., Beaty, J., Drasgow, F., Gibson, W.M., Pearlman, K., Segall, D.O., & Shepard, W. (2006). Unproctored internet testing in employment settings. *Personnel Psychology, 59*, 189–225.

Tokar, D. M., Fisher, A. R., & Subich, L. M. (1998). Personality and vocational behavior: A selective review of the literature, 1993–1997. *Journal of Vocational Behavior, 53*, 115–153.

Tonidandel, S., Quinones, M. A., & Adams, A. A. (2002). Computer-adaptive testing: The impact of test characteristics on perceived performance and test takers reactions. *Journal of Applied Psychology, 87*, 320–332.

Tornow, W. W. (1993). Perceptions or reality: Is multiperspective measurement a means or an end? *Human Resource Management, 32*, 221–230.

Totterdell, P., Spelten, E., Smith, L., Barton, J., & Folkard, S. (1995). Recovering from work shifts: How long does it take? *Journal of Applied Psychology, 80*, 43–57.

Tourangeau, R., & Yan, T. (2007). Sensitive questions in surveys. *Psychological Bulletin, 133*, 859–883.

Towler, A. J. (2003). Effects of charismatic influence training on attitudes, behavior and performance. *Personnel Psychology, 56*, 363–381.

Tracey, J. B., Tannenbaum, S. I., & Kavanagh, M. J. (1995). Applying trained skills on the job: The importance of the work environment. *Journal of Applied Psychology, 80*, 239–252.

Triandis, H. C. (1995). A theoretical framework for the study of diversity. In M. M. Chemers, S. Oskamp, & M. A. Costanzo (Eds.), *Diversity in organizations* (pp. 1–36). Thousand Oaks, CA: Sage.

Triandis, H. C., Kurowski, L. L., & Gelfand, M. J. (1994). Workplace diversity. In H. C. Triandis, M. D. Dunnette, & L. M. Hough (Eds.), *Handbook of industrial and organizational psychology* (2nd ed., Vol. 4, pp. 769–827). Palo Alto, CA: Consulting Psychologists Press.

Trice, H. M., & Beyer, J. M. (1993). *The cultures of work organizations.* Englewood Cliffs, NJ: Prentice Hall.

Trice, H. M., & Sonnenstuhl, W. J. (1988). Drinking behavior and risk factors related to the work place: Implications for research and practice. *Journal of Applied Behavioral Science, 24*, 327–346.

Truxillo, D. M., Donahue, L. M., & Kuang, D. (2004). Work samples, performance tests, and competency testing. In J. C. Thomas (Ed.), *Comprehensive handbook of psychological assessment* (Vol. 4, pp. 345–370). Hoboken, NJ: Wiley.

Turner, A. N., & Lawrence, P. R. (1965). *Industrial jobs and the worker: An investigation of response to task attributes.* Cambridge, MA: Harvard University Press.

Turner, M. E., & Horvitz, T. (2001). The dilemma of threat: Group effectiveness and ineffectiveness under adversity. In M. E. Turner (Ed.), *Groups at work* (pp. 445–470). Mahwah, NJ: Erlbaum.

Turner, N., Barling, J., Epitropaki, O., Butcher, V., & Milner, C. (2002). Transformational leadership and moral reasoning. *Journal of Applied Psychology, 87*, 304–311.

Turner, S. M., DeMers, S. T., Fox, H. R., & Reed, G. M. (2001). APA's guidelines for test user qualifications. *American Psychologist, 56*, 1099–1113.

Turnley, W. H., & Feldman, D. C. (2000). Re-examining the effects of psychological contract violations: Unmet expectations and job dissatisfaction as mediators. *Journal of Applied Psychology, 84*, 594–601.

Tyson, P. R., & Vaughn, R. A. (1987, April). Drug testing in the work place: Legal responsibilities. *Occupational Health and Safety*, 24–36.

U.S. Department of Justice. (1998). *Bureau of Justice Statistics Special Report on Workplace Violence 1992–1996.* Washington, DC: The Bureau.

U.S. Department of Labor. (2004). *www.doleta.gov* (accessed 9/27/04).

U.S. Department of Labor. (2006). *The Department of Labor's 2005 findings on the worst forms of child labor.* Washington, DC: Bureau of International Labor Affairs.

Van Buren, M. (2001). *The 2001 ASTD state of the industry report.* Alexandria, VA: ASTD.

Van De Water, T. J. (1997). Psychology's entrepreneurs and the marketing of industrial psychology. *Journal of Applied Psychology, 82*, 486–499.

van Dyck, C., Frese, M., Baer, M., & Sonnentag, S. (2005). Organizational error management culture and its impact on performance: A two-study replication. *Journal of Applied Psychology, 90*, 1228–1240.

Van Eerde, W. (2000). Procrastination: Self-regulation in initiating aversive goals. *Applied Psychology: An International Review, 49*, 372–389.

Van Eerde, W., & Thierry, H. (1996). Vroom's expectancy models and work-related criteria: A meta-analysis. *Journal of Applied Psychology, 81*, 575–586.

Van Iddekinge, C.H., Raymark, P.H., & Roth, P.L. (2005). Assessing personality with a structured employment interview: Construct-related validity and susceptibility to response inflation. *Journal of Applied Psychology, 90*, 536–552.

Van Velsor, E., Ruderman, M. N., & Young, D. P. (1991). *Enhancing self objectivity and performance on the job: The role of upward feedback.* Paper presented at the 6th annual conference of the Society for Industrial and Organizational Psychology, St. Louis.

Vancouver, J.B. (2005). The depth of history and explanation as benefit and bane for psychological content theories. *Journal of Applied Psychology*, *90*, 38–52.

VandeWalle, D., Brown, S. P., Cron, W. L., & Slocum, J. W. (1999). The influence of goal orientation and self-regulation tactics on sales performance: A longitudinal field test. *Journal of Applied Psychology*, *84*, 249–259.

VandeWalle, D., & Cummings, L. L. (1997). A test of the influence of goal orientation on the feedback-seeking process. *Journal of Applied Psychology*, *82*, 390–400.

Vecchio, R.P. (2003). Entrepreneurship and leadership: Common trends and common threads. *Human Resources and Management Review*, *13*, 303–327.

Verdi, B. (2000). Psychologists seek protection under the union label. *The Industrial-Organizational Psychologist*, *38(1)*, 31–35.

Vinchur, A. J. (2007). A history of psychology applied to employee selection. In L.L. Koppes (Ed.), *Historical perspectives in industrial and organizational psychology* (pp. 193–218). Mahwah, NJ: Erlbaum.

Vinchur, A.J., & Koppes, L.L. (2007). Early contributors to the science and practice of industrial psychology. In L.L. Koppes (Ed.), *Historical perspectives in industrial and organizational psychology* (pp. 37–58). Mahwah, NJ: Erlbaum.

Viswesvaran, C., & Schmidt, F. L. (1992). A meta-analytic comparison of the effectiveness of smoking cessation methods. *Journal of Applied Psychology*, *77*, 554–566.

Viswesvaran, C., Schmidt, F.L., & Ones, D.S. (2005). Is there a general factor in ratings of job performance? A meta-analytic framework for disentangling substantive and error influences. *Journal of Applied Psychology*, *90*, 108–131.

Vroom, V. H. (1964). *Work and motivation*. New York: Wiley.

Wagner, R. K. (1997). Intelligence, training, and employment. *American Psychologist*, *52*, 1059–1069.

Wagner, S. H., & Goffin, R. D. (1997). Differences in accuracy of absolute and comparative performance appraisal methods. *Organizational Behavior and Human Decision Processes*, *70*, 95–103.

Wainer, H. (2000). *Computerized adaptive testing* (2nd ed.). Mahwah, NJ: Erlbaum.

Waldman, D. A., Ramirez, G. G., House, R. J., & Puranam, P. (2001). Does leadership matter? CEO leadership attributes and profitability under conditions of perceived environmental uncertainty. *Academy of Management Journal*, *44*, 134–143.

Walker, C. B., & Rumsey, M. G. (2001). Application of findings: ASVAB, new aptitude tests, and personnel classification. In J. P. Campbell & D. J. Knapp (Eds.), *Exploring the limits in personnel selection and classification* (pp. 559–576). Mahwah, NJ: Erlbaum.

Wallace, S. R. (1965). Criteria for what? *American Psychologist*, *20*, 411–417.

Wanberg, C. R. (1997). Antecedents and outcomes of coping behaviors among unemployed and re-employed individuals. *Journal of Applied Psychology*, *82*, 731–744.

Wanberg, C. R., Kammeyer-Mueller, J. D., & Shi, K. (2001). Job loss and the experience of unemployment: International research and perspectives. In N. Anderson, D. S. Ones, H. K. Sinangil, & C. Viswesvaran (Eds.), *Handbook of industrial, work, and organisational psychology* (Vol. 2, pp. 253–269). London: Sage.

Wanberg, C. R., Kanfer, R., & Banas, J. T. (2000). Predictors and outcomes of networking intensity among unemployed job seekers. *Journal of Applied Psychology*, *85*, 491–503.

Wanberg, C. R., Welsh, E. T., & Hezlett, S. A. (2003). Mentoring research: A review and dynamic process model. In J. J. Martocchio & G. R. Ferris (Eds.), *Research in personnel and human resources management* (Vol. 22, pp. 39–124). Kidlington, UK: Elsevier.

Wanek, J. E. (1999). Integrity and honesty testing: What do we know? How do we use it? *International Review of Selection and Assessment*, *1*, 183–195.

Wanous, J. P., Sullivan, S. E., & Malinak, J. (1989). The role of judgment calls in meta-analysis. *Journal of Applied Psychology*, *74*, 259–264.

Warr, P. (2007a). Some historical developments in I-O psychology outside the United States. In L.L. Koppes (Ed.), *Historical perspectives in industrial and organizational psychology* (pp. 81–107). Mahwah, NJ: Erlbaum.

Warr, P. (2007b). *Work, happiness, and unhappiness*. Mahwah, NJ: Erlbaum.

Warr, P., Allan, C., & Birdi, K. (1999). Predicting three levels of training outcome. *Journal of Occupational and Organizational Psychology*, *72*, 351–375.

Warr, P. B. (1987). *Work, unemployment, and mental health*. Oxford: Clarendon.

Warr, P. B., & Payne, R. L. (1983). Social class and reported changes in behavior after job loss. *Journal of Applied Social Psychology*, *13*, 206–222.

Weekley, J. A., & Gier, J. A. (1989). Ceilings in the reliability and validity of performance ratings: The case of expert raters. *Academy of Management Journal*, *32*, 213–222.

Weekley, J. A., & Jones, C. (1997). Video-based situational testing. *Personnel Psychology*, *50*, 25–49.

Weick, K.E. (2001). *Making sense of the organization*. Maldon, MA: Blackwell.

Weiss, D. J., Dawis, R. V., England, G. W., & Lofquist, L. H. (1967). *Manual for the Minnesota Satisfaction*

Questionnaire. Minneapolis: Industrial Relations Center, University of Minnesota.

Weiss, H. M. (1990). Learning theory and industrial and organizational psychology. In M. D. Dunnette & L. M. Hough (Eds.), *Handbook of industrial and organizational psychology* (2nd ed., Vol. 1, pp. 171–221). Palo Alto, CA: Consulting Psychologists Press.

Werner, J. M., & Bolino, M. C. (1997). Explaining U.S. court of appeals decisions involving performance appraisal: Accuracy, fairness, and validation. *Personnel Psychology, 50,* 1–24.

West, M. A. (2001). The human team: Basic motivations and innovations. In N. Anderson, D. S. Ones, H. K. Sinangil, & C. Viswesvaran (Eds.), *Handbook of industrial, work, and organisational psychology* (Vol. 2, pp. 270–288). London: Sage.

Westin, A. F. (1992). Two key factors that belong in a macro-ergonomic analysis of electronic monitoring: Employee perceptions of fairness and the climate of organizational trust or distrust. *Applied Ergonomics, 23,* 35–42.

Wherry, R. J. (1957). The past and future of criterion evaluation. *Personnel Psychology, 10,* 1–5.

Whetten, D. A., & Cameron, K. S. (1991). *Developing management skills* (2nd ed.). New York: HarperCollins.

Whittington, D. (1998). How well do researchers report their measures? An evaluation of measurement in published educational research. *Educational and Psychological Measurement, 58,* 21–37.

Wiener, R. L., & Hurt, L. E. (2000). How do people evaluate social sexual conduct at work? A psychological model. *Journal of Applied Psychology, 85,* 75–85.

Wiesen, J. P. (1999). *WTMA: Wiesen Test of Mechanical Aptitude* (PAR edition). Odessa, FL: Psychological Assessment Resources.

Wiesenfeld, B. M., Raghuram, S., & Garud, R. (1999). Managers in a virtual context: The experience of self-threat and its effects on virtual work organizations. In C. L. Cooper & D. M. Rousseau (Eds.), *Trends in organizational behavior: The virtual organization* (Vol. 6, pp. 31–44). New York: Wiley.

Wigdor, A. K., & Sackett, P. R. (1993). Employment testing and public policy: The case of the General Aptitude Test Battery. In H. Schuler, J. L. Farr, & M. Smith (Eds.), *Personnel selection and assessment* (pp. 183–204). Hillsdale, NJ: Erlbaum.

Williams, C. R., & Livingstone, L. P. (1994). Another look at the relationship between performance and voluntary turnover. *Academy of Management Journal, 37,* 269–298.

Williams, K. M., & Crafts, J. L. (1997). Inductive job analysis. In D. L. Whetzel & G. R. Wheaton (Eds.), *Applied measurement methods in industrial psychology* (pp. 51–88). Palo Alto, CA: Consulting Psychologists Press.

Williamson, L. G., Campion, J. E., Malos, S. B., Roehling, M. V., & Campion, M. A. (1997). Employment interview on trial: Linking interview structure with litigation outcomes. *Journal of Applied Psychology, 82,* 900–912.

Willness, C. R., Steel, P., & Lee, K. (2007). A meta-analysis of the antecedents and consequences of workplace sexual harassment. *Personnel Psychology, 60,* 127–162.

Wilson, M. A. (2007). A history of job analysis. In L. L. Koppes (Ed.), *Historical perspectives in industrial and organizational psychology* (pp. 210–241). Mahwah, NJ: Erlbaum.

Woehr, D. J. (1994). Understanding frame-of-reference training: The impact of training on the recall of performance information. *Journal of Applied Psychology, 79,* 524–534.

Woehr, D. J., & Huffcutt, A. I. (1994). Rater training for performance appraisal: A quantitative review. *Journal of Occupational and Organizational Psychology, 67,* 189–205.

World Health Organization (2007). Carcinogenicity of shift-work, painting, and fire-fighting. *The Lancet Oncology, 8,* 1065–1066.

Wright, P. M. (1990). Operationalization of goal difficulty as a moderator of the goal difficulty–performance relationship. *Journal of Applied Psychology, 75,* 227–234.

Wright, T. A., & Cropanzano, R. (2007). The happy/productive worker thesis revisited. In J. J. Martocchio (Ed.), *Research in personnel and human resources management* (pp. 269–307). Oxford, UK: JAI.

Wright, T. A., & Wright, V. P. (1999). Ethical responsibility and the organizational researcher: A committed-to-participant research perspective. *Journal of Organizational Behavior, 20,* 1107–1112.

Yeatts, D. E., & Hyten, C. (1998). *High-performing self-managed work teams.* Thousand Oaks, CA: Sage.

Yoo, T-Y., & Muchinsky, P. M. (1998). Utility estimates of job performance as related to the Data, People, and Things parameters of work. *Journal of Organizational Behavior, 19,* 353–370.

Yorges, S. L., Weiss, H. M., & Strickland, O. J. (1999). The effect of leader outcomes on influence, attributions, and perceptions of charisma. *Journal of Applied Psychology, 84,* 428–436.

Yost, E. (1943). *American women of science.* New York: Stokes.

Youngblood, S. A., DeNisi, A. S., Molleston, J. L., & Mobley, W. H. (1984). The impact of work environment, instrumentality beliefs, perceived labor union image, and subjective norms on union voting intentions. *Academy of Management Journal, 17,* 576–590.

Yukl, G. (1994). *Leadership in organizations* (3rd ed.). Englewood Cliffs, NJ: Prentice Hall.

Yukl, G., & Falbe, C. M. (1991). The importance of different power sources in downward and lateral relations. *Journal of Applied Psychology, 76*, 416–423.

Zaccaro, S.J., Kemp, C., & Bader, P, (2004). Leader traits and attributes. In J. Antonakis, R. Sternberg, & A. Ciancola (Eds.), *The nature of leadership* (pp. 101–124). Thousand Oaks, CA: Sage.

Zaccaro, S. J., & Klimoski, R. J. (2001). The nature of organizational leadership: An introduction. In S. J. Zaccaro & R. J. Klimoski (Eds.), *The nature of organizational leadership: Understanding the performance imperatives confronting today's leaders* (pp. 3–41). San Francisco: Jossey-Bass.

Zakon, R. H. (2004). *Hobbes' internet timeline* (v7.0). Retrieved February 10, 2004, from *http://www.zakon.org/robert/internet/timeline*

Zalesny, M. D. (1985). Comparison of economic and non-economic factors in predicting faculty vote preference in a union representation election. *Journal of Applied Psychology, 70*, 243–256.

Zedeck, S. (1992). Introduction: Exploring the domain of work and family careers. In S. Zedeck (Ed.), *Work, families, and organizations* (pp. 1–32). San Francisco: Jossey-Bass.

Zedeck, S., & Cascio, W. F. (1982). Performance appraisal decisions as a function of rater training and purpose of the appraisal. *Journal of Applied Psychology, 67*, 752–758.

Zedeck, S., & Goldstein, I. L. (2000). The relationship between I/O psychology and public policy: A commentary. In J. F. Kehoe (Ed.), *Managing selection in changing organizations* (pp. 371–396). San Francisco: Jossey-Bass.

Zedeck, S., Outtz, J., Cascio, W. F., & Goldstein, I. L. (1995). Why do "testing experts" have such limited vision? *Human Performance, 8*, 179–190.

Zeidner, J., & Johnson, C. D. (1994). Is personnel classification a concept whose time has passed? In M. G. Rumsey, C. B. Walker, & J. H. Harris (Eds.), *Personnel selection and classification* (pp. 377–410). Hillsdale, NJ: Erlbaum.

Zellers, K. L., & Tepper, B. J. (2003). Beyond social exchange: New directions for organizational citizenship behavior theory and research. In J. J. Martocchio & G. R. Ferris (Eds.), *Research in personnel and human resources management* (Vol. 22, pp. 395–424). Kidlington, UK: Elsevier.

Zhao, H., & Seibert, S.E. (2006). The big five personality dimensions and entrepreneurial status: A meta-analytic review. *Journal of Applied Psychology, 91*, 259–271.

Zhao, H., Wayne, S.J., Glibkowski, B.C., & Bravo, J. (2007). The impact of psychological contract breach on work-related outcomes: A meta-analysis. *Personnel Psychology, 60*, 647–680.

Zhou, J., & George, J. M. (2001). When job dissatisfaction leads to creativity: Encouraging the expression of voice. *Academy of Management Journal, 44*, 682–696.

Zickar, M. J. (2001). Using personality inventories to identify thugs and agitators: Applied psychology's contribution to the war against labor. *Journal of Vocational Behavior, 59*, 149–164.

Zickar, M. J. (2003). Remembering Arthur Kornhauser: Industrial psychology's advocate of worker well-being. *Journal of Applied Psychology, 88*, 363–369.

Zickar, M.J., & Gibby, R.E. (2007). Four persistent themes throughout the history of I-O psychology in the United States. In L.L. Koppes (Ed.), *Historical perspectives in industrial and organizational psychology* (pp. 61–80). Mahwah, NJ: Erlbaum.

Zieky, M. J. (2001). So much has changed: How the setting of cutscores has evolved since the 1980s. In G. J. Cizek (Ed.), *Setting performance standards: Concepts, methods, and perspectives* (pp. 19–52). Mahwah, NJ: Erlbaum.

Zimmerman, B. J. (1995). Self-efficacy and educational development. In A. Bandura (Ed.), *Self-efficacy in changing societies* (pp. 202–231). New York: Cambridge.

Author Index

Page references in *italics* indicate References section

Subject Index

Page references in **bold** indicate where the entry is defined in the margin.